Medical Law and Ethics in Nigeria

Malthouse Law Books

Abdulrazaq, M T, *Revenue Law and Practice in Nigeria*
Adah, C E, *The Nigerian Law of Evidence*
Asuzu, C., *Fair Hearing in Nigeria*
Bambale, Y Y, *Crimes and Punishments under Islamic Law*
Bambale, Y. Y., *An Outline of Islamic Jurisprudence*
Bambale, Y. Y., *Islamic Law Relating to Property and Commercial Transactions*
Beredugo, A.J., *Nigerian legal system: an introductory text*
Emiri, F, & Deinduomo, G., *Law, Oil and Development Challenges in Nigeria*
Emiri, F. & Deinduomo, G., *Law and Petroleum Industry in Nigeria*
Emiri, F., *The Law of Restitution in Nigeria*
Emiri, F., *Law and Medical Ethics in Nigeria*
Fogam, P, *Law of Contract*
Emiri, F., *Equity and Trusts Law in Nigeria*
Goldface-Irokalibe, I.J., *The Law of Banking in Nigeria*
Igweike, K, *Nigerian Commercial Law: Agency*
Igweike, K, *Nigerian Commercial Law: Contract*
Igweike, K, *Nigerian Commercial Law: Hire Purchase*
Ikoni, U.D., *An Introduction to Nigerian Environmental Law*
Ladan, M.T., *Introduction to Jurisprudence: classical and Islamic*
Maidoh, D.C., Oho, F. *et al., Judicial Administration and Other Legal Issues in Nigeria*
Mowoe, Kehinde, *Constitutional Law in Nigeria*
Okoh, Sheriff E. E. *Succession under Islamic Law*
Olong, Adefi *M., Administrative Law in Nigeria: an introduction*
Olong, Adefi M., *The Nigerian Legal System: an introduction*
Omorogbe, Yinka, *Oil and Gas Law in Nigeria*
Omotesho, Aboaba, *The Law of Tort in Nigeria: Selected Themes*
Sagay, I, *Law of Succession and Inheritance*
Sagay, I, *Nigerian Family Law: Principles, Cases, Statutes and Commentaries*
Utuama, A A, *Nigerian Law of Real Property*
Utuama, A A, *The Law of Trusts and their Uses in Nigeria*
Utuama, A. A., *Planning Law in Nigeria*
Uvieghara E E, *Labour Law in Nigeria*
Uvieghara E E, *Sale of Goods (& Hire Purchase) Law in Nigeria*
Yakubu J A, *Administration of Justice in Nigeria*
Yakubu J A, *Law of contract in Nigeria*
Yakubu J A, *Press Law in Nigeria*
Yalaju, J.G., *Media law in Nigeria*

Medical Law and Ethics in Nigeria

Professor Festus Oghenemaro Emiri
Professor of Jurisprudence and Dean of Law
Delta State University,
Oleh Campus, Delta State of Nigeria.

m a l t h o u s e

Malthouse Press Limited

Lagos, Benin, Ibadan, Jos, Port-Harcourt, Zaria

Published by

Malthouse Press Limited
43 Onitana Street, Off Stadium Hotel Road,
Surulere, Lagos, Lagos State
E-mail: malthouse_press@yahoo.com
malthouse_lagos@yahoo.co.uk
Tel: +234 (01) 802 600 3203

First Published 2012
ISBN 978-978-8422-33-4

Distributors:

African Books Collective
Oxford, United Kingdom
Email: abc@africanbookscollective.com
Website: http://www.africanbookscollective.com

Dedication

To:
Mrs Omotunde (*nee* Akapo)
(an outstanding student of my first Medical Ethics class at the Lagos State University, Lagos, in 1993)

Acknowledgements

This work is a product of my interest in ethics. The idea of writing a book on medical ethics law was first suggested to me in 1989 by Olufemi Abayomi Akerele Esq (deceased) when I was assigned to supervise his long essay at the Lagos State University. At that time, his long essay, entitled Legal Implications of Recent Biomedical Phenomena, was considered challenging. I was fortune to have the quiet encouragement of Prof. Mike Ikhariale, about five years later, who assigned me to teach both gender law and medical ethics, in the Faculty at the undergraduate level. This book was my teaching draft between 1993 and 1997. I greatly benefited from the opportunity to teach the course and the interaction it made possible between my students and I, though the book shape has since changed.

During the intervening years to this work being published, I incurred many other debts of gratitude. Several friends encouraged and commented on drafts of the book, and unfortunately these comments are unavailable in this final product. Notwithstanding, they all contribute to what (immodestly, if you so think) makes this work more rounded. They include Professors Yomi Dinakin, Maduabuchi Dukor and A D Badiaki. Especially grateful I am to Mr. 'Bode Richards, who took over responsibility for much of the editorial and logistic challenges with Malthouse Press.

This work was made less tasking by the wonderful shield given by Professor Patrick Mouboghare and Dr. A.O. Giwa from unexpected constant distractions at the Delta State University, Oleh Campus, during my sabbatical years, between 2004 and 2006.

Table of cases

R v. Flattery (1877) 2 QB.D 410; 334

Statutes

Nigeria

Convention on Psychotropic Substance 1971; 388
Helsinki 1994 Declaration on bio-medical research; 22
Helsinki Declaration of 1964; 33, 147, 148, 152, 155, 300
Lisbon Declaration of 1981; 33, 43
Oslo Declaration of 1970; 33, 34
Sydney Declaration of 1968; 33
Tokyo Declaration of 1975; 33, 34
Tribunal Miscellaneous Offence Decree 1988; 389
Venice Declaration of 1983 of the International Code of Medical Ethics. Rule 9; 20

Table of Contents

Chapter 1

Framework for Medical Ethics

The interaction between medicine, law and philosophy is no doubt real. Bio-technology ability to cause life, and prolong it throws up many ethical questions, resolution of which can hardly be by sheer appeal to individual conscience of the doctor considering the multi-dimensional facets in which medical services are rendered and the fact that there is hardly moral solidarity on the many ethical issues in medicine.[1] The provision of medical services brings together the doctor, patient and at least the relatives or friends or both of the patient concerned with the relief of his illness. Ethical problems therefore which arise in the course of the patient's treatment will require considering the various parties ethics and values, and to a large extent should appeal to certain model(s) they recognise. Since individual consciences of the parties work in different ways. For, while there may be moral solidarity on fundamental principles, such as the sanctity of life, conflict does exist as to the content of life, i.e., the content of the principle. Some who hold to the principle may in the same breadth justify abortion, euthanasia, and a host others, while others who hold to same principle may argue that abortion and euthanasia are outside the range of the fundamental principle. This is why ultimate decisions in medicine require more than merely the intuitive judgment of the doctor who comes face-to-face with ethical problems in practice. Whatever decision the doctor reaches on treatment choice must necessarily conform to the general framework of law, which ultimately shapes morality.

Medical law is an area largely dominated by common law principles formulate by the court, because Parliament is often reluctant to legislate on the many sensitive issues that modern medicine brings to the fore.[2]

But even at this, common-law framework itself is not without its dangers. Many of the moral issues that arise in modern medicine defy legal classification and

---

[1] MDA Freeman, Introduction: Legal and Philosophical Frameworks for Medical Decision—making, in Freeman (ed.) *Medicine, Ethics and the Law* (London, Stevens and Sons, 1988) chapter 1; Mason & McCall Smith, *Law and Medical Ethics*, 4th ed. London, Butterworths, 1994. p. 5; O F Emiri, Human Factor in Medicine in O.F. Emiri (ed) *Cross-cutting Issues in Ethics, Law and Medicine*, Lagos, ACLHC, 2000) chapter 1.

[2] There are indeed few areas of medicine that have been legislated upon. The Medical Council Act 1998, sets out the general framework for regulating medical practice, guided by the basis philosophies of the Hippocratic Code and its several refinement over the years by the World Medical Council in the form of Physician Oath.

skill of lawyers. While precedent does play an important role in the areas of property, commerce, obligations and other traditional legal areas, it is often helpless where novel moral issues are in question. If as some suggest, such penumbra areas should be resolved by appeal to moral principles, here again the role of the courts may be implicated. Courts do not really appear to be the place for shaping public morality and good. While it may be possible to stretch legal concept to capture analogous relationship in medicine, we just must admit that many such comparison are misfits. An example is the case of *Moore* v. *Regents of the University of California*.[3] Here the California Supreme Court was faced with how to classify blood samples taken from the plaintiff. The defendant University, developed it into a cell line with potential commercial value running into millions of dollars. The issue for determination bordered on whether the unauthorised use was a violation of the plaintiff's property within the property bracket, protected by the tort of conversion? If yes, could it be classified as stealing, or some other kindred property offences? If no, would the plaintiff at least claim a private law entitlement within the two entitlement bracket of property or liability rules?[4] These are no mean issues for determination, because their classification are by no means simply; more so when classification determines to a large degree causes of action, defences and remedies.

Often, the nature of ethical dilemma triggered by modern medicine touch on sensitivities of human nature that 'the formulation of social and moral policy becomes an enterprise which the courts have neither the means or right to perform,'[5] because these are areas also where it is difficult to argue seriously that the man on the street cannot proffer solutions to questions.

Since the courts and lawyers can hardly reach moral consensus on the many ethical issues, would it make sense to turn these issues over to the legislature with or without the assistance of research and reform body? Can the Law Reform Commission do the job? Hardly, since law reform bodies are populated by lawyers, it is plausible to argue that their reasoning will equally suffers from the limitations associated with transposing legal concepts into novel, often moral problems. With a view of finding some consensus in medical ethics, some advanced jurisdictions have resorted to establishing hospital standing ethical committees composed of lawyers, doctors, philosophers, theologies and other disciplines.[6] No matter how laudable the creation of such structures may be, it is hardly disputable that they amount to no more than 'debate houses,' promoting different perspective to the many ethical issues of medical treatment. They can hardly shape responsibility. While we must admit

[3] (1990) 793 P. 2d 479 (Cal. Sup. Ct).

[4] Calabresi and Melamed, Property Rules, Liability Rules, and Inalienability: One View of the Cathedral (1972) 85 *Harv. L.R.* 1089 (an innovative way of analysing entitlements introduced by Guido Calabresi and A. Douglas Melamed); see also Symposium: Property Rules, Liability Rules, and Inalienability: A Twenty-Five Year Retrospective (1997) 106 *Yale L.J.* 2081-2215.

[5] *Bland* v. *Airedale NHS Trust* [1993] 2 WLR 316 at 360 and 362, per Lord Mustill. See also *Gillick* v. *West Norfolk & Wisbech Area Health Authority* [1986] AC 112, per Lord Diplock.

[6] Ian Kennedy, Professor of medical law at University of London and President of the Centre of Medical Law and Ethics, has suggested the establishment of such standing committees in England.

that law continues to be an indispensable tool in the resolution of moral issues in medicine, we must admit that 'it is not a neutral tool wielded in an apolitical way by disinterested players'. It is very much a social product, a reflection of the power of particular interest groups, economic, religions and professional. The political economy of decision making in the area of medical law comes sharply into focus when health resources allocation is questioned.'[7]

Since most ethical questions in medicine involve matters of right and wrong, it has been suggested by some commentators that that throws medical discourse into the mould of moral philosophy. By this analysis it is suggested that our finding the basic philosophical foundation for decisions in medicine can help explain most of our hitherto dilemmas. It is tempting to think that the emergence of the Hippocratic based Code of medical practice is the starting point of a universal principle on which decisions are made. Here again we cannot pretend that philosophy has the answer. Different philosophies proffer different solutions and identifying a starting point or a consensus has been difficult. The ranges of discourse have spanned from Utilitarianism to Kantianism. The former is rooted in the concept that the maximisation of welfare is the signpost for determining ethical positions of right or wrong.[8] On the other hand, the latter emphasises our taking rights seriously. Here again we must admit the limitations of philosophy.[9]

It is virtually impossible in medicine to talk of utility in the sense of defining happiness or welfare in terms of either quality or quantity. Can we empirical state as categorical truth that a little happiness derived by psychiatric patients is better or not, than a lot of happiness experienced by a small group of terminally ill patients? This is an area where we are forced to accept the limitation of Bentham–Mill utilitarian philosophy. Is the Kantian ethos with emphasis on the rights of individual the solution? Classical Kant argument proceeds on the basis that we should not treat others as a means to an end. It accordingly encourages total benevolence. But here again is the problem. While not doubting that benevolence is ideal and pervades many areas of medicine, it will be too high an ideal to suggest that it is the motivating force in medical practice.[10] What all this show is that moral philosophy has its limitation. Its analysis often only provides guidelines and not particular answers because of the very nature of the inquiry, namely, an inquiry involving moral questions. That notwithstanding it can and does provide a basis tool for rational decision-making.

Today, most decisions in medicine can be explained by the concept of personal autonomy. This is primarily mirrored by concepts such as informed consent and self- determination, as the thread underlying most discourse on medicine and care-giving. Autonomy explains the liberalisation of abortion – the mother's right to

---

[7] See MDA Freeman, Introduction: Legal and Philosophical Frameworks for Medical Decision–making, in Freeman (ed.) *Medicine, Ethics and the Law* (London, Stevens and Sons, 1988) chapter 1.

[8] J S Mill, *On Liberty* and *Utilitarianism* (Bantam, New York, 1993).

[9] Immanuel Kant, *The Metaphysics of Morals* (M. Gregor ed., Cambridge Univ. Press, Cambridge, 1996).

[10] Mason & Smith, above n. 1 at 6.

autonomy. Autonomy argument to some extent also informs medical decision in the areas of surrogate motherhood and even euthanasia. But autonomy argument can easily run into counter-argument on the ground that some may not share its philosophy, because it is essentially individualistic. Ethics it can be argued should not promote individualism in a manner that ignores a social dimension to life which itself enriches the life of the individual. It is for this reason that a logical application of the autonomy concept must admit certain limitation to accommodate the expectations of others – society and the state.[11] Or what good would we be promoting in medicine if we advocate only the patient rights, altogether ignoring the feelings of the patient's relatives, the medical doctor who is at the centre – stage, and other care-givers and institutions, such as the state? Hardly any!

Closely related to it is the equal combative and self-assertive theory of rights. While it is admitted that the concept of 'rights' permeates most of the moral position endorsed by decisions in medicine, in the sense that most recognised position in law are couched in rights, *rights-analysis* hardly can explain the subordination of certain rights to other where there exist a clash of rights.[12] Emphasis on patient's rights, would invariable mean the subordination of the rights of others, even when they also have vested interest in treatment and care-giving. For example, do doctors and nurses who give medical services not have rights that should be protected? It is contestable that the autonomy of the patient's rights does relieve them of duty to treat to the best of their ability in accordance with the Hippocrates principle.[13]

The English Warnock Report is an example of how difficult it can be in our pluralistic society to draw a philosophical or moral basis for issues fundamental to society. The report shows a vicissitude between utilitarian considerations, deontological philosophy and at times swings to paternalism and Kantianism. The internal inconsistency of following a particular policy basis merely shows that wrangling is a natural result in the resolution of moral issues. That being the case, we may be forced to an intuitive guide, the doctor's first guide on ethics. Though intuition may enjoy little appeal in moral philosophy, its usefulness is hardly contestable, especially in the field of medicine 'where the practical fact is that each doctor-patient encounter is played out on a different pitch.. the goal-post moving imperceptibly with each consultation within that relationship.'[14]

---

[11] For general reading, see O. F. Emiri, Euthanasia and Treatment Cessation: A Paradox (1996) *Essence of Philosophy* 55; D.T. Meyers, *Self, Society and Personal Choices* (1989); T.E. Hill, The Importance of Autonomy in Hill (ed.) *Autonomy and Self-respect* (1991).

[12] See for example rights conflict in *Airedale NHS Trust* v. *Bland* [1993] 1 All ER 821, [1993] 2 WLR 316, [1993] 12 BMLR 64, an artificial feeding case involving a persistent vegetative state patient. Following a right analysis the House of Lords was of the view that a conflict between the principles of sanctity of human life and that of self-determination did not lead to a moral impasse. Lord Goff for example in [1993] 2 WLR 316 at 367 f said, 'to this extent, the principle of the sanctity of human life must yield to the principle of self-determination.'

[13] *Okonkwo* v. *MDPDT* (1999) 9 NWLR (pt 617) 1 CA, (1999) 6 NWLR (pt. 786) 1 SC - where the argument was at least advanced that a patient's right does not relieve the doctor of his duty to treat the patient to the best of his professional ability.

[14] Mason & Smith, above n. 1 at 7.

The value of intuition is that though it may be difficult to articulate on logical grounds, its correctness is hardly doubted. For example, intuition tells us that the principle of sanctity of life should be upheld, but hardly tells us why it should be so, especially in the face of contending moral argument for ending life. Again we are forced to admit that while the doctor's intuitive stance may be his first guide to morality, morality is itself shaped by other outside influences from which intuition is not immune to.

Despite the limitations of the various moral concepts, one thing emerges clearly from them — they sharpen our awareness of the many contending moral issues that are often thrown up by medical treatment. They serve as useful tools of argument for what is considered right or wrong - pointers of how ethics should develop. They enrich our quest for humanism in the practice of modern medicine.[15] Our discussion in this book will reveal how these concepts are played out in the various arguments and policies that underlie the vast array of medical topics.

Basis of medical responsibility

The general basis for physician's liability is fault-based. [16] This is considered proper because it is 'one of means whereby doctors are made to show a sense of responsibility, and justly claim to professional freedom.'[17] However in jurisdictions as New Zealand, a no-fault-system has been introduced. Under the system, a patient who suffers injury from medical treatment or diagnosis is allowed to recover compensation without needing to connect his injury to fault of the doctor. There are numerous rationales for the no-fault compensatory regime. Generally under a fault regime, a patient who suffers injury is unlikely to have his claim vindicated because physician's faults are often difficult to prove. Also, it has been suggested that direct litigation based on fault can create a situation of defensive medical practice, which itself is not beneficial to the patient, physician and society. Worse still, it is an established fact that most medical injuries are really medical accidents, rather than the result of negligence, thereby dimming the chances of recovery for patients who often rely on negligence. Since the essence of a patient's claim for medical negligence or breach of contract is to recover financial compensation through litigation, it invariably means that factors that make litigation a gamble, translates to a frustration of the patient's remedy. Generally, litigation is often protracted, expensive, with uncertain results. A fault regime promotes defensive medicine. This is so because every successful claim would amount to a dent in the professional competence of the doctor.

---

[15] See Freeman, above n 1. at p. 5, Emiri above n 1 at p. 91

[16] Sheila McLean, No Fault Liability and Medical Responsibility in MDA Freeman (ed.) *Medical Ethics and the Law* (London. Stevens & Sons, 1988) 147 and see generally the Royal Commission on Civil Liability and Compensation for Personal Injury (Pearson Commission) Recommendation, Cmmd. 7054 of 1978.

[17] This was the position of the medical profession in England before the Pearson Committee made its recommendation in 1978, see Cmmd. 7054 report para 1342.

To avoid the unpleasantness, doctors may be forced to engage in excessive diagnosis for fear of liability claims, thereby placing the patient at more risk, while stretching his finances. The situation only short-changes the patient. Litigation runs the risk of damaging doctor-patient relationship, so if possible should be avoided. These disadvantages of the fault regime are what make the construction of a relatively non-combative and non-contentious compensatory regime attractive. That medical accidents are more common than cases of medical negligence makes imperative a modification of the legal process in such a way that a patient can get compensation for medical accident outside the present 'no-recovery' for accidents without fault, combative system. A change in this direction could remove defensive medical practice and provide the patient with a better compensatory mechanism for medical harm suffered. Such a state-funded compensatory scheme, can enhance patient's care and rights respect. If properly managed can further provide a speedy and appropriate compensation for medical injuries.[18]

New Zealand Accident Compensation Act, 1982, appears to provide a model close to a state sponsored compensatory regime for medical accidents.[19] Under the Act, personal injury includes, physical and mental consequences of any injury or accident, be it medical or surgical, dental or first aid accidents, incapacity resulting from occupational diseases or industrial deafness and, actual bodily harm (including pregnancy and mental or nervous shocks) arising from any act or omission by any person within the description of sections 128, 132 and 201 of the Crimes Act 1961. It further states that the following are excluded from the definition of personal injury, namely (i) damage to the body or mind caused by cardio-vascular or cerebra-vascular episode or (ii) damage to the body or mind caused exclusively by disease, injection or the ageing process.[20] Commendable as it is, the Act has its drawbacks. Its distinction between *accident* and *disease* is illogical and prevents a robust compensation for all injured persons regardless of the causes giving rise to it.[21]

One thing must be appreciated. The term accident is not an uncomplicated concept. In ordinary usage, it could mean any unexpected mishap. In the context of medicine, an accident may be described as any injury to the human system which is unexpected and not designed by the person who causes the injury. That being the case, it can be difficult to distinguish between a harm caused by sickness and one

---

[18] McLean, above n. 16 at 150; For general reading see also T. Ison, *The Forensic Lottery* (Staples Press, 1967); C Wood (ed.) *The Influence of Litigation on Medical Practice* (Academic Press, 1977) both cited by McLean, above n. 16 at 160 n. 9

[19] The Act was amended by the Accident Compensation Act, 1982. For general reading on the operation of the New Zealand model, see C.R. Cripps, Medical Practitioners Liability for Personal Injury Caused by Negligence (1978) *NZLJ* 29; R Mahoney, Informed Consent and Breach of the Medical Contract to Achieve a Particular Result; Opportunities for New Zealand's Patient Personal Injury Litigators to Peck Out of the Accident Compensation Closet (1985) 6 *Otago L. Rev.* No1, 103.

[20] Section 2 of Accident Compensation Act, 1982. As a result of economic realities, the scope of recovery under the 1982 Act was narrowed in the Accident Compensation (Amendment) Act 1992. The 1992 Act restricts recovery for 'medical misadventure'. For reading on the amended legislation, see R Mahoney, New Zealand's Accident Compensation Scheme: A Reassessment (1992) *Amer. J. of Comp. Law* 159.

[21] McLean, *above* n. 16 at 151

caused by accident in medical cases. It is in this context therefore the suggestion that the Act's definition of medical misadventure to include accidents, that excludes sickness, defeats the policy thrust of its 'no-fault' compensatory regime. The distinction appears to be a result of a reasoning designed to exclude some forms of injury from the scheme, which gives little regard to the intention of the legislature – a commitment to compensating on the basis of the consequences of an accident and not the cause of it. This is what makes the distinction unfortunate.[22] The philosophical underpinning for the Act is a desire to abolish an elusive search for fault, with a view to fix liability. It is on this basis that it can be said that 'medical misadventure' ought to be treated as wider than its present confinement to medical negligence. To equate medical misadventure with negligence (i.e. a failure to exercise care and skill of a competent doctor) as the New Zealand Act does, is to defeat the generous regime introduced by the Act. Though they both may sometimes occupy the same square, they need not always be.[23] Medical misadventure or mishap can safely include negligence, failing to make accurate diagnosis, failing to attend to a patient, and situations such as leaving swabs behind after surgery, but is not necessarily limited to these.

Compensation payable under the Act comes from the Accident Compensation Corporation. Compensation under the scheme does not bar an action by a patient for any injury not covered under it. In effect an action for damages for negligence or breach of contract is still maintainable for personal injury not considered accident within the statutory framework. Whether failure to make disclosure to a patient is within the definition of accident would to some extent depend on whether the doctor know or ought to know what risk would result from non-disclosure. If yes, then it cannot be said to be unexpected, and so may not be within the meaning of accident under the Act.

The New Zealand no-fault scheme however should not be confused with a strict—liability regime. A crucial distinction between both is the identity of the person or organisation funding the compensation award. Some have suggested that strict liability would completely shield the doctor from compensation burden, whether it be the result of misadventure, medical accident or negligence. The suggestion will only throw all the burden on the state, a thing that is hardly desirable. That type of situation is not what the Act enacts or in any way intends. If anything, there is justification for restricting classes of injuries for which compensation is payable. Since the state is the party that make compensation, there is good reason to argue that it should have a right to restrict the types of harm that will attract compensation. That is what the New Zealand Act does, by excluding disease. Whatever the merits or otherwise of the New Zealand model, it is instructive of how the burden of medical responsibility can be made temperate for a more conducive patient/doctor relationship.[24]

---

[22] Ibid.

[23] See *Re Monday* [1984] 4 NZLR 339 and *Re Stafford* [1984] NZACR 783

[24] Ian Kennedy & Andrew Grubb, *Medical Law*, 2nd. edn., London: Butterworths, 1994, 539

Institutional framework for medical services

It is hardly contestable that a patient in the framework of a hospital health care may receive treatment not only from doctors but also from other caregivers such as nurses, pharmacists, physiotherapists, social health workers, and many others. The organisation and regulations on these professions are found in their various legislation and rules of professional ethics regulating them.[25] Our discussion however will focus primarily on the institutional framework for doctors, because the doctor's position is more pointed to the context of this book, and its basis principles can analogically apply in a wide context to the other professions.[26]

The Medical and Dental Practitioners Act (MDPA) 1988, do not use the phase 'doctor', rather it uses the phase 'medical practitioner' and 'dental surgeon' to describe its registered members. Accordingly our discussions here would treat both under the generic description of doctor, because of its wide conventional usage. Section 8 provides that a person shall be entitled to be fully registered as a doctor if (a) if he possesses a qualification approved by the Medical & Dental Council and (b) if he holds a certificate of experience issued pursuant to s.11 of the Act. Such a certificate is usually issued the doctor after the compulsory housemanship of one year or such other time as may be specified. The Council will only recognise a qualification issued by an institution whose course of training is designed for persons seeking to become doctors if the institution is properly organized and equipped for the training.[27] In pursuance of its statutory function of determining the standard of medical knowledge and skill,[28] the Council may permit provisional registration of medical graduates to practice as doctor on what is often referred to as housemen on compulsory apprenticeship in a recognized medical centre.[29] With the recent enactment of the National Health Insurance Scheme (NHIS) Act, a doctor may be engaged in the practice either as a general practitioner or hospital doctor within the NHIS scheme or outside the scheme as a private practitioner.[30]

National Health Insurance Scheme (NHIS)

A doctor within the scheme is one who provides services within the framework of publicly funded medical care. Under the scheme, a doctor may practice as a general practitioner or hospital doctor. The scheme recently introduced in Nigeria is a social

---

[25] See for example, Nursing and Midwifery (Registration) Act, 1779, Cap N143, LFN 22004, which establishes the Nursing and Midwifery Council of Nigeria for the registration,discipline of members. See also Pharmacists Council of Nigeria Act, 1992, Cap P17, LFN, 2004.

[26] Note that in Nigeria the medical and dental professions are regulated under a common umbrella, see Medical and Dental Practitioners (MDP) Act, 1988, Cap, LFN 2004; see also *Code of Medical Ethics in Nigeria for Medical and Dental Practitioners*, revised edition of January 2004, published by Medical & Dental Council of Nigeria.

[27] s.9 Medical and Dental Practitioners (MDP) Act, 1988, Cap, LFN 2004.

[28] s.1 (2) (a) Medical and Dental Practitioners (MDP) Act, 1988, Cap, LFN 2004.

[29] s.12 Medical and Dental Practitioners (MDP) Act, 1988, Cap, LFN 2004.

[30] See National Health Insuranc Scheme (NHIS) Act, 1999.

health programme designed by government to complement sources of health financing and to improve access to health care for the majority of Nigerians. The preamble to the Act states that its objective is to ensure access to good health care services to every citizen and to offer protection to families from financial hardship of huge medical bills.[31]

By s.1 a beneficiary under the scheme described, as an insured person is entitled with his dependants to the benefit under the scheme-good quality and cost effective health care services. A registered beneficiary under the scheme is expected to enjoy easy access to a wide range of health care that includes diagnostic test, family planning, hospital care, dental care, even prescribed drugs and many more. Section 18 provides that the services to be enjoyed are defined curative care; prescribed drugs and diagnostic tests; maternity care for up to four live births; preventive care, including immunisation, family planning, ante-natal and post-natal care; consultation with defined range of specialists; hospital care in a public or private hospital in a standard ward during a stated period for physical and mental disorders; eye examination and care, excluding tests and the provision of spectacles; and a range of prosthesis and dental care as defined. By subsection 3, the term 'defined curative care' is construed to mean as defined by the Council, i.e. the Governing Council of the NHIS. What that means is that the type of curative care a beneficiary can receive may well be restrictive or expansive depending on what range the Council decides. A similar caveat is placed on consultation with specialists and care related to prosthesis and dental care. Even where the care required is maternal in nature, the beneficiary can only enjoy it to a maximum of four children. Hospitalisation in a public or private hospital during physical or mental illness is similarly restrictive. It is not made to depend on cure. It depends on a stated period of time, presumable to be determined by the Council. These restrictions are to some extent at variance with the proclaimed objectives of the scheme set forth in the preamble and s.5.

The Act establishes a scheme known as the National Health Insurance Scheme [NHIS] for the purpose of providing health insurance which will entitle insured persons and their dependants [loosely referred to as beneficiaries] to good quality and cost effective care.[32] By virtue of section 16 an employer with a minimum of ten employees may enter into the Scheme by paying contributions deducted from its employees' wages. Once that is done, all persons from whom deductions are taken from together with their registered dependants become beneficiaries. Deductions so made by the employer are to be remitted to a designated Health Management

---

[31] See also s.5 which repeats a similar objective but goes further to include the following: as policy objective, to limit the rising cost of health care services; ensure equitable distribution of health care cost; improve and harness private participation in health care services, etc.

[32] S.1 of NHIS. Note the scheme is made a body corporate by s.1 (2) (a). Responsibility for the management of the scheme is entrusted to its Governing Council [s.2]. The functions of the Scheme are set out in s.6. They include registration of health maintenance organisations[HMO] and health care providers [HCP]; sustaining the Scheme by appropriate regulation as the proper regulatory body charged with the management of it etc.

Organisation (HMO) in such manner directed by the Council[33] The Act also allows a person not liable to make contribution, (presumable because his employer chooses not to register under s.16 or is not within traditional employment structure) to apply for registration as a voluntary contributor under the Scheme [34] It is in consideration of these contributions (capitation payment in respect of the contributor or such approved fees stated by the Council) that the Health Care Provider (HCP) comes under obligation to provide the care of the beneficiary.[35]

The structure of the Scheme shows that the Council approves and registers HMOs under the Scheme who shall function as private or public health maintenance insurance organisations if they satisfy registration requirements of the Council.[36] Upon registration they shall function to collect contribution from the contributors; make capitation payment to the HCP, and render returns of its activities to the Scheme. [37] The HMO is only authorised to contract a registered HCP for the purpose of rendering health care services under the Act. It is also responsible for ensuring that contributions received are properly kept as stipulated by the Council. It is further expected to establish a quality assurance system to ensure qualitative health care is given to contributors by HCPs in carrying out its functions under the Scheme. The Scheme provides a list of accredited health care providers/hospitals, (HCPs) from which a beneficiary can choose to register with. In the event of sickness the beneficiary will receive treatment at his HCP facility by presenting his identity card. HMOs act as financiers of the scheme. Essentially they are insurance companies set up to facilitate the provision of medical services to contributors/beneficiaries.

On the other hand, a HCP may be a licensed government or private hospital or health care giver. A doctor who wishes to be on the scheme's list may apply for listing with it. Once listed, the relationship between the General Practitioner (GP) and the Scheme may takes on one or all of the following characteristics – (a) contractual- creates a contractual relationship between the GP and the Council for the provision of medical services. It has been suggested that is the proper relationship created under the arrangement because the GP, from the nature of services he renders can hardly be construed an employee of the Scheme, (b) the relationship may also takes on a statutory flavour within the realm of public law. What that mean in effect is that duties and rights of the parties get construed in the context of the NHIS Act (c) the relationship may take on a hybrid character, not wholly contractual or statutory, but something in between both.

In *Roy* v. *Kensington & Chelsea Family Practitioner Committee*[38] the court in England was faced with the issue of defining the boundaries of medical services

[33] s.17 (1) NHIS Act, 1999.
[34] s.17 (3) NHIS Act, 1999.
[35] see s.18 NHIS Act, 1999 for a detail of the health care services
[36] s.19 NHIS Act, 1999.
[37] s.20 NHIS Act, 1999.
[38] [1990] 1 Med LR 328, on appeal to House of Lords [1992] 1 AC 624

provided under the English National Health Service Act 1977. The Dr Roy brought an action in debt against the defendant Family Practitioners Committee for work done. He based the debt claim on a breach of contract. The Committee reduced his practice allowance by 20 per cent on the ground that he was devoting less than satisfactory time to his practice as a GP engaged under the NHS. It was not disputed that he had been absent from his practice by reason of family, sickness and holiday, but it was conceded that there was no complain from patients against him about the time devoted to his practice in the context of adequate care to them. They received treatment from the locum employed by him as his practice manager. Roy contended that his relationship with the Committee is contractual, to provide general medical services to NHS patients and that by employing a locum in his absence he had perfected the obligation. Meanwhile the Committee had reduced his practice allowance by 20 per cent, and so he contended that the reduction was a breach of contract. He accordingly claimed a refund of the money deducted. The sought to have the claim struck out as an abuse of process on the basis that that the relationship between the parties was a matter only of public law. White, J stated that though there were contractual echoes in the relationship between the doctor and the committee those were deceptive, and that the claim is an abuse of process. It was accordingly struck out.[39] The rights and duties of the parties were dependent on statute and the duty which the committee discharged was a public law function. That being so, the court would not substitute its judgment for that of the committee. The plaintiff can only vindicate his claim for deduction by way of an action for judicial review.

The English Court of Appeal held the lower court wrong, stating that the relationship between the parties was contractual. According to Balcombe LJ, (Nourse and Neill LJJ agreeing) the application by the GP to the Committee, as the NHS employer in the locality and its acceptance by it, constitute a contract.

Curiously, in reaching the decision the Court of Appeal did not refer to an earlier judgment of the Employment Appeal Tribunal in *Wadi* v. *Cornwall & Isles of Selly FPC*[40] to the effect that, the relationship is one of contract. Accordingly the House of Lords in the *Roy* appeal sought to resolve the conflict.[41] The Law Lords stated that the relationship is governed by statute and that it is erroneous to import into it contract principles. Roy was said to acquire a bundle of rights under the statute, which he could vindicate against the Committee for payment. Of interest Lord Lowry said that the Committee has no right to withhold payment to the GP under the scheme from the Secretary of State who administers it. In his Lordship's view, it is a mere conduit pipe for the payment. The House of Lords therefore

---

[39] See [1989] 1 Med L.R. 19.

[40] [1985] ICR 492.

[41] See [1992] 1 AC 624, [1992] 1 All ER 705. Note under the English NHS the Committee merely administers on behalf of the district health authority the scheme on its behalf. This may be likened to the functions of HMO's under s.20 (g) and the Zonal Health Insurance Offices (ZHIO) under s.22 (e) established by the Council under the NHIS Act 1999 in Nigeria.

refused to strike out the claim even though according to Lord Bridge, the relationship was probably not contractual. 'Nevertheless, the terms which govern the obligation of the doctor on the one hand, as to the services he is to provide, and of the family practitioner committee on the other hand, as to the payment which it is required to make to the doctor, are all prescribed in the relevant legislation and it seem to me that the statutory terms are just as effective as they would be if they were contractual to confer upon the doctor an enforceable right in private law to receive the remuneration to which the terms entitle him'.[42] According to Lord Lowry, the court had jurisdiction to entertain the doctor's action because it was concerned with a private right. It was one for an ascertainable sum of money and the existence of any dispute as to entitlement meant that the doctor was alleging a breach of his private law rights through a failure by the committee to perform their public duty.[43]

This raises certain conceptual and procedural issues. If the relationship is statutory, it should follow that a GP who disputes any aspect of the relationship will either have (a) a specific statutory remedy, say an appeal to the Secretary of State against a particular matter or (b) enjoy the right of judicial review of administrative action. It is suggested that a curious analysis of the Nigerian statute on health insurance show no significant departure from the English, and so *Roy* may well summarise the legal position between the GP and Scheme. Section 26 makes explicit that a statutory arbitration board shall be established under the scheme for the purpose of considering complaint by any aggrieved person on any matter relating to violation of any of the provisions of the Act; against any agent of the scheme or HCP An ordinary reading of the provision, gives the impression that it only covers as it were, complains by contributors. This should be so considering the persons against who complaints can be sought against – agents of the Scheme or HCP. But it is suggested that the arbitration jurisdiction is more expansive. The power as conferred by section 26(2)(b) extends to all cases relating to a violation of any of the provisions of the Act.[44]

The Act, unlike the English model does not contain provision that the GP shall give treatment personally. Under the English model, the GP is required to give personal care to the patient even though he could use a deputy to provide general medical services so long as he ensures that steps are taken by him to continue the patient's treatment. Before employing a deputy to provide the services, the GP shall take reasonable steps to satisfy himself that the person is competent to discharge the duties for which he is employed. That notwithstanding the GP will be held vicariously liable for all acts and omissions of his deputy or any one acting for the

---

[42] [1992] 1 AC 624 at 630.

[43] Ibid., at 654.

[44] This certainly should cover complains within the bracket of Dr. Roy aforesaid. As an omnibus provision it covers complain either way, from and against all relevant parties under the Scheme, beneficiaries, the Scheme and its operatives such as its Council, ZHIO, etc., HMOs and HCPs, as far as it relates to a violation of the Act.

deputy. The English Act provides that the GP shall only employ a deputy after obtaining the consent of the necessary NHS authority. However where the deputy is also on the NHIS list, he alone would be personally liable for his acts and omissions. The GP is required to make known to his patients such times and places when he would be available. He is also required to keep a record of the patient's illness and treatment. He is prohibited from charging the patient a fee, save in exceptional situations where the Act or regulation made thereunder permits charging, e.g., where he makes an examination at a place other than the usual hospital, such as, at the police station. Even though the Nigerian NHIS Act do not explicitly contain these stipulations, it is reasoned that regulations when made by the Council, in pursuance of the objectives of the Act, would incorporate these acceptable features of the English practice.[45] Under the English model, in addition to being on the list, the GP may also apply to be placed on the list of specialists. Generally, a GP may withdraw his services by giving a 3 months notice to the Scheme. A doctor's name would be removed from the list if he dies, ceases to be a registered medical practitioner or is removed by the NHIS for professional incompetence and the like e.g. breach of the terms of his NHIS employment.[46]

Hospital Doctor

The hospital doctor working in an NHIS hospital is not subject to the statutory framework that govern the GP service under the Scheme. His legal relationship remains that of an employee with the NHIS service provider, the HCP, and is governed by general contract of employment between him and his employer.[47]

Whether contract or tort principles or both govern the NHIS service rendered to a patient by the GP or hospital doctor is the subject of some controversy. Some scholars are of the view that following the House of Lords decision in *Pfizer Corporation* v. *Ministry of Health*[48] - which decided that if services are provided pursuant to statutory obligation, the implication of contract would be inconsistent with a statutory regime - gives the impression that NHIS services should be defined only in the bracket of its statutory framework. Flowing from it, the doctor—patient relationship is to be governed exclusively by the NHIS Act and any other relevant statute and regulations make under the powers conferred by the Act.[49] It however

[45] See s.6 (j) of the NHIS Act, empowers the Scheme to do such things as are necessary for the purpose of achieving the objectives of the NHIS Act.

[46] See Roy's case [1992] 1AC 624.

[47] For discussion on the statutory intervention in matters of general contract of employment of doctors in England see, M Siddall, Not As Well As Can be Expected (1992) 142 *New LJ* 763; B Raymond, Employment Rights of the NHS Hospital Doctor in C Dyer(ed.) *Doctor, Patients and the Law* (1992) both cited in Kennedy & Grubb, above n. 24 at 45 and on the nature of the changed NHS medical services provided in England, see D Hughes, The Reorganisation of NHS; The Rhetoric and Reality of the Internal Market (1991) *54 MLR* 88.

[48] [1965] AC 512.

[49] A.P. Bell, The Doctor and the Supply of Goods and Services Act 1982 (1984) 4 *LS* 175, see also Lord Pearson Committee Report[*The Royal Commission on Civil Liability and Compensation for Personal Injury*, 1978 Report, Cmnd 7054.

must be admitted that, such a position does not put an NHIS patient in a less favourable position to a private patient, because the same legal and factual considerations determine when a breach of duty in contract or in tort or both is raised under the NHIS and common law rules.[50]

The other contrary position is that the relationship can be both contractual and statutory contemporaneously. This is attractive for two main reasons; (i) the existence of a statutory duty is not necessarily inconsistent with a contract to provide services.[51] It is plausible to envisage situations where a doctor's statutory duty to provide medical services can be performed within a framework of contract for valuable consideration while rendering services within statutory context. (ii) it is also conceivable for consideration to move from the patient to doctor on the basis that the doctor would apply for listing with NHIS.

In the provision of services the English Act incorporates several standards of treatment to reflect the particular circumstance of individual patient. For example, different treatment regimes are prescribed for first time patients, the aged, children and those that have not regularly visited their doctors for a long time. Provisions on standard treatment for these exceptional patients are regulated under the Act. Take as example a first-time patient: the doctor is in addition to rendering usual medical services requested, under obligation within a time frame specified, to invite the patient for consultation. During consultation, the doctor is required to undertake physical examination, make a medical record of the patient's history and access what manner and extent personal medical services would be required. Regulations along similar lines by the Council under the NHIS Act in Nigeria would be recommended.

The general tenor of the Act

A doctor who renders services creates a doctor-patient relationship once there is a factual request by the patient and a corresponding undertaking by him to treat. But in certain exceptional cases, the relationship may come into being without a request. That notwithstanding, in all cases the relationship will only arise when there is an undertaking by the doctor. A no-request accompanied with an undertaking would usually arise in emergency situations or where the patient is unconscious. This may also arise where a doctor is employed by a third party to treat or examine the patient e.g. an occupational doctor who examines an employee. It is expected that regulations when made by the Council in Nigeria under the Act, would generally regulate the circumstances of request, undertaking and termination of the relationship under the NHIS Scheme. Whatever, regulated standard of care should ordinarily follow the traditional *Bolam* principle.[52]

Where a doctor is employed by a third party to treat a patient, in which case there is no request by the patient, the duty of care remains intact, as though the

---

[50] See Pearson Report, above, n. 22.

[51] See *Roy* case [1992] 1AC 624.

[52] See *Bolam* v. *Friern Hospital Management Committee* [1957] 2 All ER 118, [1957] 1 WLR 582; see also *Tharke* v. *Maurice* [1986] 1 All ER 497 and Lord Nathan, *Medical Negligence* (1957).

relationship were created by request. However in the context of no-request the question that could become controversial is whether the doctor is under a duty to make disclosure to the third party who employs him. The ambit of the duty to disclose and the extent is generally circumscribed by the doctor's duty of confidentiality. In *Green* v. *Walker*[53] confidentiality and breach of duty of care were the issues. G was the employee of an offshore company. As a condition of his employment he had to undergo medical examination as to fitness. Dr W, who examined him issued a report to his employer stated that he was fit and employable without restriction. Things however turned out badly. One year after the report, G was diagnosed with lung cancer. G for himself, and his daughter, sued W claiming damages for negligence on the grounds that, if he had carried a proper diagnosis he should have discovered the early stages of cancer, which could have helped him take early preventive actions. The doctor's failure in this respect was said to reduce his chances of survival and life expectancy. While the suit was pending G died. W then moved for summary judgment, on the grounds that no relationship exists between him and G, because G's employer was the person who employed him. The issue before the court centred on whether W had a duty to G, in the character which required him to perform the examination with standard medical care and skill and further, to report his findings to G, even if it constitute a threat to his health. The court held that the examination by the doctor was sufficient to create a doctor-patient relationship. Accordingly, the doctor was expected to exercise the care and skill expected of a professional doctor of his calling. He was also under a duty to make disclosure to the examinee, G, of any finding which raise danger to his health.

Though the issue has not specifically being decided by the English courts, it is suggested that the English courts would follow the ratio in *Green* v. *Walker*.[54] The Nigerian position should be no different. That notwithstanding, whether failure to disclosure to the examinee would amount to a breach of duty depends on the nature of the doctor's undertaking. Where for example, a doctor undertakes examination in circumstances where he covenants to make disclosure only to the third party who engages his services, say in pursuance to insurance, there ought to be no obligation to disclose to the examinee. But it can be argued that such an undertaking is fundamentally inconsistent with the doctor-patient relationship, laced in trust and confidence.[55] Arguing from that perspective, it would be strong to state that all such undertakings are void for attempting to remove the very essence of medical treatment and examination. This argument is attractive especially when considered in the context that request by a patient is not a prerequisite to raise the doctor-patient relationship. All that is required is the undertaking of some sort to provide medical services.

The English Unfair Contract Terms Act, 1977 fortifies the argument. Section 2 of the Act, expressly stipulates that a person cannot by reference to any contract

[53] (1990) 910 F 2d 291 [5th Circ.CA].
[54] (1990) 910 F 2d 291 [5th Circ.CA].
[55] see Kennedy & Grubb, above n. 24 at75, see also *Thomsen* v. *Davidson* [1975] Qd R 91 at 97.

exclude his liability for death or personal injury resulting from his negligence. If restriction of the doctor's undertaking would not shield him for personal injury and death arising from negligence, it necessarily should follows that a violation of the disclosure duty to the examinee cannot be excluded by contract with say, an employer in an occupational treatment. From that perspective, it is suggested that a doctor who discloses information to the patient may be adopting a safe course. However, it can be argued that the absence of legislation similar to the English Unfair Contract Terms Act in Nigerian is warrant for excluding the argument of a duty to disclose. If this position is accepted, a Nigerian doctor would have no obligation to make disclosure if he has expressly agreed to restrict the information to the third party.[56] However, a strong case for disclosure relying on arguments along the lines of *Green* case and the English Unfair Contract Terms Act, 1977, as discussed above, may dictate disclosure as safe practice for the Nigerian doctor.

Noteworthy of mention also is the fact that the doctor-patient relationship may also be raised even where the patient is incompetent, as where he is unconscious or mentally retarded.[57]

Medical malpractice procedure

Our discussion here will be concerned with means other than court litigation for handling cases of medical malpractice. What is focused on therefore is the professional procedure for accountability of the doctor under the professional rules of the Medical and Dental Council [the Council]. Generally there are two ways of ensuring accountability outside recourse to courts for the medical malpractice. They are (a) the professional self-regulation method and (b) public procedure for holding doctor's accountable. The Medical and Dental Practitioners [MDP] Act, 1988,establishes the Council as the body responsible for; determining and reviewing the standards of knowledge and skill for persons seeking to become members of the profession. Accordingly it is empowered to establish and maintain a register of members; review and prepare from time to time a statement of code of conduct considered desirable for the practice of the profession and any other functions conferred on it[58] In pursuance of these powers the Council have made several regulations on professional conduct[59]

The 2004 Rules was informed by the experience of the Council in the course of Preliminary Investigation [PI] by its Medical and Dental Practitioners Disciplinary Tribunal [Tribunal] and judgments of the Nigerian Court of Appeal and Supreme Court on matters of professional discipline of members. Interestingly, this new Rule

---

[56] But cf. *Smith* v. *Eric*[1989] 2 All ER 514.

[57] See *Re F: mental sterilisation* [1989] 2 All ER 545, (the court held that the relationship may arise without request by the patient. and that it could involve services rendered during emergencies. See also Nield J in *Barnett* v. *Chelsea & Kensington HMC*[1968]1 All ER 1068.

[58] See s. 1 (2) Medical and Dental Practitioners Act (MDPA) 1988.

[59] For example Medical and Dental Practitioners (Disciplinary Tribunal and Assessors) Rule 1966. See also Code of Medical Ethics in Nigeria (Rules of Professional Conduct) issued 1st January 1990, revised 1st January 2004.

has been styled Code, to reflect its intended legal status; that of making it more solemn and respectable in consonance with the intention to give the document the right legal status. The Code is intended to enhance the practice of the profession within the framework of conscience, dignity and its Codal provisions.[60]

The accountability of doctor's to the public is discharged primarily through the procedure for handling complaint from the public against medical doctors. In pursuance of the MDP Act, the Tribunal is established, charged with the responsibility of considering and determining any case referred to it by the Investigating Panel [IP]. The IP is charged with the duty of (a) conducting preliminary investigations into cases where it is alleged that a member in his capacity as doctor, misbehaves or for any other reason is subject to proceedings of the Panel. In carrying out this function it is vested with powers to compel persons by subpoena.[61] Complains are carefully investigated in the vast majority of cases. It may not always result in a reference to the Tribunal via the President of the Council. It may end with a letter of advice or admonition to the doctor concerned. If in the course of its investigations it adjudges that a doctor's conduct is prima facie infamous, it shall prepare appropriate charges and forward it to the Secretary of the Council.[62] The report is what forms the basis on which the President of the Council will use to set up the Tribunal.[63] The Tribunal operates like a court. If it finds the doctor guilty, it may make any of the following orders: (a) that the name of the doctor be removed from the register of members, or (b) suspend the doctor from the practice of medicine, or (c) admonish the doctor.[64] In addition to the Council procedures above, some well-run hospitals have ethics committees that internally handle patients' complaints within their facilities.[65]

The Medical and Dental Council

Our discussion in this section would be concerned with an analysis of the Medical and Dental Practitioners Act, 1988, (the Act), the Medical and Dental Practitioners (Disciplinary Tribunal and Assessors) Rules, 1966 (the Rules) and Code of Medical Ethics, 2004.The centrality of the Council is emphasised by the very first provision of the Act. Section 1 provides for the establishment of the Council with the enormous powers and duties of general superintend of the profession in Nigeria. It is charged with the responsibility of (a) determining the standard of knowledge and skill for persons seeking to become doctors and to review same from time to time (b) ensuring the establishment of and maintenance of register of members and the

---

[60] See Introduction to Code of Medical Ethics in Nigeria (Rules of Professional Conduct) issued lst January 1990, revised lst January 2004 at 3.

[61] S. 15 MDPA 1988.

[62] S. 3 of Disciplinary Rule.

[63] S. 5 of Disciplanary Rule.

[64] S. 16 (2) of the Act. For detail reading, see C. Ham, *et al.* (eds.) *Medical Negligence and Accountability* (1988); E.S. Akpata, *Medical Ethics*, Lagos: Lagos Univ. Press, 1982.

[65] R.E. Klien, *Complaint Against Doctors* (1973); A. Grubb (ed.), *Challenges to Medical Care* (1992).

publication of members list from time to time (c) reviewing and preparing from time to time a statement code of conduct and (d) any other functions conferred on it by the Act. Its composition reflects both streams of the profession, medical and dental practitioners.

As part of its statutory functions, it is empowered to appoint a Registrar, who shall prepare and maintain on behalf of the Council, the names, addresses and qualification of members. In the exercise of this function he is required to divide the register into three parts, namely; (a) fully registered members (b) provisionally registered members (c) persons granted limited registration under section 13.[66] Section 13 provides that the Council may grant limited registration to any person who is employed in an approved hospital or institution in Nigeria in the capacity of a doctor if he intends to be in the country for a limited period in the employment in question. Council may also grant such limited registration if a person has passed the assessment examination, of the Council, following some qualification obtained outside Nigeria that is acceptable to the Council. A curious reading of the word "and' between subsection (a) and (b) would seem to give the impression that the general tenor of section 13 applies to doctors who are trained outside the country, who subsequently take up employment in Nigeria. The mere fact of a foreign doctor's employment in an approved hospital is not sufficient. The Council must further be satisfied that he possesses a request medical qualification for purpose of medical practice. In addition the applicant for limited registration may be required to pass any assessment examination by the Council required of him. Whether such examination is required is at the discretion of the Council. Subsection (2) specifically states that limited registration shall terminate at the time permitted by Council or such time as the doctor's employment ceases. As to whether the employment of such a doctor when terminated by his employer should automatically be the basis of the withdrawal of his limited registration is a matter solely to be determined by the Council. Its decision is made conclusive by subsection (6). A limited registered doctor is not permitted to open or manage on his own a private hospital. What this mean is that although he can manage a public hospital, if that constitute part of his terms of employment, he cannot on his own establish and operate a private clinic of his own.[67] He is however liable for all his acts and omissions under his employment as a doctor, even though the Act states that he would not be accorded the status of a fully registered doctor in all other matters under it. Accordingly he cannot enjoy for example the privilege of being a Council member. The duty of the Registrar includes making necessary alteration to the register, removing the name of a registered member who have died, or becomes insane.

A person who holds a qualification approved by the Council and has a certificate of experience issued in pursuance of section 11 shall be eligible for full

[66] S. 6 MDPA 1988.

[67] S. 13 (5) MDPA) 1988.

registration[68] As a general rule, the Council recognises a university degree in medicine or dentistry from a recognised institution.[69] Section 11 makes it mandatory for the doctor to obtain a certificate of competence from a recognised institution. The mandatory training leading to the certificate is usually referred to as *housemanship.* The time period is usually one year, although it may be longer or shorter than one year, because the Council may by regulation specify the length. Prior to full registration, a person who has obtained a recognised medical or dental certificate from a university may be granted provisional registration pending the mandatory training on competence under section 11.

Section 17 makes it an offence for any person who is not a doctor to hold himself out as one. Under section 19, the Council is vested with the power to make regulations, rules, or such orders incidental and supplementary to the Act. In pursuance, of this power, the Council made the Rules.[70]

The first Schedule to the Act is a supplementary provision relating to the Council. It makes provision for matters such as qualification and tenure of members, and proceedings of the Council .The second Schedule is supplementary provision relating to the Disciplinary Tribunal and Investigating Panel. The Attorney General under the schedule is responsible for making rules as to the selection of members of the Tribunal and procedure to be followed in receiving evidence. For purposes of advising the Tribunal on question of law, the Council shall on the nomination of the Chief Justice of Nigeria appoint an assessor to the Tribunal.

The Rules govern the procedure for trial.[71] The Tribunal has similar powers as a court of law. Its proceedings shall be in public. It has power to adjoin cases, order payment of costs, pronounce on guilt, refer to the Attorney General for necessary action any person who makes false statement before it and extend time to do anything under the Rule.

The Code as previously stated replaces the 1980 Rule on ethics. Unlike the previous 48 sections of the old Rule the Code has 70 sections. It is divided into 8 parts. Part A deals with preliminary matters. It contains the preamble and general matters. Part B deals with professional conduct. Part C discusses question of malpractice. Next is a section on improper relationship with colleagues and patients. It is followed by a part dealing on aspects of private practice. Part F deals with self-advertisement and related offences. The G part deals with conviction for criminal offences. The final part is styled miscellaneous.

Part A

This part begins with the usual preamble tradition. It set out the objective of the Code: namely to preserve the primacy of the profession and its acclaimed esteem.

---

[68] S. 8 MDPA) 1988.

[69] S. 9 MDPA) 1988.

[70] The Rule is made pursuant to the Council's power under the repealed MDPA 1963. The Rules continue to apply despite the repeal of the 1963 Act to all matters of discipline and assessment but with necessary modification in the context of the 1988 Act and the 2004 Code of Ethics.

[71] Rule 3-6 provide for reference of prima facia case to the Tribunal.

Immediately following the preamble is rule 2 on induction of new members. It is an innovation not contained in the old rule. It fills a lacuna under the 1988 Rule. By this stipulation, the Registrar of the Council is enjoined to administer on new members at an induction ceremony the Physician Oath. The solemn occasion can in a far-reaching manner leave a lasting ethical impression on new members that can greatly improve standards. Rules 3 and 4 specifically demand from member's allegiance to the profession and respect for colleagues. As supplementing and amplifying the three classes of registered members under section 6 (3) of the Act, it includes as a fourth category the registration of specialists[72] Section 6 (b) prohibits a member from practicing for any year if he defaults to pay practice fees. This is a superfluous stipulation because s.14 of the Act already so stipulates. Rule 7 is an improvement on the 1988 Rule in that it provides a comprehensive guideline for non-indigenous doctors. It recognises the value of exchange programme doctors. In recognition of their value, rule 7 (d) states that should an exchange programme doctor wish to remain to practice after the expiration of his programme, the Council will assess him further for retention as a limited registered member or request him to sit for a proficiency examination.

Rule 8 is in *pari materia* with rule 5 of the 1988 Rule. It incorporates by reference the Venice Declaration of 1983 of the International Code of Medical Ethics. Rule 9 restates general ethical principles, such as that which requires the doctor to promote the health of his patient, uphold the dignity of the profession etc [73] Rule.10 is in *pari materia* with rule, 7 of the old Rule. It list the rights and responsibility of members.[74] It states that only persons who have undergone the course of training designed to make them doctors in an approved institution by the Council can be licensed to practice. As an improvement on the old Rule (the 1988 Rule does not make a specific provision on this matter) section 11 deals with clinical etiquette. It states for example that treatment procedures should respect the appropriate privacy of the patient and be empathetic. The doctor must avoid smoking in the clinic and ought to guard against acts or omissions that could provoke allegations of impropriety. Rule 12 is a classification of hospital. Noteworthy of mention, it discourages the establishment of hospitals as strict business enterprises or as limited liability companies under relevant laws. The rationale for this must be the fact that the ethics of the profession requires an injection of qualities such as empathy, maintenance of honour, fidelity, trust and the likes, which may be difficult to incorporate into the main purpose of the agency philosophy of maximising owner value in business. Where a member is connected with a company that provides medical services, he is enjoined to ensure that the organisation complies with the provisions of the Code on ethics. Because this may prove difficult for him, the section advises that its members should consider the inherent dangers of associating

---

[72] But cf. S. 6 MDPA 1988, which stipulates three categories of practitioners in the order of fully registered members, provisionally registered membera and, limited registered members.

[73] A similar stipulation is found inRule 6 of the 1988 Rule.

[74] Rule 7 of the old Rules of make a similar stipulation.

with such business enterprises. The section further contains a description of hospital facilities, defines a clinic, primary health care, medical centre, general, specialist and teaching hospital.

Rule 13 prohibits the practice of specialty without registration of specialist qualification with the Council. Rule 14 advises against the practice of self-medication save for minor ailment. Accordingly, rule 15 advises a colleague who gives treatment to another not to expect the usual fee charged ordinary patients. Rule 16 — 18 deals with matters connected with good team spirit among doctors.

One of the finest innovations of the Code is the provision on informed consent. This is contained in rule 19. Its inclusion is informed by recent judgments of the courts, especially *Okonkwo* v. *Medical and Dental Practitioners Disciplinary Tribunal*[75] in which the Supreme Court explicitly recognised the patient right of self determination and autonomy [76] The section contains an approved proforma consent form suggested for use in the treatment of patients. Interestingly it states that the majority age for consent purposes is 18.[77] Rule 20 carries further the frontiers of informed consent into the area of termination of medical services at the request of the patient or his relative. The patient right to terminate treatment even against good medical advise is preserved without prejudice if he returns for help to the same doctor.

Rule 21 — 24 deal with matters connected with modern biomedicine. Section 21 enjoins members to familiarise themselves with new frontiers in medical advancement.[78] It advises caution in research areas as cloning, genetic engineering, etc by doctors. In an era of information technology, members are advised to make appropriate arrangements for their patient's privacy and the protection of their personal information by rule 22. Rules 23 and 24 also advise necessary caution in the area of assisted reproduction and HIV/AIDS treatment and research.

Part B

This part broadly regulates professional conduct especially in relation to allegation of infamous conduct in a professional respect. Specifically, rule 26 states that a failure to adhere to rules 1- 25 will amount to infamous conduct. Rule 27 requires all members to cooperate with the disciplinary organs of the profession. Rule 28 incorporates a duty of care on the part of the doctor to his patient. It lists what shall amount to professional negligence. Recurrent negligence is viewed with severity.

---

[75] (1999) 6 NWLR (pt. 786) 1. The preamble of the 2004 Code of Ethics proclaims that the Code was enancted to bring medical practice more in line with recent court decisions.

[76] See chapter on informed consent

[77] It is arguble whether this stipulation of age alters the general majority age of 21. While general majority age remains 21, for specific matters like informed consent to medical treatment, the court should ordinarilly accept 18 provided in the Code of Ethics. Unfortunately, the Code does not mention the mature minor rule in *Gillick* v. *West Norfolk and Wisbech Area Health Authority* [1985] 3 All ER 402. This notwithstanding, there is good reason to think the mature minor principle in *Gillick* would be applied in Nigeria. For detail discussion see *infra*.

[78] *Crawford* v. *Charing Cross Hospital* [1953] TLR 1, per Lord Denning.

Accordingly, a member who appears more than once before the Disciplinary Tribunal and is found guilty would not be given the option of merely being admonished. Rule 29 states that such a member shall be suspended for not less than 6 months. Where however he is habitually negligence the practitioner's name shall be struck out of the list of members. Rule 31 incorporates the Helsinki 1994 Declaration on bio-medical research.[79] But beside this, it contains a proposal for national drug approval process. It is a codification of ethically permissible limits to pre-clinical testing, new drug application, and the likes.

Part C

This part categorises the following as malpractice, namely; issuance of false medical certificate, deceit to patient with of view of extorting fees, aiding a non-doctor to practice medicine or dentistry, advertising and acting as commission agent to health workers like chemist, nurse etc, and allowing a member to be influenced by considerations of religion, race, politics, nationality or social standing in the treatment of a patient.

Part D

This part deals with what are considered improper relationship with colleagues and patients. Rule 40 prohibits what can broadly be considered maintenance in law. A doctor must not instigate a patient to institute lawsuits against colleagues. A doctor is by rules 41 and 42 enjoined to refer a patient to a better skilled or better-equipped facility if a patient's ailment is beyond his skill or facility.[80] Rule 48 treats as a serious offence, adultery and other improper association with a patient. Sanction for breach is made to attract the removal of the member's name from the register. In this connection any finding of fact made in proceedings in the High Court or an appeal from a decision in such proceedings shall be conclusive evidence before the Disciplinary Tribunal of the allegations against a doctor. For example, if in a divorce suit before the High court, a doctor is a cited party and adultery is proved against him in connection with treatment of a patient, that will constitute conclusive evidence of improper and indecent behaviour to person of the opposite sex under the Code for purposes of trial before the Tribunal.

Part E

This part is concerned with particular aspects of private practice. By rules 49 and 50 only consultant and general practitioners of above 10 years practice engaged in full time employment in the public service can own or run private practice during their spare time.

Part F

This part in the main proscribes self-advertisement and touting.

[79] See Appendix F.

[80] *Okonkwo* v. *MDPDT* (1999) 9 NWLR (pt 617) 1, (1999) 6 NWLR (pt. 786) 1.

Part G

Under this part conviction by a court of competent jurisdiction, which in the opinion of the Disciplinary Tribunal incompatible with the status of a doctor may be sufficient ground for striking a member's name from the register. Rule 60 states that unlawful abortion shall constitute a grave offence. Any doctor who aids criminals in his practice either by commission or omission will be guilty of an infamous conduct.

Part H

Under this part doctors are advised to avoid alcohol and drug offences and improper financial transactions and purchase of patronage.[81] Rule 67 absolutely prohibits torture, whether by physical, psychological or chemical means. By this prohibition it would be unethical for a doctor to cause restrain of a suspected drug trafficker with a view to force his urine or excrement. It invariably follows that a doctor who allows himself to be used in executing a sentence of court that amounts to torture may be exposing himself to breach of the Code, e.g. in the cutting of say, the hand or limb of a criminal pursuance to court order, as in the case of Babagingabi in the Zamfara State.[82] Rule 68 prohibits doctor-assisted suicide or euthanasia. Rule 69 is an expression of the conditions which in the opinion of the Council may render it unsafe to practice the profession. These include senile dementia, drug addiction etc. Section 70 is the last rule. It provides for the enforcement of sanction of the Council. If the Tribunal finds a member guilty, the sentence would be published in a gazette of the Federal Republic of Nigeria and four national newspapers. Notification of publication is to be deposited with the permanent secretaries of the federal and all states ministries of health and the National President of the Nigerian Medical Association or Nigerian Dental Association, depending on whether the erring member is a medical or dental practitioner. Where the member is merely suspended, the Registrar shall in addition to the publication requirement, direct the suspended member to complete on a monthly basis an approved proforma to the effect that he maintains compliance with the sentence until the period of the suspension expires.[83]

Some scholars have expressed the view that generally the profession has been too lenient with doctors on matters bordering on infamous conduct.[84] Whether that is the case or not, it is suggested depends on a distinction being drawn between serious and not too serious malpractice and whether the Council should concern itself not only with serious misconduct, but also with cases not so serious. This is an area where balance is required. Some argue that it would be unfair to expose a doctor

---

[81] Rules 64-66.

[82] The hand of Babagingabi who said to be amputated by a doctor on the orders of a Sharia court judge purnisment to conviction for stealing a cow in 2001.

[83] For an explanation of the word 'infamous conduct in a professional respect, see *Allinson* v. *General Council of Medical Education* [1894] 1 QB 750; *Doughty* v. *General Dental Council* [1989] AC 164, [1987] 3 All ER 843; *Marten* v. *Royal College of Veterirnary Surgeons' Disciplinary Council* [1964] 1 QB 1, [1965] 1 All ER 949; *McEniff* v. *General Dental Council* [1980] 1 All ER 461, [1980] 1 WLR328; *McCoan* v. *General Medical Council* [1964] 3 All ER 143, [1964] 1 WLR 1107; *Denloye* v. *Nigeria Medical Council, MDPDT* v. *Okonkwo* (1999) 9 NWLR (pt 617) 1, (1999) 6 NWLR (pt. 786) 1

[84] Brazier, *Medicine, Patients and the Law*, 2n ed., 1982

who though competent, acts incompetent in an isolated case to discipline. Good as the argument may be, it conversely may be unfair to leave the aggrieved patient, the victim of the isolated malpractice with no remedy. This is what commends the New Zealand state sponsored compensation regime.[85]

History and evolution of medical ethics

Medicine is a primary science suggested to date as far as the creation of man.[86] Creation account of the Bible, other Holy writings and mythologies of indigenous people around the world, generally acknowledge God as responsible for creation. The story of the Bible tells that soon after the creation of the physical universe man was created. Seeing the need for him to have a companion God made him a wife. To accomplish this He made the first man fall into a deep sleep. While asleep, God took one of his ribs to build into a woman.[87] It has been suggested that this very act was the first surgery in human history; and has been considered the birth of medicine or surgery or both. Together as a couple, God gave them health, dietary and ethical rules for their benefit.[88] Later another of our common ancestor, Noah, was given further dietary regulations.[89] When the Jews became organised into a nation in a covenant relationship with God, additional dietary and health rules were given them.[90] However there appears little in the records suggesting that during the period medicine was practised as a profession.[91]That notwithstanding, it can be said that to

---

[85] New Zealand Accident Compensation Act, 1982 and Accident Compensation (Amendment) Act 1992; see also C.R. Cripps, Medical Practitioners Liability for Personal Injury Caused by Negligence (1978) *NZLJ* 29; R Mahoney, Informed Consent and Breach of the Medical Contract to Achieve a Particular Result; Opportunities for New Zealand's Patient Personal Injury Litigators to Peck Out of the Accident Compensation Closet (1985) 6 *Otago L. Rev.* Nol, 103.

[86] See Code *of Medical Ethics in Nigeria* issued by the Medical and Dental Council of Nigeria, (revised January 2004, edition); a code that make stipulations on rules of conduct for medical and dental practitioners. The preamble states that 'the medical profession has been from time immemorial, and universally still remains, the most learned and the only noble among the original three learned professions.'

[87] *Holy Bible*, Genesis 2: 21-23, contains an account of creation, and how the first man, Adam, rib was constructed into the woman, Eve. Some commentators however, argue that this account is no basis for the birth of medicine, because in their view, it is rather more related to the art of sculpture.

[88] Ibid., Genesis 1:29,30.

[89] Ibid., Genesis 9:2-4.

[90] For example, the Holy Bible in Leviticus 11:4 prohibited among the Jews the eating of animals such as pigs, and others susceptible to parasitic infection. Deuteronomy 23:6-14 required that human excrement be covered, thereby protecting the people from air-borne diseases. The moral principles in Leviticus chapter 18 protected them from sexually transmitted diseases. Laws on quarantine stated in Leviticus 13:1- 59; 14:36, 38 protected others from infections diseases.

[91] The practice of medicine seems to have been founded in Egypt. Egyptian physician embalmed Jacob the father of Joseph. (Gen. 50 1-3). The account that states that Joseph had a body of physicians' is an indication that the practice of medicine was not unfamiliar to the Egyptians people, especially in the nobility courts.

the extent that the various rules were designed to promote good health of the people, it is the very foundation of the practice of preventive and or public medicine.[92]

In the then world the practice of medicine was generally unscientific, more closely related to religion, superstition or magic. Most of the then healers knew very little of the human anatomy.[93] In ancient civilization it was not uncommon for people to associate several of their ancestral gods as having curative spirits and powers. The Babylonians for example associated the god Ea with healing. It was their god of healing. In Rome (as in Egypt) men and women slept in the temples of Isis and Serapis to receive healing. Blood transfusions in primitive form were not unknown to them. The familiar and common symbol of medical facilities of a staff with snake wound around it is said to be a symbol associated with the Greek healing god, Aesculapius. It is also suggested to be association with the Roman god, Mercury.[94] That ancient civilisations were familiar with medicine is further shown by the Code of Hammurabi, King of Babylon's first dynasty, about 1663 B C E. The Code contained provision for physicians' fees and has references to a 'bronze operating knife'. These references suggest that the Babylonians also practiced medicine as a profession. Unfortunately, the then practice of medicine and superstition were closely connected and difficult to separate.[95] The famous physician, Imhotep (2900 BC), was even made the god of healing.[96]

Greek physician, Hippocrates, who is however considered to be the founder and father of modern medicine systemised the practice. He recognised the need for a code of practice for the physician and his pupil. It is reputed that he had no connection with the temple hospitals of his time, which were controlled by the priest of Aesculapius. He practiced medicine as a modern science, while instructing his students on ethics.[97] His teaching on ethics is what has largely been translated to become the Physician Oath. The Oath together with legislation, common law and principles of equity, learned writings, and case-laws presently constitute the basis of ethical rules for the medical profession.

Africans medicine was connected with the practice of magic. The Yoruba's and Igbo's in Nigeria considered Osanyin and Agwu respectively, as their gods of medicine. Traditional doctors claim their healing power from the gods or dead ancestors. Modern medicine as we know it today may not have radically changed the faith of some in traditional medicine and its appeal to the god's.[98]

---

[92] Modern day practice of medicine that emphasises preventive medicine as the basis for 'health for all' is implicit recognition that prevention by little medical care can prevent the development of serious illness.

[93] J. Orr, *The International Standard Bible Encyclopaedia*, 1960, Vol. IV, p. 2393.

[94] *Insight on the Scriptures*, Vol. I. at .629-634, 1988, published by Watch Tower Bible and Tract Society of Pennsylvania. See also E.B Idowu, *African Traditional Religion*, Lagos, SCM Press, 1976, 197-198.

[95] Ibid., at 630-1.

[96] The *Guinness Encyclopaedia* 1993, Guinness Publishing, at 248.

[97] A copy of the Hippocratic Code is contained in Appendix.

[98] Idowu, above, n. 94 at 200-2.

Medicine is concerned with diagnosis, prognosis and treatment. Diagnosis assists the physician in treating the cause of sickness. It provides him with relevant information that assist in determining most appropriate management strategy. The profession is an imperative because sickness or disease is a part of living. Religionists explain sickness on the basis of disobedience by man against his creator's will. They attribute it to the fall of man in Eden. On that construction, we can say that sickness is as old as life. This explains why most civilizations one way or the other linked medicine to religion, rooted in the belief that sickness originates from disobedience to the will of G(g)od. If sickness is so caused, then the gods were considered to have the cure for all sickness. Physicians in the primitive stages of the profession were therefore trained in temples and sacred homes of gods. The objective, as that of today's medicine, is to attempt care for, or reduce sickness.

Development of medicine through civilisation

Let us consider a brief history of the progress of medicine through civilisation.

(i) ***Egyptian medicine*** is said to be first effective example of organised medicine. Imhotep practised organised medicine with pupil instruction. He became known as the Egyptian god of medicine. Papyrus documents reveal that he was a physician, priest and court official. Egyptian medicine was sophisticated to a large extent in the areas of observation, diagnosis and treatment. They were reputed to have a community health scheme, where patients were observed, diagnosed and treated for no-fees, as the practice of medicine and its expenses were borne by the community. This no doubt resembles a public health service scheme of our time. Priestly class also developed and ran specialist practice of medicine. Textbook for diagnosis and cure were published and rules of professional ethics were evolved for the practitioners. For example, the priest caste-physician had rigid rules enjoining them to undertake experimental treatment. Doctors were required to follow laid down procedure in standard textbook, and were fined if they followed unorthodox practices, which result in injury to patient. Penalties were enforced on the defaulting physician.[99] Though it remains unclear how organised medicine spread from Egypt to Babylon, it is hardly contested that its practice was somewhat organised. Imhotep is said to have made a special study of trauma arising from building activities of worker in the pyramid under his supervision in Egypt.

(ii) ***Babylonian medicine*** The Code of Hammurabi (1900 BCE) indicates that basis element of medical ethics was laid down for doctors. For example, the Code contains provisions for payment of fees and the rates chargeable. The rates depend on several factors, such as the state of patient, ability to pay fees, result of the medical

[99]Mason & Smith, *Law and Medical Ethics*, 4th ed. London, Butterworths, 1994, p. 4 and Guinness Encyclopaedia, *above*, n.96 at 227; see also A.W. Bensley, The Origin of Orthopaedics (1982) 75 *J Roy. Soc. Med* 648, cited in Mason and Smith *above* n. 1 at 4.

treatment. There are also indications in the Code that Babylonian physicians practiced surgery.[100]

(iii) ***Greek medicine*** Greek medicine was probably influence more by philosophy than religion. Its medicine developed at a time that coincided with the emergence of Greek philosophy, rooted in the search for logical and ethical foundation for worldly phenomena. It is therefore not surprising that ethical rules were developed for its physicians. The profession was largely influence by Greek philosophers, like Heraclitus (540-480 B C), and Parmenides (515 BCE) who in their search for knowledge, emphasised the place of logical coherence, observation and rationality. The result was that the then hitherto strong link between superstition, religion, and priestly influence on medicine in other civilizations was de-emphasised. In its place rationality, diagnosis and empirical experiments were practiced. At its peak, Grecian medicine was a rational science, clearly separated from religion. Naturally, just as Greek philosophers ran schools of thoughts; its physicians also formed schools of medicine, with pupil instruction in the profession and ethics.

The Greek philosopher and physician, Hippocrates of Cos (460-370 B C E) is considered to be the father of modern medicine. He set out a code of ethics for pupil, essentially summarised in what is known as the Hippocrates Oath. Basically it opens with a solemn oath by the pupil swearing by Apollo, the physician, and the gods and goddess of medicine, Aesculapius, Hygiene and Panacea, to observe the oath. He swears to consider dear as his parents his medical instructor and if need be, in turn instruct his master's children in the art of medicine without charging a fee. Further, the pupil swears to always treat his patient to the best of ability, and never to do any harm to him, either in the form of prescribing a deadly drug or advice, which may cause death, or cause abortion. The primacy of treatment consideration to any other is stressed by the oath. It states that a pupil shall only enter a house to treat, and must eschew all other intentions, such as ill doing, seduction and pleasure of love with women. He is also under oath to keep professional secrets and confidence, while striving to maintain the dignity of the profession. The teachings of Hippocrates are in the collection known as the Hippocrates Corpus, reputed to be his teaching written down by his followers. He was known to have advocated moderation as a key to good health.

With the decline of the Roman Empire, civilisation moved away from Greece to Arabia and others parts of the world. Not surprising the Hippocratic Oath influence also declined in use. But with the emergence of organised university medical school instruction, the Oath regains its prominence in medical instruction. The present Physician Oath, otherwise known as the Declaration of Geneva of 1948, as amended at Sydney in 1968, largely draws on the Hippocrates Oath and is suggested to be a re-write of it in modern language.[101]

---

[100] Above n. 96.

[101] The Physician Oath is now an integral part of the Code/Rules of professional conduct for medical and dental practitioners in Nigeria. See a copy of the rules in appendix.

(iv) ***Jewish medicine*** The Jews believed in one God and used the Bible as their sacred book. Though the Bible was written primarily as a book of faith, it contains basis concept of medicine and other form of treatment that Jews subscribed to. Sickness was considered concomitant of imperfection resulting in death, passed onto humans from the sin of Adam. Jewish practice of medicine was basically preventive. For example, its Law Code prohibited immorality, which can lead to sickness and death. That its code mentions sicknesses such as tuberculosis, boils, piles, eczema, leprosy, etc indicates that Jewish practice of medicine was probably advanced. Its strong emphasis on the isolation of infectious patients, and regulation of sewage disposal gave birth to the modem principles of public health medicine.[102] Though the Bible does not mention herbal remedies used by Jewish physician, it is reasonable to expect that they employed herbal medication such as those also used by Egyptians, like honey, garlic, oil, vinegar and wine. Its practice of care for the sick carried over into Christianity probably constitutes the underlying ethical practices of nursing, charity, devotion to the less fortunate, equality and the likes, in modern medicine.[103]

Era of transformation

With the decline of Roman Empire, civilisation moved westward to areas like France and Italy. One result of this was the establishment of medical schools in and around France and Italy. The twelfth and thirteenth centuries witnessed the return of classical learning in philosophy, law and science. In Europe, teachers set up schools and the "lost' learning of the ancient world was moved out of Arabia into Europe. It was greatly assisted by its translation from Arabic into Latin. By 1200 CE, universities (with medical schools) were established in Paris, Bologna and Oxford. By 1500 CE, there were more than 70 universities in Europe.[104] Those desirous of becoming physician were required to undergo formal schooling and training in medicine, hence the learned title 'doctor' was coined for the physician.[105] The medical faculties taught most aspects of medicine, (except surgery, because the Church then prohibited the shedding of blood). Instruction included study based on physiology, and empirical knowledge, occasionally mixed with some superstition.[106]

Since then there has been great strides in medical science. Let us mention a few. Andreas Vesalius' (1514-1564) book *De Humani Corporis Fabric* (On the Fabric of

---

[102] *Aid to Bible Understanding* (1971 Watchtower Bible and Tract Society of Pennsylvania) 451.

[103] Mason and Smith, *above* n.1 at 5; see also A Rendle Short, *The Bible and Modern Medicine* 40-41; Manual of Tropical Medicine 5.

[104] See, *above*, n. 99 at 406. In cities like Montpellier, in France, and Bologna in Italy with universities, it is said that by the 14th century, these universities medical instructions included training in anatomy, with the dissection of corpses. So while surgery was prohibited by the then established ecclesiastical and royal decrees because; it was considered tantamount to blood-shedding, the prohibition did not possibly extend to corpse. By implication it can be suggested that knowledge of human anatomy was known at the time.

[105] M King Roper, Ethics: Lawyers and the Title Doctor, (1980) 6 *Akrow L.R.* 7.

[106] Ibid.

Human Body) described accurately the human anatomy. William Harney (I578-1677), discovered the true nature of heartbeat and blood circulation. Dutchman Anton Van Leevwenhoek used the invention of microscopes in medical research on spermatozoa, blood cells and microbes. Edward Jenner (1796-1823) discovered vaccination cure to smallpox. Frenchman, Louis Pasteur (1822-95) demonstrated that diseases are caused by bacteria. Horace Wells (1815-48) pioneered pain control by anaesthesia. The period also witnessed interesting developments with the introduction of another profession into medicine - nursing, by Florence Nightingale (1820 - 1910). The nursing profession brought about a reduction in death rate in hospital around Europe. The 19th century saw the introduction of preventive medicine and sewage control. The next century witnessed the introduction of technology in the diagnosis and treatment of patient. The discovery of x-ray by German physicist Wilhelm Konrad Rontgen (1945-1923), the place of vitamins by Sir Frederick Gmoland Hopkins (1861-1947), chemotherapy by Paul Ehrlich (1854-1915) changed the landscape of the practice of medicine. Today, with the aid of technology, physicians have been able to transplant organs, carry out prenatal screening and other biomedical experiments that have improved medicine. Paradoxically however, these have also raised attendant ethical questions, many of which will task us and are addressed in the pages of this book.

Introduction of medicine into Nigeria

Most of the early explorers to the African continent during the colonial period were medical doctors. Foremost amongst these were David Livingstone, Mungo Park, John Kirk and Schnister. The first crop of doctors that came to Nigeria were Portuguese. Dutch, West Indies and British followed them. In 1472, it was reported that the expedition of Fernando Gomes to Lagos included some medical personnel. However organised medicine began with the establishment of the Medical Examination Board in 1787. It was later replaced in 1902 by the West African Medical Services. Doctors who served under the schemes were primarily government official, and were specifically mandated to care for government officials.[107]

Today the medical and dental professions in Nigeria are regulated by the Medical and Dental Practitioners Act, 1988 (hereinafter referred to as the Act or MDPA).[108] The Act establishes the Medical and Dental Council of Nigeria (the Council) as the official body of the profession statutorily charged with overseeing the practice. It is also charged with supervising medical education. As part of its function, the Council keeps an official register of members. It is empowered to

[107] *Above*,n.99 at p. 40-406; see also A Adesola, Vice-Chancellor of the University of Lagos Opening Speech at workshop on medical ethics in 1982, in E. S. Akpata, *Medical Ethics* (Proceedings of Workshop) Lagos: Lagos University Press, 1982, at 3.

[108] Decree No 23 of 1988 (now Act) repeals the Medical and Dental Practitioners Act, 1963. See Laws of the Federation, 2004.

make rules for its Investigating Panel and Disciplinary Tribunal responsible for the enforcement of its rules and general ethics for practitioners. The Registrar of the Council maintains and keeps a register of all practitioners. Whenever an allegation is made against a member, the Council is empowered to establish an Investigation Panel, to investigate the allegation against the member If a *prima facie* case is made out, the case is sent to the Disciplinary Tribunal for responsible adjudication. When so acting, the Tribunal acts and or serves as the court for medical discipline and conduct.[109] An Assessor is appointed to advise the Tribunal on questions of law. The Tribunal's verdict is expressed or couched in the form: that an allegation of infamous conduct in a professional manner is established or not established, as the case may be. If the verdict pronounced is one of guilty, the member may be suspended and or his name may be erased from the register of members.

An infamous conduct in a professional respect for which a practitioner may be held liable has been described by Lord Esher MR in *Allison* v. *General Council of Medical Education and Registration* as follows:

> "If it is shown that a professional man in the pursuit of his profession, has done something with regard to it which would be reasonably regarded as disgraceful or dishonourable by his professional brethren of good repute and competency then he is guilty of an infamous conduct in a professional respect."[110]

It is an absolute requirement that the alleged infamous conduct must arise out of or pertaining the physician's profession. So if the infamous conduct has no relevance whatsoever to his acts and or omissions in a professional respect no liability can arises.[111] In view of the fact that the Council is empowered to review from time to time a statement of its code of conduct for members, it can be said the scope of matters embraced within the term "infamous conduct in a professional respect" as it relates to its Rules are not closed.[112]

Sources of Medical Ethics

A dictionary defines ethics as a system of moral principles or rules of conduct.[113] The root word for ethics is derived from the Greek term *ethos*, which denotes

---

109 *Dr. Denloye* v. *Medical Dental Practitioner Disciplinary Committee* [1968] All NLR 298; *Okonkwo* v. *Medical & Dental Practitioners Disciplinary Tribunal* (1999) 9 NWLR (pt 617) 1 (A), (1999) 6 NWLR (pt 786) 1 (SC).

101[1994] QB 750 at 760-1, per Esher MR; For similar description see *IBWA* v. *Imano Ltd.* (1988) 3 NWLR (pt 85) p. 633; Re a Solicitor, Ex. p. Law Society [1912] I KB 302; *Graham* v. *A-G of Fiji* [1936] 2 MER 992; *Ex. p. Mechan* [1965] NSWR 30 (Australia); *Legal Practitioners Disciplinary Tribunal* v. *Idowu* [1971] NLR 128 at 137-138, per Ademola C JN; *Hennessy case* [1946] Lancet (1) 616 at 622.

111 See dissuasion in chapter on rules Professional Conduct.

112 Ibid.

113 *Oxford Advanced Learners Dictionary of Current English.*

custom and or habits. Sources of medical ethics in Nigeria are to be found in the following:

(i) Received English law: This comprises of English common law and doctrines of equity and statutes of general application in force in English on January 1, 1900, that are incorporated into our legal system.[114] The term common law means the unwritten laws of England developed from common practice or custom considered uniform, and binding even though not enacted by Parliament. In it narrow juristic sense, it means that body of law administered by the courts of common law before the Judicature Acts 1873-1875. In a general sense the term equity means a liberal and humane interpretation of law as far as is possible without actual antagonism to law itself.[115] In a juristic sense, it is that special and peculiar department of the English legal system which was created, developed and administered by the Courts of Chancery or Equity, before the Judicature Act 1873 - 1875.

(ii) ***Local statute*** These are laws enacted by the Nigerian legislature. Local statutes that regulate and touch on medical practice include the Medical and Dental Practitioner's Act 1988. It establishes the Medical and Dental Council and regulate it operations. Other local statutes that are connected with it include: The Poison and Pharmacy Act cap 152 of 1965; The Dangerous Drug Act Cap 48; The Indian Hemp Decree No 17 of 1966; The Food and Drug Act; The Pharmacist Act No. 26 of 1964

iii) ***Learned writings and articles*** A practitioner is expected to possess and exhibit reasonable degree of skill expected of fellow practitioners. To do so, he is expected to keep abreast with new technique in medicine by reading learned writings, in the form of books, journals and the like. In *Bolam* v. *Friern Hospital Management Committee*,[116] the court observed: that though it may not be reasonable for a doctor to be expected to read every journal, if it is shown in a learned journal that a procedure is wrong and yet a doctor pigheaded continues with the practice, he will be liable for malpractice or negligence. That does not mean that a medical man can obstinately and pigheaded continue to carry on with some old technique if it has been proved to be contrary to what is really substantially the whole of informed medical opinion. If he does he would open himself to liability for malpractice. In *Crawford* v. *Charing Cross Hospital*[117] even though an anaesthetist failed to read an article in the medical journal the

[114] See s.16 of Federal Supreme Court 1960; s.13 High court of Lagos Act, 1955; s.13 High Court of Western Region, 1955; s. 28 (b) High Court law of Northern region, 1955; s.13 High court of Eastern Region. The State (Creation and Transitional Provisions) Decree of 1967, s.15 specifically provides that all existing law in the region out of which a state is created shall have effect in the state, subject to modifications necessary to bring it in conformity with the provisions of the statute.

[115] O. F. Emiri, *Equity and Trust in Nigeria*, Lagos, Malthouse Press, 2006.

[116] [1957] 2 All ER 1118.

[117] [1953] TLR 1.

Lancet describing risk in an operation, the court did not hold him negligent for adopting a procedure that he would have avoided if he had read the article. Lord Denning warned that

> It would be putting too high a burden in a medical man to say that he must read every article in the medical press...the medical man duty is limited to taking reasonable steps to keep himself abreast of modern developments in technique...failure to read a particular article may be excusable while disregard for a series of warning in the medical press could perhaps be cogent evidence of negligence.

Both cases underscore the fact that when a medical technique becomes notorious to medical practitioner through learned articles, any doctor who acts in disregard of it would be liable in a claim for negligence or malpractice.

(iv) ***Rules of Professional Conduct*** The Medical and Dental Practitioners Act No 23 of 1988 empowers the Medical and Dental Council to make rules for professional conduct of its members. The objective of the rules as stated in its preamble is to preserve the primal position of the practice in society. The Rule state in part:

> Our profession has been from time immemorial and universally, it still remains the most learned and the only noble among the original three learned professions - the primary three learned professionals being the physicians, the scribe (lawyer) and the priest. It is the primal duty of every doctor to maintain this primal position in society.[118]

The rule stipulates conducts that are unprofessional and the attendant penalties thereto. Some of the infamous conducts for which a doctor can be guilty include: adultery, improper sexual association with a patient, divulging professional secrets, advertising his services, dishonesty in financial matters, negligent conducts, issuance of false professional certificate, improper attitude towards members of an Investigation Panel and disregard for the health of his patients and many others.

(v) ***Hippocrates teachings and Physician Oath*** Far back as the 5th century B C E, the father of modem medicine, Greek physicians Hippocratic (460 - 377 B C E),

---

[118]. See preamble to the *Rules of Professional Conduct*, 2004 revised edition, published by the Council, rule 1. Though the rules state that the profession of medicine is the primal learned and noble profession, most lawyers would contest the statement. While it is hardly contestable that the practice of medicine is one of the three learned professions, it could be an over statement to suggest that it is primal. It appears that even before the creation of Eve from the rib of Adam, suggested as surgery, law was the first to be ordained. Physical laws sustain all physical creation. What is more, soon after creation of the man, God gave him laws regulating his obligations, including the widely known prohibition on the forbidden tree and or fruit. That would suggest that law was the first. The creation of the material universe and the subsequent appearance of man on earth followed creative day order. Coupled with positively charge by law to keep the beauty of the garden and abstain from eating a fruit of good and bad puts medicine after law.

during the golden age of Pericles, recognised the need for a code of conduct for doctors-called the Hippocrates Oath.[119] To bring it in line with modern practice and language, the General Assembly of the World Medical Association in Geneva, Switzerland in September 1945 replaced the Hippocrates Oath with the General (Physician Oath) Declaration.[120] The Oath substantially re-enacts the Hippocrates Oath, preserving its essence, especially the obligation of medicine rooted in humanitarian service and the preservation of life. As a general rule, on graduation medical students subscribe to the Oath. By that solemn ceremony, they covenant to abide by its dictates in the pursuit of their chosen profession.[121] By so doing the importance of the Physician Oath is indelibly imprinted on their heart, mind and soul.

(vi) ***International Declarations on Ethics by World Medical Association*** (WMA) The body is the amalgamation of all the world's medical associations. Accordingly its declaration on ethics represents shared standards that are binding, or at least strongly persuasive in matters connected with code of conduct or ethics. The following are the principal declarations of the body:

(a) Helsinki Declaration of 1964.[122]
(b) Sydney Declaration of 1968.[123]
(c) Oslo Declaration of 1970.[124]
(d) Tokyo Declaration of 1975.[125]
(e) Lisbon Declaration of 1981 (amended in Indonesia 1995).[126]

The *Helsinki Declaration* condemned the medical crimes of Nazi Germany in guise of medical research. It expressly states that all clinical research involving human objects must conform to normal and general scientific principles. Flowing from it, all consideration must be given to risk-benefit factors and doctors are enjoined to be weary in performing clinical research where the personality or the subject is liable to be altered either by drugs or experimental procedures.

The *Sydney Declaration* states the criteria for determining the moment or time of death. It was necessitated by the emergence of modern medical techniques that have capacity of reversing death and the dying process. It set the criteria for the pronouncement of death, now generally associated with the death of the brain. It further stipulates that brain death certification should

---

[119] See Appendix for full text of Hippocrates Oath.

[120] . See Appendix for full text of General (Physician Oath) Declaration of 1948.

[121] See I Okolo, Medical Ethics in Nigeria, in B.C Umerah (ed.) *Medical Practice and the Law in Nigeria* (Lagos: Longman) 19_

[122] See Appendix.

[123] See Appendix.

[124] See Appendix.

[125] See Appendix.

[126] Appendix

involve clinical report by two or more physicians, in the form of clinical judgment or electroencephalograph test. It also addresses some of the ethical problems of organ harvesting and transplantation. The *Oslo Declaration* of 1970 is a statement on therapeutic abortion.

The *Tokyo Declaration* of 1975 provides guide to practitioners in cases of torture and inhuman treatment, or punishment of persons.

(vii) Case-laws: Appeals from the decisions of the Medical and Dental Tribunal lies in the fist instance to the Court of Appeal, from where further appeal may lie to the Supreme Court. To the extent, that these courts exercise appellate jurisdictions over the Tribunal's verdicts, to that extent and purpose, their decisions are binding on the Tribunal and generally constitute sources of professional ethics. Without pretence the 2004 Code in its introduction positively acknowledge that the revision of the Code was necessitated by a desire of the Council to reflect courts decisions on matters of professions ethics.[127] Though appeals from the Tribunal do not lie to high courts, they nonetheless may exercises supervisory jurisdiction on the Tribunal by means of its prerogative power of mandamus.[128]

Rationale for Medical Ethics

Medical ethics sometimes referred to as medical jurisprudence or forensic medicine, is the application of medical knowledge to law, ethics and morality. It involves knowledge of law and ethics in the treatment of patients. Science is changing the world into a better place in many respects. In our time, medical science has grown beyond the widest imagination, thereby throwing up many ethical questions. Every informed person is aware of the amazing accomplishments of scientists in many fields.[129] It has dramatically increased our knowledge of the universe and of living things. Studies of the human body have opened up improved ways of treating illness and injuries. Rapid advances in electronics have ushered in the computer age. Scientists have performed astounding feats, even sending men to the moon and back.

---

[127] See introduction to Code, it states that 'this particular edition has undergone some major modifications, informed by the experience of Council in the course of preliminary investigations by the...Investigating Panel, sittings of the...Tribunal, and rulings of the Court of Appeal in the professional disciplinary matters that have been to Council.' For example in *Denloye* v. *Medical and Dental Practitioners Disciplinary Committee* [1968] 1 All NLR 298 it was held that proceeding of a Tribunal must observe and conform with principles of natural justice, and any violation will render its proceeding null and void and of no effect whatsoever. The court also stated that the jurisdiction of the Tribunal do not extend or cover matters within the exclusive jurisdiction of regular courts, such as questions relating to adjudging a person guilty of a criminal offence. See also *Okonkwo* v. *MDPDT* (1999) 9 NWLR (pt 617) 1; (1999) 6 NWLR (pt 786) 1 (SC). These and other decisions undoubtedly form part of the sources of medical ethics.

[128] Ese Malemi, *Administrative Law in Nigeria.*

[129] *Life-How Did It Get Here?* at p.10, published by Watchtower Society Pennsylvania.

Many years when some doctors practised surgery and the dissecting of corpses, they frightened their contemporaries. The Church was quick to persecute them for what it considered to be murder or, at least, blood-shedding.[130] Such a thing considered a feat many years is now common place. Today, organs and tissues can and are transplanted from one person to another. It is now possible to deposit semen in the vagina and procure pregnancy without physical sexual intercourse. Advances have also been significant in genetic engineering. Dying human have been revived by procedures considered impossible some hundred year ago. All of these developments in medical science are bound to have corresponding legal implications. Consider some.

In September 1987, for the first time, doctors transplanted foetal tissues into the brain of two adults suffering from Parkinson's disease. The tissues were obtained from a spontaneously aborted 13-week old foetus. The transplant operations were carried out in La Raza Medical Centre, Mexico City.[131] The issues raised by it can be as many as: what is the legal status, if any, of a foetus; should abortion be permitted if it is for the benefit of a third party; what is the proper limits of foetus experiment; and many others. Also it is reported that in 1985, nearly 8,000 kidneys and 20,000 corneas were transplanted globally. A thinking person may question the morality of permitting the formation and promotion of human spare parts business. Genetic engineering may also raise its own questions. For example, in 1989, the heart of a baboon was transplanted into a child. Some may question it as being beastly.

If a person's genes are said to be made-up of one pair inherited from one's father and the other part from the mother to create a unique person, then if the set-up is altered by a progress of genetic engineering, would it be plausible to argue that the personality of the patient is altered to such an extent that affects, say, criminal responsibility? If recent discovery and or proposition on genes that suggest that certain genes are responsible for some anti-social behaviours is correct, for example, some studies associate schizophrenia, alcoholism, and homosexuality to certain gene formation, then a patient who undergoes a gene alteration may somehow be able to raise defences within the bracket of accident, compulsion, and the like under the Criminal Code. That would possibly require a reconstruction of our theories of criminal responsibility and punishment. These and many other related issues call for the formulation of 'new' rules of ethics for medicine.

Shared Common History

The practice of law and medicine share many things in common. Apart from their primal positions, they are both ancient in origin and learned. Physicians are

---

[130] The Roman Catholic Church was then critical of the practice of singing in mediaeval times

[131] Texas San Diego Newspaper Union of October 1978. *Awake* July 22, 1978 p. 3-4; see also A O. Akerele, Legal Implications of Some Recent Biomedical Phenomena, unpublished long essay, 1989, Faculty of Law, Lagos State University, Lagos, at. 3-6.

commonly called 'doctors'. It is of interest to note that in Continental jurisdictions, degrees in law are awarded as doctoral degrees. History has it that the first doctorate degree was awarded in civil law in the twelfth century in Bologna, Italy. Doctorate in medicine was first awarded in the fourteenth century. In keeping with this practice, continental legal systems continue to award doctoral degrees in law. Other common history between both professions is noticeable in their noble nature and care for the anxieties of others: who consider them 'demigods' to life problems.

Determining the province of Medical Ethics

To aid the physician cope with the moral dilemmas now posed by the practice of medicine, which have increasingly made question of life and death, more complex and controversial, the need for medical jurisprudence or ethics cannot be questioned. This is made more compelling by the fact that there is now more than ever an emphasis on human rights, which invariably dictates respect, guarantee, and protection of humanist elements in medical treatment. The public and professional concern for ethics in the practice of medicine is brought about by the scope of modern medicine. An example is that of *Airedale N H S Trust* v. *Bland*.[132] A young boy was admitted in a hospital with severe brain problems which put him in a vegetative state. For purposes of argument, let us assume that the doctors considers future medical care useless, in that it would only succeed in mutilation, pain; and expenses, without a hope of recovery. If on the other hand his relatives keep urging the hospital to do everything possible until the patient may die or recover, that will certainly raise many ethical questions, answers to which are by no means common, depending on individual beliefs, wishes, values and fears. No question about it, harmonising the divergent answers may be problematic, because there is hardly moral solidarity on matters of ethics. That being the case, the business of medical ethics is to attempt to help the doctor to quickly see the moral questions his treatment may throw up, and help all the interested party in the management of a patient to arrive at the best decision possible. Medical ethics thus reveal to the physician that being ill and healed are complex phenomena, which involves the patient person as an individual, as much as his organs and tissues.[133]

Though a study of ethics can create in a physician a sound moral character, it cannot pretend to cover the countless dilemmas he would face in his practice. An attempt to resolve these within a single framework was responsible for the emergence of the Hippocrates Oath, now replaced by the Physician Oath. But the truth of the matter is that both have proved grossly inadequate in resolving the practical and clinical dilemmas that a physician faces in his day to day practice.

Recourse to a court moral standard has also not proved fool-proof. A critical appraisal of case law in the context of ethics reveals that there have been no

---

[132] 1993] 1 All ER 21 (HL).

[133] Tim Hackler, Medicine and the Human Factor, *Topic*, issue no.197 at 51 (quarterly magazine of the United States Information Service of American Embassy).

coherent principles on which the courts have based its value judgments. The situation is compounded, by the reluctance of courts getting involved in making moral decisions. For example, Lord Bridge in *Gillick* v. *West Norfolk* and *Wisbech AHA*, expressed the reluctance this way, when he said:

> ..in cases where any proposition of law implicit in a departmental advisory document is interwoven with question of social and ethical controversy, the court should, in my opinion, exercise its jurisdiction with the utmost restrain, confine itself to deciding whether the proposition of law is erroneous and avoid either expressing *ex cathedra* opinion in area of social and ethical controversy in which it has no claim to speak with authority or proffering answers to hypothetical questions of law which do not strictly arise for decision.[134]

This is not surprising, ethics is an area of life that affects the lives and interest of a large section of the society and lay persons, as well as the courts and lawyers are well fitted to decide what is right or wrong.[135] Many of the issues that arise from biomedical advances defy the skill of lawyers. Appeal to legal precedents could be unhelpful, because most are novel, not covered by traditional appeal to previous judgments. While precedents can play an important role in solving legal puzzle in the areas of property, law of obligations and commerce, ethical questions are usually novel in character. Therefore attempts to categorise medical questions into familiar legal compartment may not be free of distortions.[136] To illustrate, would it be proper to import into the question of surrogate motherhood, principles of contract, such as offer, acceptance etc? How should we classify an agreement to purchase a human organ for transplant purpose? Would the principles governing sale of goods law readily apply? May be, we find consolation in the views expressed by Lord Bridge in *Gillick* [137] that the court must be circumspect in making decision on questions of ethics.

Can legislation be trusted with the task of determining the province of medical ethics? When called to decide whether or not it was legal to permit a hospital to withdraw artificial hydration and nutrition from a persistent vegetative patient in *Airedale N H S Trust* v. *Anthony Bland*,[138] Lords Browne Wilkinson and Mustill, expressed concern with leaving ethical issues with courts rather than Parliament. Lord Browne Wilkinson said:

> I have no doubt that it is for Parliament not the court to decide the broader issues which this case raise...Where a case raises wholly new moral and social issues, in my judgment it is not for the judges to seek to develop new, all embracing, principles of law in a way which reflects the individual judges moral stance when society as a whole is substantially divided on the relevant moral

[134] [1985] 3 All ER 402 at 427.

[135] See Lord Reid in *Petitt* v. *Petitt* [1970] AC 777; and see also Reid, *The Judge as Lawmaker*.

[136] M D.A Freeman, *Medicine, Ethics and the Law: Current Legal Problems*, London: Stevens & Sons, 1988, p. 1.

[137] [1985] 3 All ER 402.

[138] [1993] All ER 821, [1993] 2 WLR 316.

> issues...If Parliament fails to act, then judge-made law will of necessity through a gradual and uncertain process provide a legal answers to each question as it arises. But, in my judgment, that is not the best way to proceed.[139]

Lending credence to His Lordships view above, Lord Mustil added:

> The formulation of the necessary broad social and moral policy is an enterprise which the courts have neither the means nor in my opinion the right to perform. This can only be achieved by democracy through the medium of Parliament.[140]

This however may not be an all solution to the moral questions in medicine. Who can claim that Parliament is ever well informed of ethical questions that arise from bio-medical advancement in society? To enable it do what his Lordships advocate above, it would be necessary for it to be equipped with research and an advisory body of relevant professionals, composed of lawyers, doctors, philosophers, theologians and other disciplines, to advise Parliament on every conceivable ethical problem in medicine. A thing hardly available to it at all times. Even at this, meaningful consensus on ethical question is difficult, if not, impossible to achieve.[141]

In an attempt to provide an institutional framework for advice on ethical question, Jimmy Carter, former President of the USA, in 1980 established the Commission for Study of Ethical Problem in Medicine and Bio-medical and Behavioural Research.[142] The Commission headed by Professor Alexander Capron, in its five years of existence before President Ronald Reagan defunded it in 1985, made very useful comments on many biomedical ethical questions. Its contribution covered areas such as, in vitro fertilisation, defining the criteria of death, genetic engineering and experiments, decisions to forego, or prolong life-sustaining treatments and many others. For example, its recommendations on the criteria for determining death, either on cardiopulmonary or neurological grounds, when published in the Journal of American Medical Association was widely applauded by the profession and has since widely been adopted by many states in the United States of America. Both the American Bar Association (ABA) and the American Medical Association (AMA) welcomed its translation into the Uniform Determination of Death Act.[143] The English and Nigerian jurisdictions, on the other hand have been slow in developing any institutional framework for analysing medical ethical problem. As if a wake from slumber however, England set up the Warnock Committee to advise on infertility treatment and embryo research and experimentation. Interestingly, institutional framework for advice on medical ethics in the form of national commissions exists in countries such as, France and

---

[139] Ibid., at p. 380.
[140] Ibid., at p. 382.
[141] Stephen Tomline, *The Place of Reason in Ethics.*
[142] 1 Kennedy & Grubb, *Medical Law* (2nd ed. London: Butterworths, 1994) at 24-31.
[143] Ibid.

Denmark.[144] Their importance in advancing bio-medical ethics where they exist, is good reason why jurisdictions like Nigeria lacking similar commissions should consider the desirability of establishing same.

Non-existence of the commissions in some jurisdictions is additional reason why turning moral questions to Parliament for decision making may not be advisable. Legislation, where it exist, in this area have often woefully lagged behind advance in bio-technology. So an attempt to use it as a ready guide for doctors is dubious in the least.

While, lawyers, judges, philosophers and others, may debate ethical questions and proffer divergent answers, we must acknowledge that the doctors make the decision and often in an *ex-parte* emergency situation. Since medical ethics ought to be the universal principle on which the doctor makes his decision, a search for a credible, solid philosophical foundation is desirable.[145] Determining it has not been easy. Why? Most teachers of philosophy advocate different ethical theories, each claiming to be undisputedly correct, thereby making the subject more controversial than comprehensible.[146]

The Utilitarian School of Jeremy Bentham, advanced by John Stuart Mill, for example, urge that we perform acts which will have the best overall result by reducing pain, and maximise happiness.[147] However commendable it seem, it has its shortcoming in helping us solve the moral question in medicine. Medical treatment can hardly be considered a distribution of happiness in terms of quality or quantity. To use the illustration of Mason & Smith, is a little happiness derived by large numbers of mentally subnormal patients any greater or less than a lot of pleasure experienced by a small number of livers transplant recipients? [148] Do we not most times subscribe to a doctor inflicting pains in the course of management of a patient (may be in the form of a painful operation) to bring about relief to ailments? At the time of operation, no doubt, pain is maximised and happiness minimised for the patient. The reverse only occurs later when the patent, at least begins the recovery journey. Consequently, utilitarianism can hardly be the philosophical foundation sought for the many decisions in medicine.

Intuitionalism on the other hand, urges that we simple recognize a course as morally good by it having certain empirical properties and then generalise the results of that isolated moral intuition. This school argues that moral rules are mere rules of thumb-mere summaries of part judgment of individual action.[149] It a concept close to our conception of conscience, which in reality is the doctor/patient first practical guide on matters of ethics. By equating ethical decision of biomedical questions with

---

[144] Ibid.

[145] Mason & Smith, above, n. 1 at 5, 6

[146] Stephen Tomline, above n. 141.

[147] *Introduction to Morality.*

[148] Mason and Smith, above n. 1 at 3.

[149] D.C. Emmons, Justice Reassessed, (1967) 4 *American Philosophical Quarterly* 144 at 147.

'common sense' moral judgment, which in most cases it is not, moral intuitionism is as unhelpful as utilitarianism.

The subject of medical ethics is a comparatively young subject which crosses formal legal boundaries of criminal law, human rights, tort, contract and family law jurisprudence. The topics in medical jurisprudence range from question of medical negligence, confidentiality, consent to treatment, death, transplantation; psychiatry, toxicology and pre-natal treatments, etc. A cursory look at its scope, and case-law decisions would seem to indicate that the philosophical foundation for decision making have swung as a pendulum between the principles of autonomy of person and appeal to human right and dignity, (wherein lies the best-interest concept).[150]

Kennedy and Grubb are of the view that the unifying and underlying philosophical and legal theme on the subject is located in respect for human rights.[151] The learned writers are to a certain extent justified in their proposition, especially in the context of discussions on the right of autonomy, self-determination, informed consent and treatment choices, reproductive medicine, research, death and the dying process and medical malpractices, virtually the major part of the subject. The difficult with the approach however is that an attempt to classify factual issues, such as transplantation and in vitro fertilisation (IVF), as human rights issues appears illogical.[152] While admitting, that human rights is not altogether irrelevant in determining the ethical basis of decisions in medicine, as the prohibition against invasion on a persons body can be captured in term of rights against self-invasion, rights appeal can be too individualist in application. What is more, the analysis hardly explains what happens when rights come in conflict. When it does, a moral impasse is created requiring a solution not usually based on primacy of one against another, but a weighing of their competing morality.[153]

Questionable, if all the intellectual coherence of the subject were to be summarized on the basis of rights, we would need to determine whose rights are being referred to. Is it that of the patient, his relatives, doctor, or the state? If we answer; the patient's rights, then it would only be natural to ask further, does the physician not also have rights in choosing his patient and management course in accordance with his Oath? If we translate his Oath as requiring him to use the best of his ability to do good or cure, it logically translates to mean for him a 'right to treat', if the intention is to cure. No doubt it invariably would justify his trampling on the patient's right to refuse treatment or objection to particular medical method of treatment. This situation no doubt would be grotesque to imagine in the context of modern democracy and trends in ethics that recognise autonomy of the patient.[154] Same can be said on insistence of an appeal to patient's rights. An analysis

---

[150] This is not meant to be an exclusive list of the scope of study of medical ethics, but it merely captures the possible range of subjects that concern a book of this nature.
[151] Kennedy & Grubb, above n. 142 at3.
[152] Ibid.
[153] Mason & Smith, above n. 1 at 7.
[154]Lord Donaldson in *Re T* [1992] 3 WLR 782 (CA).

along that line would be an unduly assertive position that may not satisfy society's quest for a consensual foundation for decision in medicine.

Noteworthy of mention is the fact that in Nigeria issues of human rights has been classified into two broad categories; common law rights and constitutional rights.[155] A common law right it is suggested is not as sacrosanct as a constitutional right. Generally most of the rights known to the subject of medical ethics are common law in nature, even though some judicial authorities have read constitutional flavour into many. In *Okonkwo case*[156] for example, the right of informed consent (a common law right) was elevated by the Supreme Court to the constitutional right to dignity of human person, personal liberty and freedom of conscience. Several examples abound in many other jurisdictions of similar attitude. Some jurisdictions have moved the patient's right to reproduce into the mould of fundamental right to procreation. In the course of our discussions through the pages of this book we shall encounter many such cases. Through legal activism, several common law rights are upgraded to constitutional rights. Consider a hypothetical case. Assuming a patient carries a card, which states in unequivocal terms that he does not wish blood to be administered to him in any circumstances. The patient's wish would no doubt be respected by a hospital, because he would in essence by so doing be exercising his common right of self-determination or a right to informed consent. Assuming further that the hospital, knowing of the terms of the stipulation, disregards them and insist on transfusing blood. The patient can argue that forced transfusion is an abuse of his common law right of self-determination or autonomy. It is also possible to argue that to the extent that medical treatment is not meant to treat tissues or organs only, but the whole person, an unlawful treatment amounts to degrading treatment prohibited constitutionally. The constitutional guarantee of the right to dignity of the human person may have been violated by such forced transfusion. In fact medical science, now more than ever, appreciates the importance of treating the 'whole-person', recognising the separate but interrelated nexus between the body, mind and spirit of a patient.[157] Accordingly, the healing of the body in the face of a broken mind or spirit is but partial victory, if not a complete defeat to treatment of a patient. By upgrading common law rights into constitutional (as has been done in same jurisdictions) a new dynamism is injected to ethics.

Notwithstanding all that has been said, the underlying ethics that more closely capture the philosophical foundation for ethics in medicine seem to be the concept

[155] Per Karibi-Whyte JSC in *First African Trust Bank Ltd.* v. *Basil Ezegbu* (1992) 9 NWLR (pt.264) 132 and *Doma* v. *Ogiri* (1997) 1 NWLR (543) 656.

[156] *MDPDT* v. *Okonkwo* (1999) 9 NWLR (pt 617) 1; (1999) 6 NWLR (pt 786) 1 (SC)

[157] See M A. Casberg, (1967) 7 *Journal of American Medical Association* 150 and G.F. Begley, (1970) 12 *Texas Medicine* 25. See also *R.* v. *Bourne* [1939] I KB 687, [1938] 3 AII ER 615, where Lord MacNaghten equated the term 'health', not only with life, but also with well-being and welfare of a patient. In *Okonkwo* v. *Medical & Dental Practitioners Disciplinary Tribunal* (1999) 9 NWLR (pt 617) 1, the Court of Appeal equated the right of an adult to refuse treatment as not different from matters related to and with freedom of thought, conscience and religion.

of 'autonomy of the patient'. The early development of the subject recognised its importance. It has generally found expression through tort principle, rooted in the philosophy that no physician no matter how good intended should examine or treat a patient against his consent. This is a concept derived from the law of tort, the first legal contact subject with medical ethics in its embryonic stage of development. The Kansas Supreme Court in *Naterson* v. *Klineetal* recognised this fact when it said:

> Each man is considered to be master of his own body, and he may, if he is of sound mind, expressly prohibit the performance of life-saving surgery, or other medical treatment. A doctor might well believe that on operation or form of treatment is desirable or necessary, but the law does not permit him to substitute his own judgment for that of the patient by any form of artifice or deception.[158]

Also in *R* v. *Hallstron Ex p. W* (No. 2), the English Court of Appeal reinforced the principle, saying

> There is no canon of construction which presumes that Parliament intends that people should against their will, be subjected to treatment which others however professionally competent, perceive, however, sincerely and however correctly, to be in their best interest.[159]

It is this philosophy that forms the cornerstone for most of the subject of medical ethics, such as, IVF treatment, abortion, informed consent, medical confidentiality, etc. A close analysis of these subjects reveals a close alignment with the libertarian philosophy of J S Mill. Its essence can be summarised this way:

> The sole end for which mankind are warranted, individually or collectively, in interfering with the liberty of action of any of their numbers, is self protection... The only purpose for which power can be rightfully excised over any member of a civilized community, against his will, is to prevent harm to others. His own good, either physical or moral, is not a sufficient warrant. He cannot rightfully be compelled to do or forebear because it is better for him to do so, because it will make him happier, because, in the opinion of other, to do so would be wise or even right. These are good reasons for remonstrating with him, or reasoning with him, or persuading him, or entreating him but not for compelling him, or visiting him with evil in case he do otherwise. To justify that, the conduct from which it is desired to deter him ought to be calculated to produce evil to someone else. The only part of the conduct of anyone, for which he is amenable to society, is that which concerns others. In the part, which merely concerns himself his independence is of right absolute over himself, over his body and mind, the individual is sovereign. The only freedom which desires the name is that of pursuing our own good in our own way so

[158] See also Glanville Williams, *Textbook of Criminal* Law, 2nd edn; 25.1 and 14, 1981 statement of The World Medical Association, known as the *Declaration of Lisbon*, *Schloendorff* v. *Society of New York Hospital* (1914) 105 NE 92 at 93, per Cardozo J.

[159] [1986] 3 All ER 306 at 314. See also *Malette* v. *Shulman* (1990) 47 DLR 18; *Okonkwo* v. *MDPDT* (1999) 9 NWLR (pt 617) 1; (1999) 6 NWLR (Pt 786) 1 (SC)

> long as we do not attempt to deprive others or impede their efforts to obtain it. Each is the proper guardian of his own health whether bodily or mental and spiritual.[160]

In effect as long as the patient insists on autonomy to his body or refuses treatment, no one can override his wish and or rights. His autonomy can only be overridden in very exceptional cases. The welfare of others is not sufficient. But its scope is moderated by other factors, such that require a balancing with the legitimate expectation of society and economic considerations, amongst several others. *Airedale NHS Trust* v. *Anthony Bland*[161] illustrates the interplay. The appeal to the House of Lords had to do with the withdrawal of artificial feeding of a patient who was in a persistent vegetative state. The court held the withdrawal lawful. In arriving at this conclusion, it considered several factors justifying its position. Lord Goff, considered the fundamental principle of the sanctity of human life and the principle of the patients right of self determination, concluding that to the extent, that both rights conflict in the instance case, to this extent, the principle of sanctity of human life must yield to the principle of self- determination.[162]

His Lordship's statement is implicit recognition that the interest of society is a legitimate factor in reaching a decision. In the views of the court the patient's autonomy could be ascertained through substituted judgment, using 'best interest' as test for his choice. Applying the test, it reasoned that the patient's relative's wishes in the instant case could be treated as the unconscious patient's wish. Describing the nature of the right his Lordship added:

> It is established that the principle of self determination requires that respect must be given to the wishes of the patient, and for present purpose perhaps more important, the doctors duty to act in the best interest of his patient must likewise be qualified...the same principle applies where the patient refusal to give his consent has been expressed at an earlier date, before he became unconscious or otherwise incapable of communicating it...I wish to state that in cases of this kind, there is no question of the patient having committed suicide nor therefore of the doctor having aided or abetted him in doing so. It is simply that the patient has, as he is entitled to do, declined consent to treatment which might...have the effect of prolonging life.[163]

Statement such as the above indicates that the philosophical foundation to which appeals are made in cases of medical dilemma is the principle that the patient is the sovereign over his body. His wish, whether rational or otherwise is to be respected by all. Where he is unable to tell his wish, treatment must be given in his best interest.[164]

---

[160] J.S. Mill, *On Liberty* (1859), chapter 1, Everyman edition.) pp.72-73,75, cited with approved by the Wolfendon Committee in its report on Homosexual Offences and Prostitution, Cmnd 247. 13, 16, 224, 227, 257.

[161] [1993] 2 WLR 316; (1993) 12 BMLR 64.

[162] Ibid.at367, per Lord Goff

[163] Ibid. at 367, see also per Hoffman LJ, pp. 351 H — 352 A (CA).

[164] Ibid at 370 C-D per Lord Goff (HL).

Logical extension of the right may make permissible abortion right, euthanasia, and more. How far the courts would allow it lead to an irresistible respect of the patient's wish in all forms of medical treatment only time will tell. Meanwhile, it seemingly provides the foundation for analysing most ethical issues in medicine.

Chapter 2

Reproductive medicine

Introduction

Reproductive medicine is important in thinking about who we are, and who we say we want to become. Ethical questions about reproductive medicine are many and varied because they throw up issues at the heart of contemporary social, economic and political struggles over sexuality, reproduction, gender and the family.[1] In this respect a discussion on sexuality and marriage is so integral to the human nature that it can create emotional tension in discourse. Public attitude to sex and marriage can easily reveal what our thinking are - whether orthodox or unorthodox. Whatever position we take, one thing is certain – medical science is rapidly changing to accommodate the changing world's view of sexuality. In this area legal response has largely been dominated by the libertarian philosophy of Mill – which emphasises private autonomy and consent.[2] The great divide of consent and no-consent, on the other hand has largely influenced criminal and marriage laws. Generally, criminal law sanctions the offender in any non-consensual sex relationship;[3] only rarely does it do the same for consensual intercourse. If it does, it usually would be on grounds of public policy.[4] It is also from this premises that the law constructs marriage as a consensual relationship between a man and a woman for life to the exclusion of all other persons.

Sexuality and marriage

Lord Penzance in *Hyde* v. *Hyde* defined a valid marriage as a voluntary union of a man and woman to the exclusion of all others.[5] This definition is still considered valid for marriages celebrated under most marriage statute and the Matrimonial

---

[1] M. Stanworth, *Reproductive Technologies, Gender, Motherhood and Medicine* (1987) p. 3; D. Morgan, Technology and the Political Economy of Reproduction in MDA Freeman (ed) Medicine, *Ethics and the Law* (London: Stevens & Sons (1988) chapter 2; Mason & Smith, *op. cit*, chapter 2.

[2] J.S. Mill, *On Liberty* (Everyman ed, 1859) pp. 72-73.

[3] This explains why rape, indecent assault and other kindred offences are punishable by law. See for example section 357 of the Criminal Code, Cap C38 Laws of the Federation of Nigeria (LFN) 2004. For a more detailed discussion on sexual offences in Nigeria, See Okonkwo & Naish, *Criminal Law in Nigeria*, Ibadan Spectrum Books. 1990

[4] See prohibition of intercourse with a girl less than 13 years, prohibition of incest, homosexuality, etc., in sections 214-227 of the Criminal Code, LFN 2004.

[5] *Hyde* v. *Hyde* (1866) 114 LT 188.

Causes Act.[6] Thus for a marriage to be valid it must be between two persons of different sexes. The law does not allow for marriage of persons of the same sex. Section 5 (1) (a) of the Matrimonial Causes Act states that a marriage would be violable if either party to the marriage is incapable of consummating the marriage.[7] A marriage is consummated when there is sexual intercourse between the parties by the male organ fully penetrates the female organ.[8] By this understanding a valid marriage can only be one celebrated between two persons of the opposite sex. Consummation may be prevented if (i) the parties are same sex biological or (ii) if the male partner is incapable of having and sustaining erection because of impotence. (iii) if both or either party wilfully refuses to consummate the marriage.

Determining the sex of the parties may sometimes be difficult. By means of scientific advancement it is now possible to change the sex of a person or improves on a person's sexuality. A person may possess both male and female features, a state referred to as transsexuality.[9] A transsexual person may possess both testis and ovary. Question of sex allocation can become relevant in law to determine questions on impotence and responsibility for sexual offences, succession and possibly matter relating to medical certificate or evidence.[10] Some who have vagina, have features of an upper part protruding as large penis-like clitoris. If such a person should undergo a sex change, it would be necessary for the court to determine sex allocation. That was the issue presented to the court for determination in *Corbett* v. *Corbett*.[11] The petitioner sought a declaration that his marriage with the respondent was void on grounds that the respondent at the time of marriage was a man and not a woman. The facts were that the respondent biologically a man, underwent a surgical operation which involved the removal of his testicles and the construction of a vagina. Thereafter he lived as a woman. Subsequently he married the petitioner. The court (Ormrod J) held the marriage void because the respondent was treated as a man despite the sex change. In his Lordship's view, the sex of a person is determined at birth and since the respondent was a man at birth he was biologically a male. He further gave the following as guideline for sex allocation: that to determine sex for the purpose of marriage, the court would consider three determining factors, namely: (i.) the person's chromosomal features or make-up; (ii) the pre-operative gonadal feature/compliment; and (iii) the genital feature. Using these as guideline his Lordship was of the view that more weight ought to be given to the genital features at birth. Sadly it was held that notwithstanding the validity of the marriage or the sex of the 'wife,' she was physically incapable of consummating the marriage by artificial cavity. If all three features are in agreement, i.e. point to a particular sex that would be held to be the sex of the person. Using these criteria, he held that the

---

[6] Matrimonial Causes Act, 1970, Cap M7, LFN 2004

[7] Ibid.

[8] *S* v. *S* (no.2) [1962] 3 All ER 55.

9 John Glaister: *Medical Jurisprudence and Toxicology*, 9th edn. London: Livingstone p. 359.

[10] Ibid.

[11] [1970] 2 All ER 33, [1971] P. 83, but cf. *SV* v. *SY* [1962] 3 All ER 55.

respondent was a man because all the features were congruent of male particulars. It must be noted that the court did not decide what the position of law would be if chromosomal and gonadal features show transsexuality with no clear male or female genital. May be in such a case the court would hold the person incapable of consummating a marriage on the ground that he is neither wholly male nor female.[12]

A transsexual person may not demonstrate any anatomical or physiological abnormality, but may suffer from an intense desire to be identified and accepted by one of the sex groups – either male or female. This is what often causes them distress and sometimes depression. A transsexual person is different from a homosexual. While a homosexual is often content with his own sexuality and the method by which he expresses it, the transsexual is different. In his imagination nature is mistaken, and if anything desires to correct the mistake. Where the transsexual desires a change in sex, this can only be accomplished by radical surgery. This process includes castration in both males and females, a process that has remained questionable on legal and ethical grounds[13] While some jurisdictions expressly have legislation that regulate matters of consent for transsexual change in sexual preference, the position in most common law jurisdictions is regulated either on the basis of a tacit understanding between medicine and law or on the basis of the doctrine of necessity or genuine medical treatment.[14] Generally a person's sex is determined from the genital organs, from gonads or from chromosomal make up or from external characteristics such as physic. This is where controversy may crop up, especially as to what weight to place on one or several of these factors because they vary from person to person. Some men may have genitalia that are congenitally malformed or are masculinised women, referred to as the adrenagenital syndrome. At the other end, some women may exhibit rudimental female genitalia with chromosomal male features. Some writers are of the view that faced with conflict of evidence, transsexuals should be assigned to the sex they are likely able to support in society; thereby subordinating the chromosomal sex features to the upbringing in society of the transsexual.[15]

How has the court treated these matters? These were the issues that arose for determination in *Corbett* v. *Corbett*.[16] *Corbett* was followed in *R* v. *Tan*,[17] though

---

[12] S.5(1) (a) of Matrimonial Cause Act 1970.

[13] See for example DW Meyers, *The Human Body and the Law* (1970) p. 66, cited in Mason & Smith *op. cit.* p. 42 n.10. Meyer has argued that the invasive nature of the castration surgery is such that consent in law is impossible to cover, because in his view it is tantamount to maiming at common law and or statute. Note that while translation from male to female can be so accomplished by the construction of artificial vaginal, the reverse from female to male is still biological impossible; see for general discussion, A Rogers, Legal Implications of Transsexuality (1993) 341 *Lancet* 1085; M. Roth, Transsexuality and the sex Change Operation: A Contemporary Medico-Legal and Social Problem (1981) 40 *Med. Leg. J.* 5.

[14] Sweden for example puts 18 as the age of consent for sex change, see A Cremona-Barbaro, Medical-Legal Aspects of Transsexualism in Western Europe (1986) 5 *Med. Law* 89.

[15] Mason and Smith, *op. cit.*, 43

[16] [1970] 2 All ER 56; [1971] P. 83.

[17] [1983] QB 1053; [1983] 2 All ER 12.

criticised as an unfeeling judgment that refused to consider the total sexual ambience of the individual. It has also been subject to criticism of commentators. For example, Finlay suggests that disputes in the context of *Corbett* case ought to be determined on the basis that transsexual marriages are valid if it is found that the transsexual is capable of fulfilling the essential role of the sex that he or she has assumed.[18] Generally every man is presumed capable of consummating a marriage until the contrary is proved by permanent de facto incapacity. Impotence is the inability of a man to have and sustain penis erection which makes it incapable for him to have sexual intercourse. Impotence is relevant in law for purposes of marriage in proceeding relating to nullity and divorce, paternity disputed or matters connected with sexual offences. A complete absence of penis is prime facie evidence of impotence. Malfunction or impartial development of it may also be evidence of impotence, depending on the degree of malfunction or underdevelopment, as in cases of transsexual. A marriage is rendered voidable if a husband is incapable of consummating the marriage due to impotence.[19] Medical evidence may be required by the court to determine capacity to consummate. For example in *Fajemisi* v. *Fajemisi*, [20] where impotence was alleged, the husband was examined by a medical doctor to determine the state of his organ erection. Also in *Ogunmuyiwa* v. *Ogunmuyiwa*,[21] Taylor CJ ordered medical examination of the husband respondent to determine his potency.

The Matrimonial Causes Act does not define what constitute 'consummation' of a marriage. It is for this reason that resort is made to case law interpretation. Its ordinary meaning in relation to marriage is to make a marriage complete by sexual intercourse. To achieve it the male organ must fully penetrate the female organ. Neither the rupture of the hymen or the emission of semen is required.[22] Once there is penetration a marriage is consummated. It is immaterial for how long it last or whether one of the parties is sterile or that the satisfaction derived therefrom was low due to malfunction of sexual organ or terms imposed by a party e.g. the use of family planning devices. In *W (otherwise) K* v. *W* [23] and *R* v. *R*,[24] where penetration was transient it was held that there was no consummation and or penetration. These cases do not align with the position that rape is complete with penetration no matter how slight and is contrary to *S* v. *S*, considered a better authority.

---

[18] H.A. Finlay, Sexual Identity and the Law on Nullity (1980) 54 *ALJ* 115; J Taite, The Law relating to Consummation of Marriage when one of the spouse is a post-operative transsexual (1980) 15 *Anglo Amer. LR* 141; J.M. Thomson, Transsexualism-A Legal Perspective (1981) 6 *J. Med. Ethics* 92.

[19] S.5(1) (a) of Matrimonial Cause Act 1970.

[20] (unreported) suit 1/190/67 of 2/4/70.

[21] [1965] 1 All NLR 660.

[22] See sec. 6 of Criminal Code. In *R* v. *Hughes* (1884) 9 Cox to prove rape it is not necessary that the victim a virgin human was broken or injured or that there was emission of semen – *R* v. *Allen* (1839) 9 C &. P 312; *R* v. *Cox* (1832) 5 C &. P 297.

[23] [1967] 3 All ER 178.

[24] (1952] 1 All ER 1194.

In *S* v. *S (No.2)*;[25] the wife had a malformed vagina that did not permit full penetration by the husband's organ and it reduced the consequential satisfaction. The court held that there was penetration and consummation of the marriage. The use of contraceptives or other family planning devices or coitus interruption e.g. withdrawal before emission of semen do not prevent consummation.[26] It is in this respect that the House of Lord's decision in *Cower* v. *Cower*[27] that intercourse must be ordinary and complete and that the use of contraceptives constitutes an impediment which frustrated consummation is therefore unfortunate. Whatever, it can be argued that it is reconcilable with *S* v. *S* on the grounds that an impediment or frustration of a act does not necessarily mean a absence of the thing itself. It only makes the thing difficult to achieve or reduces its satisfaction if it is a thing that is subject to pleasure, such as intercourse.

Consummation may be relevant in paternity disputes, because pregnancy is no irrefutable evidence of consummation. It can be brought about by artificial insemination or from adultery.[28] In deciding paternity cases considerable value may be placed on blood test. Blood of all person generally fall within four broad grouping – O, A, B and AB. But it must be admitted that this is of limited usefulness considering the fact that about 90 per cent of all blood groups belong to O and A and the remain to B and AB. The real value of blood test is that it can provide exclusion evidence, but is incapable of furnishing inclusive evidence that a person is the biological parent of a child.[29] Potency or otherwise may be an issue in the proof of sexual offences. Below puberty, a boy is presumed incapable of having sexual intercourse. Since puberty means the attainment of virility rather than power of coitus, which may and is usually earlier than puberty or virility. An equation of power of coitus with virility under the Criminal Code on grounds of age is unfortunate.[30] It confuses two separate and distinct things as one. The Criminal Code fixes the age for attainment of virility as above 12 years.[31] Accordingly, all boys above 12 years are presumed capable of having sexual intercourse. It is noteworthy however that the Code does not fix the limit when a man ceases to be sexually potent. This is reasonable, because spermatozoa have been found in men over ninety years. Since impotence is the inability to have sexual intercourse, it follows that an impotent man cannot be guilty of the offence of rape and other sexual offenses that involve the use of the male organ. Such a person may however be successfully

---

[25] [1962] 3 All ER 55.

[26] See *Baxter* v. *Baxter* [1948] AC 2 74.

[27] [1945] 2 All ER 197.

[28] *L* v. *L* [1949] 1 All ER 141; *Clark* v. *Clarke* [1943] 2 All ER 540.

[29] G.O Obi, Haematology and Legal Medicine in S. Akpata (ed) *Medical Ethics*: Proceedings of Workshop: Lagos Univ. Press (1982) p. 51.

[30] J. Glaister *op. cit.* p. 358.

[31] S. 30 the Criminal Code provides that a male person under the age of 12 is presumed in law to be incapable of sexual intercourse. This is an irrefutable presumption of law.

charged and convicted for sexual offences that do not involve carnal knowledge, eg. being an accessory to rape offence.

A woman, on the other hand, is primarily sterile if she is past ovulation. While the general rule is that a woman can only become pregnant during the menstruation period of her life, in some rare cases it is possible for pregnancy to occur after the usual signs of menstruation have ceased. The law does not fix the age when a woman becomes sterile nor does it state when she ceases to be. That notwithstanding, it can safely be said as a statement of fact that children who have not yet commenced menstruation may not be capable of bearing children. It is therefore unfortunate that the English rule on perpetuities of vesting for contingent gifts proceeded on the basis that a girl less than five year could give birth in *Re Gaite*[32] and in *Re Dawson*[33] the judicial reasoning proceed on the assumption that a woman aged over 60 years could give birth to a child. Both decisions have been criticised by Bartin Leach[34] on the grounds that they ignore biological realities. In his words, the cases can only be explained on the grounds that the 'judicial world is populated by fertile octogenarians and precarious toddlers'. While his criticism may be true of *Re Gaite*, same cannot in all probabilities be said of *Re Dawson*, because it may be possible for a woman who has stopped menstruation to be pregnant.

The Matrimonial Causes Act provides that if consummation of a marriage is impossible because either or both parties wilfully refuse to consummate it the marriage would be dissolved.[35] Since a wilful and persistent refusal to consummate a marriage is a question of fact to be determined from the evidence of the parties, medical examination is generally unnecessary except to prove impotence.

Blood test

The courts can under its discretionary, inherent powers order blood testing in a paternity dispute to determine the biological father of a child.[36] Blood testing in pursuit of this purpose has its limitation. It can only provide conclusive evidence of paternity in the negative sense. It can prove that a man is not the biological father of a child. In the positive sense, it can only prove that a particular man is the father of a child if the blood contains unusual characteristics.[37] Though there is no express power in Nigeria which authorities the court to order a blood test in a paternity dispute, the English Family Law Reform Act 1980, expressly authorities an English

---

[32] [1949] 1 All ER 459.

[33] (1888) 39 Ch. D 155.

[34] B Leach, *The Rule Against Perpetuities*, 2nd ed.p89

[35] See S. 15 (2) (a) and the cases of *Owobiyi* v. *Owobiyi* [1965] 1 All NLR 625 in which the English cases of *Horton* v. *Horton* [1947] 2 All ER 871 and *S* v. *S* (otherwise C) [1954] 3 All ER 736 were considered by Taylor CJ.

[36] For a general discussion, see M. Hayes, Use of Blood Test in Pursuit of Truth (1971) 87 *LQR* 86.

[37] S v S [1971] 3 All ER 107; *W* v. *Official Solicitor* [1971] 3 All ER 107, but cf. F v F [19] P. and In Re L [19] p.

court to so order. Section 20 (11) of the 1980 English Act provide that the court 'may give direction for the use of blood test'.[38]

Even though there is no express Nigerian legislation on the matter, it is reasonable to suggest that the practice in both Nigeria and England will be no different and that an analysis of the use of the statutory power in England would provide a useful road-map for the practice in Nigeria. The fact that the English Act employs the phrase 'the court may direct the use of blood test' is indicative of the fact that there should be no automatic resort to it wherever there is a paternity dispute. The section only confers discretion on the courts. Though the Act does not spell out the circumstances for its order, it is settled that in exercising the discretion the court must attempt to balance any conflict between its desire to act in the best interest of the child and the interest of justice. Let us see how the courts have exercised the jurisdiction:

In *W* v. *Official Solicitor*,[39] the husband had obtained a decree nisi on the grounds of his wife's adultery with a named co-respondent, a coloured man. The co-respondent disappeared before the divorce petition was heard. In effect it meant that a blood test could only point in one direction – that the husband is not the child's father. It could not show the identity of his father. The trial court and the English Court of Appeal (Lord Denning MR dissenting) refused to exercise its discretion that the child be tested to determine his paternity. The House of Lords reversed the Court of Appeal decision. According to Lord Reid the issues raised required balancing two often-conflicting interest: that of the child's best interest and the interest of justice. His Lordship said,

> But here there is or may be a conflict between the interests of the child and the general requirements of justice. Justice requires that available evidence should not be suppressed, but it may be against the interest of the child to produce it.[40]

Accordingly, the House of Lords ordered testing even though there was only one possible identifiable father. The case illustrates that a blood test may be ordered even if there is only one identifiable father if considerations of justice so dictate. In this case the litigation turned around who should be responsible for the child's maintenance. That put the interest of justice ahead of the interest of the child. When a similar question of who should bear responsibility for a child's maintenance was raised in a paternity case in *S* v. *S*[41] the court was of the view that it was a case for a rightfully exercise of the discretion to order blood test. A husband was granted divorce on the ground of his wife's adultery with the co-respondent. Meanwhile the wife sought an affiliation order against the co-respondent in the magistrate court, which adjourned the matter pending the High Court trial on the legitimacy of the

[38] S. 20 (11 of (English) Family Law Reform Act, 1980.

[39] [1970] 3 All ER 107.

[40] Ibid. at 112.

[41] [1970] 3 All ER 107, Note the case and *W* v. *Official Solicitor* were both decided together by the House of Lords.

child. The House of Lord's was of the view that the High Court and the Court of Appeal were right in those circumstances in ordering a blood test, because it could help to establish as between the two men who was the father of the child.

Where however blood test is merely required to prove a wife's adultery or it will result in harmful effect on the child the court will not make an order. In *M(D)* v. *M(S)*,[42] the wife obtained a maintenance order on the ground of desertion that resulted from the couple separation. After the separation, she conceived and gave birth to a child. The husband denied the paternity of the child and the wife refused to allow a blood test to be taken. Five years later the wife cohabited with another man as wife and had children. Five year after this the husband petitioned for divorce alleging that ten years before the wife had committed adultery with an unknown man and as a result gave birth to a child. In order to establish the truth of his allegation, the husband asked for blood test to be taken. Lord Denning MR was of the opinion that 'these adults should fight out their own battle without bringing the infant into it'.[43] His Lordship's view enjoyed the support of Lord MacDermott. In *S* v. *S*,[44] Lord Denning summarised the position of law this way:

> If I had reason to believe that the applicant for a blood test was of a fishing nature, designed for some ulterior motive to call in question the legitimacy, otherwise unimpeached, of a child who had enjoyed a legitimate status...the court...would be justified in refusing the application.

It is reasonable to expect that similar principles will apply to DNA testing relating to paternity.[45]

The Acquired Immune Deficiency Syndrome (AIDS)

This deadly disease has been described this way by a commentator[46]

> AIDS is about loss of control – control of one's own bowels and bladder, one's arms or legs...AIDS is the moment to moment management of uncertainty. It's a roller coaster ride without a seat belt. Once this ride begins, there is never a moment when the rush of events that swirls you stops long enough for you to get your bearings. AIDS is like motion sickness except you realise that you'll never stop moving one way or another, you'll be dealing with AIDS for the rest of your life.

No doubt the AIDS crisis is a triumph of anxiety and uncertainty. Unfortunately every aspect of this deadly disease resonates with uncertainty. Many

---

[42] [1969] 2 All ER 243.

[43] Ibid. at p. 245, per Lord Denning MR.

[44] [1971] 3 All ER 107 at 115.

[45] For general discussion see O. F. Emiri, Legal issues in DNA Testing in Emiri (ed) *Crosscutting issues* p. 23.

[46] M Callen, Persons with AIDS, Remark at the Annual meeting of the American Public Health Association, Las Vegas, Nevada, 1986, reprinted in *Surviving And Thriving With AIDS: Hints for the Needy Diagnosed* in Callen (ed.) 1987 p. 39 cited in W. B. Rubenstein, *Law and Empowerment: The Idea of Order in the Time of AIDS* (1989) 98 *Yale LJ* 946.

year after its discovery, scientist still debate the causative relationship between it and the human immune deficiency virus (HIV).[47] They are unable to explain why the virus lay dormant and harmless for years and why it is then suddenly activated. Nor have they satisfactorily explained the differing physical manifestation of HIV infection or predict what infections will afflict which of us, when or how. More worrisome is the fact that there have only been limited successes in finding curative experimental drugs, and those claimed to be potent are dubious. AIDS may be transmitted by a single act of heterosexual intercourse. It is not confined to the homosexual and drug community. It may also be transmitted through the transfusion of infected blood or blood products or through congenital infection i.e. to an infant born from an infected mother.[48] The HIV virus, which is itself symptomless, is transmittable. After a lay incubation period put at maximum of about 10 years, about 30-40% of those infected with the HIV virus will invariable develop clinically to AIDS or pre-AIDS. The mortality rate of full-blown AIDS is probably 100% and hopes of a cure are dim.[49] A person is said to be HIV positive when his blood contains anti-bodies for the AIDS virus. But this does not in itself prove that the person has AIDS, because the clinical definition of a person with AIDS requires the sufferer to have developed one of a number of secondary illnesses resulting from the destruction of the sufferer's immune system by the virus.[50] This is so because a person HIV positive may not look or feel ill, more so when the virus is probably symptomless and only 30-40% of those who tested positive to it will develop AIDS.[51] On thing however is clear, anyone who develops AIDS is likely to die. It is said that the fact that a person test positive to the HIV virus does not mean he is infected, because HIV antibodies may be present in the blood stream when the virus itself is not. However, no reliable test is available to distinguish between infectious and non-infectious suffers. It is for this reason that both groups are treated identically – as carriers. Some are of the view that to the extent that a carrier may remain asymptomatic for up to 10 years from time of initial infection, it mean that a carrier may infect anyone before he is diagnosed, which invariable means that present statistics on the AIDS pandemic is likely to be gross under-estimates.

Society's response to AIDS remains somewhat controversial; being dictated by a mixture directed at the protection of the sufferer's right to privacy and some form

---

[47] Rubenstein, *above* n. 46; M.Y. Schechter, et. al, HIV-1 and the Aetiology of AIDS (1993) 341 *Lancet* 658

[48] Note that the role of breast feeding in the transmission of AIDS is currently uncertain. See for example, European Collaborative Study: Mother-to-Child Transmission of HIV Infection (1988) 2 *Lancet* 1039.

[49] R O'Dair, Liability in Tort for the Transmission of AIDS: Some Lessons from Afar and the Prospect for the Future; Baruch, AIDS in the Courts: Tort liability for the Sexual Transmission of Acquired Immune Deficiency Syndrome (1987) *Tort and Insurance LJ* 165 AT 167 N. 4; Mason and Smith, *op. cit*, pp. 20-21

[50] Stauter, *United States* v. *Moore*: AIDS and the Criminal Law-The Witch Hunt Begins (1989) 22 *Akron LJ* 50, cited in O'Dair, *above* n.49.

[51] Some scientific studies now reveal that there is a 100% causative relationship between HIV and AIDS. Dr. Roberts Gallo, a co-discoverers of the AIDS virus suggest that 90% of all HIV carriers will die – *Scientific American* (1987) 265, 39 – 48; see also Stauter, *above* n 50 at p. 506.

of coercive control of its spread.[52] Our discussion will focus on the legal aspects of the AIDS pandemic in the context of its legal classification and the doctor-patient relationship.

AIDS and legal classification

It has been suggested that the legal system already has formalised categories that are equipped to deal with AIDS-related legal issues and that the practical differences between AIDS related issues and other traditional categories are relatively easy to assimilate in the legal process.[53] While it is not in doubt that most AIDS-related issues will show certain degree of novelty, it appears that there already exists institutional and conceptual framework for dealing with the issues. Analogous situations abound, especially from cases involving sexual transmission of genital herpes, from cases involving school children infected with hepatitis B virus, to efforts to round up prostitutes to stem the spread of syphilis and certain statutes and cases relating to discrimination against the disabled.[54]

Carrier's liability to sexual partner

While most cases on liability for sexual transmission of disease have often concerned a defendant who actually know that he is infected, there exist the possibility that such liability may also extend to persons in high risk groups. Suppose, a man who was previously a homosexual begins a relationship with a girl, questions

---

[52] Most jurisdictions threaten quarantine or at least endorse restriction of freedom of those who pose an unreasonable threat to public safety and health. In Cuba for example, testing positive for HIV may lead to compulsory detention. For a general reading of the vacillating policies dictated by social and political considerations, see the following R Bayer & C Healton, Controlling AIDS in Cuba. The Logic of Quarantine (1989) 320 *New Engl. J. Med.* 1022; L Gostin, Public Health strategies for controlling AIDS: Legislative and Regulatory Policy in the United States (1989) 261 *J. Amer. Med, Ass* 1621; H. Watchirs, HIV/ AIDS and the law: The Need for Reform in Australia (1993) *I J. Law Med* 9; P. Illingworth, AIDS and Liberation (1990) 4 *Journal of Bioethics* 340; Bayer Aids and Liberation: A response to Illingworth (1992) 6 *Journal of Bioethics* 23; M Morris, American Legislation on AIDS (1991) 303 *BMJ* 325; all of which are cited in Mason & Smith, *op. cit*, pp. 22-23, n. 20, 1 and 3.

[53] See H Dalton's work, *AID and the Law: A guide for the Public* in Dalton (ed) (S. Burns & Tale AIDS law project, 1987) a collection of twenty essays discussing amongst others medical background, government and private sector responses, health care issues and problem of special groups. But cf Bubenstein, *above* n. 1, a reply to Dalton's work in which the writer argues that it is difficult to pigeonhole AIDS related litigation within present legal paradigm

[54] Dalton, above n. 53 at XIII; see also *School Board of Nassan County* v. *Airline* (1987) 107 S. Ct. 1123 (the American Supreme Court held that a teacher with tuberculosis a contagious disease could be considered handicapped within s. 504 of the Vocational Rehabilitation Act of 1973). See also the following American cases that treat HIV infection as handicap within the 1973 Act. *Doe* v. *Cetinella Hosp. Civ.* 87 – 2514 (D.C. Cal. June 30, 1980); *Ray* v. *School Dist of Desoto County*, 666 F. Supp. 1524 (M.D. Fla. 1987); *Thomas* v. *Atascaders Unified School Dist.* 662 F. Supp. 376 (C.D. Cal. 1986); *Local 1812* v. *Dept of State*, 662 F. Supp 50 (DOC 1987); *Accord District 27 Community School Board* v. *Board of Educ.* 502 NYS 2d. 325; 336 Supp. Ct 1986); see also Belinsky & Solomon, Doctors and Patients; Responsibility in a confidential Relationship in *AIDS and The Law*, Dalton (ed) above n. 53 at p. 201 – 209, where the writer draws analogy from *Tarasoff* v. *Regent of the Univ. of Cal.* 17 Cal. 3d. 425; 551 p. 2d 334, 131 Cal. Rptr. 14 (1976) on the duty of psychotherapist to protect third persons from the dangerous acts of their patient to as applying to cases involving contagious diseases.

may be raised as to whether he owes a duty of disclosure to his present partner. Assuming that he gets infected in the course of the relationship, where there is no disclosure to her of her partner's previous sexual conduct, will the law allow her to sue? Should the fact that any compensation recoverable would be of little value to her, because she has relatively a short time to live influence recoverability or its amount? If she has dependants, will the desire to compensate her dependants be an incentive for recovery? More generally, should the court in assessing compensation, if any, consider the social and economic disadvantages that result from infection with the HIV virus?[55]

Generally, liability for transmission has revolved around questions on criminal and civil liability for assault. In determining liability the courts have been concerned with the fact of consent to sexual intercourse. Once it is established that the claimant consents to intercourse, no claim for sexual assault will succeed. The nature of the act or identity of the defendant is irrelevant. Whether such consent is vitiated by a failure on the part of the defendant to disclose his sexual status would amount to assault is no different from matters related to identity. It does not go to the question of consent, which should be the very essence of the claimant's complain for a sexual offence.[56] To the extent that the cases do not consider the possibility of alternative action in negligence based on breach of a duty to disclose risk of infection, these cases can hardly serve as guide in AIDS—related litigation concerning liability for infection. The prospect of negligence is however dimmed by judicial attitude of construing medical negligence within the narrow confines of the concepts of informed consent and self-determination.[57]

In *Kathleen* v. *Robert*,[58] the plaintiffs complain was that she caught herpes as a result of sexual intercourse with the defendant. She sought a claim in damages on three grounds against the defendant, namely: (i) that by falsely stating that he had no venereal disease, which was untrue in material particulars, the defendant committed the tort of deceit or (ii) that being aware of his infection but deliberately omitting to disclose its existence, the defendant committed the tort of battery, or (iii) that by unreasonably failing to disclose the fact of his infection when he knew or ought to know that he was infected, the defendant committed the tort of negligence. The Court of Appeal for the State of California stated that if any of the facts above could be proved the cause of action would succeed. Noteworthy of mention, is the fact that the court explicitly stated that the same principle would apply to AIDS infection cases.[59] It will appear that grounds (i) and (iii) would stand chances of

---

[55] Socially a carrier may suffer isolation. Economically, a carrier may find it difficult to attract credit.

[56] See A Aguda, *Law and of Criminal Procedure*, London: Sweet & Maxwell 1980, see also *R* v. *Clarence* (1888) 22 QB. D 23

[57] *Sidaway* v. *Governors of the Bethlehem Royal Hospital* [1985] AC 871 at 894, per Lord Diplock and 898, per Lord Bridge.

[58] 198 Cal. Rept. 273.

[59] Ibid. at p. 276, see also Hermann, AIDS, Therapeutic Confidentiality; and Warning Third Parties (1989) 48 *Maryland L.R.* 54.

success under the English common law, but ground (ii) will run into counter-argument, because consent to a physical act can only amount to battery if it is non consensual. The effect of the California decision is that there exists a duty on any carrier who knows of his infection to make disclosure to his sexual partner. If he belongs to a high risk group, such as, a (former) drug abuser or homosexual, he would come under a duty to disclose by a construction of the reasonable test relating to a person who 'know or ought to know' of his infection. Would a reasonable man, for example one who belong to a high risk group not be expected to undergo medical testing to enable him warn potential sexual partners? If we answer in the affirmative, then it would be easy to impose a duty to disclose on person within the high risk bracket.

However, O'Dair is of the view that an extension of the duty to disclosure to persons within the high risk group may well be an analogy the court would be reluctant to make, because possibility exist that mandatory AIDS testing for such a group may be construed as unjustified infringement of their group interest.[60] What is more, since there is a 'window' period within which the antibodies may not be revealed even with testing it follows that mandatory testing may not in all event further the 'neighbourliness' duty of care to a defendant's sexual partner.[61] An alternative requirement that imposes a duty on the high risk person to disclose circumstances making intercourse with him risky appears to place too much moral burden on the defendant. This should be so when we consider such a requirement from the context of the fact that AIDS can be contacted also from even a single heterosexual contact. Unless there exists such a reciprocal duty of disclosure on the part of the plaintiff it would be unfair to impose it on high-risk defendant persons. We must acknowledge the fundamental difference between risk and an actual event itself. It is discriminatory to put a group of persons under a duty simply because of their sexual difference when a similar duty is not imposed on other who are at risk of infection from their traditional sex preference. The only people not at risk are those entering life long monogamous relationships where neither partner has had any previous sexual experience.

In an AIDS relating litigation where a claimant seeks compensation on the grounds of breach of duty to disclose or care, it is possible for the defendant to raise constitutional issues as defence. It can be argued that the claim amounts to a violation of his right to privacy. Such an argument was put forward by the defendant in *Kathleen* v. *Robert*.[62] The defendant stated that the claimant's action violated his constitutional right to privacy. The California Court of Appeal was however unimpressed with the argument. In reply, it stated that right to privacy

---

[60] O'Dair, above n. 49 at. p 222 - 223

[61] Some researches state that the window period may be within 9 months to 3 years. See O'Brien, Mandatory HIV Antibody Testing Policies: An Ethical Analysis (1989) 3 *Journal of Bioethics* 273 at 276. For a summary of the neighbour principle on care, see Lord Atkin in *Donoghue* v. *Stevenson* [1932] AC 562 at 580; see also *Grant* v. *Australian Knitting Mills* [1936] AC 85.

[62] 198 Cal. Rept. 273.

would be overridden in the interest of public health. The American use of tort as a means of deterring socially undesirable conducts however may suffer limitation when an attempt is made to transpose it into the classical common law model of the English type. While the American courts have no difficulty in awarding punitive damages, the English practice is to rarely award punitive damages because tort law essentially is used as a compensatory tool only.

Vindicating an AIDS—related case within the bracket of negligence is not free of controversy. Every claim in negligence requires the claimant to prove a duty, a breach of the duty of care and resultant damages. Assuming that the claimant in an infection case is able to scale the first two requirements, the third can become problematic. The reason is not unconnected with the need to show a causative link between the breach and the injury. How can this be a problem for an infected claimant? Let us consider what happens when the HIV virus enters the body. Scientists tell us that virus are not living organisms. They are rather mobile genetic codes or message capable of disrupting the functions of normal healthy cell. When the virus enters the body it re-programmes the normal healthy cells. It destroys the body's ability to fight infection by reprogramming the white T4 cells on which the body depends for the production of antibodies to fight diseases. The result is that the body becomes incapable of fighting infection by the production of antibodies. Rather it produces further virus. The triggered virus is what later develops within a maximum period of 10 years to full-blown AIDS, an often terminal condition.[63] Herein lies the difficulty for the claimant. He will need to show clearly that the resultant AIDS is not the damage itself, but the HIV infection, for if it were otherwise the resultant damage may be treated as one outside present limitation period of 6 years for tortuous acts and omissions. Will we treat HIV virus infection as within the definition of physical injury? If HIV is asymptomatic, it means that the infected claimant may well enjoy normal life and may not have suffered physical injury within the contemplation of the law. This is likely to be so because essentially it would mean that the complaint of a claimant is not that he has already suffered physical injury, but that he or she risks developing AIDS in some future time. In effect any finding that the infection with the virus is itself physical injury and therefore actionable damage can only be treated as policy consideration or purposive interpretation of injury motivated by a desire to compensate the claimant for injury. Maybe what make sense in this context is to construe physical injury to include injury to health, thereby treating the virus infection as actionable damage on the ground that an infected person probably losses the chances of living to full age in good health. These are wider policy matters that require interplay of medicine, law and ethics in the face of the damaging effect of the infection.

[63] .O'Dair, above n 49 at pp. 226 – 228, see also Darby, Tort Liability for the Transmission of the AIDS virus: Damages For Fear of AIDS and Prospects of AIDS (1988) 45 *Wash. & Lee L.R* 185.

Privacy and confidentiality in doctor-patient relationship

Our discussion here will focus on what a doctor should do if his HIV positive patient refuses to disclose his sexual contacts, past and present. *W* v. *Egdell*[64] was a case that revolved around the confidentiality issue. The plaintiff had been detained in a mental hospital after killing several people. The defendant doctor who was engaged by his solicitor to provide medical report on his condition made an unfavourable one which was not used by the plaintiff. The defendant however took it upon himself to provide copies of it to the hospital and the Home Secretary. In an action against him for breach of confidence, the English Court of Appeal held that the defendant did not breach any confidence. The interest of the public – its health and safety far outweighed the interest of preserving the doctor—patient confidence. *X* v. *Y*[65] was another such case relating to public safety and confidentiality. The plaintiff health authority sought an injunction to restrain the publication by a newspaper of information obtained by them in breach of confidence that two identified doctors were practicing whilst being treated for AIDS. The argument of the defendants was that disclosure was necessary to protect public health and safety, and further, that it was a matter that could generate public interest in full and informed debate if members of the public knew of the facts. Rose J (sitting as a court of first instance) ordered the injunction on the grounds that there was already sufficient information in the public domain to allow for the requisite debate without a necessary disclosure of the doctors identity.

The present legal position in America is that in certain exceptional circumstances, the doctor may warn a patient's contacts that they may be at risk from his patient's sexually transmitted disease if warning is considered proper in the interest of public health.[66] Common law also recognises that the equitable duty of confidence is subject to overriding public good and interest.[67] In this respect *Tarasoff* v. *Regents of the University of California*[68] is very instructive. The patient told his therapist of his intention to kill a named person, the plaintiff's daughter. But he did not warn the intended victim who was eventually murdered by the patient. In a claim by the plaintiff, on behalf of his daughter's estate, claiming compensation for breach of a duty to warn her the Supreme Court of California held that, if the therapist knew or ought to know that his patient posed a serious danger to an identifiable individual, that was sufficient to put him under a duty to take reasonable steps to protect that individual. Since he failed to do so, he was held liable.

Several questions can be raised about what *Tarasoff* decides in the context of AIDS related litigation. By analogy, will its principle apply only where the intention of the patient is revealed? Or does it extend to perceived intention of the patient, as discerned by the therapist? Is the duty to warn owed only to identify victims of the

---

[64] [1989] 2 WLR 689.

[65] [1988] 2 All ER 648.

[66] *Davis* v. *Rodman* 227 S.W. 612 at 614 (1921); *Gammill* v. *United States* 727 F. 2d . 950 (1984).

[67] *Beloff* v. *Pressdram* [1973] 1 AII ER 241 at 260; *Schering* v. *Folkman Chemicals* [1981] 2 WLE 848.

[68] (1976) 17 Cal. 3d; 345; 551 P. 2d 334; 131 Cal. Rptr. 14.

patient's wrong? Or does it also extend to foreseeable victims? These questions are important because, if we are to extend the principle into the area of AIDS, it could well restrict or expand the ambit of duty a doctor owes to the patient's sexual contacts. In the AIDS context the resolution of these questions would tell us whether a doctor owes such a duty only to a known partner or to foreseeable partners. In the United States, writers have been debating whether the *Tarasoff* principle ought to extend to AIDS related cases[69] Some are of the view that its expanded application to AIDS cases could cause damage to the doctor—patient confidential relationships. The beneficial value of such disclosure has also been questioned. The partner of the HIV patient may already be positive by the time a supposed warning is given. On this ground it can be argued that costs of imposing such an onerous duty on the doctor is not worth its supposed benefit. But there exist also counter-argument for imposing a duty. Consider for once: the partner of the HIV patient may be particularly vulnerable, believing that she is in a monogamous heterosexual relationship and so not within any foreseeable risk. It is on this ground that there appears good reason why the unsuspecting partner ought to be warned. Warning can also be a preventive step in transmitting AIDS congenitally, as the woman may then choose not to become pregnant for fear of the risk of passing it onto her baby. It will be reasonable no doubt to hold in favour of a duty being owed to the HIV positive current partner and any child of that person infected *in utero*.[70]

Tarasoff principle as it is presently understood suffers severe limitations if we attempt to use it for purposes of drawing similar parallels in AIDS related litigation. Under English common law in the context of a duty to warn, 'Good Samaritan' law is restrictive in nature. Generally, the common law does not make liable a person for failing to do a good or moral act, save where certain rare relationship exists between the parties, such as those arising from blood or contract. The classical example often given to illustrate the proposition is that no liability is incurred if a man who can swim sees a neighbour drowning and yet refuses to help him. English courts, unlike its American counterpart, have long adopted the view that while a man is under a moral duty to act as a Good Samaritan, there is no legal duty to do so. This would logically mean that while a doctor may have a moral duty to warn the HIV positive patient's sexual partners, there is no legal duty to do so. It is not out of order to argue that because all sexual intercourse carry some risk of AIDS infection, the doctor should have no duty to warn past partners or the contact of past partners, or foreseeable partners of the HIV positive patient. Anyone who engages in the act of intercourse, whether with an AIDS patient or non-AIDS person ought to know of the inherent dangers such act may possible bring with it. A no-duty to warn argument also finds justification from the unnecessary burden it seeks to put on the

[69] Hermann, Therapeutic Confidentiality, and Warning Third Parities (1989) 48 *Maryland LR* 54; Psychotherapist Duty to Warn: Ten years After Tarasoff (1985) 15 *Golden Gate U.L. Rev.* 271; Howe, Ethical Problems in Treating Military Patients with Human Immuno-deficiency Virus (1987) 3 *Jo. Contemp. Health Law and Policy*, 111.

[70] O'Dair, above, n.49 at p. 239.

doctor. Warning past partners and their contact can be a difficult requirement. How is the doctor expected to gather information about their whereabouts, more so when such warning may not prevent their infection; if they are already infected from contact with the patient?

This brings us again face-to-face with the value of warning. Some of those not yet infected by the patient may not take serious the doctor's warning. In any event, why should it be the doctor's duty to shield persons from a risk they choice to voluntarily run? Foreseeable partners may well be unidentifiable members of a large class of people at risk of the carrier's conduct, that the doctor ought not to owe a duty. This notwithstanding, there is ultimately good reason why a doctor should owe a duty to warn his patient's known sexual partner. Our society have increasingly come to view medical care giving as a social entitlement, and in that context it is not unreasonable to impose a duty to warn on a professional whose duty is to provide care.[71] What position the courts would adopt will depend on how it considers care-giving through medicine. If a duty to warn exists, the doctor is required to put reasonable effort to discover from the HIV patient the identity of his partner. Negligence in this respect is raised if the director does not take reasonable steps expected of a professional in his calling. The prevailing guideline issued by the General Medical Council of England for example, requires a doctor to make some attempt to persuade his patient to disclose his HIV status to his spouse or sexual partner.[72]

Belifsky and Solomon are of the view that the American courts application of the *Tarasoff* principle on liability, with its extension[73] to cases involving contagious diseases[74] imposes a duty to inform or warm known sexual partners of a patient HIV status. It is respectfully suggested that their arguments and parallel analysis are merely propositional, drawn analogically from an analysis of the authority. There should be no serious objection to a contrary position, that seek to distinguish the *Tarasoff* principle being inapplicable to AIDS related litigation.

AIDS and Employment

This is an area where ethical issues relating to AIDS takes on an emotive response, because employment is closely connected with discrimination. Generally in America, discrimination statutes are interpreted to forbid discrimination of carriers.[75]

---

[71]Ibid.

[72]See, *Statement of the General Medical Council to Registered Practitioners*, September 8, 1988, cited in O'Dair, *above* n 4 at p. 245 n. 62, see also *Gillick* v. *West Norfolk & Wisbech AHA* [1986] AC 112; [1985] 3 All ER 402 – where a similar disclosure duty was imposed in matters of contraceptive.

[73] Belifsky & Solomon, Doctors and Patients in *AIDS and the Law*, Dalton *et al.* (eds) London, Yale Univ. Press. 1987

[74] Query? Is AIDS like a contagious disease that can be spread by social contact? HIV virus is not a contagious disease spread by casual contact. For discussion see W.E. Parmet, AIDS and the Limits of Discrimination Law (1987) 15 *Law Med. Hlth Care* 461 and A Orr, Legal AIDS: Implications of AIDS and HIV for British and American Law (1989) *J. Med. Ethics* 61, cited in Mason and Smith, *op. cit.* P.25 n.19.

[75] See for example S. 504 of (USA) Vocational Rehabilitation Act of 1973 (discrimination against disabled).

Some American courts have held that disability law prevents employers from requiring HIV testing as a condition of employment.[76] Handicap discrimination statutes are interpreted to forbid discriminatory use of tests. What this mean is that employees who are members of a protected group may not be singled out for special testing not uniformly administered on all employees. However there is no general prohibition of non-discriminatory medical testing.[77] In England, like Nigeria, there are no such discrimination laws directly related to medical or physical disability. That being the case, it can be said that an employer may refuse to engage a known carrier even though it can be argued that such an act may constitute indirect discrimination on grounds of sex, if the claimant can show disproportion in the rate of infection based on gender. An employer, of course, should be able to escape liability if he can show that a carrier does not fit his employment.[78]

The major ethical question in this context (testing) relates to confidentiality of the result of testing. If from a pre-employment testing an employer discovers that the prospective employee is a carrier, would it be ethical to inform him of his status? If testing is considered non-discriminatory because it is required for all employees, can the employer use a HIV positive result as the basis for terminating an employee's contract of service? These are weighty ethical matters that are yet to be tested by the litigation process. While there are no doubt ethical argument that can be advanced that HIV positive should not of itself be a ground for terminating a contract of employment, counter arguments are also conceivable that it ought if the condition may affect job performance and public acceptability of the employee if engaged in duties directly touching on members of the public.

The Politics of AIDS

The recent years have witnessed the efforts of people with AIDS (PWAs) coming together to forge a common front to deal with the anxiety of the AIDS crisis. PWA politics and empowerment movement in America dates to the second Annual AIDS Forum held at the National Lesbian and Gay Health Conference in Denver in June 1983. The purpose of the PWA empowerment movement is as summarised by their Mission Statement:[79]

> We are people with AIDS and AIDS Related Complex (ARC) who can speak for ourselves to advocate for our own causes and concerned...we do not see ourselves as victims. We will not be victimised. We have the right to be treated with respect, dignity, compassion and understanding. We have the

---

[76] A Leonard, AIDS in the Workplace in AIDS and the Law.

[77] Ibid.

[78] For general reading, see N Fagan & D Newell, AIDS and Employment Law (1987) 137 *NLJ* 752; I Kelly, The AIDS Virus at Workplace (1991) 141 *NLJ* 88.

[79] Sometimes PWA go beyond just lobbies, especially in the United States of American and some European states where they have become vocal. Sometimes they have taken their anger against government and society's inaction by engaging in civil demonstration, picketing and the like, eg, the March 1987 march in New York around Wall Street.

> right to lead fulfilling, productive lives, to live and die with dignity and compassion.

The Denver Principles calls on health care professional to empathise with them and not simply treat and deal with AIDS intellectually. PWA movement's aside, empowerment and collectivisation have become forceful lobbies in some jurisdictions, especially on issues of importance to them. The result is that most enacted AIDS legislation and practice directives show and reflect concern for them.[80] These notwithstanding, the public still exhibits fear of AIDS, believing that it is contagious and highly infectious. True, AIDS is a deadly disease, but there exist a need to evolve an ethical framework of regulation able to deliver compassion, rather than quarantine laced with contempt and hatred.

[80]Statement of Purpose of the National Association of PWA in *Surviving and Thriving with AIDS: Hints for the Newly Diagnosed*, p. 130 (M. Callen ed.1987) cited in Rubenstein *above.*

Chapter Three

Bio-Technology and Reproduction

Introduction: the politics of reproduction

A conservative notion of family is implicit in the recent resistance to new biotechnology relating to the family and sexuality. For supporters of the traditional family values, no new forms of family outside the confines of traditional marriage should be permitted. For opponents of the legally defined family new forms of households should be encouraged.[1] For example, Artificial Reproductive Technique (ART) has the potential of separating sex from reproduction and so further separating biological from social parenthood. When governments encourages such technique, it invariable suggest that our hitherto construction of 'private sphere' of law within the boundaries of privacy is expanding.[2] These techniques throw up issues relating to parental rights and responsibilities, the up-bringing, care and control of children conceived and born in the crest of bio-technology, and the appropriate role of state agencies overseeing the boundaries of the technology. The *Gillick* litigation[3] is one such social question generated by technology. The issue raised in the case no doubt revealed the capacity of medicine to penetrate the private space of the family and supersede the familial regime of parental control.

ART explicitly means that it is no longer necessary to achieve reproduction through physical contact of sex. This makes it look like some form of technological incest, thereby minimising the repugnancy which might otherwise attach to the process, and of course by extension it legitimises research and experimentation on foetus. Not all persons however share the fears and concern for the family introduced by modern technology. For example, some commentators argue that the fear is unfounded, because it is rooted in perceived language and perceptual

[1] For general reading see, M.D Davis, Moral and Maternal: The Family in the Right in R. Levitas (ed.), *The Ideology of the New Right* (1986); J. Lewis, The Politics of Motherhood in the 1980s: Warnock, Gillick and Feminists (1986) 13 *J. Law & Soc.* 321, L. Moran, A Reading in Sexual Politics and Law (1986) 8 *Liverpool LR* 83; D Morgan, Technology and the Political Economy of Reproduction in MDA Freeman (ed), *Medicine, Ethics and the Law*, London: Sweet & Maxwell (1988) 23.

[2] N Rose, Beyond the Public- Private Division: Law, Power and The Family in P. Fitzpatrick & A. Hunt, *Critical Legal Studies* (1987) 61, cited in Morgan, *above* n 1 at 48 n 10.

[3] *Gillick* v. *West Norfolk & Wisbeck AHA* [1986] AC 112.

solidarity. Yoxen,[4] for example, argues that the language of nature is often used to imply a shared agreement about common standards where none really exists. He argues that science is nothing but the transformation of nature. Because we choose to select only a bit of that external world which we call nature, we fear a more incursive entry into our construction of nature because it questions when and with whom members of our species may reproduce in ways that may re-order our live, sexual relations, our basic satisfaction, our kinship, our sense of meaning to life and our conscience.[5] From this premise he encourages a reconstruction of our view of the world so as to have a more robust view of nature as ever expanding. If we do, then we are better able to appreciate new reproduction techniques as further threshold exposition of true nature, and fewer objections would greet most new techniques. Writing far back in 1932, Aldous Huxley in his book, *Brave New World*[6] describes how in the future science and technology would be used as though they had been made for man, not as though man were to be adapted and be enslaved to them.

Reproduction technique however appears set to take us in the opposite direction. The range of reproductive technique can be broadly divided into three division, namely: (a) old, (b) new and (c) the speculation techniques. Into the mould of the old we can list the IUD and most contraceptive devices, abortion, sterilisation, vasectomy and the Caesarean including episiotomies. Under the new techniques we can list most sex selection techniques such as amniocentesis, foetal monitoring, pre-conception sex selection, IVF, surrogacy, embryo transfer, embryo freezing, organ transplant, development of artificial placenta and cloning. The futuristic and speculative group comprises of the seas of cloning, parthenogenesis – (the production of embryo from egg unfertilised by sperm) and the development of artificial placenta or artificial womb. Biotechnology relating to reproduction remains controversial because they crystallise issues at the heart of contemporary social and political struggles over sexuality, reproduction, gender relations and the family.[7]

Artificial insemination

The technique envisages the entry of the male sperm into a woman's egg outside her body. Fertilisation takes place in a Petri dish-tube, test-tube of popular imagery.[8] The first external fertilisation was noted in 1879, using a rabbit. The first external human fertilisation occurred in 1968.[9] After fertilisation, the fertilised embryo is re-implanted into the recipient's womb and the eggs begin the process of cell division. Success of the implantation producing pregnancy depends on the timing of the

---

[4] E Yoxen, *Unnatural Selectio n* (1986) p 4-6, cited in Morgan *above* n 1 at p. 49 n. 20.

[5] Morgan above n 1 at p. 26.

[6] A Huxley, *Brave New World* (1932).

[7] M Stanworth, *Reproductive Technology, Gender, Motherhood and Medicine* (1987).

[8] D Morgan, Technology and the Political Economy of Reproduction in MD Freeman (ed.)*Medicine, Ethical and Law: Current Legal Problems* ((1988) p.9 at 29-30.

[9] Ibid.

implantation, the quality of the embryo, the fallopian tube of the recipient and sometimes the uterine environment. But it must be said that success rate in the in vitro fertilisation (IVF) technique is fairly low; although there is a direct relationship between multiple pregnancies and the number of pre-embryo transferred. If one embryo is transferred, success rate is likely put at 8 per cent. If it is two embryos it raises to 20 per cent and with three can move as much as 30 per cent.[10] Most IVF programme involves the use of super ovulatory drugs and monozygotic twinning. IVF can be time-consuming, physically and emotionally draining. It is for this reason that some suggest that the method should only be used as last alternative if there is no other satisfactory technique to procure pregnancy.

Women who undergo IVF are often given super hormonal drugs to stimulate the production of more than one egg or human chorionic gonadotropin (hcg) to induce ovulation when the follicles containing the eggs are determined to have opened sufficiently. The eggs are removed at the optimum ovulation process, usually the fourth day. In recent times, scientists have developed the Gamete Infra-Fallopian Transfer (GIFT); Peritomeal Oocyte and Sperm Transfer (POST) and vaginal intro Peritoneal Sperm transfer (VISPER) techniques. GIFT is presently more popular. It involves mixing an egg or eggs from the ovaries with sperm and placing the egg back into the recipient women's fallopian tube immediately so that fertilisation takes place in the body rather than in a petridish. The only difference between it and IVF is that in GIFT because fertilisation takes place in the body what happens to the eggs and sperm cannot be observed and recorded, meaning that any possible abnormalities may be difficult to correct.

Medical advances have thus made possible the production of children to couples who hitherto were unable to bear children. Medically assisted reproduction is therefore the response of medicine to the desire of women to have children. Childlessness is now to a large extent conquered by medicine. There are many reasons why a couple who desire children may be childless. It could be the result of infertility,[11] genetic deficiency [12] or some other medical reasons,[13] or no reason

---

10 Ibid. The first fertilisation of human egg in 1968 produced Louise Jay Brown as first test tube baby. She was born in Oldham, England. Though IVF gave birth to what is now known as assisted reproduction technology (ART) it has now grown to include all forms of fertility treatment that involve the use of both eggs and sperms.

11 Infertility is the involuntary, significant reduction of reproduction capacity. According to the Canadian Law Reform Commission, Working Paper 1992, p. 65 on medical assisted procreation, in North America infertility is the inability of a woman to become pregnant after one year of unprotected intercourse. The World Health Organisation standard is two years. See Kennedy & Grubb, *op. cit*, 758.

12 It arises where one of the couple carry a deleterious gene or both carry Recessive characteristics e.g. the chromosomes are altered or diseased With illness like down's syndrome, mental disease etc., which may be transferred to their offspring's.

13 This include cases where the woman is unable to carry a baby due to anatomical problems e.g. blockage of the fallopian tube or ovum abdominal adhesion.

whatsoever.[14] Sometime a couple unable to bear children because of infertility undergo treatment therapy for the purpose of determining the nature and the parties responsible for the state of childlessness.[15]

For women fertility therapy usually involves test on hormonal dysfunction by x-ray investigation. For the male partner therapy may involve seminal and blood test and analysis. If investigation reveals that it is the woman that is responsible for the childless state reproduction may be medically assisted by hormonal drug therapy or surgery,[16] if need be. By bio-technological devises as in vitro fertilisation (IVF) and gamete infra-fallopian transfer (GIFT) can be used as additional measures to produce pregnancy.[17] If investigation, points the other way, i.e., to the male partner, and it is shown to relate to the level of sperm count, drug therapy may be employed.[18] If it does not produce pregnancy, artificial insemination by donor (AID)[19] or artificial insemination by husband (AIH)[20] may be employed to assist reproduction. This is one area where modern medicine shows that it is not only concerned with the preservation of life, but with remedying malfunction of the human body. In the next two chapters, we shall only consider medically assisted reproduction technique known as artificial insemination and surrogate motherhood. This is not borne out of reasoning or presumption that the other management procedure for the treatment of infertility and childlessness, (e.g., drug therapy and surgery) are less important in producing pregnancy. We have chosen to exclude or give less attention to them because they raise less moral and legal questions, and when they do, we can analogically apply principles drawn from other sections in this book, such as discussions on informed consent, research, and the like to meet with the issues they raise.

Simply stated artificial insemination (Al) is the deposit of semen in the vagina, the cervical canal, or the uterus of a woman by instruments to bring about

---

14 Because there exist opportunities of adopting children's a couple may choose it as option to pregnancy associated with maternity deaths. It is estimated that the mortality rate arising from pregnancy in Africa is as high as 25%.

15 Where viral infection or abnormal ovulation is the cause of the childless state, drug therapy may employed as appropriate management.

16 Blockage of the fallopian tube is possibly the most significant anatomical problem of an infertile woman. The usual management regime involves is clearance of the fallopian tube blockage by surgery.

17 This is a medical method used as the ultimate treatment management, where drug therapy and surgery have not succeeds in producing pregnancy. IVF, in vitro fertilisation, is the standard treatment of childlessness. Fertilised ovum from a laboratory is transferred into the embryo of the woman. GIFT, gamete infra-fallopian transfer resembles IVF in many respects.

18 The amount of sperm required to fertilise the female egg for reproduction is still subject to medical controversy.

19 AID, artificial insemination by donor, is a procedure whereby donated semen (not from the parties) is injected into the woman uterus to produce pregnancy.

20 AIH, artificial insemination by husband is similar to AID, different only in the sense that the donated semen is not from a stranger, but the husband. It is for this reason that AIH is considered less objectionable on moral and legal grounds, than AID.

pregnancy without physical intercourse. The methods can be either through heterologous insemination (the semen used is obtained from a third party, usually described as AID [21] or homologous insemination, the semen being obtained from the husband.[22] Since the semen used may either be obtained from the woman's husband or from a donor, the establishment of semen banks is a natural reflection of the reality of AI. Whether in the future the law would permit advertisement for potential donors, as is the case with blood would depend on classification of the AI procedures. A call for donation from persons considered genius or desirable, with a view to building a generation of specially endowed persons may well raise ethical issues connected with eugenics in medicine.

Since it may now be possible for a sterile or even impotent husband to impregnate his wife through Al it has been suggested by some commentators that the hitherto procreative rule that there cannot be babies without sex is no longer truth in our time. AI also has special appeal for women convenience. A sterile woman can now have a baby by a surrogate thereby saving herself the trouble of carrying a baby to term. She can even enter into agreement for her husband's semen to be deposited with another woman who will have the baby for her. If her fallopian tube is bad she could ask medical doctors to remove an ovum from her which her husband or donor could fertilise. The fertilised egg can then be inserted in her womb or that of some other woman by arrangement and or agreement.

These wonders are not without their dark sides. Our concept of family is bound to be reconstructed. Public policy considerations and morality issues would surely be raised if a man donates his semen to a woman not his wife. For example, we need to ask questions like, should it be considered adultery? If so, should the donor be treated as a proper cited-party in a matrimonial proceeding? All of these could call for a new definition of what is considered "immorality".[23]

Though to some extent most ART [AI and surrogate motherhood (SM)], can be accomplished without medical intervention, IVF technique requires medical supervision. While Al and SM have been with us for a longer time, IVF is a more recent development. It has been suggested that IVF is a technique developed in the

---

21 Mason & Smith, *op. cit.*, 51 suggest that there is a movement to replace the acronym AID, with the term DI (donor insemination) because of its close resemblance with AIDS and the HIV infection.

22 Kennedy & Grubb, *op. cit.*, 759.

23 ART is spreading. Though Nigeria and many other developing countries do not have legislative framework in place regulating these techniques along the pattern of the English Hunan Fertilisation and Embryology 1990 Act, or statement of self regulating issued by the Medical and Dental Council of Nigeria in this area, the general tenor of articles 67 and 68 prohibiting torture and euthanasia should suggest caution by the doctor. Whatever the English 1990 Act can serve as a useful guide on how to develop an ethical framework in Nigeria. Whether or not legislation is required to regulate this developing area of medicine is the subject of controversy. The Canadian Ontario Law Reform Commission considered the desirability or otherwise of regulation in its paper titled, Human Artificial Reproduction and Related Matters, 1985, cited in Kennedy and Grubb, *op. cit.*, pp. 762-768. Surrogate Motherhood (SM) on the other hand is regulated in England by the Surrogacy Arrangement Act 1985. For reading on ethical issues, see S Jennings, Virgin Birth Syndrome (1991) 337 *Lancet* 559.

1970s. In recognition of some questions IVF may raise the United Kingdoms set up a committee on Human Fertilisation and Embryology (commonly referred to as the Warnock Committee) to study and make recommendations on the procedure. Its recommendation crystallised into the Human Fertilization and Embryology Act, 1990 (HFEA) which set out most of these issues.[24] Let us begin by considering the various methods of AI and the regulatory framework of the HFEA.[25]

Artificial Insemination by Husband (AIH)

This method of AI is considered less objectionable on moral grounds, though ultra-orthodoxy could question its procedure on grounds that it does not produce pregnancy by natural, physical sexual contact. On this basis it can be said that it alters the course of nature. The objection takes on weighty consideration especially in the context where the AIH procedure is combined with some other bio-technological devices that raise complex issues. To illustrate: by improved medical methods, it is now possible to preserve the semen of a husband in a "bank". What would it be like, if after death of the husband his wife undergoes AIH and bears children? Such a procedure could raise questions like, how should the children be treated, as progeny of the deceased? If so, should the birth affect testamentary dispositions? Answers to these questions are not easily reconcilable with established legal rules. If parenthood is determined by the genetic make-up of a child, then it would be proper to treat the child as the progeny of the deceased husband. But the answer may not be altogether satisfactory because this common law rule when formulated did not envisage the novel practice of preservation of semen in a bank for use after the death of a donor. It was formulated to deal with situation then prevailing. The transposition of the example here is therefore novel to it.[26] This is why some are of the view that ART raises issues fundamental to parents, children and third parties that it would be improper to leave it to the uncertain, evolutionary development by the courts.

In an effort to answer some of these question section 28(6) (b) of HEFA specifically excludes the donor from paternity. Section.28 (2) makes provision for married women, while section 26 (3) permits the procedure for parties in a common

---

24 See discussion in chapter 1

25 The Act. Came into effect in lst August 1991 in UK. See Ontario Law Reform Commission Report, *Human Artificial Reproduction and Related Matter* (1985) for a detail discussion for argument for and against regulation.

26 The problem of an unexpected childbirth can affect issues of succession. The medieval case of *Noys* v. *Mordaunt* (1808) 33 *ER* 273 illustrates the difficulties this may raise. Even though the case had nothing to do with bio-technique of reproduction, but was rather concerned with certain complex devises, the court was forced to formulate the doctrine of election in equity, the exact ambits which still remain controversial. See *Johnson* v. *Calvert* (1993) 851 P. 2d 776 (Cal. Sup. Ct) for discursion; see N. Cragg, Mistakes in Wills and Election in Equity (1990) 106 LQR 487

law marriage, what can safely be regarded as cohabitation.[27] The Act however makes no provision for single women. Essentially, it stipulates that the husband of a woman inseminated with the sperm of another man by a person licensed to do so will be treated as the father of the child, provided he consents to the process. The rule will be inapplicable if the husband does not consent to insemination. Noteworthy of mention, section 26 (1) state that the husband of a consensual donor inseminated is "for all purpose" to be treated as father of the child. This stipulation is intended to resolve any paternity disputes that mat arise. Specifically, section.26 (6) excludes the donor from paternity.[28] By so stating, the Act places a seal of finality on the claim by a child to the estate of the deceased man. To the extent that implantation is not consensual, the child can hardly be considered the deceased progeny. Thus while the process is not expressly prohibited by the English statute, it only settles the probate and succession issues that the procedure may generate. The subsection does not cover the related questions of the man who is reported missing but thought to be alive by the wife. In such a case it can be argued that paternity could be established.

Some commentators draw attention to bizarre application of long-term prisoners seeking permission to use AIH to impregnate their wives before release.[29] Whether the request is within general prisoners rights is not without controversy. Its resolution would depend on whether prison is construed to cover all physical moral and emotional restrains. If it only covers physical restrain, then there should be no objection to the request, particularly when conjugal prison visit is permitted.

Since AIH can produce pregnancy, without physical consummation of a marriage it follows that an application for dissolution of a marriage under the Matrimonial Causes Act, 1970[30] on grounds of non-consummation of a marriage can still be sustain, even if a woman is pregnant.

To produce pregnancy through AIH it is not uncommon to implant one or more fertilized egg in the woman's womb which may result in multiple birth for which the couple may not be emotionally and financially ready for. Blastocyst-transfer technique has been devised to cut down on such multiple births.

Artificial Insemination by Donor (AID)

AIH, as a procedure similar in all respect with AID, except that in AID, the donated semen is not from the woman's husband. It is often resorted to if a husband is

---

27 S. 28 (6) (6) of 1990 Act. The rationale of the rule is not face from absurdity. If such a child is treated as born into a single parent family, would it not be deceitful to register its surname as that of the supposed father? See *Leeds Teaching Hospitals NHS Trust* v. *A* [2003] 1 FLR 1091

28 Human Fertilization and Embryology Act, 1990 (HFEA).

29 Mason & Smith, *op. cit.*, p. 52.

30 S.5 (1) (a) of the MCA 1970 provides that non-consummation of a marriage shall render it violable. Pregnancy is therefore not prima facie evidence of consummation of a marriage. In *B* v. *B* [1952] 2 All ER 76 however, AID was held to constitute approbation by a party seeking dissolution of marriage.

infertility. Sperm obtained from a donor is injected into the woman. Because many couple who use AID are loath to abandon all hope of husband/wife offspring, some doctors mix the semen of the husband with that of a donor so that the couple can still symbolical feel that the ovum fertilised is that of the husband. The procedure has been described as artificial insemination by husband and donor (AIHD). Some suggest that it is tantamount to an invasion of the sanctity of marriage. This issue was considered in *Oxford* v. *Oxford*.[31] The court adopted a reasoning that the essence of adultery or immorality is not expressed in the moral turpitude of physical sex outside the marriage, but rather it is the voluntary surrender of the reproductive facilities of the body to another, equally as reprehensible as adultery, and is tantamount to it. But the Scottish Court thought otherwise in *Maclennan* v. *Maclennan*.[32] It stated that since AID does not involve any physical sexual contract it is not adultery It is however plausible to argue that if AID is employed by a woman without her husband's consent it would amount to an unreasonable behaviour for the purpose of dissolution of marriage. In fact the reasoning in *Doornbos* v. *Doornbos* was on the footing that the surrender of the woman's reproductive facilities without her husband's consent amounts to adultery.

That notwithstanding, the acceptance of AID by a couple could be interpreted as testimony of strength and bond in the face of physical difficulties. It probably explains why HEFA makes illegal AID without license and the parties consent. Mutual consent by couple to accept AID as treatment for infertility is not free from other difficulties. Some of these include but are not limited, to the following:

(i) **Information.** It is expected that a hospital facility that performs AID would keep a register of information relating to the identity of the donor.[33] The desirability of this cannot be over emphasised. The preservation of information would help prevent donation by closely related persons, either by blood and or marriage to the couple. Since it is expected that AID would be employed only where there is close resemblance of race between the parties and donor, so as not to raise social issues, a hospital facility must be careful not only in keeping information, but also in observing this minimum safeguard. If information is kept, then the next question would be who should be entitled to access it and under what circumstances? Under the Act a child aged 18 born through the method may require the Authority

---

31 (1921) 58 DLR 57.

32 [1958] SC. 105.

33 31 of the English 1990 Act. requires the Human Fertilization and Embryology Authority (HFEA) to keep a register of information relating to the donor, patient who receive infertility treatment and the children born from the semen donated. The license holder (usually an infertility treatment research and storage centre — often a hospital facility) is under a statutory duty to sends the information to the HFEA. Note the Act also regulates fertility donated genetic materials (sperms, eggs or embryo) and their storage. While it does not directly regulate surrogacy arrangements because it is regulated under the Surrogacy Arrangement Act of 1985 in UK, the HFEA provides general guidelines on matters involving the use of gamete in surrogacy.

(HFEA) to establish whether or not he was born by infertility treatment.[34] If the answer is yes, then he may seek information the Authority may deem] fit to disclose. The Authority in that respect may disclose to him whether the person he proposes to marry is related by blood to him or her. This provision however does not require the Authority to give any information as to the identity of the donor, it only authorises access to information about a child genetic background.[35] It is noteworthy that far back as at 1947, the English Public Morality Council on AI stated as part of it guideline to doctors (i.e. before the 1990 Act), that any who undertake AI must keep all relevant documents relating to it confidential. It is possible to envisage that in the near future, permission to access limited information about genetic background could provide fertile grounds for breach of confidentiality claims especially in circumstances where others who access it employ it for unlawful purposes. Danger to family life and public morality of certain facts cannot be glossed over.

(ii) **Single women request** One moral issues AID may generate include a request by single woman for it. Noteworthy, cohabitees can under the 1990 Act request for AID treatment. But the real problem relates to single women or lesbian couple who are not covered by the Act. Whether they should be allowed to use AI would depend on how it is viewed. If it is considered merely a just means to satisfy the desire of a woman to bear children then there would be little objection to exclude single women or lesbians from it. They too equally may feel the same desire to bear children like any married couple. It could be argue that if single parents are able to get impregnated by natural means with little objection, it would be discriminatory to deprive them of the artificial method if they so desire it. On the other hand, it is arguable that the medical team that performs AID are not engaged in a morally colourless act and so there remains strong objection to the process. That being so, a physician who participates in it is expected to consider the wider social and ethical issues of the resultant effect of the treatment – the production of babies. He should not therefore be unmindful of the disadvantages babies could face when eventually born into single parent or lesbian families.[36] This brings to the fore the best interest need of a child.[37]

As a general guide for AI treatment, the Royal College of Obstetricians and Gynaecologist in 1947, suggested that the practice should be employed only where there exist a close relationship of race and character between the donor and

---

[34] S. 31 of HFEA Act, 1990.

[35] The position should be contrasted with the Adoption Act 1976, S. 51, which give a child 18 a legal right to access information about parents.

[36] Whether or not single parent families are less stable than regular families is itself not free from controversy, considering the rising rates of divorce worldwide. See S Jennings, Virgin Birth Syndrome (1991) 337 *Lancet* 559.

[37] Case law and indeed S. 13 (5) of the 1990 Act require the best interest of the child is to be considered as paramount factors in the management of infertility cases so that the resultant pregnancy and birth of the baby would be into a home that is prepared to love to love the baby.

husband.[38] This is sensible because it creates race, colour and ethic affinity between husband and child born through the process thereby creating a better climate for social acceptability of child. To illustrate, imagine that a black couple consents to AID and for some unknown reason the woman is implanted with semen from a white donor. Birth of the child can constitute an embarrassment to the couple with adverse social effect. If it is the result of a doctor's negligence, a cause of action will certainly lie against him.

As general rule, which accords with common sense, the parentage of a child born through AID by consenting parents is awarded to them.[39]

In Vitro Fertilisation (IVF)

IVF is usually employed if there is a blockage of the woman's fallopian tube. It is a medical process, which involves the implantation of an embryo in the woman womb. The process involves the use of instrument to harvest eggs from the woman's ovaries. The eggs are then put in a test-tube where it is fertilised -in vitro fertilisation. The fertilised eggs are placed in the woman where it grows into foetus and then a baby. IVF is popularly referred as test-tube baby technique.[40] It is the collected ova from the woman that is fertilised with the husband's sperm in a laboratory (test tube). The procedure used closely resembles AIH. It therefore poses less ethical problem which can safely be brought within the category of AIH. In rare cases the sperm used may be donated if the husband's sperm cannot produce pregnancy. In that case IVF resembles AID and the ethical questions remain the same. If the woman is unable to produce eggs from her ovary, or the eggs produced carry an x-linked genetic disease in which case it would be medically advisable to have ovum donated to her, she too would have it donated to her. Donated ova may be obtained from another woman by surgery during a sterilisation treatment. Because ova can prove difficult to find, some hospitals offer free sterilisation for their donation. Once harvested, there is a need to use them because if they are preserved (cryopreserved), medical evidence indicates that they could suffer a risk of chromosomal abnormality. But once it is successfully harvested and fertilised in the laboratory with the sperm, subsequent implantation into the woman hardly runs the risk. If a birth result, the woman who carries the pregnancy to term is considered the mother

---

38 S. 28 (3 allow common law cohabitees to request for AID treatment from her partner. It has been suggested that provisions such as these which seek to equate cohabitation with marriage in certain respects is evidence of gender sensitivity.

39 See General Council Report of the Public Morality Council on Artificial Human Insemination 1947. See also *Higgins* v. *Memorial Hospital Jacksonville Inc.* (1998) August Journals law publication, where fertilisation occurred using the ova of Mrs. Higgins, a white woman and sperm of Mr. Higgins a black and the procedure was consider legal. Noteworthy of mention the parties were a couple. This general common law rule is enacted in s. 28 (2) of the 1990 Act].

40 This new revolution in baby making is available in Nigeria. The *Guardian* newspaper of Thursday, June 10, 1999, revealed that Providence Hospital, Lagos is one of such fertility treatment centres in Nigeria.

of the child whether the fertilisation results from a donation or from her husband.[41] The position accords with common sense and morality, because it is the couples that actively commissions the process and so are treated as parents. It remains sensible even if the ovum and sperm are donated. Once fertilised and implanted into the wife it is natural to consider the couple as the parents of the baby.[42]

Outside the ethical issues IVF treatment raises in the context similar to AID and AIH as stated above, the following are additional, namely (a) genetic defects from manipulations (b) eugenic ((c) sex relocation (d) burden on the national health resource (e) unethical request and (f) multiple birth problems and several others. Transfer of fertilized embryo into the woman's womb involves manipulation which way result in an abnormal foetus. This could mean that the resulting birth could suffer from defects caused by the manipulation of an otherwise natural process.

Negligence by the hospital, or doctor or any other persons connected with the treatment in this respect would raise legal liability. To employ a judicial word, a *Damascus sword* can slice through if things go wrong with the process.[43]There exists danger that the process could be used in pursuit of eugenics and for sex selection. By altering the percentage of male-female bearing spermatozoa with processed specimen it is claimed that sexes can be selected. While the procedure is supported by some on grounds that it has potentials in a drive to eliminate prophylaxis of x-linked diseases and is ethically preferable to embryonic selection or abortion, it is considered too simplistic to justify eugenics on moral grounds. In most developing countries that are patrilineal, the birth of male children is preferred. According to one record, out of the abortions in a Bombay hospital in India, only one was a male foetus. This indicates that sex relocation can be subtle gender discrimination against women. No wonder the Government of India is introducing legislation designed to criminalise pre-conception sex determination services.[44] IVF treatment is also an expensive medical treatment, with a low rate of success worldwide. It is estimated that an average treatment cost would be between $5,000 to $10,000. In many developing economies, public funding for such medical procedures could be considered an unnecessary burden on the public purse. However when considered in the context that a successful birth is unquantifiable in money term, a good case can be made for public spending in this respect.

---

41 See per Lord Simon in the Ampthill Peerage [1977] AC 547 (HL) at 577 and s. 27 (1) of 1990, Act and the Victorian (Australia) legislation, Statute of Children (Amendment) Act, 1984 and sections 5 (1) and 7 (1) of Australia Artificial Conception Act 1985.

42 This common law position is fortified by sections. 27 and 28 of the 1990 Act

43 S. 44 of the 1990 Act stipulates that the persons who cause an injury or damage to the birth of a child conceived through the process shall be liable for it. Liability is not diminished by the fact that one or both parent did not know of the risk of their child being born abnormal.

44 See G Nandan, India to Ban Prenatal Sex Determination (1993) 306 *BMJ* 353, T Marteau, Sex Selection (1993) 306 BMJ 1704; The Lancet 'Jack or Jill' (1993) 341 Lancet 727, all cited in *Mason* v. *Smith op. cit.* p. 52.

The process sometimes has resulted in multiply births because it requires an introduction of multiple gametes into the woman. Where multiple births occur, possibility exists that the couple may not be ready for it emotionally and financially. So rather than bring them joy the birth could cause a certain degree of anxiety.

It appears that the most burning issue the technique brings to fore is its request by single women. Some consider it tantamount to causing virgin pregnancy and birth.[45] On this ground, it raises ethical objections.

Section 14 of the English HEFA, 1990 provides that an embryo can legally be stored for up to five (5) years. By this stipulation a woman who does not want a disturbance of her social or economic life or status, may simply request that the embryo created should be preserved until she is ready to have a baby. Woman past menopause can therefore have babies. Single women and lesbians can bear children without needing to get involved in heterosexual intercourse. These possibilities are legally permissible by analogical interpretation of section 14. But it by no means answer the ethical questions the procedure throws up in a satisfactory manner. The greatest objection to IVF remains religious. Most orthodox religions consider it as an attempt by science to play the position of a creator and thus deny the glory of creation to God.[46]

Conceptual and practical issues in IVF and embryo donation

Medical technique in this process envisages the entry of male sperm into a woman's egg outside her body. Fertilisation takes place in a petridish, often referred to as test tube. It is reported that the first external fertilisation occurred in 1879 using a rabbit.[47] The first fertilisation of human eggs was in 1968. Louise Jay Brown was the first test tube baby. She was born in Oldham, England[48] in 1978. She was conceived in a laboratory through a process called in vitro fertilisation (IVF). An egg extracted from the woman is united with a sperm of a man in a glass dish. After fertilisation, the fertilised embryo is re-implanted into the recipient womb and the egg begins the

---

[45] S Jennings, Virgin Birth Syndrome (1991) 337 *Lancet* 559.

[46] The Rome Catholic church, like most other orthodox religious groups do not support the practice of AI. See the publication, Man, Medicine and Morality, for the expressed view of the church. Similar views are expressed in Judaism and Islam. See Rabbi Immanuel Jakobivits, Human Fertilisation – A Jewish View (1987) *Medical Science Law* 15 and Aminah Nolley, (1987) *Medical Science Law* Vol. 27 No.3, where the Muslim scholar questioned the rationale of British Muslim doctors who take part in AI fertility treatment. For detailed discussion and a feminist perspective, see M. McGuire & N.J. Alexander, Artificial Insemination of Single Women (1985) 43 *Fertil Steril* 1982; S. Jennings, Virgin Birth Syndrome (1991) 337 *Lancet* 559; S. Golombok, & J. Rust, The Warnock Report and Single Women: What about the Children (1986) 12 *J.Med. Ethics* 182.

[47] Morgan, above n 1 at p. 29

[48] Ibid, see also *Awake*, Sept. 22, 2004 (Infertility: The Treatments, The Question) p. 3, published by Watchtower Bible and Tract Society of New York Inc.

process of cell division. In the case of the first test tube birth, the fertilised embryo was re-implanted in the mother two and half days after fertilisation. At the time the egg cell had subdivided into eight microscopic cells that were inserted into the mother's uterus to develop normally.[49] Success of re-implantation depends on its timing, quality of the fallopian tubes and the uterine environment. IVF gave momentum to what is now known as assisted reproductive technology (ART) which has grown to include all forms of fertility treatment that involve the use of both egg and sperm.

Essentially ART involves fertility treatment in the following bracket, namely:[50]

(i) artificial insemination (Al). This a procedure by which semen is deposited into the female reproductive organs other than by natural means. Generally it is an option employed before resort is had to any of the other methods below;

(ii) gamete intra-fallopian transfer (GIFT). It is a procedure that involves removing eggs from a woman's ovary. It is then combined with sperm. The unfertilised eggs and sperm are introduced into the recipient's fallopian tube;

(iii) intracyto-plasmic sperm injection (ICSI). It is a procedure by which a single sperm is injected directly into an egg (IV) in vitro fertilisation. It involves removing eggs from a woman's ovaries and fertilising them outside the body. The fertilised eggs (embryos) are later transferred into the recipient's uterus through the cervix;

(iv) zygote intra-fallopian transfer (ZIFT) is a procedure by which eggs are collected from a woman's ovary and fertilised outside her body. The fertilised egg is later introduced into her fallopian tube through a small incision in recipient's abdomen.

How far ART will go is yet unknown. Fertility treatments sometimes involve many questions that go to our definition of humanity and personhood. These may take the shape like this: is it ethical for a woman to give birth to a baby from an egg donated by another woman? What if the donated egg comes from an embryo that has been frozen? What about the enormous cost that it often involves? It is estimated that about 100,000 children are born annually by ART. Each treatment cost several thousands of dollars – often not less than $10,000 per cycle of treatment. It has been suggested that ART will become more widespread because it addresses many of the causes of infertility and it aligns with modern life-style that emphasises pursuit of personal goals unlimited by traditional methods of reproduction.

But ART is not without its risks. These include the following: (i) human error; fertility clinics may make mistake in the mixing of sperm and embryos. Conceivably, a conception of a baby that is of a different race to the parents can be embarrassing to the couple; (ii) multiple births: as a result of multiple embryos implanted can cause multiple births, with attendant risk of premature birth, low

[49] *Awake*, above n 48.

[50] Ibid.

birth weight, still birth and sometimes long-term disability; (iii) birth defects: it has been suggested that IVF increases the chance of a risk of birth defects, such as heart, kidney problems; (iv) recipient's health: complications from hormonal treatment or a multiple-foetus pregnancy may have damaging effect on the mother.

It is no wonder why ART raises a number of questions. Most orthodox religious consider ART techniques that replace the marriage act, i.e. physical intercourse, immoral. Going by that proposition, it can be reasoned analogically that a technique that aids marriage act, such as surgery to correct tubal blockage and the use of hormonal drugs are not objectionable. But a treatment that requires fertilisation in a test tube will be, because it does not encourage or aid the marriage act.

No doubt the various ART techniques can challenge our social norms, moral, and ethical values and legal systems. Whatever position one takes is most likely to be influence by what a person's conception of the status of embryos is, which invariable depends on answer to the question – when does life begin? Is it at conception or later during pregnancy? Person who hold orthodox views that life begin at conception would have trouble resolving whether it is ethical to fertilise more than one egg to be introduced into the recipient. If they get to the point where some eggs are not introduced into the woman, then they must consider the illogical and contradictory position of keeping or destroying the surplus stock of embryos. If these materials are considered 'persons', then next, who should bear the heavy responsibility of destroying them if not needed? What should happen to any stored embryos if the couple divorce or one of them is dead or unwilling to have more children? The traditional view leaves no room for the use of unused embryos for stem cell research.

Legal rules however are not that absolute in application. Generally, it is established that life begins not at conception, but later on during pregnancy or actual birth.[51] It is this legal position that allows for embryos research and make legally permissible conduct that otherwise would have been criminal, such as liberal abortion, etc.

ART regulation by statute

The function of medicine is no longer exclusively associated with the preservation of life, but it now extends to include remedying the malfunction of the human body. The development of IVF technique raised concerns that led to a call for regulation. In response the English government set up a committee of inquiring into human fertilisation and embryology.[52] The Committee was chaired by Baroness Warnock and it came to be popularly called the Warnock Committee.[53] The framework of

---

[51] See general discussion on abortion and embryos research.

[52] I. Kennedy & Grubb, *Medical Law: Text with Materials*, 2nd edn. (London: Butterworths 1994) p. 759.

[53] Report of the Committee of Inquiring into Human Fertilisation and Embryology 1984 (Cmnd 9314).

the Human Fertilization and Embryology Act, 1990 was the result of the recommendation of the Warnock Committee. The 1990 Act has been described as "reflecting the fine balance between assisting the infertile and the fear of what could flow from the technologies as they are developed."[54]

Before discussing the main provisions of the Act, we shall consider argument of alternative ways to regulate ART other than by legislation. It has been suggested that the many questions raised by ART can be answered within the framework of the common law, the existing statutory rules and professional rules of conduct for medical personal that render an exclusive statutory regime in the form of the English HEFA, 1990 unnecessary. Pursuing this argument, it is suggested that ART technique should be allowed to grow without legislative fetters in such a manner that the common law can regulate it on a piecemeal basis. On the other hand, it can be argued that the fundamental questions raised by ART for parents, children and third parties should not be left to the uncertain, vicissitudes of evolutionary legal development e.g. the status of artificially conceived children. Considering the fact that the dictates of science when followed to its logical extremes can create horrors and that private ordering may be motivated by pure selfish interest there is the need for a degree of state intervention through legislation. There exist sound philosophical and practical reasons for introducing some control that limits free rein of science and individual wishes Regulation is desirable in the interest of broader social values. For example it may be desirable to regulate or prohibit teenagers from donating ova for IVF uses, because a women's ability to produce ova are not limitless. However whatever position is taken by the state should take into consideration many factors, such as personal wishes, a flexible perception that permits reasonable scientific developments, etc. It is suggested that areas for prohibition and or regulation should be skilful marked with clarity that reveals enlightenment.

The 1990 Act regulates donated genetic materials (sperm, eggs or embryos) or other materials involved in the creation of an embryos) or other material involved in the creation of an embryo outside the human body. Its regulation includes and covers storage of these materials. It, however, does not directly regulate the practice of surrogacy in so far as it does not involve the use of donated genetic materials or IVF techniques. Surrogacy in the main is regulated by the (English) Surrogacy Arrangement Act, 1985. The main provisions of the 1990 Act establish the Human fertilisation and Embryology Authority (HFEA) charged with the function of implementing the legislation. Its primary functions includes; to licence treatment service centres, provide framework for the storage of gametes and embryos and research on embryos, monitor the activities carried under statutory licence, maintain

---

54 Kennedy & Grubb, above , n.4 p. 763, see also the following analysis of the Warnock Committee recommendation, B. Dickens, Reproduction Law and Medical Consent (1985) 35 *Toronto L.J.* 255 and A. Capron, Alternative Birth Technologies: Legal Challenges (1987) 30 *UC Davis Law Rev*; See *R (Quintavalle)* v. *Secratery of State for Health* [2003] 2 AC 687 on question whether the Act which contemplates an embryo created by fertilisation, extends to embryos created by cell nuclear replacement in an unfertilised egg.

a code of practice for activities carried under the Act and to report to the Secretary of State on its activities.

The statutory scheme of regulation can largely be divided into the following three categories, namely,[55]

(i) **prohibited activities** - these are activities that cannot be licensed. They are illegal and criminal activities under the Act. They include activities such as cloning

(ii) **regulated activities** - these are activities which are prohibited unless carried in pursuance of licence granted by the Authority, e.g., the creation of embryo *ex utero* or the storage of gametes of embryos.

(iii) **unregulated activities**- these are activities not regulated or prohibited by the Act and so can lawfully be undertaken even without licence, e.g., treatment of a couple using the sperm of the male partner, commonly referred to as artificial insemination by husband (AIH).

A few interesting highlights of the Act are:

(i) Access to infertility treatment is not limited to married couples or heterosexual couples. However section 13 (5) introduces a caveat, namely that "a woman shall not be provided with treatment services unless account has been taken of the welfare of any child who may be born as a result of the treatment (including the need of that child for a father) and of any other child who may be affected by the birth." By this the doctor is expressly enjoined to consider wider social issues of the treatment.

(ii) Proprietary ownership of gametes and embryos is vested in the person who provides it. Schedule 3 of the Act requires that a gamete provider shall at the time it is procured indicate in writing what use it should be put to. The implication is that it gives the provider proprietary right over it.[56]

(iii) Section 31 imposes a statutory duty on the Authority to register information and give access and or information relating to gamete donors, patients receiving infertility treatment and any children born as a result in certain cases.

(iv) Sections 27 to 29 make provision that govern the status of children born by ART.

---

[55] For a detail analysis of the Human fertilisation and Embryology Act, 1999, see Kennedy & Grubb, above n 52 at pp. 769 – 829. See also *Quintavalle* v. *Human Fertilisation and Embryology Authority* [2005] UKHL 20 (HL) on whether pre-implantation genetic diagnosis (PGD) and human leukocyte antigens (HLA) typing are activities with the Act

[56] See *Davis* v. *Davis* (1992) 842 SW 2d 588 and para. 4 of schedule 3 of the 1990 Act on how disputes over the fate of frozen embryos should be treated in cases of marital breakdown.

Chapter Four

Surrogate Motherhood (SM)

Simply put, surrogate motherhood is a process wherein a woman and her husband enter into a contract or arrangement with another woman by which she permits that other to be implanted artificially with her husband's semen with a view of carrying the resulting pregnancy to term for them. The child is expected to be surrender to the couple. In some cases the eggs of the couple are fertilised *in vitro* thereafter implanted in the surrogate woman who arranges to give the baby to the genetic parents – being the couple. SM closely resembles AI or IVF save that unlike them it involves the active cooperation of an otherwise involved woman in the process of pregnancy and birth.[1] It is common practice for the surrogate mother to be promised a financial reward for her inconvenience that would naturally follow nine months of pregnancy. The surrogate mother may or may not be related to the commission couple.

Surrogate practice is not novel, as it may appear. Ancient Israelites practiced it.[2] When Abraham and Sarah had difficulties bearing children, Sarah suggested that her Egyptian slave-girl, Hagar, should be used as a surrogate mother to help them bear a child.[3] The only material difference between the Abram–Sarah surrogate motherhood and the modern reproduction technique of SM, is that while the former involved physical sexual contact, the later need not involve physical contact. In fact it is usually completed by AI. Not only did the Jews practise SM, they also had a version called brother-in-law marriage.[4] The Jewish canon law permitted a brother in-law to marry the wife of his deceased brother for purposes of bearing children for him to preserve his name.[5] That practice can be referred to in our times as 'surrogate fatherhood'. Going by this it could be suggested that they practised both surrogate motherhood and fatherhood. Similar custom and practices were not uncommon to most African patrilineal families prior to modernity. [6]

---

[1] Mason & Smith, *op. cit*, p. 67.

[2] Peter Singer & Deane Wells, *New Ways of Making Babies: The Reproduction Revolution* (1984) pp.107-108, see also S. Roberts, Warnock and Surrogate Motherhood: Sentiments or Arguments? in P. Byrne (ed.) *Rights and Wrongs in Medicine*,1986.

[3] The Holy Bible, Gen.—

[4] Ibid., Deuteronomy 25: 5, 6.

[5] Ibid, Genesis 38:8,9; Gen. Chapter 39 Ruth chap. 4.

[6] The Igbo in Eastern part of Nigeria practice marriage and children rites akin to the Jewish Customs.

The English Warnock Committee describes SM this way:

> Surrogacy is the practice whereby one woman carries a child for another with the intention that the child should be handed over after birth. The use of artificial insemination and the recent development of in vitro fertilisation have eliminated the necessity of sexual intercourse in order to establish a surrogate pregnancy. Surrogacy can take a number of forms. The commissioning mother may be the genetic mother, in that she provides the egg, or she may make no contribution to the establishment of the pregnancy. The genetic father may be the husband of the commissioning mother, or of the carrying mother, or he may be an anonymous donor. There are thus many possible combinations of persons who are relevant to the child's conception, birth and early environment. of these various forms perhaps the most likely are surrogacy involving artificial insemination, where the carrying mother is the genetic mother inseminated with the semen from the male partner of the commissioning couple, and surrogacy using in vitro fertilisation where both egg and semen come from the commissioning couple, and the resultant embryo is transferred to and implanted in the carrying mother.[7]

It follows from the description above that SM can be accompanied in two ways:

(i) by an infertile couple arranging for a surrogate to carry a pregnancy for them by an implantation of the husbands semen in the surrogate mother, or

(ii) embryo created from the gametes of the couple is implanted in the surrogate

While some commentators draw a line of difference between the two procedures above, in that they consider the former as partial or complete surrogacy, and the latter as womb leasing, it would appear that both raise identical moral issues.[8]

There are many reasons why a couple may use SM. SM is often employed as a management method for infertility if a woman has no uterus or if her pelvic is damaged beyond what can be remedied surgically. It may also be employed where pregnancy in the commissioning mother is medically not advisable, for example if pregnancy may result in extreme abnormal behaviour in the woman or because she may suffer from excessive miscarriage that makes it traumatic for her to carry a pregnancy. In some case however, SM may however be used for the sake of convenience by a commissioning mother who can bear children with minimal discomfort. For example, a woman could choose not to be pregnant because she

---

[7] Warnock Committee of England was set up to consider legal framework for regulation of human fertilisation in 1984. For reading on ethical questions, see WJ Winsdale, Surrogate Mothers: Private Right or Public Wrong (1981) *J Med Ethics* 153; IM Mady, Surrogate Mothers: The Legal Issues (1981) 140 *Amer J Law Med* 323; B Cohen, Surrogate Mothers: Whose Baby Is It? (1984) 10 *Amer J Law Med* 243; I Davies, Contract to Bear Children (1985) *J Med Ethics* 61; R Macklin, Is Anything Wrong With Surrogate Motherhood? (1988) 16 *Law Med Hlth Care* 57; JG Hogg, Surrogacy-Nobody's Child (1991) 21 Fam Law 276;RA Charo, Legislative Approaches to Surrogate Motherhood (1989) 16 *Law Med Hlth Care* 96, S Sloman, Surrogacy Arrangement Act 1985 (1985) 135 *NLJ* 978.

[8] Warnock Committee 1984 reports par. 8.1. and Mason &. Smith, *op. cit*, 67-68.

imagines that her social and economic fortunes may suffer from pregnancy or natural conditions associated with it.

SM bears some resemblance with adoption of children even though it would appear to be more fulfilling than it in the sense that the resultant child is usually genetically related to the couple.[9] From this perspective it can be predicted that when it becomes more readily available adoption would decrease, because it satisfies in a biological manner the urge of couple to become parents. A child born from SM is genetically related to the commission parents because it is wholly formed from their eggs, a womb is merely leased for it incubation. Since the genes are wholly so formed all that takes place in the womb is multiplication of the cells to form body parts. The surrogate mother's gene does not form any part of the child and so the child is not genetically related to her. Herein lies the fundamental difference between it and adoption. An adopted child usually bears no genetic relation with its adopted parents.

Moral questions

In most cases where SM is practised a commissioning fee is usually paid to the surrogate mother for purposes of reimbursement and in some cases as profit consideration for the arrangement. In *A* v. *C*[10] a couple in cohabitation entered into a contract with a prostitute friend for SM in consideration of a fee of £3,000. When the child was born, the surrogate mother changed her mind. She refused to hand over the child to the commissioning couple. The father's application for access to the child was granted, although the court in its judgment described the surrogate agreement as contrary to public policy. The decision to grant access was reversed by the English Court of Appeal. Both judgments, that of the Family Division and the Court of Appeal, were painfully short, the facts not fully reported. It is difficult to know exactly why the contract was declared void for being contrary to public policy. However, it seem that the agreement was declared void because it was thought that the arrangement was susceptible to exploitation especially in the context of anxiety resulting from childlessness, a thing treated as publicly reprehensible. This is the very objection of many concerned people to SM. They frown at the idea that a woman should rent and or hire her womb for the purpose of making money. For these ones SM is no different from prostitution which involves the use of a woman's body for the purpose of making money. Also, the arrangement to hand over the baby to the commissioning parents has been likened to selling babies which is expressly forbidden in many jurisdictions.

---

[9] D Brahams, Surrogacy, Adoption and Custody (1987) 1 *Lancet* 817; S P de Cruz, Surrogacy, Adoption and Custody: A Case Study (1988) 18 *Fam Law* 100.

[10] [1978] 8 Fam Law 170. See also Re AC (a minor) [1985] 8 Fam Law 170; *Re an adoption application (surrogacy)* [1987] Fam 81, [1987] 2 All ER 826. See also D Brahams, above n. 9; S P de Cruz, above n. 9.

Let us use the experience related by Nuel Keane, an American lawyer engaged in SM to map out some of the dark side of the process.[11] He relates the story of three sets of couple he assisted in arranging surrogacy for a fee. Though all turned out to be happy at the end in that babies were born the traumatic process between commission and the handing over of the children were not fee of moral questionings. Bill and Bridget was an infertile couple who through the contact of Keane got Diana as a surrogate mother. Diana looked a responsible woman who could bear them children. It was agreed that she was to be reimbursed for her expenses in bringing the agreement to fruition. As soon as Diana became pregnant she requested the couple to send her money to travel from Tennessee in Kentucky to Boston, New York; when the money got to her she claimed she was robbed of it. The couple sent her another. Soon thereafter, her car needed to be fixed. She incurred extra medical expenses. She constantly phoned asking for money from the couple and when she did, it was clear that she was either drunk or stoned on drugs. To make matters worse, sometimes when she phoned, she threatened to kill herself if the money she asked for is not sent. Of course the anxious commissioning couple complied with all her request.

Shortly before the birth she asked for $3,000 to do a computer course. In all the commissioning couple spent over $12,000. As though the couple trauma were not over, two weeks before birth, she phoned that she was in jail on a drunk-driving charge. She needed bail. The couple travelled to meet her in Tennessee so that nothing goes wrong for safe birth only to further discover that she is in fact a lesbian. Happily, the baby was born safely. Diana did not stop to demand money under threat. She threatened to hold up or oppose adoption proceedings by the commissioning couple if she is not given money. As things worked out, she did not succeed and she moved out without a forwarding address from Tennessee. Whatever the happy commissioning partners had their baby whose status at the time of writing of Keane story was in 'legal-limbo' because adoption proceedings were pending. This experience is just one of many things that can go wrong with SM. Though it ended happy for Bill and Bridget, the journey was tortuous. Others may not be as fortunate at the end as they were. It is clear from this experience that it could be used as a means to exploit anxious couple with an urge to become parents. This explains why some argue that SM is contrary to public policy and why jurisdictions with regulation prohibit commercial surrogacy. To reduce the vagaries of the arrangement, it is suggested that the terms of the agreement should be

[11] Noel Keane, *"Surrogate Mother"*, cited by Kennedy & Grubb, *op. cit.*, p. 821-823.

properly worded.[12] A typical example of how and what terms the agreement should contain, is found at Appendix F.[13]

The debate continues whether surrogacy should be permitted. In *A* v. *C*[14] the English Court of Appeal held surrogate agreement contrary to public policy. At the court of first instance (the Family Division) Comyn J stated:

> ...the agreement between the parties I holds as being against public policy. None of them can rely upon it any way or enforce the agreement in any way. I need only give one of many grounds for saying that, namely, that this was a purported contract for the sale and purchase of a child.

The publicity given to the birth of 'Baby Cotton' to a surrogate mother in England in 1985 in *Re C (a minor)*,[15] provided the court another opportunity to consider the legal framework of SM. The commissioning couple Mr. and Mrs. A who lived in America were in their 30's. Mr. A was fertile, but Mrs. A was not, but they strongly desired to have a baby of their own to live with them in their country home. In furtherance of it, Mr. A contracted an American agency to procure a surrogate mother for them. The agency got a surrogate in England. Soon thereafter Mr. A travelled from America to England. There his seminal fluid was taken and inseminated to a surrogate mother who he did not physically meet. The implantation was successful and resulted in the birth of a baby. The surrogate agreement contained a clause for payment to the surrogate mother and that at birth the baby would be handed over to the commissioning couple, Mr.& Mrs. A. In anticipation of the birth of the child, the commissioning couple travelled to England in 4th January 1985. On that day the baby was born. But alas, the London Borough of Barnet obtained a 'place of safety order' that the baby should remain in the hospital to be cared for by the hospital nurses. The application was brought under the Children and Young Persons Act, 1969, (s. 28) on the grounds that the baby would be abandoned by the mother. Two days later the commissioning couple issued a wardship summons. The fact was that the surrogate mother voluntarily relinquished her parental right, abandoned the baby in the hospital soon after its birth. On this strength the local authority supported the application of Mr. A that the baby be given to him and his wife for care and upbringing. Lately J so directed, but he refused to determine the legal nature of the agreement. He stated:

> First and foremost, and at the heart of the prerogative jurisdiction in wardship, is what is best for the child or children concerned that and nothing else.

[12] The surrogate agreement may contain provisions such as those preventing ant-social behaviour by the surrogate mother, address questions of paternity of the child, especially for purposes of subsequent adoption proceedings, time frame for nursing and return of the baby to the commission couple and so on.

[13] The agreement is that used by the Infertility Centre of New York, where Noel Keane works as a leading advocate and Executive Director in the surrogacy centre.

[14] [1978] 8 Fam law 170.

[15] [1985] FLR 846. See also Re an adoption application (surrogacy) 1987] Fam 81, [1987] 2 All ER 826.

> Plainly, the methods used to produce a child as this baby has been, and the commercial aspects of it raise difficult and delicate problems of ethics, morality and social desirability. These problems are under consideration elsewhere. Are they relevant in arriving at a decision on what now and, so far as one can tell in the future is best for this child? If they are relevant, it is incumbent on the court to do its best to evaluate and balance them. In my judgment, however, they are not irrelevant.
>
> The baby is here. All that matters is what is best for her now that she is here and not how she arrived. If it be said (though it has not been said during these hearing) that because the father and his wife entered into this arrangement it is some indication of their unsuitability as parents, I should reject any such suggestion. If what they did was wrong (I am not saying that it was), they did it in total innocence. It follows that the moral, ethical and social consideration are for others and not for this court in its wardship jurisdiction.[16]

Tactically, Latey J, refused to hold that a surrogacy arrangement is contrary to public policy, unlike Comyn J in *A* v. *C*. His Lordship did not consider the fact that the commissioning couples were part of a commercial surrogacy agreement strong enough to debar him from making wardship award in their favour.

In response to the legal uncertainty of the status of surrogate agreements and the grave ethical questions the case raised, the English Parliament enacted the Surrogacy Arrangement Act, 1985. The Act is an attempt to adopt a moderate stance. It does not prohibit it, but discouraged it, declaring commercial surrogacy contracts illegal.[17]

In *Re an Adoption Application (surrogacy)*,[18] Latey J had another opportunity to consider; the nature of surrogacy and certain statutory provisions on adoption. Mr. and Mrs. A applied for the adoption of a child. The facts are laden with emotion. Through advertisements Mr. and Mrs. A met with Mr. and Mrs. B to arrange for surrogacy. Mr. and Mrs. A were a devote couple who desired to have a child. They had done everything to enable them but Mrs. A could not as a result of medical problems. They tried adoption but to no avail. They listened to a radio programme and Mrs. A watched a television program about surrogacy. Meanwhile Mr. and Mrs. B had two children, and as a couple desired no more, though Mrs. B enjoyed pregnancy despite sickness. Mrs. B heard, saw and read about surrogacy and was deeply moved about the plight of childless couple. So after discussion with her husband who agreed to surrogacy, Mrs. B put an advertisement in a magazine to which Mr. and Mrs. A responded. They all (Mr. And Mrs. A and Mr. And Mrs. B), agreed that Mrs. B should become surrogate mother for Mr. and Mrs. A. As a result of the arrangement, Mr. A and Mrs. B had sexual intercourse on few occasions and in due course a child was conceived. It was in no sense a love affair. It was physical

---

[16] Ibid., p. 852.

[17] For desirability of regulation surrogacy by legislation, see RA Charo, Legislative Approaches to Surrogate Motherhood (1989) 16 *Law Med Hlth Care* 96, and S Sloman, Surrogacy Arrangement Act 1985 (1985) 135 *NLJ* 978 for a detail discussion of the English Surrogacy Arrangement Act 1985.

[18] [1987] Fam. 81; [1987] 2 All ER 826.

congress with the sole purpose of procreating. As soon as there was conception intercourse ceased. It was agreed between the parties that since Mrs. B was to lose her employment during the period of pregnancy, a fee of £10,000 was to be paid by the commissioning couple to her. There were indications that Mrs. B turned down other request from a couple offering very large sum to choose the coupe because she sympathised with them.

The commissioning couple paid £5,000; the balance was due when the baby was born. When due Mrs. B refused to accept the balance £5,000 because she had obtained money from the sale of her story. She and a professional writer co-authored a book: *Surrogate Mother, One Woman's Story* from which she made money. It was written pseudonymously with care to conceal the identity of the child. When the child was born, all the parties were supremely happy. When born in the hospital, Mr. and Mrs. A were present. Two days later, the child and mother, Mrs. B, went to the home of Mr. and Mrs. A. The four of them spent a week together, before Mrs. B left. The child thrived with commissioning couple, who kept contact with Mrs. B. Two and a half years later the commissioning couple applied for adoption of the child. The issue therefore was whether or not the payment of £5,000, would invalidate an award of adoption, for contravening section 50 (1) of the Adoption Act, 1976, which prohibits profit or financial reward for adoption purposes. Latey J had no hesitation in awarding them adoption. He held that the surrogate arrangement did not contravene the Adoption Act, 1976. The payment did not constitute an element of profit or financial reward. In His Lordships view it was meant simply to compensate the surrogate mother for the inconvenience of pregnancy. He stated:

> The first question, therefore, is whether in the present case there has been any 'payment or reward' within the meaning of section 50 of the Adoption Act, 1976 – 'for adoption'; to put it conveniently albeit in precisely. This is a question of fact to be decided on the evidence. Mr. and Mrs. A and Mr. B have all given evidence. All are transparently honest. They did not make notes. They did not take legal advice. Not surprisingly, their recollection of the precise sequence of events and what was discussed and when is not clear. What was wanted was a baby and that Mr. and Mrs. A should have it from birth to care for and bring up. And that it was upon this that they were all concentrating. It was only after the payments had been made and the baby was born that any of them began to turn their minds in any real sense of adoption and the legalities. In my judgment there was no payment or reward within the meaning of Section 50 (1) of the Adoption Act 1976.[19]

It is noteworthy, that Latey J expressed confidence in the commissioning couple. He said that even if the payment were construed as profit, he was still willing to

[19] Ibid., p. 831. But cf. with the view of New Jersey Supreme Court in case of *In the Matter of Baby M* (1988) 537 2d 1227. For a discussion on the connecting issues between surrogacy, adoption and custody issues, see also D Brahams, Surrogacy, Adoption and Custody (1987) 1 *Lancet* 817; S P de Cruz, Surrogacy, Adoption and Custody: A Case Study (1988) 18 *Fam Law* 100.

make the award for adoption by allowing some profit retrospectively in the overall interest of the child. Also of note, is the fact that although the proceeding in the case was one for adoption, surrogacy arrangement was not expressly frowned at by the court even though pregnancy in the case was brought about by natural intercourse.

In *Re P (Minor) (Wardship: surrogacy)*,[20] the English Family Division of the High court, had an opportunity to state its views on the validity or otherwise of surrogate agreements. The case was heard before the President of the Division, Sir John Arnold. Here the surrogate mother offered her services to a married professional man who donated sperm by AI and it was agreed that he would pay a lump sum to adopt the child. During the pregnancy, the surrogate mother developed misgivings about the child and when she gave birth to twins in October 1986 her disinclination hardened. After a period of indecision, and despite her concern and regrets for having disappointed the commissioning couple, decided to keep the children; she refused to hand-over the twin to the married professional man. She and the man independently approached the local authority that applied to court to make the children wards of the court and to deal with the matter of adoption. As at the date of the hearing for custody, the woman had cared for the twins for 5 months. After considering the family set-up of both parties and the fact that the twins have an Asiatic background like their father and the social problems the woman would encounter in keeping the children in an English village, the court still made an award in favour of her. It was strongly influenced by the degree of maternal bound that had already arisen between the twins and her. His Lordship considered less deserving the fact that the child would live in an English village racially different from them with their mother. He said:

> The court's duty is to decide the case, taking into account as the first and paramount consideration, the welfare of the child or children, and if that consideration leads the court to override any agreement that there may be in the matter, then that court is fully entitled to do.[21]

Again, it is noteworthy to state, that the President of the Family Division, Sir John Arnold, did not criticise surrogate arrangement. On it he stated:

> ...One possible view about that matter is that there is, or may in certain circumstances be, an element concerning the surrogacy agreement which is repellent to proper ideas about the procreation of children, so as to make any such agreement one which should be rejected by law as being contrary to public policy. It is not necessary in this case, for the reasons, which I have indicated, to come to any conclusion upon that point. The existence of the agreement is relevant to this extent, that plainly one of the factors which has to be taken into account in determining the welfare of the children lies, is the factor of the character of the rival custodians who were put forward for consideration and it might be that the willingness of these persons to enter into a surrogacy agreement would reflect upon their moral outlook so

---

20 [1987] 2 FLR 421 (Fam. Div.).

21 525 A 2d 1128 (NJ Sup Ct, 1987).

> adversely as to disqualify them as potential custodians at all, but I do not think that factor enters into the present case.[22]

Let us see how American law has responded to surrogacy. *In the Matter of Baby M*,[23] the court was asked to determine the validity of a surrogate contract for which consideration was placed at $10,000. For the fee a woman agreed to be inseminated with the semen of another woman's husband, and thereafter surrender the child to the natural father and his wife. The wife was then to adopt the child and the natural mother would be forever separated from her child. Thus in February 1985, William Shern and Mary Beth Whitehead entered into the surrogate contract which contained a recital that Shern's wife, Elizabeth is infertile and that Whitehead is willing to provide a child as mother, with Stern as the father. Mrs. Whitehead's husband, Richard, was also a party to the contract, promising to do all acts necessary to rebut the presumption of paternity under the Parentage Act. Although Mrs. Stern was not a party to the agreement the contact granted her sole custody in the event of Mr. Stern's death. The fee of $10,000 was agreed to be paid to Mrs. Whitehead and a further fee of $7,500 to the Infertility Centre of New York (ICNY) for arranging the contract.

After several AI over a period of months Mrs. Whitehead became pregnant and on March 8, 1986 Baby M was born. She refused to hand-over the child. Even in the face of court order she absconded with the baby. The trial judge considered the matter on grounds of strict law alone in the context of adoption law. On this strength he concluded that a valid contract existed between the parties which was breached and that state interest (*paren patriae*) dictated granting custody to the commissioning couple because that would be in the best interest and welfare of the child. On appeal to the New Jersey Supreme Court, the decision of the trial court was reversed. The Supreme Court considered the legal issues from the background of the relevance, if any, of adoption law and the attitude of the court to commercial surrogacy agreement. It held that the surrogacy agreement was contrary to adoption law and public policy and so null, void and of no legal effect. Wilentz CJ said:

> Our law prohibits paying or accepting money in connection with any placement of a child for adoption...Excepted are fees of an approved agency (which must be non-profit entity) and certain expenses in connection with child birth...Mr. Stern knew he was paying for the adoption of a child. Mrs. Whitehead knew she was accepting money so that a child might be adopted, the Infertility Centre knew it was been paid for assisting in the adoption of a child. The actions of all three worked to frustrate the goals of the statute. It strains credulity to claim that these arrangement, by those in the surrogacy business as an attractive alternative to the usual route leading to an adoption, really amount to something other than a private placement adoption for money.

---

[22] Ibid., p. 426. See also 525 A 2d 1128 (NJ, 1987).

[23] 525 A 2d 1128 (NJ, 1987).

The Chief Judge considered the legal consequence of Mrs. Whitehead agreement to surrender the child to the Stern's family inconsequential because the whole arrangement was contrary to public policy in his view. He stated:

> Putting aside the issue of how compelling her need for money may have been, and how significant her understanding of the consequences, we suggest that her consent is irrelevant. There are, in a civilized society, some things that money cannot buy. In America, we decided long ago that merely because conducts purchased by money was voluntary did not mean that it was good or beyond regulation and prohibition. *West Coast Hotel Co.* v. *Parish* 300 US 379,57 CST 578,81 LEd 703 (1937) — there are, in short, value that society deems more important than granting to wealth whatever it can buy, be it labour, love or life. Whether this principle recommends prohibition of surrogacy which presumably sometimes results in great satisfaction to all the parties, is not for us to say. We note here only that, under existing law, the fact that Mrs. Whitehead agreed to the arrangement is not dispositive.

His Lordship considered the contract one that totally disregarded the interest of the child. He referred to it as a 'bare contract for the sale of a child', or at its very least, 'a sale of a mother's right to her child', the only mitigating factor in the case being that the purchaser was the father. Noteworthy, the Supreme Court however did not find objectionable a voluntary non-commercial surrogacy agreement provided it does not compel the surrogate mother to hand over the child. As though by a reverse twist however, the court awarded custody to the commissioning couple on the basis of the best interest of the child.

So far the cases show sympathy for SM, so long as it is not used for purposes of exploitation. The cases reveal a rough mapping of the moral and ethical problems SM raises. Let us consider some of these in the context of the response of law (legislation, principles and authorities).

Ethical issues

Gender exploitation

It can be argued that when put in its raw state SM is nothing than exploitation of women for the benefit of men.[24] It aids a man to procreate by buying with money a woman womb. It is objectionable on the grounds that the law ought to resist this form of purchase of the woman's procreative facilities just to satisfy the urge of a man to have children. 'It is the sale of a child, or at the very least, the sale of a mother's right to her child'[25] But it can be countered on the ground that the urge to

---

[24] *In the Matter of Baby M*, 525 A 2d 1128 (NJ, 1987). See also GJ Annas, Fairy Tales Surrogate Mothers Tell (1986) 16 *Law Med Hlth Care* 27; S Dodds and K Jones, Surrogacy and Autonomy (1989) 3 *Bioethics* 18.

[25] See *in the Matter of Baby M*, 525 A 2d 1128 (NJ, 1987). See also I L B Andrews, Surrogate Motherhood: The Challenge for Feminists (1988) 16 *Law Med. Hlth Care* 72 and S. Doddo and K James, Surrogacy and Autonomy (1989) 3 *Bioethics* 18.

bear children through surrogacy usually involves not only a male commissioning partner but also an active female commissioning partner. The Biblical case of Abraham and Sarah is an example. In fact it was Sarah who actively urged for it. In modern times, there are strong indication that surrogacy is often requested for by women, especially if they are infertile. It was so in *Re an Adoption Application (surrogacy)*[26] and many others.[27] From this perspective it can be said that the gender exploitation objection only sees one side of the coin. It does not see the other side that prohibiting it can be paternalistic. In this respect it can be suggested that it constitute male aggression against the woman in that it seek to prevent and deny women their right to control their bodies. Autonomy principle makes her sovereign over her body. That being so restriction that amounts to depriving her using her body for any purpose, including making money may derogate on women sovereign right.

Sale of babies

Some have questioned SM on the ground that it is tantamount to sale of a child, criminalised in almost all jurisdictions.[28] It is suggested that the process implicates maternal responsibilities in that the child is handed over to a commissioning couple and that to that extent is radically different from adoption. It was on this basis that the learned Chief Judge in *Baby M* stoutly differentiated SM from adoption. In his view the following are the differences: First, and perhaps most important, is that surrogacy is motivated by payment of money of some kind, but adoption merely relieves the natural mother of the financial burden of supporting her child. Secondly, the process in surrogacy involves the purchase of a woman's reproductive capacity at the risk of her life which is absent in adoption. Thirdly, the mechanism of adoption does not result in the child going to the highest money bidder, unlike in most cases of surrogacy. Fourthly, the mother's consent to surrender her child in adoption is revocable, unlike surrogacy where it is irrevocable. Whether or not His Lordship's classification is exhaustive or in fact factual is not itself free from controversy. Suffice to say that, this was the main plank for the court's argument that SM is akin to sale for a child in *Baby M*.

A critical analysis of the argument however would seem to suggest the opposite. The upsurge in SM is an indication that couples prefers it to adoption. It enjoys several advantages over it. The child is genetically related to the commissioning couple, wholly formed from their eggs. On this basis it can hardly be classified as a sale arrangement. When a contract of surrogacy is made, the surrogate mother need not be under any financial pressure. In most cases the contract is entered into before implantation by AI or by natural intercourse. In fact, some of the cases show that its

---

[26] [1987] Fam 81, [1987] 2 All ER 826 *See In the Matter of Baby M*, per Wilentz CJ (*supra*).

[27] See the facts of the cases discussed under this chapter, and the related question whether surrogacy is tantamount to the use of a woman's body, including her reproductive facilities as she pleases, including renting her womb if she so chooses?

[28] Purchase of babies is prohibited by s.57 of the English Adoption Act 1976. See s. 50 of America's Adoption Act. 1958.

purpose is not sale *per se* or reward, but an urge to help childless couple. In this respect the story of Mrs. B in *Re an Adoption (Surrogacy)* [29] is instructive. She said in evidence:

> I wanted to help a childless couple. My own children are very precious to me and I sympathised greatly with any couple who are unable to have children of their own so much so that I was willing to have another pregnancy in order to give someone else that joy...The money represented only my loss of earnings, expenses in connection with the pregnancy, and emotional and physical factors. I emphasise that I did not go into the arrangement for commercial reasons, nor did I accept the money to hand (the child) over. I would have done that in any event. In fact, overall, I was marginal worse off. That does not bother me since my motive was not financial.[30]

On this strength the objection to SM that it is akin to a sale transaction cannot be a categorical truth in many respects.

Corruption of public morality

By this it is argued; that a surrogate agreement is no more than a criminal conspiracy to corrupt and outrage public morals and decency. It is here reasoned that an arrangement that permits the use of a woman's body for a fee is against public policy and ought to be prohibited as no materially different from prostitution. But is this a valid reasoning? Does it involve as in cases of prostitution physical (pleasure) contact for money consideration and the surrender of reproductive facilities for a similar purpose?

In most cases pregnancy is by AI. While not unmindful of the peculiar facts of *Re an Adoption Application (surrogacy)* [31] where pregnancy resulted from physical sexual intercourse between the commissioning father and surrogate mother, it is a recognised fact that most SM do not involve physical intercourse. *Re an Adoption*, was exceptional to the conventional Al method. Even at that, the report tells us it was with the consent of the surrogate mother's husband, and that it was not a love affair. It ceased soon after conception was achieved. So it was not really a case of wife leasing. Whatever, at the end of it all, all the parties were supremely happy. Not one was hurt. So its counter argument may proceed like this: why should we imagine that some figment-public decency was hurt by the arrangement. It is useful to remind ourselves of one of the most quoted reference in modern medical jurisprudence, that of JS Mill:

> The only purpose for which power can rightfully be exercised over any member of a civilised community against his will is to prevent harm to others. His own good, either physical or moral, is not sufficient warrant. He cannot

[29] [1987] Fam 81, [1987] 2 All ER 826.
[30] Ibid., 84.
[31] [1987] Fam 81, [1987] 2 All ER 826.

> rightfully be compelled to do or forebear because it would be better for him to do so, because it would make him happy or because, in the opinion of other to do so would be wise, or even right.[32]

The arrangement does not seem to have hurt her society. Even after putting her story in her book, titled, "*Surrogate Mother and Woman's Story*", care was taken to conceal the identity of the child. His Lordship, Latey J, was also mindful of this fact in that he also tried to do same in his judgment. It would appear therefore that only an over stretched imagination would consider private surrogate arrangement indecent to public morality. May be, the Biblical injunction of the Pharisees Gamilel should be a guide in this respect. "Let them be". If SM is good enough, it would thrive, if it is not, it would suffer natural death. But for now all we need do is to regulate its nature and scope in a manner that shows tolerance.[33]

Social distress

The stories related by Keane, a leading American Attorney on SM in his book, *The Surrogate Mother*, testifies to the fact that the journey from arrangement to conception, birth and handing over of the child may cause grieve to the parties. A child who becomes aware of his conception and birth through SM could also feel distressed. It is for this reason that most surrogate mothers' identity are kept confidential. However the intervention by commercial intermediaries could increase risk of disclosure of supposed confidential information. This is to some extent cared for by the provision of donor's anonymity under the Human Fertilisation and Embryology Act, 1990 (England). It provides for example, that if SM is brought about by AI the Human Fertilisation and Embryology Authority shall keep a register of information on the identity of the gamete donors, patient's who receives the fertility treatment and a record of children born by the treatment method. Section 31 requires a license-holder (i.e. a fertility centre licensed by the Authority under the Act) to supply such information to the Authority.[34] Under the Act certain information are classified as confidential. Disclosure is restricted and can only be made in circumscribed circumstances. By so doing, the Act provides the necessary protection of information. Where however pregnancy is not brought about through AI but by physical contact it would be advisable to include in the surrogate agreement provision for limited access to information or a confidentiality bond.

---

[32] JS Mill, *On Liberty and Representation Government*, Blackwells, Political Text (1 Ed 1948) p. 8.

[33] See Warnock Committee (minority) Report, Cmnd 9314, 1984, Expression of Dissent A, which suggest that surrogacy should reman a treatment option. There is evidence of support for this position in Australia, see N Swan, Australia Ethics Committee Approves Surrogacy (1990) 301 *BMJ* 254. But cf. Surrogacy Parenthood Act 1988 of Queensland that expressly prohibits and criminalises the process.

[34] The question of who can gain access to the information and the limitation of the information that can be disclosed. See discussion, at p. For example, in *Re C* (A minor) [1985] FLR 846, where the surrogate mother was already well-known, the judge made an order restraining the press from publishing the names of the parties.

Surrogacy for convenience

The essence of surrogacy is to help childless couple. On this basis, surrogacy for mere convenience looks like an unethical expansion of the frontiers of ART. Where for example a woman capable of bearing children does not wish to undergo a period of pregnancy, but rather desires to use another woman to carry the pregnancy for her, serious ethical objection may be raised. Such an arrangement can be likened to exploitation of others, using them as means to other's selfish end. That point was taken up by the Warnock Committee. In its report, it said the following:

> In the first place we are all agreed that surrogacy for convenience alone, that is, where a woman is physically capable of bearing a child but does not wish to undergo pregnancy, is totally ethically unacceptable. Even in compelling medical circumstances the danger of exploitation of one human being by another appears to the majority of us far outweighs the potential benefits in almost every case. That people should treat others as a means to their own ends however desirable the consequence, must always be liable to moral objection.[35]

That notwithstanding, the question remains, does our liberal political economy not permit the use of others as means to ends in commerce? Is that not the very basis of the so call liberal economy or capitalism? So why is this objection vehement in surrogacy? If surrogacy is viewed as part of medical management for infertility, then there should be little or no strong objection to the procedure. The principle underlying the philosophy of JS Mill well indicates a re-evaluation of the objection.

Legal nature

One of the ethical questions the arrangement raises has been its legal nature. Section 36 of the English Human Fertilisation and Embryology Act, 1990 which makes an insertion into the Surrogacy Arrangement Act (SAA) 1985, s.1 (A), provides that 'no surrogacy arrangement is enforceable by or against any of the persons making it'. This means that while surrogate agreements are not illegal for every purpose, the court would not enforce them. In effect, parties are entitled to draw up their agreements if they so wish, but the courts would not be drawn in as arbiter in the event of dispute. The language of the legislation indicates that it does not intend to deprive surrogacy documents of all efficacies. The agreements are not declared void for all intent and purpose.[36] Thus the position in England is that non-commercial surrogacy is not illegal. Section 1 of the SAA 1985 defines a surrogate mother and the arrangement, while section 2 only prohibits commercial surrogacy. It is noteworthy

[35] Warnock Committee (minority) Report, Cmnd 9314, 1984, para. 8: 17.

[36] See per Idigbe JSC in *Buckor-Macleans* v. *Inlacks Ltd.* (1980) 8-11 SC 28 on interpretation of language used in legislation. See also per Lord Chemsford in *Parker* v. *Taswell* 27 LJ CH 812 on a discussion of the enforceable nature of surrogate contracts, see C. Sappideen, The Surrogate Mother- A growing problem (1983) *UNSW Law Rev.* 79; T. Mady, Surrogate Mothers: The Legal Issues (1981) *Amer. J of Law & Med* 324.

to mention also that to the extent that surrogacy is brought about by the use of AI or IVF techniques, it is a licensed activity under the HFEA 1990. It is not within the legislative scope of 1990 Act.

Intermediaries and advertisement

Employment of intermediaries, usually commercial surrogacy agencies, and the possible harm that can be caused by mass media advertisement for surrogate parents and commissioning couple can raise ethical questions. Some advertisements may be in bad taste to such an extent that they offend public sense of decency. Commercial surrogacy agencies may also be used to exploit. The response to it is the SAA, 1985 Prohibitions Commercial Surrogacy.[37] Section 2 expressly prohibits it. However, it is suggested that the very wording of the section does not cover non-profit agencies offering the services. It only prohibits the commercial nature of SM. Thus a non commercial agency, such as a charitable organisation is not prohibited from carrying on the object of surrogacy, so long as it does not carry it on as a commercial business. It therefore gives the impression that the Act set out to outlaw only the exploitative nature of commercial surrogacy agencies. To this end, s3 seeks to curtail the social and moral harmful effect of advertisement. It criminalises any advertisement or publication seeking for surrogate mothers, or any offer to act as a surrogate mother. *Re an Adoption Application* [38] (a case decided before the 1985 Act.) where an advert was placed seeking surrogate mothers, would now be a prohibited activity under the Act.

Custody and paternity

The arrangement may also raise issues of paternity and custody rights in the context of claims for damages in negligence and parental responsibilities. Custody would not pose much difficulty where there exists well drafted surrogacy agreement stipulating custody. A good agreement would usually address the point awarding it to the commissioning couple. But things do not always work that smooth. It is possible that the surrogate mother may change her mind and insist on keeping the child. It may also happen that the child may not be wanted either by the surrogate mother or the commissioning couple because of being born disabled or for other reasons. In a situation as this, it can be asked: who the law holds responsible for the defect of the child, especially if there exist evidence, say to the effect that, the life style of the surrogate mother could have caused the injuries. Would it matter in determining responsibility that the commission couple aggravated the situation by say, not making available money for proper medical treatment[39]? Who should exercise parental responsibility to the child when both parents (i.e. commission and

---

[37] S. 2 of SAA, 1985

[38] [987] Fam. 81.

[39] See discussion on p. .For the legal position in USA, see Uniform Parentage Act, 1973; Australia: Artificial Conception Act, 1984 (NSW); Status of Children (Amendment) Act, 1984 (Victoria); Artificial Conception Act, 1985 (W. Aust.).

surrogate parents) do not want the child? These are many of the nutty legal questions that the law might need to resolve.

If the procedure used to produce pregnancy and birth is AI or IVF, sections 27-29 of the HFEA, 1990 can be helpful in resolving paternity questions. It provides that the surrogate mother irrespective of whether the embryo is the product of her body is to be treated as the mother of the child. This stipulation in section 27 (1) follows earlier Australian legislation on the matter of award of paternity.[40] If she is married and conception is by AI her husband is the father of the child. Thus the woman of the commissioning couple is not the mother of the child. The surrogate mother's husband shall in law be treated as the father of the child, unless evidence shows that he did not consent to the procedure. The commissioning couple are not treated as the parents even if conception results from the use of their gamete.

The fact that sections 27-29 award paternity to the surrogate parents of a child is not conclusive on custody matters relating to where a child should live and grow up. The provision of the English Children Act 1989 empowers the court to award parental responsibility on the basis of the welfare and advancement of the child. This means that there is no legal fetter on the basis for which the court may award custody. The 'best interest' principle is paramount. If the welfare and advancement of a child dictates making an award to a person other than the surrogate parents, say to the commissioning couple, the court would so do without hesitation. Resolution of the issue could be made less controversial if the parties to a surrogate agreement agree on allocation of parental responsibility. A properly drafted agreement would contain one, usually allocating it to the commissioning couple. Where on the other hand, the agreement does not specify allocation of custody, it is suggested that the commission couple should take quick steps to apply for it to prevent *legal limbo* on the child's status. To do so in jurisdictions with adoption legislation like U.K., the following steps are advised (i) they must seek to adopt the child under the relevant adoption laws, such as the Adoption Act, 1976 of England;[41] (ii) they should seek a parental order pursuant to any relevant law that allocate paternity. For example, under section 30 of the HFEA, 1998;[42] and (iii) apply for wardship of the child under the courts inherent power to allocate wardship over a child. When all these three steps are taken and resolved in the commissioning couples' favour, then only have they completed the legal framework for the allocation of parental responsibility.

Even at this, when all the parties agree, the court in the interest of the child may yet not make an allocation to the commissioning couple. The fact however is that if the parties to the surrogate arrangement all agree, it makes it easier to succeed in seeking allocation of parental responsibility. Requirement (i) above shows a level of seriousness on the part of the applicants. By it the parties show that they intend that

---

[40] Ibid. See also *Leeds Teaching Hospitals NHS Trust* v. *A* [2003] 1 FLR 1091

[41] S. 28 (4) of HFEA 1990.

[42] An application under the Act is necessary to rebut the presumption of parentage stipulation under Ss. 27-29 of the Act, so that the child may be treated in law as the child of the commissioning couple. An order under s. 30 is tantamount to an adoption.

the child is an accepted person to their household. Requirement (ii) is important because in some jurisdictions, like the UK, the court is authorised to make an order granting parent status to persons other than the surrogate mother if pregnancy results from placing of an embryo or sperm or eggs or AI of a commission husband; or if the gamete of the commission husband or his wife or both are used to produce pregnancy in the surrogate mother. That is what section 30 of the UK HFEA,1998 provides. The relevance of an application pursuant of requirement (ii) become compelling with hindsight of sections 27-29 which ordinarily allocate parent status to the surrogate mother and her husband, as against the commission couple. An application for wardship under (iii) above is a necessary requirement because the courts from medieval times have acquired jurisdiction over all minors. Flowing from it, it is imperative that all application for adoption ought proper to be made to it.

Difficulties are only likely to arise if there is a disagreement between the parties to the agreement. Where this is the case, the court is not empowered under section 30 of the 1990 Act to make a parental order to the commission couple because in the circumstance the surrogate mother cannot be said to relinquish parentage. In determining custody the court considers as paramount the welfare of the child which may dictate that either or neither the surrogate mother or commissioning couple should be awarded the responsibility.[43] In making an order the court would normally allow the other party's visitation rights. If in an extreme case both or all of the parties reject the child, say because of some form of disability, the court may make an allocation order to a third party in the best interest consideration of the child's welfare and advancement.

Contract and tort liabilities

The above notwithstanding, issues relating to breaches of contract and tort can arise from surrogacy arrangements. The parties' agreement may care for matters bordering on breach of its term. Since the courts are generally reluctant to get drawn into surrogate disputes it is expected that even in the face of well drafted agreements it would not mediate to enforce contractual stipulations on breach of contract. Some have therefore suggested some level of court involvement in this bewildering area of advancement in medicine more so when public concern and morality need to be balanced with the principles of autonomy of contract. From the surrogate mother, things can go wrong: She may wish to abort the pregnancy or alternatively live a life-style that could cause serious damage to the foetus. If the surrogate mother decides to have an abortion for good or no reason, can the commissioning couple prevent her? If *Paton* case[44] marks the boundaries of permissible intervention, it would follow by analogy that the commission couple cannot prevent her. This is predictable so because if it were otherwise, the law may be guilty of putting the commissioning couple in a higher pedestal than a spouse in matters relating to

[43] See *Re P.* (Minor) (Warship surrogacy) [1987] 2 FLR 421.

[44] *Paton* v. *British pregnancy Advisory Service* [1979] QB 276, [1978] 2 All ER 987 (a husband cannot by injunction prevent his wife from undergoing an abortion).

abortion rights. Sensibly the legal position would be that a commissioning couple cannot prevent a surrogate mother from obtaining an abortion. The position is fortified by appeal to self autonomy of the surrogate mother. Autonomy appeal in fact has been a spring board for a demand to de-criminalisation of abortion in many jurisdictions. If this is anything to go by, it is a signal that commissioning couple cannot veto by an order of injunction the decision of a surrogate to seek abortion.

As the law stands, the couple cannot be compensated for distress and shock that results from a breach of a surrogate agreement. All they may get as damages if possible, would be for loss of bargain, usually fixed as the expenses paid. Even this may be difficult especially with hindsight of section 1A of SAA, 1985, which makes surrogate agreement unenforceable. So, those who enter into surrogate agreement are pretty much on their own. They must learn to be content with wherever the benefit or burden swings. That notwithstanding, it is arguable that a tortuous claim for negligence may lie against the surrogate. If the argument is attractive, the couple may recover for nervous shock and distress. But again to do so the necessary elements of negligence must be proved – a duty of care, breach of the duty of care and resultant damages not being too remote. That can be a difficult hurdle especially in conservative jurisdictions that do not use tort law as a private legal regime to adjust socially disapproved conducts, but rather to compensate for injury. If the surrogate mother wilful or negligently causes damage to the foetus a claim for wrongful life or birth may lie. Even this is speculative for the present.

On the part of the commissioning couple it is also possible for some things to go wrong. For example, they may refuse to pay the agreed fees to the surrogate mother or refuse to take care and custody of the child born by their commission. The first problem is not likely to arise because the couple are usually anxious for a child and would likely be prepared to do all in their power to keep faith with the arrangement and if need by to surpass contractual expectation. The story of Bill and Bridget, commissioning couple, with surrogate mother Diana in USA told by Noel Keene in the book, *The surrogate mother*, is illustrative that commissioning couple are not likely to breach the agreement. Notwithstanding, it is not out of place to imagine that some unscrupulous couple may behave otherwise. Where this happens, it is only legitimate to allow the surrogate mother to recover in contract the agreed fees and expenses thereto in maintaining the pregnancy and or child, if birth results; subject to regulation by statute. If the couple refuse the child the surrogate mother may recover maintenance for the upkeep of the child. Whether or not these legal questions shall be so resolved depends on the legal regulatory framework in place in the relevant jurisdiction. In Nigeria, there is no legislation in force, so the common law position would provide the signpost for the resolution of the issues.

The bewildering nature of ART suggests some level of legislative regulation to reduce ethical confusion and controversy. An attempt to "dam" the controversy through case–law does not appear to meet the expediency of the situation. The basic reason being that the legal system's loyalty to principles of precedent is not well fitted to deal with novel issues that ART litigation can throw up. Case law runs too slow in pace as against the rapid movement in ART. Its evolutionary guide will be outstripped by medical advances. These inherent weaknesses of case-law development have prompted some jurisdictions to seek legislative guide. The English Adoption Act 1976, Surrogacy Arrangement Act 1983 and the Human Fertilisation and Embryology Act, 1990 are examples of attempts to provide a general legal framework for the regulation of ART. As our discussion has so far shown the English experience has been a mid-way approach, between prohibition and criminalisation on one hand, and liberty in the other hand. As a system of regulation it avoids both extremes. It is suggested that Nigeria should put together a body of relevant professional to plot the way forward in regulating this growing area of medical advancement.

ART and foetus

Just before we bring this discussion to an end in this chapter, it must be mentioned that a legal thread on which it seem the resolution of much of the legal difficulties surrounding SM and in fact most ART procedures rest is the legal nature or status of a foetus. The legal pendulum swings between treating it as person and property. It can safely be said that a foetus is neither of them but a hybrid. This was the issue before the Tennessee Supreme Court in *Davis* v. *Davis*.[45] It was a divorce action between Mary Sue Davis and Junior Lewis Davis. It revolved around the disposition of crypogenically preserved products of IVF. The parties in the divorce suit agreed on all the terms of the dissolution of their marriage but disagreed on the question of custody of seven stored frozen embryos. Mrs. Davis asked that it be implanted in her. The husband objected on the grounds that it be frozen until he makes up his mind whether or not he wants to be a parent outside the confines of marriage. The trial court granted Mrs. Davis custody on the basis of a reasoning suggesting an ascription of personhood to it. From the premise he stated that the best interest of it would be better served by granting her custody. She was granted the right to have them implanted in her to facilitate pregnancy. But the Court of Appeal reversed the decision. It vested control of the stored embryo to the parties' joint control. Mary Sue Davis dissatisfied with it sought a review of the decision in the Supreme Court. The Tennessee Supreme Court granted the review, not because it disagreed with the legal reasoning of the appellate court, but (i) because it wanted to settle some of the legal and ethical issues raised in the case, and (ii) because the appeal decision which granted the parties joint custody, did not provide a useful guide in the event that the parties do not agree on what to do with the stored embryo.

Before the matter came up for first hearing before the Supreme Court the positions of the parties were altered. Mary Sue Davis re-married (now Mary Sue Stowe) and moved out of the State of Tennessee. She therefore no longer wanted an

---

[45] (1992) 842 SW 2d 588 (Tenn. Sup. Ct.). For case discussion, see C Corns, Deciding the Fate of Frozen Embryoes (1990) 64 *L Inst J* 273. See also GF Smith, Australia's Frozen 'Ophan' Embryoes: A Medical, Legal and Ethical Dilemma (1985/86) 24 *J Fam Law* 27, cited in Mason and Smith, *op. cit*, at 65 n. 13.

implantation, but wished to donate them to childless couple. Junior Davis was also remarried and he vehemently opposed the wish of Mary for donation. He preferred that it be discarded or destroyed. This was another impasse. The court however was of the view that the impasse and change in legal position of the parties was immaterial to the outcome of the case. Noteworthy at the time the parties signed up for the IVF programme they did not specify what should be done with the unused embryo, neither was there in place a legislation governing disposition of such unused embryo. In the absence of statutory regulation and precedent from cases, learned works only guided the Supreme Court. It held that Junior Davis interest was not procreative and so was far out weighed by the wishes of Mary Sue Davis in procreation because she wished the embryo donated to some childless couple. The court however recognised the fact that if she had desired to have the embryos implanted in her the scales may become close or even, thereby making the dispute more difficult to resolve.

The case afforded the court an opportunity to resolve some issues relating to the legality or otherwise of IVF and other ART techniques. It explicitly disapproved the trial court proposition ascribing personhood to foetus, recognising the potential damaging effect such ascription would pose for medicine. Daughtrey J said:

> Left undisturbed, the trial courts ruling would have afforded pre-embryos the legal status of 'persons' and vested them with legally cognizable interest separate from those of their progenitors. Such a decision would have doubtless have had the effect of outlawing IVF programs in the State of Tennessee. But in setting aside the trial court judgment the Court of Appeal, at least by implication, may have swung too far in the opposite direction.

The reasoning is undoubtedly sound in principle. If embryo is granted the status of person, then in one go, the law would have outlaws most ART techniques, such as AI, IVF and to a large extent SM obtained through fertilisation. This would be so because it would in effect mean that once fertilised, it cannot be destroyed. If the position were so, there would exist a legal obligation to implant a foetus to produce birth. Any implantation which causes it harm becomes actionable. Its freezing or storage or a research would automatically be wrongful. The Supreme Court prevented such a slippery slope.

Even though the authorities reveal that an embryo is not 'person' in law, it is not altogether useless. Legal policy indicates that it is entitled to some form of protection in the context of personhood. It is accorded a degree of respect higher than body tissues, even though not as that accorded persons. The reason is not unconnected with the fact that it has potential to become a person and so is symbolic in many respects even before it develops real features of personhood. The court was not unmindful of this in *Davis*. It stated:

> We concluded that pre-embryos are not strictly speaking, either 'persons' or 'property', but occupy an interim category that entitles them to special respect because of their potential for human life.[46]

Philosophical questions and ART

Let us raise a few additional ethical questions ART raises.[47] It is said that categories of language and thought respond to change. This invariable means that if technology in medicine continue at its fast pace of development we shall be constrained to develop new vocabulary to more properly capture concept of birth, parenthood and families. The supposed security and certainty of traditional gender relations and family forms considered cornerstone of civilisation insulated from the technological stock market is bound to require redesigning. Much of our hitherto settled ways of thinking could be questioned in such a manner that touch our deep chords of anxiety and create fear in minds. If, as some commentators have suggested, fertility is closely related to the general position of women and men in society and that it is much a social construction as well as a biological fact, then in essence there is no pure biology in the social world. Flowing from this proposition, it is arguable that because women are defined by the medical and other professions almost exclusively as mothers, the pursuit of fertility treatment takes the shape of raising in us fears and anxiety over most ART techniques. From this premises feminist construct medicalisation and professionalization of childbirth and rearing as connected with power relation between the sexes.[48] This explains why new ART procedures can cause anxiety for men who define and construct reality in the real world by seeing women through the perspective of child bearing. Report that in 1984 a woman in California, USA gave birth to baby developed from an egg donated by another woman must thus be frightening news from that construction.[49] Motherhood is a male scientific achievement and is conducted according to male devised rituals and regulation and so is kept in check by them from slipping to a scientific state that re-defines the perspective of women in the eyes of men.

But as the position of men and women slowly change by ART techniques, the possibilities of separating sex from reproduction and rearing, and by extension, the de-emphasising and replacement of the privilege given to heterosexual relationships is bound to confront and strike at the root of present male devised regulations. These techniques have increased women capacity to control their bodies. Techniques that include certain forms of cloning and parthenogenesis take on new dynamics in that

---

[46] Ibid.

[47] D Morgan, Technology and the Politics of Reproduction, in MDA Freeman (ed.) *Medicine, Ethics and Law*, London: Stevens & Sons, 1988, p. 23.

[48] Ibid. at 40; see also Andrea Dworkin, *Right Wing Women: The Politics of Domesticated Females* (1982), Lucy Bland, *Marxism Today* (1985) p. 21; JO Scott,(ed) *Violence in the Family* (1980); L Doyal and L Pennell, *The Political Economy of Health* 19881); L Moran, A Reading in Sexual Politics and Law(1986) 8 *Liverpool L. Rev.* 83; M Mazor and H Simons (eds.) *Infertility: Medical, Emotional and Social Considerations*(1984);R Arditt, RD Klein and S Mindens (eds) *Test-Tube Women* (1984

[49] *Awake* Magazine, Sept. 22, 2004, p.3.

women can reproduce without the need of the patriarchal genetic. For the present, AID and IVF make possible reproduction without most of what we know as the family structure. But not to be overcooked is that these technologies may present contradictory choices for feminism. It is arguable that these liberating possibilities are offered by medicine at the potential price of making women bodies more available and accessible to medicine, thus giving doctors and researchers greater power to control women's lives.[50] There is some force in this counter-argument. What, for once consider: Who can tell with confidence that when reproductive engineers develop an artificial womb they might not place the cultured embryo directly into the mother womb machine, thereby dispensing with natural wombs? Not to be overlooked is the possibility that including single women and lesbians in infertility treatment programme could increase marital, childcare and welfare problems, thereby threaten normal family life. This possibility was long recognised by the Warnock Committee, when it stated:

> From the evidence, many believe that the interest of the child dictate that it should be born into a home where there is a loving, stable, heterosexual relationship and that, therefore, the deliberate creation of a child for a women who is not a partner in such a relationship is morally wrong.[51]

It assumes that behavioural and emotional problems are bound to afflict children reared by single women and lesbians. This argument is hardly empirical and some feminist scholars think that it is the other way. Perhaps it is the quality of family relationship and the pattern of upbringing that matters for psychosexual development and not the sexual orientation of the mother. Poverty and isolations of single parent families may make it easier for 'fatherless families' to become socially problematic, but that it is by no way conclusive.[52]

Whatever, it is hardly contestable that the past history of the development of medical technologies is sexist, classiest and racist in orientation. This is what explains why the questions of reproductive freedom or rights remain at the background of much of the ART debate.

---

[50] Doyal and Pennell, above n. 48.

[51] Warnock Committee Report, Cmnd 9314, 1984.

[52] S Golombok, A Spencer and M Rutter, Children in Lesbian and Single Parent Households: Psychosexual and Psychiatric Appraisal (1983) 24 (4) *J. Child Psycho. Psychat.* 551.

Chapter Five

Fertility treatment

Fertility control is widely known today as family planning. It is a matter of interest to states and individuals for many reasons. These range from resource allocation, micro and macro economic planning and developmental issues. There are basically two types of fertility control measures: permanent, and the other less permanent.

Permanent fertility control

Sterilisation is mainly a permanent fertility control technique. Surgical operation is employed to permanently impair a patient's ability to reproduce. In men it is achieved by the male *vars deferens* being cut and tied, a process usually referred to as vasectomy. It makes a man sterile. In women it is done by cutting off the fallopian tube which aids the carriage of ova between the ovary and the womb. It prevents permanently, the ability to become pregnant. Because the procedure is almost impossible to reverse,[1] sterilisation is said to be open to objection on the grounds that it completely interferes with the individual reproductiveness. A change of mind would not reverse it.

Non-permanent fertility controls

Non-permanent fertility control generally takes the form of contraceptive. Contraceptive may be in the form of condom and contraceptive pill. Generally outside the use of condom, other forms of contraceptive require some level of physician's involvement either in terms of prescription or in application.[2]

All forms of contraceptives are designed to prevent pregnancy or the formation of an embryo in the women. However, there are some forms of contraceptives that are intercceptively designed to work after an embryo is formed in the womb of woman. This is the class to which the intro-uterine device (IUD) belongs. IUD is

---

[1] It has been reported that in some rare cases a form of microsurgery may be employed to reverse sterilisation. See AK Banergee and A Simpsn, Reversing Vasecomy (1990) 304 *BMJ* 1130. Generally most orthodox religions frown at fertility control measures. For the Catholic position see, J Poole, Time for the Vatican to Bend (1992) 339 *Lancet* 1340; and for the Islamic view see, DAR Verkuyl, Two World Religions and Family Planning (1993) 342 *Lancet* 473.

[2] It is considered by medical personnel that where such hormonal medication contains high estrogens, it may cause some risk to the patient.

therefore on emergency contraceptive in the sense that it is administered when an embryo is formed, with a view of disposing it. It is for this reasons that serious ethical and legal objection has been raised against IUD. The legal framework of sections 228-230 of the Criminal Code criminalises any thing used to procure a miscarriage and or cause abortion in a woman.[3] To the extent that IUD is capable of procuring the removal of the embryo, it is within the context of law a procuring medication that produces miscarriage or abortion. Any physician who prescribes or administers it to a woman may in effect be exposing himself to criminal sanction. In *R* v. *Price*,[4] the defendant was convicted for criminal abortion for inserting IUD in a woman who was pregnant with a view to procuring miscarriage. The term, to procure miscarriage was construed synonymous with abortion. However in the Indian case of *R* v. *Ademma*[5] the defendant was charged for procuring abortion of a woman who was one month pregnant. The trial court acquitted him on the ground that there was nothing which could be called a rudimentary foetus or child in her that was aborted by the IUD or capable of being aborted by it. On appeal, the Madras Court of Appeal ordered a re-trial, stating that the offence would be committed anytime from conception. It said:

> The term miscarriage is not defined in the Penal Code. In its popular sense it is synonymous with abortion and consists in the expulsion of the embryo or foetus i.e. the immature product of conception. The stages to which the ovum or embryo may have assumed are immaterial...Section 312 requires proof of pregnancy and the intended expulsions of the immature contents of the uterus are established. The word 'with child' means pregnant, and it is not necessary to show that quickening, i.e. perception by the mother that the movements of the foetus have taken place, or that the embryo has assumed a foetus form.[6]

It therefore follows that conception begins with the elementary formation of the embryo or foetus and that thereafter the implantation of anything designed to disturb the natural development to birth is sufficient to sustain a charge under the Code. It is accordingly immaterial to a charge being sustained that the insertion of IUD took place just a month after conception. Since legislation, authorities and legal commentaries to a large extent do not draw any line of distinction between miscarriage and abortion, it would be unsafe for a doctor to recommend IUD to a patient.[7]

---

[3] Criminal Code, Cap. Laws of Nigeria 2004.

[4] [1969] 1 QB 541, [1968] 2 All ER 282. Note that the conviction was set aside on appeal on other grounds, namely misdirection.

[5] [1886] ILR IX Mad 369, a decision of the Madras Court of Appeal, interpreting s.312 of the Indian Penal Code, a provision in *pari materia* with our Criminal Code, s.229).

[6] Ibid. 370.

[7] See *Hall* v. *People* 201 P. 2d 382 (1948) (SC Col.) *Scot* v. *State* 117 A 2d 831 (1955) Sc. Del.), *R* v. *Trim* [1943] VLR 109 (Australia).

Some however have argued that *R* v. *Price* is not an authority for stating that IUD treatment is criminal abortion, because in their view the case was decided before the enactment of the English Abortion Act, 1967. These commentators argue that it only establishes that in some cases IUD may be regarded as an instrument used to procure abortion. IUD may only be construed as abortion if a woman is truly pregnant, not necessarily when an embryo is formed, because it is reasoned that there cannot be a miscarriage if there is no 'true carriage' in a woman.[8]

In support for the position, commentators cite *R* v. *Dhingra*,[9] a case that was unfortunately disposed off summarily. It involved a charge under the Offences Against the Person Act, 1961, section 58. The charge was brought against a doctor who fitted a contraceptive coil in his secretary some 11 days after they had intercourse. The judge, having heard gynaecological evidence that implantation could not have occurred, withdrew the case from the jury on the ground that the woman could not be said to be pregnant 'in the true sense of the word'. The reasoning would seem to have proceeded on the basis that until the embryo becomes a viable foetus (usually fixed as from the 12th week of conception) a woman is not truly pregnant.[10] Further argument in support of the non-classification of IUD treatment as abortion is morally based. It looks morally less reprehensible to use IUD than destroy a foetus by abortion. Notwithstanding, some ethicist would insist that to employ IUD is to interfere by artificial method with the natural courses of creation and to this extent is morally wrong, warranting its classification as abortion[11] Whatever may be the arguments and distinction between 'true pregnancy' and 'mere pregnancy,' it is safer for a doctor not to prescribe IUD, under the present legal framework of our criminal jurisprudence.[12]

Fertility control is classified as medical treatment. Lord Fraser in *Gillick* v. *West Norfolk and Wisbeck Area Health Authority*[13] said:

> These and other provisions show that Parliament regarded advise and treatment on contraception and the supply of appliances for contraception as

---

[8] But cf. IJ Keown, Miscarriage: A Medico-Legal Analysis [1984] *Crim LR* 604.

[9] (1991) *Daily Telegraph*, 25 January, p5. See *Royal College of Nursing of The UK* v. *Dept of Health and Social Security* [1981] AC 800 whether s. 1 of the Abortion Act which legitimates abortion in certain circumstances when pregnancy is terminated by a registered medical practitional includes termination by a nurse.

[10] Where to draw the line between true pregnancy and pregnancy may not be as easy to resolve as simply distinguished by the judge in *R* v. *Dhingra*.

[11] It is probably for this reason that Catholic faith, condemns some, if not all, types of fertility control or treatment. See J Poole, Time for the Vatican to Bend (1992) 339 *Lancet* 1340; and DAR Verkuyl, Two World Religions and Family Planning (1993) 342 *Lancet* 473.

[12] There is no doubt that aside this form of interceptive contraceptive, displanting contraceptive of the menstrual extraction meant to destroy or dislodge an implanted embryo method is clearly criminal abortion. See D Crystal-Kirk, Embryo Arrest: The 'No-man's Land' between Contraception and Abortion (1989) 57 *Med-Leg J* 111; JO Drife, Deregulating Emergency Contraception (1993) 307 BMJ 695; K McK Norrie, Post Coital Anti-pregnancy Techniques and the Law in AA Templeton and D Cusine (eds) *Reproductive Medicine and the Law* (1990).

[13] [1984] QB 581, [1984] 1 All ER 365, on appeal [1986] AC 112, [1985] 1 All ER 402, HL.

essential medical matters. So they are, but they may also raise moral and social question on which many people feel deeply, and in that respect they differ from ordinary medical advice and treatment.[14]

Non-Surgical Permanent Fertility Treatment Contraceptive

Except for cases of contraceptive that may invite criminal sanction[15] and those raising product liability, the main ethico–legal questions it raises are those relating to its provision to minor and mentally ill patients.

Contraception, Children and the mentally ill

When consulted by a minor seeking fertility treatment the doctor is often faced with a three dimensional problem - question of consent, confidentially and public morality and or decency policy. He immediately has to make a mental summation of the advantages and the disadvantages of the treatment sought from him. He may consider questions such as, is the patient too young to understand sex, especially its connection with pregnancy and child caring? If she is, and yet insists on having sexual experience, should she be protected by contraception to save her from the trauma of an eventual pregnancy or venereal disease? What possible harm would she experience if allowed free sexual expression? What if it results in pregnancy and she seeks an abortion, would the doctor's failure to provide early preventive treatment have done her more harm than good?

After a consideration of these possible questions he has to make a decision whether or not to give the treatment requested. In making the decision the doctor is likely to have considered not just the patient's interest,[16] but also that of the society, public morality and decency. If a decision to give contraceptive treatment and advice is arrived at, he is expected to further consider the difficult questions of the facts of consent and the issue of medical confidentiality. The former is material in the provision of the treatment, because the doctor needs to be sure that there is in fact *real* consent. For example, whether or not the patient though a minor is legally capable of giving consent to treatment without parental consent is material. He ought to be mindful of this fact because lack of legally required consent can expose a doctor to civil and criminal liability as well as professional discipline. Consent investigation by him can help determine what is best for the minor, by no means an easy issues to resolve.

The House of Lords decision in *Gillick* examined these issues in the provision of contraceptive for minor. The Law Lords held that provided a minor has attained sufficient maturity and understanding of a treatment requested, her consent alone is

[14] [1985] 1 All ER 402 at 407.

[15] E.g. contra-gestation such as IUD.—

[16] *Gillick* v. *West Norfolk and Wisbeck Area Health Authority* [1984] QB 581, [1984] 1 All ER 365, on appeal [1986] AC 112, [1985] 1 All ER 402, HL.

sufficient and valid. The facts of the case resulted from a circular published by the Department of Health, stating that doctors could, in limited circumstances, provide family planning treatment to minors without parental consent. Mrs Gillick, thought this was a very offensive circular. She sought to have it declared unlawful by the court. She had five daughters who were minors. So she sought an assurance from her local health authority that her daughters would not be given advice and treatment on contraception without her consent and knowledge. When the authority refused to give the assurance sought, she sued it and the Department of Health. She sought the following orders: (i) a declaration that the advise contained in the circular is unlawful, because it amounted to an advise to doctors to commit the offence of causing or encouraging unlawful sexual intercourse by girl under 16, contrary to section 28 (1) of the Sexual Offence Act, 1956 or the offence of sexual intercourse with a girl under 16, contrary to section 6 (1) of the Act; and (ii) a declaration that an advice and treatment on contraception given to a child below the age of 16 is unlawful for being inconsistent with her rights as a parent consent-giver.

The trial court (Woof J) relied on the Canadian case of *Johnston* v. *Wellesley Hospital*[17] to reach a decision that a person below the age of 16 is capable of consent to the provision of treatment and advice on contraception, provided she is of sufficient mental maturity and understanding of the implication of the treatment. The judgement was reversed on appeal, by the English Court of Appeal.[18] The Court of Appeal based its decisions on the inseparable duties and rights of parents to reserve consent for children. But that was not the end of the matter. The defendants, backed by the British Medical Association, dissatisfied with the decision of the Court of Appeal, appealed the matter to the House of Lords.[19] By a majority of 3-2, the House restored the judgement of the trial court. It held that a minor could receive treatment and advice on contraception, if she is mature to understand the implications of the treatment requested for even without parental knowledge and consent. By this decision the House of Lords introduced the concept of *mature minor* principle in the English medical jurisprudence.

Lord Scarman rejected the argument of Mrs. Gillick that the provision of contraceptive would directly assist in the commission of sexual crimes. He said:

> The only effect of the provision of the means of contraception is that in some cases it is likely to increase the likelihood of a crime being committed by reducing the inhibitions of the persons concerned to having sexual intercourse because of their fear of conception or the contraction of disease.

---

[17] [1984] QB 581, [1984] 1 All ER 365 See *Johnston* v. *Wellesley Hospital* (1970) 17 DLR (3d) 139. See also A. Bainham, Handicapped Girls and Judicial Parents (1987) 103 *LQR* 334.

[18] [1986] AC 112, [1985] 1 All ER 830, CA.

[19] [1986] AC 112, [1985] 1 All ER 402, HL see J. Morgan, Controlling Minors Fertility (1986) 12 *Monash Univ. LR161*, P Gerber & A. Rahemtula, Who Has The Rights to Advise Children on Birth Control (1986) *Med J. Austral* 419.

Lord Fraser also rejected the principle of parents 'absolute authority' over minor children as *consent givers*. In his Lordship view, the resolution of the question borders on the resolution of who between the minor and parent, should exercise veto consent, a question that ought properly to turn on the resolution of what is the best interest of the child. From the issue framed by His Lordship, the substratum of Mrs. Gillick's claims were made to turn not on the construction of the legislation relating to sex, but rather on best interest consideration of the child. Citing *Re P. (a minor)*,[20] where the court ordered a local authority to fit a contraceptive appliance in a girl aged 15; pregnant for a second time, His Lordship concluded that it might be desirable in some cases in the girl's interest to give contraceptive advice and treatment without parental consent. In Lord Fraser's view, a doctor would be justified in proceeding without parent's consent or even knowledge if he is satisfied that: (i) the girl (although under 16 years of age) will understand his advice; or (ii) he is unable through persuasion to convince her to inform her parents or if she refuses to allow him to inform her parents that she is seeking contraceptive advice; or (iii) she is very likely to begin or to continue having sexual intercourse with or without contraceptive treatment; or (iv) if the doctor forms the opinion that unless she receives contraceptive advice or treatment her physical or mental health or both are likely to suffer or (v) that her best interest require him to give her contraceptive advice, treatment, or both without the parental consent. He however sounded this advice to the profession:

> The case ought not to be regarded as a licence for doctors to disregard the wishes of parents on this matter whenever they find it convenient to do so. Any doctor who behaves in such a way would, in my opinion, be failing to discharge his professional responsibilities.

The *Gillick* decision is not free of controversy. It appears to take a narrow, simplistic view of the consequences of a minor seeking contraception advice and treatment. It glosses over many social issues that do not readily get resolved from the contentious nature of adversarial litigation process. Consider for example, some possible social issues: How does a doctor establish sufficient maturity of a minor that excuses his not seeking parental consent? Even at that, is sex and contraception one of the things a minor needs as necessaries? If we answer yes, a dubious answer, further questions would need to be addressed. Is the possible danger of say, cervical cancer a minor may expose herself to as a result of premature sexual activity not sufficient reason for an illiberal regime of regulation of minor request for contraception? One only hopes that this does not implicate law as a discipline concerned with *right* at the expense of losing the *left*. Whatever, the decision serves

[20] (1981) 80 LGR 301.

as a useful guideline for doctor, patients, parents and the public on matters of consent to general medical treatment.

Contraception advice and treatment of the mentally ill is in many respects as those of minors. Generally similar principles apply to both. This is so because in both cases the patient treatment raises question of consent. In line with *Re C*[21] it would be safe to suggest that the five guidelines given by Lord Fraser in the *Gillick* case with relevant amendment, would also regulate the provision of advice and treatment to mentally handicapped patient.

Product liability from the use of contraception

The underlining principle on defective product liability remains as formulated by Lord Atkin in *M'Alister (Donoghue)* v. *Stevenson*.[22] Whether or not a manufacturer, supplier, (including a physician who makes prescription) would be liable or not for defective products depends on the common law principle of negligence. A defective contraceptive may result in liability to the manufacture if it is shown to be defective or if it exposes the user to intolerable risk without a direction or warning as to the risk. As in all tort of negligence, three elements must be proved to raise liability – a duty of care, breach of the duty of care and resulting damages.

In determining whether a contraceptive drug is badly manufactured, the court would consider whether the manufacturer has carried out all reasonable research (including clinical experiment) which accords with scientific knowledge available. In certain cases, a manufacturer can escape liability for a defective drug if he can establish that the state of scientific and technical knowledge available at the relevant time was not such that would have enabled it to discover the defect in the drug. The manufacturer who makes the plea would escape liability on the basis that the state of art at the relevant time of manufacture could not have revealed the risk.[23]

There are however a great number of cases, especially on matters of contraception where a drug though not defective, causes injury because it is not accompanied with sufficient warning of possible risk or lacks sufficient relevant direction for use, e.g. where dosage prescription is insufficient. In determining liability the court would consider the following point aptly stated by Robins JA in *Buchan* v. *Ortho Pharmaceuticals (Canada) Ltd* namely:

> In determining whether a drug manufacturer's warning satisfies the duty of making adequate and timely warning to the medical profession of any dangerous side-effects produced by its drug of which it knows, or has reason to know, certain factors must be born in mind. A manufacturer of prescription drugs occupies the position of an expert in the fields; this requires that it be under a continuing duty to keep abreast of scientific developments pertaining to its products through research, adverse reaction reports, scientific literature

---

[21] [1993] *The Independent*, 15 October p. 34; [1994] 1 All ER 819.

[22] [1932] AC 562 at 599 (HL).

[23] Already s. 4-(I) (e) of the UK consumer Protection Act, 1987 has incorporated this degree in the statute. This degree is commonly called "development risk" or "a state of the art defect..."

> and other available methods. When additional dangerous or potentially dangerous side-effects from the drugs use are discovered, the manufacturer must make all reasonable efforts to communicate the information to prescribing physicians...Whether a particular warning is adequate will depend on what is reasonable in the circumstances.[24]

In this respect the state of art risk or defect is a defence open to the manufacturer. Warning must be addressed to persons likely to be injured by the use of the drugs. If it is a specialised drug intended to be dispensed only by specialist prescription, a warning to the experts will do.[25] In addition to the common principle, a manufacturer is under a statutory duty to ensure that his drug complies with the relevant statute regulating consumer protection laws.[26]

Sterilisation

As previously stated, surgical control usually involves in men the cutting of a male vas (vasectomy) and in women the cutting of the fallopian tube. Most ethical objections to surgical control through sterilisation centre on its irreversible nature. In addition, the ethical questions may also involve legal issues relating to informed consent, its non-therapeutic uses and liability for failure of the procedure to prevent pregnancy.

Legal questions of consent

If consensual sterilisation is considered objectionable, non consensual sterilisation must be repulsive. If practised as state policy for control of population, dangers of compulsion and the like could become additional worries. Whether or not an individual can give consent to a programme of sterilisation is governed by general principles of informed consent. However this proposition has its caveat. In *Bravery* v. *Bravery*, Lord Denning said:

> An ordinary surgical operation which is done for the sake of a man's health with his consent is of course perfectly lawful because there is just cause for it...Likewise with a sterilisation...But when it is done, without just cause or excuse, it is unlawful, even though the man consents to it. Take a case where a sterilisation operation is done so as to enable a man to have the pleasure of sexual intercourse, without shouldering the responsibilities attached to it. The operation then is plainly injurious to public interest.[27]

---

[24] (1986) 54 OR (2d) 92.

[25] *Rirton Marine Ltd* v. *Washington Iron Works* [1974] SCR 1189, *Murphy* v. *St. Catharine General Hospital* (1964) IOR 239, 41 DLR (2d) HCJ).

[26] In England the Consumer Protection Act 1987. A. H Hudson, Instructions As to the Use of Consumer Goods (1981) *LQR* 550, ss.4-5 of Food and Drugs Act, Cap 150 LFN, 1990; Food Products (Advertisement) regulation 1996 of NAFDAC, s.4; .9 of Consumer Protection Council Act, 1992.

[27] [1954] I WLR 1169 (CA).

His Lordships view has been criticised for being too restrictive and out of alignment with the liberal philosophy of J S Mill which informs many decisions in medical ethics. The parallel that sterilisation operation enables a man to enjoy sex (pleasure) without responsibility as being injurious to the public is controversial. Condom can do it, and yet there is generally no serious objection to its use as a fertility control method. No wonder, Sir Raymond Evershed and Hodson LJJ, disagreed with the statement of Lord Denning quoted above. Hodson LJ. said:

> In our view these observations are wholly inapplicable to operations for sterilisation as such, and we are not prepared to hold in the present case that such operations must be regarded as injurious to the public interest.

This view seem to more properly represent the current position of law,[28] a position that now enjoys statutory backing in England,[29] New Zealand[30] and some other jurisdictions.

Questions have been raised whether in determining factual consent the doctor would be acting in line with good practice to disregard entirely the wishes and views of persons proximate to the patient by virtue of marriage, contract or blood relationship. The social value of seeking their views cannot be over emphasised. For example, it may be desirable to seek a spouse's opinion to a sterilisation request so that domestic and social harmony are not disrupted. That notwithstanding, the legal position is that their views or wishes are legally irrelevant. *Paton* v. *British Pregnancy Advising Services*[31] is authority for the proposition. In determining consent, the only relevant person is the patient. However, sterilisation without spouse consent, may be basis for a finding on grounds of 'intolerable behaviour' for purposes of divorce under the Matrimonial Causes Act, 1970. If request for sterilisation is from a mature minor, the principle in *Gillick* case [32] remains valid. Consent by the mature minor alone would do. Where consent is absent the operation is strongly objectionable because it brings to an end, a basic human function – procreation. That being the case, nothing short of full consent would do. Basically, the same principles as discussed in the chapter on "informed consent" apply here. The only difference here is that the principles apply in a more particular way to sterilisation. Decisions of the court in this respect have largely been influenced by the elevation of non-consensual sterilisation to the status of 'basic human right to procreate'.[33] By this, the courts treat

[28] For a summary of the Canadian position, see *Cataford* v. *Moraine* (1978) 114 DLR (3d) 585.

[29] The purport of National Health Service Act is to classify sterilisation for contraceptive purpose as a proper, just cause, not one contrary to petition interest. This is the prevailing viewpoint of law.

[30] S. 61A of the New Zealand Crimes Acts 1961 that stipulates no one shall be liable for the purpose, which includes rendering a patient sterile.

[31] *Paton* v. *UK* (1980) 3 EHRR 408; *Paton* v. *British Pregnancy Advisory Service Trustees* [1979], QB 276, [1978] 2 All ER 987

[32] [1979] QB 2 76, [1978] 2 All ER 987.

[33] *Skinner* v. *Oklahoma* (1942) 316 US 535, *Re. D A minor (Wardship: sterilisation)* [1976] 1 All ER 326, [1976] Fam 185; *Re Eve* (1986) 31 DLR (4th) 1; *HG (specific issue order: sterilisation)* [1993] 1 FLR 587 at 592.

the right to procreate as a basic common law human right, that can only be taken away with full consent or if impossible, in the best interest of the patient.

Argument on rights is hinged on the ground that there is a fundamental right to free procreation. This right it is claimed includes the fundamental right to bear children, a fundamental right to chose not to have children and a right to choose means of contraception. In fact counsel for *Eve* argued that a court ordered sterilisation would constitute an infringement of her right to liberty and security of the person under s.7 of the Canadian Charter of Rights and Freedoms. In recognition of this, LaForest in *Re Eve*[34] said that what was at stake in the case was a consideration of fundamental human rights. Also in the English case of *Re D (a minor) (wardship: sterilisation)*[35] the judge referred to the basic human rights of a woman to reproduce, concluding that it would constitute a violation of a girl's right to sterilise her without her consent for non-therapeutic reasons.

Our discussion so far has been on non-consensual sterilisation of minor and incompetent adult. By so doing we have excluded competent adults not because its discussion is less important but because non-consensual sterilisation of adult is a rare phenomena. If it does occur, it would generally be governed by principles of informed consent. It may only occur in emergency treatment cases, a fact widely acknowledged. For example, in its Working Paper 24 (1979) the Law Reform Communion of Canada states:

> Sterilisation as a medical procedure is distinct because except in rare cases, if the operation is not performed, the physical health of the person involved is not in danger, necessity or emergency not normally being factors in the decision to undertake the procedure. In addition, to its being elective it is for all intents and purposes irreversible.[36]

A doctor involved in non consensual sterilisation of incompetent adult and minor must proceed with caution for three reasons, namely (i) the procedure involves matters of values, (ii) its implications are always serious and (iii) unlike other surgical treatments, is usually sought for non-therapeutic reasons. Let us consider a few authorities on the matter.

Re D (a minor)(wardship: sterilisation) [37] was a case involving a minor, 11 years old with an IQ of 80. It is said that the rating did not necessarily make her unfit to cope with life, marry and raise children. She was suffering from a rare condition known as Sotos syndrome, but her condition was improving. Heilbrow J relying on medical evidence, held that sterilisation was not in her best interest especially considering the irreversibility of the operation and the significance it may bear on her as a young person. Significantly the court expressed the view that a decision to

---

[34] (1986) 31 DLR (4th) 1 at 32.
[35] [1976] 1 All ER 326.
[36] Ibid., see also 1979 Working Paper of the Canadian Law Reform Commission.
[37] [1976] Fam 185, [1976] 1 All ER 326.

sterilise is outside the scope of the clinical judgement of a single doctor. Her Ladyship also raised basis issues of human rights, treating the right to procreate as a basis right.

Re D represented the English position until the cases of *Re B (a minor wardship sterilisation)*[38] and *Re F (a mental patient sterilisation)*[39] doubted it. Even the Canadian Supreme Court in *Re Eve*, quoted with approval *Re D*. Noteworthy of mention however is that the Canadian case of *Re Eve* was decided before the later two English cases of *Re B* and *Re. F*. That notwithstanding it is suggested that *Re Eve* and *Re D* more properly represent current ethics and law.

Re Eve was a Canadian case having to do with a child who lived with her mother while attending local school. When she was 21, her mother sent her to a school for retarded adults. While there she got close to a male student and they both talked about marriage. However, when the school discovered this, it brought the affair to an end. Her situation troubled her mother under whose care she was. The girl was attractive and attracted to men and her mother feared that she might innocently become pregnant. She was also concerned about the emotional effect pregnancy and a subsequent birth might have on her, because in her view she could not adequately cope with the duties and responsibilities of a mother. The mother's concern was heightened by the fact that she herself was approaching 60. So she decided that Eve should be sterilised. The medical evidence revealed that Eve 24, suffered from an extreme expressive aphasia. While she might be able to carry out the mechanical duties of a mother, under supervision, she would be incapable of being a mother in any other sense. She had no proper appreciation of marriage, the consequential relationship between intercourse, pregnancy and birth. Expressive aphasia is a condition in which the patient is unable to communicate outwardly thought or concept perceived. The Supreme Court of Canada held that even though it had jurisdiction to authorise sterilisation under its *paren patriae* jurisdiction, such a jurisdiction was circumscribed by the principle that the court must act in the best interest of the patient. Having distinguished between therapeutic and non-therapeutic sterilisation, it concluded that non-therapeutic sterilisation should not be authorised under the *paren patria* jurisdiction. LaForest J said:

> The grave intrusion on a person's right and the certain physical damage that ensures from non-therapeutic sterilisation without consent, when compared to the highly questionable advantages that can result from it have persuaded me that it can never safely be determined that such a procedure is for the benefit of that person. Accordingly, the procedure should never be authorised for non-therapeutic the purposes under the *parens patria* jurisdiction.[40]

---

[38] [1988] AC 199, [1987] 2 All ER 206 (HL).
[39] [1990] 2 AC 1, [1989] 2 All ER 545 (HL).
[40] (1906) 3 DLR (4th) 1 at 32.

Having so said, the court then drew a guideline on matters of consent for therapeutic sterilisation. LaForest J further said:

> Since these issues may arise in cases involving application for sterilisation from therapeutic purposes...I will venture a few words about them. Since bearing emergency situations, a surgical procedure without consent ordinarily constitutes battery, it will be obvious that the onus of proving the need for the procedure is on those who seek to have it performed. And that burden, though a civil one must be commensurate with the seriousness of the measure proposed. In conducting these procedures, it is obvious that a court must proceed with extreme caution, and wise as MacDonald J noted, it would open the way for abuse of the mentally incompetent. In particular, in any such proceeding, it is essential that the mentally incompetent have independent representation.[41]

In effect, all request for therapeutic sterilisation on minors and mentally incompetent must be sought for from the court under its *parens patria* jurisdiction. Additionally, the burden of proof requires something beyond balance of probability for civil litigation. It thus put it between balance of probabilities and proof beyond reasonable doubt. The reason for this high burden of proof is rooted in 'the seriousness of the measure proposed': Even at that, it is suggested that there is the additional requirement of independent representation in all cases involving the mentally incompetent.

Noteworthy of mention, the Canadian Supreme Court stated that its *parens patria* jurisdiction, akin to the English wardship jurisdiction is a proper procedure in cases within the bracket of *Eve*, i.e. incompetent adult. She in fact was 21. This may seem to re-enforce the thinking that in making decisions on the legality or otherwise of sterilisation, the same principles apply both to incompetent adults and minors. Whether a similar jurisdiction would apply in England, and by extension Nigeria, is doubtful. Authorities in England and commentators have increasingly doubted the correctness of using wardship jurisdiction for adult patients.[42]

Also the distinction drawn between therapeutic and non-therapeutic sterilisation and imputation of principle of human rights in the sterilisation context made by the Canadian Supreme Court remains controversial. These matters were considered by the House of Lords in *Re B (a minor)(wardship sterilisation)*.[43] A local authority was in charge of the care of a mentally handicap and epileptic 17 years old girl, who had a mental age of 5 or 6. She could not understand the connection between sexual intercourse and pregnancy and birth and if pregnant, would be unable to cope with it and the baby. From her mental state, it was legally impossible for her to give consent to a marriage. Unfortunately, she was exhibiting the normal sexual drive and inclination of a girl of 17. Expert opinion advice that she should not be permitted

---

41 See discussion on jurisdiction at and MDA Freeman, see also *Re F* (HL decision at n. 47).
42 (1986) 31 DLR (4th) 1 at .
43 [1988] AC 199; [1987] 2 All ER 206.

to become pregnant, but preventing it would somehow be a difficult task because of her possible reaction to contraceptive. The drugs reacted badly on her when administered with her routine, necessary drugs meant to control her mental instability and epilepsy. This was complicated by the fact that it was extremely difficult to place her on a course of oral contraceptive pills. On these ground the local authority applied to make her a ward of court, and for leave to sterilise her. The application was supported by her mother. But the Official Solicitor acting as her guardian *ad litem* opposed it. The trial court granted the application, and on appeal to the English Court of Appeal, the appeal was dismissed; hence the further appeal to the House of Lords. The House of Lords upheld the decision of both courts. It authorised sterilisation on the ground that it was in the best interest of the patient, minor.

On the issues classifying sterilisation procedure as a basic human right and the relevance, if any, of the distinction between therapeutic and non-therapeutic sterilisation, the court said: (Lord Hailsham):

> We were invited to consider the decision of Heilbron J in D (a minor) (wardship: sterilisation) 1976 Fam 185, 193, where the judge rightly referred to the irreversible nature of such an operation and the deprivation which it involves of a basic human right, namely the right of a woman to reproduce. But this right is only such when reproduction is the result of informed choice of which this ward is incapable. I have no doubt, whatsoever, that the case was correctly decided, but I venture to suggest that no one would be more astonished than that wise, experienced and learned judge herself if we were to apply these proper consideration to the extreme and quite different facts of the present case. We were also properly referred to the Canadian case of *Re Eve* (1986) 31 DLR (4th) 1. But whilst I find La Forest J's history of the *parens patriae* jurisdiction of the Crown (at 14-21) extremely helpful, I find, with great respect his conclusions (at 32) that procedures of sterilisation 'should never be authorised for non therapeutic purposes' totally unconvincing and startling contradiction to the welfare principle which should be the first and paramount consideration in wardship cases. Moreover, for the purposes of the present appeal, I find the distinction he purports to draw between therapeutic and non therapeutic purposes of this operation in relation to the fact of the present case above as totally meaningless, and, if meaningful, quite irrelevant to the correct application of the welfare principle.[44]

Lord Hailsham speech implicitly recognises the implication of basic human right in sterilisation, though in their view it is a right only the informed, presumably, the competent can enjoy. Whatever, the implicit recognition is all that is required to employ it as 'canon-further' for developing the law in a more robust manner, His Lordship caveat above notwithstanding. It is therefore not ambitious to suggest that the human right to procreate proposition survives *Re B*.[45] The House only quarrelled

[44] [1988] AC 199, [1987] 2 All ER 206 (HL).

[45] Ibid.

with the usefulness if any, of making a distinction between therapeutic and non-therapeutic sterilisation. Lord Hailsham refused to agree with the Canadian Supreme Court distinction in *Re Eve*. Lord Bridge treated the distinction as a 'sweeping generalisation that is entirely unhelpful'. Lord Oliver also did not consider the distinction any useful in determining the primary and paramount question of whether sterilisation is in the best interest or welfare of the patient. An analysis of the House of Lords judgment reveal that it ruled as irrelevant in determining issue of sterilisation considerations of eugenic, convenience of the care-givers to the patient, and any other related matters. It was categorical in holding that the relevant and paramount consideration is the 'best interest' principle. What is best for the patient is the cornerstone

Both decisions (that of the House of Lords in *Re B* and the Canadian Supreme Court in *Re Eve*) may appear contradictory. But it is possible to reconcile them because only their conclusions differ. Both applied the same best interest test. From this perspective, any conflict is reduced to application of principles to facts. It is suggested that *Re Eve* was more of a generalisation of principles, while *Re B* represented particularisation on the facts before their Lordship. Whatever, the conclusion in *Re. B* has been severely criticised, especially on gender grounds.

In the view of Freeman,[46] the case exhibits an intolerable degree of gender discrimination. He argues that if the request for sterilisation was for a 17 year old boy, the House of Lords would have reached a different decision. It would have refused sterilisation as unhelpful in protecting him. While it is hardly contestable that the learned writer's argument has much force that commends it, counter argument is not nonsensical either. Fact of life would seem to dictate that reproduction generally has little adverse effect on boys, unlike girls. An unplanned birth for a girl is more likely to derail her, than a boy. It is for this reason that the only ethico-legal basis for compulsory sterilisation of a boy conceivable would be rooted in punitive or eugenic considerations, hardly for purposes of protection, as in the 17 year old girl in *Re B*. Since sterilisation for punitive or eugenic purposes is open to more serious objections than for protective purposes, the House of Lords conclusion in Re B may find some justification on grounds not rooted in discrimination.

---

[46] M. Freeman, For Her Own Good (1987) *LS Gaz.* 949, See also K Mck Norrie, Sterilisation of the Mentally Disabled in England and Canadian Law (1989) 38 *ICLQ* 38; R. Leed D. Morgan, Sterilisation and Mentally Handicap: Sapping the Strength of the State (1988) 15 *Law L Soc.* 229: JES Fortin, Sterilisation, the Mentally Ill and Consent to Treatment (1986) 51 *MLR* 634; A Grubb & D. Pearl, Sterilisation and the Courts (1987) 46 *CLJ* 439; j. Montgomery, Rhetoric and Welfare (1989) 9 *Ox J of Leg St* 395; J. Goldham, The Right to Reproduce (1989) 63 *Law Inst.J.* 708. L.Appleby & C. Dickens, Mothering Skills of Women with Mental illness (1993) 306 *BMJ* 348; but cf. J.A Robertson, Procreative Liberty and the Control of Conception Pregnancy and Children (1983) 69 *Van. L.R* 405 and A. Thomas, For Her Own Good – A Reply (1987) 84 *LS Gaz* 1196. On eugenics for sterilisation see P.R. Reilly, Eugenic Sterilisation, United States in A. Willians (eds) *Genetics and the Law – III (1985)* Ch. 17, K McKnorrie, *Family Planning Practice and the Law* (1991).

Re B[47] has been severely criticised as not representing good law. In *Re D*, Heilbron J (rightly in our view) refuses to authorise sterilisation because of its irreversible nature and on the ground that it would amount to a deprivation of a basic human right, namely the right of a woman to reproduce. But in *Re B*, the House of Lords distinguished *Re D*. While it is valid to accept that the two cases have material difference, the basic principles of irreversibility of the operation and human rights issues alive in both cases were fundamentally the same. On the question of the basic human right to reproduce, Lord Hailsham stated:

> To talk of the basic right to reproduce of an individual who is not capable of knowing the causal connection between intercourse and child birth, the nature of pregnancy, what is involved in delivery, unable to form material instincts or to care for a child appears...wholly to part company with reality.

For Lord Oliver[48] the right 'is of value only if accompanied by the ability to make a choice or indeed to appreciate the need to make one.'

It is humbly suggested that the Law Lords were too dismissive of the argument based on rights without giving it serious considerations. Though in *Re B*, the judges did not deny that a right to reproduce existed, they however thought it meant nothing to her. The validity of the right cannot be denied.[49] The right exists simply by virtue of our being human. It is one right that enhances our humanity. The Law Lords in failing to see the germaneness of the right lost the very essence of the issues in contention. What the court should have done was to adopt a conception of rights as very important protectable interest, and where it considers it to conflict with other rights, adopt a stance that maximises the fulfilment of the right and minimises its violation.

The conclusion of the House of Lords took many things for granted that may not have been valid. It assumed that she was fertile, which may not have been the case. Was there any empirical fact to show that the sterilisation ordered would protect her from sexual exploitation? Hardly. If anything, it could only prevent pregnancy if she is fertile. It assumes without more that she was mentally retarded. But did it do an analysis of what constitutes mental retardation? If the 70 marks of intelligence quotient is used as the cut-off mark for general average intelligence, we may be surprised that more persons than we imagine will be considered retarded. It is suggested that because diagnostic procedures are fallible and the denial of a person's rights can be injurious, it is necessary to adopt a conservative approach requiring irremediable moral incompetence before an individual's right should be denied.[50]

---

[47] [1988] AC 199; [1987] 2 All ER 206 at 213.

[48] Ibid. at 219.

[49] Re D (1976) 1 All ER 326; *Eisenstadt* v. *Baird* 405 US 438 at 453 (1972); see also McLean, The Right to Reproduce in T Campbell *et al* (eds.) *Human Rights*, Blackwell, 1986. p. 99; Kingdom, The Right to Reproduce in M. Ockleton (ed) *Medicine, Ethics and Law* p. 54.

[50] D Meyers, Alienable Rights: A Defence (Columbia Univ. Press.) 1985 at. 141.

Somewhat sad in *Re B* was the haste with which the case was rushed to a conclusion. It rushed through court just before her 18th birthday, when she would attain majority.[51] At 18 she would no longer be subject to wardship jurisdiction, and so a court-ordered sterilisation would have been foreclosed - hence the rush. This only raises the question of the competence of the court to order involuntary sterilisation on a retarded adult. She would have been 18 years a few months to when the case was decided. The House of Lords rushed the case because it doubted whether there was any *parens patriae* jurisdiction in the High Court after majority. If she had reached majority the court would have become handicapped to authorise sterilisation without her consent - hence the hurry. The court was not in doubt that it would have been prevented from doing what it really wanted to do – sterilise her. Lord Hailsham[52] after expressing doubt whether there was a residual *parens patriae* jurisdiction said, "in twelve months time it would be doubtful what legal courses would be open." But for Lord Oliver,[53] he stated that the jurisdiction would not come to an end on majority for a retarded person. Whatever, this gives an impression that the Law Lords did not properly avert their minds to the serious human rights issues that were raised, but rather were more prepared to make orders based on expediency. It is for these reasons that *Re B* represents a slippery slope away from *Re D*. Sadly, by implication it reveals how the 'best interest' test can be used to play out inalienable human rights and possibly mask gender power. According to Freeman,[54] *Re B*, is suspect because (i) it puts the retarded girl's best interest ahead of her basic human rights (ii) it refuses to treat 'best interest' as the equivalent of 'best medical treatment and (iii) for not taking her rights seriously and (iv) the 'best interest' test lacks sufficient guideline, thus creating enormous latitude for subsequent decision makers to justify further invasion of rights.

Unfortunately, *Re B*, left open the question of how to determine the best interest of the patient. Two years later in *Re F (a mental patient: sterilisation)*[55] the court attempted a mapping of the principle. F an adult of 36 suffered from serious mental disability, probably as a result of an acute infection of the respiratory track, which inflicted her when she was about 9 months old. She had been a voluntary in-patient in a mental hospital since age 14. She suffered from mental disability, which put her verbal capacity at 2 and her general mental capacity at 4 or 5. She was unable to express her views in word and her mother was the only relative she had who regularly visited her. They both had a strong bond of affection and F was

---

[51] M D A Freeman, Sterilising the Mentally Handicapped, in MDA Freeman (ed) *Medicine, Ethics and the Law* (1988) 64.

[52] [1987] 2 All ER 206 at 212.

[53] Ibid. at 218. This position is contrary to the ratio in *T* v. *T* (1988) 2 WLR 189, where the court held that the *parens patriae* jurisdiction does not exist for retarded adult; See also *Sparkman* v. *McFarlin* 532 F 2d 172 (1977) rev. (1978) 435 US 349; and also B. Hoggett, The Royal Prerogative in Relation to Mentally Disordered. Resurrection, Resuscitation, or Rejection in Freeman (ed) *Medicine, Ethics and The Law*, 1988 p. 85.

[54] Freeman, above n. 51 at 78 — 79.

[55] [1990] 2 AC 1, [1989] 2 All ER 545 (HL).

making progress; although there was no prospect of any development in her mental capacity. While in the hospital she developed a relationship with P, a male patient. The relationship appeared to have involved sexual intercourse, about twice a month, from which she derived pleasure. The relationship was entirely voluntary on her part and it was suspected that pregnancy could result from it. However, because of her mental disability, she would not be able to cope with pregnancy, labour or delivery. She could hardly understand these features of womanhood, and she lacked ability to care for the baby if she eventually has one. It would therefore from a psychiatric view be disastrous for her to have a child. The use of pills as contraceptive was not advised because of the risk it would cause to her physical health. She could not also use IUD as there was a danger of infection arising from it. She would not be able to describe the symptoms to enable quick remedial measures. The trial judge, Scott-Baker J, on the facts as they stood held that it was in the best interest of F to be sterilised by legation of her fallopian tubes.[56] The English Court of Appeal affirmed the decision. On procedure to be adopted for requesting sterilisation, the court said that in all cases an application for approval to the High Court is a pre-requisite.

The legal basis for the decision was not appealed against to the House of Lords. Rather the appeal to it was only concerned with questions of law and legal procedure applicable. In very categorical terms, the House of Lords stated that the *parens patria* jurisdiction no longer exists in the English legal system and that application procedure for sterilisation are governed by way of seeking court declaration. It also disapproved a procedure that makes the court consent-giver on behalf of a patient to such operations. The logical application of this conclusion is by no means pleasant. It would dictate that a doctor can on his own offer sterilisation treatment without court approval on an incompetent adult if in his judgement it is in his patient's best interest.

Going by the court's analysis of best interest, the requirement would be satisfied if the treatment or surgical operation is undertaken for any or all of these three purposes, namely: (i) to save life; or (ii) to improve health or life; and (iii) to prevent deterioration of physical or mental health. More disturbing is its conclusion that in deciding what best interest ought to mean for the patient the doctor should act in accord with principles set out in *Bolam case*. On this, Lord Goff, had this to say:

> In making decisions about treatment, the doctor must act in accordance with a responsible and competent body of relevant professional opinion, on the principles set down in *Bolan* v. *Friern Hospital Management Committee* (1957) 2 All ER 118 (1957) I WLR 582. No doubt, in practice, a decision may involve others beside the doctor. It must surely be good practice to consult relatives and others who are concerned with the care of the patient.[57]

[56] See also HG (specific issue order: sterilisation) [1993] 1 FLR 587, *Re E* (a minor) (medical treatment [1991] 2 All ER 585, [1991] 7 BMLR 117.

[57] [1990] 2 AC 1 at.

This is rather an unfortunate parallel. *Bolam case* was concerned with questions of breach of duty in negligence. That being the case it would hardly be a relevant authority in matters connected with sterilisation, an area of social medicine. Sterilisation conceivably relates more with questions of values, social policy and the likes. It therefore is unadvisable to constitute the doctor as the only relevant authority. Social medicine requires balancing the interest of all persons connected with the medical procedure proposed such as the patient, relatives and the community. So why should even the doctor be a relevant reference, if the sterilisation sought is non-therapeutic? Simple logic would dictate that less, or no weight whatsoever should be given to his opinion in this context. Unfortunately, the House of Lords thought otherwise. Rather it gave to doctors what would seem to be a limitless power to make sterilisation decisions for patients on the basis of best interest. The caveat/direction that the doctor must seek court approval is not any consoling. Why because, present adversarial litigation process hardly provides the forum for resolution of the varied ethical, legal and social questions sterilisation raises. In fact, Lord Goff himself doubted the wisdom of applying the *Bolam's* test, when he said that for a court to automatically accept the expert (doctor's) opinion, would be a denial of the function of the court. He even suggested that the court should only attach weight to it. If anything, it is implicit recognition that the court acknowledged the limitation of the *Bolam's* rule in this context.

Whatever, two subsequent cases, *Re M (a minor (wardship: sterilisation)*[58] and *Re P. (a minor (wardship: sterilisation)*[59] are pointers that the judicial safeguards interpreted by reference to *Bolam's* standard are not effective, because of their vagueness. In *Re M*, the court in reaching a decision authorising sterilisation for an incompetent adult was influenced by the fact that if the patient becomes pregnant, abortion may be recommended because of envisaged risk of foetal handicap. Even though the judge, Bush J, unequivocally stated that eugenic considerations were irrelevant in arriving at the patient's best interest test, an analysis of the case indicates that that was indeed the real reason for the decision. Why, we may ask was the court afraid of the possible birth by the patient of a handicap baby, if it is not reasoned that steps should be taken to prevent as far as possible future production of say, imbeciles. Rightly, Margaret Brazier, in her critique of the case describes it as one of 'eugenic barred from the front being let in at the back'.[60]

In *Re P*, Castham J authorised sterilisation because in his view it was a last resort to prevent the patient from unscrupulous exploitation by men, having heard evidence from Professor Robert Winston, a world-renowned expert in tubal surgery that sterilisation is now reversible. The rationale for authorising sterilisation as last resort, rather than a convenient method of contraceptive remains questionable.[61]

---

[58] [1988] 2 FLR 49 (tubal ligation), per Brush J.

[59] [1989] 1 FLR 182 (tubal ligation), per Easthan J.

[60] M. Brazier, Sterilisation: Down the slippery slope? (1990) 6 *Professional Negligence* 25.

[61] See also the cases *of Re W. (mental patient) (sterilisation)* [1993] 1 FLR; and attempt to set out guideline to determine the best interest principle in practice note of official solicitor reported in [1993] 3 All ER 222;

Essentially, the *Bolam's* best interest test proved an unsatisfactory guide in both cases. Suspicion of possible foetal handicap was interpreted in *Re M*, as sufficient to tilt the scale against the patient. In *Re P*, possibility of the patient's exploitation by men was used as basis that sterilisation is in her best interest. It is submitted that the best interest test were merely used as smoke-screen to further gender power relations. Rather than this vague criterion, what is needed is a legal regime that can properly blend the social, ethical and legal implication of sterilisation.

Therapeutic and non-therapeutic sterilisation

It would be sufficient here to state that the distinction has not been considered useful in England, although the medical and social implications of both may be different.[62] It is however important to mention that if it is for non-therapeutic purpose the unbridled power of the doctor to make decisions on the basis of best interest, should be more circumscribed. This should be so because it is an area of social medicine where the views of the doctor should be accorded less weight by the court in arriving at a decision whether or not to sterilise.

Sterilisation and the medically handicapped

Sterilisation for eugenic or other social control purposes has long been part of medical history. Erroneously it is widely believed that it began with Nazi Germany. Sadly however, as an ideology it can be traced as far back as 1869 to an ivory tower, University of London.[63] Also in 1897 an attempt was made in Michigan to pass a law mandating involuntary sterilisation. In 1907, Indiana became the first American state to pass a compulsory sterilisation law. It is reported that by the 1930s a majority of American states had involuntary sterilisation laws.[64]

Though most of these were struck down as unconstitutional or for being repugnant to 'due process' or 'equal protection under the law or for being 'cruel and unusual' punishment, the U.S. Supreme Court in *Buck* v. *Bell*[65] gave a stamp of approval to sterilisation for eugenic. Buck was a feeble minded girl. Her mother was also alleged to be feeble-minded. Buck intelligence was said to be less than average. Her proposed sterilisation under a Virginia statute was challenged on due and cruel punishment process grounds. The court rejected the due process argument. It held that sterilising her was also not cruel because it makes it safe for her to be released to the community. Justice Holmes said:

---

and the case of *Dept. of Health A Community Services (NT)* v. *JWB & SMB* (1992) 66 ALJR 300, which summaries the Australia position of best interest principles.

[62] See discussion on the view from the various jurisdictions at

[63] M D A Freeman, Sterilising the Mentally Handicapped, in MDA Freeman(ed) *Medicine, Ethics and the Law* (1988) p55. It is said that the founder of the eugenic movement was Sir Francis Galten of the University College, London in the 1880's.

[64] Ibid.

[65] 274 U.S.209 (1927).

> We have seen more than once that the public welfare may call upon the best citizens for their lives. It would be strange if it could not call upon those who already sap the strength of the state to make lesser sacrifices, often not felt to be such by those concerned. In order to prevent our being swamped with incompetence, it is better for all the world if instead of waiting to execute degenerate offspring for crime or let them starve for their imbecility, society can prevent those who are manifestly unfit from continuing their kind... *Three generations of imbeciles are enough* (emphasis is_mine).[66]

The statement made no pretence that eugenic was considered constitutional. It is suggested that even though such naked use of negative eugenics became old fashioned, its policy survived with refinement in modern medicine.

In *North Carolina Association for Retarded Children* v. *State of North Carolina*,[67] the plaintiff association challenged a state statute that authorised voluntary and involuntary sterilisation. Though the court agreed that there was a duty to institute sterilisation proceedings if its use is in the best interest of the retarded person, it stated that in certain rare cases it would be proper to embark on involuntary sterilisation if it is in the best interest of the retarded or the state or both. Unfortunately, it is reported that hundreds of thousands were sterilised in America (USA) under most states compulsory programme raising serious ethical questions. For a moment consider: who were the persons who suffered under the programme? Very sadly the majority were mainly young women, often poor, from socio-economically and culturally deprived environments. If anything, it shows what underlie sterilisation in modern medicine is the politics of oppression against poor women. It is therefore surprising that attempts are made to rewrite history by associating forced sterilisation exclusively with Nazi Germany.[68] Maybe the reason if not located in mischief, is designed to show its danger in modern medicine, especially when pursued as a state project. Nazi Germany was probably the first government that vigorously pursued it as state policy in the 1930's. It created 'hereditary health courts' made up of judges and physicians to enforce the 'law on the prevention of hereditary diseases on future generation'. It is reported that a variety of medical and anti-social habits were sufficient for forced sterilisation under this policy, such as, hereditary blindness or deafness, alcoholism, etc. The policy later degenerated to a point where it was aimed at racial groups and people considered undesirable by Nazi definition. Gypsies (i.e. children of French North Africans occupation troops after World War 1), Jews and religious groups, especially Jehovah's Witnesses were designated anti-social and were sterilised and or persecuted.[69] Some have suggested that sterilisation was also pursued as state policy

---

[66] Ibid. at p. 207. For an analysis of the illogical and inherent contradiction in his Lordships statement, see Freeman, above n 53 at pp. 57-58.

[67] 420 F Supp. 451 (1976).

[68] Freeman, above n 63 at p. 587.

[69] See F Ptaftlin & L Gross (1982) 5 *In. J of Law and Psychiatry* 419. Cited in Freeman above n 53.80 ft nt 31.

in India under Indira Gandhi's government as a population control devise. A similar charge has been made against China.

Liability for failed sterilisation

Generally actions for damages are confined to personal injuries or property. The loss of a person was not thought a proper subject of compensatory damages under the common law.[70] It took Parliamentary intervention in the form of Fatal Accidents legislation to provide remedy for the loss of a breadwinner.[71] But beginning in the 1980s, courts entertained claims by parents against physicians for wrongful birth of children. Paradoxically while death is not actionable, what would seem an obvious blessing, 'birth,' is made the subject matter of compensation. These litigations are premised on the rather disruptive effect an unplanned child brings to a parent. In allowing compensation for wrongful birth the court has been driven between balancing two paradoxical matters–the blessing of childbirth and the financial burden resulting from an unplanned birth.

Litigation in this respect can broadly be classed into three types (i) action for wrongful birth brought by a handicapped child; (ii) action for wrongful birth by parents; and (iii) an action for wrongful conception. The first two actions are usually raised if a child is handicapped, while (iii) is connected with situations where parents complain of the disruptive effect the birth of a healthy unplanned baby brings to them. That notwithstanding, some commentaries do not make the distinction, choosing to put them together. We shall however stick to the distinction because it enables us more properly to capture the various conceptual and practical ethical issues that each raises. The first category we would describe as wrongful life, the second as wrongful birth and the third as wrongful conception. Once we are mindful of the categories, we can better appreciate the discussion.

Wrongful life

Essentially it is an action instituted by a handicap child against a physician for alleged negligence which deprives his mother the opportunity of an abortion which would have prevented his birth with handicap. The court is generally dismissive of these actions. In *McKay* v. *Essex AHA*,[72] the plaintiff child was born severely disabled because his mother contracted German measles during pregnancy. It was suggested that the test on the mother to detect rubella was negligently performed,

---

[70] Andrew Grubb, Conceiving – A New Cause of Action? p. 121 the next page for further reading.

[71] See 1846 fatal Accident Act and subsequent enactment on fame subject mailer for further reading see Tedeschi, On Tort Liability for Wrongful Life (1968) 1 *Israel L.R W* 513; Teff, An Action for Wrongful Life Action Really Dead (1987) *JSWL* 306; WVH Rogers, Legal Implication of Ineffective sterilisation (1985) 5 *LS* 296; Mark, liability for failure of Birth control methods (1976) 76 *Colum. L. Rev* 1187, C. Symmons, Policy factors in Action for Wrongful Birth (1987) 50 *MLR* 269, Robertson, civil liability Arising from wrongful Birth following an unsuccessful sterilisation Operation (1976) 4 *An J Law & Med* 131.

[72] [1982] 2 AII ER 771. But see the Congenital Disabilities (Civil Liability) Act 1976 (UK) which provides that such action can be instituted if negligence occurs not during pregnancy, but before conception which impairs either parents in their ability to have a healthy child.

and that if it was properly done it would have been easy to know that the child might be handicapped. Failure in this respect, it was alleged deprived the mother of having an abortion. The English Court of Appeal struck out the claim on the grounds that (i) some measure of life is better than none; (ii) that the action is contrary to public policy; (iii) that the existence of such actions might encourage abortion and put doctors under a duty to do so in manners detrimental to public health; and (iv) that it was difficult for the court to calculate the amount of damages recoverable if the claim were to be upheld, especially in the context of comparing the non-existence of a child with its handicapped existence.

The American jurisdiction response is rather ambivalent. In the initial stages, claims within the bracket were dismissed.[73] Recently however, some courts have implicitly recognised a claim to damages for the extra cost of maintaining a handicapped child. Noteworthy, damages to compensate for mere existence, including pain and suffering are not recoverable.[74]

Wrongful birth

The birth of a handicapped child often brings direct pains to its parents. Action by parents for a wrongful birth is equivalent of a wrongful life action. This would usually result from a negligent sterilisation or a negligently performed abortion. For example, in *Scuriaga* v. *Powell,*[75] the plaintiff, a single parent action for wrongful birth was for pain, suffering, loss of earning and impairment of marriage prospect. The action succeeded, because the abortion was negligently performed.

Wrongful conception

Usually action relating to wrongful conception arises from the birth of a healthy child as a result of a failed sterilisation operation or other failed contraceptive measures.[76] Claims instituted by parents would usually seek compensatory damages for physical injury caused to the mother during pregnancy and at birth, and financial loss to the parents in raising the child. Essentially claims within the bracket result from failed contraception. If negligence arises from a failed female contraceptive operation, the male partner can hardly point to any physical injury to him, and so the claim takes the appearance of financial loss, if any.[77]

It has been suggested that claims for wrongful conception were the first to appear among the three categories. Far back as 1961 in *Waters* v. *Park,*[78] the plaintiff

---

[73]Grubb, *op cit. Glactman* v. *Casgrave* (1967) 386 NE 2d 807; *Bomman* v. *Allan* (1979) 404 A 2d 8; *Curlender* v. *Bio-science Laboratories* (1980) 165 Cal. Rptre. 477.

[74] *Turpin* v. *Sotini* (1982) 643 p. 2d 954; *Procanik* v. *Cicle* (1984) 478 A 2d 755.

[75] (1979) 123 SJ 406; Noteworthy the claim was not for the cost of raising the child though handicapped. It was for her pain, loss of earning and the impairment of her marriage prospect as a result of negligently performed abortion.

[76] Grubb, *op. cit.*, p. 124.

[77] Ibid.

[78] *The Times*, July 15, 1961, reported by Grubb, *op. cit.*, p. 144 n. 20 (unreported) April 29, 1977 reported by Grubb, *op. cit.*

who underwent a failed hysterectomy and sterilisation instituted an action against the physician for wrongful conception. The court held that the defendant was not negligent in failing to advise the plaintiff of the risk of a failure. He complied with a competent body of professional practice. A similar claim was made by a plaintiff woman in a failed tubal ligation operation in *Williams* v. *St. Helen's and District HMC*.[79] Her action was dismissed because failure to disclose was treated as not negligent in the circumstance.

The spate of these litigations became common when vasectomies became common medical treatment. If a vasectomy performed on a man and or sterilisation procedures on a woman fails, a wrongful conception cause would be raised legally. But that is not the end of the matter. Litigation in this context raises serious ethical questions that go to our very humanity that should not be waved aside lightly. Ognall J in *Jones* v. *Berkshire AHA*[80] drew attention to this when he said the following:

> I pause to observe that speaking purely personally, it remains a matter of surprise to me that the law acknowledges an entitlement in a mother to claim damages for the blessing of a healthy child. Certainly it is that those who are afflicted with a handicapped child or who long desperately to have a child at all and are denied that good fortune would regard an award of this sort of contingency with a measure of astonishment. But there it is that is the law.

Certainly it raises public policy issues that go to the root of gratitude for the birth of a healthy baby. If recovery is allowed, we may ask questions such as, where do we draw the line? Should it only apply to parents claim for pain and suffering and whatever injury is directly suffered as a result of failed birth control measures, in which case the amount recoverable is likely to be minimal? Or should it extend to cover future cost to parents for the upkeep of the child, in which case the amount recoverable is likely to be enormous? These were the matters considered by the English court in *Udale* v. *Bloomsbury AHA*.[81] In the views of Jupp J, it was contrary to public policy for the court to award upkeep cost, thereby making the physician the financial father of the child. The policy issues raised by his Lordship extend to consideration of the child's feelings and the wider issue of womanhood. For instance, how would a child feel to learn as he grows up that his life was considered a mistake for which the parents are reaping a windfall from the physician? What is more, a wrongful conception claim appears tantamount to an unnatural rejection of womanhood and motherhood, matters that cannot be easily pushed aside. The birth of a child should be a thing for rejoicing, not litigation.

---

[79] p. 144 n. 22, see also *Thake* v. *Maurice* [1986] 1 All ER 497; *Udale* v. *Bloomsbury AHA*, July 2, 1986; *Emeh* v. *Kensington AHA* [1985] 3 All ER 1044; *Eyre* v. *Measday* [1986] 1 All ER 488; *Gold* v. *Harringay HA.* [1987] 2 All ER 888.

[80] July 2, 1986, cited in Grubb, *op. cit*, p. 144 n. 25, see also *Gold* v. *Harringay HA* [1987] 2 All ER 888, per Lloyd LJ.

[81] [1983] 2 All ER 522; (1983) 1 WLR 1098.

But public policy argument and appeal of Jupp J in *Udale* was rejected by Pain J in *Thake* v. *Maurice*.[82] A claim for wrongful conception to recover the upkeep of an unplanned child succeeded. A similar position was taken in *Emeh* v. *Kensington & Chelsea AHA*.[83] The English Court of Appeal rejected the public policy argument in *Udale*. Waller and Purchas LJJ were unimpressed by the use of public policy as the striking mechanic against claims for wrongful conception. Waller LJ said 'the court should not be too ready to lay down lines of public policy.'[84] Purchas LJ stated for his part that 'I see no reason for the courts to introduce into the perfectly ordinary, straight forward rules of recovery of damages…some qualification to reflect special social positions.'[85]

An analysis of the cases reveal that a wrongful conception claim may arise for the following four factual settings

(i) from negligence arising from pre-operation counselling. For example the essence of the claims in *Waters*[86] and *Williams*[87] were that the physician should have counselled the patient on the possibility of failure in the sterilisation operations
(ii) negligent failure to disclose inherent risk that would influence the patient consents to a sterilisation operation. In *Thake*[88] the claim concerned a negligent failure to inform the patient that a sterilisation operation had risk of failure which may influence her to seek alternative measure.
(iii) the claim may also arise from a failure to advise a patient that alternative contraceptive measure exist which is less likely to fail than that the patient is to undergo or has undergone. In *Dendaus* v. *Yackel*[89] the patients claim was that there was a medical procedure that she could undergo which had a lower failure rate and
(iv) sometimes a failure to give advise to a patient may be the basis for a wrongful conception claim. In *Venner* v. *North East Essex AHA*,[90] one of the patient's allegation was that the physician failed to advise her that if she ceased to take her contraceptive pills prior to undergoing surgical sterilisation she or her husband should in the meantime take alternative contraceptive to prevent pregnancy. Interestingly on the facts Tucker J. found that the physician had warned her. It is suggested that if the physician had not, it should not ordinarily be a ground for a claim because there should really be no need for a warning when it is obvious that a failure will result in pregnancy.

---

[82] [1986] 1 All ER 497, per Peter Pain J.
[83] [1984] 3 All ER 961.
[84] Ibid., 1051, per Waller LJ.
[85] Ibid., 1056, per Purchas LJ, in his view only parliament has the right to change the social position on the matter.
[86] Above n. 78.
[87] Above n. 79.
[88] Above n. 82.
[89] (1980) 5 WWR 273 (British Columbia Supreme Court), see also *Palmer* v. *Eadie* (unreported English Court of Appeal decision of May 18, 1987, cited by Grubb, *op. cit.*, p. 144 n. 46.
[90] Unreported, February 1, 1987, cited by Grubb, *op. cit.*, p. 144 n. 49.

Wrongful conception claims may not only be directed against the physician. In *Troppi* v. *Scorff*[91] the Michigan Court of Appeal found a pharmacist liable for negligence when he used tranquilizers to fill the patient's prescription for birth control pills which resulted in the patient becoming pregnant.

Requirements for wrongful conception claims

For a patient to succeed in a claim for wrongful conception he or she must establish the following:

(i) that the physician did not give any warning or did not counsel on alternative procedure. Since litigation is likely to take place after some relatively long time from the act complained of, both the patient and the physician may be confronted with evidential questions of proof. This requires recollection of the exact encounter and since both accounts are likely to be self-serving, the courts will generally be wary of it. In this struggle to recount events, the patient is likely to be at advantage. He suffers the damage directly and because his encounter with the physician is more likely to be less frequent, he invariable should remember more of the events. The physician on the other hand does not enjoy those advantages. He encounters many patients. Unless something striking about the patient or his illness is present he would likely not recollect the events that took place. May be, his patient case note or file would be his only help. According to Ognall J in *Jones* v. *Berkshire AHA*,[92]

> 'To the doctor the patient was one of hundreds, if not thousands of patients, and therefore there could in common sense be no possibility of their bringing to mind the actual meetings, still less the full gist of what passed between any one of them and the plaintiff. But to the plaintiff on the other hand this was a matter of special importance.'

Under such circumstances the physician is most likely going to rely upon his usual and or standard practice at the time to put forward an argument against negligence or breach of contract.[93] Alternatively, he could rely on the consent form signed by the patient which may contain express warning of the risk of failure,[94] or record stating that warning has been given by him to the patient.

(ii) the patient must also establish that the physician's failure to warn and or counsel on alternative procedure is negligent or amounts to a breach of contract for which damages should be assessed. Since most sterilisation operations are often carried out privately, there exists the likelihood that a contract will be in place

---

[91] (1971) 187 NW 2d 511.

[92] July 2, 1986 (unreported) cited by Grubb, *op. cit.*, p. 144 n. 25.

[93] *Thake* v. *Maurice* [1986] 1 All ER 497 where the physician argued that he gave the usual standard warning.

[94] See *Eyre* v. *Measday* [1986] 1 All ER 488.

between the patient and the physician.[95] Where a contract exists between the parties, a physician may be sued for breach of contract for failing to disclose a risk of reversal. In *Thake*, the court rejected the argument of the patient that a failure to disclose risk of reversal concerning a vasectomy amounted to an express or implied contractual guarantee that the patient will be sterile.[96] Nourse LJ was of the view that a physician 'cannot be objectively guaranteeing the success of any operation or treatment unless he says as much in clear and unequivocal terms.'

It is also conceivable to argue that a failure to warn can amount to a misrepresentation. But to do so, as is implicit from the statement of Nourse LJ in *Thake*,[97] the physician's statement must be clear and unequivocal about the irreversibility of the operation, a difficult thing for any professional person to say. This is what makes a claim within the bracket of misrepresentation unlikely of success.

Negligence appears to take the front burner in wrongful conception claims. In jurisdictions with stricter rules requiring the physician to disclose risk a prudent patient would wish to know, a failure to make such disclosure will amount to negligence.[98] In England the practice as traced out in *Bolam*[99] requires that the physician should exercise the 'reasonable skill and care of the ordinary competent medical practitioner.'

What this mean in effect is that if a physician complies with this duty in accordance with what a competent body of medical opinion is, he would not be liable for negligence.[100] No action against him would succeed even if disclosure would be expected by other parameters if in the opinion of a competent body of medical opinion disclosure would not be required. This preposition however appears weakened by the statement of Lord Bridge in *Sideway* to the effect that in some circumstance a non-disclosure in compliance with professional practice might result in a patient lacking information which is obviously necessary to an informed choice.[101] This may well be what could make such a non-disclosure negligent.

It is suggested that *Sideway* extends the law slightly beyond *Bolam*, and so if a patient were to ask questions, it would seem that the physician's duty to disclose would become more onerous. Subject to a therapeutic reason for withholding

---

[95] A contract document will likely be absent in National Health Scheme treatment and so the patient's only resort will be not for breach of contract but for negligence. The national health insurance scheme being proposed in Nigeria is not likely to be different on the legal stations.

[96] [1986] 1 All ER 497, Similar conclusion were reached in *Eyre* v. *Measday* [1986] 1 All ER 488 on a female sterilisation operation.

[97] [1986] 1 All ER 497 at 512.

[98] Ibid.

[99] *Bolam* v. *Friern Hospital Management Committee* [1957] 2 All ER 118, [1957] 1 WLR 582. See also *Sard* v. *Hardy* (1977) 379 A 2d 1014 (Maryland Court of Appeal), *Gray* v. *Welsor* (1985) 11 DLR (4th) 706 (New Brunswick Court).

[100] In *Sideway* v. *Governors of Bethlehem Royal Hospital* [1985] 1 All ER 643, [1985] AC871 (HL) it was suggested that a physician's duty to disclose inherent risk in a medical procedure is the same in relation to treatment or diagnosis.

[101] [1985] 1 All ER 643 at 663 per Lord Bridge. See also Lord Templeman at 666.

answers because it is, for instance, considered proper to withhold information in the patient's best interest or health, the physician comes under a duty to answer as truthfully as he can. A word of caution, disclosure according to Kerr LJ must 'depend upon the circumstances, the nature of the inquiry, the nature of the information which is available, its reliability, relevance, the condition of the patient.'[102]

(iii) Finally, the plaintiff must show that the defendant's negligence caused the damage suffered. The plaintiff can scale the hurdle if he can show either of this: that as a result of non-disclosure he consented to the operation or that if proper disclosure was made the patient would have more readily have prevented the harm or injury. The first is like an argument that if the patient knew of the reversibility of the sterilisation operation he would not have consented to it.[103] The alternative argument is like saying that non-disclosure of the reversibility of the operation prevented the patient from readily noticing her pregnancy which would have been aborted to avoid birth.[104] Accordingly, the plaintiff in the first case is required to show that he refused the medical procedure and in the second that she refused to undergo an abortion. Where the plaintiff's argument is within the first, the court will hold that a failure to inform the patient of a reversal risk would have resulted in the patient not consenting to it if satisfied that that would be the course a 'reasonable patient'' would adopt. This is an objective approach.[105] It has however been suggested that the objective test is rather onerous for the patient, because in deciding the matter it is the testimony of the patient that should be the governing consideration.[106] It is the patient that is immediately affected, not the reasonable man on the street. Whatever, it is suggested that by the application of a reasonable evidential tool the court may blur the objective and subjective test in the interest of justice.

In developing countries where children are seen as family treasures, it could be hard to imagine litigation for the failure of sterilisation that results in the birth of a child. An award of damages to the parent would seem double compensation. Children are an entitlement and source of happiness to parents. So to compensate them for a failed sterilisation, is like awarding damage to parent who have benefited from a failed procedure that works for their good. At law however, a patient can recover damages for failed sterilisation if he or she can establish that the method failed as contraception due to negligence of the doctor or as a result of breach of contract. The fact that pregnancy results after sterilisation is not sufficient for liability. It may be explained as one of the things that can happen in nature.

---

[102] *Blyth* v. *Bloomsbury HA*, *The Times*, February 11, 1987 cited by Grubb, *op. cit.*, p. 146 n. 93, see also *Gold* v. *Haringay HA* [1987] 2 All ER 888.

[103] *Gold* v. *Haringay HA* [1987] 1 FLR 125.

[104] *Thake* v. *Maurice* [1986] 1 All ER 497.

[105] *White* v. *Turner* (1980) 120 DLR (3d) 260 at 266.

[106] *Sard* v. *Hardy* (1977) 379 A 2 d 1014 at 1025.

In *Emeh* v. *Kensington & Chelsea & Westminster Area Health Authority*[107] the court had to determine whether a woman who refused to undergo an abortion after a failed sterilisation negligently performed which resulted in an unwanted child or pregnancy can succeed in a claim for wrongful conception. The plaintiff, a mother of three normal children, had an abortion to terminate a fourth pregnancy and at the same time underwent a sterilisation operation to prevent further pregnancies. The operation was performed negligently by two doctors employed by the defendants' health authority. Some months later, the plaintiff became pregnant, although she did not discover the fact until she was some 20 weeks pregnant. She then decided that she did not want any more abortion but would continue with the pregnancy. She later gave birth to an abnormal child and instituted an action against the defendants for damages for loss of future earnings, maintenance of the child, pains, suffering and loss of amenities including the extra care which the child would require. The court awarded her substantial damage for the birth of the child following failed sterilisation, despite the fact that abortion was an available option. Slade LJ said:

> By their own negligence they faced her with the very dilemma which she had sought to avoid by having herself sterilised. For the reason which I have attempted to give, I think that they could, and should, have reasonably foreseen that if as a consequence of the negligent performance of the operation she would find herself pregnant again, particularly after some months of pregnancy, she might well decide to keep the child. Indeed, for my part I would go even a little further save in the most exceptional circumstances. I cannot think it right that the court should ever declare it unreasonable for a woman to decline to have an abortion, in a case where there is no evidence that there were any medical or psychiatric grounds for terminating the particular pregnancy.[108]

On the quantum of damages recoverable, Purchas LJ, cited with approval the decision of the Supreme Court of Minnesota in *Sherlock* v. *Stillwater Clinic*[109] that:

> We hold that in cases such as this an action for wrongful conception, may be maintained and that compensating damages may be recovered by the parent of the unplanned child. These damages may include all prenatal and postnatal medical expenses, the mother's pain and suffering during pregnancy and delivery, and loss of consortium. Additionally, the parents may recover the

[107] [1985] QB 1012, [1984]3 All ER 1044 (CA) JH Scheid, *Benefit* v. *Burden*: The Limitation of Damages in Wrongful Birth (1984) 2 *J Fam. Law* 57; A.B Humwitz, Tert II The Wrongful Birth Cause of Action 1983) *Annual Survey Amer Law* 675, D Brahams, Damages for Unplanned Babies- A Trend to be Discouraged (1983) 133 NLJ 643; A Mullis, Wrongful Conception Unravelled (1993) 1 *Med. Law Rev.* 320, A Grubb, Damages for Wrongful Conception (1985) 44 *CLJ* 30.

[108] Ibid., at p. 1023.

[109] (1977) 260 NW 2d 169 at 170-171.

reasonable costs of rearing the unplanned child subject to offsetting the value of the child's aid, comfort and the parent's life expectancy.[110]

The heads under which damages can be awarded remain controversial. Brook J in *Allen* v. *Bloomsbury Health Authority*[111] while admitting that the relevant principles in assessing damages was considered by the House of Lords, observed that the principle gleaned from the numerous decisions of the English Court of Appeal, shows that damages could only be awarded for the following heads:(i) damages for foreseeable loss and damage plaintiff mother suffers in consequence of the doctors negligence. In *Emeh* v. *Kensington & Chelsea & West-minister Area Health Authority* the court awarded damages under this head;[112] (ii) general (and any associated financial special damages for discomfort and pain associated with the continuation of pregnancy and delivery, with a set-off, respecting the benefits of avoiding pain, suffering, and financial loss which she would have undergone for an abortion[113] as underlined in *Thake* v. *Maurice*,[114] and *Gandiner* v. *Mounfield*, [115] (iii) damage for economic loss associated with her physical injury. This category is satisfied either by showing that there is loss suffered because at the time the unplanned child is born she has another growing child to feed, cloth, house, educate and care for until the child becomes an adult; or that there is loss suffered because she has lost earning or incurs other expenses because of her obligation towards her child, which she sought to avoid by sterilisation as underlined in *Emeh* and *Thake* cases; (iv) damages for wear and tear in bringing up the child. This head of recovery is to be set-off by the benefit the child gives the parent as underlined in *Thake case* (v) general damages for foreseeable additional anxiety, stress and burden in bringing up a handicapped child. *Emeh case* awarded damages under this head. Even with this, assessing damages remains problematic because the court has to fix a money value that represents loss. In *Lindsay* v. *Greater Glasgow Health Board*,[116] a whopping sum of £50,000 was the settlement obtained out of court in a suit for wrongful pregnancy or conception.

Wrongful conception litigation can also arise in the context of a breach of contract. Sterilisation being, an elective surgery, is not covered by the English NHS scheme and the Nigerian NHIS Act. That being the case, it is not unusual for the parties to contract for it. To avoid litigation a doctor should pay special attention to the terms of the contract so as not to unnecessarily expose himself to lawsuit. Whether an action for breach of contract will succeed depends on the terms of the contract as illustrated in *Thake* v. *Maurice*[117] and *Eyre* v. *Measdey*.[118] In *Eyre* v.

[110] [1993] 1 All ER 651, [1992] 13 BMLR.
[111] [1993] 1 All ER 651, [1992] 13 BMLR 47.
[112] [1984] 3 All ER 1044, [1985] QB 1012.
[113] *Supra.*
[114] [1989] 1 All ER 497 at 508, [1986] QB 644 at 682, per Kerr LJ.
[115] [1989] 5 BMLR 1, 5-6 per Scott-Beker J.
[116] [1990] Scohsman, 14 March p.8 (Scottish case settled out of court).
[117] [1986] QB 644, [1986] 1 All ER 497 (CA).

Measdey,[119] the plaintiff and her husband, not wishing to have more children consulted the defendant gynaecologist with a view of the plaintiff undergoing a sterilisation operation. The defendant explained the nature of the operation to them. He said it was irreversible without informing them that there was a small risk (1%) of pregnancy reoccurring even after the operation. As a result the couple believed the operation was full proof to pregnancy. About a year after the operation, (1979) the plaintiff became pregnant and gave birth to a child. In an action, the plaintiff claimed against the defendant for breach of contract, contending that the representation was to the effect that the operation was full proof and that failure to warn her of the risk of pregnancy was a breach of the contractual term or express or implied warranty. The English Court of Appeal held the defendant not liable in damages. Slade LJ, was not in doubt that the relevant contract between the parties was embodied in the oral conversation between the parties, but in his view liability would depend on the meaning of the phrase used, 'irreversible' and the inference a bystander hearing their discussion would draw. He said:

> There has been some discussion in the course of argument on the meaning of the phrase 'irreversible' and as to the relevance of the statement, undoubtedly made by the defendant to the plaintiff that the proposed operation must be regarded as being irreversible. However I think the reference to irreversibility as simply meaning that the operative procedure in question is incapable of being reversed, that what is about to be done cannot be undone. I do not think it can reasonably be construed as a representation that the operation is bound to achieve its acknowledged object, which is a different matter altogether...On the facts of the present case, I do not think that any intelligent lay bystander (let alone another medical man) on hearing the discussion which took place between the defendant and the other two parties, could have reasonably drawn the inference that the defendant was intending to give any warranty of this nature.[120]

The reasoning and conclusion of Slade LJ on the phrase irreversible and the reasonable inference that can be drawn from the parties discussion is difficult to reconcile with the facts of the case. The phrase 'irreversible' cannot in the circumstance of the case have related to operative procedure. It indeed should have only one reasonable meaning in the light of the parties' discussion, that the operative procedure would achieve a full proof to pregnancy. A reasonable bystander would have considered the use of the term as some form of guarantee or warranty that the operation will have the effect of preventing pregnancy. It is for this reason that the conclusion is with respect, absurd.

The case should be contrasted with *Thake* v. *Maurice*[121] The plaintiffs, a married couple, not wishing to have any more children, consulted the defendant to perform a

---

[118] [1986] 1 All ER 488 (CA).
[119] Ibid.
[120] Ibid.
[121] [1986] QB 644, [1986] 1 All ER 497 (CA).

vasectomy on the 1st plaintiff. He signed a contract form stating that he consented to the operation. The operation was performed on him in 1975. In 1977, his wife, the 2nd plaintiff became pregnant. She only recognised this fact when it was too late for an abortion. In 1978, she gave birth to a baby girl. The plaintiffs sued the defendant claiming that he breached the contract to sterilise the first plaintiff, or alternatively, damages in that he was induced to enter the contract by a false warranty or innocent misrepresentation that the operation would render 1st plaintiff permanently sterile. Further and in the alternative, they claimed that the defendant failed to warn them of the small risk that 1st plaintiff may become fertile again. There was no suggestion that the defendant had not performed the operation properly. At the time of the operation it was medically known that in rare cases the effect of the operation was naturally reversible.

Though the trial court, and the English Court of Appeal reached diametrically opposed conclusions on the matter of breach of contract, it was held that the failure of the defendant to warn of the possibility of a natural reversal of a vasectomy operation was proof of negligence for which damages were recoverable. The court's explanation of the phrase 'irreversible' accords more with good sense. In the views of Neill LJ, the phrase must be understood to be a therapeutic assurance only, and since medicine is not an exact science, in the circumstance, the reference that could be drawn was not one of a guarantee, may be a probability assurance only.

To avoid unnecessary explosion to possible liability claims, doctors are advised to draw up contracts containing clauses explaining the risk of reversal, and excluding all and any liability in the event of failure. Well-drafted clauses can minimise, if not altogether eliminate liability, even though it is a controversial point whether the courts would uphold a clause that seeks to exclude liability in a manner that destroys the very essence of medical treatment.[122]

As a final note before leaving the subject, it should be said that in the minds of some informed persons the rationale for wrongful pregnancy litigation remains questionable. Counsel for the defendant in *Udale* v. *Bloomsbury Area Health Authority*[123] succinctly listed some of these in his address. They are as follows: (i) that public policy ought to discourage the award of damages for the birth of a normal child which results from a failed sterilisation. Consider for a moment, how a child will feel and react if it gets to know that a court had publicly declared him unwanted by his parents and worse, that his upbringing is being paid for by a medical doctor because of his negligence. Parental respect may be jeopardised, with detrimental effect to society; (ii) fear of lawsuit could bring unbearable and intolerable pressure to bear on doctors, a fact recognised by the English Law Commission in its report on Injuries to Unborn Children.[124] Such suits could place the

---

[122] See 1990 NHS Guide to consent for examination or treatment, which states that certain stipulations shall be void if they seek to remove the substratum of examination or treatment. Contrast with *Worster* v. *City & Hackrey Health Authority* (1987) *Times*, 22 June.

[123] [1983] 2 All ER 522, [1983] 1 WLR 1098.

[124] Law Commission No.60 August, 1974 Cmmd 5709 par. 89.

doctor under a subconscious pressure to advice abortion in doubtful cases because of fear of an action of damages for wrongful pregnancy; (iii) if a couple institutes a lawsuit for wrongful conception, they in effect represent that the child is unwanted, unbeneficial to them. In that respect the proper order ought not to be award of damages to the parties, but custody to a third party who would welcome the child, possibly with a set-off allowance for the woman in consideration of her trouble in carrying the pregnancy to term. Otherwise we would in effect be giving them a 'free child', while at the same time giving them money. The proper thing is for the court to award parenthood to persons other than the parents, damages would only then be to the parents for the womb leased, the 'eggs donated' and other consequential losses due to the pregnancy, no more.

These counter arguments notwithstanding, the courts have recognised the validity of wrongful pregnancy litigation,[125] stating that no public policy prevents the award of damages from wrongful or failed sterilisation.[126] As a middle way of assuaging the pains, distress and anxiety of the patient, the doctor and society, it is suggested that a public-sponsored fund should be established in support of damages which may be awarded against doctors for wrongful birth/life or conception cases. Until such a legal framework is established, it is suggested that courts should be circumspect in awarding damages, taking into consideration the many social issues, especially those raised by defence counsel in *Udale case*. That way the court would be paying attention to the competing interest of the parties.

---

[125] *Udale* v. *Bloomsbury A.H.A.* [1983] 2 All ER 522.

[126] *Allen* v. *Greater Glasgow Health Board* (25 Nov. 1993) unreported, reported in part in Mason & Smith, *op. cit*, p.83.

Chapter Six

Abortion

Introduction

Pregnancy and abortion are of interest to lawyers and doctors because of the many controversial questions they throw up. These include, but are not limited to questions on succession of estates, allocation of criminal responsibility for abortion or infanticide, wilful negligence, paternity disputes, sentencing and even medical evidence. Pregnancy is usually for a gestation period of forty weeks. In some rare cases it may be slightly more or less.[1] Pregnancy may occur at different ages for different women. Some about 13 years and others after menopause had been able to become pregnant. Abortion is the termination of pregnancy. The Nigerian law makes no distinction between abortion, premature labour, and miscarriage. Criminal abortion may occur at any stage of pregnancy. Section 228-230 of the Criminal Code is the provision dealing with criminal abortion. Procuring abortion by the administration of poison on a woman is a felony. Section 228 makes it an offence for any person with intent to procure abortion to administer on a woman any poison. Section 229 makes it an offence for a person to administer poison on herself, with intent to procure her miscarriage. Section 230 punishes any person who unlawfully supplies to another anything, knowing that it is intended to be used to procure an abortion. Basically, this is directed at hospitals and chemists who supply to young girls abortion drugs/poison. Sections 228-230 are similar to the provisions of sections 58 and 59 of the Offences Against the Persons Act, 1961. The latter provisions are wider in scope than those of the Criminal Code, in that the offence is not limited to the administering of poison or any noxious substance, it extends to the use of any instrument intended to cause miscarriage.

A noxious thing is any thing that can produce the effects of effecting a miscarriage in a pregnant woman.[2] This may depend on a large extent on the quantity of the substance used.[3] Therefore a harmless substance when taken in

---

[1] In *Edet* v. *Essien* (1932) 11 NLR 47. The Nigerian courts judicially noted the fact that gestation period is a period of nine months.

[2] *R.* v. *Hollis* (1873) 28 LT 455.

[3] *R* v. *Hannah* (1877) 13 Cox 547.

excess may become noxious if its excessive consumption can result in effecting a miscarriage. For example, alcoholic beverage can be treated as a noxious substance when consumed in excess with the intention to produce a miscarriage. If it is proven that the substance is administered with intent to procure a miscarriage, and that the substance is a poison or a noxious thing, it would be immaterial for the defendant to argue that as a matter of fact the substance cannot or is incapable of procuring an abortion.[4]

If in the process of procuring the miscarriage, the woman dies, the person who administers the substance will also be liable for unlawful homicide if the necessary intent to kill is proven.[5] For example, if it can be proved that death resulted from the prosecution of an unlawful purpose (administering of a poison or noxious thing to produce miscarriage) and that the act is of such a nature as is likely to endanger human life from which death results, the offender would be rightly convicted for homicide.[6] If the necessary intent for murder is not proved, the administrator of the substance may be successfully prosecuted for manslaughter. The controversial question however is whether a woman who successfully procures miscarriage on herself with or without the aid of another can be successfully prosecuted for attempted suicide?[7] That would depend on whether by so procuring the miscarriage the law can read an intent to kill herself. It is respectfully suggested that conviction will be difficult because her action can only at best be treated as a necessary intention to procure a miscarriage. That death may result from her action does not go to show an intention to kill herself. She naturally would not intend such a thing. Since a child does not have separate existence until birth from the mother, death of a foetus is not actionable as unlawful homicide.[8]

Section 297 provides a defence and or protection to a person (medical practitioner) who with surgical instrument operates on any person for her benefit or upon an unborn child for the mother's life, if the operation is reasonably performed in good faith and with reasonable care. The ambit of this or similar provision was discussed by the English court in *R* v. *Bourne*.[9] An eminent obstetrician surgeon was charged with criminal abortion on a girl under 15 years of age. She became pregnant as a result of sexual rape assault on her by some soldiers. The defendant admitted performing the surgery. His counsel submitted that he had not acted unlawfully because the defendant in carrying out the operation acted to protect the young girl's health that could be gravely endangered if the pregnancy was not terminated. He

---

[4] *R* v. *Cramp* (1880) 5 OBD 307; *R* v. *Spicer* (1955) 39 Cr. App. R. 189.

[5] S. 316 (1) to (6), state the six necessary interests to find a charge for murder.

[6] S. 316 (3) of Criminal Code (CC) Law.

[7] S. 327 CC makes it an offence for any person to attempt to kill himself.

[8] S. 307 CC states that a child becomes a person capable of being killed when it has completely proceeded in a living state from the body of its mother. See *R* v. *Wright* (1841) 9 C p. 754, *R.* v. *Sellis* (1837) 7 Cd P 850.

[9] [1939] IKB 687[1938] 3 All ER 615.

further submitted that it was near impossible to draw any distinction between danger to the life of the young girl and danger to her health. Prosecution countered it, submitting that the law only makes surgery lawful if it is performed to save the mother's life and no more. MacNaghter, J directed the jury that the proper test to be applied was whether the defendant's act was done in good faith for the purpose of preserving the girls life, and that if in the surgeon's opinion a delivery cannot result without death to the mother, the surgeon is entitled to save the mother's life. He further directed that if a pregnancy was likely to make the mother a physical or mental wreck, then the surgeon operating for that purpose must be seen as operating to preserve the life of the mother. The jury accordingly discharged the defendant. It found that the pregnancy could wreak havoc on the young girl. By this decision, the court widened the scope of what was previously regard as justifiable abortion. The phrase 'life of the mother' was treated as inclusive of her 'physical or mental health'.

The conclusion has been applauded by some writers because in their views it attempts to align abortion regulations in line with social realities, and contemporary practice.[10] The English Abortion Act, 1967 incorporates the ratio in *R* v. *Bourne*.[11] The Act liberalises abortion. It provides that an abortion shall be lawful if carried out in the following circumstances: if the continuance of a pregnancy would involve risk to the life of the pregnant woman; or injury to her physical or mental health; or any existing children of her family greater than if the pregnancy were terminated; or if there exists a substantial risk that the child if born would suffer from such physical or mental abnormalities that it could be seriously handicapped.[12] Practically, the Act widened the scope of justifiable abortion beyond the rule in *R* v. *Bourne*. Justifiable abortion under it includes matters relating to family size or (family planning) and by implication, selective abortion directed to eliminate handicapped births.

Family planning no doubt is an interesting social topic for governments. It is said that over half of developing countries are presently pursuing family planning with a view to making their population manageable. The reasons are varied. But for sure, are closely related to resources allocation, infrastructure, employment and the like, all of which are close to the hearts of governments, individuals and the family. It raises questions such as whether it is ethical to permit the termination of life as a means to control family size. Would it be tantamount to state sponsored murder? If not, does the policy encourage in the long run respect for life? Could other family planning procedures that do not involve abortion achieve the aim? [13] Advanced

[10] Glaister, *op. cit*, p. 383 described the trial as less a criminal trial than a co-operative effort by judge, jury, council, and witnesses to create law out of strong but ill-defined feelings".

[11] [1939] 1 KB 687.

[12] [1939] 1 KB 687.

[13] S. 1 of the Abortion Act, 1967 applicable in United Kingdom.

prenatal tests, either in the form of ultrasound[14] or amniocentesis[15] makes it possible for doctors to diagnose sex, physical or mental impairment of the unborn. The English abortion Act permits an abortion if prenatal testing reveals substantial physical or mental abnormality. Ethically unignorable is the message such permissible abortion can send to disabled members of our society. It likely makes it harder for them to root out negative feelings selective abortion confronts them with.[16]

It should be noted that the legal position on abortion in Nigeria remains *R* v. *Bourne*.[17] The English position is wider, its boundaries marked by its Abortion Act, 1967. Nigeria's position since the enactment of the Criminal Code, as interpreted in *Bourne* case represents our law on abortion, a position sometimes criticised by writers and medical practitioners.[18] Of interest, it can be asked, if the conditions for permissible abortion exists as circumscribed in Nigeria, or as permissive in England, who can exercise the right? Will the consent of say, the husband be required? If yes, what if the parties disagree? Can the husband seek injunction to stop an abortion of his partner?

These questions were raised in *Paton* v. *Trustees of British Pregnancy Advisory Committee & Ors*.[19] A woman who had consulted two doctors was advised to have an abortion. Her husband attempted to restrain the proposed abortion by injunction. He claimed to be entitled to have a say as to the destiny of the foetus of their marriage. The court held that since a foetus had no rights known to law or equity, the husband could not acquire any right to restrain his wife from having an abortion. It thus laid to rest the question of who can rightfully exercise the choice to have a legal abortion – the pregnant woman alone. The social implication of the conclusion in an African family setting to say the least is repulsive.

R v. *Bourne*[20] makes lawful therapeutic abortion. The Abortion Act 1967 of England is considered a compromise measure enacted by Parliament as a stop gap between pro and anti-abortion pressure. S.1 (1) of the Act states that a person shall

---

[14] Ultrasound is a non-invasive procedure wherein high-frequency sound waves are used to form an image of the baby in the womb.

[15] Amniocentesis is an invasive procedure wherein a syringe of a simple amniotic fluid in which a baby in the womb is suspended is taken out for chemical testing to detect any foetal defects.

[16] Family control method include the following, sterilisation in men or in women, birth control, pills, diaphragm and spermicide, cervical cap, sponge, intrauterine device (coil), condoms, rhythm method based on menstrual cycle calculation, hormone implants and withdraw of penis just before ejaculation.

[17] [1939] 1 KB 687; *Royal College of Nursing of the UK* v. *Dept of Health and Social Security* [1981] AC 800; Jennifer Fitzgerald (1995) 4 *Queensland Law Society Journal*.

[18] Ss. 228-230, 297 of Criminal Code or applicable in Southern Nigeria or the Penal Code applicable in Northern Nigeria.

[19] (1980) 3 EHRR 408. See also J.L Caldwell, Abortion: The Father's Lack of Standing [1988] *NZLR* 165; P.T. O'Neill and J. Watson, The Father and the Unborn Child (1975) 38 *MLR* 174.

[20] [1939] 1 KB 687. See also W.O. Chukudebelu and P.C. Nweke, Abortion and the Law in *Medical Practice and the Law in Nigeria* (Longman) 1989.

not be guilty of the offence of abortion when termination is advised in good faith by two registered medical practitioners of the opinion that continuing pregnancy involves risk to life of the pregnant woman or injury to her physical or mental health, or any existing children in her family, greater than if the pregnancy were terminated, or there is a substantial risk that if the child were born it would suffer from such physical or mental abnormalities as to be seriously handicapped. As though further liberalising abortion, section 1 (2) provides that in determining the risk of injury to a woman or her existing children's health, account may be taken of the pregnant woman's actual reasonable foreseeable environment. Also by s. 37 of the Human Fertilisation and Embryology Act, (HFEA) 1990 (a legislation that amends the Abortion Act 1967) it is provided that:(1) Subject to the provision of the section, a person shall not be guilty of an offence under the law relating to abortion when a pregnancy is terminated by a registered medical practitioner if two registered medical practitioners are of the opinion, formed in good faith: —

(a) that the pregnancy has not exceeded 24 weeks and that the continuance of the pregnancy would involve risk greater than if the pregnancy were terminated, or injury to the physical or mental health of the pregnant woman or any existing children of her family or

(b) that the termination is necessary to prevent grave permanent injury to the physical or mental health of the pregnant woman or

(c) that the continuance of the pregnancy would involve risk to the life of the pregnant woman, greater than if the pregnancy were terminated or

(d) that there is a substantial risk that if the child were born it would suffer from physical or mental abnormalities as to be seriously handicapped.

(2) In determining whether the continuance of a pregnancy would involve such risk of injury to health as is mentioned in paragraph (a) or (b) of subsection (1) of this section, account may be taken of the pregnant woman's actual or reasonable foreseeable environment.

(5) No offence under the Infant Life; (Preservation) Act 1929 shall be committed by a registered medical practitioner who terminates a pregnancy in accordance with the provision of the Act (i.e. the Abortion Act 1967)

So rather than limit the circumstances in which abortion is permissible, s. 37 of the Human Fertilisation and Embryology Act, 1990 has the effect of significantly liberalising it. Subsection (4) of the section, amends section 5(1) of the Abortion Act 1967 in the following manner, stating:

> No offence under the Infant Life Preservation Act 1929 shall be committed by a registered medical practitioner who terminates a pregnancy in accordance with the provisions of the Act.

The legal effect of all these provisions make it doubtful if there can be any illegal abortion in England once the relevant regulations (1967 and 1990 Acts) are complied with. By the power conferred on the Secretary of State to make regulation under the Abortion Act 1967, the Abortion Regulation 1991[21] was made. By virtue of s.2 of the Regulation, a certificate by the medical practitioners opinion recommending abortion is required to be given before the commencement of abortion, or if not reasonable practicable, one shall be issued not later than 24 hours after termination of pregnancy. It is therefore not a surprising thing to find that there has been rare conviction under the Act. Only *R* v. *Smith* is reported.[22] In summarising the legal position, Scarman LJ said:

> The Act (Abortion Act 1967) though it renders lawful abortions that before the enactment would have been unlawful, does not depend on the basis principle of the common law as declared in R v. Bourne, namely that the legality of an abortion depend on the opinion of the doctor. It has introduced the safeguard of two opinions: but if they are formed in good faith by the time the operation is undertaken, the abortion is lawful. This great social responsibility is firmly placed by the law on the shoulders of the medical profession. (Insertion is mine).

Under the English law, lawful grounds for abortion are categorised into 4 as spelt out in s. 1 (1) of the 1967 Act or s. 37 of the 1990 Act. In reaching a decision whether the continuance of a pregnancy would involve greater risk than termination, the relevant consideration is a comparative analysis of the risk inherent in terminating the pregnancy immediately and the risk to the mother if the pregnancy goes full term. Also relevant for consideration under the four broad categories is risk to the pregnant woman's 'physical and mental health'. Determining risk to physical health certainly is not problematic, but same cannot be said of mental health. In a narrow perspective, mental health risk is the fear of the pregnant woman developing mental illness resulting from the continuance of pregnancy. In this respect psychiatrist evidence is all that would do. The contrasting view is that mental health is not necessarily restricted to psychiatric illness, but a state of complete general mental, physical and social well being, not just the absence of disease. Convention medical practice supports this wider perspective, as doctors generally do not require psychiatric opinion in reaching a decision as to whether the mental health of a pregnant woman is at risk.

The provision requiring the doctor to consider the effect, physical or mental, of a pregnancy to the existing children of a pregnant woman is disguised economics. For a doctor to determine economic factors is absurd and to say the least inconsistent with his calling. Why should he take poverty into account in arriving at his decision? In developing states, the phrase 'family' has wider connotation than in English.

---

[21] [1978] 2 All ER 987. See also *Dehler* v. *Ottawa Civil Hospital* (1979) 101 D&R (3d) 686; *Paton* v. *United Kingdom* [1980] 3 EHRR 408; *Royal College of Nursing of the UK* v. *Dept of Health* [1981] AC 800.

[22] [1974] 1 All ER 376 [1973] 1 WLR 151 (CA) See also *Wall* v. *Livington* [1982] 1 NZLR 373 (NZCA) but cf. C v. S [1988] QB 135, [1987] 1 All ER 1230 (CA). See also D Munday *et al*, Twenty-one Years of Legal Abortion (1989) 298 *BMJ* 1231.

Therefore if he must consider the children of the family, he would in effect be referring to biological children, dependent relations, etc. Certainly, except in affluent families, every extra child could adversely affect the economy of the family. This is what makes absurd the provision as a ground for abortion. It can be argued that this is exactly the intention of Parliament, hence the provision that he should consider the actual or reasonable foreseeable environment of the patient.

In calculating the 24-week time-limit, it is suggested that in less developed communities where women are less meticulous about monthly circles calculation should begin from the first day a woman last sees her monthly circle.

Noteworthy is the fact that the Act permits abortion for eugenic reasons. Pre-natal scanning (which can be likened to a window in the womb) has largely opened-up the womb with some degree of precision, that enables us determine degrees of disability an unborn child may suffer. Thus, if there exists a risk of physical or mental abnormalities, abortion is permissible under the Act. Not to be overlooked is the adverse message it can send to the less-able or handicap. It gives the impression that they are merely tolerated, because they have been fortunate to be born. If we knew of their state while unborn, we should have prevented them from entering the world by terminating their mother's pregnancy. It is more painful for them to know that it is the course their mothers would have taken if they knew all the facts.

In *Rance* v. *Mid-Downs Health Authority*,[23] the plaintiffs were a married couple. When 1st plaintiff was 26 weeks pregnant, she had an ultrasound scan in a hospital administered by the defendant. The radiographer taking the scan thought that the scan showed a possible abnormality in the foetus and so marked the case file with a question mark 'E Spine'? Later that day, she discussed her suspicions of abnormality with the consultant radiologist of the hospital, who decided that no further action should be taken because there was 'no firm evidence of abnormality'. When the baby was born, it suffered from spinal bifide. The plaintiff subsequently discovered that the spinal bifide may have shown up on one of the scans taken. As a result the plaintiff commenced action against the health authority and the consultant radiologist, claiming that the defendants were negligent in not ascertaining whether the factors were abnormal when the possibility was raised by the radiographer, thereby denying her of the possibility of having the pregnancy terminated. The defendants denied negligence, contending that even if the abnormality had been discovered it would have been an offence to terminate the pregnancy in the 26th week under section 1 of the Infant Life (Preservation) Act 1929 because the 'child was capable of being born alive.' Destruction before it had an existence independent of its mother was unlawful unless it was necessary to preserve the mother's life. Brooke J decided for the defendants because His Lordship was satisfied that the child was capable of being born alive at the time any hypothetical abortion would have taken place, which itself would have been unlawful. The case revealed the

[23] [1991] 1 QB 587 [1991] 1 All ER 801, per Brooke J.

unsatisfactory state of abortion law in England prior to the 1990 HFEA which amended the 1967 Abortion Act.

The legal position in Nigeria however remains that abortion can only be legally performed for therapeutic purposes (in the mother's welfare) as outlined in *R* v. *Bourne*).[24]

The American position was summarised by the Supreme Court in *Roe* v. *Wade*[25] and *Doe* v. *Bolton*.[26] Any limitation on a pregnant woman's access to abortion by legislation constitutes an infringement on her constitutional right to privacy.[27] They further decided that same rule will apply to minors although their parents may be informed of an abortion request. Parents are not however granted veto power. During the first trimester of pregnancy, she has absolute liberty on grounds of rights to individual privacy to seek abortion on the advice of her doctor. The liberty is limited by state intervention during the second trimester in the interest of the health of the mother (not the foetus). State interest can be expressed by specifying what facilities should be used for the abortion. After the 2nd trimester, at what time the foetus becomes viable, (assessed at 24th-28th week of pregnancy), the state acquires a compelling interest in the health of the foetus. At that stage abortion can only take place if the pregnancy threatens the life and or health of the mother. Daughtrey J in *Davis* v. *Davis* said:

> A woman and her doctor may advice on abortion within the first three months of pregnancy but after three months, and before viability, abortion may occur at a properly regulated hospital facility. Moreover after viability, abortion may be chosen to save the life of the mother.[28]

In Australia therapeutic abortion is permissible.[29] In Canada abortion is more liberalised[30] and, like America, is more of a constitutional than philosophical matter.[31]

---

[24] *Supra.*

[25] 93 S. Ct. 705 (1973), 410 US 113 (1973), 35 L Ed 2d 147 (1973). For discussion, see NK Rhoden, Trimesters and Technology: Revamping *Roe* v. *Wade* (1986) 95 *Yale LJ* 639; I Loveland, Abortion and the US. Supreme Court (1992) 142 *NLJ* 974; W Dellinger and GB Sperling, Abortion and the US. Supreme Court: The Retreat from *Roe* v. *Wade* (1989) 138 *Univ Penn LR* 83; J Bopp and RE Coleson, What Does *Webster* Mean (1989) 138 *Univ Penn LR* 157.

[26] 93 S. Ct. 739 (1973)

[27] Compare M.L. McConnell, Abortion and Human Rights: An Important Canadian Decision (1989) 38 *ICLQ* 905

[28] 842 SW 2d 588 (Tenn Sup Ct, 1992). For the position in Northern Ireland, see S. Kingman, Northern Ireland's Abortion Law Criticised as Unclear (1993) 307 *BMJ* 284.

[29] *Tremblay* v. *Daigle* (1989) 62 DLR (4th) 534.

[30] *R* v. *Morgentaler* [1988] 1 SCR 30 at 56, per Dickson CJ, 'forcing a woman, by threat of crminal sanction, to carry a fetus to term is a profound interference with a woman's body and thus a violation of security of the person.' For discussion of the case, see M.L. McConnell, Abortion and Human Rights: An Important Canadian Decision (1989) 38 ICLQ 905; (1987) 62 DLR 4th) 634, 6—— See also ; *C* v. *S* [1988] QB 135, [1987] 1 All ER 1230, *Medhurst* v. *Medhurst* (1984) 46 OOR) (2d) 263, where Reid J of the Ontario High Court held that a father cannot act as the foetus next of kin. *Whalley* v. *Whalley* (1981)

Ethical issues in abortion

Other interest

Most abortion discourse largely centre on the interest of the pregnant woman, the foetus[32] and in some rare cases state interest.[33] Discourses on the rights of other parties, as that of the doctor, and the expectant father rarely enter. This should not be understood to mean that these third parties have no interest in pregnancy. In determining whether to permit abortion, there is need to consider the doctor's assessment, the views of the father of the foetus and those of other relevant health workers in the health delivery system.

The place of the father

The legal position in virtually all jurisdictions is that the expectant father has no right whatsoever in the determination of whether or not a pregnant woman should have an abortion. In traditional societies the proposition would be considered strange.

In *Paton* v. *Trustees of British Pregnancy Advising Services*,[34] the court stated that a father cannot prevent a mother (his wife) from seeking an abortion. Sir George Baker of the Family Division of the Queens Bench, said:

> The two doctors have given a certificate. It is not and cannot be suggested that that certificate was given in other than good faith and it seems to me that

---

122 DLR 3d 317 (BCSC); *Mack* v. *Brandouburg* (1988) 61 Alta LR (ld 235 (QB), *Doe* v. *Doe* 314 NE 2d 128 (Mass 1974); *Jones* v. *Smith* 278 So 2d 339 (Fla Dist. Ct. Amp. 1973), *Wall* v. *Livingston* [1982] 1 NZLR 734 (NZCA) based more on statutory interpretation than common law.

31 In *Webster* v. *Reproductive Health Services* 109 S Ct. 3040 (1989) the Supreme Court of America while demonstrating its unwillingness to over turn Roe v. Wade, was prepared to make minor incursion into it – that state legislation restricting availability of abortion were not necessarily unconstitutional. On the issue whether state funds could be used for abortion *Harris* v. *McRae* 100 S Ct. 2671 (1980) decide that state funds should only be available in limited cases to preserve life of the mother or in cases of pregnancy from incest or rape. J.H. Ely, The Wages of Crying Wolf: A Comment on *Roe* v. *Wade* (1973) 82 *Yale LJ* 920.

32 Mason ans Smith, *op. cit*, p.116. See discussion on the legal status of foetus at p. 117 and legal problems associated with the present state of the law which; ridiculously "make it more profitable for the defendant to kill the plaintiff (an unborn child) than to injure it, (American) jurisdiction which permits liability for negligent injury to foetus. See *Amadio* v. *Levia* 50 A 2d 1085 (Pa 1985). Even in England there appears to be some move by the courts to invest foetus with some form of identity; possibly within the present legal consortium that foetus has no rights whatsoever. See the obiter statements in *Re T (Adult: Refusal of medical treatment)* [1992] 4 All ER 649 at 653, [1992] 9, BMLR 46 at 50 and *Re S (Adult: Refusal Of medical treatment)* [1992] 4 All ER 671, [1992] 9 BMLR 69, [1992] 3 WLR 806, cases criticised by learned writers e.g. see Barbara Hewson, Ethical Triumph, or Surgical Rape? (1993) 137 *SJ* 1182.

33 See statement of Daughtrey J in *Davis* v. *Davis*, 842 SW 2d 588 (Tenn Sup Ct, 1992).

34 [1979] QB 276, [1978] 2 All ER 987. [1979] QB 276 [1978] 2 All ER 987 (QBD). See also JL Caldwell, Abortion: The Father's Lack of Standing [1988] *NZLR* 165; PT O'Neill and I Watson, The Father and the Unborn Child (1975) 38 *MLR* 174. On the legal status of the unborn child, see DM York, The Legal Personality of the Unborn Child [1979] *SLT* 158.

> that is the end of the matter in English law. The 1967 Act (Abortion) gives no right to the father to be consulted in respect of the termination of a pregnancy. True, it gives no right to the mother either, but obviously the mother is going to be right at the heart of the matter consulting with the doctors if they are to arrive at a decision in good faith unless of course, she is mentally incapacitated or physically incapacitated (unable to make any decision or give any help) if for example, in consequence of an accident. The husband, therefore, in my view, has no legal right unforeseeable at law or in equity to stop his wife having this abortion or to stop the doctor from carrying out the abortion...The Supreme Court of the United States has reached the same conclusion, that a husband, or an illegitimate father, has no right to stop his wife nor the woman *who is pregnant by him,* from carrying a legal abortion (Planned Parenthood Central Missouri v. Danforth, Attorney–General of Missouri; (1976) 428 US 52 (insertion is mine).

Paton dissatisfied with the decision appealed to the European Commission of Human Rights. The main plank of his appeal was that Article 8 of the European Convention on Human Right, which permits respect of family life vested in him the right *qua* father on implantation to prevent an abortion. The Commission rejected his appeal.[35] The Canadian position is no different. In *Tremblay* v. *Diagle*,[36] counsel for the applicant father argued that to the extent that a potential father contributes to conception to that extent he should be vested with an equal say in the destiny of the foetus. The court in reply to the argument said:

> There does not appear to be any jurisprudential basis for this (application) argument. No court in Quebec or else where has ever accepted the argument that father's interest in a foetus which he helped create could support a right to veto a woman's decision in respect of the foetus she is carrying...We have been unable to find a single decision in Quebec or elsewhere which would support the allegation of 'father's rights' necessary to support this injunction. There is nothing in the Civil Code or any legislation in Quebec which could be used to support the argument. This lack of legal basis is fatal to the argument about father's rights.[37]

The 'no-father right' principle has been stretched to include the proposition that he cannot in any way act on behalf of the unborn to enforce its rights. The reason for this conclusion is based on the premise that a foetus has no legal right until it is born. It constitutes an integral part of its mother.

Sir George Baker P in *Paton* recognised that an exception was made to the settled principle in the American case of *White* v. *Yup*.[38] But His Lordship said that position was different. *White* v. *Yup*,[39] involved a wrongful death claim. It was the complaint of the plaintiff that the negligence of the defendant caused the foetus to

---

[35] [1980] 3 EHRR 408 (E Com. HR).
[36] (1989) 62 DLR (4th) 534.
[37] (1989) 62 DLR (4th) 634 (Can Sup. Ct.).
[38] (1969) 458 P 2d 617.
[39] Ibid.

be still-born. The action was held maintainable by the American court. In England, however, a foetus has no right of action. Therefore a father cannot also act as the foetus's next of kin. It can be suggested that since the principles in *Paton* and the other cases referred to above were all decided on the interpretation of statutory provisions relating to abortion law, the principle should not apply to common law rights. Such an argument is, however, absurd because the broad principles decided in the *Paton* type litigation are of universal application.

Re F (in utero),[40] fortifies the universality of the cases. A local authority applied to protect an unborn child by making it a ward of court. It considered the dangerous behaviour of the mother inimical to the child's development. Without drawing a line of distinction between whether the legal position is founded on statute or common law principles, the English Court of Appeal rejected the local authority's application stating that it has no jurisdiction to ward an unborn child. May LJ said:

> In the absence of authority I am driven to the conclusion that the court does not have the jurisdiction contended for. I respectfully agree with the dictum from the judgement of Baker in Paton v. Trustees of BPAS. I also agree with the comments made by Heilbron J in her judgement in C v S.

Although only May LJ expressly confirmed the soundness of *Paton* and *C* v. *S*, the other judges (Staughton and Balcombe LJJ) did not doubt them either. *Paton* and *C* v. *S* therefore expresses the universal principle on the legal status of a foetus.[41] In matters of abortion, the pregnant woman's right is paramount; she alone has the right to determine the fate of her foetus. It is suggested that this should be an area of law that requires judicial rethinking. To exclude the father who has contributed to conception in the decision-making process is not altogether desirable. Some balance need to be struck. While the law ought to accord primary consideration to the right of the mother, the views of others should not be treated as irrelevant either.[42] If their wishes conflict, precedence can be given to the mother. The maintenance of matrimonial harmony is compelling reason for a consensus resolution framework. For example in the State of Pennsylvania (sections 320-329 of Pennsylvania Abortion Control Act, 1982) requires a woman seeking abortion to provide evidence that her husband has been consulted. The constitutionality of the provisions were considered in *Planned Parenthood of SE Pennsylvania* v. *Casey*,[43] and struck down for being unconstitutional. The United States Supreme Court took the view that the statutory requirement infringes on the woman's right to bodily

[40] [1988] Fam 122, [1988] 2 All ER 193. See also *Re Baby R* (1989) 53 DLR (4th) 69.

[41] Cv S [1988] QB 135, [1987] 1 All ER 1230.

[42] The position of Paton case is the prevailing jurisprudence in common law jurisdiction. See Australian case of *AG of Queensland (ex-p Kerr)* v. *T* (1983) 46 ALR 275 (High Ct.), Canadian case of *Borowski* v. *AG of Canada* [1987] 4 WWR 385 (Sask.CA), American case of *Roe* v. *Wade* 410 US 113 (1973), Quebec case of *Tremblay* v. *Daigle* (1989) 62 DLR (4th) 634 (Can Sup. Ct.).

[43] (1992) 122 5 Ct. 2791 (US Supt. Ct.).

integrity. Unfortunately, the decision brings us back to where we do not want to be. If anything, it reinforces the rule that in matters of abortion the only relevant person to consult in determining whether to terminate is the mother. According to the European Commission of Human Rights the reason for the rule is rooted in the fact that she is the one primarily concerned with the pregnancy, its continuation or termination. More so her right to private life is in issue.

The Doctor

The conscience of a doctor should not be overlooked in the whole process. Generally most religions discourage abortion. It is therefore not uncommon to expect to find a doctor who refuses to take part in an abortion procedure. In the circumstance, would it be proper to override his conscientious objection? It is therefore suggested that the law ought to tolerate and respect his conscience.[44] In line with that s. 4 of the English Abortion Act, (1967) state as follows:

> (1) Subject to subsection (2) of this section no person shall be under a duty, whether by contract or by any statutory or legal requirement to participate in any treatment authorised by this Act to which he has a conscientious objection. Provided that in any legal proceeding the burden of proof of conscientious objection shall rest on the person claiming to rely on it.
>
> (2) Nothing in subsection (1) of this section shall affect any duty to participate in treatment which is necessary to save the life or to prevent grave permanent injury to the physical or mental health of a pregnant woman.

The effect of the provision is that a doctor may refuse to take part in an abortion procedure. That notwithstanding, under the Act he has a duty to give advice on abortion. Doing so, he may advise the patient to seek abortion elsewhere on grounds of his conscience. Such advice could pose a challenge to the fiduciary relationship that underlie the doctor-patient relationship, more so when chances exist that a second refusal may delay termination, a thing that can prove risky to mother and foetus. Noteworthy, the wording of subsection (2) imposes a duty on a doctor to participate in all cases of emergency or life-threatening situations notwithstanding his conscientious objection. In effect, emergency or life threatening situations overrides conscientious objection in this context.

The same rules apply to nurses in a hospital facility,[45] in fact with greater force; because they often play a greater role in the process. The phrase 'no person participates in any treatment' in section 4 includes all persons proximate to the abortion process —- doctor, nurse and may be pharmacist depending on whether he is closely connected with the therapeutic term. It is suggested that the provision on conscientious objection, using the proximate test does not cover persons in clerical,

---

[44] J Warden, Abortion and Conscience (1990) 301 *BMJ* 1013. See also BD Weinstein, Do Pharmacists Have a Right to Refuse to Fill Prescriptions for Abortifacient Drugs (1992) 20 *Law Med Hlth Care* 220.

[45] See *Royal College of Nursing of UK* v. *DHSS* [1981] AC 800 [1981] 1 All ER 545 (HL).

secretarial or administrative positions in a hospital facility. This should be so because they hardly perform duties connected with the process in a manner that can affect the health of the mother. Its scope was tested in the English Court of Appeal in *R* v. *Salford Health Authority, ex p. Janaway*,[46] affirmed subsequently in *Janaway* v. *Salford Area Health Authority*.[47] Mrs. Janaway was in the employment of the respondent health authority as secretary/receptionist. It was at Irlam Health Centre, working for a Dr. Baroah. She was asked by Dr. Baroah to type a referral letter referring a pregnant woman for an appointment with a consultant, with a view of him forming an opinion as to whether to perform an abortion. Mrs. Janaway, a Roman Catholic holding the belief that abortion is morally wrong, refused to type the letter. It was eventually hand written by another doctor in the health centre. She was later told that her refusal was a breach of the authority's disciplinary rules. She was asked to give a firm assurance that the conduct would not be repeated in future.

Her reply was to the effect that she would continue to refuse such demands. She claimed protection under section 4 (1) of the Abortion Act. 1967. The authority sought legal advice, on the strength of which it wrote her stating that her refusal was not covered by s.4 (1). Her employment was then terminated. Her appeal against the authority's decision to the Employment Appeal Tribunal was dismissed.

With leave of court she appealed for judicial review by way of an order of *certiorari* to the High court. Nolan J dismissed her case. On further appeal to the English Court of Appeal (Slade, Balcombe and Stockier LJJ) the decision of Nolan J. was affirmed and her appeal dismissed. With leave she appealed to the House of Lords. She claimed the protection of section 4 (1), arguing that the phrase 'participate in any treatment authorised by the Act', covered taking part in any arrangement preliminary to and intended to bring about medical or surgical measures aimed at terminating pregnancy, which includes the typing of a letter. The authority on the other hand, contended that the phrase is limited to taking part on the actual procedure undertaken at the hospital for abortion purposes. The House of Lords held that merely typing a letter could not be construed as aiding an abortion. Typing a letter is an act of carrying out her obligation to her employer. She was too distant from the actual treatment. Accordingly her appeal failed and was dismissed.

As a final word on the discussion it must be said that abortion authorised for eugenic reasons as permitted by the U.K. Abortion Act, offends the strict interpretation of the Physicians Oath. Since the desirability of abortion for eugenic may in some cases be real, there may be a need for balancing.

Relationship between homicide and abortion

It would appear that both concepts are not related because the Criminal Code defines homicide as the unlawful killing of a person,[48] while abortion is associated

---

[46] [1988] 2 WLR 442 (CA).

[47] [1989] AC 537 [1988] 3 All ER 1079 (HL).

[48] Section 234 of Criminal Code Law.

with miscarriage of a foetus. Since a foetus by definition does not qualify as a person because it has no separate existence from its mother, it is impossible to describe its termination as the killing of a person, more so when it has no legal rights.[49] That notwithstanding, both are connected in that though injuries to a foetus would not qualify as homicide, if the injured foetus is subsequently born but dies as a result of the pre-natal injury, that could amount to murder or manslaughter depending on the circumstances. That was the ratio in *Keeler* v. *Superior Court of Amador County*.[50] Mrs. Keeler while driving home was blocked by the petitioner who assaulted her. As a result she sustained personal injuries. A caesarean section was performed and her foetus examined *in utero*. Its head was found to be severely fractured. It was delivered still-born. The pathologist evidence was that the cause of death was skull fracture and that the death was cursed by the injury to her abdomen by the force the petitioner applied to her. The petitioner was charge for murder in that he killed a human being to wit: Baby Girl VOGT, with malaise aforethought. The California Supreme Court dismissed the charge. Mosk J said:

> We conclude that in declaring murder to be the unlawful and malicious killing of human being the legislature in 1950 intended that to have the settled common law meaning of a person who had been born alive, and did not intend the act of feticide– as distinguished from abortion to be on offence under the law of California.[51]

The sad reality of the common law makes it more profitable to kill a foetus than to injure the foetus. This is so because no criminal charge for murder of a foetus would be successful, but a civil claim for damages to an injured foetus has a slim chance of success. To remedy the ugly situation, some jurisdictions have defined homicide to be 'the unlawful killing of a human being, or a foetus with malice aforethought.'[52] The Nigeria and English laws are yet to make the amendment. Noteworthy, however, section 309 of the Criminal Code states that if a child dies in consequence of any act done before or during birth, the person who does the act shall be deemed to have killed the child. May be we can stretch this provision to cover the kind of situation that arose in *Keeler case*.[53]

---

[49] By virtue of s. 235 of Criminal Code Law, a child can only 'become a person capable of being killed when it has completely proceeded in a living state from the body of its mother.' In effect, feotus is not vested with personhood. See also *Paton* v. *British Pregnancy Advisory Service Trustees* [1979] QB 276; [1978] 2 All ER 987. But cf. G.R. Dunstan, The Moral Status of the Human Embryo: A Tradition Recalled (1984) 10 *J. Med Ethics* 38.

[50] (1970) 470 P. 2d 617 (Cal Sup. Ct).

[51] Ibid.

[52] Section 187 of the California Criminal Code's definition of murder as amended in 1970. See also *Keeler* v. *Superior Court of Amador County* (1970) 470 P. 2d 617 (Cal Sup. Ct); *Commonwealth* v. *Lawrence* (1989) 404 MRS 378.

[53] (1970) 470 P. 2d 617.

Chapter Seven

Biomedical research and experiment

From the inception of medicine, biomedical research and experimentation proceeded with the use of human as objects without question. However with increasing awareness of the attendant harm it portends coupled with human rights questions it raises have necessitated cautiously. For example, the preamble to the Anatomy Acts 1832 and 1871 states one danger resulting from the practice. It states as follows:

> And whereas the legal supply of human bodies for such anatomical examination is insufficient fully to provide the means in order further to supply human bodies for such purposes, divers great and grievous crimes have been committed, and lately murder, for the single object of selling for such purposes the bodies of such persons murdered.[1]

It is clear from the above preamble that the use of human in unveiling information about the cause of death with a view to acquiring knowledge of diseases which affect the body, by means of post-mortem examination can trigger murders. Many years ago, unscrupulous criminals killed others and sold their corpses to medical schools for experiment. *Burke and Hare case* [2] illustrates the type of horrors it triggered. In modern times and under guise of human experiment, Nazi Germany and Japan were known to have engaged in genocidal acts and human mutilation in medical laboratories without regard for human dignity and decency. The world rose up to condemn them by enacting an international ethical code on research, the Nuremburg Code on medical treatment, which metamorphosed into the Helsinki Declaration of 1964.[3] In some jurisdictions ethical codes have been enacted by national medical associations to address these human dignity issues. An example is the guidelines issued by the Royal College of Physician's of London and the Medical Research Council in 1992. In Nigeria the Helsinki Declaration is an incorporal part of the code of conduct for doctors.[4]

Benefits of medical research and experiment can be immense. It provides the medical world instructive knowledge of the nature of disease which affects the human body. Such knowledge would otherwise have been difficult to obtain

[1] See Preamble, Anatomy Act 1832 (England) and Anatomy Act Nigeria.

[2] *Oxford Dictionary of Law.*

[3] See Appendix and E.O. Amaku, Human Experimentation and the principles of Informed consent, ed. By E.S. Apata, *Medical Ethics*, Lagos University Press, 1982 p.113-115.

[4] See Appendix.

without the use of human as research object. This explains why ethics cannot totally condemn and frown at human experimentation. Therefore what is here required is a sort of balance between the contending issues, i.e., need for continuing human objects for experiment and the question of dignity of the objects.

The Helsinki Declaration does not define the term 'research' or 'experiment'. That notwithstanding, in this chapter both words would be use interchangeable as though equivalent, even though they are not necessarily synonymous. Experiment as the name implies is more of finding solution. It is speculation. Research on the other hand, is closely connected with a deepening of knowledge as an end-point. Research is clinical if its object is to improve the medical condition of a patient. It is non-therapeutic where the object is not aimed at furthering medical knowledge on a particular medical subject. If any biomedical research involves risk of some sort to the patient, e.g. dizziness, headache, etc., it is generally considered good ethics for the researcher to seek alternatives objects other than humans, unless it is absolutely necessary to use humans. Even at that, the reason for research must be to discover further information on a serious disease that is beneficial. Importantly, the patient must give consent to the proposed research. It is for this reason that the court imposes a greater duty of care on the researcher than a doctor engaged in routine treatment.

Research and experiment

Research is an investigation directed to the discovery of some fact by careful, critical or scientific inquiring.[5] Thus a research project is one which can be rightly described as a scientific enquiry, systematic in design aimed at contributing to knowledge. Experiment on the other hand involves more of speculation designed to find out what a cause is. No matter how well tried a treatment outcome may be, no doctor can full-proof know how a particular treatment would turn out in the case of an individual patient. It is to thus a truism that every treatment therapy is more or less an experiment. While it is possible to modify an experiment if it does not meet expectation, research on the other hand is aimed at a particular course until the programme proves unsatisfactory. Such a programme may be invasive or non-invasive, and it is sometimes difficult to draw the line between both. It is considered invasive if a programme requires whole or part entry into the body. On the other hand, it is non-invasive if a research does not involve entry into the body. Sometimes research may involve only observation, with no form of intervention, e.g., certain research in psychology.

Research often involves a life object. Since biomedical research aims to contribution to knowledge and health care, it is only normal to expect that the objects of research are human or in some case animals. Therapeutic research aims at improving the health of the patient or a group of persons suffering same ailment as the patient. Non-therapeutic aims to deepen knowledge, which in turn aids treatment

---

[5] *Shorter Oxford English Dictionary.*

at some future date. Example of this is the discovery of X-ray by German Physicist Wilhelm Konrad Rontgen (1842-1923), which today is a valuable tool in medical investigation.

Biomedical research and experiment are propelled by a desire to make medicine an exact science, eliminate useless and unreliable therapy and quack medicine. In its early stages research was largely unregulated, until the Nuremberg trials revealed the horror perpetrated by the Nazi in guise of research that necessitated a global concern to regulate research.[6] Since every research involves risk of some sort, researchers are required to do all in their power to minimise the risk. The Helsinki Declaration[7] broadly spells out the broad guidelines required to be observed by researcher. For example, a doctor is under positive duty to evaluate the risk/benefit ratio. According to the guideline issued by the Royal College of Physician, if the risk is above minimum permissible,[8] the patient shall only be involved in the process if the following five requirements are satisfied: (i) the risk must be small when compared with that already suffered by the patient as a result of the disease; (ii) the disease must be of a serious nature; (iii) knowledge gained from the research must hold out prospect of great practical benefit; (iv) there must be no other means of obtaining that knowledge and; (v) the patient must give a full factual informed consent. These five principles do not apply to research on animals—generally regulated by the Cruelty to Animal Act, 1876.[9] Whether a research is therapeutic or non-therapeutic will make little difference on the standard expected to be exhibited by the researcher.

Before commencing a research which involves human object, a doctor ought to satisfy himself that the five cardinal requirements are satisfied. Next he is expected to consider the fact of the patient's informed consent. Consent will only be treated as informed if the patient is properly told by the researcher of the intended procedures and the possible risk related to it. In effect it requires the doctor to discharge his duty of full and frank disclosure to the patient. In clear and unambiguous manner the doctor is expected to explain the purpose of the experiment and its benefit to the patient and or society, the risk involved so that the patient may choose to participate in the programme or opt out of it. It is only after this explanation to the patient and the patient's agreement to take part or be involved in the process that consent can be treated as full and factual.

---

[6] For a detail of the catalogue of repulsive medical research carried on the German. See Joy Katz, *Experimentation with Human Beings* (1972) in which he sets out the major elements in the trial of Dr. Karl Braudt and others before the Nuremberg Military Tribunal (pp. 292-306).

[7] See appendix. See also guideline issued by the Royal College of Physicians in 1992 and H. Beecher, Ethics and Clinical Research (1966) 274 *New Eng. J. Med* 1354; Working Party Report of English Institute of Medical Ethics, titled *Research and Children* (1986); Little, *Human Guinea Pigs in Moral Dilemmas of Modern Medicine* (1985) ed. M. Lockwood.

[8] Minimal risks involve sampling and build reaction from treatment.

[9] The Cruelty to Animals Act 1876 is a statute of general application in Nigeria. However, by virtue of s. 424 of the Criminal Code which makes criminal a range of offences dealing with offences of cruelty to animals, it is suggested that the force of the 1876 Act is now taken over by the Criminal Code.

Fact of consent is a paramount requirement. It is designed to safeguard venerable patients because the doctor occupies an unequal position to his patient. The reasons are obvious. The doctor by virtue of his training has better knowledge of medicine than his client. In some states in America and Canada, informed consent requirement are statutory in nature. Some such regulations go as far to specify the amount of disclosure and explanation necessary. A doctor who fails to observe the basis principles of informed consent exposes himself to actionable damages. Hall JA of the Saskatchewan Court of Appeal in *Halushka* v. *University of Saskatchewan* said:

> There can be no exception to the ordinary requirement of disclosure in the case of research as there may well be in ordinary medical practice. The researcher does not have to balance the probable effect of lack of treatment against the risk involved in the treatment itself. The example of risk being properly hidden from a patient when it is important that he should not worry can have no application in the field of research. The subject of medical experimentation is entitled to a full and frank disclosure of all the facts, probabilities and opinion which a reasonable man might be expected to consider before giving his consent.[10]

The plaintiff was a university undergraduate in the University of Saskatchewan. Not able to find summer vacation job, the employment office of the university advised him that he could earn $50 by participating in a test at the university hospital. He accordingly went there. He was told that the test had to do with research on an anaesthetic agent *Fluoromar*, and that it will last a couple of hours. He was further told that the test is safe and so that there was nothing to worry about. The procedure for the test was explained to him. He executed a consent form for the purpose. On the day of the test, the procedure followed was described to him except that the catheter after being inserted in the vein of his arm will advanced towards his heart. The test made him unconscious for four days. He was discharged after ten day in the university hospital, and paid $50, the bargain fees. As a result of the adverse effect of the test drug on the plaintiff the defendant decided to withdraw the drug for having too narrow a margin of safety. Plaintiff brought the action on two grounds, namely trespass to his person and negligence. The hospital was held liable. On the degree of information or disclosure or both required, Hall JA said:

> The respondent was not informed that the catheter would advance to and through his heart but was admittedly given to understand that it would be merely inserted in the vein in his arm. While it may be correct to say that the advancement of the catheter to the heart was not in itself dangerous and did not cause or contribute to the cause of the cardiac arrest, it was a circumstance which, if known, might very well have prompted the respondent to withhold his consent. The undisclosed or misrepresented facts need not

[10] (1965) 52 WWR 608 at 616 (Sask CA)

> concern matters which directly cause the alternate damage if they are of a nature which might influence the judgment upon which the consent is based.[11]

The court stated that explanation must cover all possible research procedure. Procedural explanations are generally construed strictly based on prima facie presumption in favour of the patient.

Special cases

Treatment of children

By their very nature children are less experienced than adults. They depend on competent adult, usually parents or persons in *locus parentis* for major decision making. The 1992 Guidelines for the Ethical Conduct of Medical Research Involving Children by the British Paediatric Association recognises that research involving children can be a worthwhile project. Yes, if it holds prospect of benefit to children; is well arranged and conducted; does not duplicate earlier works; is not undertaken primarily for finance or professional advantage; involves statistical appropriate number of subjects and is properly reported.[12] May be because non-therapeutic research can sometimes be an important means for promoting child health the said guideline does not stipulate that this form of research is itself unethical without more.

While it is necessary in some cases to have children participate in research to enable the medical world come to a more enlightening cause and care for paediatric diseases the court are usually jealous of such arrangements and so would readily intervene if benefit is outweighed by pain, risk and burden. In accord with this position, the World Health Organisation Conference, Manila, Philippines, September 1981, enjoins doctors to consider the following question in every research proposal: (i) are the objectives of the research valid?; (ii) is the question at hand a priority problem?; (iii) is the question peculiar to children alone?; (iv) has studies been done in vitro or in animals and found safe?; (v) can the research be done utilising adults?; (vi) what is the risk—benefit ratio?; (vii) is the research scientifically sound and significant?; (viii) is the procedure safe and consistent with the research design?; (ix) has the legal guardian given consent?; (x) is the child's privacy and confidentiality protected?; (xi) for children (6 year and above) is the assent of the child sought and obtained?[13]

The above questions are pertinent in view of the Declaration of Helsinki and the common law doctrine of informed consent. It is important to ask what objectives the research aims at achieving. The Nazi regime in Germany for instance mutilated

---

[11] *Supra*

[12] Guidelines for the Ethical Conduct of Medical Research Involving children (British Paediatric Association) 1992, Ch 6. See also C. Hudges, Legal and Ethical Issues in Research in the United Kingdom: Children, the Elderly and Mentally Incapaciatates (1992) 6 Phar. Med. 309, cited in Kennedy & Grubb, *op. cit*, 1053

[13] WHO.

the organs of Jews, non-conformist and its perceived enemies under the inhuman guise of medical research. This was unequivocally condemned by the Helsinki Declaration 1964.[14] The Declaration in positive terms restated the ethical position this way:

> 'all research must conform to morals and science. Any research, which is immoral, contrary to good judgment, is prohibited. Clinical research on children should elucidate the cause and or cure of diseases affecting children. The researcher must show its propriety–in terms of effect and consequence. He should, for example, show that the world proportion of children that have contacted the disease, or will contact it is enormous enough to cause concern and that, contact of the disease is crippling in effect or terminal.'[15]

Children for many reasons need protection from the world around them. They are more venerable to deceit; they are the leaders of the future, to mention a few. For children to be used for research purposes, it must be shown that the disease investigated is peculiar to children, and that finding cures can only be done with child as experiment objects. If alternative experiment *in vitro* or in animals is safe, no good reason for the participation of children in experimental process will exist.

The risk—benefit ration to the particular child and other children is an important consideration. Any experiment capable of altering the personality of a child is not permissible. The term personality in this context is widely interpreted. For example, any experiment capable of permanently changing a child's anatomy, facial or body structure or function of the organs, falls within the category. An experiment that weighs more on the scale of risk than benefit is clearly contrary to the Helsinki Declaration. It must be scientifically based on proposition with known foundation. Mere hypothesis would not do. That is why it is imperative that the procedures should be known scientifically to be generally safe and sound.

Because parents are the proper guardians for children, the law requires them to provide children with necessaries, including medical care. Child neglect, dependency, and protection statutes typically require parents to provide children necessary medical care. The United State Supreme Court in *Parham* v. *J. R.* recognised this when it said:

> Our jurisprudence historically has reflected Western civilisation concepts of the family as a unit with broad parental authority over minor children. Our cases have consistently followed that course; our constitutional system long ago rejected any notion that a child is 'the mere creature of the State' and, on the contrary, asserted that parents generally have the rights coupled with the high duty, to prepare children for additional obligation...The law's concept of the family rest on a presumption that parents possess what a child lacks in maturity, experience, and capacity for judgment required for making life's

---

[14] Appendix.

[15] Ibid.

difficult decision. More important, historically it has recognised that natural bonds of affection lead parent to act in the best interest of their children.[16]

Some jurisdictions have stretched the requirement to include parents submitting to compulsory medical treatment for their children.[17] Compulsory treatment has been construed to include objectionable procedures considered good for the child to which the parents object - for example, blood transfusion. When parents refuse such treatment, some have wrongly imagined that refusal can be the basis of prosecution for criminal abandonment. The correctness of such proposition is doubtful.[18] States *paren patrie* jurisdiction in the welfare of children should not override parental concern and wishes.[19] It is therefore absolutely necessary for the researcher to seek and obtain consent from the legal guardian before any experiment can be carried on children.[20]

The confidential particulars of children used in a research must be respected. From the days of Hippocrates until the present, members of the medical profession have bound themselves not to divulge professional secrets. The legal basis for the rule is rooted in the confidential and fiduciary nature of the doctor-patient relationship. If the child patient is a mature minor within the *Gillick* classification, it would be necessary in addition to seeking the parent consent, to also seek the mature minor consent.[21] This is reasonable because nature minors are generally responsible for their criminal and civil wrongs.[22] That fortifies the *Gillick* mature minor consent

---

[16] (1979) 442 US 584.

[17] In *Re President and Director of Georgetown College Inc.* (1964) 331 F. 2d 1000, Justice Skelly Wright ordered the transfusion of a minor's mother because in the court's view her refusal to transfusion would mean a choice to voluntary abandon her child who relies on her for living. With respect, the judgment is wrong. For discussion and critique of the case, chapter on informed consent.

[18] Note, the Refusal of Life Saving Medical Treatment vs. The States Interest in the Preservation of Life: A Clarification of the Interest at Stake (1980) 58 Wash. Univ. L. Q 85 at 102; A. Usel, The Right to Die (1989) 103; Clarke, The Chance to Refuse or withhold Medical Treatment, The Emerging Technology and Medical Ethical Consensus (1990) 13 Creighton L. Rev 995; *Fasmire* v. *Nicolean* (1990) 551 N.E, 2d 77 (N.Y.C.A); see also comments that although blood transfusion is a standard in medicine and emergency to save life in cases of acute anaemia and blood loss, experts think it is more of a medical problem than a solution. Seminar on Non-blood medical management and alternatives to blood transfusion, at Lagos Univ. Teaching Hospital (LUTH) on 19th August 2010, reported in the *Guardian* newspaper of August 20th, 2010, at p. 5.

[19] Rhoden, The Judge in the Delivery Room: The Emergence of Court-ordered Caesareans, 74 *Cal. L Rev.* (1986). See also *McFall* v. *Shimp* (1978) Pa D & C 3d 90, *Sidaway* v. *Bethlehem Royal Hospital* [1985] AC 871.

[20] Goldstein, medical care for the child at Risk: On State Supervision of Parental Autonomy; (1977) 86 *Yale L.J.* 6; C. Hodges, Legal and Ethical Issues in Research in the UK; Children, the Elderly and the Mentally Incapacitated (1992) 6 *Pharmaceutical Med* 304. See also on research on children, BM Dickens, The Modern Function and Limits of Parental Rights (1981) 97 *LQR* 462; A McCall Smith, Is There Anything Left of Parental Rights in E Sutherland & McCall Smith (eds) *Family Rights* (1991) chp 1; Institute of Medical Ethics (England): Medical Research with Children: Ethics, Law and Practice (1986) Bull. No 14 p.8; RB Redmon, How Children Can be Respected as Ends and Still be Used as Subjects in Non-Therapeutic Research (1986) 12 *J Med Ethics* 77.

[21] *Gillick* v. *West Norfolk and Wisbech A.H.A* (1984); on appeal (1986); revsd (1986)[1985] 3 ALL ER 402

[22] See S.28 of Criminal Code (defence of immaturity).

requirement. According to the Tennessee Supreme Court in *Cardwell* v. *Bechtol*: 'recognition that minors achieve varying degrees of maturity and responsibility has been part of the common law for well over a century.'[23]

Dworkin[24] summarises the necessary ethical requirements for children research as follows: (i) that the design details should meet ethical criteria for research; (ii) it must be approved by the appropriate ethical committee; (iii) voluntary parental consent must exist; and (iv) there should exist no risk and, if any, should be minimal. The researchers can only safely proceed when these factors can be resolved favourable. It is not sufficient that some of the factors can be so resolved.

If the patient is incompetent and research is necessary, consent of patient's relative or guardian is a must. Except in cases of necessity, consent is mandatory. In addition to this proxy consent, notion of 'best interest' or concept of 'substituted judgment' ought to map the boundaries of treatment and research on incompetents

Foetal experiment

Prenatal test makes possible diagnose with better accuracy of many impairments of an unborn child. Testing procedures include ultrasound and or amniocentesis. Test results can be used to diagnose foetal impairment. Paradoxically, it has also been the basis for selective abortion. Where for example impairment can result in serious disability abortion have been sought. Unfortunately tests have also been the basis for gender discrimination. It is reported that in India, out of 8,000 foetal tests 7,999 were aborted because they were of female sex. Prenatal test can also provided information as to the risk a mother may encounter during delivery. Based on such data doctors may advise a caesarean or a vaginal delivery. In *Re S*,[25] prenatal test was what revealed that the foetus was in transverse and so could not be vaginally delivered. It was on the strength of the information that the doctor recommended a caesarean. All these are ethical matters raised by foetal experiment. Some of questions that can be asked include the following: if a foetus is shown to be impaired, who should make the decision for its abortion? The mother, or father, or both? Who determines the degree of disability that should justify abortion? Is a female gender sex disability sufficient for abortion? What message would abortion send to the less able persons in our society? Should a physician be held liable for failure to detect disability in foetus?

In *Burton* v. *Islington Health Authority*[26] it was held that a foetus has no right of action for pre-natal injury, until birth. Also in *Paton* v. *Trustee of British*

---

[23] (1987) 724 S.W 2d. 739 (Tenn) See also *R* v. *Smith* (1845) 1 Cox C.C. 260.

[24] G Dworkin, Legality of Consent on Infants and Young Children in Childhood Therapeutic Medical Research (1978) 53 *Archives of Disease in Childhood* 443 at 445; Law and Medical Experimentation (1987) *Monash U L Rev.* 189

[25] [1992] 3 WLR 806. See also *Quintavalle* v. *Human Fertilisation and Embryology Authority* [2005] UKKL 28 (HL)

[26] [1992] 3 All ER 833.

Pregnancy Advisory Committee,[27] Sir George Baker refused to grant a husband an order of injunction to restrain the wife from undergoing an abortion advised by her physicians. Common law recognises the mother as the primary person to determine the future of a foetus. However, the right has in recent times come under close scrutiny. Consequentialist arguments and wardship jurisdiction of state *parens patrae* now appear to be making inroad into the rights of the mother.

Remedy for research injury

If a research volunteer is injured, as in *Halushka* v. *University of Saskatchewan*,[28] remedy available can be compensation for damages in tort or contract. In tort, the broad basis for claim is as stated in *Bolam* v. *Friern Hospital Management Committee*,[29] modified by the House of Lords decision in *Sideway* v. *Board of Governors of Bethlehem Royal Hospital*.[30] It is also possible to claim damages in contract for breach of warranty, contract and the like, more so when contract, torts and fiduciary laws are now coming closer.[31] It has been suggested that since the society invariable gains from research, liability should not rest solely on the doctor for unethical research in all cases. A regime capable of spreading damages by way of insurance or state compensation scheme can reduce the burden of responsible researchers.[32]

Unethical research and innovative therapy

The callous atrocities committed in the laboratories of Nazi Germany and Japan led to the enactment of an international code of ethics for medical research using human objects. The first internationally accepted code was the Nuremberg Code, drawn up as a result of revelation at the war crime trials.[33] The Tribunal stated that all its members agree 'that certain basis principles must be observed in order to satisfy moral ethical and legal concepts before human beings are used in medical experiments. The few clauses in the Nuremberg Code later culminated in the Declaration in Helsinki of the World Medical Association in 1964. The Helsinki Declaration was revised in 1975.[34] Some jurisdictions have even gone further to enact the principles of the Nuremberg Code and the Helsinki Declaration into their

---

[27] [1978] 2 All ER 987.

[28] . (1965) 52 WWR 608 (1965) 53 DLR (2ed) 436.

[29] [1957] 2 All ER 118, [1957] 1 WLR 582 (CA).

[30] [1984] QB 493, [1984] 1 All ER 1018 (CA) affd. [1985] AC 871, [1985] 1 All ER 643 (HL).

[31] On the correlation between contract, tort and fiduciary claims, see OF Emiri, *Equity and Trust in Nigeria* (Lagos: Malthouse 2010)

[32] This can be from trust funds set up by foundation or government from where compensation can be paid from. C. Hodges, Harmonisation of European Controls over Research Ethics Committees, Consent, compensation and indemnity, in A Goldberg (ed) *et al*, (eds.), *Pharmaceutical Medicine and the Law*, (1991)

[33] Z. Szawarsk, Research Ethics in Eastern Europe (1982) *Bull. Inst. Med. Ethics* No. 82,13; The English text of the Nuremberg Code is published in 1992 *Bull Inst. Med. Ethics* No.82,13

[34] See Appendix.

domestic law.[35] All these codes basically express concern that research must have respect for the rights of the individual.

It is generally recognised that research though close to experiment, differs from it.[36] Traditionally, an analysis of the ethics of research follows a distinction between therapeutic and non-therapeutic research, even though it may sometimes be confusing to draw the line.[37] Therapy is distinct from research by the intention of the person engaged in it. On this ground it can be argued that research by itself cannot be therapeutic. That being so, a therapeutic research will be a research that has a therapeutic intention, as well as a research intention, toward the subject of the research. Accordingly, a non-therapeutic research is an activity which does not have therapeutic intention. In effect, a therapeutic research is an activity with a therapeutic purpose. A therapeutic research therefore serves a dual purpose, research and therapy to the subject. Practically this is difficult, especially if the primary intent of the activity is to gain new knowledge. Where however the researcher uses his clinical and therapeutic acumen in the interest of the research element of his activity, the difficulty will appear surmounted.

Usually the permissible limits of therapeutic research are judged by reference to risk- benefit ratio. A patient may only be exposed to research risk if it will bring him likelihood of greater benefit. If the patient is competent, he ordinarily is the one to determine the risk-benefit ratio for himself – having of course being properly informed. Where a patient's illness is severe, the risk of research is likely to be higher. Risk-benefit analysis is also important consideration in non-therapeutic research and activities involving incompetent patients.[38]

In a non-therapeutic research, the researcher only intention is to obtain information through systematic inquiry which contributes to general medical knowledge. Unlike a therapeutic research, the subjects may be patients and non-patient volunteers. It is arguable that since the doctor's duty to his patient is that of therapy, any non-therapeutic activity is prohibited. It would be difficult to justify non-therapeutic research on a patient using the best interest analysis, because the activity exposes the patient to additional medical intervention with risk not designed to aid his treatment. This notwithstanding, a patient with a minor illness may choose

---

[35] See for England: Guidelines issued by the Royal College of Physicians of London, *Research Involving Patient* (1990) and Medical Research Council, *Responsibility in Investigation on Human Participants and Material and Personal Information*, 1992; see also at regional level, the Council of Europe Committee Of Ministers Recommendation No. R (90) 3, 1990.

[36] B.M. Dickens, What is Medical Research (1975) 113 *Can. Ned. Ass. J.* 635; B Gaze and B Dawson, Distinguishing medical practice and research: The Special Case of IMF (1989) 3 *Bioethics* 301; For general reading on the ethical quality of certain research procedures see AV Campbell, A Report from New Zealand: An Unfortunate Experiment (1989) 3 *Bioethics* 59; R Hare, Little Human Guinea Pigs in M Lockwood (ed.) *Moral Dilemmas in Modern Medicine* (1985).

[37] See *Working Party Report on Medical Research With Children*, 1986, of the English Institute of Medical Ethics, pp33 –36, cited in Kennedy and Grubb, *op. cit.* p. 1029.

[38] See generally, *Re F (a Mental Patient: Sterilisation)* [(1990] 2 AC 1; C Hedges, Legal and Ethical Issues in Research in the United Kingdom; The Children, the Elderly and the Mentally Incapacitated (1992) 6 *Pharmaceutical Medicine* 309; see also *Re H (Mental Patient)* [1993] 9 BMLR 71.

to be a volunteer to non-therapeutic research activity, if it carries no demonstrable risk of harm to his health. Practically it will be difficult and rare to show no risk of harm. It has been suggested that non-therapeutic research on patients is only permissible where there is clear evidence of absence of risk.[39] If it is so, (which of course is likely to be rare) the patient would be in no different legal position from the volunteer who chooses to be the subject of research.[40]

If the non therapeutic research is on a healthy volunteer, the general test of risk-benefit analysis becomes an equally relevant factor in judging the ethics of the activity. In addition to it the doctor must also consider and observe the following: (i) obtain the medical history of the volunteer to enable him determine risk potential; (ii) obtain the permission of the volunteer to inform his family doctor that he is participating in the research; (iii) satisfy himself that the volunteer is not participating in any other contemporaneous research; (iv) ensure that he has available all appropriate medical equipments to meet any possible or foreseeable eventuality that may arise out of the research activity; (v) importantly, that the volunteer is sufficiently informed of the research procedure, risk and possible benefit and he is prepared to disclose any changes experienced due to the activity. A failure to observe these conditions could expose a doctor to liability for breach of contract and or a valid claim in tort as the case may be. Beyond these requirements, the core issue of valid consent must in all cases be present before any research is undertaken using the patient as object.

Recently, it has been suggested that pressure to advance in the hierarchy of science have prompted and tempted some researchers to engage in fraudulent research. Some have laid false claim to discoveries and falsified results of their experiment.[41] This has prompted the introduction of safeguard regime in many jurisdictions in the form of establishment of ethical committees with powers to regulate bio-medical research and experiments.[42] Unethical research however, must be distinguished from genuine innovative therapy which aims experimentally at cure. A research is considered innovative if it deviates from ordinary practice of medicine. That is what makes it novel or exceptional treatment - employing of new techniques. Noteworthy of mention, even an innovative therapy must conform to general standard medical practice, otherwise it will amount to unethical research. In the words of Lord Clyde in *Hunter* v. *Hanley*, innovative therapy is permitted because it aids progress in medicine. He said:

> It follows from what I have said in regard to allegation of deviation from ordinary professional practice...such a deviation is not necessarily evidence of

---

[39] Kennedy and Grubb, *op. cit*, p.1054.

[40] Ibid.

[41] See *A wake* magazine of titled, Fraud in Science.

[42] For example, the Department of Health in England has Local Research Ethics Committee on all public hospital. R. J Robinson, Ethics Committees and Research on Children (1987) 294 *BMJ* 1243.

> negligence. Indeed it would be disastrous if this were so, for all inducement to progress in medical science would then be destroyed.[43]

It is acceptable practice because it enables the doctor to apply his skill to fit the peculiarities of his patient. If it were otherwise, then medicine would be unnecessarily straight jacket application of known knowledge to the patient without considering how a therapy fits the ailment of the individual patient. Happily, it is not so. Doctors exercise discretion in the matter of developing treatment to fit patients. In *Brook* v. *St. John's Hickey Memorial Hospital*, Hunter J said:

> Too often courts confused judgmental decisions and experiments. Therapeutic innovation has long been recognised as permissible to avoid serious consequences. The everyday practice of medicine involves constant judgmental decisions by physicians as they move from one patient to another in the conscious institution of procedures, special tests, and trials and observations recognised generally by their profession as effective in treating the patient or providing a diagnosis of a disabled condition. Each patient presents a slightly different problem to the doctor. A physician is pressured to have knowledge and skill necessary to use some innovation to fit the peculiar circumstances of each case.[44]

Where a doctor however decides to use an innovative therapy it is advisable for him to seek the consent of the patient even though negligence does not automatically arise because an innovative technique is employed. According to Prowse JA of the Alberta Court (Canada) in *Zimmer* v. *Ringrose*:

> A physician is entitled to decide that situation dictates the adoption of an innovative cause of treatment. As long as he discharges his duty of disclosure, and is not otherwise in breach of his duties of skill and care e.g. has not negligently adopted the procedure given the circumstances, the doctor will not be held liable for implementing such a course of treatment.[45]

Human tissue and fluid samples

The question of who owns human tissue and fluid as sample taken from a patient for research or experiment can become controversial especially in the context of its commercialisation. For example consider the America case of *Moore* v. *Regent of*

---

[43] [1955] SC. 200.

[44] 380 NE 2d 72 (1978) (Sup. Ct. Ind.), See also sellers LJ in *Landau* v. *Wener* (1961) 105 Sol. Jo 1008 (CA).

[45] (1981) 124 DLR (3d) 215 (A16) CA) see Also *R* v. *Mental Health Commission*, Ex. p. X [1988] 9 BMLR 77 (Div. Ct.), though the case revolved around the interpretation s. 57 of the Mental Health Act, 1983 as to whether or not the treatment given by the doctor came within its scope; it is interesting to note that the case raises issues of innovative practice. The doctor prescribed Goserelin a drug manufactured by ICI for treatment of prostate cancer to a compulsive paedophile, whose sexual drive was not stemmed by routine drug of Cyproterone. Goserelin was recommended because it operates to reducing the testosterone to castrate levels. The drug succeeds in reducing the patient urge. The therapy was innovative because the drug was not sold for the purpose of reducing sexual drive, but for control of prostrate cancer. For this reason, Stuart-Smith LJ observed that it was important that the patient be told that the therapy on him is innovative and that the full implication with its use on young men had not been shunned, as trial/experiment on it had only involved its application to animals and older men.

University of California.[46] The plaintiff, John Moore underwent a hairy-cell leukaemia treatment in the university hospital. During his treatment, specimens of his blood and bone marrow were taken. Unknown to him the university hospital used them to develop a cell line which had potential commercial value running into millions of dollars. Golde established a cell line from Moore T-lymphocytes and the university applied for patent innovation, which was granted. With the patient and university assistance, Golde negotiated for commercial development of the cell line and products to be derived from it. This brought about an agreement of about $5 million dollars to the Regent of the university and Golde with the Genetics Institute and Sandoz. Moore having discovered the market potential sued all those involved in a series of suits. Moore premised his action as an invasion of his rights and for conversion of his personal property. He argued that the law of torts protects against interference with possessory and ownership interest in personal property. He theorised that he continues to own his cells following their removal from his body, at least for purposes of directing their use and that since he never consented to their use in potentially lucrative medical research, the defendants converted his property. He claimed a proprietary interest in each of the products that may be created from his cell or the patented cell-line.

The Supreme Court of California (comprising Lucas CJ, Eagelson, Kannard, Arabian, Panelli, Mosk and Broussard JJ) struck out Moore's claim for conversion on the ground of policy and that he had no limited property rights in removed cells. However, it observed that its disposal should be governed by the principle of informed consent correlative upon a fiduciary duty requiring the doctor to make full disclosure of all relevant information. The lead judgment read by Panelli J (to which all the judges except Mosk and Broussard JJ concurred) revealed the policy consideration that informed the decision. Panelli J stated:

> While we do not purport to hold that excised cells can never be property for any purpose whatever, the novelty of Moore's claim demands express consideration of the polices to be served by extending liability...there are three reasons why it is inappropriate to impose liability for conversion based upon the allegation of Moore's complaint. First, a fair balancing of the relevant policy considerations counsels against extending the tort. Second, problems in this area are better suited for legislative resolution. Third, the tort of conversion is not necessary to protect patient's rights. For these reasons we conclude that the use of excised human cells in medical research does not amount to conversion.

In the considered view of the court, extending the tort by conversion into this area of biomedicine could hinder access to necessary raw material for research purposes. It noted that thousand of human cell-lines already exist in tissue repositories. About 49 per cent of research in medical institute surveyed used human tissues or cells in their research. The advantages of the development of human therapeutic products derived from human tissues or cells or human cell-lines or

---

[46] 793 P. 2d 479 (Cal. Sup.1990).

cloned genes, is too valuable to society that suppression by law suits such as the *Moore case* would do intolerable damage to society. Noteworthy they rejected the proposition that in medical cases the court should hook and sinker swallow and import legal concepts designed for resolution of distinct societal conflict into medicine. The Court said:

> What Moore is asking us to do is to impose a tort duty on scientists to investigate the consensual pedigree of each human cell sample used in research. To impose such a duty, which would affect medical research of importance to all of society, implicates policy concern far removed from the traditional, two-party ownership disputes in which the law of conversion arose.

Mosk J in his dissenting judgment however thought that the legal concept of ownership was broad enough to give Moore some ownership rights. His Lordship noted that biological products of genetic engineering became patentable in 1980 in *Diamond* v. *Chakrabarty*.[47] In his view this drastically reduces the hitherto free access of exchange of new cell line and products among researcher. On this basis, the majority argument for free circulation of information flies out. That being so, if the patentee can seek commercial protection, there should be nothing unethical for Moore to also claim a commercial protectable interest. Concluding on the claim for conversion he said:

> It follows that the statute regulating the transfers of human organs and blood do not support the majority refusal to recognise a conversion cause of action for commercial exploitation of human blood cells without consent. On the contrary, because such statute treat both organs and blood as property that can legally be sold in a variety of circumstances, they impliedly support Moore's contention that his blood cells are likewise property for which he can and should receive compensation, and hence are protected by the law of conversion.

There is no doubt that both the lead and dissenting judgments command moral force. In England and Nigeria, the law in this respect remains unsettled. If problems like this should occur, it is reasonable to expect that our courts will resolve the question by adopting a mid-way course between the majority and minority judgment, namely: (i) that body tissues should be classified as objects between 'property' and 'no-property' for which a patient should only enjoy possession rights, ownership rights resting with the state; (ii) in the absence of overriding state interest, the patient ought to be the party to determine the destiny of the tissues and cells; (iii) where these are to be used for commercial purposes, the patient consent should be sought and the commercial property or proceeds shared between the patentee and state, provision being made for the consenting patient; (iv) unauthorised use of body tissue without patient's consent amounts to conversion or trespass as the case may be, unless there exist necessity or state interest. It is suggested that if our law resolves these contending issues in this way, our jurisprudence will have taken the good reasoning in the *Moore case*, while avoiding its doubtful slippery reasoning.

---

[47] (1980) 447 US 303.

Chapter Eight

The genetic investigation

The human body is made up of about 100 trillion tiny cells. According to available scientific evidence each of these tiny 100 trillion cells function like a walled city, with features of power plants generating cell energy, factories producing proteins, vital chemical units fostering its commerce, complex transportation system guiding specific chemicals from point to point within the cell and beyond, sentries at the barricades controlling the export and import markets, monitoring the outside world for signs of danger, disciplined armies standing ready to grapple with invader, with a centralised genetic government maintains order.[1] Each of these cells has tens of thousands of genes and DNA (deoxyribonucleic acid) which tells the cells how to function and it provides vital information on many features of the human body. From a study of this, researchers claim to have found vital link between genes and diseases. In 1986 for example, a claim was made that a certain degree of link exist between certain genes and cancer. By isolating and cloning a gene (on chromosome 13) it is believed that the hereditary eye cancer known as retinoblastoma can be prevented. Suspect genes are also being investigated for possible link to bone cancer and chronic myeloid leukaemia.[2] Genetic markers it has been suggested have been found for many other diseases. Going by this it is imagined that genetic testing can help avoid developing some of the over 3,000 known hereditary diseases and currently 50 per cent of childhood diseases that cause death.[3]

This is one reason why the United States of America agreed to support the Human Genome Project (HGP), expected to cost several billion dollars: It is expected to take 15 years or more to completion.[4] Basically the Genome Project is all about genome, which is the entire complement of the genetic materials in the chromosomes (of a person in our case). Chromosomes are composed of genes, about 50,000 to 100,000 in a human body. These chromosomes are made up of DNA, which carry

---

[1] *Newsweek*, August 20, 1979 p. 48. See article entitled, "The Secret of the Human Cell," by Peter Gwynne, Sharson Begley and Mary Hager.

[2] *Awake Magazine*, July 22, 1989, at p.19-13, "The Genetic Revolution: Great Promise with Growth Concern", published by Watch Tower Bible & Tract Society of Pennsylvania, New York.

[3] Mason & Smith, *Law and Medical Ethics*, 4th edn. p.123.

[4] *Above*, n. 2 at p. 10.

genetic information. The genome mapping project is the process whereby genes are assigned to particular chromosomes. It is expected to be a high biotechnological device that would aid in tracking diseases.

Genetic diseases are usually of three main types: (i) Chromosomal genetic disease. This relates to chromosomal altered genes which gives birth to diseases usually associated with mental illness; (ii) Unifactorial defect – it is the presence of an abnormal gene. The defect may be sex-related or x-linked, i.e. the abnormal gene is present in the x-chromosomes, without a corresponding counterpart in the y-chromosomes which determine the male sex; (iii) Multifactorial defect genes. It is reputed to be caused by environmental factor and defects of genes. The state of science today indicate that behavioural and surgical treatment can be used to remedy multifactorial gene defect and to some extent, unifactorial defects. Where medical treatment for genetic disorder is unavailable prevention is the only medical solution.

Genetic inquiry is motivated by good public health concern designed to help detect preventable diseases. Since the genome project is unique in nature and can do much good to society, it has been suggested that its potential benefits should be balanced with any dark ethical question sides. Certainly, like most biotechnology designed to save lives and alleviate suffering, it can also paradoxically be the cause of (needless) death, especially for the unborn where pre-natal investigation reveals possible defects. Discovery of an undesirable gene could be followed with a request for abortion. Genetic engineering or therapy intended to improve life then turns to be the very instrument suggesting termination of life. For example, Jeremy Rifkin is quoted as saying this:

> We want perfect babies, we want perfect plants and animals. We want a better economy. There's no evil intent here. The road to the Brave New World is paved with good intentions. Step-by-step, we are deciding to engineer part of the genetic code of living things. Two important questions emerge: If we are going to engineer the genetic code, what criteria does this society establish for determining good and bad, useful and dysfunctional genes. And I would like to know whether there is an institution anyone here would trust with the ultimate authority to decide the genetic blue print for a living thing.[5]

Ethico–legal questions

We can conveniently classify the ethical questions genetic testing raises into four: economics, eugenics, population control, and commercialism.

Economics

By current valuation the project could span over fifteen years to completion and cost untold billions of dollars. The relevant American department has already asked

[5] Above n. 2 at. p. 13.

for the sum of US$40 million for the genome project expected to gulp US$200 million per year.[6] This can be colossal sum of the resources allocated to health care. Some have questioned the worth of such resource commitment on the ground that its usefulness remains doubtful. While some geneticists consider a detailed knowledge of the human DNA to be the 'Holy Grail' that can better our understanding of human genes and diseases, others doubt its usefulness. Those who doubt claim that only a small fraction of the total genome would yield information that would have immediate medical value. It is on this basis that resources allocation to the project is suspect. The morality of committing money to a dubious project when other possible more pressing causes of diseases such as social conditions, e.g., housing, sanitation, poverty, drug addiction, poor health, etc., remain largely unaddressed is weighty.

Fears have also been expressed that making the HGP a medical social focal point could direct attention away from present contemporary issues of environment, gender and other like social issues. These arguments notwithstanding, it is suggested that from the backdrop experience of most states commitment to military expenditure with virtually no creative usefulness, no amount of money can be too much for a speculative beneficial medical technology.

Eugenics

Family information about real or possible genetic problem has the potential of encouraging abortion for eugenic reason. Quest for perfect babies being the aim of gene therapy or engineering can lead to emotional reactions to disability. Abortion for eugenics is certainly questionable. Scientific knowledge is increasingly pointing that certain diseases occur more frequently with certain racial groups, attributed to genotype. If this is reliable, then we may well progress to a stage where it will amount to discrimination to belong to a group susceptible to a particular disease. Thought like this may have influenced the Nazi policy of 'racial hygiene' under Adolph Hitler. Some commentators are of the opinion that it is rather too premature to condemn the polity without careful analysis of its underlying roots.[7] For instance, while the Nazi policy has been widely condemned, it must be noted that eugenic policy is not peculiar to Nazi. Even jurisdictions that pride human rights are as guilty as the Nazi. For example the US Supreme Court in *Buck* v. *Bell*,[8] authorised involuntary sterilisation of a mentally ill patient on ground of utility. The court said:

---

[6] Ibid., at p. 10.

[7] G Annas, *Standard of Care* (1993) p. 149-159 cited in Kennedy & Grubb, *op. cit.*, p. 4-8. See also M D A Freeman, Sterilising the Mentally Handicapped, in MDA Freeman (ed.) *Medicine, Ethics and the Law* (1988) p.55 which reveals that eugenics has its root resting far back 1869 in the University of London, and that even some American states like Michigan and Indiana passed laws authorising compulsory sterilisation for eugenic reasons. It is said that the founder of the eugenic movement in the University of London was Sir Francis Galten in the 1880's.

[8] (1927) 274 US 200.

> It is better for all the world, if instead of waiting to execute degenerated offspring for crime, or let them starve for their imbecility, society can prevent those who are manifestly unfit from continuing their kind [9]

An analysis of the statement is revelatory that cost-benefit analysis underline today's appeal of eugenics. Some have advocated it as a possible means in the search for perfect babies.[10] James Watson (a co-discoverer of DNA) is reputed to have said, 'we used to think our fate is in the stars, now we know in large measure our fate is in our genes.' Can fate be tied to our genes? If that is correct, then a person may be nothing more than an assemblage of the molecules. This will invariable mean we may not be different from manufactured goods or other objects. Humans can therefore be subject to quality control measures like manufactured products in a search for optimal species. Effectively, human can then be seen as mere articles that can be sold, purchased and destroyed. That kind of thinking could remove whatever moral objections there are to surrogate motherhood, adoption, etc.

Furthermore if the statement of John Watson were to be valid for all purposes, then behaviour becomes a product of genes raising new frontiers to questions on criminal responsibility for criminal actions. This would be a serious matter considering that some geneticist claim that the possession of the 47 xyy karyotype (extra y chromosome) can make a person more susceptible to crime. If it is so, will it not be cruel to hold a person with an extra y-chromosome responsible for his criminal action? If yes, to what degree? How do we equate it with accident? These are burning moral issues that would remain with us as long as the HGP progresses.

Population control

One purpose of genetic screening is to reveal early enough disease or likelihood of it in an unborn child. Armed with it parents can take necessary action to choose abortion or medical treatment to avoid giving birth to defective children. If a disposition towards disease or defect is one that cannot be rectified, the option available to the parents will naturally be an abortion, or carry the foetus to full term and thereafter live with the defective child. The abortion option (when preferred) raises paradoxical question of the desirability or otherwise of a project intended to

---

9 (1927) 274 US 200 at 207.

10 Huxley, *Brave New World*. For general reading see, I. Pullen, Patients, Families and Genetic Information, in E. Sutherland and A. McCall Smith (eds.) *Family Rights* (1990) chapter 3; R.F.Chadwick, What Counts for Success in Genetic Counselling (1993) 19 *J. Med Ethics* 43; S. Gevers, Use of Genetic Data, Employment and Insurance: An International Perspective (1993) 7 *Bioethics* 126; A Lippman, Prenatal Genetic Testing and Screening: Constructing Needs and Reinforcing Inequities (1991) 17 *Amer. J. Law Med.* 15; A.V. Campbell, Ethical Issues in Prenatal Diagnosis (1984) 288 *BMJ* 1633 and for general medical discussion on genetics, see A.E.H. Emery, *Elements of Medical Genetics* (6th edn. 1983). See White Paper, Human Fertilisation and Embryology: A Framework for Legislation, Published in November 1987 (CM 259) para. 37 which prohibits "the artificial creation of human beings with certain pre-determined characteristics through modification of an early embryo's genetic structure" — what journalist commonly call "designer babies".

save life being the very instrument for termination of it. It is on this ground that the project is open to serious ethical objection.

Commercialism

This could become topical in the context of who owns and can protect or patent products produced by the Genome Project. The questions raised in this context include the following: whether it would be proper to permit the establishment of business concerns for purposes of mapping and sequencing of specific areas of human genome? If yes, who should own and patent the final results? Or should discoveries be patent to government, the fund provider? Would national patent not adversely affect international co-operation on the global genome mapping project?

Admirable as the project may seem, there is a need to balance it with issues such as those of autonomy and confidentiality. Dictates of autonomy requires that all screening must be done with the consent of the patient. Confidentiality requires that the result of screening shall be treated as personal to the patient. Disclosure to third parties should only be with the patient's consent. The underlying reason for the principle is not unconnected with the fact that unauthorised disclosure of information can be adverse. For example, information that reveals disease or disposition to disease can be the cause of discrimination against a patient from others. Not to be overlooked also is the troubling effect certain information may cause the individual. For example, it could trouble an individual to learn that his genes show a disposition to say breast cancer.

Genetic counselling

There are many reasons why a person may wish to know about his genetic makeup. It may be needed for a person to make decisions on marriage, child-bearing, employment and choice of social habits. How a doctor handles it is by no means easy. If screening information exists about a patient, it can be argued that the patient acquires a right of access to it. Doctors by the very nature of their calling however owe their patients a duty to protect their patients even from themselves eg. from information that may have troubling effect on the patient. How a doctor handles this delicate situation can be challenging. It would appear settle law that the patient is entitled upon request to inspect and take copies of his medical information.[11] He is however not treated as the owners of the information. Ownership rests with the doctor. That being the case, the doctor can control its disclosure.

A failure to detect genetic abnormality after screening can expose a doctor to claims by parents and disabled children for negligent screening or counselling as the case may be. So unsuspectingly, counselling can pose dangers for him. It could place him in a position where he has to draw the line between normal and abnormal

---

[11] See *MecLnermey* v. [1991] 2 Med LR 267 (NBCA) ; *C* v. *C* [1946] 1 All ER562, *Re Kitchell and St Michael's Hospital* (1980) 112 DLR (3d) 360 (Out HC). See also I. Pullen, Patients, Families and Genetic Information, in E. Sutherland and A. McCall Smith (eds.) *Family Rights* (1990) chapter 3.

foetus. If he does, ethical responsibility for parents reaction to his advice can be unfairly shifted to him, a thing most doctors would least desire. If it is considered slippery, would allowing the parents do it be a better option? Is it not possible that such a shift can be the basis for a law suit in the nature of a claim structured on inadequacy of counsel which possibly prevents parents in making prompt decision to terminate? Who should decide? And what impact will the drawn line have on less-able members of our society? If there is revealed abnormality, should the burden of recommending abortion or suggest sterilisation rest with the doctor? What intervention will society accept as baseline for recommending abortion or sterilisation based on genetic revelations? How far should say employers be permitted to screen its workforce on the basis of genomes? These are some of the many varied problems that confront us in this respect.

In *Becker* v. *Shwartz*,[12] the New York Court of Appeal held that failure by a doctor to recommend amniocentesis to a mother of 37, who by virtue of her age had a risk of bearing a handicapped child constituted negligence, thereby raising liability for the birth of a handicapped child. Damage assessed included the cost of institutional care of the child suffering from Down's syndrome. Aside a wrongful birth claims by parents, the handicap child may also claim damages for defect. The basis for the claim will likely be that the counsellor's negligence prior to its birth resulted in his being an abnormal child, when its birth could have been avoided by an abortion advice. Though the courts are generally dismissive of actions within this bracket, possibility of success is not impossible.[13]

Since the American court in *Diamond* v. *Chakrebarty*,[14] authorised patenting of product of genetic engineering, it is suggested that the question of who can become a patentee can raise litigation controversy.

---

[12] 386 NE 2d 807 (NY 1978), see also *Noccash* v. *Burger* 290 SE 2d 825 (Va 1982), *Salih* v. *Engield Health Authority* [1990] 1 Med LR 333, *Gregory* v. *Pembrokeshire Health Authority* [1989] 1 Med LR 81, *Dumer* v. *St Michael's Hospital* 233 NW 2d 372 (Wis, 1975). See also G.G. Sarno, Recoverability of Compensation for Mental Anguish or Emotional Distress for Tortiously Causing Another's Birth (1989) 74 *ALR* 4th 798; C Dyer, Boy Wins Damages after Injury in Utero (1992) 304 *BMJ* 1400.

[13] *Gleitman* v. *Cosgrove* 296 NYS 2d 687 (1967).

[14] (1980) 447 US 303.

Chapter Nine

Neonatal treatment decisions

Neonatal treatment decision, that is, the decision about treatment for severely handicapped and premature newborns, poses ethico-legal dilemmas with increasingly sophisticated medical techniques. The paradigm of self-determination and autonomy applied to adult does not ordinarily apply in neonatal treatment decisions. The reason is that due to immaturity a neonate cannot be said to be vested with sufficient knowledge to warrant autonomy. The birth of defective neonate child forces society to choose between competing visions of what gives human life value and the role of modern medical technology in that vision.[1] It is thought that defective neonates

---

[1] For general detailed reading, see "Developments in the Law" (1990) 103 *Harv. LR* 1584 R. Weir, *Selective Non-treatment of Handicapped Newborns* (1984); D Vidyasagar & A Sarnaik (eds) *Neonatal and Paediatric Intensive Care* (1985); Rhoden, Treatment Dilemmas for imperilled Newborns: Why Quality of Life Counts (1985) 58 S. Cal. LR 1283; N Robertson (ed) *Textbook on Neonatology* (1986); Ellis, Letting Defective Babies Die: Who decides? (1982) 7 *Am. J. L. & Med* 393; Paris, Terminating Treatment for Newborns: A Theological Perspective (1982) 3 *Law, Med & Health Care* 120: Note, Medical Treatment Decision-making for Seriously Handicapped Infants: Is there a Role for the Federal Government (1988) 29 *BCL Rev.* 715 Lawton, Carder & Weisman, Recent Governmental Action regarding the Treatment of Seriously ill Newborns (1985) 11 *JC & UL* 405; Jackson, Severely Disabled Newborns: To live or Let Die? (1987) 8 J. Legal Med. 135; Koop, life and Death and the Handicapped Newborn (1989) 5 *Issues L & Med* 101; Schneider, Rights Discourse and Neonatal Euthanasia (1988) 76 *Calif. L. Rev* 151; Huefner, Severely Handicapped Infants with Life-Threatening conditions; Federal Intrusions into the Decision Not To Treat (1986) 12 *Am. JL & Med* 171, *Cantrell, Bowen* v. *American Hospital Association*: Federal Regulation is Powerless To Save Baby Doe (1986) 19 *Ind L. Rev.* 1199; Rosenblum & Grant, The Legal Response to Babies Doe: An Analytical Prognosis (1986) 1 *Issues L. & Med* 391; Stevenson, Ariagno, Kutner, Raffin & Yound, The Baby Doe Rule (1986) 255 *JAMA* 1909 Robertson, Involuntary Euthanasia of Defective Newborns (1975) 27 *Stan. L. Rev*213, Pueschei, Ethical consideration in the Life of a child with Down-Syndrome (989) 5 *Issues L.& Med* 87, Note, New Rights for Handicapped Newborns: Baby Doe and Beyond (1985) 22 *Cal W.L. Rev* 127; McLone, The Diagnosis, Prognosis and outcome for the Handicapped Newborn: A Neonatal View (1986) 2 *Issues L & Med* 15; 1 Laing, withdrawing from invasive Neonatal Intensive Care in JK Mason (ed) *Paediatric Forensic Medicine and Pathology* (1989), D O Raphael, Handicapped Infants; Medical Ethics and the Law (1988) 14 *J. Med Ethics* 5, D Brahams, Putting Arthur's Case in Perspective (1986) *Crim LR* 378, AGM Campbell, Children in a Persistent Vegetative State (1984) 289 *BMJ* 1022, r Gillon, Conclusion. The Arthur's Case Revisited (1986) 292 *BMJ* 543, H Kuhse, A modern Myth. That Letting Die is not the International Causation of Death: some Reflections on the Trial and Acquittal of Dr. Leonard Arthur (1984) 1 *J. Appl. Philosophy* 21; J Harris, Ethical Problems in the Management of some severely Handicapped Children (1981) 7 *J Med. Ethics* 117; A Whitelaw, Death as an option in Neonatal Intensive

phenomena is likely to increase with increasing drug abuse by pregnant women and the continuing spread of the AIDS virus. While advance in medicine enables society cope more with these infants, the financial and social cost invites a reconsideration of values. Unlike in common law England and Nigeria, current decisions to withhold or withdrawal medical treatment for neonates in the United States of America is controlled by federal legislation. We shall treat this subject by first considering the matter from the various jurisdictions in the following turn – USA, Britain and other Commonwealth jurisdictions. One point is worthy of note, though neonatologist can now prolong the lives of many neonates even where they have inherited degenerative diseases, they remain unable to correct the most severe handicaps. As a result the general practice amongst neonatologist has been to withhold treatment, a practice that has generated significant controversy among doctors, lawyers and other commentators.[2]

Infanticide can be described as the killing of an infant child by its mother.[3] It is punishable as manslaughter. In England the crime was created in 1922 to avoid public distaste for treating such killings as murder. Generally, legislation treats the killing of an infant, a child under the age of 12 months as infanticide. It is different from selective non-treatment of an infant. While infanticide is the causing of death, the latter is more a regime of non-treatment of an infant, which can result in its death. The latter constitutes the main discourse in this chapter. The ethics of selective treatment option of neonates rest on a distinction being drawn between an *act* on the one hand, and *omission* on the other. We will leave for detail discussion the moral relevance of the distinction until we engage in a similar discuss in the context of euthanasia in chapter 11. For now we shall only concentrate on their correlation in the context of the chapter topic.

Selective non-treatment of a child is often adopted if a baby is born defective. As a treatment option it is an indication that its parents desire that it should be allowed to die. In the process sustenance is often withdrawn as was the case in *Airedale National Health Service Trust* v. *Bland*[4] though Bland was not an infant. He was 17 years. It is in this vein that selective non-treatment closely resembles euthanasia. However it appears less graphic, raising it own unique difficulties. Selective non-treatment deals with a vulnerable life — a child who cannot give consent or express a feeling on the subject-matter. In euthanasia the adult person may to some extent be able to express his feeling on the proposal to terminate life. It

---

Care (1986) 2 *Lancet* 328; D Brahams, No obligation to Resuscitate a Non-viable Infant (1988) 1 *Lancet* 1176; G J Fairlurn, 'Kuhse, Singer and slippery slopes' (1988) 14 *J. Med Ethics* 132; J K Mason D W Meyers, Parental Choice and Selective Non-Treatment of Defective Newborns: A view from Mid-Atlantic (1986) 12 *J. Med Ethics* 67.

[2] Child Abuse Amendment Act of 1984 which amends the Federal Child Abuse Prevention and Treatment Act, 1974 (USA).

[3] See s.327A of Criminal Code, LFN 2004, Cap.

[4] [1993] 1 All ER 821, [1993] 12 BMLR 64 (HL).

is for this reason that selective non-treatment provokes emotional reactions, suggesting that it could be one dark side of medicine.

Though screening or scanning makes possible detection of most abnormality in a foetus, it is not full proof. Certain severe abnormality may not be detected, and even if it is, possibility exists that counselling of parents following it can be done negligently, and the foetus is carried to full term only to be delivered with severe defect. Rather than bring joy to the parents on delivery, the birth of a defective child can bring mixed feelings of joy and sadness. Parents are from the start saddled with the need to give intense care, a thing they may not be emotionally and financially able to do. Not to be overlooked is the effect the birth could have on the hospital, health delivery system and resource allocation. Care of defective neonates raises moral dilemma for the couple and doctor, ranging from what should be done with and to the neonate, whether it should be allowed to die by a withdrawal of life sustenance, or whether its death should be quickened by medication? If any of these decisions is arrived at, next they will be confronted with considering the legal effects of their inaction or action aimed at terminating the life of the neonate.

These questions can be troubling especially for the doctor who by the ethics of his profession ought to do all in his power to preserve and sustain life. In that circumstance, his professional calling dictates that he sustains the life of the defective neonate. But here again he has to help an unwilling parent to accept the child, who most likely feel that their child would be better off if dead than alive. How he deals in balancing his professional ethics with parents request for non-treatment aimed at causing death, is by no means easy. In arriving at a decision, a doctor is expected to consider matters such as the following: do the parents have the right to determine the life of the child? If yes, on what basis do they judge that termination of the child's life is better. Is it on the quality of life the child is expected to live? Would that not amount to a materialistic view of life? Who is in the best position to judge the quality of life of another? These are but few of the puzzling questions that confronts the doctor and parents.

The position of law is clear. Section 307 of the Criminal Code[5] states that a child becomes a person when it completely proceeds in a living state from the body of its mother. Thus, a baby has the same right of body sovereignty as an adult. It is criminal to kill it. Depending on the circumstances of a case, it would amount to manslaughter or murder. Therefore, any act or omission aimed at terminating the life of a child is criminal. This position is re-enforced by the provision of sections 301-303 and 309 which places a positive duty on any person in charge of a child to provide it necessaries of life; failing which he will be criminally responsible. Therefore, any selective non-treatment in Nigeria is criminal.

Some have however suggested that the prohibition of killing notwithstanding personhood should be understood in terms of intellectual development and capacity.

---

[5] S. 315-317 of Criminal Code, LFN 2004.

What is more, a defective neonate is seen as an unnecessary burden to the parents and society. On this basis, they argue that selective non-treatment aimed at causing death of a neonate is equivalent to, feticide or contraception. Since in those areas of medicine parents wish generally determine destiny, it is suggested that neonate non-treatment should equally be so treated. On this premise it is argued that parents' wishes, not that of anyone else or the court or law for that matter, should be primary. This viewpoint has some support with paediatric practice. For example, in the famous case of *R* v. *Arthur*,[6] Dr. Dunn's evidence was to the effect that the duty to maintain life is not absolute and that in some cases the paediatrician acknowledges that it may be better to allow a baby die in its best interest.[7] Farquharson J charge to the jury in the following terms: 'I imagine that you will think long and hard before concluding that doctors of the eminence we have heard..have evolved standards that amount to committing a crime,' recognises that the boundaries of neonatal intensive care-giving can sometimes be controversial, involving the primary consideration whether or not there is a duty of care, and if so, the extent of the duty.

There is, however, powerful counter argument suggesting continuing criminalisation of selective non-treatment. In the matter of life it is strange to give parents the privilege of playing god. Why for example, it could be asked should parent be the sole persons to determine the 'quality of life' of a child? Our experience with the abolition of twins killing in the Calabar area of Nigeria,[8] is illustrative that even parents view of life may sometimes be wrapped in fallacies.

The troubling effect and underlying message selective non treatment sends to less-able adult persons should not to be overlooked. After all would it not be better for society to allow the neonate grow up to decide for himself the serious question of quality of life? Selective non-treatment procedures assume certain facts which may not be eternal truths. Who can categorically state without fear of contradictions that we cannot learn from the lives of defective adults in our society, or are they altogether useless? Should we overlook the vital lessons of empathy that can be learnt by responding to the needs of less-able persons? The justification for selective non-treatment hinged on a fine distinction between *commission* and *omission*, which is in reality mere legal nicety as the obvious result of both is the death. Graphically put this way, selective non-treatment would amount to unlawful homicide.

---

[6] [1981] 12 BMLR 1. For an analysis of *Arthur* case, see R. Gillon, An Introduction to Philosophical Medical Ethics: The Arthur's Case (1985) 290 *BMJ* 1117; M.J. Gunn and J.C. Smith, Arthur's Case and the Right to Life of a Down's Syndrome Child [1985] *Crim L.R.* 705 and D. Brahams, Putting Arthur's Case in Perspective [1986] *Crim L.R.* 387; D. Poole, Arthur's Case (1) Comment [1986] *Crim. LR* 383.

[7] [1981] *The Times*, 6 Nov. p. 12; [1981] 12 BMLR 1at 8. See also L. Gostin, A Moment in Human Development: Legal Protection, Ethical Standards and Social Policy in the Selective Non-treatment of Handicapped Neonates (1985) 11 *Amer. J. Law Med.* 31; A. Whitelaw, Death as an Option in Neonatal Intensive Care [1986] 2 *Lancet* 328.

[8] Twin-killing practice in Calabar was opposed by Mary Slessor, now criminalised: s. 256 of Criminal Code purnishes infanticide

England

We shall now look at the cases to see how the courts have resolved these dilemmas in some jurisdictions. In *Re B (a minor) (wardship medical treatment)*[9] the English Court of Appeal approached the best interest and quality of life question by a consideration of burden—benefit analysis. It was such a bizarre case that Templeman LJ felt that it would be lamentable if the names of the parents of the child were revealed in any way to the general public. The infant suffered from Down's syndrome. She was a mongol, born with intestinal blockage, fatal unless operated upon. When the parents were informed of this they expressed the wish that it would be unkind to operate on the child. They instead preferred that she should be allowed to die within a few days, during which time she be put on sedative to keep her from pain and suffering. The parent informed the doctor of their decision with great sorrow in the considered best interest of the child. They therefore choose not to sign the consent form for an operation on the child. Their refusal prompted the doctor to contact the local authority. By order of court the baby was made a ward of court, so that the operation can be performed. However, when the child was transferred from the hospital where it was born to another hospital facility for the operation, a difference in medical opinion arose. The surgeon who was to perform the operation declined to do so when he was informed that the parents objected. He got in touch with the parents on telephone who informed him that due to the fact that the child was mongoloid they did not wish to have the operation performed. The surgeon then decided to respect the wishes of the parents. The local authority went back to the judge who gave the initial order. At this point the court ordered non-treatment. In the face of judicial indecision and medical disagreement, the question of whether to treat or not, came before the English Court Appeal.

The Court of Appeal disagreed with the court of first instance in refusing to authorise the surgical operation on the child. In its view the trial judge put too much reliance on the wishes of the parents when the real issue for determination was what the best interest of the child is. It accordingly authorised surgical treatment because in its considered view that served the best interest of the baby. Templeman LJ stated:

> The question which this court has to determine is whether it is in the interest of this child to be allowed to die within the next week or to have the operation in which case if she lives she will be a Mongoloid child, but no one can say to what extent her mental or physical defect will be apparent...But in the present case the choice which lies before the court is this: 'whether to allow an operation to take place which may result in the child living for 20 to 30 years

[9] [1990] 3 All ER 927, [1981]1 WLR 1421 (CA).

> as a Mongoloid or whether (and I think this may be brutally the result) to terminate the life of a Mongoloid child because she also has an intestinal complaint. Faced with that choice I have no doubt that it is the duty of this court to decide that the child must live.
>
> The judge was much affected by the reasons given by the parents and came to a conclusion that their wishes ought to be respected. In my judgment, he erred, in that the duty of the court is to decide whether it is in the interest of the child that an operation should take place. The evidence in this case only goes to show that if the operation takes place and is successful then the child may live the normal span of a Mongoloid child with the handicaps and defects and life of a Mongoloid child, and it is not for this court to say that life of that description ought to be extinguished.[10]

The judgment of the court reveals that by 'best interest' the court is merely referring to the 'quality of life' test, which itself is vague and meaningless as the former. For example, it does not tell whether the test ought to be determined by reference to social worth, economic cost, or the supports potential or human contentment that will be tasked by keeping the neonate alive. The phase 'best interest' does not help determine which handicap merit treatment, and which do not. May be to smoke screen selective non-treatment decisions the court have chosen deliberately to make its guidelines fluid. Whatever, 'best interest' is difficult to assess empirically. There is no generally acceptable meaning for it, especially as it continues to provide counter argument justification for termination lives. Quality is logically an evaluative property. That being the case it would not be all together right to determine it by merely different human lives. What may appear quality to an able-person may not in all respects by the measure of a less-able.

That the concept of "quality of life" is unclear and confusing is judicially recognised. Liacos J in *Superintendent of Belchertown* v. *Saikewicz* said:

> The six factor identified by the judge as weighing against chemotherapy was the quality of life possible for him even if treatment does not bring about remission. To the extent that this formulation equates the value of life with any measure of the quality of life, we firmly reject it.[11]

After *Re B*,[12] *R* v. *Arthur*,[13] came up for determination. The baby was born with apparently uncomplicated Down's syndrome. The mother told the consultant paediatrician, Dr. Leonard Arthur, that she did not wish the baby to survive, and so she rejected the baby. Dr. Arthur, a paediatrician of high repute and impeccable professional integrity then recorded in the medical notes 'parents do not wish it to

---

[10] [1981] 1 WLR 142.

[11] (1977) 370 NE 2d 64. The case had to do with whether or not a mentally handicapped patient suffering from leukaemia should have chemotherapy.

[12] (1981) [1990] 3 All ER 927, [1981]1 WLR 1421 (CA). See case discussion in D.D. Raphael, Handicapped Infants: Medical Ethics and the Law (1988) *J. Med. Ethics* 5.

[13] [1981] 12 BMLR 1.

survive. Nursing care only.' Thereafter he prescribed dihydrocodeive, a powerful analgesic and noted that the baby should be given nursing care only. Sixty nine hours later the baby died. He was charged for murder, but during the trial, the charge was reduced to attempted murder because the prosecution could not prove the cause of death. Arthur was acquitted at the end of the trial.

If Dr Arthur were a Nigerian paediatrician, he would not have been that lucky in escaping criminal liability. Section 227 of the Criminal Code which criminalises wilful neglects to provide necessaries for children under care may have caught him. So a Nigerian court could reach a decision with different conclusion to that of *Arthur's*. The prescription of 5mg of dihydrocodeine every four hours or at the discretion of the nurse in charge and nursing care only, may be construed wilful neglect. However it can be argued that since our Criminal Code only makes responsible the persons with parental responsibility, and Dr. Arthur was not such a person conviction under our Code cannot be sustained.

The medically accepted standard and legality for selective non-treatment of neonate remained remains confusing. *Arthur* case made no reference to *Re B*. This is disturbing when considered from the context that both are difficult to reconcile in their conclusions when their facts are really not materially different. An opportunity, to clearly restate the law was presented in *Re J (a minor) (wardship: medical treatment)*[14] Baby J suffered almost every conceivable misfortune. Born premature (27 weeks), it weighed only 1.1 kg at birth. It did not breathe at birth, so was put on a ventilator and given antibiotics to counteract infection while being placed on drip. His pulse rate was very low and it was uncertain if it would live. One month after birth it was taken out of the ventilator still sick and handicapped, then followed recurrent convulsion which resulted in making it oxygen-dependent for another one month. Though the prognosis was gloomy, it was discharged. It was readmitted shortly after because it had choked and had become cyanosed. Its treatment was simply traumatic for all, parent, baby and the hospital. His medical situation deteriorated to the point that Baby J was likely to develop serious spastic quadriplegia i.e. paralysis of both arm and legs. It appeared blind and deaf and mute and will develop limited intellectual ability. The question before the court was about what should be done if Baby J suffered another collapse. Scott-Baker J, the trial judge authorised the hospital to treat Baby J within certain parameters, ordering that it should not be re-ventilated in the event it stops breathing.

That was the decision the Official Solicitor appealed against to the English Court of Appeal. His appeal was hinged on two grounds, namely (i) that in *Re C (a minor) wardship medical treatment)*[15] the court gave guidelines on the approach to adopt in relation to the medical treatment of children who are dying and whose death can only be postponed for a short while (ii) that *Re B (a minor) (wardship*

---

[14] [1990] 3 All ER 930, (1990) 6 BMLR 25 (CA).
[15] [1989] 2 All ER 782, [1990] Fam. 26.

medical treatment)[16] gives similar guidelines in relation to severely, but not grossly handicapped children with a shortened but nevertheless substantial expectation of life. In his view the situation of Baby J was somewhere in between the two. He quarrelled with the absolutist approach adopted by the trail judge in authorising the withholding of treatment that could enable the child survive on the grounds of quality of life dictates.

The Court of Appeal rejected the Official Solicitor's argument, and confirmed the judgment of Scot-Baker J. It held that it would not be in Baby J's interest to re-ventilate it by machine in the event that breathing stops unless to do so seemed appropriate by the doctor's opinion in the prevailing clinical situation. Noteworthy, the court recognises that the best interest of a child is to be judge not from the context of persons enjoying normal advantages, but from the context of the handicapped child who would know nothing of a normal life. Lord Donaldson MR stated: 'The starting point is not what might have been, but what is.'

The court acknowledged that deciding the 'critical equation' of best interest of a child is not a matter which admits mathematical precision. That notwithstanding, it noted that the starting point should always be from a strong presumption in favour of a course of action which would prolong life, except for 'cabbage' cases. To avoid encroachment into criminal law jurisprudence in selective non-treatment cases, the court cleverly draw a difference between authorising termination of life, and that of inaction involving withholding treatment designed to prolong life. Lord Justice Taylor said:

> The court never sanctions steps to terminate life. That would be unlawful. There is no question of approving, even in a case of the most horrendous disability a course aimed at terminating life or accelerating death. The court is concerned only with the circumstances in which steps should not be taken to prolong life.[17]

Going by the statement above, it can be argued that the treatment procedure adopted by Dr. Arthur in *R* v. *Arthur* would be illegal, but not the situation in *Re C (a minor) (wardship medical treatment)*. *Re C* was about a moribund child who was dying and no amount of medical skill or care could do more than achieve a brief postponement of the moment of death. In the circumstance the court authorised the hospital to treat only to relieve from pains suffering and distress, so that it could die with dignity. Accordingly, it refused to authorise any treatment regime use of antibiotics or nasogastric-feeding that could prolong long. The ratio in the case seem to be that a distinction ought to be drown between 'living death', with cases where the neonate is severely, but not grossly handicapped with prospect of less life enjoyment. Where death is inevitable in the sense that the neonate is actually dying and medical treatment means a mere balancing of marginal longer life of pain

---

[16] (1981) [1990] 3 All ER 927, [1981]1 WLR 1421 (CA).

[17] [1990] 3 All ER 930 at 943, [1990] 6 BMLR 25 at 40 (CA).

against marginal shorter life free from pain, ending life with dignity is permissible, in contrast with cases where the neonate is severely, but not grossly handicapped with less enjoyment of life. The former can be treated as 'cabbage' cases in which the court ought to ready sanction selective non-treatment. The later on the other hand, as in *Re B*, the court must properly formulate the critical equation cognisant of the fact that severely handicapped may find quality of life rewarding which to the unhandicapped may seen manifestly intolerable. The court recognises that people can be amazing adaptable. But in the end there will be cases in which the answer must be that it is not in the interest of the child to subject it to treatment which will cause increased suffering and produce no commensurate benefit, giving the fullest possible weight to the child, and mankind's desire to survive.[18] But in other cases it may well find for the opposite.

American and Canadian jurisdictions

Neonatal treatment decisions became significant in the 1970s. The first courts to address the issue consistently order treatment. For example, in *Maine Medical Centre* v. *Houle*[19] and *In re McNulty*[20] the courts in Maine and Massachusetts respectively stated that the proposition on quality of life was legally irrelevant and therefore ordered that treatment be given whenever medically feasible. But by contrast, in *Re Infant Doe*,[21] an Indiana court made relevant quality of life argument. It found that the parent's decision to refuse treatment and life saving surgery was a rational choice between acceptable medical alternative. It was this case that sparked up controversy about treatment decisions for neonates. It culminated in the enactment of federal legislation designed to prevent withholding treatment in all but the most hopeless cases.[22]

The first response by the Reagan administration was the use of section 504 of the Rehabilitation Act of 1973 which forbids discrimination against an 'otherwise qualified individual with handicaps solely by reason of his handicap.' It was made to apply and prohibit decisions to withhold treatment for neonates. Using the Department of Health and Human Services (HHS), government sought regulatory

---

[18] Whether or not this fine distinction is mere hair split or substantial is not free from debate, as it would appear that view from a result position no difference exists between both. The end result of both is to terminate life. Argument making splitting distinction formed the basis of Airedale NHS Trust v. Bland case. [1993] 1 All ER 821, (1993) 12 BMLR 64 (HL); but cf. O F Emiri, Euthanasia and Treatment Cessation: A Paradox [1996] *Essence J. of Philosophy*.

[19] No 74 – 145 (Me. Super Ct. Feb 14 1974) (ordered life saving surgery for a deformed infant with brain damage dispute doctor's contrary opinion), cited in Developments in the Law (1990) 103 *Harv. L. Rev* 1387.

[20] No. 1960 (Mass. P. Ct. Feb 15, 1978) cited in (1990) 103 *Harv LR* 1387.

[21] No. GU 8104 – 004 A (Ind. Cir. Ct April 11 1982), cert denied 464 US 961 (1983) reprinted in *Declaratory Judgment in the Infant Doe Case* (1986) 2 *Issues L & Med* 77.

[22] *Above* n. 2 and Note, *above* n. 1 for a discussion on the development of federal legislation and regulation.

regime to ensure the provisions of medically beneficial treatment to these infants.[23] Unfortunately, in *Bowen* v. *American Hospital Association*,[24] the American Supreme Court invalidated s. 504 regulations because the HHS failed to show that its regulations were made pursuant to it, and that it satisfied the requirements of the Administrative Procedure Act.[25] Having killed the regulation made under the Act, government responded by another legislation-the Child Abuse Amendment Act of 1984 which amended the Federal Child Abuse Prevention and Treatment Act 1974. Essentially it was designed to prevent the 'withholding of medically indicated treatment'. By the statute, 'medically indicated treatment' is defined to mean 'reasonable medical judgment'. It provided that:

> 'treatment may only be withheld when in the doctors' opinion (i) the infant is chronically and irreversibly comatose (ii) the provision of such treatment would merely prolong dying or will not be effective in ameliorating or correcting all of the infants life–threatening conditions or otherwise be futile in terms of survival of the infant and (iii) the provision of such treatment would be virtually futile in terms of the survival of the infant and the treatment itself under such circumstances would be inhumane'.

Even when any of the above three exceptions apply the law requires cautionary provision of 'appropriate nutrition, hydration and medication'.[26]

Unfortunately, many years after the federal and state laws, together with regulations made thereunder came into force, making neonatal euthanasia criminal, medical practice is still largely at variance with them, with only a few cases challenging the legality of treatment decisions. It has been suggested that non compliance has been aided by the too poorly defined language of 'reasonable medical judgment' used in the Child Abuse Amendment Act of 1984, thereby providing insufficient guidance. The law also suffers from procedural uncertainty. Since it does not specifically include 'withholding of medically indicated treatment' within the definition of child abuse and neglect, many of its provisions may not extend to medical neglect.[27]

These aside, it contains many objectionable and controversial provisions. For example the provision requiring 'appropriate nutrition, hydration and medication' even when one of the statutory exceptions allows other forms of treatment to be

---

[23] See Developments in Law (1990) 103 *Harv. L. Rev*1387.

[24] 476 US 610 (1986) for discussion on the case, see (1986) 100 *Harv. L* Rev 100 at 285-295 (The Supreme Court, 1985 Term-leading cases).

[25] 5 USC 551-559, 701-706 (1988).

[26] It can be argued that this limitation is nonsensical. Providing artificial nutrition and hydration when treatment ought to be withheld is contradictory because even such minimal support may prolong life. It can be said that the three exceptions to the rule admits of quality of life argument for termination of treatment even though the statute makes a pretence that it is legally irrelevant.

[27] Developments in the Law (1990) 103 *Harv. L. Rev.* 13 at 1519; Freidman & Murray, State Legislation and the Handicapped Newborn: A Moral and Political Dilemma (1984) 5 *Law, Med & Health Care* 156: Rosenblum & Grant, above n.1.

withheld is simply contradictory and can sometimes be counter-productive. Would alternative measures, such as the provision of glucose and fluids to prevent painful dehydration and medication of sedation and pain relief not be more appropriate and caring than forced provision of food and water? Further, though the Act explicitly rejects a quality of life test[28] for neonatal intensive care decision making, it can be argued that its three exceptions are implicitly rooted in the philosophy.

The position in America, and some common law jurisdictions is that the court starts from a presumption in favour of sustaining the life of a neonate. Its right to live — i.e. the right to sanctity of life is first and paramount. From that position if there is any treatment available it must be given to it regardless of what the quality of life is thought to be. The British Colombia (Canada) case of *Re Superintendent of Family and Child Care Services and Dawson*[29] involved one Stephen Dawson, severely retarded in his brain. He was legally blind, partly deaf, incontinent, could not hold a spoon to feed himself, nor walk, stand, talk or hold objects. He had a life–support surgery while 5 months old, by which a shunt was implanted in his brain to draw excess cerebrospinal fluid from his head to another body cavity from where it was expelled or absorbed. Sometime while about 7 years, the shunt had a blockage and the parents though first consenting to remedial surgery, on a rethink withdrew their consent on the ground that the boy should be allowed to die with dignity rather than continue to endure life of suffering. The court rejected their argument.

Mckenzie J stated:

> I cannot accept their view that Stephen Dawson would be better off dead. If it is to be decided that it is in the best interest of Stephen Dowson that his existence cease, then it must be decided that, for him, non-existence is the better alternative. This would mean regarding the life a handicapped child has not only less valuable than the life of a normal child, but also so much less valuable that it is not worth preserving. I tremble at contemplating the consequences if the lives of disabled person are dependent upon such judgment.

Similar views were expressed in Australia by Vincent J of the Supreme Court of Victoria in *Re F.* He said:

> No parent, no doctor, no court, has any power to determine that the life of any child however, disabled that child may be, will be deliberately taken from it...(The law) does not permit them to be decision-makers concerning the quality of life, nor does it enable any assessment to be made as to the value of any human being.[30]

---

[28] Generally 'quality of life' argument is considered an invidious manner of denigrating the social worth of individuals perceived as abnormal by some. See Robertson, above n.1.

[29] (1983) 145 DLR (3d) 610.

[30] *Re F, F* v. *F* (2 July 1986 unreported) cited in Mason & Smith, *op. cit.* 154.

In America, the law does not also permit parents to make decision to terminate the life of a neonate, even if it is handicapped.[31] There is no doubt that unlike other common law jurisdictions (except for the decision in *Re Infant Doe* in America) English authorities suggest that there is no absolute obligation to preserve the life of a defective neonate. The debate however ranges on what should be the best method of diluting the present legal prohibition in almost all jurisdictions of selective non-treatment by balancing it with current medical practice that assent to it. Some have suggested that the fine distinction between killing and selective non-treatment should be abolished. In this direction legislation which authorises neo-naticide aimed at ending pain and suffering has been suggested on grounds that it would be economically efficient to deploy scare resources to other medical needs than in treating defective neonates. Like euthanasia, this may well be on area for judicial rethinking or positive legislative reform.

Much of the principles on abortion apply with necessary contextualisation to neonate treatment choices. Therefore, a consideration of conscientious objection by medical personnel in the context of abortion would necessarily apply with certain modification. Unlike abortion where the court does not consider the views of a father material, it is suggested that neonates treatment should be treated differently. Here the father wishes should be given consideration. Not to be forgotten is the warning that selective non-treatment of defective neonate calls for co-operation of all, doctors, patients, parents, courts and societies. Continued treatment of a defective neonate can and does have potentials in bringing out qualities of goodness and empathy in others that are beneficial to humanity.

Summary

By way of summary the legal position in all the jurisdictions reveal that there is no absolute obligation to preserve the life of a physically abnormal baby. Even then treatment decisions of neonates is often rooted in social, rather than medical judgment, and the often distinction between killing and letting die. Since an analysis of the controversy over control of neonatal treatment decision typically formulates the problem in terms of fundamental conflict between state intervention and

---

[31] See *Re Cicero* (1979) 421 NYS 2d 965; *Maine Medical Centre* v. *Houle* No 74-45 Sup. Ct. (Me 1974); but cf. *Weber* v. *Stony Brook Hospital* 456 NE 2d 1186 (NY, 1983) and *Re Infant Doe* I1982) GU 8204-004 A (Monroe County Cir April 12) all cited in Mason & Smith, *op. cit*, 153-154. These cases decide that selective non-treatment of handicap is permissible. *Re Infant Doe* provoke presidential reaction. Hospitals receiving Federal aid were reminded that they were prohibited from selective non-treatment for handicapped infants as they stand to loss such Federal aid if they pursue a regime of selective non-treatment.

individual, family or medical autonomy, it is suggested that an effective solution should look beyond these to the wider question of the best interest of the neonates and the critical emotional and financial stress it brings to the ultimate care-givers-the parents.

Chapter Ten

Diagnosis of death

What is death remains controversial. There is no legal definition of the term death in Nigeria.[1] The Criminal Code however defines unlawful homicide as the killing of a person.[2] Killing of another person constitutes death as it brings about that consequence. The object killed must be a person. While that may be insufficient to explain death in the sense that it forces us to describe killing, it illuminates its meaning. By equating killing with death, we can construct death as the opposite of life. Some, particularly religionist suggest that it is a change from one form of life to another. Generally it is in common parlance associated with the complete and persistent cessation of respiration and circulation. Somatic death refers to a person's death as an individual, while death of the tissues is referred to as molecular death. [3] Both are usually not contemporaneous in time, the former occurring first and then the later. While persons whose hearts and lungs may cease working may be considered dead by many, modern techniques of life saving procedure like cardiopulmonary resuscitation can now reverse the process.[4]

Some have defined death as irreversible coma and or the irreversible loss of the living matter.[5] Since modern medical science can reverse irreversible damages or coma, death can now begin to raise questions have a bearing on say criminal responsibility, organ transplantation, etc.[6] Brain death is now considered the accepted scientific definition of death. If the brain stem ceases to function, a person is considered dead. Lord Keith of Kinkel, in *Airedale NHS Trust* v. *Bland* said: "In the eyes of the medical world and of the law a person is not clinically dead so long as the brain stem retains its function."[7]

---

[1] There is no statutory definition of death in Nigeria. But the cases are instructive. They treat it as no different from a state of non-existence of a living being.

[2]. S. 315 of Criminal Code of Nigeria, 1956, Cap. LFN, 2004.

[3] J Glaister, *Medical Jurisprudence and Toxicology*, 9th edn. Edinburgh, Livingstone Pub. 1953 p. 127

[4] Generally cardiopulmonary resuscitation (CRP) procedure can combines external heart message and artificial respiration thereby prolonging heart beat and breathing.

[5] S E Ikerinwu, Death.

[6] O Ashiru, Medical Ethical in Relation to the Dead and the Dying (Thanotology) in Akpata (ed.), *Medical Ethics*, Lagos, Lagos Univ. Press, 1999, p. 117 at 119.

[7] [1993] 3 WLR 316 at 359.

Lord Goff lead judgment also corroborated the position. His Lordship said:

> ...as a result of developments in modern medical technology, doctors no longer associate death exclusively with breathing and heart beat, and it has come to be accepted that death occurs when the brain, and in particular the brain stem has been destroyed.[8]

Medically, brain death is treated as death of the whole person. That being so death is the process of dying.

Diagnosis of death include the following:

i. cessation of respiration and circulation
ii. cooling of the body
iii. general muscular placidity of the body and muscles
iv. putrefaction.[9]

Death is a painful experience. News of death of a loved one is always greeted with feelings of hurt and sorrow.[10] It is not uncommon for survivors of a dead who refuse to accept the reality of death to request post-mortem examination of the deceased[11]. Where examination is requested, the pathologist is required to give reliable information based on his examination on the body and any other laboratory investigation or test conducting in the process of examination. Usually a report will include a brief history of the incident that necessitated the examination, date and time specifying receipt of corpse, its condition, person who identified it, time of his examination, description of body parts, sex, wearing apparels, and the probable date and cause of death.

Post-mortem examination is regulating by the Anatomy Acts of 1832 and 1871.[12] Both regulate and control post-mortem examination. It stipulates who may practice anatomy, who can give permission for post-mortem examination, when an examination can be made, what particulars the post-mortem report should include, arrangement for the disposal of corpse and provision exempting physicians from civil and criminal liability for acts done pursuant to the statute.

The principal reasons for requesting post-mortem dissection are[13] (i) to determine the cause of death (ii) to furnish instruction to medical students and doctors in the

---

[8] Ibid., at 366 – 7.

[9] Putrefaction describes the stage where the body changes from the organic to the inorganic state.

[10] See Ashiru, above, ftnt.6. for a detail list of social response stages to the reality of death. These include denial, isolation, anger, bargaining, depression and acceptance.

[11] Ikerionwu, above, f.n. 5 where the view is expressed that request for post-mortem examination has increased in frequency because most African's no longer accept death as a natural phenomenon, attributing it to seen or unseen enemy works.

[12] . Both English legislation are statutes of general application, in that they were part of the Laws of England as at 1st January 1900. They apply to the extent that they are not repealed and or inconsistent with local enactment. For detail discussion on the applicability of foreign (English) statute in Nigeria, see A.D. Badiaki, *Interpretation of Statutes*.

[13] Glaister, above, .n.3at 50.

study of anatomy (iii) to assist medical science determine the causes and nature of diseases or ailments that affects the human body.

Diagnosis of death

Death is a process. Many years ago, it was associated with permanent cessation of breathing and of the beating of the heart. But we now know better. A medical dictionary defines death as a gradual dying process at the cellular level, with tissues varying in their ability to withstand deprivation of oxygen.[14] So while to the lay man the permanent cessation of breathing and heartbeat is considered death, to the doctor death is a process. For a doctor, it is the permanent state of anoxia which occurs either when respiration ceases or the heart fails. Even when in the eyes of lay persons the heart stop beating or breathing ceases, the individual cells in the body can continue to function until their residual oxygen is exhausted. The length depends on their individual oxygen consumption. It has been suggested that hairs and nails growth may continue after cessation of heartbeat. Doctors are known to harvest skin 24 hours after cessation of breathing (irreversible asystole) for transplant purposes. This is why the cessation of breathing and heartbeat is now conceived differently. Theoretically, therefore, there ought to be evidence of cellular death before a doctor makes a pronouncement of death.[15] But that is hardly the practice. Generally doctors use stethoscope to determine death. Scientifically the accepted definition of death is the death of the brain. Empirically, brain cells can withstand anoxia but for a short period – a few minutes only. This mean that if 'brain death' is the accepted diagnosis we may be left in a situation where a patient in irreversible cardio-respiratory failure is treated as *dying* but not *dead*. Death between cardiac and cerebral failure is what medically and legally qualifies as death.[16]

Cessation of breathing/respiration can be reversed by doctor's intervention. When the heart fails to distribute oxygen to the tissues the process of cellular death begins. If the patient is saved by doctor or mechanical intervention, it will be possible for a majority of the organs to recover, but not the brain because it is the most sensitive organ to oxygen deprivation and it is irreplaceable. That is what makes it possible to have a situation where the majority of body organs come back to normal function after mechanical intervention but with substantially damaged brain as controller.[17]

Though legal constrains and dictionary definition may have delayed acceptance of death as a process, modern reality reveals it is. At a philosophical level, four possible definitions of death can be identified. A commentator identifies the four as

---

[14] *Sleadman Medical Dictionary.*

[15] Mason & Smith, *op. cit*, p. 281.

[16] Ibid.

[17] R. Veatch, *Death, Dying and Biological Revolution* (1989 revised edn.) p. 16 cited in Kennedy & Grubb *op. cit*, 1373.

follows: (i) a pure formal analysis of death that gives the structure and specifies the framework that must be given content; (ii) a concept of death which attempts to fill the formal definition of death. At this level the material question is what is so essentially significant about life that its loss is termed death; (iii) identifying the locus of death i.e. what in the organism should we look for to locate death if it occurs; and (iv) identifying the criteria to determine death – that is, what technical tools do we need to apply to the locus to determine if an individual is living or dead? In the view of the commentator failing to make these distinctions has resulted in conceptual and practical difficulties in the diagnosis of death. [18]

Going by the first level of the definition of death, i.e., its formal definition, it can be stated that 'death is a complete change in the status of a living entity characterised by the irreversible loss of those characteristics that are essentially significant to it.'[19] In the case of a human, it refers to the essential characteristics that make us attribute humanness to a person, a philosophical question involving ethics and value judgment. Since personhood is often associated with concepts of being created in God's image, ability to evolve a culture, language, etc., any concept of death will have to depend on our evaluation of these qualities. Humans are complex, integrated, organism with capacities for internal regulation. This is so in two ways: (i) capacity for integrating internal bodily environment, done usually unconscious though highly complex homeostatic, feedback mechanism; and (ii) capacity for integrating one's self, including one's body with the social environment through consciousness e.g. interaction with other persons. This capacity for internal regulation is what essentially gives meaning to life. When it is lost a person can be considered dead. Going by the analysis of Veatch,[20] the irreversible loss of the embodied capacity for social interaction more approximates death. Since the death of the brain signals the irreversible loss of essential functions related to internal regulation, because it is the anatomical substratum, the locus of death is 'brain death'.

Death can either be explained by the criteria of loss of capacity for social interaction or bodily integration. In both cases brain death satisfies the test. When brain processes cease, the patient loses two functions: (i) integrating and co-ordination functions carried on primarily by the cerebellum and brain stem; and (ii) psychological function which makes for consciousness, thought and feeding. Personhood devoid of these social interaction because of brain death may be said (though debatable) to have lost the essence of living. Bodily integration on the other hand enables the living organism to organise and regulate itself. The permanent and irreversible loss of the function of the brain terminates bodily integration. So from our analysis, both the criteria of loss of capacity for social integration and bodily integration indicate the brain as locus – the organ whose death determines death.

---

[18] Ibid.

[19] Ibid., at p. 17.

[20] Above n. 17.

Using brain death as locus in both social and bodily integration is not without controversy on moral grounds. Critiques of the social integration criterion using the brain argue that there is no consensus on the essence of personhood. The argument based on essence of personhood would logically dictate that severely senile or retarded patients are not persons and so dead. That is certainly absurd. Such an argument will also treat persons in the category of *Quilan*[21] dead, a preposterous way to reason. Quilan was a woman who suffered permanent damage to the higher centre of her brain but with the lower brain functioning. Five years after being removed from the respirator that supported her breathing she remained in a PVS state but with her heart and lung functioning without need for mechanical support. The sheer implication of the personhood (social) criteria would be to treat *Quilan* as no different from a corpse. Such a conclusion certainly will shock the reasonable man.[22] Despite this controversy, it is now widely accepted judicially and clinically that death of the brain, especially the brain stem is the diagnosis of death.[23]

The brain can be divided into three parts (i) the cortex, responsible for intellectual existence. It is the portion more vulnerable to oxygen deficiency (ii) the thalamus, responsible for the regulation of our animal existence and (iii) the brain stem, responsible for control of purely vegetative functions including breathing. If this portion suffers damage it is predictable that the other parts will suffer comparable damage. It is least affected by hypoxia. Whatever, hypoxia damage to the brain is irreversible. All that can be done is to prevent further damage by supplying enough oxygen.

Brain death was first described clinically in 1969 by two French doctors.[24] For most part, the death of the brain stem signifies death because even though it is not synonymous with whole brain death, it is difficult to envisage save in rare cases, where the death of the brain stem will not simultaneously affect the rest of the brain.

There still exists some level of controversy as to whether brain death alone ought to be the diagnosis of death. To play the sage, legislation in some jurisdictions allow for other modes for determining death, by employing dual criteria. For example, the United States Uniform Declaration of Death Act 1980 states that 'an individual who has sustained either (i) irreversible cessation of circulatory and respiratory functions, or (ii) irreversible cessation of all functions of the entire brain, including the brain stem is dead.' The Victoria Federation of Australia applies a similar test. Its Human

---

[21] *Re Quinlan* 355 A 2d. 664 (NJ 1976).

[22] Presidents' Commission for the Study of Ethical Problems in Medicine and Biomedical and Behavioural Research, 1983, Medical Legal and Ethical issues in the Determination of Death, Defining Death pp. 38 —40.

[23] See *Airedale NHS Trust* v. *Bland* [1993] 1 All ER 821, per Lords Keith, Goff and Browne-Wilkinson; *Re A* [1982] 3 Med LR 303; *People* v. *Eulo* (1984) 472 NE 2d 286 (NY, CA); See also Death (Definition) Act 1983 of South Australia and Uniform Determination of Death Act, S.1, 12 ULA 31, 10 (Supp 1991) USA

[24] P. Mollard and M Goulon, Le Coma Depasse (1959) 101 *Rev. Neurol* 3.

Tissue Act of 1982 states: 'a person dies when there has occurred: (a) irreversible cessation of the circulation of the blood in the body of the person; and (b) irreversible cessation of all functions of the brain of the person.'[25] Essentially, these provisions are designed to spell out good medical practice within a legal framework for identifying death.

Legal implication of Brain Death

Applying the brain death standard can bring about the following legal implications:

Causation for unlawful killing

With the development of intensive-care technique it has become commonplace for hospital facilities to have deeply comatose and irresponsive patients with severe brain damaged maintained on artificial respirators by means of mechanical ventilation. Even though a doctor who withdraws mechanical support based on brain death definition will not be treated as acting unethical, he must weigh matters properly, especially in the context that a deceased relative who hardly accepted the clinical brain death definition could misunderstand his action. He can hardly understand how a person still conscious can be treated in medicine as dead.[26] At law the doctor who removes the patient from the ventilator is not responsible for his death. In *Re A*,[27] the parents of a child sought to have him retained on a ventilator for medico-legal reasons. But the judge made a declaration that A, who had been certified brain dead was dead for all legal and medical purposes and that the doctor who disconnected the ventilator was not acting unlawfully. The court also stated that it has no inherent jurisdiction over a dead person. Accordingly A could not be made a ward of court. Lord Lane LCJ in *R* v. *Malcherek* reaffirmed the reasoning when he said:

> ..where a medical practitioner, using generally acceptable methods, came to the conclusion that the patient was for all practical purposes dead and that such vital functions as remained were being maintained solely be mechanical

---

[25] S. 41 of Human Tissue Act, 1982 (Victoria). A similar provision is found in s. 33 of the Human Tissue Act, 1983 of New South Wales.

[26] See Report of the Conference of Medical Royal Colleges and their faculties in 1976 (England). On guide in the diagnosis of death for doctors, see Report of the Ad Hoe Committee of Harvard and Medical School (1968) 205 *JAMA* 337; Forrester (1976) 34 *Health Bulletin* 199; Jennett [1975] 1 *J. of Med. Ethics* 63, Memorandum on the diagnosis of death [1979] 1 *BMJ* (British Medical Jounal) 332.

[27] (1992) 3 Med LR 303; *People* v. *Lyons* Sup. Ct. No 56072, Alameda Co. (Cal. 1974) (victim of shooting was legally dead before being used as transplant donor); *Finlayson* v. *HM Advocate* [1978] SLT 60, per Lord Emslie LJ-G of Scottish; *R* v. *Malcherek* [1981] 2 All ER 422 at 428 – 429, per Lord Lane LCJ [1981] 1 WLR 690.

means, and accordingly discontinued treatment, that did not break the chain of causation between the initial injury and the death. [28]

What this means for example is this: if a patient injured by an assailant is in critical condition in a hospital and the doctor using standard practice is of the view that the patient is clinically (brain) dead he can discontinue treatment. When he does the patient death is not attributed to the withdrawal of treatment. The chain of causation from the injury is not broken. So the assailant remains the person criminally responsible for the death.

Responsibility and time of death

The Criminal Code states expressly that if death occurs within a period of one year (365 days) from an incident, the death will be attributed to the act causing it barring certain counter arguments of intervening circumstances.[29] This raises, though albeit, the academic or theoretical question relating to the precise time that death occurs because several legal issues may depend on it. It is too simplistic to imagine that death occurs when diagnosis is made by the doctor or when the doctor withdraws treatment, say as when he switches off a life sustaining machine. Clinical death will usually occur before the doctor withdraws treatment. So it may well be that the precise time of death is retrospectively followed by treatment withdrawal, and largely unknown or in fact unknowable. By standard practice, doctors certify death at their convenience. How does that translate to a legal problem? Assuming the victim of a violent crime is maintained solely by mechanical means for more than 365 days after the act causing his injury and thereafter the machine is switched off by the doctor, would that affect the criminal responsibility of the assailant for unlawful homicide? That is just one question. What about succession issues? If a couple gets injured in an accident and both are sustained by the ventilator when declared brain death occurs, if survivorship is made to depend on technical diagnosis of death, who would we consider to have died first with hindsight that when a doctor makes his certification of brain death is more a matter of his convenience, a state that need not coincide with the real time brain death occurs in the parties. This is likely to be more problematic in jurisdictions that allow for alternative methods in diagnosis of death such as in the United State of America and Victoria in Commonwealth Australia.[30] No doubt, it would be wholly illogical to vary the criteria to accommodate a specific situation and apply alternative methods for the

---

[28] Ibid., see also *R* v. *Potter* (1963) *Times*, 26 July V. Kitching [1976] 6 WWR 697 (Manitoba); *R* v. *Kinash* (1982) Qld R 648 (old); Skegg, *op. cit*, p. 196; *Mail Newspapers Plc.* v. *Express Newspapers Plc* [1987] FSR 90 (Ch.D).

[29] S 241 of Criminal Code, Cap LFN, 2004.

[30] See United States Uniform Declaration of Death Act, 1980 and Human Tissue ct, 1982 and 1983 for Victoria and NSW respectively in Australia.

diagnosis of death in other cases. It could implicate law to a charge of double standards.[31]

Ethical questions for the doctor

Where the patient's vital functions are being artificially maintained question concerning compliance or non-compliance with generally accepted methods for discontinuing treatment are bound to arise. The various codes of practice require testing for confirmation of brain death and repetition of testing for certainty.[32] Non-compliance with codes standard practice can raise two legal problems connected with (i) the determination of death, and (ii) the legality of the doctor's conduct. Since the legal consequences will be better appreciated in the light of practice directive or brain death diagnosis, we shall discuss it in the context of the degree of testing prescribed by the Code.[33] For purposes of convenience we shall divide it into three stages.[34] Stage 1, enjoins the doctor in testing to exclude patients with certain conditions. This includes patients suspected to be in state of deep comatose due to depressive drugs. Stage 2, requires the doctor to perform specific clinical test for confirming brain test. Stage 3, requires the doctor to repeat the testing to ensure that there has been no observer error. The interval between the test required in stages 1 and 2 is made to depend on the primary pathology and clinical cause of the disease.

If there is non-compliance with the code and question is raised on when death occurs the court will need to determine whether a patient died when the doctor so stated. True, death is a legal question, but its determination rest on medical evidence.[35] For such evidence to be acceptable there must exist demonstrable evidence that it conforms with 'generally acceptable methods'[36] If non-compliance is at stage 1, on appropriate facts the court will find that the patient was not dead at the time his death was so certified. The result may not be so for the stage 2 non-compliance, especially in circumstances where the court is of the opinion that failure to carry out a particular test is not an irresponsible behaviour by the doctor. The legal hurdle with such a conclusion is that it could run into counter-argument. If a person is legally presumed to be alive until the contrary is proven, failure to substantially comply with stage 2 certainly will raise medico-legal questions. It would appear that in this respect the court will be forced to psychologically consider the effect of non-compliance. In *R* v. *Maleherek*[37] where two sets of test were not carried out by the

---

[31] Mason & Smith, *op cit* p. 288; Skegg, *op. cit*, chapter. 9; D Lamb, Wanting it Both Ways (1990) 16 *J. Med. Ethics* 8; see also *Smith* v. *Smith* (1958) 317 SW 2d 275 (Sup Ct. Ark).

[32] See above n 12.

[33] We shall use the (English) Medical Royal College and Faculties Report in 1976 and its addendum in 1979 referred to by Johnson J in Re A [1992] 3 Med LR 303 as guide.

[34] See Kennedy & Grubb, *op. cit*, 1400.

[35] See s. 244 of The Criminal Code.

[36] Lord Lane LCJ in *R* v. *Malcherik* (1981) 2 All ER 442 at 428—429, *Bolam* v. *Friern Hospital* [1957] 2 All ER 118.

[37] [1981] 2 All ER 442.

doctors, Lord Lane CJ was of the view that 'reason were given for neither of these tests having been carried out.'[38] In effect his lordship was satisfied as to the reasons why the doctors did not carry out the tests. So if good medical reasons exist for an omission, it would be appropriate for the court to find that the patient died when he was so certified. It follows therefore that if non-compliance occurs at stage 3, the patient would be considered dead at the time the first set of test was carried out. Since the purpose of stage 3 testing is essentially confirmatory, it ought to follow that a court would in appropriate case hold that death occurs not later than the completion of the first set of tests.[39]

Non-compliance with the code or 'generally acceptable methods' also raises question of the legality of the doctor's conduct. Can he be held criminally responsible for unlawful homicide or civil negligence or both? Liability will depend on whether the conduct complained of is a breach of his duty to the patient and whether the breach is the cause of death. If as a result of non-compliance he wrongly believes that the patient is dead and he act in removing the life support machine, it is strongly believed that in such circumstances the doctor's conduct will be a breach of duty that causes death. On this ground he will be liable criminally for negligent manslaughter[40] and for civil negligence. Establishing murder within s. 244 of the Criminal Code may however be problematic because the requirement of intent to kill (a requirement under the Criminal Code) would be inconsistent with the mind of the doctor.[41]

Aside these legal issues the ethics of maintaining a patient diagnosed of brain death for the benefit of third parties is questionable. A brain dead patient is a corpse. Mason & Smith[42] indicates that there are press reports to the effect that some brain dead women were retained for weeks solely for the purpose of bringing foetus to viability for transplant purposes. Keeping a patient in such a condition for transplant purpose deserves ethical scrutiny, and could make people wonder whether emerging biotechnology is not pushing the ethical border areas of medicine into doubtful areas of morality.[43]

Death and the anencephalic

The anencephalic is a baby born with fatal neurological defect involving the absence of all or most of the cerebral hemispheres, often referred to as the 'higher brain'.

---

[38] Kennedy & Grubb, *op. cit*, p. 140.

[39] Retesting not only help eliminate error of judgment of first testing. It also ensures that the non-function of the brain stem is not just a single observation at one point in time but persist, see Dr. Pallis, *ABC of Brain Stem Death*, p. 16 – 17, cited in Kennedy & Grubb, *op. cit*, 1401.

[40] *R* v. *Majekodunmi*; *R* v. *Bateman*, *R* v. *Prentice* [1993] 4 All ER 935.

[41] For discussion as murder, see C Okonkwo, *Criminal Law in Nigeria* (Ibadan: Spectrum Books).

[42] Mason & Smith, *op. cit*, p. 289.

[43] HL Karcher, "German Doctors Struggle to Keep 15 week Foetus Viable" (1992) 305 *BMJ* 1047; A Tuffs, "Keeping a Brain-Death [regnant Woman Alive" (1992) 340 *Lancet* 1029, both cited in Mason & Smith *op cit* p. 289 n. 9.

Whether such a child should be considered brain dead has often arisen in the content of proposal to harvest their organs for use of others while the anencephalic is still breathing.[44] The legality of the procedure depends on whether the baby is treated as dead, and if so, how death is determined. Some have argued that since they lack higher brain function, anencephalic should not be considered human beings and thus their organs should be available for immediate use. Others argue that they are human beings and that killing them is murder.

Anencephalic could be used as organ donors but only upon pronouncement of death using classical brain death criteria. Thereafter it would be necessary to put the baby on a mechanical ventilator to prevent organ deterioration that could result when natural breathing ceases. But empirical clinical experiment reveals that the intervention in some rare cases could make the brain-stem strong enough to maintain independent breathing for weeks, or even months or years.[45] This indicates that anencephalic may be persons dying, but are not dead. Any argument therefore that they are dead babies is certainly controversial. Unless the criteria for death is radically altered to move beyond the traditional measure and reconstructed to include loss of higher (neocortical) function of the brain, anencephalic are not dead by present clinical death definition. The inclusion of anencephalic within the definition of death it must be admitted (if accepted) would be the first step towards a broader use of the brain death standard, a thing likely to be resisted. Though these babies have a massive defect in their brains, they still have some functions, especially at the brain stem level.[46] Any suggestion (that they are dead) will be contrary to medico-legal ethics. It would be tantamount to suggesting that the patient in the *Quinlan*[47] situation should be treated as dead for the more than ten years after her respirator was removed. That must be an absurd. Even though she was a PVS patients,[48] and so lacked the ability to think, communicate and even process any sensations of pain and pleasure as normal persons do she was still a living person. While some may consider such a life devoid of 'personhood', it does not justify treating them no better than corpses, or use them as organ donors. A medico-legal criterion that treats anencephalic as dead must also, if it desires logical coherence, treat as dead persons in a permanent comatose situation (persons dying and lacking

---

[44] For general discussion, see Kennedy & Grubb, *op. cit.*, p. 1402, G Annas, "From Canada with Love; Anencephalic Newborns as Organ Donors" (1987) 17 *Hastings Centre Report* 36; A C Capron, "Anencephalic Donors: separate the dead from the Dying" (1987) 17 *Hastings Centre Report* 5; 1988 Working Party of the Medical Royal Colleges on Organ Transplantation in Neonates, Chaired by Sir Raymond Hoffenberg.

[45] Annas, above n. 44. See *In re TACP*, 609 So. 2d 588 (Fla. 1992) - parents petition court to allow them have the organs of their anencephalic infant transplanted into another infant prior to its legal death. Application of this nature is bound to smell as slippery slope for organ-hungry opportunists. See husband's application to use wife's organs for transplant after wife's premature death in *Williams* v. *Hoffman*, 223 N.W. 2d 844 (Wis, 1974)

[46] Capron, above n 44.

[47] 355 A 2d 664 (NJ, 1976).

[48] *Airedale NHS Trust* v. *Bland* [1993], All ER 821

consciousness)[49] who are not presently treated as dead. Otherwise, it would be guilty of double-standard.

Maybe for purpose of clarity, it would be necessary to recap *Re Quinlan*.[50] In the seminal case, it was established that Karen Quinlan had no reasonable probability of ever emerging from her present comatose condition to a 'cognitive sapient state'. Under that condition the court held that 'there would be no criminal homicide in the circumstances', and that death following withdrawal of ventilatory support would 'not be homicide but rather expiration from existing natural causes.' But she did not die as anticipated. Nevertheless, if she did, there would have been no moral or legal problems because the outcome resulted from a clinical judgment taken in good faith. Thus like the anencephalic, Quinlan lacked the higher brain function. But she was not treated as dead. Her life support may be removed on good medical grounds after due deliberation based on a productive and non-productive treatment test. Withdrawal may lead to death. But that is a different matter from treating her as dead. She could be dying but not dead. If, for example she were used as an organ donor in that permanent comatose condition that would certainly have been murder. Organ harvest in her case could only have been proper if after withdrawal of ventilator she develops to the stage of brain stem death or death of the whole brain. Going by this, it would be unlawful to use anencephalic as organ donors.

Though some have argued that since an anencephalic can never develop even a semblance of personhood, and the need for their organs is real, and that many parents would be eager to have their anencephalic children used as donors in the hope that something good might come out of the tragic situation of their birth,[51] so they ought ethical be useful donors, because they are like permanent comatose patients who should be allowed to die without further treatment, the argument is not without its drawbacks. Whatever good such an argument holds, we must admit that that is a separate question or problem to which society has already respond in other ways.[52] It is certainly controversial and may be unethical to consider people in permanent coma dead, especially when the purpose is to allow removal of their vital organs for transplant purposes. It is on this ground that the use of anencephalic is objectionable.

However, considering the fact that clinical testing seem to confirm that the criteria used for diagnosing brain stem death in adult and other children is difficult to apply to neonates because of their increased resistance to brain damage, doctors should be reluctant to apply neurological criteria for determine death in children younger than

---

[49] A patient in a permanent comatose can survive for years with nothing more than ordinary nursing care in most cases.

[50] 355 A 2D. 664 (1976).

[51] 355 A2d 664 certden 429 US 922, 97 S Ct 319, L Ed 2d 289 (NJ 1976).

[52] Arthur Caplan so argued at the international group conference in London, Ontario convened by Dr. Calvin Stiller in January 1987 to discuss the issue of anencephalic as organ donors, see Annas, above n. 40.

five years.[53] The effect is that there would be insufficient information to diagnose brain death at the age of anencephalic. Since that is the case, applying brain death criteria in the first seven days of life would be unreliable. It should not be used to justify the removal of organs from neonates with beating hearts for transplantation.[54] Because such test criteria for adult and older children is inapplicable to anencephalic who have no forebrain, and so have a major neurological deficiency incompatible with life for longer than a few hours, it has been suggested that their organs could be removed when two doctors (not members of the transplant team) agree that spontaneous respiration ceases. Since the diagnosis of death in adult is that of the brain plus apnoea, by analogy the English Working Party has suggested that the absence of the forebrain plus apnoea in anencephalic should be recognised as death.[55] It is only at this point that the anencephalic can be treated as dead and used as an organ donor.[56]

---

[53] Capron, above n. 40.

[54] See Recommendation of Task Force for the Determination of Brain Death in children, Report 1987 (President's Commission), cited in Annas, above n. 40.

[55] Working Party Report, above n. 40.

[56] Ibid.

Chapter Eleven

Organ donation and transplantation

Organ is defined by the English Human Organ Transplant Act 1989 to 'mean any part of the human body consisting of a structured arrangement of tissues which if wholly removed cannot be replaced by the body.'[1] By this definition, nails, hair, blood marrow, etc., which can regenerate are excluded from the definition of what constitutes organs. While that may hold true for a construction of the Act, in a medical sense organ is wide enough to include regenerative and non-regenerative body parts. It is suggested that the Act definition is not exhaustive, more so it explicitly states that organ by its definition does not cover cases of partial removal of an organ. By its provisions, donation is only lawful where the donor and donee are genetically related.[2] It follows from this that donation can only be lawful from one relative to another.[3] From this perspective, it is discernable that the underlying policy statement of the law is to largely exclude commercialism.

A successful organ transplant involves scaling through several medical hurdles, such as:

(i) ensuring that donee body does not reject the donated organ, which is a natural reaction. The reason is simply. The body recognises self and non-self, hence it is considered more amiable that donor and donee should be genetically related to reduce the propensity of rejection when eventually transplanted with attendant suppression by medical therapy;

---

[1] S. 7 (2) Human Organ Transplant Act, 1989.

[2] S. 2, Human Organ Transplant Act, 1989.

[3] But cf. M. Evans, Organ Donation Should not be Restricted to Relatives (1989) *J. Med. Ethics* 17. For general reading on transplant programme and ethical issues, see John A Sten, Rethinking the National Organ Transplant Program; when Push comes to Shove (1994 – 95)" *J. Contemp Health Law & Polly* 197 David L. Kaserman, Fifty Years Organ Transplants; The Successes and The Failures (2007 - 08) 23 *Issues Law & Med* 45; Raja B Khauli, Issues and Controversies Surrounding Organ Donation and Transplantation; The need for Law That ensure Equity and Optimal utility of a Scarce Resources (1993) 27 *Suffolk Univ. Law Rev* 1225; Kelly A Keller, The Bed of Life; A Discussion of Organ Donation. Its Legal and Scientific History , And a Recommended Opt-out" Solution to Organ Scarcity (2002-03) 32 *Stetson Law Rev* 855; Howard S. Schwartz, Bioethical and Legal Considerations in Increasing the Supply of Transplantable Organs; From UAGA to "Baby Fae" (1984) 10 *Am. J. Of Law & Med* 397 and Gloria J.Banks, Legal and Ethical Safeguards; Protection of Society's Most Vulnerable Participants in a Commercialized Organ Transplantation System (1995) 21 *Am. J. Law & Med* 45

(ii) the next worry is that of ensuring that the donor's organ to be used is safe and healthy. For practical medical reasons it is suggested that the younger the donor the more likely the healthy state of the donated organ;
(iii) transplantation requires consideration of the question of viability. If the time difference between harvest and transplant is unnecessarily long, depending on the organ and the condition of its preservation, it may become useless for transplantation purpose. Where donor is living and proximately near the donee, say in the same hospital complex, the advantages are immerse to the technique because transportation time is reduced, in which case the warm anoxic time is reduced drastically. It also affords the transplant team the opportunity to test the health situation of the proposed donated organ before harvesting and transplanting;
(iv) Acceptance of brain death definition carries with it many of the advantages derivable from a living donor.

Though the advantage of transplant to a donee can hardly be doubted, some have questioned the legality or otherwise or rationale in law for permitting organ harvesting and transplant. In their view, put in its raw form, harvesting is equivalent to unlawful trespass, assault, and grievous harm, for which no amount of consent by the donor can relieve the doctor of criminality.[4] Such an argument would be strong in the context of equating harvesting of an organ with maiming. Since consent to a grievous assault is no defence to a charge of assault occasioning grievous bodily harm,[5] it is plausible to submit that a doctor who takes part in harvesting opens himself to criminal responsibility. But this would be preposterous and hard to justify in modern medicine.

There exists good counter-argument to that absolutist position. Organ transplant is not fundamentally different from surgical treatment or operation. Dworkin for example, argues that it is therapeutic permissible medical practice.[6] He likens a donor to a 'rescuer,' generally treated favourable at law.[7] Organ transplant is generally treated as lawful. For example, the English Human Organ Transplant Act, 1989,

---

[4] For example, s. 226 of the Criminal Code Law states that consent by a person to cause his death shall not relieve an accused of criminal responsibility for death caused.

[5] See s. 264 of Criminal Code Law.

[6] Gerald D. Dworkin, The Law Relating to Organ Transplantation in England (1970) 33 *MLR* 353. For general reading on organ donation, see J. Wallwork, Organs for Transplantation (1989) 299 *BMJ* 1291; G.D. Chisholm, Time to End Softly Softly Approach on Harvesting Organs for Transplantation (1988) 296 BMJ 1419; L.F. Ross, Moral Grounding for the Participation of Children as Organ Donors (1993) 21 *J. Law Med. Ethics* 251; M. Evans, Organ Donation Should not be Restricted to Relatives (1989) *J. Med. Ethics* 17, C. Dyer, GMC's Decision on Kidney Sale (1990) 300 BMJ 961.

[7] Generally rescuers enjoy several protection at law - *Wagner* v. *Int'L Ry* (1921) 133 NE437; 19 ALR 1, per Cardozo said: "danger invites rescue. The cry of distress is the summons to relief"; *Chadwick* v. *British Transport Comm* (1967) 2 All ER 945, (1967) 1 WLR 912; *Haynes* v. *Harwood* (1935) 1 KB 297; *Baker* v. *Hopkins* (T.E) & Sons (1959) 1 WLR 966; (1959) 2 All ER 225. See also B.A. Susu, *Law of Torts* (1996) 106.

recognises its legality, and so seeks to regulate the practice. Reference to it is implicit recognition of its benefit to society.

In all cases where an organ is transplanted the law requires that the principle of informed consent should be scrupulously observed. Even where the donor is a child within the mature minor principle of *Gillick*,[8] competence to consent would not be considered sufficient. The reason is that organ donation is a subject matter of public interest, for which the courts ought to protect the informed consent of a minor who may be swayed by irrelevant consideration to make a donation. Transplant involves serious procedures, with attendant consequences. For example if a healthy donor donates one of his kidneys, he is left with one. If something happens to his solitary kidney, his health could be greatly impaired, than if he has both kidneys. It is for this reason that it is unethical to rely on the consent alone of the mature minor, not likely to appreciate the implication of an organ donation. This naturally raises the question, who can give consent for the minor, including the mature minor? Lord Donaldson in *Re W (a minor)(medical treatment)* on this said as follows:

> Organ donations are quite different and, as a matter of law, doctors would have to secure the consent of someone with the right to consent on behalf of a donor under the age of 18 or, if they relied on the consent of the minor himself or herself, be satisfied that the minor was Gillick competent.[9]

In the context of so serious a procedure which would not directly benefit the minor, it is inconceivable that (a doctor) should proceed in reliance solely on the consent of an under-age patient, however *Gillick* competent, unsupported by parental consent. If the donor is a competent person; a doctor must ensure the patient consents to the procedure. It is suggested as safe practice for the doctor to additionally seek the opinion of other doctors. In addition, he may well need to apply to the court for guidance.[10] Therefore, to be on the safe side, a doctor involved in transplant where the donor is a minor is advised to seek consent of the minor, his parents and court before proceeding. If the donor is an incompetent adult, it is suggested that the physician should observe the principles started by Lord Donaldson above.[11] Where the patient is in a persistent vegetative state (PVS), no organs should be harvested from him because such a patient is not legally dead, using the brain-death criteria.[12]

---

[8] *Gillick* v. *West Norfolk and Wisbech Area Health Authority* [1985] 3 All ER 402, [1986] AC 112.

[9] [1992] 4 All ER 627 at 639 [1921] 9 BMLR 22 at 35.

[10] See discussion of whether proxy can effectively give consent in *Struck* v. *Struck* (1969) 445 SW 2d 145 and *Curran* v. *Bosze* (1990) 566 NE 2d 1319 (111 Sup. Ct.).

[11] *Re W* (a minor)(medical treatment) [1992] 4 All ER 627 at 639, [1921] 9 BMLR 22 at 35.

[12] It would appear that the case of *Airedale NHS Trust* v. *Bland* [1993] 3 WLR is not clear on this matter, but it is certainly safer for a doctor to avoid putting himself in a collision course with the law by attempting to harvest organ without authorisation from the court.

Agreement to donate

Commercialisation appears to occupy the centre burner on questions of ethics bordering on agreement to donate. Like surrogate motherhood, it is conceivable that unscrupulous agencies and persons will seek to catch on the technique to exploit. Danger of the poor selling their organs is real. That was the practice in England prior to the enactment of the Human Organ Transplant Act [HOTA], 1989. Mason and Smith[13] report that "impoverished Turkish donors were recruited and paid to donate kidneys to genetically and ethnically unrelated recipients." The English response to the unethical practice was the HOTA 1989. It prohibits any commercial dealing in human organs, save for the recovery of legitimate expenses involved in the operation. Unmistakably, as though that was the target of the law, section 1 stipulates that all commercial dealing in human organs is prohibited. It further prohibits all payment for supply of organs, the businesses of brokerage and advertisement of the services for human organ. The Act however did not prohibit non-commercial dealings in organs or body materials which do not fail within the definition of an organ under it.[14]

Laudable as the prohibition of commercial organ regime may seem, it is arguable that the rationale for prohibiting commercialisation is questionable. Turkish nationals, who engaged in it prior to the 1989 Act, did so because they were impoverished. That being so, the question can be asked: what is wrong if an impoverished attempts to improve his economic fortunes by dispensing with say, one of his two kidneys, when he can live full life with one? Who is the best judge as to what a person should do with his body? If the principle of body sovereignty is a cardinal signpost in medical ethics in treatment choices, then should the same concept become inapplicable for matters relating to organ donation? Is it implicit statement of the relative importance law attaches to different human lives, so that when a principle applies generally to the poor law would seek as it were, to construct exemptions? After all, who should be blamed for a state of affairs that render a group of persons impoverished? Reasoning by analogy, Dukeninier questions the rational of prohibiting commercial dealing in organs very graphically this way:

> "How can we permit men to risk their lives in driving racing cars, in entering boxing contests, and in pursuing all kinds of paid risky occupations and still object to the paid kidney donor."[15]

In *McFall* v. *Shimp*[16] the court held that it would not enforce a donation agreement just the same way equity would refuse to enforce a contract for personal service. In effect such contracts are unenforceable.

---

[13] Mason and McCall Smith, *Law and Medical Ethics*, 4th, 1994, 299.

[14] See s. 7(2) Human Organ Transplant Act, 1989 which define an organ as any part of the human body consisting of a structured arrangement of tissues which, if wholly removed cannot be replaced by the body.

[15] J. Dukeninier, Supplying Organs for Transplantation (1970) 68 *Michigan LR* 811, See also Lori Andrews, My Body My Property (1986) 16 *Hastings Center Report* (Oct. 1986) 28.

The Anatomy Acts of 1832 and 1871,[17] vest the right of disposal of the dead in the near relatives or medical director of the facility where a corpse is kept. A doctor in charge after reasonable inquiry as to the location and wishes of the relatives if they agree may authorise removal of human body organs of the deceased for therapeutic, educational, research or experimental purposes.

Replacing of organs and tissue in the human body has been referred to by some commentators as 'spare- part' medicine.[18] The first kidney transplant was performed in 1954 at Peter Bent Brigham Hospital, Boston, Massachusetts, USA. A kidney was transplanted from a twin child to the other twin. Now major body parts including heart, bones, bone marrow, liver, including genes, to mention a few have since been successfully transplanted. In 1974 Dr Christian Bernard transplanted a heart in South African hospital.[19]

The legal, moral and ethic issues that such technological advance may potent was echoed by J.G Castell this way:

> "sooner or later we may be shocked to see newspaper advertisement reading like this: Buy a human egg, rent a wombs shop for a super baby, grow a new heart, kidney and liver, wake up in the 3000 AD."[20]

It raises issues connected with:

- how to determine extent of consent. In this respect, it can be asked whether or not proxy consent is sufficient;
- how to balance state interest (*parens patriae*) with that of individual autonomy;
- legality of commercialisation of human spare-part medicine and its relationship with cannibalism;
- how it affects determining the moment of death and places criminal responsibility for homicide. For example, consider the case of one Roger Ragland.[21] He exhibited all neurological signs of brain death for 12 hours. The hospital received his family's permission to use his kidney for transplant, so he was put on a respirator to continue blood and air circulation through his body tissues. But alas! He recovered and came back to life. The question can well be asked, if in the interval his kidney had been harvested for transplant purpose, would the hospital authority have been responsible for his death?

---

[16](1978) 10 Pa. D & C 3r 90.

[17] The Acts are statutes of general application apply to Nigeria since they were enacted before 1900 to the extent that they are not repealed or Inconsistent with local enactment. The English position on this subject is now regulated by Human Tissue Act. 1961.

[18]Paul Matthews, Whose body? People as property (1983) *CLP* 914.

[19] 1989, February 5 *Journal of American Medical Association.*

[20] J.G Castell, Legal Implication of Biomedical Science and Ethnology in the 21st century; *Osgoode Law School Journal* 15

[21] Reported in the *San Diego Union* newspaper October 1, 1970.

The *Dallas Morning News* also reported an interesting case having a bearing on heart transplant.[22] It tells of a defendant standing trial for homicide. He shot and killed one Samuel Mitchell Allen. He however argued, that his shot was not the cause of death, but the hospital harvesting of the deceased's heart for transplant purposes. His argument was rejected by trial Judge William Hayes. His Lordship rejected the defendant's argument, holding that death is an issue of fact. A person dies if based on usual and customary standard of medical practice, he is certified dead. In this case, the defendant having suffered irreversible cessation of brain function was medical dead. Any removal thereafter of any body organ cannot be attributed to be the cause of death.[23]

Further ethical question that could further arise are now discussed below.

Public policy considerations

Public policy is associated with the infinite moral value usually appealed to by the courts in its desires to prohibit course of conducts that are shocking. To most orthodox, it is repulsive to imagine that body parts can be taken from A and fixed in B. They equate such medical feats as no more than cannibalism. Contracts for sale of body spare parts may also be disturbing. Consider for example, would it be ethical for a person who lives below the 'poverty line' to contract for the harvesting of one of his kidneys for money considerable?

Should such contracts be prohibited as contrary to public policy and morality? How should we treat middlemen who set up shops and broker body spare parts, acting as agents for buyers and suppliers? The harmful effects of these bring to our minds horrible acts that necessitated the enactment of the Anatomy Acts of 1832 and 1871 in England. The Act was enacted at a time when there was great concern about crimes which were being committed in order to procure bodies for the purpose of anatomical dissection. The facts of the case of William Burke and William Hare[24] are gruesome to recall. Burke was an Irish navy who lodged in Hare's lodging house in Edinburgh in 1827. Both of them sold the body of a fellow lodger who died to a surgeon for anatomical dissection. Thereafter they killed other persons in the lodging house. It is reported that they murdered at least fifteen (15), selling their bodies to a school of anatomy. In 1828 the body of a victim was found in a surgeon's premises. Burke was tried and convicted for murder, while Hare was used as 'Crown witness'. Burke was hanged on January 28, 1829, while the mob screamed 'Burke him' meaning kill him. The incident gave rise to the Anatomy Act, 1932, which regulates the supply of bodies to medical school.

No wonder the preamble to the Anatomy Act reads:

---

[22] *Dallas Morning News*, USA of 27/5/74.

[23] See also *Airedale NHS* v. *Anthony Bland* [1993] 3 WLR 316 where death was defined to mean brain death.

[24] See a report on it in *The Oxford Companion to Law*, David Walker, Oxford: Clarendon Press, p. 161

> Whereas knowledge of the cause and nature of sundry diseases which affect the body, and the best methods of treating and curing such diseases, and of healing and repairing divers wounds and injuries to which the human frame is liable, cannot be acquired without the aid of anatomical examination.
>
> In addition, whereas the legal supply of human bodies for such anatomical examination is insufficient fully to provide the means of such knowledge.
>
> And whereas, in order to further supply human bodies for such purposes, divers great and grievous crimes have been committed, and lately murder, for the single object of selling the bodies of the persons so murdered.
>
> And whereas therefore it is highly expedient to give protection, under certain regulations, to the study and practice of anatomy, and to prevent as far as may be, such great and grievous crimes and murder as aforesaid, be it therefore enacted by the King's Most Excellent Majesty.

The Owerri Riot in Nigeria in 1997, popularly known as 'Otokoto' episode, is a reminder of the grave danger that can arise if organ donation and use is unregulated. Grave crimes of murder were alleged committed in Owerri, Eastern Nigeria, because it was lucrative to sell whole body parts.[25] If spare of the body becomes marketable for transplant, then the world may yet wait to see more horrible crimes than those committed by William Burke and his accomplice.

Consider something a little more extreme. If a man, being father of a large family, living unhappily because of being poor, decides to sell his body parts for a lucrative sum, and the said sale facilitates his eventual demise, but at which time the consideration of sale passes to his next-of-kin to improve their standard of life, should the law prohibit such a conduct? Is it suicide? What is immoral if a man must die to give his heirs a better life, which they cannot have in his lifetime? Is such a person any different from a 'rescuer' or some form of 'good Samaritan?' Is he not at least better than a paid 'suicide-bomber' who causes his death and goes down with the lives of others? Who should be the final arbiter of how a man should live – himself, society or the state? The questions that can arise from this are numerous.

It was reported in the press that a German company carrying on business of organs transplant charges as much as $45,000.[26] The interesting thing about the report is that the company is 'drowning in offers' from all over the world. The proliferation of such companies around the globe would certainly be worrisome. The reaction on the face of this may suggest that transplant is offensive to public morality and good, or at best that the practice must be restricted severely. But that is like looking at the hole in the doughnut and not seeing the delicacy itself. Conservative reason as manifest in *A* v. *C* may stall medical progress. In *A* v. *C*[27] Commy J held that an agreement between H and X whereby H would artificially inseminate X and the child born handed over to H was void for being contrary to public policy. If the court would hold such agreement repugnant to public policy, then one can only

[25] Otokoto was widely reported in the newspapers in 1983.
[26] Femi Akerele, long essay in LASU, 1988.
[27] [1978] 8 Fam. Law 170.

imagine what judicial attitudes would be to spare-part medicine. Happily, the court is embracing changes and more than ever before in attempting to align law with medical advancements.[28]

Genome and criminal responsibility

Genome studies are revealing the basis for potential disease and it has been said that certain predominant genes are responsible for schizophrenia, alcoholism and even abnormal sexual behaviours. A casual link at least is being established between behavioural traits and the genes of a person. If genes determine so much of our personality, then gene transplant holds the possibility of altering biological, physiological, psychological and behavioural characteristics. That being so, a person whose genes are manipulated could become a different person. Such could raise question of whether criminal responsibility principles should be altered. All legal system have to some degree or other incorporated the simple moral ideal that no one should be convicted of a crime unless some measure of subjective fault can be attributed to the person.[29] Therefore act or omission that occurs independently of the exercise of a defendant's will not be the basis for criminal responsibility.[30] It can be argued that where gene transplant occurs and the defendant can successfully show (by medical evidence) that this have resulted in a change in personality with criminal propensity, the defendant should be able to plead the excusing defence of accident. Conceivably, a successful plea can constitute foundation for further litigation in other branches of law.

The fact of Consent

No doubt, the ultimate judge of what can be done to a patient's or person's body is the patient himself.[31] However, considering the gravity of transplant, it is imperative that consent must be real from both the donor and donee.[32] Consent in form only is insufficient.[33] There is no factual consent if the decision to donate is not that of the donor, but someone else. For example, if he is persuaded by others to arrive at the decision, the court would hold that there is an absence of consent. It is therefore an absolute requirement that the patient must not be under an influence that overbears the independence of his decision. Lord Donaldson MR gave an indication of how to identify undue influence and its effect:

---

[28] See Lord Goff in *Airedale NHS* v. *Anthony Bland* (*supra*).

[29] Okonkwo & Naish, *Criminal Law in Nigeria* (Sweet & Maxwell (1964) p 71. See especially, s. 24 of the Criminal Code Law, which provides that a person shall not be criminally responsible for any act which occurs independently of the exercise of his will.

[30] S. 24 of Criminal Code.

[31] This right of self-determination is firm fixed in common law. See Cardozo J in *Schloendorff* v. *Society of New York Hospital* (1914) 67 DLR (4th) 321.

[32] Such a proposition is disceranable from Lord Donaldson MR statement in *Re T* [1992] 3 WLR 782 where he said obiter that "the more serious the decision, the greater the capacity required."

[33] See *Chatterton* v. *Gerson* [1981] QB 432, *Re T* [1992] 3 WLR 782, *MNDPT* v. *Okonkwo* (*supra*) where the fact of consent was discussed extensively.

> When considering the effect of outside influence, two aspects can be of crucial importance. First, the strength of the will of the patient. Second, the relationship of the 'persuader' to the patient.[34]

Any attempt by a "proxy" to give consent on behalf of a donor as in *Mcfall* v. *Shimp*[35] is void. That explains why the court rejected an application to force a competent man to give his dying cousin a life–saving bone marrow for transplant. The judge treated the application as having no precedence in the common law. He expressed his resentment this way:

> For our law to compel defendant to submit to an intrusion of his body would change every concept and principle upon which our society is founded. To do so would defeat the sanctity of the individuals and would impose a rule which would know no limit, and one could not imagine where the line would be drawn. For a society which respects the rights of one individual, to sink its teeth into the jugular vein or neck of one of its members and suck from it sustenance for another member, is revolting to our hard-wrought concepts of jurisprudence. Foreseeable extraction of living tissue causes revulsion to the judicial mind. Such could raise the spectre of the Swastika and the Inquisition, reminiscent of the horrors these portend.[36]

However, by contrast, the Kentucky Supreme Court in *Struck* v. *Struck* [37] held that parents could give consent on behalf of their child to the removal of a kidney from their incompetent adult son for transplant into their competent son suffering from kidney failure. Its reasoning is unclear, and difficult to reconcile with the concept of self-determination. May be, it can be explained on the basis that parents being the next of kin of an incompetent child are the lawful medical attorneys, his health care proxies; who can make health care decision for and on behalf of the patient. A charge however can be made that such reasoning treats the incompetent child as a means to an end. He was required to use his body to rescue his brother. Some rights commentators have suggested that the case should not apply to situations where the donor is competent. The right of self-determination only evaporates where it is shown conclusively that the incompetent donor cannot make any rational decision, or weigh information and balance risk. In *Re C*,[38] the court held that the right to decide medical treatment for a patient suffering from mental illness rested with the patient because he could weigh information and balance same despite her illness. Whatever, the reasoning of the Kentucky Supreme Court in *Struck's* which treats a donor as the means to an end is open to powerful moral and legal objections.

---

[34] In *Re T* [1992] 3 WLR 782 at 797.

[35] (1978) Pa D & C 3d 90.

[36] (1978) Pa D & C 3d 90 at 92.

[37] (Ky. 1969) 445 S.W. 2d 145.

[38] Per Thorpe J, *The Independent* newspaper of 14/10/93 p. 34 (unreported).

Causation issues

Causation is important in assigning liability for harm, injuries or other losses. Causation link can be crucial in transplant in locating the moment and cause of death. If a person is dead there can be no (or less) objection to the removal and preservation of the properties of the living matter in his body. The fact that molecular life remains for a relative short time after the occurrence of somatic death makes it possible to preserve vital body organs like kidney, liver, heart and others after cessation of respiration and circulation. To preserve such vital organs the patient may be maintained on a ventilator. At the stage where a patient's brain ceases to function, no legal objection can be raised against harvesting, save where a contrary valid wish is expressed by the deceased while alive and competent.

Because it is now well settled that death is the irreversible cessation of brain function, it has become easy to dispel argument such as put forward by defendant who shot Samuel Mitchell Allen.[39] Allen was certified dead after an electro-encephalogram, (an instrument that records brain wave activity) showed no sign of life in him. At that stage, he was brain dead. So any harvesting of his organ could not be the cause of death.

Legal response to organ donation[40]

The discovery of immune suppressive drugs capable of reducing the biological reaction that may cause a patient's body to reject transplanted organs has increased the use of transplant in medical treatment. This advance however confronts us with the question of supply of solid organs. Inadequate supplies and or equitable basis for distributing the scare resources have remained problematic. Most discourses on transplantation have generally focused on kidney transplant, while paying less attention to transplantation of other solid organs[41] because kidney transplantation

---

[39] See f. n. 17.

[40] For detailed reading, see 'Schwartz, Bioethical and Legal Considerations in Increasing the Supply of Transplantable Organs From UAGA to Baby Fae' (1985) 10 *Am. J. L & Med* 397; Cohen, Increasing the Supply of Transplant Organs: The Virtues of a Future Market' (1989) 58 Geo Wash. L Rev 1; Duckenminer, Supplying Organs for Transplantation (1970) 68 *Mich. L. Rev*811; Childress, Ethical Criteria for Procuring and Distributing Organs for Transplantation (1989) 14 *J. Health Pol. Polly & Law* 87; Demetrius, transplantation: The Relatives' View (1975) 1 *Jo Med. Ethics* 71; R. Vratch, *Death, Dying and the Biological Revolution* (rev. ed 1989); Martyn, Wright & Clark, Required Request for Organ Donation: Moral, Clinical and Legal Problems (1988) *Hastings Centre Rep. April-May* 1988 at 27, Hansmann, The Economics and Ethics of Markets for Human Organs (1989) 14 *J. Health Pol Pol'y & L* 57; Brans, Transplantable Human Organs: Should their Sale Be Authorised by States Statutes (1977) 3 *Am. J.L & Med* 183; Note, Regulating the Sal of Human Organs (1985) 71 *Va. L. Rev.* 1015; Blumstein, Government Role in Organ Transplantation Policy (1989) 12 *J. Health Pol. Pol'y & L* 5; Note, Compulsory Removal of Cadaver Organs (1969) 69 Colum. L. Rev. 693: D. Mathieu, (ed 1988) *Organ Substitution Technology: Ethical, Legal and Public Policy Issues* (1988), D. Cowan, J. Kantorowitz, J. Moskowitz & R. Rheinstein (eds) *Human Organ Transplantation: Societal, Medical-Legal Regulatory and Reimbursement* (1987).

[41] Such other Solid organs include heart, heart-lung, kidney, liver, lung and pancreas.

has had a longer history of success and it constitutes the majority of solid organ transplant.[42] Furthermore, many of the issues associated with renal transplantation are more clearly defined than those surrounding other transplant procedures.[43] It is in this respect that an analysis of the ethico-legal and medical issues surrounding cadaveric kidney transplantation can illuminate the discussion of similar problems involving other transplantable organs.

It is important to note that the kidney is a 'paired' organ and so can be donated by a living individual to another unlike most other solid organs. That however does not prevent kidney transplant procedures in cadaveric cases. In fact most of kidney transplantation from living donor to another and from cadavers to living may raise slightly different ethical and legal issues. We can state with little fear of contradiction that both can be grouped under one heading. Both raise questions of informed consent though in slightly different context. That notwithstanding our discussion here will focus on the legal and regulatory framework for transplantation from cadavers.

(i) American jurisdiction

In response to shortage of transplantable organs in the United States, the American Bar Association and the National Conference of Commissioners on Uniform State Laws endorsed the Uniform Anatomical Gift Act (UAGA) in 1968.[44] Section 2 (a) of the Act grants any competent adult the right to state whether he wishes to donate his organs for transplantation after death. Also section 3 states that any such individual may donate all or part of his body for transplantation or research purposes, and that the donor may even specify a particular donee as beneficiary of the organ for therapy or transplantation. Section 2 (e) provides that where the decedent expresses such a desire, his wishes shall be honoured over any familial objections. By 1973, all the fifty states as well as the District of Colombia had enacted some version of the UAGA. It has been suggested that the Act's aim is to increase supply of donor organs.

The UAGA however suffers from certain defects rooted primarily in psychological barriers to donation. First, it does not adequately address the question of people's unwillingness to approach death in a national manner. It is a fact of life that most persons are unwilling to confront their own mortality long enough to consider organ donation. It is this same fear that makes the majority die intestate; talk more of considering the matter of organ donation. Secondly, even if people were to respond to mortality in a rational rather than emotional manner, distrust of

---

[42] it is estimated that in the United States Kidney transplant is more than of all solid organ transplantation. See statistic of American Council on Transplantation. See statistic of American Council on Transplantation for transplant performed in 1988 in its report titled US Transplant Stat Sheet (1989), cited in Developments in the Law (1990) 103 *Harv L Rev* 519 at 1616 n.10.

[43] (1990) *Harv. L. Rev* 1519 at 1616.

[44] See Uniform Anatomical Gift Act, 8A ULA. 15 (1983) hereafter (UAGA), amended in UAGA (1987). 8A ULA. 2 (Supp 1989) – for discussion see Sadler, Sadler & Stason, The Uniform Anatomical Gift Act: A Model for Reform (1968) 106 *JAMA* 2501, cited in (1990) *Harv. L. Rev* 1519 at 1617 n.15.

doctors may prevent many from making organ donation decision. People can easily feel that if they express a wish to make donation doctors may certify them dead very readily for transplant purposes. It has been suggested that 'although the UAGA prohibits the doctor who determine the potential donor's time of death from being a member of the transplant team, and it is widely known that a doctor cannot give permission to harvesting even after death, fears that doctors might do *something* to the potential donor before a person is really dead or might hasten death in some way is responsible for either lukewarm or outright rejection in patient's willingness to sign donor cards'.[45]

Even though signed donor-card deserves respect like living-will cards, within the bracket of the *Malette* v. *Shuman*[46] type, the practice in the United States suggests that doctors have often required permission from the next-of-kin or relatives to perfect the decedent wishes. This appears unnecessary and somewhat weakens the legal validity of a signed organ donor card. It is plausible to suggest that this practice can be halted by creating a cause of action for failure to respect a donor's wishes.[47]

With a view to addressing the issue of inadequate supply of organs and the shortcomings of UAGA, the American Congress in 1986 added section 1138 to title XI of the Social Security Act. Under the section, to be eligible or remain eligible for any federal Medicaid funds hospitals are required to establish written protocol practice for the identification of potential donors. The essence of it is to create awareness, so that patients can, ahead of or in anticipation of death, give thought to possible donation. But this again suffered certain set backs due to the routine familial inquiry which somewhat shifted the locus of decision making from the individual donor to the family.[48] Under the routine familial inquiry, the doctor is required to inform the family of a choice to donate, especially if a patient is identified as a potential organ donor. Even if a patient is not considered a potential donor, he may request that his organ be used for transplant purpose at death. Thus under the present legal regime in USA a patient or his family after death may consent to harvest of organ provided it is not for commercial purposes.

(ii) England

The general common law rule is that the next of kin of a decedent wishes will prevail against that of the decedent. Organ donation of a cadaveric is now largely regulated in England by statute, especially the Human Tissue. Act (HTA) 1961. By

---

[45] (1990) 103 *Harv. L. Rev* 1519 at 1618. Note s.4 (a) and (b) of UAGA requires that a donor indicates his donative intent in a document, usually a card which he can carry with him, considered similar to an advanced medical directive card or the willing will.

[46] (1990) 67 DLR (4th) 321 , see also *Re T*[1992] 4 All ER 649; (1992) 9 BMLR 46.

[47] For example, in the state of Missouri, there is legislation which imposes liability on a doctor if he acts contrary to a patient's advanced directive regarding the termination of life support. See Missouri Anno . See also PDG Skegg. Liability for the Unauthorised Removal of Cadaveric Transplant Material (1974) 14 *Med. Sci. Law* 53; I.M. Kennedy. Further Thoughts on Liability for Non-Observance of the Provision of the Human Tissue Act 1961 (1976) 16 *Medical Science, Law* 49

[48] (1990) 103 *Harv. L. Rev.* 1519 at 1620-1621.

section 1 (1) the removal of organs would be authorised if there is a specific request to that effect by the deceased. The provision is similar to section 2 (a) of the American UAGA. Donation may be for therapeutic, educational or research purposes. Similar to the American 'routine familial inquiry'[49] policy under section 1138 of the Social Security Act, section 1 (2) of the English HTA provides that if there is no express authorisation by the deceased under section 1(1), the decedent's organs may be removed if the person lawfully in possession of the body has after making 'such reasonable enquiry as may be practicable', come to a conclusion that the deceased if given the choice while alive would have expressed no objection to the harvesting of his organ; or that no surviving spouse or surviving relative would object to the body being so dealt with. Once he forms that opinion, he can lawfully make a donation of the decadent.

Under the American UAGA, donative intent of a donor must be in writing, usually in form of a card which the donor can carry with him.[50] This requirement is designed for quick identification of a donor. Doctors are expected to respect the wish. There is however no similar requirement for a patient who make a donation under s.1 (1) of the HTA. The operation of section 1 (2) of the HTA remains controversial. The wording of the sub-section has occasionally been difficult to implement. Who for example, should be treated as a 'person in lawfully possession' of a deceased? It can be argued that the word 'possession' should be interpreted not in terms of physical holding, but in terms of who ought to have possession of the decadent. In this respect possession takes the meaning of one who ought, in the absence of the deceased's wish, would have the right of disposal of the body. An interpretation in this manner would vest the right of possession in the deceased next of kin. However, if the physical possession analysis is adopted, then in practical terms it would be the hospital facility where the patient dies. While the later interpretation is widely supported by the legal profession and the British Medical Association, an isolated application of it, without considering the context of the former can gravely hurt the feelings of the deceased next of kin thereby inflicting further unnecessary emotional suffering on them, a thing which should be avoided if possible.[51]

What constitutes 'reasonable enquiry' raises practical issues of value judgment. If 'possession' is construed in the sense of physical hospital facility holding and not in the sense that gives it to the deceased next of kin, then it is suggested that the *Bolam* test would be the benchmark for judging reasonableness.[52] Where for example a doctor prolongs the life of a patient so that he can make the necessary enquiry for donative purposes, reasonableness may be judged by such factors as continued viability of the patient's organs, length and depth of enquiry and the likes. It has

---

[49] The routine familial inquiry under the Social Security Act requires health professorial to inform the family of a deceased of its option to donate organs once a patient has been identified as a potential organ donor (and is physically unable himself to consent).

[50] An organ donor card is required under S 4 (a) and (b) of UAGA, 8AULA, 15, 43-44 (1983).

[51] For a general discussion of the shortcomings of HTA, see Mason & Smith, *op. cit,* pp. 300-302.

[52] *Bolam* v. *Friern Hospital Management Committee* [1957] 2 All ER 118 [1957] 1 WLR 582.

been suggested that the wording "any surviving relative" under section 1 (2) admits of too wide a class of potential persons from whom enquiry may be made. Interpreting the wording in a way that requires enquiry only from any relative who can be reasonably contacted or is available would be more effective and practical.[53] Though the HTA aims to make more available solid organs for transplant, inadequate supply still resists.[54] The reason in England, like in America, is not unconnected with the fact that legislation has not sufficiently succeeded in making most of the potential donors, actual donors[55]

(iii) Other jurisdictions

Organ donation in many advanced jurisdictions is largely regulated by legislation. Most of the federating units in Australia have enacted statute that fairly follows the English Human Tissue Act 1961.[56] There is no legislation in Nigeria regulating the practice, whether by cadaver or living donors. So to a large extent the common law position is preserved, namely, in the absence of specific instructions by a deceased person, the doctor enjoys very limited rights as to the disposal of the body. The wishes of his next of kin would normally be given effect. It is suggested that our jurisdiction should also take steps to replace the common law rule by statute regulating cadaveric and living organs and tissue donation. Such a position will likely make more available organs and remove the much emotional inhibition of our people to face questions of mortality rationally. The public good effect of donation cannot be over stressed. The absence of legislation in Nigeria however does not prevent a person from making a living or cadaveric donation. That notwithstanding, the common law principle of autonomy and self-determination provides sufficient analogy that is applicable to organs, tissue donation and transplant questions. Like a living will in *Malette* v. *Shulman*,[57] nothing prevents a person from executing an organ donor card, and going further to indicate potential donees.

Conceptual and practical issues

Whatever method the donation takes, whether cadaveric or from a living donor the following issues map out the ethical questions.

---

[53] See Mason & Smith, *op. cit*, p. 301. See also s.4 of Human Tissue Act 1983 of (NSW) in Australia where next of kin are specified in order of seniority, which responsibility for consent vested in the most senior next of kin who can be contacted.

[54] According to Mason & Smith, *op. cit*, p.303, over 3,700 patients in 1988 and 4,340 in 1992 are awaiting kidney transplant in England, see also J. Wallwork, Organs for Transplantation (1989) 299 *BMJ* 1291.

[55] (1990) 103 *Harv. L. Rev.* 1519.

[56] Eg. Human Tissue Act, 1983 (NSW).

[57] (1990) 67 DLR (4th) 321; *Nancy B.* v. *Hotel-Dieu de Quebec* (1992) 86 DLR (4th) 385 (1992) 15 BMLR 95 Notable in most European countries, especially Belgium and Austria, there is a presumption that cadaveric are available for transplant unless vetoed by next-of-kin. And in Italy and Spain the presumption is somewhat coercive – see Mason & Smith, *op. cit*, p.304.

Lethal nature of organ harvest

Once we accept brain death definition and that that is sufficient for harvesting to lawfully take place, we are forced to consider the conscience of others who consider it lethal operation. Evidence exists that even some eminent doctors in all good conscience still do not accept the technical criteria of brain death.[58] Some are uncomfortable with the idea of harvesting organs from a heart-beating person simply on the grounds that brain death criteria treat such as dead. For this reason some doctors who accept ventilated donors refuse to do any harvesting until their patients are disconnected from it and has shown flat electrocardiogram.[59] How should the law address this? While it is accepted that the moment of death is a matter generally for the clinical judgment of the individual doctor, the lethal nature of the harvesting may be defused for such objecting doctors if a death certificate is issued before any harvesting is effected.[60] Such certification can serve to ease trouble conscience of objecting doctors and the emotional suspicion of some patient's relatives. Alternatively, the problem can be addressed by applying a different definition of death for transplantation purposes.[61] The reason for this is that if these safeguards are not put in place to assuage the conscience of objecting doctors and possibly the emotional suspicion of the relatives of a deceased, there may be likelihood of modern medicine confronting itself with an inherent growing apathy to its concept of brain death. The non-beating heart death test by the general public can only make for realistic brain death definition if steps are taken to diffuse the lethal posture of harvest from brain dead patients.[62]

---

[58] N. Hodgkinson, When Does a Beating Heart Die [1986] *The Sunday Times*, 7 Dec. p.l, cited in Mason & Smith, *op. cit*, p. 302 n.4

[59] Mason & Smith, *op. cit*, p.302

[60] Ibid.

[61] For example s.24 (2) of the Human Tissue and Transplant Act, 1982 of Western Australia makes no mention of death but it stipulates that two doctors must certify that all brain function must occur before any organ can be harvested from a person whose respiration and circulation is sustained artificially.

[62] Mason & Smith, *op. cit*, p. 303, reports that most Japanese are apathetic of the brain death notion, and that in fact one doctor was charged with murder for performing a cardiac transplant after using the brain death test, though the charges were later dropped; see M. Yamauch, Transplantation in Japan [1990] 30 *BMJ* 507; J. Nudesshima, Obstacles to Brain Death and Organ Transplantation in Japan (1991) 338 *Lancet* 1063.

Inadequate supply of organs [63]

Most of legislation in the various jurisdictions shows a commitment to the belief that organs should be given as gift either to specific individuals or to society at large. Donation is expected to be the result of an altruistic decision. From this perspective almost all jurisdictions prohibit the commercialisation or sale of human organs.[64] In fact the United States National Task Force on Organ Transplantation[65] in its 1986 recommendation stated that donated organs should be considered 'national resources' to be used for public good. The basic philosophy underlying most transplant legislation suggests that the legislature take as given without more that the sale of human organs is fundamentally wrong ethically. It assumes that human body parts should not be a basis of profit because it is against fundamental norms to treat it as commodity.[66] Though these statutes in the main proscribe commercial transaction in human body parts, they permit the recovery of cost associated with organ transplantation and procurement.[67]

Despite the reflexive rejection of the commercialisation and commodification of organ, it has been suggested that a system that allows for payment has good ethical argument. It could serve as an incentive that can induce many more to donate,

---

[63] For detailed reading, see Schwartz, Bioethical and Legal Considerations in Increasing the of Transplantable Organs From UAGA to Baby Fae (1985) 10 *Am J.L & Med* 397; Cohen, Increasing the Supply of Transplant Organs: The Virtues of a Future Market (1989) 58 *Geo Wash. L Rev* 1: Dukenminer, Supply Organs for Transplantation (1970) 68 *Mich.L. Rev:* 118; Childress. Ethical Criteria for Procuring and Distributing Organs for Transplantation (1989) 14 *J. Health Pol. Polly & Law* 87; Demetrius Transplantation: The Relatives' View (1975) 1 Jo Med. Ethics 71:R, Vratch, *Death, Dying and the Biological Revolution* (rev.ed 1989); Martyn, Wright & Clark, Required Request for Organ Donation: Moral, Clinical and Legal problems (1988) *Hastings Centre Rep* April-May 1988 at 27, Hansmann, The Economics and Ethnics of Markets for Human Organs (1989) 14 *J Health Pol Pol'y & L* 57; Brans, Transplantable Human Organ: Should their Sale Be Authorised by States Statutes 3 *Am. J.L. & Med* 183; Note, Regulating the Sal of Human Organs (1985) 71 *Va L.Rev.* 1015: Blumstein, Government Role in Organ Transplantation Policy (1989) 12 *J Health Pol.Poly & L* 5; Note, Compulsory Removal of Cadaver Organs (1969) 69 *Colum. L. Rev.* 693: D. Mathieu(ed 1988) *Organs Substitution Technology: Ethnical, Legal and Public Policy Issues* (1988). D. Cowan, J. Kantorowitz, J. Moskowitz & R. Rheinstein (eds) *Human Organ Transplantation: Societal Medical-Legal Regulatory and Regulatory and Reimbursement* (1987).

[64] For example USA, National Organ Transplant Act of 1984. Most states statutes make similar prohibition. See s. 397 f of California Penal Code 1988; S.4307 of New York Public Health Law, 1983, Human Tissues Act of (England), prohibits the exchange of Money, other than legitimate expenses, for the purpose of organ donation by the living. See also J. Harvey, Paying Organ Donors (1990) 16 *J. Med Ethics* 117; C. Dyer, GMC's Decision on Kidney for sale (1990) 300 *BMJ* 961.

[65] See Task Force on Organ Transplantation, US Dept. of Health and Human Services, *Organ Transplantation; Issues and Recommendation.* The Task Force was established in 1984 by the US Congress to study the problems associated with organ procurement and transplantation. See National Organ Act of 1984 cited in (1990) 103 *Harv. L. Rev.* 1519 at 1616 n.11.

[66] Note however that s.41-39-9 of Mississippi Code Ann. (1972) 2 Supp. (1988) permits its citizen to ell their body parts to hospitals or medical schools after death for post-mortem delivery, a statute the US National Task Force may have overlooked.

[67] Note, Due process in the Allocation of Life-saving Medical Resources (1975) 84 *Yale L.J* 1734 at 1736-1739.

thereby closing to a large extent the gap between potential and actual donors.[68] This it can do in three main ways:

(i) it would induce people to weight the psychic discomfort of considering donation against the tangible benefit of making one;

(ii) has potential of altering the perception of the 'organ donor card' and transforming it from a mere expression of altruism to a legally binding document;[69]

(iii) doctors will be more willing to follow the directive of an organ donor card or living will without the present inhibition that implicitly makes it expedient for them to seek family independent permission.

While the weight of philosophical, broad metaphysical and religious principles underline the proscription of commercial organ donation, it would appear that the argument is unnecessarily conclusive. Does not our society readily accept the commercialisation and commodification of nearly every aspect of modern medicine without reflexive rejection that commonly greets donation of organs? Consider for once, the commercialisation of blood and the commodification of human sperm.[70] From this perspective it can be predicted that overtime society would overcome its reflexive rejection of the notion of commodification of organs. Also worthy of attention is the immerse benefit supply of organs will generate if they are paid for. The desire to monetise what is termed 'society's moral value, the inhibition against regarding the body as a commodity'[71] should not be at the expense of limiting supply for those awaiting transplantation. Deaths resulting from unavailability of organs are not less unethical than a restrictive prohibition of commercial organ donation. It is therefore suggested that a market solution to the shortage of organs should be measured not against an ideal voluntary system that supplies sufficient organs but against the current voluntary regime that falls short of demand. While a commodification of organs can initially shock society's fundamental norms, allowing some level of payment for organs would help eliminate the tragic shortage of transplantable organs.[72]

It will be proper for legislative reform to reject the present rejection of commercial organ donation. Patients should be allowed to donate for valuable consideration under a structure that allows for the government to compensate the donor. Compensation should also be encourage by indirect ways, such as government offer

---

[68] US National Task Free recommendations, above n.64 pt. p.9.

[69] (1990) 103 *Harv. L. Rev.* 1519 at 1618. Note s.4 (a) and (b) of UGAGA requires that a donor indicates his donative intent in a document, usually a card which he can carry with him. It is similar to an advanced medical directive card or the willing will.

[70] See above n.24 see also A. Guttmann & RD Guttmann, Attitudes of Health Care Professionals and the Public Towards the sale of Kidney for Transplantation. (1993) *J. Med. Ethics* 148; JB Bigwell, Kidneys: Buy or Die (1993) 342 *Lancet* 45; J Warden, Kidneys: Not for Sale (1989) *BMJ* 1670; A Dorozynsk, European Kidney Market (1989) *BMJ* 1182.

[71] (1990) 103 *Harv. L. Rev.* 1519 at 1622, see also Brams, above n.63, and Note, above n.63.

[72] (1990) 103 *Harv. L. Rev*1519 at 1625 See *Hating Centre Report*, Ethical, Legal and Project Issues Pertaining to Solid Organ Transplantation (1985).

to give tax rebate, pay part or all of the funeral expenses and or medical bills of a donor or give the donor and his family priority if they at any time become potential transplant recipients. Since a compensatory government driven scheme would be more amiable to regulation than a private market-driven scheme, it is preferred. The reasons are obvious. Profit-driven procurement personnel may resort to overly aggressive tactics that may lead to causing people to reject donation out of a reflexive distrust of the doctor and hospital establishment. What is more, it may be politically impracticable now.[73]

Public Law perspective

An interesting feature of American constitutionalism in this context is the suggestion by some commentators that the due process and equal protection clause[74] apply to the allocation of scare organs to recipients. Notably, Note[75] has suggested that the many private hospitals who act as facilities for transplant, (said to be national resources)[76] may be deemed state agents and or actors because of government participation in their funding and operation. The reasoning for this proposition is rooted in the shortage of transplantable organs. Consider as an example, what is involved in a kidney transplant in a multi-racial society. The procurement system must attempt to obtain a racial and ethnic diverse donor pool. Thereafter the procured kidneys will have to be distributed on the basis of a procedure known as HLA antigen matching.[77] If the HLA antigen of both donor and recipient differ, the recipient's body will reject the organ. But a match reduces the likelihood of rejection. Because scientist have identified over 70 different HLA antigens and the antigens profile of various ethnic and racial groups varies considerably, the probability of two ethnic and racially different people having the same HLA antigens is rare. This is what make expedient an ethnically and racially diverse donor pool and provide a basis for treating organs as national resources.[78] So depending on the allocation system used to qualify a waiting recipient for organ transplant important ethical choices bordering on constitutionalism,[79] as the due process clause and equal protection clause, may be implicated. But it can only be so if we can identify the necessary element of 'state action'. The clauses only protect, like our constitution,

---

[73] On values that should determine the criteria for relocating the limited supply of organ to recipients, see discussion in (1990) 103 *Harv. L. Rev.* 1519 at 1630-1637, see also R.M.R. Taylor, opting In or Out of Organ Donation (1992) 305 *BMJ* 1380, E.D Chisholm, Time to End Softly Softly Approach on Harvesting Organs for Transplantation (1988) 296 *BMJ* 1419.

[74] The due process clause is the 5th Amendment to the American Constitution (US Constitution, amend V) and the due process and equal protection clause is the 14th amendment US Constitution, amend. XIVs).

[75] Note, Due Process in the Allocation of Life-saving Medical Resources (1975) 84 *Yale L. J.* 1734 at 1736-1739.

[76] National Task Force, above n.64 at 96.

[77] It is a procedure that matches the genetically pre-determined proteins found in all human tissue between recipients and donors.

[78] Above n.64.

[79] See 1999 Constitution of Federal Republic of Nigeria, Chapter II and s. 42.

individuals against state action, i.e., against conduct of the government or any entity sufficiently related to government.[80]

How can this be related to allocation of scare transplantable organs? In *Blum* v. *Yaretsky*,[81] several medicated patients challenged their involuntary transfer or discharged from a private subsidised nursing facility that was government regulated. They argued that they had been denied adequate procedural due process. The American Supreme Court held that since the decision of the private nursing facility was essentially a medical one there was no state action for purposes of the XIV amendment.

So if the decision to select a patient for transplant is taken by a private doctor whose hospital enjoy government funding in the form of the present National Health Insurance Scheme, that may not be sufficient bases for a cause of action on ground of discrimination of any sort, so long as it is a medical decision or judgment. Where however, organ transplant become managed by private hospitals that enjoy government funding and a decision to allocate an organ by a hospital admits of parameters that are not exclusively medical, a nexus between government and the hospital might seem sufficient to implicate government in the decision making of the hospital.

In *Burton* v. *Wilmington Parking Authority*,[82] a municipal parking authority leased space to a restaurateur without obtaining an agreement from it not to discriminate on the basis of race. The parking authority was held liable with the restaurateur for the latter's discriminatory conduct. In effect, if government, like the parking authority, grants a hospital or a group of doctors union to administer allocation of organs without extracting from them a promise that the rules for allocation would not discriminate against certain people, government could be vicariously liable. Although this may be logical conceptually, it is practically unlikely that a private hospital decision would be treated as that of government. This is so because even the American Supreme Court position in recently time after *Burton*[83] shows signs that suggest that governmental enforcement of a private decision does not necessarily make a decision an action of the state.[84] What is more, the mere existence of a contractual arrangement between government and a private actor or the existence of extensive government regulation does not transform a private actor to a state actor.[85] For example in *Rendell-Baker* v. *Kohn*,[86] the court held that the discharge of several employees by a private school was not state action even though

[80] See L Tribe, *American Constitutional Law*, 2nd edn 1988 s.18-1p. 1688, *Shelley* v. *Kraemer* 334 US 1 at 13 (1948) (declaring that the XI amendment 'erects no shield against merely private conduct, (1990) 103 *Harv. L. Rev* 1519 at 1637 n.155. Compare Ikpotor on state action and the enforcement of fundamental human rights provision in Nigeria, see [2004] Delta Public Rev.15

[81] 457 US 991 (1982).

[82] 365 US 715 (1961).

[83] Ibid.

[84] *Blum* v. *Yaretsky* 457 US 991 at 1009 –1010 (1982).

[85] *Rendell-Baker* v. *Kohn* 457 US (1982).

[86] 457 US 830 (1982).

the school operated under contract with the state and was extensively regulated and financed by it. Since *Blum* and *Rendell–Baker* are more recent decisions, they weaken the precedential value of *Burton.* If nothing, they suggest that only in rare cases will allocation criteria of organ by a private actor be attributable to government when non-medical criteria are used in the decision making process.

Living donors

Regenerative tissues such as blood and bore marrow presents few ethical problems in contrast with non-regenerative tissues and organ. Generally the law regulating donation and transplantation is the common law and statute. Common law principles of informed consent, principle of body autonomy and self-determination set the centre–stage for regulation. Closely connected to these is the principle that the law will not allow a person to consent to being killed or maimed.[87] Statutory regulation of live donation in England is governed by the Human Organ Transplant Act 1989. Since donation by children, the mentally incompetent and the use of foetus or neonate presents a number of thorny issues not generally encounter by cadaveric and competent (living) patient's, we shall next pay attention to them.

(i) Children

Subject to the common law right of a child, consent to treatment or medical operation resides with parents.[88] Parental consent however appears circumscribed by the requirement of benefit to the child. It is therefore suggested that if medical treatment is not geared to a child's advantage, the value of parental consent will be weakened. 'Advantage' or 'benefit' to a child is widely construed in this context. In *Struck* v. *Struck*,[89] though the donor was an adult, due to illness he had a mental age of 6. The court was of the view that it will be in his best interest for his brother's life to be saved by him making an organ donation considering the close relationship existing between the two. In the circumstance it ordered donation even though the donor could not give legal consent.

Unlike the American and may be English practice, some jurisdictions, notably Canada, has a policy of limitation. Donation by children is forbidden.[90] While an absolute prohibition on children donor may be considered extreme by some, the desirability of some level of limitation or restriction is hardly questionable. This is because a child, due to inexperience, may not fully understand what donation entails.

---

[87] See s. 226 of Criminal Code.

[88] PDG Skegg, English Law Relating to Experimentation on Children (1977) 2 *Lancet* 754, but cf. *Gillick* v. *West Norfork & Wisbech Area Health Authority* [1986] AC 112, [1985] 3 All ER 402 (on the mature minor exemption principle).

[89] 445 SW 2d 145 (Ky 1969); but cf. *Lausier* v. *Pescinski*, 226 NW 2d 180 (Wisc.1975).

[90] In Canada, the Ontario Human Tissue Gift Act prohibits donation by minor, see BM Dickens, *Medico-Legal Aspects of Family Law* (1979) p.96; Most states in Australia have greatly circumscribed the circumstances under which a minor can serve as a donor, see for example, Human Tissue and Transplant Act, 1982, ss.12 and 13 (Western Australia) and the Human Tissue Act, 1983, s.10 (NSW), For further discussion see L.F. Ross, Moral Grounding for the Participation of Children as Organ Donors (1993) 21 *J. Law Med Ethics* 251.

Even if he fairly does, which is unlikely, the law may still need to draw a distinction between cases where the recipient is the minor immediate family member and one that is not so related. Donation in cases of the former would certainly be less objectionable than the latter.

It is instructive how a policy of limitation can be structured using models from jurisdictions that either prohibit or place limitation on children donation. The Australian Law Reform Commission to some extent sets out what the parameters of such restrictions ought to look like.[91] In its report on transplant it suggested that donation for non-regenerative organs by minor should not be prohibited, but circumscribed by these rules, namely:

(i) donor and recipient should be immediate family members;
(ii) medical evidence must exist that show that unless the donation is made the recipient will die; the parents of the minor (or those *in locus parentis*) must consent to the donation; if the minor, is mature enough (using the *Gillick*[92] test) he must also consent to make the donation and;
(iii) an ad hoc committee consisting of a judge and two other persons must come to the conclusion that donation is desirable and in the best interest of the donor.

These restrictions can prove useful in protecting minor donors.

The French policy[93] requires that such a donation shall only be for the minor's brother or sister. Consent is required from the minor's legal representative. It is also required that the minor's consent must subsequently be approved by a committee of three experts, two by who must be doctors. No doubt, the French position shares a similar philosophy with the suggestion of the Australian Law Reform Commission. Whatever, the shape of the law in most jurisdictions suggests caution.

While Nigeria, as is in England, the matter remains unregulated, the English Court of Appeal in *Re W*[94] had an opportunity to clarify the law in England. Though questions of organ donation and transplantation were not directly in issue, Lord Donaldson MR said obiter that "organ donation are quite different and, as a matter of law, doctors would have to secure the consent of someone with the right to consent on behalf of a donor under the age of 18 or, if they relied on the consent of the minor himself, be satisfied that the minor was 'Gillick' competent of so serious a procedure which would not benefit the minor." From his Lordships statement, it would seem that no person below 18 can give reliable consent to donate in the absence of support from parents or the court. This is reasonable and it appears to align with current practice on minor treatment. It is suggested that the Nigerian law in this respect should not be any different.

(ii) Persistent Vegetatative State (PVS) Patients

A discussion on PVS patient is made here not because a PVS patient is any different from any living incompetent donor, but because some may confuse and equate PVS

---

[91] Mason & Smith, *op. cit*, p.296.

[92] *Gillick* v. *West Norfolk & Wisbech AHA* [1986] AC 112 (1985) 3 All ER 402.

[93] Law of 22 Dec. 1976, cited in Mason & Smith, *op. cit*, p. 217 n.3.

[94] Re W (a minor: medical treatment) [1992] 4 All ER 627, [1992] 9 BMLR 22.

patient donation with cadaveric donation. Both are fundamentally different. A PVS patient only suffers cerebral incompetence and so is no different from an unconscious patient in this respect and many more. With the present clinical definition of death includes brain stem death, i.e., cognitive death, it must be stressed that PVS patients are not persons who can be said to be dead. A PVS patient maintains his cardiovascular system and so is not dead for any purpose. So PVS donation should not be equated with cadaveric donation. A PVS patient however may be a donor within the existing legal framework when he dies, but any limiting of his life or direct killing for purpose of transplantation will be murder.[95]

(iii) Neonate and Foetus donation

Medical technology wherein foetus and in some cases neonates organs and tissues are used for transplant purposes is beginning to raise ethical questions. No doubt donation by neonates should be no different from other donors (adult and minor), that are regulated in England by the Human Tissue Act, 1961 and other regulation as spelt out in the various jurisdictions. A neonate is a person for all legal purposes. It is only different on matters connected with quality of life. But same cannot be said of foetus. It is legally not a person, even though the potentials of personhood may in certain respect justify according it something more than a 'no-status'.[96] Foetus may be involved in donation in its early stages of development as a cell or at maturity. For example, it has been suggested that brain cells of foetus may be used for brain transplant of patients suffering from Parkinson disease.[97]

Generally, organ and tissue donation legislation, such as the English and Australian Human Tissue Acts and the American Anatomical Gift Act do not make provision for foetus donation. Foetus donation is however more properly regulated by abortion legislation and the like.[98] It is in this context that foetus donation raises serious issues of morality. How? Since foetus can only be involved in transplant if it is 'viable,' it means that any statutory regulation that liberalises abortion on grounds of abnormality or defect cannot be a basis for foetus donation. Furthermore, since the general tenor of most abortion legislation prohibits procuring abortion,[99] it would necessarily follow that for foetal donation to be legal it must either come from stillborn or be moribund at birth. In case of the former, the contradictions are inherent. No foetal donor can come through that means, because for every material

---

[95] See J Downe, The Biology of the PVS: Legal, Ethical and Philosophical Implications for Transplantation (1990) 22 *Transplant Proc.* 995, cited in Mason & Smith, *op cit* p. 298 n. 9, see also British Medical Association 'Guideline Relating to The Persistent Vegetative State' reprinted in (1993) *Bull. Med. Ethics* no. 898 para 9.

[96] *Paton* v. *British Pregnancy Advisory Service Trustees* (1979) QB 276, (1978) 2 All ER 987

[97] See also Mason & Smith, *op. cit.*, p. 310.

[98] See for Nigeria: Offences Against the Person Act, 1861, (a statute of general application); England: Abortion Act, 1967; Human Fertilisation and Embryology Act, 1990; Infant Life (Preservation) Act 1929.

[99] See Offences Against the Person Act, 1861, ss. 58 and 59 prohibit procuring of miscarriage in a woman. See *R* v. *Bourne* [1939] 1 KB 687; [1938] 3 All ER 615 and O F Emiri, Human Rights issues in Abortion in Emiri (ed) *Crosscutting Issues in Ethics, Law and Medicine* (Lagos: ACLHC 2000) p. 36.

purpose it is not viable. In the case of the latter, foetal donor can only be limited to anencephalic foetus, which as previously discussed, implicates morality on grounds that anencephalic are persons within medico-legal definition of cognitive or somatic death.[100] Since the anencephalic is a living person, it will be legally wrong to equate it with a cadaveric for purpose of transplant. It must be allowed to die naturally. Any killing or limiting of its existence for purpose of transplant will be murder.

So either way it is difficult to obtain viable foetus for transplant. A dead neonate or abortus can only be used for transplant if it is reanimated in order to provide undamaged organs. To provide this by-pass in England, where the donor is an anencephalic, it is stipulated that harvesting shall only be permitted if 'two doctors not part of the transplant team agree that spontaneous respiration has ceased'[101] This is nothing but a widening of the boundaries of the diagnosis of death to make available organs that would otherwise have been legal difficult to procure, even though the stipulation can still be said to be no more than a restatement of general diagnosis of death, i.e., cessation of respiration. Since most organs are sensitive to 'warm anoxia,' this criterion will still require some form of 'reanimation ventilation.' This again raises ethical questions as to reanimation length of time for transplant purposes considered less objectionable.

Some of these issues and principles were discussed by the Florida Supreme Court in *Re TAC*.[102] T, born anencephalic lived for just nine days. Her parents sought to have her declared dead so that her organs can be used to save lives. Though the circuit judge found as a fact that she was not brain dead, he nevertheless authorised the harvesting of a single kidney on the ground that it would not hurt her. The decision was upheld on appeal by the District Court of Appeal, despite the fact that she was then dead at the time of the appeal. A further appeal to the Florida Supreme Court was entertained on the ground of the public importance of the issues raised in the case. Essentially it endorsed the previous decisions of the two lower courts-that authorised harvesting the kidney of the anencephalic, T. Noteworthy of mention, the Supreme Court acknowledged that an anencephalic does not meet the traditional definition of brain death and it further stated by its conclusion that matters of anencephalic donation should be governed by strong utilitarian rather than strict deontological principles.[103]

---

[100] See discussion, *infra* (on diagnosis of death).

[101] Ibid, see also Report of the Working Party of the Conference of Medical Royal Colleges and their Faculties in the United Kingdom on Organ Transplantation in Neonates (1988).

[102] 609 So 2d 588 (Fla. 1992).

[103] See J R Salaman, Anencephalic Organ Donors (1989) 298 *BMJ* 622; D A Shewman, A M Capron, W J Peacock & B L Schulman, The Use of Anencephalic Infants as Organ Sources (1989) 261 *J Amer Med Ass* 1773, W F May, Brain Death: Anencephalic and Aborted Foetuses (1990) 22 *Transplant Proc.* 885, L S Rothenberg, The Anencephalic Neonate and Brain Death: An International Review of Medical, Ethical and Legal Issues (1990) 22 *Transplant Proc.* 1037, but cf. M Harrison, Organ Procurement for Children; The Anencephalic Foetus as Donor (1986) 2 *Lancet* 1383; A Davies, The Status of Anencephalic Babies Be used as Donor Bank? (1988) 14 *J Med Ethics* 150.

Ethical questions bordering on consequentialism would be implicated if a woman merely chooses to carry to term or near it a pregnancy a foetus simply for the purpose of providing transplantable organs. It would at first glance appear to suggest using or viewing or both life as a 'means' rather than an 'end'. But if so, is the reverse not paternalistic? Can counter-arguments be advanced that to prevent a woman from carrying an anencephalic to term will in very direct ways deprive potential recipients of organs the opportunity to receive them? A charge based on discrimination can also be made against the prohibition. For example, it can be argued that any such prohibition strikes at the fundamental procreative right of the woman. It could also implicate law for seeking to control a woman's body when at the same time it permits expression of the right to autonomy, even to the extent that a competent patient may refuse life-saving treatment. Why it could be asked, should the case of a pregnant woman be different? These arguments and counter-arguments probably suggest that this is another area of medicine requiring the application of utilitarian principles rather than sheer deontological philosophies in mapping ethical boundaries.[104]

[104]On values that should determine the criteria for relocating the limited supply of organ to recipients, see discussion in (1992) 305 *BMJ* 1380 , E.D. Chisholm, Time to End Softly Softly Approach on Harvesting Organs for Transplantation (1988) 296 *BMJ* 1419. Mason & Smith, *op. cit*, p. 310 where the learned authors appear to suggest a similar approach.

Chapter Twelve

Euthanasia or Mercy Killing

Because medical science can now prolong life, it can confuse us as to where death begins. We therefore are forced to look at new perspectives that distinguish between death as we used to know it and death in which the human body lives in some fashion but the brain or a significant part of it does not.[1] This process has become topical in medical ethics considering that the majority of persons now die in hospital facilities where they are likely to meet their end in a sedated or comatose state. For many patients at the threshold of death, a desire to die is understandable. This desire is implicitly recognised as lawful in law by the recognition of the principle that a competent adult does have a right to refuse medical treatment even if the effect of it would mean death. For the incompetent, the law generally recognises the principle of substituted judgment, on which basis a third party may be allowed to exercise the incompetent's right of autonomy.[2] Substituted judgment principle aims at ascertaining the incompetent patient's choice as if he were competent.[3] Our discussion in this chapter will separate the law about the ending of life for the incompetent and competent patient and the vexed question of whether termination of life-sustaining treatment is itself distinguishable from mercy killing, commonly referred to as euthanasia.

The *Oxford Companion of Law* defines the term 'euthanasia' to mean 'the causing or hastening of death, particularly of incurable or terminally ill patient, and at their request.'[4]

It goes further to describe the attendant legal rule governing euthanasia and to distinguish if from similar legal phenomena, stating:

> Generally it (euthanasia) is treated as illegal and not distinguishable from murder, largely because of the difficulty of distinguishing in legal rule and in fact between criminal and justifiable causing of death. A narrowly

---

[1] Veatch, An Ethical Framework for Terminal Care Decisions: A New Classification of Patients (1984) 32 (9) *J. Am. Geriatrics Society* 666 cited in the Matter of Claire Conroy (1985) 486 A. 2d 1209 (NJ Sup. Ct)

[2] *Airedale NHS* v. *Bland* (1993) 1 ALL ER 821; (1993) 3 WLR 316

[3] Skegg, Law, Ethics and Medicine, 72; *Wilson* v. *Pringle* (1987) QB237; Re Eve (1986) 2 SCR382 (Supreme Court of Canada); Re F(1990) 2AC1; John Roberson, Organ Donation by Incompetent, and the Substituted Judgment Doctrine (1976) 76 *Columbia L.R* 48

[4] David M. Walker, *The Oxford Comparison of Law* (Oxford Press, 1980) p. 441.

distinguishable case is of refraining from seeking to prolong life in cases of great pain or inevitable death, which is generally considered morally and legally permissible.

Euthanasia as a practice in today's medicine is generally acceptable and wide spread. Pioneer heart transplant surgeon Professor Christian Bernard admitted that it is standard medical practice.[5] Its rampancy was also recognised by Lord Goff in *Anthony Bland* case, where His Lordship said: 'It is of course well known that there are many responsible members of our society who believe that euthanasia should be made lawful'.[6]

It is suggested that if the right of self-determination is stretched to logical conclusion, suicide, euthanasia and abortion will become unquestionable legal. Some have sought to draw a line of distinction between voluntary and involuntary euthanasia. The former is a situation where the patient at his request is killed, especially to relieve suffering from incurable illness. It is involuntary when life is ended without the patient or his proxy invitation. Like voluntary euthanasia, the motive may be to relieve pain and suffering, but its moral justification (if any) is paternalism – what is considered best for the patient, a victim of pain. This will be the case where a doctor causes death in the absence of either a personal or proxy invitation to do so.[7] The momentum in favour of voluntary euthanasia is considerable strong. The decriminalisation of suicide and attempted suicide in many jurisdictions is a pointer. The growing recognition of living wills, respect for the patient's right to refuse treatment and or sustenance, and the general judicial attitude to the ending of life for cases of terminally ill and incurable patient, coupled with liberal legislation in some jurisdictions legalising euthanasia, are pointers as to how the law is likely to develop in the future. Like Cory J has noted, 'dying is an integral part of living...the right to die with dignity should as well be protected as in any other aspect of the right to life.'[8] Generally the argument in favour of giving effect to the patient's right to terminate treatment and sustenance will in the future more likely prevail against counter-arguments especially where the patient illness is incurable or terminal.

Literally euthanasia means a good death. Over the years however the phrase have been modified and is associated with an active attempt to end life on the prompting (usually) of the patient. Generally most doctors do not find objectionable euthanasia in the original sense of good death, i.e., symptom free death with dignity. But its modified meaning does not enjoy similar acceptability. For example the World Medical Association in connection with the second meaning states:

---

[5] C Bernard, *Good LfelGood Death*, Prentice Hall Press, 1987.

[6] *Airedale NHS Trust* v. *Bland* [1993] 3WLR 316, [1993] 1 All ER 821; (1993) 12 BMLR 64.

[7] Mason & Smith, *op. cit*, p. 316; H. Palmer, Dr Adams Trial for Murder [1957] *Crim. L.R.* 365, *R* v. *Arthur* [1993] 12 BMLR 1; *R* v. *Cox* [1992] 12 BMLR 38.

[8] *Rodriguez* v. *A.G. of British Columbia* [1993] 3 WWR 553.

> 'Euthanasia that is the act of deliberately ending the life of a patient, either at his request, or at the request of his close relative is unethical. This does not prevent the physician from respecting the will of the patient to allow the natural forces of death to follow its course in the terminal phrase of sickness.'[9]

The statement makes a distinction between active and passive euthanasia. The former requires specific action on the physician's part in ending life. The later is concerned with non-treatment of terminal condition.[10] The distinction merely makes pronounced the distinction often drawn in law between 'acts' and 'omissions'; raising moral issues whether both are essentially different in characters and result. But, reviews of the authorities in the subject have turned around related questions of self-autonomy, the wish of the patient and the quality of life.[11]

It raises many medico-legal questions connected with the purpose of medical care, legal classification and distinction between act and omission, rules of causation, patient's consent, autonomy and choice, moral interest of the society in preserving or terminating life, and also the *proprietary* of using the civil court system to make declaration on matters bordering on criminality.

Ethical issues

(i) Purpose of Medical Care

Generally medical care aims to achieve four things, namely: (a) to cure sickness when it occurs; (b) to prevent the re-occurrence of illness; (c) where the sickness cannot be cured, to prevent its further deterioration; (d) and to relieve pain or suffering or both in the body and mind of a patient.[12] It follows therefore that where medical care is not administered to achieve any of the above aim(s), it is all together useless and ought to be discontinued.

Reasoning along similar line, the Master of Rolls in *Anthony Bland* case said: 'I doubt if it has ever been an object of medical care merely to prolong the life of an insensate patient with no hope of recovering where nothing can be done to promote any of these objects.'[13] It is therefore plausible to ask whether there is justification on moral grounds to hasten the death of a patient suffering from incurable sickness? If in the circumstance hastening of death relieves pain and further suffering, should death be encouraged on the basis of furthering one of the aims of treatment? While the court seem to say in one breath that any hastening of death will be wrongful, it at the same time appears to recognise though hypocritically that ending life in those circumstances is proper. For instance, the court permitted a hospital to discontinue

---

[9] World Medical Association [1967] Lancet 1305.
[10] Roger Leng, Death and the Criminal Law (1982) 45 *MLR* 206.
[11] *Airedale NHS* v. *Bland* [1993] 3WLR 316, [1993] 1 All ER 821; (1993) 12 BMLR 64.
[12] *Bland case* [1993] 3WLR 316, per Thomsd Bringham MR.
[13] *Bland case* [1993] 3WLR 316 at 336.

medical care in *Auckland Area Health Board* v. *AG*[14] when it was clear that further treatment will not advance any medical objective. Thomas J of the High Court of New Zealand authorised a hospital to discontinue medical care to a patient suffering from Guillian-Barre' syndrome where treatment and care were only administered with the sole purpose of maintaining the patient life, not geared to cure or improve the condition of the patient. His Lordship said:

> In my view, doctors have a lawfully excuse to discontinue ventilation when there is no medical justification for continuing that form of medical assistance. To require the administration of a life support system when medical function or purpose are served only to defer the death of the patient is to *confound* the purpose of medicine.[15]

Noteworthy of mention, his Lordship justified euthanasia for incurable cases like cancer and passed the responsibility of deciding the desirability or otherwise of euthanasia to doctor's judgment of what constitutes the best interest of the patient in the circumstance.

Going by his reasoning, if a doctor thinks that it is in the patient's best interest to die he lawfully can trigger euthanasia not by actively fostering death but by ceasing to prolong life by withdrawal of treatment. The case therefore seeks like many others to draw a distinction between withdrawal of treatment and actively hastening death by positive acts. While the former will be lawful in certain situations, the latter is prohibited. Active trigger of death and treatment withdrawal however are hardly distinguishable morally and in effect. May be as safeguard from preventing the 'best interest' approach slipping into morally dangerous terrain, His Lordship, added as caveat to it a further requirement: 'that in all such cases the doctor must adhere to medical procedures which safeguard against possible medical error of individual judgement'. This would in effect mean that all a doctor need do not to act unlawful is to seek medical opinion from at least another physician as to whether the opinion he has reached on the patient's best interest is corroborative. Sir Stephen Brown, P in *Airedale NHS Trust* v. *Bland* also thinks that a second opinion by another doctor grounds the best interest test safer when he said: 'I would expect that in all similar applications there would be not merely be one medical opinion but at least two responsible medical opinions.'[16]

Lord Donaldson MR reviewing *Auckland Arch Health Board v. AG* in *Re J*[17] also said:

> It surely was never intended that it (i.e. medical treatment) be used to prolong biological life in patients benefit of the prospect of returning to an even limited exercise of human life. Nothing in the inherent purpose of these scientific

[14] [1993] 1NZLR235.
[15] [1993INZLR235 at 253
[16] Unreported 13/8/92 (High Court of New Zealand) referred to in *Bland* case [1993] 3WLR 316 at p336.
[17] *Re J* (a minor) [1993] Fam. 15, [1992] 4 All ER 614.

advances can require doctors to treat the dying as if they are curable. Natural death has not lost its meaning or significance. It may be deferred, but it need not be postponed indefinitely. Nor surely, was modern medical science ever developed to be used inhumanly. To do so is not consistent with its fundamental purpose. Take the case of a man riddled with cancer, in constant agony and facing imminent death. Is he to be placed upon a respirator? On the contrary it has been generally accepted that doctors may seek to alleviate a patient's terminal pain and suffering even though the treatment may at the same time possibly accelerate the patient's death. As I perceive it, what is involved is not just medical treatment, but medical treatment in accordance with the doctor's best judgement as to what is in the best interest of his or her patient. They remain responsible for the kind and extent of the treatment administered and, ultimately, for its duration... But with a patient such as Mr. L, where life is being prolonged for no therapeutic or medical purpose or, in other words, death is merely being deferred, the doctor is not under a duty to avert that death at all costs. If, in my judgement, the proper medical practice would be to discontinue the life support system, and that would be in the best interest of the patient, he may do so subject to adhering to a procedure which provides a safeguard against the possibility of individual error."[18]

Following similar reasoning courts have authorised treatment cessations[19] in severe cases where medical treatment do not further any medical purpose. In *Airedale NHS* v. *Bland*, the House of Lords authorised the cessation of medical treatment to a 17 years-old patient in a persistent vegetative State (PVS). Similar conclusion was reached by the Quebec Superior Court in *Nancy B* v. *Hotel-Dien de Quebec*.[20] The patient suffered from Guillain Barre's syndrome, which severely impaired the patient's intellect and made survival dependent on a respirator. Informed medical opinion appeared to agree with legal position on cessation of treatment, if not outright euthanasia.

In *Bland* case, Sir, Thomas Bingham cited the informed position in Canada and England as supporting treatment cessation, where no useful purpose would be advance by medical treatment. Recognising that treatment cessation is itself proper the Law Reform Commission of Canada recommended in its report that: 'A physician should not incur any criminal liability if he decides to discontinue or not initiate treatment for an incompetent person, when that treatment is no longer therapeutically usefully and not in the person's best interest.'[21] Also the British Medical Association Ethics Committee states that

'feeding gastrostomy tubes for nutrition and hydration as medical treatments are warranted only when they make possible a decent life in which the patient

[18] Ibid.

[19] *Nancy B* v. *Hotel-Dien de Quebec* (1992) 86 DLR (4th) 385. See also In *Re J* [1991] Fam. 33, In *Re B* (1981) 1 WIR 1421, In Re C [1991] Fam 26.

[20] *Nancy B* v. *Hotel-Dien de Quebec* (1992) 86 DLR (4th)

[21] .Report on Euthanasia, Aiding Sucide and Cessation of Treatment p. 27

> can reasonably be though to have a continued interest...There is no justification for continuing medical intervention in such a state and the working party feels that the individual concerned is most appropriately treated as an incompetent patient with terminal condition.'[22]

The preponderance of these opinions suggests that where medical treatment is not in the best interest of a patient, hospital authorities will be justified in discontinuing or in not initiating treatment. The effect would allow death with least pain and suffering. Such action is legally permissible. It is classified as treatment cessation. But where same result of death is effected by the introduction of an active positive hastening of death by a doctor, classified as euthanasia, it is prohibited and considered murder. That brings us to the next ethical question having to do with the prohibition of euthanasia. While paradoxically permitting treatment cessation, euthanasia is treated as unlawful, thereby raising question that revolve around what constitutes act and omission.

(ii) Distinction between Acts and Omission

As previously stated, a commentary states:

> 'Generally it (euthanasia) is treated as illegal and not distinguishable from murder, largely because of the difficulty of distinguishing in legal rule and in fact between criminal and justifiable causing of death. A narrowly distinguishable case is of refraining from seeking to prolong life in cases of great pain or inevitable death, which is generally considered morally and legally permissible.'[23]

This being so, the question can be raised whether turning off of a life-support machine for a patient is murder? Answer to the question would require asking whether there is any moral or ethical difference in not starting the machine in the first place, and starting it only to stop it thereafter? Its relevance has a bearing on the philosophical foundation for fixing criminal or civil liability or both. Generally in law, a defendant is held responsible for the consequence of his action. To so do a nexus must exist between his act or omission and the resultant effect. Cases for the test of responsibility or fault have turned on matter of causation.[24] In this regard it is important to classify a defendant's course of conduct whether it is an *act* or *omission*. The reason for this classification is not only a matter for legal history, but is also one related to criminalisation policy. Generally a defendant is responsible for the consequence of his conduct attributable to his act. On the other hand, conduct

---

[22] British Medical Association Report, 1991, and 1991 report of the Institute of Medical Ethics.

[23] David M. Walker, *The Oxford Comparison of law* (Oxford Press, 1980) p. 441.

[24] HLA Hart and AM Hanore, Causation in the Law: A Surveyof Common Sense Principles (1956) 72 *LQR* 58; Notes of an Address on Special Problem of the Law of Torts, p. 11, reprinted in (1957) 71 *LQR* 402 at 413.

classified as omissions attracts less responsibility or no responsibility. Criminal policy have mainly concerned itself with the punishment of harmful act, leaving to the conscience of the individual and society to judge what constitutes harmful omission, without necessarily assigning sanction to it. Omission is only made punishable in law where there exists a legal duty to act. That being so, omissions which trigger responsibility, are rare.

In all cases where it is shown that medical treatment serves no medical purpose, and ought to cease or not initiated, the court fixes the limit of liability. Causative rules demand that a defendant is responsible for the consequences of his action. So to fix responsibility it becomes relevant to see what results from the act of the defendant. If stopping a life-support machine, such as an artificial respirator would mean death of the patient, then the defendant who stops it would be responsible for murder of the patient. But if on the other hand, the defendant omits to activate the respirator which causes the death of the patient, it will hardly be criminal, unless there is a legal duty to initiate or activate the respirator. These issues are relevant in all the cases where the court have authorised treatment cessation in the best interest of patients.[25]

By classifying treatment cessation as conduct within the bracket of omission, treatment cessation authorisation becomes easier and more compatible to decree. For example in *Anthony Bland*, having held that the discontinuation of his life-sustaining treatment was more related to a conduct within the bracket of omission to act, rather than a positive act, the relevant question turned on whether there was a duty to continue medical treatment. The artificial feeding process by a nasagostric tube inserted through his nose and drawn into his stomach was also in issue, even though the majority judgment largely reveals that it was either glossed on or at best made secondary to the distinction between the divide of acts and omissions. Since no duty to act existed in the case as the court reasoned because medical treatment could no longer meet any of the objectives of treatment, it become less graphic to describe what happens with the ventilator as not sufficient warrant to attract responsibility. That exactly was the position adopted. By the fiction of 'best interest' of the patient the court stated that further treatment not serving the purpose of medical care was not in the patient's best interest. Accordingly the duty to sustain life at that point evaporates. When it does the hospital's proposed conduct of turning off the ventilator can then be classified as omission, a thing legally permissible.

In arriving at such a conclusion it becomes necessary for the court to make less graphic the consequences of the proposed conduct. The House of the Lords had to reformulate the issues for determination. Even though the simplistic approach to the issue would have been: 'Whether it is in the best interest of the patient to die?' the Law Lords formulated the issue in this less graphic way: 'Whether it is in the best

---

[25] *Airedale NHS Trust* v. *Bland* [1993] 3WLR 316 ; *Nancy* v. *Hotel de Quebec* (1992) 86 DLR (4th) 385.

interest of the patient that his life should be prolonged by the continuation of medical treatment?'

By so doing, the resultant consequences of a discontinuation of the artificial feeding of the patient was not equated with 'starvation', but rather with life support ventilator. From that perspective, the hospital request to discontinue treatment likened to cutting a mountaineer's rope or severing the air pipe of a deep-sea diver, as argued by Mr. Munby for the patient, was made to look like something else-less pointed. The request was rather made to take the form of an omission to act where no duty to act exist.

Even at that counter-argument can be advanced that if a conduct whether classified as an act or omission results in harm, in this case death, no good would be achieved by drawing a distinction between both with a view to authorising harm. The moral issues are the same. If by positive act a doctor stops a respirator or administers a lethal drug to quicken death both would result in the patient's death. Lord Goff alluded to this fact when his Lordship admitted that a 'charge of hypocrisy' could be made in trying to distinguish both. If the doctor by discontinuing treatment is entitled in consequence to let his patient die, should it then be unlawful to put him out of his misery straight away, in a more human manner, by a lethal infection, rather than let him linger in pain until he dies?'[26]

It is respectfully submitted that the courts drew the distinction simply to make it less inhibitive to authorise euthanasia, smoked-screened as treatment cessation.

(iii) Sanctity of life versus right of self-determination

No doubt the community where a patient lives has an inherent interest in the preservation of a patient's life. The interest of society is usually expressed by legislation designed to protect life, prohibiting homicide and kindred offences This however is to be balanced with cherished societal human values of autonomy and self-determination of individual. These values no doubt are necessary for the preservation of freedom. It is however conceivable that both interest of the sanctity of life and self determination can sometimes come in collusion. For example, a patient who refuses life-saving treatment is exercising his right of self-determination. But if he is allowed to die as his chooses, his action may constitute a breach to the sanctity of life principle, equally cherished by the state and society. In America, state interest is expressed in the form of *paren patria* jurisdiction. Both principles no doubt are rational, but where they conflict the right of self-determination prevails.[27] The legalising of suicide in some jurisdictions is pointer that the primacy of self-determination can lead to an ethical slippery-slope. If the right remains uncircumcised by reasonable limits it could provide 'canon-further' for active euthanasia by less-able patients.

---

[26] *Airedale NHS Trust* v. *Bland* [1993] 3WLR 316; *Nancy* v. *Hotel de Quebec* (1992) 86 DLR (4th) 385.

[27] *Airedale NHS Trust* v. *Bland* [1993] 3WLR 316. See also *Re T. Adult* [1992] 4 All ER 649; (1992) 9 BMLR 46.

(iv) Naturalist issue

Moralists would argue that life is a sacred great gift from God that must be treasured at all and every cost. So to the extent that euthanasia treats life with no regard it is considered unethical. If death is inevitable however, some moralist may have fewer objections if the patient refuses to lengthen the dying process. What appears more objectionable to them is the hastening of the dying process. Christian moralist will cite the case of King Saul. When he was fatally injured and death was eminent, his armour bearer refused his request to help him 'die with dignity,' rather than from the hand of a considered unclean enemy.[28] David prescribed death penalty for the person who claimed to have done the mercy–killing of King Saul.[29] Why? Because euthanasia is considered a crime against the giver of life, God.

(v) Doctor as decision–maker

Faced with request by a patient requesting euthanasia, what should the physician do? By ethics of his practice he is enjoined to preserve life. If he accedes to the patient request he could be liable for murder. Hastening of death is not legally permissible. In *R* v. *Adams* [30] and *R* v. *Cox*,[31] the courts held that no physician has the right deliberately to cut the tread of life by hastening death of a patient. In both cases doctors who administered lethal injection to patients at their request were held responsible for unlawful homicide. Even if a doctor believes in euthanasia he is by the ethics of his profession not permitted to hasten the dying process. The fact that his motive is kindly and somewhat moral will not make his action legal. That is irrelevant in law. It is the intent to kill or cause grievous bodily harm which constitute the *mens rea* for homicide. The reason leading to formation of the intention is generally immaterial.[32] It follows therefore that even though the practice may be accepted by even prominent doctors as standard medical treatment, any who practice it stands risk of conviction for homicide, and possible civil claim by survivors of the patient.

A case can however be made for a physician's kind motive. Modern medicine now recognises the concept of treating first the person as a patient, and then his well being. That may be what the court alluded to in *Anthony Bland* that where treatment amount to extensive manipulation of the patient that shocks sense of decency, in other words, amounts to what can be described as mortification, further treatment may be withdrawn to preserve the dignity of the dying person.[33] Even at

---

[28] 1 Samuel 31:4 (Holy Bible).

[29] 2 Samuel 1:6-16(Holy Bible).

[30] Unreported, 8/4/57, per Devlin J.

[31] Unreported 18/9/92, per Ognall J. See also *Barber* v. *Superior Court of State of California*, 195 Cal. Rptr. 484.

[32] See s316. Of Criminal Code Law.

[33] *Airedale NHS* v. *Bland* [1993] 3 WLR 316 at 394, per Lord Mustill. *Re Conray* (1985) 486 A 2d 1209 at 1249, per Handler J.

that we are confronted with the question of who ought to make the decision or determine when treatment amounts to mortification. This is the point where the doctor may be implicated. Who should determine the moment of mortification and or best interest of the patient? Should it be the doctor or the surrogate-decision maker?

What should the doctor do when faced with such a situation? The President of the Family Division in *Bland* case advised that he should apply to court for authorisation to cease treatment. This brings us to the issue of the procedure for bringing such applications.

(vi) The role of courts

Where should choice of medical treatment decisions be made? Are courts the proper forum for making treatment choices? Some doubt the courts as proper forum. Lord Goff said, 'the law does not feel able to authorise euthanasia.'[34] It mean the court have no legal power to authorise euthanasia because it is to every intent and purpose illegal. However if the nature of the treatment can be classified within the bracket of treatment cessation the court can be the forum where permission ought to be sought and obtained. Be that as it may, treatment cessation application can also trigger questions such as, whether the proposed conduct can be put into effect without committing a criminal offence and particularly the offence of murder?[35] Usually the applicant would seek a declaratory relief to cease treatment by not continuing treatment or by withdrawing the artificial feeding process. Where the declaration is granted as requested it does not automatically decide what effect authorisation can legally have. The possible effects of a decree authorising cessation were well summarized by Lord Mustill into three categories namely:

(a) it can change the legal status of the proposed conduct, in the sense that it legalises it;

(b) it can also creates a new common law rule exception to the charge of murder. This would amount to opening new frontiers to criminal law. Court authorisation to cease treatment would be treated as a new defence to a charge for unlawful homicide. It requires incorporating developments in medical science into criminal legislation;

(c) it further can reassure the medical doctor that the proposed conduct is lawful, so shall attract no civil or criminal responsibility.[36]

---

[34] *Airedale NHS* v. *Bland* [1993] 3 WLR 316 at 350, per Lord Goff.

[35] Ibid, at 389, per Lord Mustill.

[36] Ibid, at. 391-2See also *Finlayson* v. *HM Advocate* (1978) SLT (Notes) 60 (Scottish Case); Malcherek 91981) 2ALLER422; *Re. Quinlan* (1976) 355 A 2d 664 D. Casswell, Rejectivly Criminal Liability for life – Shortening Care (1990) 6 *J of Contemporary Health Law and Policy* 127 and *R.* v. *Bodkin Adams* (1957) CLR 365 (ccc), per Devlin J; both cited in Kenendy & Grubb, *op. cit*, 1205 - 1207

Even at that, more serious ethical questions may yet be asked arising from the application. Consider: if the physician in good faith considers it in the best interest of the patient to cease treatment and he according does so before seeking court authorisation. If charged with murder, will it be proper to convict if the facts show that the court would have authorised treatment cessation if an application were made before ceasing treatment? Even if an application was made at the proper time, i.e., before withholding or withdrawing treatment, can the court in its civil jurisdiction make a declaration on whether on the facts a charge for unlawful homicide should be dismissed simple because the doctor had good reasons to cease treatment? If so, can the declaration constitute a defence to a criminal charge of murder? If it does, will it be proper for courts to use its civil jurisdiction to make declaration of criminality, a preposterous thing it should not do? Anyone familiar with the way the legal system operates knows too well that both are separate spheres that hardly mix. Attempt to use the civil court to make pronouncement on crimes is absurd. It will be considered novel and can be dangerous because the age long distinction between criminal and civil matters is recognised not just for administrative convenience. That was what His Lordship meant when he said:

> "I recognise that strong warnings have been given against the civil court usurping the function of the criminal court. Notwithstanding the objection there exist a few cases where the civil court have made declarations that constitute defence in criminal charges."[37]

In a jurisdiction like Nigeria where all criminal offences and their defences are codified, it will prove difficult to use court's civil declarations as defences for criminal charges unless such declarations are already recognised by the statute in question. For example, the defence for murder under the Criminal Code can hardly accommodate a situation where a doctor can plead court authorisation. That being the case a doctor who obtains such authorisation and proceeds to withhold treatment may expose himself to a charge. Defence if any, must therefore be structured in such a way that it can be accommodated by section 306 of the Code. In that case the doctor's defence will be under the provisions of the Code structured on the facts of authorisation as pointing to a lack of intention to kill. This no doubt is an unpleasant way to raise a defence.[38]

Another troubling question that remains unresolved is whether such a civil declaratory can constitute estoppel to further prosecution of a doctor. It ought to be. The House of Lords thought so.[39] Compton J in *Barber* v. *Superior Court of State of*

---

[37] Ibid., at 366, per Lord Goff (lead judgement). See *Imperial Tobacco Ltd.* v. *Attorney-General* [1981] AC 718 at 741, 752; *Royal College of Nursing of the United Kingdom* v. *Department of Health and Social Security* [1981] AC 800; *Barber* v. *Superior Court of State of California* (1983) 195 Cal. Rptr. 484; In *Re Gardner* (1987) 537 534 A 2d 947.

[38] *Aoko* v. *Fagbemi*, (1961) 1 ALLNLR400 (HC) constitutional requirements for crime; no common law offences; section on murder in Criminal Code and make the arguments.

[39] *Airedales case*, [1993] 3 WLR 316 at p. 366, per Lord Goff, and at 390, per Lord Mustill.

California, endorsed a similar view. He said: 'a murder prosecution is a poor way to design an ethical and moral code for doctors who are faced with decision concerning the use of costly and extraordinary life support equipment.'[40]

Usually it will be reasonable to expect that court declarations would constitute complete bar to criminal prosecution. If it does not, it is suggested that that would be a good ground for the Attorney-General to enter a *nolle proseque* to a criminal charge.

(vii) Deciding what constitutes best interest

To justify treatment cessation the preponderance of authorities suggests that it must be in the best interest of patient to cease treatment. But who decides what is "best interest", especially if the patient cannot express a wish or never did express one before becoming incompetent? Whose standard should be used in judging the quality of life? Should it be the patient, or the doctor or the community? What index should be used in deciding what constitute best interest of the patient? It no doubt brings us face to face with the problem of formulating the 'critical equation.'[41] The fact that a patient suffers severe pain ought not to be the exclusive reason why treatment must cease. On the scale of equation, pain is just one factor to be considered. Handler J in *Re Conroy* said:

> 'Clearly, a decision to focus exclusively on pain as the single criterion ignores and devalues other important ideals regarding life and death. Consequently, a pain standard cannot serve as a significant concern that bear on the decision to forgo life-prolonging treatment.'[42]

The moral and legal distinction between euthanasia and treatment cessation remains controversial. The former remains unlawful unlike the latter. In *Frenchary Health Care NHS Trust* v. *S*, for example the English Court of Appeal [43] held that it is in the best interest of a patient whose gastronomy tube was accidentally dislodged during a PVS treatment not to be replaced. Also in *Auckland Area Health Board* v. *A. G*, [44] the New Zealand court held that where no medical benefit would result to a patient the doctor can withdraw treatment even if the resultant effect is death. In *Auckland* the patient, suffering from Guillain-Barre syndrome had his brain disconnected from his body leading to complete sensory loss and paralysis. He was kept alive by means of a ventilator, unlike *Bland* case where the patient was kept going through an artificial feeding process. The question presented to Thomas J was very pointed, similar to that put before the trial court in *Bland* case by the Official

---

[40](1983) 195 Cal. Rptr. 484 at 486 See also Canadian Law Reform Com mission Working Paper of July,1983, suggesting that criminal sanction should not accompany a court sanction treatment cessation.

[41] See *Re J* (A Minor) (Wardship: Medical Treatment) [1991] Fam. 33 at 46, per Donaldson of Lymington MR.

[42] (1985) 486 A 2d. 1209 at 1248.

[43] [1994] *Times*, 19 February.

[44] [1993] 1 NZLR 235, [1993] 4 Med. LR 239.

Solicitor, namely: whether or not the doctor by his proposal to withdraw the artificial ventilation support would not make himself criminally responsible for homicide under the law? In the traditional manner of making euthanasia less graphic by masking it to appear as treatment cessation, Thomas J reformulated the issue to the effect that: the question was whether a doctor is under a duty to continue medical treatment which has no medical benefit notwithstanding that the effect of so doing would result in death of the patient. Using common sense reason he held that no 'real life' was being enjoyed by the patient, but a mere 'manifestation of life', which should end without medical assistance. The doctor was lawful excused to discontinue treatment in the circumstance.

Simply put, all the cases show that allowing a patient to die by withholding or withdrawing treatment in certain circumstances is permissible if it is in a patient's best interest, or if medical treatment will serve no further beneficial purpose, but actively assisting a patient to die is criminal. If the facts fit into the classification of the former it is advisable for the doctor to seek court permission before ceasing to treat in all cases.

Terminal care and dying: ethical questions

Terminal illness is one that will eventually lead to death. This does not mean death must take place within a fixed time. Its definition has become controversial because of the difficulty of separating the dying from the terminal ill. Dying process is said to begin as soon as we are born. Terminal illness begins when:

(i) diagnosis of illness is made and remedial conditions are eliminated or;
(ii) death is eminent within a proximate time or;
(iii) medical treatment is directed not to cure but to prevent further deterioration or is administered for palliative purposes.[45]

No doubt the diagnosis and the prognosis of terminal illness can be subject to much uncertainty, thereby making the ethical problems which result from it difficult to deal with. Terminal illness cuts across all age groups, children, adolescents, adults and the elderly. The range of illness that come within its bracket include cancer, lung and heart disease, AIDS, stroke or multiple sclerosis and in children congenital defects and some form of inherited diseases.

Ethical concerns

Clinical problems relating to treatment of terminal patients is bound by ethical questions that can broadly be considered under three main categories:[46]

---

[45] K Calman, Ethical Implications of Terminal Care, in Freeman (ed) *Medicine, Ethics and the Law*, London: Stevens and Sons, 1988, p.103.

[46] Ibid., at p. 107.

(i) the third person's view of ethics. This brings to the fore issue relating to aggregates, population, communities or special groups invariably tied to matters of justice and utility;
(ii) the second person's view of ethics. This is an ethical value system that arises between the individuals, such as doctors and patients. Key ethical concepts that are primary here are those of compassion and respect for autonomy; and
(iii) The first person view of ethics, concerned with issues of morality and integrity of each individual health care professional, like the doctor and nurse.

Noteworthy of mention is the fact that the legal principle of autonomy or self-determination which generally underlies medical ethics is crucial in understanding the various questions raised in the treatment of the terminally ill. Autonomy is also itself related like the other three categories to the wider questions such as those that question our mortality. Whenever clinical case of this nature arises people are quick to ask 'why me?' And for the case-giver, each time the patient dies his mortality is questioned and life considered uncertain. These moral and spiritual questions can hardly be divorced from the legal issues that merit consideration. Let us now discourse the ethical issues using our three categories.

The third person's ethics

This is an area that tasks the twin ethical value system of justice and utility. Medical facilities available are often distributed unequally. Equally related to the matter of justice above is the fact that certain terminal illnesses are better served than others. For example, the public perception is that illnesses such as cancer and AIDS deserve more support from the public health purse than stroke.

From the utility standpoint we are required to weigh the utility cost of the care of the terminal ill against the background of diminishing public health resources. For examples the question may be asked, how do we justify putting up enormous resources for the care of say a cancer patient at the expense of lesser resources to the care of malaria and anti-smoking campaign that could prevent certain form of cancer.

The second person's ethics

This is a stage in ethics that involves the patient and his professional care-givers, the doctors and nurses. Communication must be geared to build confidence in the patient. Even if truth of patient's condition must be disclosed to him or relatives it should take place in an atmosphere that recognises need for compassion and respect of patient right of autonomy. In the context of autonomy the doctor is bound to consider the issues of euthanasia and the associated question of living. Compassion also requires that the doctor and other care-givers are aware of the different cultural and religious values of the patient and should be non-judgmental; but rather treat all with fairness.

The first person's ethics

This is an aspect that calls on the health care professional to bring to bear principles of compassion, justice and the ability to be non-judgmental. He may find his value system to be a variance with that of the patient or his relatives. But he must in the ultimate ensure that the patients is the decision-maker, even if he reaches one based on advice from others, e.g. relatives, priest, lawyer, etc.

The ending of life: incompetent patient

In the New Jersey case of *Re Conroy*[47] the issue for decision revolved around the circumstances under which life-sustaining treatment may be withheld or withdrawn from an incompetent, institutionalised elderly patients with severe and permanent mental and physical impairment with a limited life expectancy. We shall use this phrase 'termination of treatment' to refer to both withholding and withdrawal of treatment without distinction, a position that also enjoys judicial recognition. According to the court, whether treatment is withheld from the start or withdrawn later makes no difference to the end result, death.[48] The court recognise that if a distinction is made between both doctors might be reluctant, in some cases to make the usual decision to commence treatment because once started withdrawal will become legally problematic. But if as the court do (making no distinction between both) doctors will be encouraged to err on the side of preserving life knowing that a reasoned decision to withdraw treatment can be made later.[49] The New Jersey Supreme Court in *Re Quinlan* also expressed a similar reasoning when it stated:

> 'there must be a way to free physicians, in the pursuit of their healing vocation from possible contamination of self-interest or self-protection concerns, which would inhibit their independent medical judgment for the well-being of their dying patients. We would hope that this opinion might be serviceable to some degree in ameliorating the professional problems under discussion.'[50]

This notwithstanding it can still be argued with some force that withholding and withdrawal are morally distinct. The taking away of that which is used for life-support and not beginning a therapy when a new crisis in the management of a patient begins are two different things that ought to be kept distinct. On moral grounds we are not obligated to help others even if it is in our power to do so, but we are morally obligated not to interfere with life-sustaining routines.[51] Arguments along this line bring to the front burner issues related to the legal policy of responsibility in cases for acts and omission.[52]

---

[47] 464 A 2d 303 (NJ, 1983), CA; 486 A 2d 1209 (NJ, 1985) SC. For discussion on the case, see N Rhoden, How Should We View the Incompetent? (1989) 17 *Law Med Hlth Care* 264; HL Hirsh and MK Cuneo, Who Shall Live, Who Shall Die: Who Decides? (1986) 5 *Med Law* 111.

[48] *Airedale NHS* v. *Bland* (1993) 1 ALLER821

[49] *Re Quinlan* 355 A2d 664 (NJ 1976)

[50] 355 A 2d 664 (NJ, 1976).

[51] JM Finnis,Bland: Crossing the Rubicon? (1993) 109 LQR 329

[52] Ibid.

The *Conroy* court held that life sustaining treatment could be terminated if any of the following tests is satisfied, namely: (i) the subjective test. Under this test life-sustaining treatment can be terminated if it is clear that the patient would have refused treatment. This test focuses on what the patient would have done, rather than on what the average, reasonable person would do.[53] (ii) the objective test – This test focuses on the patient's best interest. It requires that a surrogate decision-maker evaluates the burden and benefits of sustaining the patient's life.[54] Where the burden outweighs the benefit derivable from continued treatment, treatment may be terminated. The court was of the view that the governing principle to determine 'best interest' is an analysis of pain. This position has been criticised as being somewhat parochial in that it unduly glosses over a whole range of relevant and material human values.[55] In its place it has been suggested that the quality of life test which includes matters like dignity, the invasive nature of continuing treatment, the medical value of treatment on the patient and matters such as personal privacy will provide a more accurate measure of a patient's best interest than one that exclusively focuses on pain.

To prevent an excessive appeal to treatment termination, the New Jersey Supreme Court in *Conroy* required that a state 'ombudsman' shall oversee the decision-making procedure with a view to guard against abuses.[56] While this is appreciated, we must not also loss sight of the fact that this supposed safeguard can become an unnecessary burden. If the court properly scrutinises the appointment of the surrogate decision-maker with reference to the patient's family, that ought to do because at that stage the court can confidently assume that the decision will most likely reflect the real or best interest of the patient, the governing test.

Our discussion shall use *Conroy* as the road-map to navigate this section of our discussion because to a large extent it represents the position of the law at least in the United States of America, and by extension the common law position. What is more, the American jurisdiction reports more of such litigation. Furthermore *Conroy* bring into one fold the hitherto thinking that artificial nutrition and hydration are not medical treatment.[57] Prior to it courts have likened the administration of food and water as different from more traditional forms of medical treatment such as artificial feeding by means of a nasogastric tube.[58]

---

[53] Cf. Smith, In Re Quinland: Defining the Basis for Terminating Life Support Under The Right of Privacy (1976) 12 Tulsa LJ 150 where the writer argues that permitting a guardian to make medical decisions for incompetent interferes with the patients rights of privacy.

[54] *Airedale NHS* v. *Bland* (1993) 1 ALLER821

[55] *Re Conroy* (1985) 486 A2d 1209 at 1248

[56] The New Jersey Supreme Court in *Re Conroy* while commending the appoitment of a guardian to art as prevy for the incompetent patient, also required the appointment of an ombudsman to investigate before a decision to withdraw treatment is taken by the doctor and patients relatives.

[57] *Re Conroy* (1985) 486 A 2d 1209 (NJ)

[58] Cf at what stage does natural feeding become medical treatment? See Schrieber J in *Re Conroy* dissenting judgment that artificial feeding is significantly different from bottle-feeding

Ms. Claire Conroy[59] was an elderly incompetent diabetic, severely malformed with an intellectual capacity only marginally above that of a person in a persistent vegetative state (PVS). Permission to remove her nasogastric tube was sought and granted by the trial court on the ground that no valid purpose was served by needlessly prolonging a useless life. Even though the patient died, an appeal was taken to the New Jersey Court of Appeal. In the appeal court's view the death following the removal of the feeding tube which led to the patient's dehydration and starvation was nothing but implied active killing. The court was not prepared to condone active euthanasia. On further appeal to the Supreme Court of New Jersey, it reversed the appellate decision, holding that 'artificial feeding is equivalent to artificial breathing by means of a respirator—both prolong life through mechanical means when the body is no longer able to perform a vital bodily function on its own.[60] Let us consider the position before *Conroy.*

Legal Development Before Conroy

One point needs to be stressed here. Our discussion on the incompetent patients generally should in principle also include minor children. While to a large extent the position of the law as to incompetents in the United State of America and English common law are same in material content, some differences exist on the question of decision—making if the incompetent is an adult. The difference is not related to the type of decision that may be made or its basis, but who can be a decision—maker. While most American states jurisdictions provide for family members as substitute decision makers either as of right under relevant family consent statutes or by application to court for appointment as guardians, these possibilities do not exist in England.[61] In *Re F*[62] the House of Lords vested decision-making in the doctors.

The question whether life-sustaining treatment may be withdrawn from an incompetent, comatose patient was first addressed by the New Jersey Supreme Court in *Re Quinlan.* [63] Karen Quinlan had lapsed into what is called irreversible coma following drug overdose. She suffered cortical damage that resulted in total loss of cognitive functions. At that time there was no known cure or treatment for her condition and experts believed that her survival depended on the continued use of artificial respirator. Her diagnosis was that of being in a 'chronic persistent vegetative state' with no reasonable chances of recovery. Since she was unable to

---

[59] 464 A 2d 303 (NJ, 1983), CA; 486 A 2d 1209 (NJ, 1985) SC.

[60] Ibid at 1236, per Schreiber J. See also RS Dresser and EV Boisaubin, Ethics, Law, and Nutritional Support 91985) Arch Intern Med 122, cited in Mason & Smith, *op. cit*, at 340 n. 2.

[61] Skegg, *Law, Ethics and Medicine*, pp 72, 73 where the writer posits that no one can consent to medical treatment on behalf of an incompentent adult. See also *Re T* (adult: refusal of treatment) (1992) 4 All ER 649, per Lord Donaldson MR; *Airedale NHS Trust* v. *Bland* (1993) 1 All ER 821, per Lords Goff and Mustill, where the Law Lords seem to state that 'substituted judgment' test has no place in English Law, but in the USA, citing *Re Quinlan* (1976)70 NJ 10 and *Belchertown School Superintendent* v. *Saikewicz* (1977) 373 Mass 728, as American case illustrations.

[62]Re F (mental patient: sterilisation) [1990] 2 AC 1, [1989] 2 WLR 1025.

[63] 355 A 2d 664 (NJ, 1976).

make any treatment decision for herself, her father sought to act as her substitute decision-maker. He sought court permission to discontinue the artificial respirator treatment. The court was required to pronounce on whether the incompetent can refuse life sustaining treatment. The court held that the discontinuation of treatment was not criminal homicide in the circumstance and that death following withdrawal of ventilatory support was not homicide, but rather 'expiration from existing natural causes. The Supreme Court of New Jersey ruled that the right to refuse life-sustaining treatment is a constitutional right that extends to incompetent as well as to the competent. While it is a fact that she did not die as anticipated, even if she did, there will still have been no legal problem. This is so because the outcome would have been a good faith-clinical decision after due consideration of the benefit or no-benefit treatment test.[64]

Quinlan has been followed in many cases where the courts have faced the same issue. In *Superintendent of Belchertown State School* v. *Saikewicz*,[65] *Quinlan* was followed and the court held that the constitutional right to privacy encompasses the right to refuse medical treatment and the right may be exercised. It also makes needless the moral and practical fiction of employing the substituted judgment doctrine.

Convoy also goes beyond the cases decided before it on the question of the decision-making procedure. In *Quinlan* the court removed itself from the decision-making process. The process requires the concurrence of the guardian, family, doctor and the hospital ethics committee as a prerequisite to termination of treatment.[66] The attitude of abstaining from judicial intervention was discarded in *Conroy*. It considered the *Quinlan* procedure inappropriate for nursing home patients who are often vulnerable due to their usual mental and physical impairment. In recommending more stringent procedures the court may not have been unmindful that the role of the doctor in the nursing home is limited unlike a usual hospital. In clear unequivocal terms it decided that before treatment may be discontinued under any of its three test (the subjective, limited objective and pure objective test) an applicant seeking a decision to terminate must notify the state office of the Ombudsman.[67] On receipt of the request the Ombudsman shall treat it as an abuse (a presumption bias) and begin an investigation of the grounds for the application. Thereafter he will cause a report within 24 hours to be made to the relevant government agency that operate or regulate the health or nursing home and the Commissioner of Human Service. Investigation before the Ombudsman may be by public or private hearing. The application must also contain a prognosis of the patient's condition from two unaffiliated doctors independently appointed by the Ombudsman. Once this procedure is applied, the guardian, with the concurrence of

---

[64] Mason & Smith, *op. cit*, at 336.
[65] 370 NE 2d 64 (Mass, 1977).
[66] 355 A 2d 664 (NJ, 1976)
[67] (1985) 486 A 2d 1209 (NJ)

the attending doctor and the Ombudsman may terminate life if they believe in good faith that any of the three tests is satisfied. This is a radical departure from the procedure in *Quinlan.* Going by *Conroy*, termination need no application to court as long as the procedure outlined above are followed.

The English Common Law position

As previously stated the position in England is substantially the same with that of the United States of America. There is no known Nigerian case on this subject and so the position traced out in these jurisdictions may serve as useful guide in showing direction. In the matter of the ending of life the centre stage is set by the criminal law's prohibition of murder, with tort and family law at its fringes on matters connected with negligence, battery, care of children, etc. While the stage is played out on the basis that life is sacred, the court have shown that this is by no means absolute. [68] In *Airedale NHS Trust* v. *Bland*, [69] the House of Lord decided that in case of an incompetent patient the governing test to be used by the decision-maker whether to terminate treatment is that of the 'best interest' of the patient.

Some commentators argue that the decision ought to turn on whether a treatment is ordinary or extra-ordinary. This argument within moral theology makes a distinction between obligatory and non-obligatory care. It is said that ordinary care is obligatory for the patient to accept and for others to give and provide. Extra-ordinary care is optional. In everyday language the distinction is between common and unusual care. [70] Whatever the distinction it is hazy and in many cases difficult to state with clarity. For example the Supreme Court of Delaware in *Severns* v. *Wilmington Medical Centre* recognising the difficulty asked the questions: 'Are medicines a part of such life sustaining systems? If so, what medicines? Is food or nourishment a part of such life-sustaining systems? If so, to what extent? What extra-ordinary measures? What measures (or equipment) does the medical profession regard as not extra ordinary under the circumstances? What ordinary equipment is used?'[71]

An analysis of Bland case

The distinction between common and uncommon treatment has little significance to a moral analysis of whether treatment should be withheld, withdrawn or continued. For example, an argument that proceeds on the basis that unusual treatment meets with a lower success rate of cure than common treatment does not really say much about the moral significance about the distinction. Rather the moral analysis here should turns on question of success rate and not the usual or unusual nature of the procedure. It has been suggested that the distinction is unhelpful because it

---

[68] *Airedale NHS Trust* v. *Bland* (1993) 1 All ER 821

[69] [1993] 1 All ER 821; (1993) 12 BMLR 64.

[70] See Mason & Smith, *op. cit*, 324

[71] (1980) 421 A 2d 1334.

represents a conclusion reached in the light of the consideration of a number of factors and it is these factors that any proper analysis of the doctor's (patient's) duty should concentrate upon.[72]

Whatever, *Airedale NHS Trust* v. *Bland* represents the position of the law in England. The traditional approach is that a positive act directed to cause death is generally unlawful, but in certain circumstances the law will permit the causing of death by omission, as in the case of withdrawal or withholding of medical treatment. The fact that a patient is severely handicapped if he were to live or will find life burdensome will not prevent treating termination of the patient's life as murder, i.e., the doing of some positive act to hasten death. Consent of the patient is no defence to a charge of murder, no matter how well motivated the intention is.[73] It is however submitted that a defence can be raised if the drug administers which hasten death is designed to relieve pain and suffering when hopes of a cure have evaporated in the treatment of a patient.[74] The reason for this is that in such a case the doctor cannot be treated as showing an intention to bring about death. Lord Goff in Bland on this stated that: 'a doctor may, when caring for a patient who is, for example, dying of cancer, lawful administer painkilling drugs despite the fact that he knows that an incidental effect of that application will be to abbreviate the patient's life. Such a decision may properly be made as part of the care of the living patient, in his best interest."[75]

In *Bland* the court was forced to make a distinction between acts and omissions when called upon to decide whether it is lawful to withdraw life support in the form of hydration and nutrition to a hopeless (PVS) patient that could lead to death. Their Lordships were of the opinion that while murder is the positive causing of death with an intention to do so, withdrawal or withholding treatment classified as omission is different. Like *Conroy* the court was forced to examine the ethical and practical difference between withholding and withdrawal of treatment. For example it had to re-examine the ambits of what constitutes lawful omission within the structure of criminal law. It had to decide how to place removal of the nasogastric tube that provided the patient hydration and nutrition within the divide. But Lord Browne-Wilkinson for his part admitted that such a withdrawal is a positive act, similar to switching off a ventilator in the case of a patient being sustained by it. But in his judgment he did not so classify the withdrawal. He was of the view that that will in itself introduce into law an intolerable distinction he was not prepared to make. In justifying this position, he Lordship gave an example: 'If instead of removing the nasogastric tube, it was left in peace but no further nutrients were provided for the tube to convey to the patient's stomach, that would not be an act of

---

[72] R Gillan, Enthanasia, Withholding life prolonging Treatment, and Moral Difference between Killing and Letting Die (1988)14 *J. Med. Ethics 115*

[73] *Criminal Code Law*

[74] *R.*v. *Cox* (1992) 12 *BMLR* 38

[75] *Anthony Bland*, per Lord Goff.

commission.' His Lordship reasoning therefore proceeded on the basis that the withdrawal here was not what caused death since by itself the nasogastric tube does not sustain life. This is what makes it possible to merely classify it as permissible omission that may cause or justify death or the ending of life.[76] In the views of Lord Goff, withdrawal that is the switching off of the life support machine was in substance not an act but an omission, and does not constitute a breach of duty because the doctor was not obliged to continue treatment in a hopeless case. Unfortunately these views appear to place 'duty' as the basis for analysing the legality of treatment decision on the ending of life without a detailed analysis of the question of responsibility. That was why Lord Mustill, who disagreed with the majority thought that the act-omission dichotomy is unhelpful in determining the serious questions of the ethical basis for ending the life of an incompetent.

If Bland decides that duty is the basis for analysing the legality of decision to end life, then it forces us to consider the content of the 'duty'. Generally, treatment decision for the incompetent adult and minor by the substitute decision maker ought to be motivated by the 'best interest' principle. This is what properly forms the bedrock of the content of the duty. In the *Bland* case the House of Lords relying on its earlier decision, *Re F*,[77] asked the question whether it was in the best interest of Anthony Bland to continue to receive treatment and not whether it was in his best interest to die. By so framing the question the court became concerned with whether any real benefit could come to the patient by the continuation of treatment. Since he was a PVS, no medical treatment could cure or improve his condition. He could not therefore possibly benefit from a continuation of medical treatment. It was thus possible to rationale that continuing treatment would be invasive and non-dignifying for Anthony Bland.[78]

On the other hand, Lords Mustill and Keith were of the opinion that the best interest principle should be weighed within the context of the relative values of benefit and burden. This would make more graphic the proposed decision. It places in the centre burner the question of weighing the patient's life, whether to live or die. It has been suggested that even though Lords Mustill and Keith endorsed the general 'best interest' test, they recoiled with a caveat to avoid the logic implication of the case. They stated that for a PVS patient there exists the need to proceed on the basis of weighing the various interest of the patient because the patient being permanently insensate, can have no interest especially in the context of continuing treatment.[79]

The best interest of the incompetent remains a decision for the doctor.[80] In the case of a minor, the decision is that of the parents in consultation with the doctor. If the patient is incompetent the doctor would be expected to use good judgment in

---

[76] *Roger Leng*, above n.10
[77] *Re F*, *F.F* (2 July 1986, unreported) Supreme Court of Victoria
[78] *Airedale NHS Trust* v. *Bland* (1993) 1*All ER* 821
[79] Kennedy & Grubb, *op. cit.*, p. 1225.
[80] This follows *Re F* (*supra*) approach.

determining the best interest by reference to the *Bolan* test.[81] In *Bland* Lord Browne-Wilkinson said: '(this is the) stage where the responsible doctor comes to the reasonable conclusion (which accords with the view of a responsible body of medical opinion) that further continuance of an intrusive life support system is not in the best interest of the patient.'[82]

Some commentators argue hat the ratio in *Bland* only applies to PVS patients. As support for this they cite *Auckland* case, which was cited and approved by the House of Lords in *Bland*. The Auckland case involved an insensate patient. In *Auckland AHB* v. *Attorney-General* [83] the 59 year old patient suffered from extreme Guillain-barre syndrome, an illness that affects the nervous system. Although he could not be considered to be 'brain dead,' his brain was unable to communicate with his body because both were disconnected. He was living but impaired, so he could not move a muscle or limb. He was therefore lifeless and motionless and there was no prospect of his recovery. He was kept alive by an artificial ventilatory support system to achieve breathing. In the circumstance his doctor with the support of the patient's wife decided to withdraw the life support system. The question before the court was whether the doctor's action amounted to culpable homicide. Thomas J stated that the critical question was whether the doctor was under a duty to provide or continue with the life support system or whether he had a lawful excuse for discontinuing it. His lordship by analogy took the position that medical intervention would be construed as 'necessaries of life' if it accomplishes any of the following: prevent, cure, or alleviate pain, suffering or disease. [84] Since the prognosis of the patient showed no signs of recovery, he adopted the position that the life-support system was not a necessary of life. His Lordship also justified the withdrawal of the life-support on the grounds that there was no medical justification for continuing treatment, because treatment 'has no further medical function or purpose and serves only to defer the death of a patient is to confound the purpose of medicine.' In other words, if treatment is not designed to prevent, cure or alleviate a disease condition there will exist legal justification in withholding or withdrawing treatment. On the question of causation, his lordship queried the thinking that wherever the doctor withdraws a life-support system which results in death he should be treated as causing death. In his view, provided the doctor is not under a duty to provide medical treatment (because it is not considered a necessary of life) or he has a lawful excuse for declining or continuing treatment, the doctor would not be treated as causing death. Certainly the patient in this case was like *Bland*, insensate, because he was incapable of responding to his

---

[81] *Bolan* v. *Friern Hospital Management Committee* (1957)2 *All ER* 118, (1957)1 *WLR* 582.

[82] *Airedale NHS Trust* v. *Bland* [1993] 1 All ER 821.

[83] [1993] 1 *NZLR* 235 (New Zealand High Court).

[84] Ibid; see also on the proposition that necessaries of life includes medical treatment. *R* v. *Senior* [1899] 1 QB 283; *R* v. *Burney* [1958] *NZLR* 745; *R* v. *Books* [1902] 9 BCR 33; *R* v. *Moore* [1954] *NZLR* 893; *R* v. *Tutton* (1989) 48 CCC (3rd) 129.

environment. The New Zealand case was cited with approval by the House of Lords in *Bland*.[85] That is said to be implicit recognition that the legality of withholding or withdrawing treatment spelt out in *Bland* should remain restricted to PVS insensate patients.

But such a proposition can be countered by reference to the American case of *Conroy* where the patient was not insensate and yet the court considered it legal to terminate treatment.[86] Even though Lord Mustill in *Bland* [87] when reviewing *Re J* [88] on the question of whether 'quality of life' could be a basis for ending life, expressly rejected the idea on the grounds that 'if correct would validate active as well as passive euthanasia and thus require a change in the law of murder,'[89] there are indications that quality of life can be the basis for withholding or withdrawing treatment. His Lordship himself admitted so when he stated that the fact 'that a patient is in great pain may give him or her a powerful motive for wanting to end it, to which in certain circumstances it is proper to accede.' [90] He however warned that that will not legalise withdrawal of treatment on the ground of incapacity or infirmity when comparing the quality of life with that of others. Notable on the quality of life issue, both Lords Goff [91] and Browne-Wilkinson [92] expressly reserved to make comments, thereby giving the impression that they are undecided on the issue. It can be argued with some confidence that if a patient is not insensate i.e. not PVS, the courts may still authorise withdrawal of treatment if the patient's circumstances are extreme. In doing so the court may have to insist on a very high threshold of 'intolerability' or 'extremity.' It can be said as concluding statement, that the law in this context remains unsatisfactory. It is another illustration of the wide gap that exists between modern biotechnology and the law. To use the words of Lord Mustill, 'the law has been left behind by the rapid advance of medical technology.' [93]

---

[85] See the judgment of Lords Goff and Mustill in *Bland* [1993] 1 All ER 821.

[86] In *Re Conroy* 486 A 2d 1208 (NJ 1985); *Re Dinnerstein* (1978) 380 NE 2nd 134 (App Ct. Mass) (patient suffered from degenerative disease of Alzheimer in PVS state); *Re Sprin* (1980) 405 NE 2d 115 (Mass Sup. Ind Ct); *Re John Storar* (1981) 420 NE 2d 64 (NY CA) see also Steffen J of Nevada Supreme Court in *Mackay* v. *Bengstedt* (1990) 801 P. 2nd 617 (on the issue of quality of life for a competent adult).

[87] [1993] 1 All ER 821.

[88] Re J a minor medical treatment [1992] 9 BMLR 10, [1992] 2 FLR 165 [1992] 4 All ER 614, see also B Polland, Killing and Dying – Not the Easy Way Out (1988) 149 *Med. J. Austras* 312; R Gilon, Euthanasia, Withholding Life-prolonging Treatment and Moral Difference Between Killing and Letting Die (1988) 14 *Jo Med Ethics* 15; T.B. Brewin, Voluntary Euthanasia (1986) 1 *Lancet* 1085; G. Gillet, Euthanasia, Letting Die and the Pause (1988) 14 *Jo Med Ethics* 61; but cf. M. Parker, Moral Intuition, Good Deaths and Ordinary Medical Practitioners (1990) 16 *Jo. Med. Ethics* 28.

[89] [1993] 1 All ER 821 at 891, per Lord Mustill.

[90] Ibid.

[91] [1993] 1 All ER 821 at 870 per Lord Goff.

[92] Ibid., at 884, per Lord Browne-Wilkinson.

[93] Kennedy & Grubb, op cit p. 1268, see also the view of Taylor LJ in Re J (supra) above n. 54.

Ending of life for the competent patient

As a general rule a competent patient is entitled to refuse medical treatment, even life-sustaining treatment.[94] Unfortunately the English courts admit of two exceptions to the rule, namely: competent minor[95] and pregnant women.[96] Commentators have criticised these exemptions.[97] A competent person is at liberty to refuse treatment even if the result of it will lead to his death.[98] The position in the United States of America however has been limited by anxieties concerned with the state interest in the preservation of life and preventing of suicide. In this respect *Mckay* v. *Bergstedt*[99] is instructive. The patient, a 31 year-old competent quadriplegic sought to vindicate his right to die. It was evident that he became quadriplegic at 10 due to a swimming accident. Faced with the sorrow of the death of his father, he sought to be released from the life of paralysis held intact by life-sustaining properties of a respirator. He could enjoy limited life from his wheelchair amputation, read, watch television. But he despised about life without the attentive care and love of his devoted father. On this basis he petitioned the court as a non-terminal competent, adult quadriplegic for an order permitting the removal of his respirator by a person who could also administer a sedative and thereby relieve pain that would otherwise precede his demise. He further sought an order of immunity from civil and criminal liability for anyone that provides the assistance and for a declaration absolving him of suicide in the removal of the life-support system. The court granted the orders sought (Steffen J delivered the judgment, Young CJ, Rose and Mowbray JJ concurred; Springer J dissenting). The court while admitting that there is the need to balance the right of autonomy against state interest,[100] stated that where the quality of life is so dismal, the individual right must prevail over that of the State. The patient right prevailed over that of the State. The patient was said to enjoy a pre-eminent right under common law to withdraw his consent to a continued medical

---

94 [1993] 1 All ER 821 at 888, per Lord Mustill. To prevent this, the House of Lords in its legislative capacity in the wake of Bland set up in 1993 a select committee to investigate the ethico-legal issues surrounding treatment decision to end life. *Airedale NHS Trusts* v. *Bland* [1993] 1 All ER 821 at 860 per Lord Keith, at 866 per Lord Goff, at 881-882 per Lord Browne-Wilkinson and at 889 per Lord Mustill; Cruzan v. Director, Missouri Dept of Health 110 S Ct 2841 at 2846 497 US 261 (1990) quoting *Union Pacific R Co* v. *Botsford* 1141 US 250 at 251 (1891).

95 *Re W (a minor: medical treatment)* [1992] 4 All ER 627.

96 *Re an Adult: Refusal of Medical Treatment)* [1992] 4 All ER 671 per Stephen-Brown p.

97 See discussion on informed consent, chapter see also Kennedy & Grubb, *op. cit.*, p.1270.

98 *Airedale NHS Trust* v. *Bland* [1993] 1 All ER 821; *Nancy B* v. *Hotel-Dieude Quebec* (1992) 86 DLR (4th) 385 (Que. Sup.Ct.); *McKay* v. *Begstedt* (1990) 801 P 2d 617 (Nev. Sup.Ct).

99 (1990) 801 P.2d 617 (New Sup.Ct).

100 State interest have been defined and confined to the following 4 criteria (i) preserving the sanctity of all lives; (ii) preventing suicide; (iii) protecting innocent third parties who may be adversely affected by the death of the party seeking relief; and (iv) preservation of the integrity of the medical profession. See *Re AC* (1990) 573. A 2d 1235 (DC CA); *Brophy* v. *New England Sinai Hospital* (1986) 497 NE 2d 626 (Mass. Sup. Ind. Ct) PVS can refuse artificial feeding); Re Farrell (1987) 529 A 2nd 404 (patient has no right to compel doctors to violate accepted professional standard in exercise of his right of autonomy.

regimen involving his attachment to a respirator. It said: 'in so ruling, we attach great significance to the quality of Kenneth (Bergstedt's) life as he perceived it under the particular circumstances that were afflicting him.'[101]

On the question whether the proposal amounts to suicide the court applied the act and omission test. Suicide involves affirmative action. In this case, the patient did not seek an affirmative measure to terminate his life, he desired only to eliminate the artificial barriers standing between him and the natural process of life and death. The patient did not wish to commit suicide. He desired only to live for as long as the state of his health would permit without artificial argumentation and support. According to Steffen J, 'society had no right to force upon him the obligation to remain alive under conditions considered to be anathema. To rule otherwise would place an unwarranted premium on survival at the expense of human dignity, quality of life, and the value that comes from allowing death a natural and timely entrance.'[102]

The question of protecting third parties did not arise. On the preservation of the integrity of the medical profession, his Lordship stated that though it is under a duty to heal, when treatment has the effect only of delaying death in a bodily environment essentially bereft of quality, the profession's integrity will not be threatened by a competent adult refusing life-extending treatment. As support for this proposition, his Lordship cited the conclusion of the President's Commission, established by the USA Congress in 1978, consisting of doctors, ethicist, lawyer and others to consider matters relating to medical treatment.[103] In this context, the exercise of the patient's common law right to refuse life-sustaining attachment to a respirator did not present an ethical threat to the medical profession.

In has been suggested that the (near) absolute nature of the right to refuse treatment is tactic recognition of state sponsored suicide. But in *Bland* case, Lord Goff put the matter in its proper perspective when he said,

> 'I wish to add that in cases of this kind, there is no question of the patient having committed suicide, nor therefore of the doctor having aided or abetted him in doing so. It is simply that the patient has, as he is entitled to do, declined to consent to treatment which might or would have the effect of

---

[101] Steffen J in *McKay* v. *Bergstedt* (1990) 801 P 2d 617.

[102] Ibid.

[103] President's Commission for the Study of Ethical problems in Medicine and Biomedical and Behavioural Research Deciding to Forgo Life-Sustaining Treatment p. 3, US Govt. Printing Office, 1983 states: "The voluntary choice of a competent and informed patient should determine whether or not life-sustaining therapy will be undertaken, just as such choices provide the basis for other decisions about medical treatment. Health care institutions and professionals should try to enhance patient's abilities to make decisions on their own behalf and to promote understanding of the available treatment options...Health care professionals serve patients best by maintaining a presumption in favour of sustaining life, while recognising that competent patients are entitled to choose to forgo any treatment, including those that sustain life." Cited in *Mckay* v. *Bergstedt* by Steffen J.

prolonging his life, and the doctor has, in accordance with his duty, complied with his patient's wishes.'[104]

So a distinction must be drawn between suicide and choosing how to be treated.

Noteworthy of mention is that while the patient enjoys the right to chose and control his medical treatment, as a matter of public policy he cannot compel a health care provider to violate general accepted professional standard. For example, if a patient choice of treatment is one the hospital or doctor find to be contrary to its or his moral and ethical principles it may take steps to transfer the patient to another facility of the patient's choice.[105] So a patient who refuses a treatment offered by the doctor should be prepared to look for another doctor who will comply with his request. The right to refuse treatment must be subject to the overriding principle of public policy. Therefore if a patient for example, refuses routine hygiene services such as washing and change of bandages by the nurses which itself endangers the health and safety of the hospital facility, his refusal may be overridden. This justification, it must be noted, only applies to nursing services.[106]

Questions have sometimes been asked whether the right of the patient to refuse treatment extends to the patient's request to the doctor to exceed treatment proposed on the ground that the patient is exercising his right to chose. This may arise in a situation where the patient request a particular treatment considered in the doctor's reasonable judgment useless to the patient. It is respectively suggested that if the doctor's judgment is reasonably formed using the *Bolan* test[107] of reasonableness and the medical procedure suggested by the patient does not serve a medical interest,[108] the doctor will not be under any duty to comply with the patient's request.[109] But if the reason for refusal to comply with the patient's request is because in relative terms the cost of providing the treatment is considered enormous to benefit the patient will derive, the patient's choice of treatment should be respected. This should be so even if the cost may become burdensome to tax-payers.[110] Whatever, this is an area of medicine that requires the balancing of many practical issues.

---

[104] *Airedale NHS Trust* v. *Bland* [1993] 1 All ER 821 at 866, per Lord Goff.

[105] See RE Farrell (1987) 529 A 2d 404 (NJ Sup Ct) per Garibaidi J, *Brophy* v. *New England Sinai Hospital* (1986) 497 NE 2d 626, per Liacon J.

[106] See Kennedy & Grubb, *op. cit*, p.1277 and Law Commission Report on Mental Incapacitated Adult and Decision-Making Treatment and Research (consultation Paper No 129 para 3.25) refers to by Kennedy & Grubb, *op. cit*, p.1277.

[107] *Bolan* v. *Friern Hospital Management Committee* [1957] 2 All ER 118 [19570]1 WLR 582.

[108] Medical treatment should be directed to cure illness, where illness cannot be cured to prevent further deterioration, and to relieve pain and suffering in the body and mind-In Re JHL unreported High Court of New Zealand case of 13/8/92, per Thomas J; *Airedale NHS Trust* v. *Bland* [1993] 1 all ER 821; *Mckay* v. *Bergstedt* (1990) 801 P 2d 617 (Nov. Sup. Ct), per Steffen J.

[109] See *Re J* (a minor) (wardship: medical treatment) [1992] 4 All ER 614.

[110] Per Lord Browne-Wilkinson in *Bland* case [1993] 1 All ER 821 it is not for a judge in reading a view of what is for the benefit of the one individual whose life is in issue to take into account... allocation of limited financial resources.

Physician-assisted suicide (PAS)

We will begin this section on the moral and legal issues surrounding doctors-assisted suicide with the story of Jack Kevorkian, an American doctor best known for his zealous advocacy of individual right to doctor—assisted suicide.[111] In 1989 he invented a device called the Thanatron,[112] which can administer an anaesthetic and a lethal injection of potassium chloride through an intravenous line. The potassium chloride will cause the heart to cease beating, while the anaesthetic makes the death painless. Janet Adkins a 54-year-old woman suffering from Alzheimer used the machine to snuff—out her life. Kevokian was charged for murder but the charge was dismissed. He was later judicially restrained by court from using the suicide machine. When he refused to comply, the Michigan State Medical Board revoked his medical license. Without his licence he no longer would have access to the drugs needed for the machine. Undeterred, he built a new machine not requiring drugs under medical prescription. He invented a new machine, the Mercitron, consisting of a tank of carbon monoxide and a facemask used to inhale the gas.

With the machine he assisted over a dozen deaths in Michigan following which the Michigan legislature passed a law temporarily prohibiting assisted suicide pending further investigations by a state commission. He was eventually jailed for assisting suicide and the American Medical Association also condemned his action for violating the doctor's primary commitment to healing. But others noted that he brought much needed attention to the moral and legal issues surrounding doctors assisted suicide. Still some others suggest that his approach challenge society's conception of death as an emotive matter, thereby making us see death in a more rational manner.

This section of our discussion will make a distinction between doctors-assisted suicide and euthanasia, i.e. mercy killing. Doctors-assisted suicide is a situation where a doctor assists the patient in bringing about his death. It is the equivalent of aiding and abetting suicide by the doctor. On the other hand, euthanasia is a request to the doctor by a patient that he should be killed painless. In the case of the former the doctor is merely an accessory, while in the later he is the perpetrator. In practical terms both can be illustrated this way: if a doctor places poison close to the patient so that he can administer on himself the doctor would have assisted suicide as an accessory. But, if rather than do so he injects the poison into the patient, he becomes a perpetrator of murder. Though, on moral grounds, the distinction is of little significance, legal punishment for both are different.

The social value of denying the doctor's right to help a patient in bringing about death was one of the issues in *Attorney-General* v. *Able*.[113] The executive committee

---

[111] Microsoft @Encarta(R) Encyclopedia99.© 1993-1998 Microsoft Corporation. Also cited in L. Weir, The Morality of Physician-Assisted Suicide (1992) 20 *Law, Medicine & Health Care* 116.

[112] *Thanaton* has a Greek root, meaning death machine.

[113] [1984] 1 All ER 277, [1984] QB 798.

of a society established to promote voluntary euthanasia published a booklet entitled 'A Guide to Self-Deliverance', which it sold on request to members of the society. The booklet aimed to overcome the fear of dying and to reduce the incidence of unsuccessful suicide. It set out in detail several methods of what it termed self-deliverance that could have deterred some people from committing suicide. The Attorney General took the view that the booklet constituted an offence under s. 2 (1) of the English Suicide Act, 1961 and so sought a declaration that future supply of it should cease. Woolf J held that the publication can constitute an offence under the Act.

Though the case was not directly in all fours with doctors-assisted suicide, it implicitly makes it unlawful for a doctor to assist suicide. The social value of the prohibition has been challenged by some who urge for a change.[114] As the law stands a doctor will be unable to help his patient bring about death if the patient is unable to do so himself. All he could do is to withhold or withdraw treatment in the structure permitted in the *Bland* equation.[115] Outside that confine, he is like all others-helpless.

Argument against and for PAS

Arguments against PAS are as follows:

(i) *Doctor's duty.* It is said that the doctor occupies a position in society and especially in relation to his patient of confidence and trust. The patient entrust to him his health care, a trust that will be eroded if doctors become involved in PAS, because if they do, their position may gradually slope from one providing health care to one snuffing-off life, the very opposite of their primary duty. The Hippocratic Oath positively states 'I will neither give deadly drugs to anybody if asked for it, nor will I make a suggestion to this effect." Thus by moral stipulation of their calling PAS is unethical. On this ground, it has been suggested that treatment designed to bring about death is contrary to the doctor's primary duty to cure.

(ii) *Moral insignificance of distinguishing between PAS and euthanasia.* It is said that on moral terms there is no difference between an accessory to death and the perpetrator of death. Both are designed to bring about the ending of life. In both cases the doctor uses his skill as doctor to cause death.

(iii) *Unlawfulness of patient's request.* It is said that PAS is a thing a patient should not be morally and legally permitted to request, because suicide is immoral and by asking the doctor to assist the patient is directly asking the doctor to commit a crime. In this respect a distinction is made between negative and positive moral rights.[116] When a patient seeks for example, the withdrawal of an artificial

---

[114] Wanzer *et al*, The Physician Responsibility Towards Hopelessly Ill Patients: a Second Look (1989) *New Eng. J. Med*

[115] *Airedale NHS Trust* v. *Bland* [1993] 1 All ER 821.

[116] *R* v. *Weir* above.

life-sustaining machine he is exercising a negative moral right or liberty, a right to refuse medical treatment. In cases of this sort the doctor ought to comply with the patient's request. Where on the other hand, the patient seeks to exercise a positive moral right, such as a right to commit suicide, his claim is in effect different from a situation where he seeks to be let alone by the doctor. Rather he is seeking to impose a duty on the doctor to help him accomplish his desire of self-destruction. Such a claim lacks moral merit and so should not impose any duty whatsoever on the doctor.

(iv) *Damages the reputation of the medical profession.* PAS could create doubts in the patient's mind of the doctor's commitment to cure and provide effective treatment for the patient's current medical condition.

(v) *Sacredness of human life.* The theocratic survival of our predominantly secular law and religions (transcendental) arguments are in support of treating life as a sacred gift from God for which no doctor should arrogate to himself the right of PAS.

Formidable as these arguments are they are not absolute in nature. While the doctor's primary duty is to cure or heal that is only one of the goals of medicine. Also important to the profession is the prevention of deterioration of illness, minimising pain and suffering of the patient and the discontinuation of unnecessarily invasive treatment designed merely to keep a patient alive in a bodily environment. These are also legitimate aims of medicine. When the quality of life of a patient becomes deplorable an insistence on the ancient Hippocratic Oath becomes questionable. Furthermore, equating PAS and euthanasia on moral grounds involves a less appreciation of the difference between them. In PAS the doctor does not cause death. It is the patient who causes his death. He only enables him to do so himself. It is on this basis different from euthanasia. What is more, the moral argument about the distinction between acts and omissions in the context of withholding or withdrawing medical treatment can with very minor adjustment also apply here. In a PAS situation, the doctor can be treated as respecting the patient's right of autonomy to refuse medical treatment even if the effect will be the ending of his life. On the question of the unlawfulness of patients requesting PAS from the doctor, it must be conceded that such request do not place the doctor under any moral obligation to act. It must also be remembered that since the doctor is more likely to be in close attendance to the patient, he is usually the first person the patient would naturally request assistance from. There is therefore less force in the argument that it is unlawful to make such request of the doctor. The request can be to anyone. But since the doctor is more readily available and ought to be an expert in medical matters, he most likely would be in a better position to advise on what procedures can quickly bring about the ending of life.[117]

---

[117] Ibid.

Damage to the profession's reputation and a feeling of distrust can only be good argument if there are widespread abuses of PAS. The courts or the legislature, even the doctor's regulatory bodies can prevent that by express stipulations of the conditions that will make it legal for PAS. By so doing the doctor-patient relationship of confidence will not be threatened. Argument about the sacredness of life is certainly theocratic. The state is legally permitted to end life in many circumstances e.g. in the quelling of riots, in execution of death sentence on criminals, etc. These are said to be good reasons for treating the sacredness as not immutable. What then would we say of a patient with chronic, progressively deteriorating or terminal condition with a prognosis of no hope of recovery? Should this not also be good reason for displacing the argument on the sanctity of life? If as in *Bland*, [118] the sanctity of life argument will accept a displacement by the patient's right of self-determination or autonomy, a similar analogical argument could be made for PAS. Sometimes PAS can be justified as a compassionate way for doctors to respond to current medical reality of alleviating patient's pain and suffering. That a large section of society support euthanasia, talk less of PAS was even admitted by the court in *Bland* case.[119]

In his formidable argument, Professor Robert Weir presents five reasons for legalising PAS.[120] According to the learned writer 'the realistic limits of physicians to heal all their patients and effectively relieve suffering' represents the ethical case for PAS. Our admitting this limitation requires that we address medical reality as they currently exist in patients. Some are with terminal conditions, other with chronic and degenerative diseases. Many of these find life intolerable and as last resort request PAS to bring about death. Their situation calls for compassion from all, more especially from the doctors who treat them. Rather than sheer appeal to an ancient Hippocratic Oath there is now a need to reconstruct illness in the light of present realities.

Two, while most sicknesses involve psychologically and physiological pains and suffering, many of these can be managed with empathic support, medication, medical intervention, nursing care and the rest. But where there is no alleviation of pain and suffering by the methods designed to manage it and the suffering portend to be life running in such cases it may be ethical to employ PAS.

Three, most patients desire to control their living, dying and death. We all make life choices everyday that suit our desires. One such desire is to be relieved of suffering. In reaching a decision to withdraw treatment for *Anthony Bland*,[121] the House of Lords drew on the supposed desire of the patient, the fact that he was a football lover, an energetic young man and the like to draw the conclusion that he

---

[118] [1993] 1 All ER 821.

[119] Ibid.; see also the opinion of 12 doctors who published the article on the provision of health care for the hopelessly ill - Wanzer *et al.* above n. 81; see also article by Weir, above n.78.

[120] R Weir, above n.78.

[121] *Airedale NHS Trust* v. *Anthony Bland* [1993] 1 All ER 820.

would not have desired to be PVS and in its stead would prefer to die with dignity. Even if the patient as a result of illness is treated as no longer enjoying autonomy of choice, his treatment choices can be determined by inquiry as to how he lived while sensate. By substituted judgment, his choice can be known. It means in effect that a patient who requests PAS is merely exercising his right to autonomy. In this respect the desire to remain autonomous and in control (in extreme cases) sometimes includes a request for help from a doctor-a request for help in exercising control over one's final exit.[122]

Very convincingly, the learned writer draws attention to the invasive nature and harm continuing medical treatment can pose in cases where the prognosis shows little hope of recovery. Ethically a doctor should avoid intentional or negligent harm to the patient. Since the ultimate harm is the death of the patient, he is by correlation enjoined not to kill or assist in the patient's death. That however is not all the harm that can be visited on the patient. Invasive treatment, the impairment of mental and psychological welfare, physical injury and technology abuse qualify as harm. When as in *Anthony Bland* case treatment requires feeding through an artificial machine which sometimes brought about complications in his digestive system requiring medical intervention considered invasive, it was only proper to treat it as harmful to the patient. Such a condition can be worse than death. Whether the doctor should play any role in facilitating the harmful, invasive treatment to preserve the patient in a bodily environment in order to help prevent another harm, his self-destruction is the issue. A patient by requesting PAS gives an indication that harm from invasive treatment is worse to him than the ultimate harm of death. In such rare cases it would be best to endorse PAS for the sake of the patient and those who love him.

The motive for PAS may range from preservation of the patient's quality of life, compassion for a patient in intolerable situation, desire to help patient's family emotionally and financially and of course occasional eccentric desire for publicity by doctor, as the example of Jack Kevorkian. It is hard to say whether the position taken by Jack Kevorkian is not one motivated for publicity. Whatever the motive, it cannot be disputed that in some case the motive for PAS is purely compassion. While some doctors will not on moral grounds accept PAS, others do, especially if the plea to help is for compassionate reasons designed to help a patient out of an intolerable situation. It is suggested that either moral choice to help or not to help, if rooted in compassion is ethical depending on the facts of the individual case. [123]

Since PAS can be open to abuse, it is suggested that if law recognises it, in rare cases where it is desirable, certain safeguards must be put in place to check possible abuses.[124] Safeguard procedures may use as model the *Conroy* [125] requirements and caveat, such as, inquiry by state Ombudsman and any other stringent requirements.

---

[122] Weir, above n. 78.

[123] Weir, *op. cit*, see Law Reform Commission (Canada), 1983 Working paper Report to the Minister of Justice on Euthanasia, Aiding Suicide and Cessation of Treatment, 1983 p.35.

[124] Ibid.

It can be argued with some force that section 34 of the 1999 Constitution which protects the dignity of the person is implicit prohibition of any law which prevents a person making a choice, albeit, through his doctor to end his life when continued treatment will be nothing but indignity to person. In *Rodriguez* v. *Attorney General of British Columbia*,[126] a similar issue arose for determination. The petitioner suffered from lateral sclerosis and incurable progressive disease affecting the nervous system; leading to extensive muscle wasting. The sickness has as general symptom prior to it speech, chewing and swallow difficulties. The petitioner wished to avoid these future stress and loss of dignity caused by such a death and so he proposed that a doctor should assist him to end his life with dignity. She also applied for an order declaring invalid s.241 of the Canadian Criminal Code which makes aiding and abetting suicide a criminal offence on the ground that it conflicts with the constitutional protection of bodily integrity. Her application was dismissed by the Canadian Supreme Court. The court took the position that it is improper to make fundamental change in long-standing policy by mere appeal to general constitutional principle. The law prohibiting aiding and abetting of suicide is a valid and desirable legislation that fulfils the government objective of reserving life and protecting the vulnerable. McLachin J of the Canadian Supreme Court however read a dissenting judgment. His Lordship stated that since the legislature has decriminalised suicide but not its aiding and abetting, the effect was to deny to some people the choice of ending their lives if they are physically unable to do so themselves. This is what deprives the petitioner of her security of the person i.e. the right to make decisions concerning her body which affects only her in a way that offends the principles of fundamental justice thereby violating s.7 of the Canadian Charter of Rights and Freedom (our own s.34 of the 1999 Constitution). He according struck down the provision of the Criminal Code that makes it an offence to aid and abet suicide.[127]

His Lordship debunked the proposition that the state has an interest in absolutely forbidding anyone to help another end his life. He stated that simply causing death is not what the law criminalises. This is so because where death is caused for good excuse there is legal justification, e.g. killing in self-defence. So criminal culpability depends on the circumstances in which the death is brought about or assisted. Since law has long recognised that if there is a valid justification for bringing about death of someone, the person who does so will not be held criminally responsible — in the case of the petitioner there is justification – the justification of giving her the

---

[125] In *Re Conroy* 486 A 2nd 1209, 98 NJ 321 (NJ 1985).

[126] (1993) 82 BCLR (2nd) 273 (Can. Sup. Ct).

[127] A similar reasoning was used by the Supreme Court of Canada in *R* v. *Morgentaler* (1988) 1 SCR 50 to stroke down the abortion provision of the Criminal Code. Parliament set a scheme authorising therapeutic abortion, the effect of which was to deny or delay therapeutic abortion to some women. It was struck down using s.7 of the Charter because it deprived some women the right to deal with their bodies as they chose thereby infringing their security of the person, in a manner which did not comport with the principles of fundamentals justice.

capacity to end her life which able-bodied people have as a matter of course. The justification is her clear desire to end her life at a time when in her view, it makes no sense to continue living. Conclusively his Lordship stated that in his view the law does not only authorise passive assistance – the withdrawal of support necessary to life, but also authorises active assistance – the provision of a means to permit a person of sound mind to choose to end his or her life with dignity. Noteworthy of mention also is the fact that Sopinka J, like McLanchlin J concurred that the Criminal Code infringes the patient's right to bodily integrity under s. 7 of the Chapter, even though he reached a different conclusion on the facts of the case. His Lordship, joined the majority in dismissing the appeal.

Whether a court in Nigeria will adopt the majority position or that of the dissent judgment of McLaction J in a similar situation would depend on how it perceives the merits of the intellectual struggle that characterised the various judgments in *Rodriguez*[128] Even if policy argument are to favour PAS[129] it will not likely go unregulated to prevent abuse. Regulation should take the *Conroy*[130] Ombudsman safeguard structure or any other thought fit, such as those suggested in *Rodriguez*[131]

Euthanasia practice in some jurisdictions

Our discussion will begin with a review of the jurisprudence in Netherlands, because it throws in a lot of light on the moral and legal basis for the judicial attitude on the subject.[132] Article 293 of the Netherlands Penal Code[133] prohibits the taking of life of another person at his request, what can be referred to as voluntary euthanasia. Notwithstanding this express prohibition the courts beginning with *Arrondissement-strechtbank* [134]to *Hoge Raud*[135] have interpreted the Code as providing a defence to a charge of voluntary euthanasia. The exact understanding of the prohibition and judicial interpretation came up for review before the Netherlands Supreme Court in *Ankasus*[136] The case involved the killing of an elderly woman, one Mrs. B, at her request by her doctor. In the view of the Supreme Court culpability or otherwise

---

[128] (1993) 82 BCLR (2nd) 273.

[129] Netherlands is one country where PAS is permitted.

[130] *Re Claire Conroy* 464 A 2d 303 (NJ, 1983), 486 A 2d 1209 (NJ, 1985).

[131] See for example the approach suggested by McEachern CJ of the British Columbia Court of Appeal in *Rodriguez* case wherein he suggested that the procedure should involve a petition to a superior court with two medical reports as part of the material needed to ground an application.

[132] For a general discussion of the law see J. Keowu, The Law and Practice of Euthanasia in the Netherlands (1992) 108 *LQR* 51 Margaret Battin, Voluntary Euthanasia and the Risk of Abuses: Can We Learn anything from the Netherlands? (1992) 20 *Law, Medicine and Health Care* 133.

[133] Title XIX of Penal Code list Voluntary euthanasia as one of the serious offences against human life. See also Art. 287, and 294 that prohibit intention killing and assisting suicide.

[134] District Court judgment in 1973, cited in Keown above n.97.

[135] Supreme Court judgment in 1986, also cited in Keown, above n.97.

[136] Supreme Court judgment of Nov 27, 1984, cited and discussed in Keown, above n. 97.

depended on a proper evaluation of whether 'according to responsible medical opinion measured by the physician standard of medical ethics' a situation of necessity existed. Necessity as defined under the Netherlands Penal Code takes on two meanings, psychological compulsion and emergency.[137] In the view of the Supreme Court the lower court that convicted the doctor for unlawful homicide did not do a proper evaluation of the defence of necessity, which involves (i) weighing whether and to what extent according to professional medical judgment an increasing disfigurement of the patient's personality and or further deterioration of her already unbearable suffering were to be expected; (ii) whether it could be expected that soon she will no longer be able to die with dignity under circumstances worthy of a human being; (iii) whether there was still opportunities to alleviate her suffering. On these grounds the case was referred back to the Hague Court of Appeal to objectivily consider the culpability of the defendant in the context of the defence of necessity. After a re-consideration, the Court of Appeal on September 11, 1986 acquitted the doctor on the basis that he acted according to good medical ethics after considering the patient's condition. By a Bill passed into law in 1993, Netherlands formally recognised the medical current practice on euthanasia, but requires the doctor to report death to the local coroner.[138]

Following *Anthony Bland*[139]the question whether voluntary euthanasia should be permitted was presented before the House of Lords Select Committee on Medical Ethics in 1993. It was charged with recommending whether or not to change the law on the subject. No change has come, so the legal position in *Bland* remains the current position in England. According to Lord Goff[140] voluntary euthanasia is unlawful even if motivated by humanitarian desire to end suffering however great that may be. However when considered in the context that English common law permits the withholding or withdrawal of life-serving treatment in appropriate cases, a charge of hypocrisy can be made against the prohibition of euthanasia. Lords Goff, Mustill and Browne-Wilkinson admitted the fact.[141] A critical mind may ask if a doctor by discontinuing treatment is entitled in consequence to let his patient die, why should it be lawful to put him out of his misery straight away.[142] Both have one effect-to produce death. But as previously discussed the justification for the difference in judicial thinking is attributed to the great dichotomy between acts and omissions. This explains the conclusion in *R* v. *Cox*.[143] Dr Cox patient was an elderly

---

[137] See Art. 40 Emergency in this context includes a choice situation to the defendant to break the law in order to promote a higher good.

[138] Ibid.

[139] [1993] 1 All ER 821, See (Kennedy & Grubb, *op. cit*, p. 1315 and (1993) 307 *BMJ* 1511.

[140] Ibid. at p per Lord Goff, see also *R* v. *Cox* [1992] 12 BMLR 38, per Orgnall J, see also the views of Lords Mustill and Keith in *Airedale NHS Trust* v. *Bland* [1993] 1 All ER 821 at 861; Roger Long, Mercy Killing and the Criminal Law Revision Committee (CLRC) [1982] *NLJ* 76.

[141] [1993] 1 All ER 821 per Lord Goff, per Lord Browne-Wilkinson, at p. Lord Mustill.

[142] Ibid., Lord Goff.

[143] [1992] 12 BMLR 38.

woman suffering from an incurable disease. She experienced great pain which was uncontrollable by the use of drugs. Repeatedly she requested her consultant, Dr. Cox and others to kill her. Dr. Cox administered a lethal dose of potassium chloride on her and she died immediately. Dr. Cox was prosecuted and convicted for attempted murder. Orgnall J while admitting that it is lawful for a doctor who genuinely believes that a certain treatment is beneficial to his patient, either therapeutically or analgesically to administer a drug or treatment even if it carries risk to life, he held that he must never use such drug with the primary purpose of hastening the moment of death.

Even though the House of Lords in *Bland* confirmed the *Cox* approach, it would appear that it was less enthusiastic in recognising the illogical distinction between withdrawal of life-saving treatment and the taking of active step to end life; preferring that reform of this be left to Parliament.[144] Unfortunately Parliament has not had the muscle to legalise euthanasia for strong emotional and religious reasons.

Ending of life and anticipatory decisions

This section is concerned with situations in which a patient while competent makes treatment decisions about possible future health care in the event of when he no longer can make choices either as a result of incompetence due to accident or supervening illness or emergency. In a normal hospital setting one can conceive of it in situations where the patient signs a consent form usually before a medical operation or surgery. Some of the forms in ordinary medical setting states that the patient consents to surgery and that the doctor may use certain extra-ordinary procedures if deemed necessary to heal the patient while in coma as a result of anaesthetics. It has been suggested that if this type of anticipatory consent were properly appreciated earlier by commentators and the courts, conjecture as to its legal effect would have been more settled.[145]

Anticipatory consent may take different forms. It could be in the form of an advance medical directive (AMD) document. The essence of the document is to specify the type of health care treatment a person wish or does not wish to receive. A proxy medical directive (PMD) specifies a surrogate as the person to make such decision if the patient becomes unable to do so. Both AMD and PMD may be combined in a single document.[146] The term 'living will' is sometimes used to refer to

---

[144] Bland (1993) 1 *All ER* 821; *ER* 821 at 867, Lord Goff.

[145] Kennedy & Grubb, *op. cit*, p.1325.

[146] USA President Commission, Deciding to Forgo Life Sustaining Treatment (1983), for general reading: G. Gelfand, Living Will statutes: The First Decade (1987) *Wisconsin LR* 737; A. Meisel, A retrospective on Cruzan (1992) 20 *Law, Medicine and Health Care* 340, D. Lanham and Fehlberg, Living Wills and the Right to Die with dignity 91991) 18 *Melb. Univ. LR* 329; D. Lanham, The Right to Choose to Die with Dignity (1990) 14 *Criminal LJ*401; D. Lanham & s Woodford, Refusal by Agents of the Life-Sustaining

both documents, which provide both for the making of an advance-directive and the appointment of a health care proxy.[147] When the document is respected, as it should be, it shows respect for autonomy. If it is one that expressly states what the patient will and will not accept, respect for it evidence the instrumental role of autonomy in promoting the patient's subjective, individual evaluation of well-being. In another sense, it reveals respect for the patient right to dignity. The document is not necessarily confined to a decision to forego life sustaining. It may extend to any treatment situation in which a patient anticipates he may lack capacity to make decisions himself. Although some have suggested that a living will is a document made by a person concerned about the loss of ability to direct care at the end of his life, indicating refusal to 'heroic' or extra-ordinary treatment to keep a patient alive, our use of it is not so restricted in the context of AMD and PMD.

Noteworthy of mention is that since a power of attorney may be general or limited, it may be employed in decision-making not only about property but also on personal matters, such as health care. When it extends to personal matters as health, it can be equated and treated as a durable advanced proxy directive. The problem however with the use of a power of attorney is that at common law it becomes void or is terminable if the donor becomes incapacitated. To circumvent this many jurisdictions in the United States of America have enacted statutes creating 'durable' power of attorney.[148] Under it the power of attorney remains valid despite incapacity of the donor. The simplicity of the power of attorney to deal with property as well as personal matters is what makes it better than the common law type.

Re T (adult: refusal of medical treatment)[149] is instructive on this respect. It was probably the first discussion in England, with hindsight of comparative developments in the American and Canadian jurisdictions. T was injured in a car accident when she was 34 weeks pregnant. She was admitted to hospital with the possibility that she may require blood transfusion. Though brought up as a Jehovah's Witness, she was not a faithful of the religion. After a conversation with her mother, who is a member, she told the hospital that she will not be willing to accept blood transfusion if it is found to be necessary in her treatment. She later signed a form of refusal to blood transfusion but it was not explained to her that it might be necessary to give blood to save her life. After undergoing a Caesarean operation her condition deteriorated and she was transferred to an intensive case unit. Because of her express refusal to blood, the consultant anaesthetics put her instead on a ventilator. Paralysing drugs were also administered. T's father and boyfriend, who were not witnesses applied that blood be administered on her despite her wishes because in the particular situation it was in her best interest to do so. At an

---

Medical Treatment (1992) 18 *Melb Univ. LR* 659; PDC Skegg, Living Wills and New Zealand Law, Bioethics Research Centre, New Zealand, Newsletter Vol. 2 No3, Sept. 1993 p.2.

147 Skegg, above n.147, D. Meyers, Medico-Legal Implications of Death and Dying (1981).

148 Ibid.

149 [1992], 4 *All ER* 649; [1992], 9 *BMLR* 46.

emergency hearing the judge authorised the use of blood. At a second hearing the judge held that T had neither consented to nor refused blood in the emergency that arose and accordingly it was lawful for the doctor to treat in whatever way they considered, even to use blood if necessary in the interest of her.

T appealed the decision. Her appeal was dismissed by the English Court of Appeal; on the ground that her refusal to blood was vitiated by the undue influence exercised by her mother. Thereafter their Lordships (Lord Donaldson MR, Butter—Sloss and Stranghton LJJ) considered the validity of a patient's anticipatory refusal to treatment. They unanimously agreed that the validity of an anticipatory refusal is valid. Lord Donaldson MR stated that if the patient had made a valid anticipatory document that covered the treatment, in the sense that it covered the emergency situation that arose in the course of her treatment it would have been valid and the doctor ought to respect it.

In effect the existence of an anticipatory document is not sufficient in itself. It must be shown to be the decision of the patient and must cover the true scope of the treatment proposed and or undertaken. If in the light of changed circumstances a doctor can infer that the patient would have reversed his decision, the doctor can deny the patient's anticipatory choice, as in *Re T.* The decision was not hers in the true sense and it did not cover the emergency situation that arose. Thus, if the factual situation upon which the choice is made fails outside the scope of the choice or the assumption upon which it is based is falsified, the choice ceases to be effective. In her case not only was her choice vitiated, it was limited in scope. It did not envisage the grave danger to her life that resulted from her treatment choice and so it was not considered unethical to override it.

In reaching its decision the English Court of Appeal considered the Canadian case of *Malette* v. *Shulman*[150] and the American case of *Werth* v. *Taylor.*[151] Malette was a case where a Jehovah's Witness woman carried a card stating in unequivocal terms that she did not wish blood to be administered to her in 'any circumstances'. The Ontario Court of Appeal awarded her $20,000 when the doctor gave her blood in order to save her life against her known wishes. Robins JA said:

> 'At issue here is the freedom of the patient as an individual to exercise her right to refuse treatment and accept the consequences of her own decision. Competent adults as I have sought to demonstrate, are generally at liberty to refuse medical treatment even at the risk of death. The right to determine what shall be done with one's own body is a fundamental right in our society. The concepts inherent in this right are the bedrock upon which the principle of self-determination and individual autonomy is based. Free individual choice in

---

[150] (1990) 67 DLR (4th) 321, (1990) 72 OR (2d) 417.

[151] (1991) 475 NW 2d 426 (Mich. CA). See also *In Re Estate of Dorome* (1987) 517 Pa 3, 543 A 2nd 452; *In the Matter of Alice Hughes* (1992) 611 A 2d 1148 (Sup NJ App. Div).

matters affecting this right should, in my opinion be accorded very high priority.'[152]

In *Werth*,[153] the plaintiff filed a civil battery suit against Taylor for authorising blood transfusion on Cindy Werth despite the plaintiff's objection. Cindy and her husband are Jehovah's Witnesses. Cindy, the mother to two children, was pregnant with twins. Just before her delivery, she filed several forms including a 'refusal to permit blood transfusion' with the Alpine General Hospital. While on admission, her husband also executed another refusal form. She delivered safely but started to bleed from her uterus and in that emergency the anaesthesiologist, Taylor ordered her transfusion despite being told that she is a witness and had refused blood. The Michigan Court of Appeal dismissed the claim on the ground that the patient's prior refusal had not been made when her life was hanging on the balance or when it appeared that death might be a possibility if a transfusion was not given. Her refusal was therefore not contemporaneous or informed in the circumstance.

In *Airedale NHS Trust* v. *Bland*, [154] the House of Lord explicitly recognised the validity of anticipation decisions to medical treatment. According to Lord Goff it will be both a tort and a crime not to respect the clear anticipatory decision or choice of a patient.[155] But as revealed from the case, for it to be valid, the following must be proved: (i) that the patient competent at the time he made the choice; (ii) the choice must be freely made; (iii) the choice must be informed in nature; and (iv) the scope of choice must relate or cover the circumstances which subsequently arise.

On requirement (i), there is no doubt that in *Re T* the patient was competent. She was a mature minor of 17. The patients in *Malette* and *Werth* were all competent adults. But in *Re T* the choice was not freely made, because it was made under the undue influence of her mother and accordingly vitiated. It would appear that the choices in *Re T* and *Werth* were not sufficiently informed in nature. In the former it appears that T's basis for refusal meant 'I refuse to have blood transfusion so long as there is an effective alternative.' In *Werth* the court found that the refusal of her husband was "wishy washy.' That was not the case with *Malette*. She was unequivocal in her refusal. On the scope of choice relating to circumstances which subsequently arise, *Malette* was very clear. Her AMD stated in part: 'I request that no blood or blood products be administered to me under any circumstances.' By implication it covered any subsequent medical treatment or emergency. But in *Re T* the court was in no doubt that T's refusal did not contemplate the grave situation that subsequently arose. In *Werth*, the Michigan court found as a fact that Cindy's refusal was made when she was contemplating merely routine elective surgery and not when life-threatening circumstances were present.

---

[152] (1990) 67 *DLR* (4th) 321, (1990) 72 OR (2d) 417 at 432, per Robins JA.
[153] (1991) 475 NW 2d 426 (Mich. CA).
[154] [1993] 1 *All ER* 821, [1993] 2 WLR 316.
[155] Ibid per Lord Keith,per Lord Goff, p.892 per Lord Mustill.

Existing law in some jurisdictions

New Zealand [156]

In New Zealand a competent patient has a right to refuse treatment. The right is protected by the New Zealand Bill of Rights Act, 1990. Section II states that 'everyone has the right to refuse to undergo any medical treatment.'[157] The right is intricately linked with the right to make an advanced directive to take effect once competence is lost. Lord Goff made that point in *Bland*[158] when he discussed the right of self-determination in the context of advance directive. He said 'the same principle applies where the patient's refusal to give his consent has been expressed at an earlier date, before he became unconscious or otherwise incapable of communicating it.'[159] In the view of Professor Skegg, 'there is every reason to believe that a suitably worded advance directive will be effective in New Zealand law, to prevent a doctor lawfully administering treatment that would otherwise be appropriate'[160]

The New Zealand Protection of Personal and Property Rights Act, 1988 authorises the appointment of others to act as a patient's proxy, or agent in matter relating to health care if the patient becomes incapable of making decisions. Section 98 states that a competent person (the donor) may authorise some other person (the attorney) to act in relation to personal care and welfare whether in general terms, or in relation to specific matters and it may be made subject to conditions and restrictions specified by the donor.[161] Since a power of attorney terminates with incapacity of the donor, the Act makes specific provision for an enduring, durable power of attorney which does not terminate with incapacity. It however places some restriction on the power of the attorney to act in particular circumstances. An attorney cannot act in care of the donor unless the donor is mentally incapable.[162] By S. 94 (1) (b) his powers are restricted to situation where the donor: (i) lacks, wholly or partly, the capacity to understand the nature, and to foresee the consequences of decisions in respect of matters relating to his personal care and welfare or; (ii) lacks the capacity to understand the nature, and to foresee the consequences, of decisions in respect of matters relating to his or her personal care and welfare, but wholly lacks the capacity to communicate decisions in respect of such matters. Also section 18 (1) (c) states that an attorney with a enduring power of attorney has no power 'to require consent to the administering to that person of any standard medical

---

[156] For a discussion see Skegg, above n.147.

[157] See also ss. 3 and 5 of the Bill of Right Acts 1990 (New Zealand) and Re S [1992] I NZLR 363 at 374; *Smith* v. *Auckland Hospital Board* [1965] NZLR 191 at 219, per T A Cresson J.

[158] *Airedale NHS Trust* v. *Bland* [1993] 2 WLR 316; [1993] 1 All ER 821; see also *Malette* v. *Shulman* (1990) 67 DLR (4th).

[159] Ibid., per Lord Goff.

[160] Skegg, above n.147.

[161] S.98 (1) of Personal and Property Rights Act (PPRA) 1988 (New Zealand).

[162] S. 98 (3) of PPRA, 1988.

treatment or procedure intended to save that persons' life or to prevent serious damage to that person's health.'[163]

In its present state these restrictions in a very considerable manner limits the value of enduring powers of attorney in the context of a refusal of medical treatment designed to prolong life in the form of treatment to save or prevent serious damage to the patients' health.[164] All the attorney can do on behalf of the patient is to prohibit non-standard medical treatment, not any standard treatment to save or prevent damage to the patient. The restrictions on the health care proxy therefore makes it more attractive for patient seeking decisions to refuse life-sustaining treatment to resort to the AMD, properly worded, rather than rely on the New Zealand version of a health care proxy. Because of the otherwise advantages a proxy could have far and above the advance directive type, in that it enables the patient to choose a proxy whom he has confidence than the advance directive that can be inflexible in changing circumstance, it has been suggested that the restrictions on proxy under the New Zealand should be reconsidered by the Law Commission, the Medical Council and the Bioethics Research Centre of New Zealand with a view of incorporating into it flexible and acceptable features of both AMD and the health care proxy.[165]

(ii) United States of America[166]

The first living will statute in USA was the California Natural Death Act, 1976. Following the California style, 13 states and the district of Colombia have enacted their own natural death statutes. These statutes formally establish the requirements for directive to physicians. Though they vary as to penalty for breach, some treating failures to respect the directive as unprofessional, other do not. Under the California statute a directive will only be binding if signed by a qualified patient, technically defined to be someone who has been diagnosed as terminal in condition. At the time the document is signed the patient is also required to be fully competent. The California statute was enacted partly in response to the situation presented in *Re Quinlan*[167] (an application to remove the patients' respirator). The Act does not apply or cover cases within the *Quinlan* bracket. It only covers patients who are at the verge of death. In effect it excludes people for whom the greatest concern is expressed about a prolonged and undignified dying process. They are outside the statute because their death cannot be said to be imminent within the contemplation of the law. Such patients are only in an intolerable health state. To remove this unfortunate exclusion some states statutes do not have the imminent death requirement. The triggering event that brings to operation most living will statutes

[163] See also s.98 (5) of PPRA, 1988.
[164] Skegg, above n.147.
[165] Ibid.
[166] For a discussion and further reading, see report of President' Commission, above n.147, G. Gelfand, above n.147; Kennedy & Grubb, *op cit* p.1337.
[167] 70 NJ 10, 355 A 2d 647 on appeal 429 US 922 (NJ. 1976).

however still remains imminent death. It is suggested that if these laws are designed to permit the natural death of persons who desire ending their lives, then the requirement that death be imminent whether or not treatment is withdrawn nullifies the purpose of the legislation

Because of the criticism of the limited application of most natural death statutes, a second generation of statutes permitting the creation of durable power of attorney for health care decision emerged[168]. The first of this was the California Durable Power of Attorney Health Care Act, 1983, currently known as the California Civil Code.[169] Most state jurisdictions have also followed and trailed the California statute. No sooner a third generation of statutes emerged, combining the provisions relating to living will (i.e. the National Death statutes with the option of appointing proxy decision-maker i.e. the durable power of attorney type), this was again been followed by a fourth generation of legislation of a somewhat different nature, vesting decision-making power in the patient's family members in circumstances where the patient has not made an advance directive.[170]

Following the far-reaching decision in *Cruzan*[171] where the United States Supreme Court drew no distinction between withdrawal of medical treatment and artificial hydration and nutrition; and that advance directives are beneficial in furthering a patients choice,[172] most states began the process of enacting or amending existing legislation to do the following: (i) take account of artificial hydration and nutrition by equating them with medical treatment; and[173] (ii) give effect to patient's advance directives where previously there was no such legislation.[174] Interestingly, the Federal Government of the United States by the Patient Self-determination Act, 1990 enjoins all health care providers who enjoy federal funding to advise patient at the time of admission or treatment, of their rights under state legislation to make an advance directive. It further requires them to put in place policies regarding patient's advance directives. Health care providers are also required to make out documents stating whether the patient does execute one or not.

(iii) England

In England there is no direct legislation on the subject, the provisions of the Enduring Power of Attorney Act 1985 notwithstanding. The Act provides that a power of attorney may survive the maker's incompetence. It however does not

---

[168] Ibid see also Natural Death Act, 1976 of California State first living will statute in the American jurisdiction, now known as the California Health and Safety Code (ss. 7185 – 7194.5); California Durable Power of Attorney Health Care Act, 1983 now California Civil Code (ss 2430-245). President Commission, above n. 147.

[169] Kennedy & Grubb, *op. cit*, 1338.

[170] See ss.2430-2445, Cal. Civil Code.

[171] *Cruzan* v. *Director, Missouri Dept of Health* (1990) 497 US 261.

[172] O'Connor J. even went as far as stating that the American Constitution may actually protect a patient's right to have his wishes respected as reflected in an advance directive.

[173] State of Ohio, see Kennedy & Grubb, *op. cit*, 1339.

[174] New York and Massachusetts, Kennedy & Grubb, ibid.

cover decisions on medical treatment. The position of the law remains that living wills are recognised at common law if they satisfy the requirements in *Re T.* The debate is thus engendered as to whether there is an additional need for legislation to give effect to living wills, and if so, what the provisions should look like. It has been suggested that living wills in the medical process could be helpful in bring certain hitherto ignored perspective in treatment. For example, it can provide a better mechanism for the regulation of the participation of the patient's relatives in health care management of a patient.[175] The document can also be useful when the patient encounters several or different doctors in the course of his treatment. It could give the doctor a helpful indication of the patient's wishes and; enable the patient have more say on his treatment.

While is can hardly be doubted that the use of advanced directive may lead to better practices in the decision making about life-sustaining care, it is not without its pitfalls. A regulation derived from, say, professional rule, custom or positive legislation requiring doctors to keep living forms, discuss and or offer them to patients can rock the crest of the doctor-patient relationship of confidence and trust in health care. It could result in a situation where patients may less trust the doctor in rendering standard treatment aimed at cure. If a mutual distrust arises in this respect, possible discussion about life-sustaining care is bound to be adversely affected.

(iv) Other jurisdictions

There is no living will statute in Nigeria, but there is reason to believe that the fundamental ratio in *Okonkwo* v. *MDPDT*[176] will make a suitably worded living will effective at law. Most jurisdictions in Australia have enacted living will statutes.[177] Many jurisdictions in the Canadian federation also have enacted legislation on living wills.[178] Noteworthy of mention, in the absence of express legislation on living wills, the common law recognises the validity of the concept.

Some conceptual and practical issues in the ending of life

This section will show that even though courts have given to the emerging imperative of patient's autonomy in the form that right to refuse medical treatment is valid, paradoxical judicial decisions have failed as a practical matter to prevent the

---

[175] For example the tortuous effort to find *Anthony Bland's* decision as to whether to withdraw treatment in Bland [1993] 1 All ER 821 from his relatives and the substituted judgment approach would be minimised if AMD is employed by the patient.

[176] (1999) NWLR.

[177] Natural Death Act, 1983 (South Australia); Natural Death Act (Northern Territory) (for discussion see D. Lanham and B. Fehberg, above n.147. Medical Treatment Act, 1988 (amended 1990) (Victoria) discussed by Lanham & Woodford, above n.147, all cited in Kennedy & Grubb, *op cit* 1339.

[178] Consent to Treatment Act, 1992 and Substitute Decisions Act 1992 (both of Ontario) The health Care Directive Act, 1992 (Manitoba).

frustration of the concept by doctors and family relatives. It will also reveal that in cases of incompetent patients the standards employed by the courts are practically unrealistic, conceptually confusing and incoherent.[179] Most of the decisions suffer from serious internal conflict that rarely justify their results.[180] In both *Quinlan*[181] and *Saikewicz*,[182] the court used the legal standard of 'substituted judgment'. By this the decision-makers are said to arrive at a decision the patients would have made, in both cases that they would choice non-treatment if they were able to choose. But what was the evidence of this before the court? In *Quinlan* available evidence was scanty. The court was of the opinion that most people would choose end of life in *Quinlan* situation. But did that make it *Quinlan* decision? What most people would desire is certainly different from what a particular person wishes. So a statement of most people desire or wish was not certainly the wishes of Quinlan. The substituted judgment test was made more ridiculous in *Saikewicz* where the patient was retarded. No one, including the patient himself could have located his wishes.[183]

It is generally admitted that the courts seeking to release the incompetent from invasion treatment thought undesirable, have widely employed the 'substituted judgment' and 'best interest' test. As stated above the application of the substituted judgment test is itself problematic. The courts have adopted different amount of particularised evidence concerning previous expression of the patient's attitude towards life-sustaining treatment. At one extreme, in *Re Storer (Eichner)*[184] and in *Re Westchester County Medical Centre (O'Connor)*[185] the New York Court of Appeal adopted strict evidential requirement for the application of the concept of substituted judgment. Under the restrictive approach what is required is clear unequivocal evidence of the patient's previously expressed preferences. But herein lies the problem. Generally people are shy to confront matters of mortality. So in effect getting to know previous statements of an incompetent patient's preference would in most cases be practical elusive. In the absence of such clear and convincing evidence patients in the *Storar* and *O'Connor* situation will be forced to endure intrusive, unbeneficial treatment that a similarly situated competent patient would not choose.[186] What a paradox.

To prevent this unfortunate result, some courts adopt a more liberal approach. The evidence required under this approach includes such things as remote and infrequent statements by the patient, his prior religious beliefs, lifestyle choices etc. Even at this, the approach can even be ridiculous. In *Saikewicz* where the patient had never been competent, it would amount to mere conjunction for the court to

---

[179] Developments in the Law Medical Technology and the Law (1990) 103 *Harv. LR* 1522 at 1643.
[180] Nancy R Rhoden, Litigating Life and Death (1988) 102 *Harv. LR* 375.
[181] 355 A 2d 664 (NJ, 1976), per Hughes J.
[182] 373 Mass 728, 370 NE 2d (1977) (patient terminally ill).
[183] Rhoden, above n.181 at 376.
[184] 52 NY 2d 363, 420. NE 2d. 64, 438 NYS 2d. 266 cent denied 484 US 858 (1981).
[185] 72 NY 2d 517, 531 NE 2d 607, 534 NYS 2d (1988).
[186] Developments in the Law, above n.180 p.1641.

know his wishes on life-sustaining treatment because he had never had one. That notwithstanding, purporting to apply the substituted judgement standard the court stated that treatment should be based on the decision the incompetent would have made 'if he were competent'. This was nothing but a legal fiction. It is nonsensical to say in the least to assume that the never-competent patient is competent and then to base decisions on what he would decide. The actual and hypothetical patients have different histories and understanding of the world and so is a different person altogether. In this context substituted judgment merely masquerades a patient's choice, when the basis for the decision will be more readily explainable using the best interest principle.[187]

Even where it is based on evidence of a once-competent patient's preference, we must admit that an aggregation of random statements made over years on specific tragedies is not a reliable guide to decision making because: (i) such verbal statements lack the indicia of commitment and thoughtfulness attributable to actual choices; (ii) preference can radically change overtime; (iii) informal statements are likely to be too general in character. Non-verbal statements are no better. With them are associated interpretation problem. Statements and conducts are susceptible to different interpretation depending on how it is perceived by different persons. For example, one can explain the incompetent's refusal to artificial feeding on many grounds. It could be a reflection of anger, pride, or depression. By allowing family and friends (some of whom are selfish and unloving) to rely on intuitive personal knowledge of the patient can in some cases fail to protect the incompetent

In place of the substituted-judgment test some courts have adopted the 'best interest' principle. But then the question, what is the decision-maker to consider as benefit and burden to the patient from continued treatment? Is he expected to take into account matters relating to the patient's consent, medical condition, degree of pain, invasive nature of treatment, prognosis, loss of dignity, risks, side-effects of

---

[187] Ibid., for criticism of the substituted judgment standard, see also McLent & Saiki, Patient Attitudes to Decision Life-Sustaining treatment (1986) 146 *Archives Internal Med.* 1013; McCrasy & Botkin Hospital Policy on Advance Directives. Do Institutions Ask Patients About Living Wills? (1989) 162 *JAMA* , 411; Wilkler, Patients Interest: Clinical Implications of Philosophical distinctions (1988) 36 *J. Am. Geriatrics Society* 951; R. Veatch, Death, Dying And The Biological Revolution: Our Last Quest For Responsibility (rev. ed. 1989) p.114; Aras, The Severely Demented, Minimally Functional Patient: An Ethical Analysis (1988) 36. *J. AM Geriatrics Society* 938; Minow, Beyond State Intervention in the Family: For Baby Jane Doe (1985) 18 *U. Mich J.L Ref.* 933; Rhoden, above 45; Dresser, Life, Death and Incompetent Patient: Conceptual Infirmities and Hidden Values in the Law (1986) 28 *Ariz. L.R*; 73, Lo & Dornbrand, Guiding the Hand that Feeds: Caring for the Demented Elderly (1984) 321 *New Eng. J. Med.* 402. Buchanan, The Limits of Proxy Decision-making for incompetents (1981) 29 UCLA L.Rev Veatch, Limits of Guardian Treatment Refusal: A Reasonableness Standard (1984) 9 *AM Jo. L & Med.* 427; Ramsey, The Saikewicz Precedent: What Good for an Incompetent Patient, Hastings Center Report. Dec. 1978 at p.30, citing in Rhoden, above 181 at p.386 n.50; Burt, Withholding Nutrition and Mistrusting Nurturance: The Vocabulary of in Re Conroy (1987) 2 *Issues L & Med.* 317; Presidents Commission For The Study of Ethical Problem in Medicine & Biomedical 7 Behavioural Research: Deciding to Forgo Life-sustaining Treatment. 135, (1983).

treatment, quality of life and the interest of the patient's family and the like?[188] When family interest is used for example as a factor, the court will invariably be importing considerations that shift the focus of inquiry from the patient to the best interest of the family. Aside this, the best interest standard suffers two serious defects (i) there is no shared societal consensus about the constituent elements of quality of life (ii) the relevant factors may be misapplied or improperly evaluated eg. healthy persons may subjectively devalue the life and worth of a disabled or a person suffering from a debilitating, degenerative illness as of little worth when that may not be how others, including the patient think.

Dissatisfied with either standard, hybrid approaches have been adopted by some courts. The substituted judgment standards is used when adequate basis exist to determine the patient's preferences. If it is impossible, decisions have turned on the best interest test. In this category the courts have devised two forms of best interest- the limited objective and pure objective best interest test. While this hybrid approach is commendable in that it enables the court to avoid sheer application of substituted judgment in an absurd manner, it is submitted that the combination of both the substituted judgment and best interest standards abuses the legal basis for decision-making on treatment termination. They in effect turn the process into a 'right' not of the patient, but that of a third party.[189]

The procedure for termination of medical care for the incompetent is still subject to controversy. In *Saikewicz*, the Massachusetts Supreme Judicial Court took the view that the ultimate decision making responsibility is that of the courts. That being the case prior judicial approval to terminate life-sustaining treatment is a must.[190] But some other courts have rejected the approach, adopting instead other forms of extra-judicial safeguards.[191]

Following *Quinlan*, most courts have affirmed the right of the competent and incompetent to terminate medical treatment. Often ignored however, is the fact that most medical decisions on treatment are still left largely in the hands of doctors.

---

[188] See *In Re Conroy* 98 NJ 321 at 365-366, 486 A 2d 1209 at 1232 (1985) *In re Guardian of Grant* 747 p.2d 445 at 457, 109 Wash. 2d 545 at 568 (1987); *Cruzan* v. *Director, Missouri Dept. of Health* 109 S. Ct. 3240 (1980). On fears of using the quality of life index as a licence for eugenics and euthanasia, see R. Lipton, The Nazi Doctors: Medical Killing and Psychology of Genocide (1986) pp.30-79, 96-133; citing in Developments in the Law, above 44 p. 1652 n.70.

[189] Developments in the Law, above n. 180.

[190] *Superintendent of Belchertown State School* v. *Saikevicz* 373 Mass. 728; at 739 370 NE 2d 417 at 434-435 (1977), but cf in re Spring. 380 Mass 629 at 636-637; 495 NE 2d 115 at 120-121 (1980) (where the Mass. Sup. Ct stated that Saikewicz does not require prior judicial approval).

[191] *J F Kennedy Memorial Hospital* v. *Bludworth* 452 So. 2d 921 at 926 (Fla. 1984), In *Re Storer (Eichner)* 52 NY 2d 266 at 276 cert. Denied 454 US 858 (1981); *In re Guardianship of Grant* 109 Wash. 2d 545 at 565-567; 747 p. 2d 445 at 456-457 (1988) (en. Banc) modified on other grounds 757 p. 2d 534 (Wash. 1988) (agreement between doctor and family); *In re Quinlan* (*supra*) (hospital ethics or prognosis committee); *In Re Guardianship of Barry* 445 So.2d 365 at 372 (Fla. Dist.Ct. App. 1984) and In re LHR 253 Ga. 439 at 446, 321 SE 2d 716 at 722-723 (1984) (diagnosis by attending doctor, supported by two other independent doctors); In re Conroy (supra) (requires approval of state Ombudsman for termination of treatment for elderly in nursing homes).

Courts still fail to appreciate the ingrained tradition of doctor's authority that can frustrate in practical terms the patient's right of self-determination. Traditionally, doctors are hostile to patient's participation in decision-making. This situation is worse in developing countries like Nigeria, where doctors are known to insist on professional autonomy even at the expense of depriving patients their right of autonomy.[192] For example, if a doctor insist that the decision to use a respirator is purely a medical one, he would have in technical terms at least, disrespected the patient's 'right' to terminate treatment if he so chooses. Inadequate communication also pervades the decision making process for the incompetent patient. Empirical studies reveal that doctors often limit care to the incompetent in the absence of family instructions.[193] Conflict between patient and doctor may arise from the professional bias of doctors in favour of continued treatment, although with the changing face of medicine, this may well shift the powerful pressure on doctors to terminate treatment.

Aside this practical situation that may derogate the patient right of self-determination, the conceptual incoherence of 'the substituted judgment standard with a relaxed evidential requirement, the narrow applicability of that standard with a strict evidential requirement, and the indeterminacy of the best interest standard' combine to more derogate the right. [194] To reduce this problem it has been suggested that a framework should be established for discussion and dialogue by all parties in the decision making process. Only then can the advance in biotechnology fuel rather than frustrate medical self-determination.[195]

A doctrinal analysis of the right of self-determination has been minimal. Generally the majority of courts ground the right to refuse treatment or sustenance under the common law doctrine requiring that doctors respect the informed consent of the patient. Based on the common law principle of individual autonomy, the doctrine seeks to vindicate the right of every person to determine what will be done to his body. The informed consent concept is rooted either or both in tort theories of battery and or negligence. Under the former, a doctor who treats or sustains without consent commits battery for which the patient may recover compensatory damages without proof of harm. Emerging judicial pronouncements are now shifting the defining standard of professional conduct under negligence. Unlike the 'harm

---

[192] Davidson, Hackler, Caradine & McCord, Physicians' Attitude on Advance Directive (1989) 161 *JAMA* 1415 at 1419; Bertel & Delhanco, Choices About Cardiopulmonary Resuscitation in the Hospital: When Do Physicians Talk with Patients? (1984) 310 *New Eng.J.Med.* 1089; Brennan, Silent Decisions: Limits of Consent and the Terminally Ill Patient (1988) 16 *Law, Med. & Health Care* 104; Wit & Pearlman, Consent in Medical Decision Making: he Role of Communication (1988) 3 *Jo.Gen.Internal.Med*9, all cited in Developments in the law, above n. 180.

[193] Zinberg, Decisions for the Dying: An Empirical Study of Physicians' Responses to Advance Directives (1989) 13 *Vt.L. Rev* 445, Brennan, Ethics Committee and Decisions to Limit Care: The Experience at the Massachusetts General Hospital (1988) 160 *JAMA* 803.

[194] Developments in the Law, above n 180.

[195] Ibid.

principle' in battery which is the non-consensual touching *per se*, the 'harm' in negligence is the failure to observe a reasonable degree of care and skill in not informing the patient and obtaining his consent.[196]

Both competent and the incompetent's right to refuse treatment and sustenance can be rooted in common law battery. Even though incompetent cannot fulfil the function envisioned by the doctrine of informed consent, it is nonetheless battery to treat or sustain the incompetent without consent, whether or not he is unaware of the contact. Except in emergency, the doctor is required to obtain consent from an authorised third party if he does not want to be exposed to a law-suit for battery. Noteworthy of mention, in the United States of America, some courts have based the right to refuse medical treatment and sustenance on the due process clause and the right of privacy.[197] The Supreme Court of Nigeria also adopted a constitutional perspective in the *Okonkwo* v. *MDPT*[198] case fuelling the proposition that the American approach is on wings in Nigeria.

---

[196] See R Faden & T Beauchamp, *A History and Theory of Informed* Consent (1986) p. 17; Oddi, The Tort of Interference with the Right To Die: The Wrongful Living cause of Action (1986) 75 *Geo. L.J.* 625.

[197] Cruzan v. Director, Missouri Dept. of Health 110 S. Ct 284, 497 US 261, (1990); Developments in the Law: The Interpretation of State Constitutional Rights (1982) 95 *Harv.L.R* 1322.

[198] (1999) 6 NWLR (pt 786)1 (SC).

PART TWO

Medical Practice

Chapter Thirteen

Medical malpractice

Introduction

Medical malpractice is all about medical errors or negligence, an issue which invariable turns on an analysis of the reasonable doctor.[1] Litigation and dispute in this context are often emotive. For one thing an otherwise private arrangement is submitted to third party scrutiny. Since negligence invariable mean analysing a doctors course of diagnosis, or advise or treatment by a reasonable standard of his professional colleague, it may well be that a proof is itself a verdict of some form of incompetence or moral blameworthiness on the doctor's part. It is only natural that no doctor will like to be cut within the web of a malpractice suit. Liability is judged by an objective standard as a measured of professional conduct. Though liability is generally fault based, there is really no correlation between doctor's negligence and moral blameworthiness. We just must admit that mistakes or errors are part of our human nature. Some mistakes may be negligent, other not. It can result from mistake or mere error. Some may cause harm, others no harm.

Questions have sometimes been asked whether the objective standard is not itself a doctor's based standard. Why? The alleged negligence is judged on the basis of the conduct of a reasonable doctor. It is submitted however that that in itself does not make it exclusively medical standard because the ultimate decision is not doctor-

---

1 For general reading see, Picard, The Liability of Hospitals in Common Law (1981) 26 *Mc Gill LJ* 997; GHL Fridman, Hospital Liability for Professional Negligence (1980) 4 *Leg. Med. Q* (Canada) 80; W P Whippy, A Hospital's Personal and Non-delegable Duty of Care for its Patients —Novel Doctrine or Vicarious Liability Disguised (1989) 63 *ALJ* 182; J Bettle, Suing Hospital Direct: Where Tort was it Anyhow? (1987) 137 *NLJ* 573; A Montrose, IS Negligence an Ethical or Sociological Concept? (1958) 21 *MLR* 259; Picard, *Legal Liability of Doctors and Hospitals in Canada* (2nd ed. 1984); M Brazier, *Medicine, Patients and the Law* (2nd ed. 1992); N Terry, The Malpractice Crisis in the United States: A Dispatch from the Trenches (1986) 2 *Professional Negligence* 145; *N* v. *Dokkum*, The Evolution of Medical Malpractice Law in South Africa (1977) 41 *J. of African Law* (175; L R Walker (*et al.*) The Effect of Malpractice Litigation on Patients Access to Speciality Physician Services (1990) II *J.Leg.Med* 199; B Dickens, The Effect of Legal Liability on Physicians Services (1991) 41 *Univ.Tor.L.J.* 168 R Smith, The Epidemiology of Malpractice (1991) 301 BMJ 621; JDJ Harvard, Doctors and Medical Negligence (1990) 300 BMJ 343; M A Jones, Medical Negligence – The Burden of Proof (1984) 134 *NLJ* 7; RBM Howie, The standard of Care in Medical Negligence (1983) *Juridical Rev* 193; G Robertson, *Whitehouse* v. *Jordan – Medical Negligence Retired* (1981) 44 *MLR* 457.

based. A growing number of cases reveal that judges recognise that, although the doctor's standard serves as a guide, it is not the ultimate benchmark of measure. The court, not the doctor is the final judge of what is negligence or malpractice. In arriving at a decision judges pay attention to the emerging emphasis on individual rights and other policy issues that enter into medical treatment.

Malpractice operates on two basis principles: (i) the patient consents to treatment; and (ii) treatment undertaken without proper care and skill.[2] If a patient does not consent to treatment, it will be actionable assault and or battery to treat. This primary proposition will not be discussed in this chapter. If a doctor fails to exercise proper care and skill in his treatment he would be liable to compensate the patient for any harm resulting by an action in negligence. Our discussion would rather focus on this aspect, namely the (ii) category above.

Noteworthy of mention, the doctor's liability may be either contractual and or delictual. Negligence remains the most common basis of liability in medical malpractice, whether the claim lies in contract or delict. But medical malpractice is not limited to award of damages flowing from professional negligence. It can and does embrace other causes, such as breach of medical confidentiality,[3] failure to carry out a treatment already agreed upon by the doctor i.e. breach of contract.[4]

While the United States of America has the highest vibrant number of litigation in this respect, the English jurisdiction exhibits a conservative approach to malpractice litigation.[5] This is because the English assumes a generally protective attitude to the medical profession believing that its position will reduce incidence of combative practice, which invariable increases the cost of health care. In *Hiske* v. *Cole* [6] Lord Denning stated that in order to find a doctor liable for negligence his conduct should be one deserving of censure or be inexcusable in the circumstance. What this mean is that the courts should be circumspect to find or rarely should find negligence against a doctor. This follows the traditional pattern of protection traced out in Tindal CJ charge to a jury in 1838:

> 'Every person who enters into a learned profession undertakes to bring to the exercise of it a reasonable degree of care and skill. He does not undertake, if he is an attorney, that at all events you shall gain your case, nor does a surgeon undertake that he will perform a cure, nor does he undertake to use the highest possible degree of skill. There may be persons who have higher education and greater advantages than he has, but he undertakes to bring a

---

2 M Brazier, *Medicine, Patients and Law* (2nd ed. 1992) p. 21 – 22 cited by Kennedy & Grubb, *op. cit*, p. 397.

3 See discussion on informed consent.

4 Dokkun, above n. 1 p. 177.

5 Strauss, *Doctor, Patient and the Law* (3rd edn. 1991) p. 243.

6 (1968) 112 SJ 483; see also *Okonkwo* v. *MDPRT.*

> fair, reasonable and competent degree of skill, and you will say whether in this case, the injury was occasioned by the want of such skill in the defendant.'[7]

Nigerian judges have also used similar language and standard in fixing doctor liability.[8] It is submitted that the standard for fixing doctor's liability, the practical difficulty in linking a patient's injury to treatment coupled with a jurisprudence that judges doctor's conduct against that of his professional colleagues and the expense of litigation, all operate to inhibit medical negligence litigation in a manner that the American system with its contingency fees and its sympathetic juries, does not.[9]
Medical malpractice is the failure by a medical man to exercise reasonable degree of skill and care. It is the failure to exercise the standard of care that a reasonable man should exercise in a given circumstance. For a doctor it is his failure to exercise a reasonable degree of skill and care expected of an average medical doctor. The tort of negligence was recognised as a tort head in *Donoghue* v. *Stevenson*.[10]

A doctor who is negligent exposes himself to disciplinary action from the Nigerian Medical and Dental Council,[11] to action for civil and criminal negligence. If his negligence results in death of a patient he may in addition be charged for murder (culpable homicide punishable by death)[12] or manslaughter. Charges for murder are however likely to be rare. Usually a charge for manslaughter is more plausible going by the nature of doctor's work. To lead to conviction for manslaughter the Nigerian court have held that the degree of negligence required is one higher than that required for a civil actionable negligence. In *R* v. *Akerele*,[13] the Privy Council approved the statement of Lord Hervart in the English case of *R* v. *Bateman* [14] that the degree of negligence required in criminal cases must go beyond that for civil liability. It requires showing 'such disregard for the life and safety of others' to amount to manslaughter. In *Akerele* of about 47 children the doctor administered injection 10 died. The prosecution case was that the drug, a mixture of powder sobite in sterile water was overdosed. The court held that negligence was not established because the consequence of the mixture only took place at a later date. If the charge, however, was for rash or negligent act not resulting in death, the degree of negligence will have been slightly lower.[15] In *Dabholkar* v. *King*,[16] the Privy Council

---

7 *Happier* v. *Phipps* (1838) 173 ER 581.

8 *Okonkwo* v. *MDPRT* (1999) 6 NMLR(pt786)

9 Mason & McCall Smith, *op. cit*, 191; Strauss, above n. 5; W A Harland & R S Jandoo, The Medical Negligence Crisis (1984) 24 *Medicine, Science and the Law*, 123.

10 [1932] AC 562.

11 LFN, 2004

12 S. 244 list the 6 necessary intent to substantial a charge for murder.

13 (1941) 8 WACA 56.

14 1925) 133 LT 730 at 732.

15 S. 343 of the Criminal Code states that any person who gives medicine or medical and surgical treatment in a rash or negligent manner as to endanger life or is such as is likely to cause harm to a person shall be guilty of a misdemeanour.

16 [1948] AC 221 (East African case).

when construing an East African provision similar to section 234 of the Criminal Code stated that although the negligence which constituted the offence (under s.222 of Tanganyika (Tanzania) Penal Code is higher than that for civil actionable wrong, it nonetheless is not as high as that for manslaughter. Flowing from this, three degrees of negligence can be constructed, namely: (i) the highest degree required for prosecution of manslaughter; (ii) the intermediate degree for rash and negligent acts; and (iii) the lowest degree required for civil liability.

Section 230 of the Code gives the legal underpin for doctor's liability, namely: that a doctor who undertakes to treat must use reasonable care because by his calling he holds out himself as possessing requisite skill.[17] Noteworthy, the section applies to all persons who undertake treatment of others, except in cases of necessity. Our criminal law deals ruthlessly with any unqualified person who holds himself out as a doctor. It requires such a person to demonstrate the requisite skill of a qualified doctor. The test for judging responsibility in this respect is not the fact of the person's qualification, but the fact of the person's conduct considered negligent. Therefore if an unqualified person exhibits the same degree of skill and care that a doctor would have demonstrated he would escape liability. In *R* v. *Lawant*,[18] the defendant was acquitted on a charge for manslaughter because the court found that although unqualified, he exhibited the proper degree of skill. He sterilised his instruments used in treating tonsils. But in *R* v. *Ozegbe*[19] the defendant was held liable for manslaughter because he performed an operation with no proper knowledge of surgery and in an incompetent manner. It is not uncommon in developing countries to see quacks offering their services to the public claiming falsely to be qualified doctors. The court have attempted to deal decisively with them.[12] In sentencing one of such culprits, the court said: 'It is extremely dangerous for an ignorant mountebank like the accused to dabble in medical science for which he is least qualified. This type of offence is very common nowadays and a deterrent sentence is required in this case.'[20]

The legal basis for doctor's civil liability is founded on the ground that the public entrust itself to their care and so are entitled to demand and expect a reasonable degree of skill and care. The question whether or not a doctor is negligent will therefore depend on the facts of each case. Whatever the facts the following three requirements must be established: (i) that the doctor owes a duty of care to the patient; (ii) that the duty is breached; and (iii) the result is damage.

Interestingly, equitable principles of fiduciary law are now reforming doctor's liability for malpractice. In Canada and United States fiduciary principles are redefining matters of human and personal interests. For example in *Norbery* v.

---

17 S. 230 provides that every person who except in a case of necessity, undertakes to administer surgical or medical treatment must posses reasonable skill and use reasonable care in acting.

18 [1961] WNLR 133.

19 [1957] WNLR 152.

20 C.O. Okonkwo, *Medical Negligence and the Legal Implications*, p. 119.

Wynrib[21] at least three judges took the position that the doctor-patient relationship is fiduciary. They applied it to protect the interest of a woman patient receiving medical care free from sexual harassment and exploitation by her doctor. When so harassed she was adjudged entitled to equitable compensation. She received an award for damages, including punitive damages by way of equitable compensation for the emotional pains caused her by the doctor's sexual acts in breach of his fiduciary duty. McLachlin J, with whom L'Heureux and Dube JJ. concurred said that fiduciary principles 'are capable of protecting not only narrow legal and economic interests, but can also serve to defend fundamental human and personal interests.'[22]

What this means is that outside the traditional common law basis for liability, equity can provide supplementary far-reaching vista to liability. Whether liability under equity would cover all or most areas of malpractice is however not clear.[23] If the statement of the court is anything to go by, equitable liability can and should only be raised where a malpractice is one that can affect human and personal interests, eg., cases of sexual harassment and exploitation, blatant disregard of patient's treatment choices in such a manner as to indicate callousness on the part of doctors. It is suggested that this head will not readily apply to general cases of malpractice that have little bearing on human and personal interest connected with dignity of the person, such as wrong diagnosis, wrong treatment and the likes.

Let us now consider the basis two ways to fixing liability under contract and or delictual.

Contractual liability

The law of contract may provide a remedy for an express or implied warranty given by a doctor. Generally it is an implied term of contract that a doctor will exercise reasonable care and skill in the treatment of his patient. If he fails to do so, he will come under an obligation to compensate the patient for damages caused by his breach of contract.[24] The law implies a contract in every circumstance when a patient submits himself to a doctor for treatment. In *La Fleur* v. *Cornelis*, [25] a plastic surgeon was held bound to an express contractual warranty he made to his patient. The warranty was said to arise when he imprudently said to the patient: 'there will be no problem, you will be very happy.'

---

[21] (1992) 92 DLR (4th) 449; see also A Mason (extra-judicial), The Place of Equity and Equitable Remedies in the Contemporary Common Law World (1994) 110 *LQR* 238 at 247-248.

[22] Ibid., at 499.

[23] *State* v. *Okechukwu* [1965] 9 ENLR 91 at 94.

[24] D Giesen & 1 Fahrenhorst, Civil Liability From Medical Care: Principles and Trends (1984) *J. of International Legal Practitioner* 84; *Myers* v. *Abrahamson* 1951 (3) S A 433 (C) and (1952) (3) S A 121 (C).

[25] (1979) 28 NBR 2d 569 (NBSC), discussed in M A Jones, *Medical Negligence* (1991) p. 18, cited in Mason & MaCall Smith, *op. cit*, 195.

Noteworthy of mention, damages for breach of contract, unlike damages for delict, are not intended to recompense the patient for injuries suffered but rather to put him in the position he would have been if the treatment was properly performed. Though the general rule laid down by the House of Lords in *Addis* v. *Gramophone Co Ltd*[26] is that if damages fall to be assessed for breach of contract rather than in tort, it is not permissible to award general damages for frustration, mental distress, injured feelings or annoyance occasioned by the breach, there are exceptions to the rule. Where the contract that is breached is itself a contract to provide peace of mind or freedom from distress, damages may extend to injured feelings, mental distress, and the like.[27] Since medical treatment can be likened to a contractual arrangement designed to provide peace of mind or freedom from distress it has been held that damages in this context may be awarded for patrimonial loss, discomfort, pain, mental distress and so on.[28]

Whether the Nigerian courts will adopt this approach to damages is not certain. But the South African courts have held that contractual damages for medical negligence will not go as far as cover mental distress. Prior to *Administrator, Natal* v. *Edouard*,[29] damages were awarded for inconvenience, discomfort or loss of time if they are directly connected to the breach complained of.[30] But in *Administrator, Natal* v. *Edouard* [31] the court overruled earlier decisions on this point. It stated that damages should only to be awarded for patrimonial loss, and not for discomfort, pain, suffering and loss of amenities of life caused by the birth of a child resulting from a breach of contract to perform a sterilisation operation.[32] By so doing the South African courts took the position that common law contractual damages cannot be awarded for any form of intangible loss, even if the contractual arrangement is one designed to provide convenience, comfort and basic enjoyment of life. Since this attitude can and does have a suffocating influence on medical litigation, in the sense that it is overtly restrictive of the patients right to claim damages, especially in a setting that subverts the reasonable expectation that treatment or medical contract designed to give peace of mind may be breached and the realistic damages expected to flow from his will not be awarded, it has been suggested that the English approach, rather than the South African should be adopted by our courts.

---

26 (1909) AC 488 (1908-10) All ER Rep. 1; see also *W* v. *Egdell* [1989] 1 All ER 1089, per Scott J.

27 *Jarvis* v. *Swans Tours Ltd* [1973] 1 All ER 71 [1973] QB 233; *Heywood* v. *Wellers* (1976) 1 All ER 300 (1976) QB 446; *Cox* v. *Phillips Industries Ltd* [1976] 3 All ER 161 [1976] 1 WLR 638 per Lawson J.

28 *Jarvis* v. *Swans Tours Ltd* (*supra*) [1945] AD 354, *Bennett* v. *Shaw* (1902) 19 SC 248 at 251; *Reed* v. *Eddels* [1920] OPD 69, cited in *Dokkum*, above n. 1 at 178 ft nt 69, cited in *Dokkum*, above n 1 at 178 ft nt 19.

29 [1990] (3) SA 581 (A).

30 *Dokkum*, above n.1.

31 [1990] (3) SA 581 (A)

32 SA Strauss & MJ Strydom, *Die Suid-Africaamse Gemeskundige* (1967) p.1 cited by Dokkum, above n.1 at 171

If a doctor commits a breach of contract the patient will be legally exempted from his obligation to remunerate the doctor for his service. In addition the patient may also claim damages if the breach has led him to incur extra cost, for example, consulting another doctor for a more proper treatment.[33]

To raise liability the patient will need to prove the following: (i) the contract or at a minimum, a prior doctor—patient relationship; (ii) the negligent act complained of or an intentional breach of the contract; (iii) a link between the injury and the treatment, i.e. causation; and (iv) resulting damages. Whatever, the same act complained of may also be the basis of a claim in delict.

Delictual liability

To come within this bracket, the patient must prove damages suffered through a wrongful or negligent act of the doctor. To do this he will need to show: (i) the existence of a duty of care; (ii) the breach of that duty i.e. the specific nature of the duty breached; (iii) the particular ground of negligence alleged and; (iv) causation, i.e. that is a casual link between the act complained and damages suffered. To show the existence of a duty of care the patient would need to set out the facts that could have been foreseen by the doctor which raises the duty of care. The onus of this lies on the patient. This he can do by establishing that the defendant: (i) ought to foresee the possibility of his conduct that causes the injury or loss; (ii) that the doctor ought in the circumstances to take reasonable steps to guard against the loss or injury; and (iii) that the doctor negligently failed to take the reasonable step expected.

Whether there exist a casual link between injury and act complained of is a legal question that raises issue of foreseeability. Damages are only recoverable if they are foreseeable and not too remote. Generally for personal injuries the patient is entitled to claim for: (i) actual pecuniary loss, e.g. loss of earning or medical expenses for consulting another doctor; (ii) pain and suffering; and (iii) prospective loss, eg. future medical bills. Since these are most likely to be treated as special damages, the patient is under an obligation to particularise them. Because negligence is the gist of most malpractice litigation, it is the common denominator for liability in medical malpractice, whether the claim is structured in contract or tort. It is for this reason that our next discussion will focus on it.

Proof of negligence

Duty of care

Proof of negligence begins with the patient proving a duty of care. It is imagined that this will be little problematic for him. The duty arises from the circumstances of

---

[33] *R* v. *Bateman* (1925) 94 LJ KB 791, per Lord Hewart CJ; *Barnett* v. *Chelsea & Kensington Hospital Management Committee* [1969] 1 QB 428,; [1968] 1 All ER 1068.

the fact that one person holds out himself as possessing special skill and knowledge based on which others consult him. In the context of medicine, the doctor owes a duty to use reasonable care and skill in the administration of treatment. To raise the duty no contractual relation is necessary, nor is it necessary that he services should be rendered for a consideration or reward. In effect the duty arises at common law from the doctor's undertaking to give treatment. Lord Denning MR said:

> 'Whenever they accept a patient for treatment they must use reasonable care and skill to cure him of his ailment...I ask can there be any difference between hospital authorities that accept a patient for treatment and railway or shopping authorities who accept a passenger for carriage? None whatever. Once they undertake the task, they come under a duty to use care in the doing of it, and that is so whether they do it for reward or not.'[34]

The only problem may be in identifying the precise moment that the duty of care comes into being. This is because many persons may have a role to play in the patient's treatment, eg., pharmacists, nurses, midwives, physiotherapists. These professionals, generally regulated outside the tenor of doctor's ethics can introduce complication into identifying the precise moment.[35]

Standard of care

Generally negligence is a failure to act the way a reasonable man in the circumstances of the defendant will act, or doing some act which a reasonable man in the circumstance would not do. Standard of care is judged by the action of the man in the street, i.e. the ordinary man. In the context of medical treatment, negligence is judged by the standard expected of a reasonable doctor in the position of the defendant. An inquiry to determine whether a defendant is negligent is an inquiry whether the doctor's conduct amount to a breach of duty of care that he owes his injured patient.

McNair J in *Bolam* v. *Friern Hospital Management Committee*,[36] summarised the position of law traced from a long line of cases from *Lamplier* v. *Phipos*[37] to *R* v. *Bateman* this way:

> 'A doctor is not guilty of negligence if he has acted in accordance with a practice accepted as proper by a responsible body of medical men skilled in that particular act...Putting it the other way round, a doctor is not negligent, if he is acting in accordance with such a practice merely because there is a body of opinion that takes a contrary view. At the same time that does not mean that a medical man can obstinately and pig-headedly carry on with some old

[34] [1951] 2 KB 343, per Lord Denning MR.

[35] This matter will be the subject of discussion when considering the institutional framework of medicine.

[36] [1957] 2 All ER 118 at 121, [1957] 1 WLR 582 at 586.

[37] (1838) 8 C & P 475 at 478.

> technique if it has been proved to be contrary to what is really substantial the whole of informed medical opinion. Otherwise you might get men today saying: I don't believe in anaesthetics. I don't believe in antiseptics. I am going to continue to do my surgery in the way it was done in the eighteenth century. That clearly would be wrong'. [38]

The summary above has widely been referred to as the *Bolam* test. It was followed by the Privy Council in *Chin Keow* v. *Government of Malaysia*,[39] *Whitehouse* v. *Jordan*,[40] and a host of many others and the Nigerian Supreme Court in *Okonkwo* v. *MDPT*.[41]

If a doctor holds himself as possessing specialist qualification or expertise, a higher standard would be required of him. So if he undertakes a treatment that require special skill which he does not have, he could be guilty of negligence if he fails to exhibit the care expected of a specialist doctor with requisite qualifications and experience. In determining if a doctor is liable for negligence, policy matters are often considered, such as availability of equipment, prevailing knowledge at the relevant time, etc. If negligence is sought to be raised from a mistake in diagnosis, the court will employ the standard of the ordinary skilled doctor. Negligence may take a variety of form. Mis-diagnosis, negligent surgery, negligent advise or failure to warn of potential risk inherent in a treatment procedure, negligently allowing a dangerous patient to be at large, inadequate supervision of inexperienced staff, etc.[42] Let us particularise some of the facts that can raise negligence.

(i) Approved Practice

If the act complained of is one within the range of usual or approved practice, the alleged conduct is judged by what is considered normal medical practice. Lord Clyde in *Hunter* v. *Hanley* said the following:

> 'To establish liability by a doctor where deviation from normal practice is alleged, these facts require to be established. First of all, it must be proved that there is a usual and normal practice. Secondly it must be established that the course the doctor adopted is one which no professional man of ordinary skill would have taken if he had been acting with ordinary care.' [43]

---

[38] (1925) 94 LJ KB 791 at 794.

[39] [1967] 1 WLR 813.

[40] [1981] 1 All ER 267, [1981] 1 WLR 246 at 276-7 per Lord Edmund-Davies, see also *Maynard* v. *West Midlands Regional Health Authority* [1985] 1 All ER 635, per Lord Scarman; *Sidaway* v. *Board of Governors of the Bethlehem Royal Hospital and Maudslen Hospital* [1985] AC 871, [1985] 1 All ER 643.

[41] pt

[42] Dokkum, above n 1 at p.181-182; see also S Maclean, Negligence – A Dagger at the Doctor's Back, in P Robson & Watchman (eds) *Justice, Lord Denning and the Constitution* p. 104; *Roe* v. *Minister of Health* [1954] 2 QB 66.

[43] [1955] SC 200 at 206 (Scottish case).

Simply as the formulation may seen it is not free of controversy. One, who sets the standard of care that the doctor must comply with considered usual practice? Is it the court or the medical profession? Two, what if there are more than one type of medical procedure considered usual in the circumstance? If that is the case, what are the liability implications of choosing a treatment procedure not generally accepted by a responsible body of opinion within medicine?

It has been argued that if the legal standard of care is that of the medical profession, it would mean that the profession would not only be offering evidence of good practice (a factual matter) but will also at the same time be determining what doctors ought to do (a legal matter).[44] The prevailing view is that the medical profession sets the stage for the standard. It is the initial inquiry point from where the standard admits of other policy matters and so eventually ends up as a legal standard. Before a conduct is adjudged usual or approved, the courts must first rightly regard the practice as professionally tenable. By so doing, the courts while looking at the 'nucleus' from medicine, ultimately puts in value judgment of its own. According to Lord Denning MR, 'the law will not allow the medical profession to play God.' [45]

In *Rogers* v. *Whitaker*, the Australian High Court said:

> 'In Australia it has been accepted that the standard of care to be observed by a person with a special skill or competence is that of the ordinary skilled person exercising and professing that skill. But that standard is not determined sole or even primarily be reference to the practice followed or supported by a responsible body of opinion in the relevant profession or trade.' [46]

It is the court that ultimately decides if a course of conduct is acceptable or not. Yes, expert professional evidence of custom will be relied upon by the court and in a majority of cases will be overwhelming, but that's how far it can go. No doctor can rely on it with complete certainty. For example, the Supreme Court of Canada in *Reibi* v. *Hughes*, said:

> 'To allow expert medical evidence to determine what risks are material and hence, should be disclosed and correlatively, what risk are not material is to hand over to the medical profession the entire question of the scope of duty of disclosure including the question whether there has been a breach of that duty.'

The principle was cited with approval by King CJ of the Supreme Court of South Australia in *F* v. *R*.[47]

---

[44] Kennedy & Grubb, *op. cit*, p. 449.

[45] *Sidaway* v. *Bethlehem Royal Hospital* [1984] QB 493; [1984] 1 All ER 1018 (CA); per Lord Denning MR; *Reibi* v. *Hughes* (1980) 114 DLR (3rd) 1; *Rogers* v. *Whitaker* (1992) 109 ALR 625 (1993) 4 Med LR 79.

[46] *Supra*.

[47] (1983) 33 SASR 189.

It however can be argued that *F* v. *R* and *Reibi* only apply in the context of disclosure of risk and so do not apply with same force to matters of treatment. It has been suggested also that since the general tenor of *Bolam* test was restricted in *Sidaway* to only medical treatment and not extended to disclosure, by analogy the proposition that the standard of care is legal not medical, does not apply to diagnosis and treatment. From that perspective it can be argued that the rule only applies to disclosure. Such argument it is submitted is fallacious. In fact before *Sidaway*[48] got to the House of Lords, Lord Donaldson MR of the English Court of Appeal expressed the view that *Bolam* was not fully appreciated. In his view the correct analysis of it ought to reveal that the court and not the medical profession determine the standard of care. His Lordship explicitly considered *Reibi* as good authority that covered all cases of medical treatment, advice and diagnosis. He said:

> 'I accept the view expressed by Laskin CJC (in Reibi v. Hughes) that the definition of the duty of care is not to be handled over to the medical or any profession. The definition of the duty of care is a matter for the law and the courts. They cannot stand idly by if the profession by an excess of paternalism denies its patients a real choice. In a word, the law will not permit the medical profession to play God...I think that in appropriate case, a judge would be entitled to reject a unanimous medical view if he were satisfied that it was manifestly wrong and that the doctors must have been misdirecting themselves as to their duty in law.'[49]

Several authorities show that even in matters of diagnosis and treatment, (in addition to disclosure and advice) the test is legal and ought to remain so.[50]

The next question is how to determine the standard of care where there are disagreements as to what is the appropriate course to follow. In a case where there is only one professional practice, a doctor charged with negligence can disprove it if he can show that he acted in accordance with general and approved practice.[51] Question of determining the standard of care where there are more than one professional practices arose for determination in *Bolam*.[52] The patient suffered fractures because of the administration of electro-convulsive therapy without anaesthesia by the doctor. At the same time of his treatment there were two schools of thought on the

---

48 [1984] 1 All ER 1018 (CA) per Lord Donaldson MR.

49 *Supra*.

50 *Blake* v. *Cole* (1993) 4 Med. LR 393; *Bolitho* v. *City & Hackney HA* (1993) 13 *BMLR* 11; See also A. Montrose' Is Negligence an Ethical or a Sociological Concept? (1958) 21 *MLR* 259; Fleming, *The Law of Torts*, 8th ed. 1992 p.121; See also on value of customs in other professions outside medicine; *Cavanagh* v. *Ulster Weaving Co. Ltd* [1960] AC 145, [1959] 2 All ER 745; *Thompson* v. *Smiths Ship Repairers (North Shields) Ltd* [1984] QB 405, [1984] 1 All ER 881; *Edward Wong Finance Co. Ltd* v. *Johnson, Stokes & Master* [1984] AC 296 (Solicitors held negligent even though they followed normal customary conveyancing practice in Hong Kong).

51 *Whiteford* v. *Hunter* [1950] WN 553, per Lord Potter; *Vancouver General Hospital* v. *McDaniel* (1934) 152 LT 56.

52 [1957] 2 All ER 118; [1957] 1 WLR 582.

subject of anaesthesia in such treatment. One held the view that the relevant drugs should be used. The other, that such drugs only increased risk. The court held that the doctor was not negligent if he acted in accordance with the practice accepted by a body of responsible doctors. Negligence did not become proved simply because the doctor employs a procedure for which some members of his profession take a contrary view.

A judge's preference for one body of distinguished professional opinion to another also professionally distinguished is not sufficient to establish negligence of a doctor whose actions have received the seal of approval of those whose opinion truthfully expressed were not preferred. In *Maynard* v. *West Midlands Regional Health Authority*,[53] the trial judge preferred the opinion (alternative) of a body of medical experts to that chosen by the doctors notwithstanding the fact that the doctor's procedure was also supported by other medical opinion, considered reasonable. The negligence alleged against each doctor was that contrary to the strong medical opinion, which should have led them to diagnose tuberculosis, they held back from a firm diagnosis and decided that the patient should undergo the diagnostic operation, mediastinoscopy. This was an operation which carried risk even when properly performed, such as damage to the left laryngeal recurrent nerve. Unfortunately this occurred in the instant case with resulting paralysis of the left vocal cord. Two distinguished doctors in the treatment of chest disease gave different medical opinion. Lord Scarman of the House of Lords was not in doubt that the facts was not about mistake or carelessness in performing the operation. The operation was performed properly. So, negligence if raised at all would turn on alleged error in judgment in requiring the operation to be undertaken. The doctors were held not negligent.

In the realm of diagnosis and treatment, negligence is not established by preferring one respectable body of professional opinion to another. Failure to exercise the ordinary skill of a doctor (in the appropriate speciality, if he is a specialist) is what is necessary.[54] Going by this, if the court is unable to select between two or more alternative, the doctor will be liable for negligence because in that case he will not have acted in accordance with a practice accepted as proper by a responsible body of medical men, following the *Bolam* test.[55]

Since a doctor need to carry out his duty in accordance with practice accepted by his colleague, it follows that he has a duty to keep himself informed of major developments in the practice of medicine. This does not mean that he must know all that should be known in a particular area of his profession. In *Crawford* v. *Board of Governors of Charing Cross Hospital* the patient suffered injuries (bronchial palsy) as a result of his arm being kept in a certain position during an operation. Six months prior to the operation, an article appeared in an English widely read medical journal,

53 [1985] 1 All ER 635, per Lord Scarman.

54 *Bolam* v. *Friern Hospital Management Committee* [1957] 2 All ER 118, [1957] 1 WLR 582.

55 *Bolam* v. *Friern Hospital* [1957] 2 All ER 118, [1957] 1 WLR 582.

'Lancet' showing the dangers of the type of procedure used for the patient. The patient brought an action against the anaesthetist for negligence, alleging that if he had read the journal in question, he would have avoided the treatment procedure employed which resulted in his injury. The court found in favour of the doctor. His action did not amount to negligence. But Lord Denning said:

> 'It would, I think be putting to high a burden on a medical man to say that he has to read every article appearing in the current medical press, and it would be quite wrong to suggest that a medical man is negligent because he does not at once put into operation the suggestion which some contributions or other might make in a medical journal. The time may come in a particular case when a new recommendation may be so well proved and so well known, and so well accepted that it should be adopted, but that was not so in this case...The medical man's duty is limited to taking reasonable steps to keep himself abreast of modern developments in technique...failure to read a particular article may well be excusable, while disregard of a series of warning in the medical press could perhaps be cogent evidence of negligence.'[56]

Because the practice of medicine is becoming more and more scientific, it would be dangerous for a doctor to practice by coasting along only on the basis of long practice. He will need to keep abreast with modern technique.[57]

(ii) Innovative treatment

Sometimes an innovative treatment may only amount to a deviation from an established or approved medical treatment. If negligence is to be raised in this context it must be shown that there is a usual and normal practice, that the doctor has not adopted the practice and that the practice adopted by him is one that no professional man of ordinary skill would have undertaken if he had been acting with ordinary care.[58] What evidence would do to establish this? Is it for the court to determine whether the deviation is justified in the sense that ordinary doctors engaged in ordinary care might adopt it? Or is the doctor's usual practice guide sufficient justification? This is by no means settled especially when judged from the backdrop of Sellers LJ statement in *Landau* v. *Werner* that 'a doctor might not be negligent if he tried a new technique, but that if he did he must justify it before the court. Successes was the best justification for unusual and non-established treatment.'[59]

This makes it risky for any doctor to try innovative treatment. There exist higher chances of raising negligence against a doctor who deviates from approved practice especially when things go wrong and an injury is suffered by the patient. In *Clark* v. *MacLennan*,[60] a gynaecologist performed an anterior coiporrhaphy

---

56 (1953) *Times*, 5 Dec., per Lord Denning, [1953] TLR 1.

57 *H* v. *Royal Alexandra Hospital for Sick Children* [1990] 1 Med LR 297, *Dwan* v. *Farguhar* [1988] 1 Qd R 234.

58 *Hunter* v. *Hanley* [1955] SC 200, Lord Clyde of Scottish Court of Session.

59 (1961) 105 Sol. Jo 1008.

60 [1983] 1 All ER 416.

operation on a pregnant woman soon after delivery when the normal practice is not to perform such operation until at least three months after birth so as to ensure its success and to prevent the risk of haemorrhage. When the operation was performed on her haemorrhage occurred, for which two further operations became necessary. In the views of Peter Pin J, where a doctor deviates from the orthodox practice, it is not enough for him to say that his decisions were based on clinical judgment. The court would make an enquiry as to whether the doctor took all proper factors into account which he knew or should know, and whether the departure can be justified on these factors. Because the defendant could not discharge the burden of justifying his departure the orthodox practice he was held liable for negligence.

It is suggested that if the case was decided on facts and burden of proof it is unimpeachable. But, its general propositions on the standard of care and the legal effect of a departure from usual practice are controversial. Mustill LJ in *Wilsher* v. *Essex Area Health Authority* [61] expressly disagreed with the proposition in *Clark* v. *MacLennan* that in certain cases there is a general burden of proof on the doctor. His Lordship's view was affirmed on appeal.[62] The proper law therefore is that the burden of proof remains that of the patient. It can shift to the doctor if the patient establishes that the procedure used is not orthodox. His suit for negligence may then succeed unless the doctor leads proper evidence of refuttal.

It follows that doctors should resort to innovative technique with caution. Whether it would not be negligence would depend on whether it is considered justified in the case in question. As a general rule the court will consider evidence of its novelty, previous trial of the procedure, dangers inherent in it, previous response of the patient to orthodox treatment, the seriousness of the patient's ailment and the patient's attitude to the novelty and risk of the unorthodox procedure.

(iii) Misdiagnosis

A mistake in diagnosis will not be treated as negligent if the doctor exhibits the proper skill and care of an ordinary doctor. He is not to be held liable simple because things go wrong. It will be a disservice to the community if liability is imposed on him for everything that happens to go wrong. It would be against community interest to make him facilitator of compensation for damages resulting from medical intervention. It would be better for all if interference with the practice of medicine is minimal. If it were otherwise, a doctor at work would forever be looking over his shoulder to see if someone was coming with a dagger-for an action in negligence against him is like 'unto a dagger'.[63]

Accordingly liability for a misdiagnosis will only be imposed if the doctor fails to exercise due care and skill. For example, a failure to conduct a test a competent

61 [1986] 3 All ER 801 at 815, per Mustill LJ.

62 [1988] 1 All ER 871 at 879, per Lord Bridge.

63 S. Maclean, Negligence – A Dagger at the Doctor's Back in P. Robson *et al*, (eds), *Justice, Lord Denning and the Constitution* p.104.

doctor would consider appropriate, or making a mistake because of failing to take a proper medical history can be considered negligent.[64] Generally, laboratory test would be expected of reoccurring symptom but extensive investigation should only be required for complicated illnesses.[65] In *Whiteford* v. *Hunter* [66] the court held the doctor not negligent when he misdiagnosed the patient of carcinoma of the bladder, because he used methods which were in common use at the time. That he did not use a cystoscope, which he did not possess and would have been difficult for him to obtain, was not considered fatal. Where however a doctor is in doubt about a diagnosis, good practice will suggest that he makes a referral to a specialist. [67]

(iv) Negligence in treatment

Here the court considers a mistake which is excusable and one that is not. Accordingly to Lord Fraser in *Whitehouse* v. *Jordan*,

> The true position is that an error of judgment may or may not be negligent, it depends on the nature of the error. If it is one that would not have been made by a reasonably competent professional man professing to have the standard and type of skill that the defendant's holds himself out as having and acting with ordinary care then it is negligence. If, on the other hand, it is an error that such a man acting with ordinary care, might have made then it is not negligence.'[68]

It follows therefore that a gross medical error will most likely be treated as negligence. This will be the case for example, of treating a wrong patient[69] using a wrong drug,[70] leaving behind inside the patient operating equipment, such as swab.[71] Goddard LJ in *Mahon* v. *Osborne* said: 'As it is the task of the surgeon to put swabs in, so it is his task to take them out and if the evidence is that he has not used reasonable standard of care he cannot absolve himself if a mistake has been made by saying: "I relied on the nurse."' [72]

---

64 *Chin Keow* v. *Government of Malaysia* [1967] 1 WLR 803; *Coles* v. *Reading* (1963) 107 Sol. Jo 115; *Barnett* v. *Chelsea & Kensington Hospital Management Committee* [1969] 1 QB 428, (1968) 1 All ER 1068; *Cavan* v. *Wilcox* (1973) 44 DLR (3rd) 42

65 *Langley* v. *Campbell* [1975] *Times*, 6 Nov. (failure to diagnose malaria after return of patient from East Africa treated as negligence). *Tuffil* v. *East Surrey Area Health Authority* [1978] *The Times*, 15 March p. 4 (failure to diagnose dysentery fatal to the doctor) both cited in Mason & Smith op cit p. 203-204.

66 (1950) 94 Sol. J 758.

67 *Okonkwo* v. *MDPT (19990 6 NWLR (pt 786)1.*

68 [1981] 1 All ER 267 at 281, [1980] 1 BMLR 14 at 30.

69 *Ibrahim* (a minor) v. *Muhammed* (2) May 1984 unreported (penis was partially amputated during circumcision) referred to in Mason & Smith, *op. cit.*, p.205 f. n. 14.

70 *Graig* v. *Mid Herts Hospital Management Committee* (1974) 118 Sol Jo 50; *Collins* v. *Hertfordshire County Council* [1947] KB 598, [1947] 1 All ER 633.

71 *Mahon* v. *Osborne* [1939] 2 KB 14, [1939] 1 All ER 535.

72 [1939] 2 KB 14 at 47; [1939] 1 All ER 535 at 559; see also *Urry* v. *Bierer* [1955] *Times* 15 July and MA Jones, Medical Negligence (1991) p. 40.

(v) Inexperienced doctors

Using the *Bolam* test it can be argued that a newly qualified doctor is required to possess the competence expected of an experienced doctor. But this may itself be too high a requirement. Expertise of a medical man should reasonable come with experience. These were the issues that arose for determination in *Wilsher* v. *Essex Area Health Authority*.[73] A newly qualified doctor who administered extra oxygen made an error in monitoring the arterial oxygen tension on the patient premature baby. It was argued for the patient that this could cause blinding condition of *retrolental fibroplasia* which occurred. The defendant hospital argued however that the standard of care expected of a junior doctor should be somewhat different from an experienced doctor. They were of the view (regrettably) that the junior doctor should undertake such a job on the basis of 'learn on the job'. It was in the defendant's view expedient in the circumstance because there was no other experienced doctor. Furthermore, it was argued that it is in the interest of the public health system to keep the hospital running. The English Court of Appeal appeared ambivalent on the question of reasonable care expected of a junior doctor. Mustill LJ for his part was however clear. In his Lordship's view the standard of care should be judged with the post occupied by him. If a junior doctor occupied specialist position, the standard of care that would be expected of him is that of a specialist. So if the junior is a house officer or a registrar undertaking specialist services of a consultant, the standard of a competent consultant will be required of him. Glidewell LJ also found the view attractive, though in his Lordship's opinion the standard would be met if the junior sought advice or consulted with the more experienced doctor when appropriate.

The Glidewell LJ's test however raises many practical questions. How will the junior know when to seek the opinion of the experienced? On what matters should this be? Must it be in all matters or only important matters? Does not the fact of inexperience also go with it difficulty of knowing when to seek advice? If we follow logically the view that standard of care is to be judged by the post occupied, will that entail that a consultant occupying a houseman or registrar post should be judged by the lower standard of a houseman or registrar? Would it not make sense to judge him by his individual competence as a consultant? These are questions that go to the root of health resources and treatment. According to Lord Denning in *Jones* v. *Manchester Corporation*: 'It would be in the highest degree unjust that the hospital board, by getting inexperienced doctors to perform their duties for them, without adequate supervision, should be able to throw all the responsibility on those doctors as if they were fully experienced practitioners.' [74]

While delegation from an experienced doctor to a junior of a specialist function is not prima facie proof of negligence by the experienced doctor, it could be so in certain circumstances, e.g., if the junior is incapable of performing the duties or is not

---

[73] [1987] QB 730, [1986] 3 All ER 801.

[74] [1952] 2 QB 852 at 871, [1952] 2 All ER 125 at 133, per Lord Denning.

properly supervised by the experienced medical man. That notwithstanding, the junior cannot throw away his personal liability if he carries out his instructed duties negligently.[75]

(vi) Danger to patient

Where there is the likelihood of a patient being danger to himself or others, the doctor is under a duty to safeguard against such dangers. In *Selfe* v. *Ilford and District Hospital Management Committee*,[76] where a patient with suicide tendency as a result of long overdose was not kept in constant supervision, the hospital was assessed for damages when he got injured from attempting suicide.

Breach of duty

In determining whether a doctor conduct amounts to negligence the court will test his conduct on the basis of the skill and care expected of an average doctor, not the skill and care expected to be exhibited by the most experienced doctor. The reason is that some may be more thoroughly educated than others.[77] The degree of care and skill required also takes into account the availability of medical materials and practice location of the practitioner. Accordingly in *Lamplier* v. *Phipos*,[78] the judge directed the jury to the effect that every person who enters into a learned profession undertakes to bring to it the exercise of a reasonable degree of care and skill. He does not undertake to perform a cure of or show the highest possible degree of skill, for others might be persons who have higher education and greater advantage than be has. All he covenants to do is to bring a fair, reasonable, and competent degree of skill to bear in treating patient.[79] The standard thus required is objective. For a specialist it is higher than that required of a pupil doctor because he is an expert in his particular speciality.[80]

A doctor is not negligent if in the treatment of a patient, he administers a drug which contrary to ordinary experience reacts disastrously on the patient. In *Roe* v. *Minister of Health* [81] the plaintiff underwent a hospital operation for minor operation. A spinal anaesthetic was given for the purpose. The anaesthetic consisted of Nupercaine injected by means of lumber puncture. Unfortunately it was contained in a glass ampoules immersed in phenol solution. Some of the phenol contaminated the anaesthetic by seeping through tiny cracks in the ampoule. That could not be detected by ordinary visual examination. When eventually

---

75 *Junor* v. *Inverness Hospital Board of Management and McNicols* (1959) *Times*, 26 March (ITL).

76 (1970) 114 Sol Jo. 935; but cf *Hidge* v. *Tameside Area Health Authority* [1981] CLY 1854, 2 PN 26 (CA) and *Thorne* v. *Northern Group Hospital Management Committee* (1964) 108 Sol Jo 484.

77 See Rule 11,pls check relevant section in Code

78 [1838] 8 C&P 475.

79 See *Bolam* v. *Friern Hospital Management Committee* [1957] 2 All ER 118; [1957] 1 WLR 582.

80 *Rich* v. *Pierpoint* [1862] 3 G & F 35; *R* v. *Akerele* (1942) 8 WACA 56; *R* v. *Ezeocha* (1946) 12 WACA 56; *R* v. *Ozegbe* [1957] WNLR 1552.

81 [1954] 2 QB 66.

administered on the patient it caused permanently paralysed of the patient from waist down. Had the anaesthetist been aware of the possibility of seeping that caused contamination he would have added a powerful colouring agent to the phenol so that the contamination of the anaesthetic will have been observed and danger to the plaintiff could have been averted. The court dismissed the action for negligence because the risk of such contamination was at that material time in medicine not appreciated by anaesthetist. A few years after the incident leading to *Roe* v. *Minister of Health*,[82] anaesthetist came to appreciate the dangers of placing ampoules solution in alcohol or spirit.[83]

Thus if an anaesthetist were to ignore such clear warning, he would be liable for negligence. Lord Denning succinctly put the matter this way in *Crawford* v. *Charing Cross Hospital*:

> 'It would be putting too high a burden on a medical man to say that he must read every article in the medical press...The medical man's duty is limited to taking reasonable steps to keep himself abreast of modern developments in technique...failure to read a particular article may well be excusable, while disregard of a series of warnings in the medical press could perhaps be cogent evidence of negligence.' [84]

Error in diagnosis is not necessarily actionable negligence because it may not be due to ignorance. What is more, a doctors give no guarantee or warranty express or implied or otherwise that he will diagnose correctly the condition for which a patient suffers. In *Whiteford* v. *Hunter and Gleed*[85] a 70 years plaintiff sued a surgeon and general practitioner for negligence in that he wrongly diagnosed his condition. Upon being told that he had 9 months to live, having been diagnosed of cancer, he wound up his business and went to America with a view to enjoying the remaining part of his life. While in America, an American surgeon operated on him for bladder complication and he got cured of his ailment which was obviously not cancer. The plaintiff claimed for pecuniary losses and mental anguish caused by the defendant's wrong diagnosis. The defendant was held liable and judgement was entered against them for £6,300 because they ought to have made microscopic and cystascopic examinations before confirming cancer in the plaintiff. *Failure to do so was negligence.* Also in *Baldwin* v. *Lord and Ors*[86] the plaintiff action succeeded against

---

82 *Supra.*

83 Macintosh, Lumber Fracture and Spinal Anaesthesia, 1951, contained such a warning. See also CO Okonkwo, *op. cit.*, p. 126

84 (1953) TLR, [1953] *Times*, 8 December, CA. See also *H* v. *Royal Alexandra Hospital for Sick Children* [1990] 1 Med LR 297; *Dwan* v. *Farquhar* [1988] 1 Qd R 234, though risk of HIV infection through blood transfusion was discussed in the medical press in March, the court held that there was no negligence for a tranfusion administered in May.

85 [1950] 94 SJ 758, [1948] Lancet vol. I, 232. But see cf. Mason & Smith, *op. cit.*, at 204 n. 6, where the learned writers suggest that 'at the time', such an error would be indefensible today; *Morris* v. *Winsburn White* [1937] 4 All ER 494.

86 [1947] vol. XV, pl. II *Med. Leg. J.* 92.

the infirmary and surgeon. He was awarded £4,000. He went for hospital operation to graft a piece of bone from his leg to his right wrist. The operation was successful. However, a tourniquet applied to the patient legs was left in position for 11 (eleven) hours; and despite administering blood transfusion he died. But in *Hatcher* v. *Black*[87] the court held that a surgeon will not be held liable simply because an operation was unsuccessful if he has brought to bear in the operation the requisite skill and care. The plaintiff a singer underwent an operation after being assured that no risk would result to her voice. During the operation a nerve was badly damaged which affected her voice. In directing the jury the judged graphically said:

> 'It would be wrong and indeed bad law to say that simply because a misadventure or mishap occurred, the hospital and the doctor are thereby liable...It would mean that a doctor examining a patient or a surgeon operating at a table, instead of getting on with his work, would be forever looking over his shoulder to see if someone was coming up with a dagger – for an action of negligence against a doctor; is for him like unto a dagger. His professional reputation is as dear to him as his body, perhaps more so, and an action for negligence can wound his reputation as severely as a dagger can his body. You may not therefore find him negligence simply because something happen to go wrong; if for instance, one of the risks inherent in an operation actually takes place or some complication ensues which lessens or takes away the benefit that was hoped for, or if in a matter of opinion he makes an error of judgement, you should only find him guilty for negligence when he falls short of the standard of a reasonably skilful medical man, in short, when he is deserving of censure...for negligence in a medical man is deserving of censure.'

A doctor will not be liable for negligence simply because he uses a course of treatment recognised in the profession even though there may be other accepted opinion differing from his choice.[88] In *Bolam* v. *Friern Hospital Management Committee*,[89] the plaintiff broke his pelvis during electro-convulsive therapy in defendant hospital. He alleged negligence because in his view the defendant failed and did not warn him of the risk of the therapy in not administering relaxant drug before the treatment and in failing to strap him down during treatment. The defendant evidence showed that some medical opinion favoured strapping down a patient both at the upper and lower limbs, while others favoured strapping the upper part only. The latter was the procedure adopted by the hospital where the defendant doctor worked. The court did not find negligence since he acted in accord with a practice accepted by a responsible body of medical men skilled in that particular act. However, the judge warned:

---

87 [1954] *Times*, 2nd July C.O. Okonkwo, *op. cit*, p. 125.

88 E N Uzodike, The Doctor and the Law Professional Negligence, in ES Akpata (ed) *Medical Ethics*, Lagos Univ. Press, 1982, p.43.

89 [1957] 2 All ER 118.

'that does not mean that a medical man can obstinately and pig-headedly carry on with some old technique if it has been proved to be contrary to what is really substantially the whole informed medical opinion. Otherwise you might get men today saying 'I do not believe in anaesthetics. I do not believe in antiseptics. I am going to continue to do my surgery on the way it was done in the eighteen century.' That clearly would be wrong."

Question of proof

To prove negligence the patient must lead medical evidence sufficient to satisfy the burden of proof. In most cases he will need to rely on the evidence of another doctor against his doctor. In practice, it is difficult to get doctors to give evidence against their colleague, a situation often referred to as doctor's 'conspiracy of silence'.[90] When considered in the context that the patient submits his safety and well-being into the hands of the doctor and that treatment may take place when he is often unconscious and or incapable of knowing what causes his injury or the medical jargon to describe the situation, proof of medical negligence becomes more problematic for the injured patient. Matters are made worse by the courts general attitude of reluctance to extend *res ipsa loquitur* to medical negligence litigation.[91] The doctor by his training and knowledge is the one who knows (most likely) what exactly goes wrong. From that perspective it would ordinarily be expected that the burden should rest on him. But that exact opposite is what the law directs. The burden is on the patient and not the doctor. Noteworthy, in the United States of America, burden of proof have largely been shifted to doctors and this has been a powerful weapon in the hands of injured patients. Some commentators have submitted that this reverse burden rule has helped in combating medical conspiracy of silence practice.[92]

Unfortunately courts within the common law system are often reluctant to apply the principle of *res ipsa loquitur* in medical negligence. *Res ipsa* is part of circumstantial evidence and it applies where a plaintiff prove facts which raises an inference of negligence in the absence of explanation. It throws the burden on the other person/defendant to displace the prima facie interference; even though there is no onus on him to establish the correctness of his explanation. The doctrine does not shift the burden of proof to the defendant. It only raises an inference of negligence on his part. If he cannot rebut the inference, the plaintiff will be treated as having established his claim for negligence. *Res ipsa* thus makes it easier for a patient to

---

90 Dokkum, above n 1 at 132; see also *F* v *R* (1983) 33 SASR 189 at 194, per King CJ, Strans, above n 5 at 245.

91 Nigeria follows the English reluctance. See a similar attitude is adopted in South Africa, see Dokkum, above n 1. The American courts however take a contrary position; see S A Strans, The Physician's Liability For Malpractice A Fair Solution in Problems of Proof (1967) 84 *SALJ* 417; Strans above n 5 p. 245.

92 This principle has been employed more in cases where swabs are left inside the body of patients. See *Easterling* v. *Walton* 208 Va. 214, 156 S E 2d 787 (1967); *Hestbeck* v. *Hennepin County* 297 Minn. 419, 212 NW2d 361 (1973); *Gould* v. *Winokur* 237 A 2d 916 (1968).

succeed. It will only applies where (i) there is no evidence as to how or why an accident occurred; (ii) the accident must be such that it would not occur without negligence; and (iii) the defendant must be in control of or linked to the situation either personally or vicariously. It only applies where the plaintiff is unable to identify the precise nature of the negligence which caused his injury and the defendant offers no explanation as to how the injury occurs. Usually, the injury should be of such a nature that does not normally happen in the circumstances unless there is negligence.[93]

Megaw LJ in *Fletcher* v. *Bench* stated what is considered to be the rationale for the law's reluctance. He said:

> 'If one were to accept the view that negligence was inevitably proved if something went wrong and it was unexplained, few dentists, doctors and surgeons, however competent, conscientious and careful they might be, would not avoid the totally unjustified and unfair stigma of professional negligence probably several times in the course of their careers.' [94]

A further reason is the uncertainties that can result from medical treatment. In medicine anything can go wrong without negligence. Sometime, it is so due to hardly avoidable mistake or error. Andrews J of the British Columbia Supreme Court captured this succinctly in *Guard* v. *Royal Colombian Hospital* this way:

> 'The human body is not a container filled with a material whose performance can be predictably charted and analysed. It cannot be equated to a box of chewing tobacco or a soft drink. Thus, while permissible inference may be drawn as to the normal behaviour of these types of commodities the same kind of reasoning does not necessarily apply to a human body. Because of this medical science has not yet reached the stage where the law ought to presume that a patient must come out of an operation as well or better than he went into it. From my interpretation of the medical evidence the kind of injury suffered by the plaintiff could have occurred without negligence on anyone's part. Since I cannot infer there was negligence on the part of the defendant's doctor, the maxim of *res ipsa loquitur* does not apply.'[95]

In *Ladlow* v. *Swindon Health Authority*,[96] the maxim was held inapplicable to raise negligence. The facts rested on *res ipsa loquitur*. The patient claimed that she regained consciousness during a Caesarean section in which she experienced pain. She failed however to establish that the intense pain occurred at a stage during which halothane should have been administered. There was no inference of negligence by the use of the anaesthetic.

---

93 Nigeria cases on *res ipsa*. See also Picard Legal Liability of Doctors and Hospitals in Canada (1984) p. 260-261; J Fleming, *The Law of Torts*, 8th ed. 1992 p. 322; D Giesen, *International Medical Malpractice Law* (1988) p. 515; Mason & Smith, *op. cit*, p. 208; *NgChun Pui* v. *Lee Chuen Tat* [1988] RTR 298 (PC).

94 [1973] unreported, cited in 4 BMJ 1117 (CA).

95 (1976) 66 DLR (3d) 676 (patient underwent an operation of a left femoral popiliteal saphenous vein by —pass graft which he claimed led to the weakness in both legs).

96 [1989] 1 Med LR 104.

Res ipsa was however established in *MacDonald,* v. *York County Hospital Corporation*[97] and *Cassidy* v. *Ministry of Health.* [98] In *MacDonald* the patient who went for treatment of a fractured ankle left hospital with an amputated leg. *Res ipsa* was raised because what happened to the patient in the absence of explanation was unusual, leading to an inference of negligence. In *Cassidy* the patient who went for operation of two stiff fingers came out with four stiff fingers. Denning LJ stated that the patient was entitled to say: 'I went into hospital to be cured of two stiff fingers. I have come out with four stiff fingers and my hand is useless. That should not have happened if due care had been used. Explain it if you can.' [99]

Some commentators suggest that the *res ipsa* rule should not enjoy extensive application in present day litigation because today's elaborate civil procedure rules dealing with inspection, discoveries and the like now operational (absent when the *res ipsa* maxim was developed) should fill the gaps designed by the invention of the rule. [100] For example the High Court of Lagos State (Civil Procedure) Rules, 2004, contains elaborate practice rules on discovery and exchange of evidence may well mean that the plaintiff/patient will more likely know what goes on in his treatment, thereby displacing the relevance of *res ipsa*.[101] When the maxim was invented in 1863 it could be said that what happened in the warehouse was unknown to the plaintiff, but he could say that barrels don't roll out of a first storey opening on to passer-by. Now the situation is certainly different, especially in the context of medical negligence. The patient should know better than the 1863 passer-by.

One point deserves mention here. It is this. The question of the fairness is raised when a competent average doctor's conduct is judged by reference to evidence of eminent doctors or the practice traced out from teaching hospitals. If the *Bolam* test is the valid basis, then the law may well be doing some disservice to the average doctor whose conduct is being investigated by reference to or reliance on evidence of eminent medical men. Their standard may not necessarily represent the standard of the ordinary doctor with due skill and care. Same argument may be advanced for using teaching hospital procedures in judging those who have not benefited from working in such centres.[102]

Causation

To succeed in an action for negligence the plaintiff must prove a direct nexus between the negligent act or omission alleged and the resulting damages. In *Barnett* v.

---

97 (1972) 28 DLR (3d) 521.

98 [1951] 2 KB 343; [1951] 1 All ER 574.

99 Ibid at p. 365 and 588, see also *Mahon* v. *Osborne* [1939] 1 All ER 525; *Holmes* v. *Board of Hospital Trustees of the City of London* (1977) 81 DLR (3d) 67; *Cavan* v. *Wilcox* (1973) 44 DLR (3d) 42.

100 *Byrne* v. *Boadle* (1863) 2 H & C 722, reputed to be the beginning of the *res ipsa loquitur maxim.* Ibid., see also Kennedy & Grubb, *op. cit.,* p. 467 and *Bull* v. *Devon Area Health Authority* [1993] 4 Med LR 117 per Mustill LJ cited in Kennedy & Grubb, *op. cit.,* p. 467.

101 See for example High Court of Lagos State Civil Procedure Rules, 2004, Orders 25 and 26 on pre-trial conference and; discovery and inspection respectively.

102 See *Malette* v. *Shulman* (1988) 47 DLR (4th) 18, per Donnelly J (Ontario High Court).

Chelsea and Kensington Hospital Management Committee[103] the court held that there was no nexus between the negligence and the death of the plaintiff because death would have nonetheless resulted to the deceased if the doctor was not negligent in the circumstances. Three (3) fellow watchmen complained of vomiting for three hours after drinking tea to a nurse on duty in the hospital. She contacted by telephone the casualty doctor who instead of seeing the patients instructed her to tell them to go home to bed and call their own doctor. The men left and after about five hours one of them died of poisoning. The deceased widow failed in her action for negligence because the evidence showed that the deceased would have died in all and any event even if he was admitted into the ward and treated with care. Her suit was dismissed because it was not established that death was caused by the doctor's negligence.

Causation remains a vexed question in law and it is generally difficult to prove it, especially in medical cases.[104] Medicine is not exact science so it is difficult to make assumption on causation. The plaintiff is required to prove that the doctor's negligence is what caused or materially caused the attendant damage. It is for the plaintiff to prove both negligence and causation. The standard of proof is balance of probabilities.[105] In *Emeh* v. *Kensington and Chelsea and Westminster Area Health Authority*[106] a married woman who already had three healthy children underwent an abortion and sterilisation operation. She subsequently learned that she was 18-20 weeks pregnant but she decided against another abortion. When the baby was born it was found to be cognitively abnormal. The sterilisation operation was found to have been performed negligently. The defence claimed that the refusal of the woman to have an abortion was unreasonable and that that broke the chain of causation thereby disqualifying her for compensation even if the surgeon had been negligent. The defence argument was rejected, including its plea of *novus actus interveniens*. Plaintiff's claim succeeded.

Also in *M* v. *London Borough of Newham*[107] the defence plea of *novus actus interveniens* was also rejected. The Master of Rolls stated that causation is a question of fact, not law. The mother and daughter sued the defendant psychiatrist who had wrongly diagnosed that the daughter had been sexually abused by the mother's boyfriend. While the diagnosis was correct to the extent that she was sexually assaulted, the assault was not from the mother's boyfriend. As a result of the report the daughter was taken into care for a year. The mother and daughter claimed they have suffered nervous shock as a result of the court's enforced separation. The court

---

103 [1969] 1 QB 428.

104 Paul Balen, Causation Problems (1994) 138 *SJ* 742.

105 *Wilsher* v. *Essex Area Health Authority* [1986] 3 All ER 801, *Houston* v. *East Berkshire Area Health Authority* [1987] AC 750, *Prendergast* v. *Sam and Dec Ltd* [1989] IMLR 36; *Emeh* v. *Kensington and Chelsea and West Minister Area Health Authority* [1985] 1 QB 1012, *M* v. *London Borough of Newham* (CA) unreported case 1994 3rd March, *The Times*.

106 [1985] 1 QB 1012.

107 (CA) unreported case 1994 3rd March, *The Times*.

affirmed *Bolam* v. *Friern Hospital Management Committee* test for determining negligence.[108] The defence argument that the causation chain was broken by the resulting court order made in wardship proceedings was rejected, because it was the inevitable result of the council (defendant's) evidence which consisted of the alleged negligent reports of the psychiatrist that formed the basis for the order. The link in the claim was therefore preserved.

The required degree of skill and care is lowered when the doctor treats in an emergency, especially outside the hospital, e.g. if he offers his services to victim of road accident while also travelling. It was reported recently that a doctor performed a surgical operation on a woman who had complication in an aircraft using basic household knife as operation instruments sterilised in alcohol. The operation was successful.[109] Under such circumstances, the degree of care and skill expected is lower. That notwithstanding, the doctor must not make the situation of the patient worse. 'Those who come to help must take care not to make things worse, the kiss of life should not be the kiss of death. But first aid need not be first class and the emergency may justify incompetence.'[110]

With a view to encourage doctors to render emergency aid, some states in the United States of America have enacted protection statutes, often referred to as 'Good Samaritan laws', to protect doctors from actionable negligence that may result from their emergency volunteer services.[111]

A plaintiff in his proof of negligence may invoke the doctrine of *res ipsa loquitur* (the thing speak for itself). The doctrine generally when applied is to the effect that the conduct complained about is indicative of negligence in that its happening is by law presumed to be prima facie evidence of negligence. When it applies, the burden of proving causation is shifted from plaintiff to the defendant.[112]

By virtue of the provisions of the English Law Reform (Contributory Negligence) Act 1945, Civil Liability (Miscellaneous) Provisions Act 1961,[113] if a plaintiff contributes to an alleged negligence his claim for damage would not be defeated by reason of his fault. Rather recoverable damage would be reduced by the court to the extent deemed just and equitable having regard to his share in the responsibility for the injury. At common law proof that the plaintiff has to any extent contributed to the injury defeats his claim for damages *in toto*. That position is now modified by the Civil Liability (Miscellaneous Provision) Act 1961. By it a plaintiff who is partly at fault will not have his claim defeated, but damages recoverable will be reduced to the extent as the court deems fit. What constitute contributory negligence is a

---

108 [1957] 2 All ER 118; [1957] 1 WLR 582.

109 Newspaper report.

110 Wilmer LJ in *Tojo Maru*

111 Ref. Kenedy Grubb.

112 *Fish* v. *Kapur* [1948] 2 All ER 176; *Cassidy* v. *Ministry of Health* [1951] 2 KB 343; *Mahon* v. *Osborne* [1939] 2 KB 14

113 Cap of law of Nigeria, 1990, s. 11. See also *Evans* v. *Bakare* [1973] 3 SC 77 and James, Assumption of Risk (1952) 61 Yale LJ 141.

question of fact and vary depending on the circumstances of each case.[114] Since *Hedley Byrne & Co.* v. *Heller & Partners*, [115] it analogically follows that a doctor can be held liable for negligence misstatement.

It has long been established as a principle of the common law that a master or principal is liable for the wrongs of his servant and or agent.[116] Clearly then, hospital homes are liable for the acts of their servants. Before *Cassidy* v. *Minister of Health*,[117] hospitals were not held liable for these because the law then did not view the hospital—doctor relationship as one of master and servant. Doctors were likened to independent contractor, not under strict rule as to direction of work. The contract engaging a doctor was seen not as a contract of service, but as an agreement to render services. Hospital obligation was considered fully discharged when it appoints a qualified doctor and no more.[118] The position was however exploded in *Cassidy* v. *Minister of Health*. Lord Denning said: "The position now is that hospitals are liable for the negligent acts of their doctors."[119]

It is not sufficient for the patient to show a breach of care, he must further adduce evidence to link the injury with the alleged negligence. Initially the common law adopted a practice favourable to the patient that somewhat smuggled the *res ipsa loquitur* maxim through the back door. In *McGhee* v. *National Coal Board*[120] it was held that negligence would be raised if the patient can establish that the treatment materially increased the risk of his injury. This 'contributory factor,' casual link concept can be likened to an attempt to bring in the *res ipsa* maxim generally rejected in the context of proof of medical negligence. But in *Wilsher*[121] the House of Lord reversed *McGhee* and all the cases that rest on it. In *Wilsher*, the patient was mother of a premature born baby. The baby was put in an oxygen chamber that was wrongly monitored. As a result the oxygen tension blinded the baby. But evidence showed that there were five possible causes for the condition. One was medical negligence but it could not be conclusively said that it was the oxygen tension that caused the particular injury. The House of Lord held that the plaintiff

---

114 *Emeh* v. *Kensington & Chelsea & West Minister Area Health Authority* [1985] 1 QB 1012.

115 [1963] 2 All ER 575; 107 SJ 454; [1963]; Lloyds Rep 485.

116 Cite works on vicarious liability *M* v. *London Borough of Newham* (unreported) (CA) unreported case 1994 3rd March, *The Times*, *Whiteford* v. *Hunter & Gleed* (1950) 94 SJ 758, HL. See Holmes, Agency (1891) 5 Harv LR 14-'common sense is opposed to making one man pay for another's man's wrong, unless he has actually brought the wrong to pass according to the ordinary cannons of legal responsibility.'

117 [1951] 2 KB 347.

118 See *Foote* v. *Greenock Hospital* [1912] SC.691; *Hillyer* v. *St. Bartholomew's Hospital* ([1909] 2 KB 820; *Strongway–Lesmere* v. *Clayton* [1936] 2 KB 11, *Powell* v. *Streatham Manor Nursing Home* [1935] AC 243, *Fold* v. *Essex C.C.* [1942] 2 All ER 237, [1942] 58 LR 357.

119 [1951] 2 KB 343.

120 [1972] 3 All ER 1008, [1973] 1 WLR 1 (HL; *Clark* v. *MacLennan* [1983] 1 All ER 416, but cf. *Ashcroft* v. *Mersey Health Authority* [1983] 2 All ER 245 (Kilner Brown J with reluctance was unable to shift the burden of proof on the doctor and held that there was no negligence).

121 *Wilsher* v. *Essex Area Health Authority* [1988] AC 1074, [1988] 1 All ER 871.

had not shown a casual link between negligence and the injury. Lord Bridge disapproved of *McGhee* as good authority on the question of shifting the onus of proof to the doctor/defendant.[122] In effect, the contributory factor test is no good law. Rather the 'but for' test is now the applicable rule. By taking a restrictive view of the decision in *McGhee* it can be said that success for the plaintiff in a medical negligence case is made more difficult.

In *Hotson* v. *East Berkshire AHA*,[123] the House of Lords had another opportunity to consider the causation test. The plaintiff was unable to establish on a balance of probabilities that the defendant's failure to treat him promptly in breach of duty would have alleviated the injuries he suffered from as a result of failing from of a tree. There was a 75% chance that his injuries would develop even in the event of correct diagnosis and treatment. The trial judge held that the matter was simply one of quantification of damages and the English Court of Appeal upheld his view that the mistreatment had denied the plaintiff a 25% chance of a good recovery, and so damages awarded was reduced. The House of Lords however declined to measure statistical chances and concluded that it was the original injury which caused the vascular necrosis, the eventual permanent injuries. His injury was held not to be one attributable to the negligence of the defendants. The chance was that of 100 people 75 would have developed a vascular necrosis and 25 would not. So on the balance of probabilities the plaintiff fell into the larger group — 75. Since there was no evidence that he was lucky to be in the group of 25 who could benefit from treatment, his injury could not be said to result from the defendant's negligence. It has been suggested that if the result would have been different if 51% of the people sustaining the sort of the plaintiff's injury could be treated with say a 20% chance of success. It would follow that on the balance of probabilities, the plaintiff could have fallen within the 51% group and so if a hospital negligently failed to treat, the plaintiff could be said to have lost that 20% chance of success. Whether this 20% loss should attract compensation in the form of 20% damages was however left open by the *Hotson* decision.[124]

The probability rule was applied by the Supreme Court of Michigan in *Falcon* v. *Memorial Hospital*[125] in a wrongful death claim. The deceased had a 37.5% chance of survival had she been treated effectively. The court held that the doctor's inaction dimmed the chances of survival and that the appropriate damages should be

---

122 Ibid., at 1092 and 883, per Lord Bridge. See however the dissenting opinion of Browne-Wilkinson VC at the Court of Appeal in *Wilsher* v. *Essex Area Health Authority* [1987] QB 730 at 779, [1986] 3 All ER 801 at 834 and J Fleming. Probabilities Causation in the Tort Law (1989) 68 Can. BR 661, cited in Mason & Smith, *op. cit.*, p. 211, which seem to suggest that Wilsher and McGhee are reconcilable on the ground that the former relates to a case where cause of injury are multi-causal, while the former to mono-causal. What that mean is that McGhee still follows the proposition that the onus is on the plaintiff.

123 [1987] AC 750, [1987] 2 All ER 909.

124 Mason & Smith, *Law and Medical Ethics*, 4th ed. p. 212.

125 462 NW2d 44 (Mich. 1990).

measured equal to the chances of survival multiplied by the total damages available for wrongful death.

Lord Mackay in *Hotson* did not reject the relevance of *McGhee* to the case because McGhee in stating that damages are recoverable for 'contributory causal link,' in the sense that the defendant increased the risk of injuring, is itself implicit that the loss of a chance to recovery is the corollary to the *McGhee* proposition, and so could be the basis of recovery for negligence. The law it must be admitted remains controversial as to the governing test. The reason is that *Hotson* was decided before *Wilsher* which gave *McGhee* a restrictive interpretation. If *Wilsher* represents the law then it is plain that its restriction on *McGhee* represents the current law. *Wilsher* decided that the defendant would not be liable if he only contributed to the injury. Logically it should follow that if the defendant merely deprived the plaintiff of a chance of recovery there can be no causal link to the injury. That would mean that *Hotson* that decides on the probability rule cannot be considered good law. Increasing the risk of the plaintiff and depriving him of chances of success are two sides of the same coin on proper analysis. To increase the risk of injury to a plaintiff is at the same time to decrease his chances of recovery. Also if *Hotson* represents the law then probabilities i.e. the 'contributory factor' and not the 'but for' rule is all the plaintiff needs prove to raise a causal link.

The probability rule in *Hotson* is not without its difficulties. It relies on statistics which are merely theoretical or hypothetical and so may not really relate to the patients' real experience. It therefore should follow as Lord Mackay put it in *Hotson* that it is only when the statistic can be personalised that the court should find a causal link. But what if the probabilities are overwhelming? In such a case the courts may likely draw an inference of a link. That would be the case in *McGhee* and not in *Hotson* and *Wilsher*. In this context the problem begins to come down to one of classification. It is like on true analysis mixing two things in one — concern to establish a causal link with negligence and question of the quantification of damages. *Hotson* appears to blur the difference and this is not good for proper legal development. [126] It confuses statistical chances with the actual effects of the defendant's breach of duty to the plaintiff.

To make matters worse the English Court of Appeal in *Bolitho* v. *City and Hackney Health Authority*[127] applied the *Bolam* test to question of causation. In determining whether a doctor would have incubated a child patient who subsequently suffered brain damage after a cardiac and respiratory arrest, the court went on a voyage to examine whether that was something a reasonable doctor would do. Since medical evidence was on both sides, it followed that a causal link was not shown between the alleged negligence and injury. This decision is unfortunate, because it confuses what should have been done (standard or breach of duty question) with what could have probably been done (a causative question).

---

[126] See *Lawson* v. *Laferriere* (1991) 78 DLR (4th) 609 (Sup. Ct of Canada).

[127] [1992] 13 *BMLR* 111.

While medical evidence as to whether that was something all competent doctors would do (breach of duty question) would likely be material in determining what could have probably been done, it cannot conclude the issue of causation.

Since causation question relate first to the need to show that the doctor conduct could cause the plaintiff harm, and secondly, that in the particular case the harm did arise from the doctors conduct, it is suggested that the *Wilsher* decision more accords with the fundamental philosophy that underpins the law, even though it may be less favourable to the patient/plaintiff. As in all cases of negligence, it must be remembered that issues of foreseability and remoteness of damages as traced in the Privy Council decision in *Wagon Mound*[128] applies.[129]

Allocating Liability – Vicarious Liability

If negligence is proved, the next question will usually turn on who pays the bill? Sometimes this again resurrects question of who is in charge. In the setting of medical operation, and in any medical setting, as a rule, the specialist doctor is responsible for his own actions and inaction. It follows that if a doctor participates in a treatment procedure with a team of specialist drawn from different specialties, he will only be liable for his own negligence and not that of other specialists, unless it is shown that he is in complete control of the procedure i.e. he exercises right of control and supervision over his colleagues.[130] The rationale for the rule is derived from the concept of the 'captain of the ship' doctrine. For example the American court in *McConnell* v. *Williams*[131] observed that until the surgeon leaves the operating room 'he is in complete charge of those present and assisting him as is the captain of a ship over all on board.'[132] The specialist doctor is master of himself. He is not under the control of the hospital to a large extent, especially in his treatment procedure. He is liable for all that work under him whether they are borrowed servants from the hospital.[133]

The captain of the ship doctrine can be problematic in application to a situation where multiple doctors are involved in a treatment. Present trend appears to restrict the application of the doctrine in America in recognition of the principle of

128 [1961] AC 388, [1961] 1 All ER 404.

129 *Emeh* v. *Kensington & Chelsea & Westminster Area Health Authority* [1985] QB 1012, [1984] 3 All ER 1044.

130 Dokkum, above n 1 p. 184; see also S v. Kramer [1987] (I) SA 887 (W).

131 361 Pa 355, 65 A 2d 243 (1949).

132 361 Pa 355 at 362, A 2d. 243 at 246 (1949).

133 *McConnell* v. *Williams* (*supra*).

independence and expertise of the doctor.[134] But the South African court appears to maintain the captain rule undiluted.[135]

Generally, using the criterion of control, an employer who stands in the position of authority vis-à-vis the employee is made vicariously liable for the wrong of his employee.[136] This form of liability will usually arise where one employs another to perform a lawful act and that other does not perform it with the required care and skill thereby causing injury to the plaintiff. In the context of medical negligence, vicarious liability can arise from two situations: (i) where the employees of the doctor are negligent; and (ii) where the employees, including the doctor of a hospital are negligent. The rationale for liability is said to be rooted in economic. It is believed that it helps spread cost, placing it on the shoulders of the party who has the economic muscle to pay. It is desirable in assuaging compensation claim to an injured plaintiff in the era of industrialisation where accidents usually occur without clear identification of the wrongdoer.

Some years ago law was reluctant to impose vicarious liability on doctors for the negligent acts or omissions of their employees.[137] That position has long been abandoned. Doctors are now held liable for the negligence of their staff. If a doctor employs anyone he comes under a duty to give him proper instruction and exercise reasonable supervision and control over him. He will be vicariously liable for the staff negligence.[138] It has been suggested that the doctors vicarious liability in this respect are two fold (i) for injury resulting from breach of duty of care/negligence by his employee in the course of employment; and (ii) direct personal liability against the doctor for failing to supervise his staff.[139] If a doctor delegate a duty to his staff he will be liable for the negligence of his staff. Where the staff however is one not employed by him or supervised by him, he may not be liable for that other's negligence.[140]

In *Hillver* v. *St Batholomew* the English Court of Appeal held the view that a hospital is not responsible for the negligence of its staff in the performance of their professional duties, as distinct from purely administrative duties. The rationale for this limitation is that the hospital neither dictates nor controls the exercise of professional judgment. According to the English Court of Appeal, the governors of a public hospital, by their admission of the patient to enjoy in the hospital the

---

134 *Marsulli* v. *Elsdon* 27 Cal App 3d 180, 103 Cal. Rptr 461 (1972) surgeon not liable for the action of anaesthetist; but cf *S* v. *Kramer* (*supra*).

135 See Dokkum, *above* n 1. p. 184; see also *Van Wyk* v. *Lewis* (1924) AD 438; *S* v. *Kramer* [1987] (i) SA 887 (W).

136 See discussion on vicarious liability.

137 Ibid.

138 J G Fleming, Development in the English Law of Medical Negligence (1959) 12 *Vanderbitt L.R* 633.

139 D Geisen & T Fahrenhorst, Civil Liability Arising From Medical Care – Principles and Trends (1984) 9 *International Legal Practitioner* 34 at 39.

140 There remains controversy whether in such situations the doctor should be vicariously liable. The captain of the ship theory suggests liability, a position contradicted by Giesen, above n.99.

gratuitous benefit of its care do, I think undertake that the patient while there shall be treated only by experts, whether surgeons, physicians or nurses, of whose professional competence the governors have taken reasonable care to ensure themselves, and further, that those experts shall have at their disposal for the care and treatment of the patient, fit and proper apparatus and appliances.' [141]

Going by this, a patient could sue a hospital for breach of contract or tort if the hospital does not employ competent staff or if it fails to supply to its staff proper medical equipment or is vicariously liable for breach for purely administrative matters. This position was a reflection of the then charitable nature of hospital treatment. The early hospitals were essentially charitable, meant for the poor. The rich could then afford treatment in their homes. All of that has now largely changed. Hospitals are now the primary institution for health care for all persons and patients come not seeking charity, but highly skilled treatment. Commencing with *Gold* v. *Essex County Council* [142] the position changed. From 1942, there has been a progression in the elimination of hospitals immunity. Consequently hospitals became liable for the negligence of doctors, nurses and even part-time anaesthetists.[143]

In this respect the courts have shifted the focus from the control criterion to one that emphasises whether the servant is a part of the master's organisation; thereby placing emphasis not on how the servant works, but rather where and when he so works. This is in response to modern social and economic realities. It thus makes difficult as escape route a hospital plea that its professional staff are free from control and supervision. As long as they are within the organisation their negligence can be thrown on the hospital. Lord Denning in *Cassidy* v. *Ministry of Health* summarised the law this way:

> 'In my opinion, authorities who run a hospital, be they local authorities, government boards whenever they accept a patient for treatment, they must use reasonable care and skill to cure him or her of his or her ailment. The hospital authority cannot of course do it by themselves, they have no ears to listen through the stethoscope and no hands to hold the surgeon's knife. They must do it by the staff they employ and if their staff are negligent in giving the treatment they are just as liable for that negligence as is anyone who employs others to do duties for him or any other corporation are in law under the self same duty as the humblest doctor.' [144]

To hold a hospital vicariously liable either via contract or tort, the plaintiff will need to prove that (i) the person who commits the negligent act is an employee of the hospital (ii) that the act is performed in the course and scope of his employment.

---

141 *Hillyver* v. *The Governors of St. Bartholomew's Hospital* [1909]2 KB 820; See also Picard, The Liability of Hospitals in Canada (1981) 26 *McGill LJ* 997.

142 [1942] 2 KB 293.

143 *Cassidy* v. *Ministry of Health* [1951] 2 KB 343, [1951] 1 All ER 574, *Collins* v. *Hertfordshire County Council* [1947] KB 578; *Roc* v. *Ministry of Health* [1954] 2 QB 66; *Gold* v. *Essex County Council* [1942] 2 KB 293.

144 [1951] 2 KB 343 at 360.

The introduction of the National Health Insurance Scheme in Nigeria and the constitutional right to health is bound to have some effect on these questions. That is what we shall now discuss.

An economic analysis of compensation regime

When a patient succeeds in an action for malpractice he would often look up to the doctor or the health authority to pay the assessed compensation. To him it does not matter who pays. Who pays is however of concern to the doctor, the health authorities, and also the public especially in an era where public hospitals and the NHIS is bring more to the fore public health resources. Though malpractice litigation is still embryonic in Nigeria, it is not unlikely to increase in the near future. Considered from the perspective of society, the issues are two: (i) the difficulty in making successful claim; (ii) the inadequate provision for compensation for medical injuries.

Empirically, the proportion of successful *medical* negligence claims is lower than those for *general* negligence. The reasons are obvious. It is difficult to prove medical negligence. The patient hardly knows enough of what has gone wrong. Doctor's conspiracy of silence and general colleague solidarity prevents the availability of relevant evidence for the patient. It is said that attempts to establish fault, cause and effect in malpractice suits turns the system into a lottery for the patient.[145] Not to be forgotten is the inadequacy of compensation regime for medical injuries. Unfortunately even though most injuries are described as cases of negligence, in truth most are not due to negligence.[146] They properly are mere errors or accidents. It has therefore been suggested in some quarters that a no-fault compensation regime, presently run in some jurisdictions such as in Sweden and New Zealand better satisfies the competing ethics for assuaging a patient loss resulting from medical injuries.

In reaction to the flood of malpractice litigations in the United States of America (a practice that have led doctors to practice defensive medicine) many jurisdictions in the USA are now attempting to curb the success rate of such law suits and the huge compensation recoverable.[147] Increasingly courts are restricting the application of *res ipsa loquitur* and by moving in the direction of increased burden of proof on the plaintiff. Some jurisdictions have adopted the practice that only the evidence of a doctor who is an expert in the particular speciality in question with comparative experience in the area would be admissible evidence sufficient to raise negligence. Furthermore, the standard of care requirement is increasingly being

---

145 See Pearson Report, Royal Commission of Civil Liability and Compensation for Personal Injury (Cmnd 7054, 1978).

146 C.Ham, R Dingwell, P.Fen, D Harris, Medical Negligence: Compensation and Accountability (1988). p.26-34, cited in Kennedy & Grubb, *op. cit*, p.512 and 528.

147 See Furrow, Johnson, Just and Schwartz, *Health Law* (2nd edn 1991) cited in Kennedy & Grubb p.539.

judged in terms of 'locality'. By so doing a rural doctor stands more chances of escaping liability.

Defences to Malpractice Litigation

Defences to malpractice litigation generally follow the same pattern as general tort defences. These are as follows:

(i) Contributory Negligence

Just as the doctor is under a duty to take reasonable care in the treatment of the patient, the patient is also under certain duties to the doctor. He must be reasonable. If he is not and his unreasonableness is the factual and proximate cause of his injury he would be treated as having contributed and his compensation will be reduced accordingly. In *Crossman* v. *Stewart*[148] the British Columbia court reduced the compensation of the patient to £26, 666 of the sum of £80, 000 assessed damages for injury that resulted in his blindness because it found that the patient had two-thirds of the blame. She obtained the prescribed drug from an unorthodox source and used them longer than prescribed. In the Quebec case of *Hospital Notre-Dame de L' Esperance* v. *Laurent*,[149] damages were reduced because the patient was passive in his treatment. Though the doctor was held negligent in failing to diagnose a fracture in the head of the femur, the patient failed to get further medical treatment for over three months.

(ii) Voluntary assumption of risk

If the plaintiff agrees, expressly or impliedly to waive the duty of care owed to him, it may be relevant in determining negligence though the court will generally be reluctant to use it as a reference considering the inequality of power relation in the doctor-patient relationship. It can even be argued with justification that the very nature of medical care underlined by public policy considerations ought to refuse voluntary assumption of risk as a defence to an action for negligence. Any such waiver should be treated as striking at the root of the essence of care and so should not be considered a defence at all, for if it were otherwise it can destroy the very soul of medical care.

(iii) Miscellaneous

The miscellaneous defence may include the defence of limitation.

---

148 (1977) 5 CCLT 45 (BCSC) cited in Piscard, *Legal Liability of Doctors and Hospitals in Canada* (2nd ed, 1984).

149 [1978] 1 SCR 605; *Robitailte* v. *Vancouver Hockey Club Ltd* (1979) 19 BCLR 158 (British Columbia Supreme Court) but cf *Foote* v. *Royal Columbia Hospital* (1982) 38 BCLR 222; *Bernie* v. *Sisters of Service* [1948] 1 WWR 103 (Alta SC), both cited in Picard, *op. cit*; see also *Schliesman* v. *Fisher* 158 Cal Rptr. 527 (Cal CA 1979); *Martinean* v. *Nelson* 247 NW 2nd 409 (Sup Ct Minn 1976).

Chapter Fourteen

Informed consent

The common law has long recognised the principle that every person has the right to have his bodily integrity protected against invasion by others. The seriousness with which the law views any invasion of physical integrity finds its justification in the fact that everyone has the right of self-determination with regard to his body. Every touching of the patient is potentially battery. It is the patient's consent, either implied or expressed, which makes the touching legally innocuous.[1] At law no treatment is to be administered to a person without his consent merely because others reason that it is for his benefit. Any one who does would be treated as a busybody that would expose him to actionable trespass.[2] A doctor who disregards a patient's right to self-determination and embarks on a treatment for which consent is not given by the patient exposes himself to the civil wrong of trespass to person and may in fact face criminal charge for assault.

Under the Criminal Code, assault is defined as any striking, touching of a person directly or indirectly without the others consent.[3] Thus any doctor who examines or treat a patient against his will would be liable for civil or criminal assault. The reason for this is that every patient is vested with the right of self autonomy. It is the patient's informed consent to treatment that constitutes authority for any treatment to be administered. Informed consent to treatment is said to have six basic elements that underlie it, especially in the context of medical experiment. They are as follows: (a) a fair explanation of the procedure to be follows, and its purposes including identification of any procedures which are experimental; (b) a description of any attendant discomfort and risk reasonably to be expected; (c) a description of any benefits reasonably to be expected; (d) a disclosure of any appropriate alternative procedures that might be advantageous for the subject; (e) an offer to answer any inquiries concerning the procedures; (f) an instruction that the person is free to withdraw his consent and to discontinue participation in the project or activity at any time without prejudice to the subject.[4] These rules were formulated to proscribe and prohibit the sort of unethical practice and medical crimes committed during

---

[1] Mason & McCall Smith, *Law and Medical Ethics*, 4th ed. London, Butterworth (1983) p. 112.

[2] Granville Williams, *Textbook of Criminal Law* (2nd ed).

[3] S. 252 of Criminal Code provides that an assault is unlawful unless it is authorised, or justified or excused by law.

[4] Defined as by DHEW rules and regulation, 1975.

Nazi regime under guise of research.[5] They apply with necessary modification to general medical treatment.

Competent adult

Lord Reid in *S* v. *McC* [6] stated that a person cannot be made to undergo even a simple medical treatment/procedure as a blood test without consent. He said:

> "English law goes to great lengths to protect a person of full age and capacity from interference with his personal liberty. We have too often seen freedom disappear in other countries not only by coup d'etat but by gradual erosion and often it is the first step that counts. So it would be unwise to make even minor concessions...It is a legal wrong to use constraint to an adult beyond what is authorised by state or ancient common law powers connected with crime and the like."

In *Sidaway* v. *Bethlen Royal Hospital*,[7] the House of Lords held that a doctor operating without consent, save in emergency or a case of mental incapacity, commits trespass and criminal assault. In *Malette* v. *Shulman*,[8] a doctor administered blood on a Jehovah's Witness patient, though he had been informed that a card in her purse stated she will not consent to blood transfusion under any circumstance. When she recovered she sued the doctor for disregarding her wish. The doctor's argued that the emergency situation resulting from her serious car injury was one that required urgent life saving blood transfusion that ought to override her medical alert instruction. He further argued that society has an interest in the preservation of life and that the particular emergency justified his disregard of the card and that he had a medical duty to save life. He reasoned that since the doctor in such emergency could not communicate the serious life-threatening nature of the situation to the patient, the patient could not make an informed refusal to the treatment deemed necessary. The Ontario Court of Appeal flatly rejected his arguments and assessed him to pay damages of $20,000 (Canadian) for trespass.

> The court said: "A competent adult is generally entitled to reject a specific treatment or all treatment or to select an alternative form of treatment, even if the decision may entail risk as serious as death and may appear mistaken in the eyes of the medical profession or of the community. Regardless of the

---

[5] See Introduction to the Helsinki Declaration appendix.

[6] [1972] AC 24 at 43.

[7] [1985] AC 871 at 87, 904.

8. *R* v. *Hallstron Ex p. W (No.2)* /1986] 2 All ER 316; *Gillick* [1986] AC 112; *Re F* (Mental Patient: sterilisation) [1990] AC 1, *Re T (Adult: Refusal of treatment)* [1992] 3 WLR 782; *Airedale NHS Trust* v. *Bland* [1993] 3 WLR; *Malette* v. *Shulman* (1990) 47 DLR 18, *Smith* v. *Auckland Hospital Board* [1965] NZLR 191 219.

[8] (1990) 47 DLR 18.

> doctors, opinion, it is the patient who has the final say on whether to undergo the treatment."[9]

Exercising the right to refuse (one form of) treatment must not be confused with suicide. They are different things. While the former is a choice how a person chooses to live and be treated, the latter is more of the exercise of the right to die. Butler – Sloss LJ succinctly drew the distinction in *Malette* case when he said:

> "Jehovah's Witness accept and take advantage of the same medical treatment as those who do not subscribe to their belief and are as anxious as anyone else to recover from any illness from which they suffer. This is not a question of a right to die. This acceptance of medical treatment in its widest sense is subject to the requirement not to accept transfusion of blood or blood derivatives."

Lord Denning made a similar distinction in *Re T*, when he said:

> "This appeal was not about the right to die but about the right to choose how to live. An adult patient who suffers from no mental incapacity has an absolute right to choose whether to consent to medical treatment, to refuse it or to chose one rather than another treatment offered. The right of choice existed whether the reasons for making the choice were rational, irrational, unknown or even non-existent" [10]

Thus rejecting a treatment suggested by a doctor and requesting alternative is quite different from suicide. The difference in law is as between apples and oranges. Rejecting blood transfusion is no suicide, especially where the patient makes request for alternative non-blood management. Since modern medicine recognises the need to treat not just the body but the whole person of a patient, his body, mind and spirit for healing to be complete,[11] it would be illogical to equate with suicide a patient refusal of blood transfusion for alternative non-blood management. Doctors are obligated to respect patient's rights to self-determination, more so where he seeks alternative that would not injury spiritual, value and emotional spirit of the patient are feasible.[12] In *Malette* case[13] the court recognised the clear and unambiguous instruction in the patient's medical alert card as an instrument that can operate even when a patient is unconscious. In effect, the card may amount to what has been

---

[9] Ibid.

[10](1992) 4 ALLER 649, (1992) 9BMLR46

[11]See Dr. M A Casberg in [1967] I American Medical Association, and Dr. G F Begley [1970] 12 *Texas Medicine* p. 25.

[12] D.T. Ridley, Accommodating Jehovah's Witness Choice of Non-blood Management, *Perspectives in Healthcare Risk Management*, [1990] pp. 17-21 (Brooklyn NY) and John J. Pais, Compulsory Medical Treatment and Freedom; Whose Law shall prevail. (1975) Summer Edition vol. X No.1 of *University of San Francisco Law Review* 25

[13] (1990) 47 DLR 18.

referred to as a 'living will'.[14] It a legal document worthy of respect. The court said: 'The card on its face set forth unqualified instructions applicable to the circumstances presented by this emergency…Those instructions should be taken as validly representing the patients wish not to be transfused.'[15]

The right of a competent adult to make in advance directive prohibiting certain forms of medical treatment in the event of unconsciousness is recognised.[16] It therefore logically follows that a person may also by extension appoint others to act as his health care proxy in the matter of his health care. *Cruzan* v. *Missouri Department of Health*[17] and *Airedale NHS Trust* v. *Bland*[18] both recognise the legal validity of living wills. Both cases, involved family attempts to remove life-sustaining medical treatment from patients in permanent unconscious state who left no clear instruction of their wishes about further life-saving treatment. In the former, the United Supreme Court accepted the proposition that a written statement by the patient of her wish whether in the form of a living will or a durable power of attorney provides clear and convincing evidence to help the court determine whether or not to continue or withdraw life-sustaining medical treatment. In the latter, the patient was diagnosed to be in a persistent vegetative state. The hospital application to withhold or withdraw medical supplies to the patient was supported by the patient's family. It was reasoned that the proposal would make it possible for the patient to end his life and die peacefully with dignity and with least amount of pain, suffering and distress. The House of Lords ordered the withdrawal on the ground that it accords with patient's wishes as can be gathered from family's evidence. Bland was allowed to die in peace. So it follows that if he had appointed a health care proxy, the wishes of his attorney would be respected. That a patient can appoint an attorney over his health matters is a well established point of law. With a view to fortify recognition of living wills or durable health care powers of attorney, some jurisdictions have enacted the right into statute.[19]

Question of ascertaining a patient refusal or consent to medical treatment is a matter of fact. This point was illustrated in *Re T (Adult: Refusal of treatment)*.[20] T whose mother is a Jehovah's Witness was admitted into a hospital when she was 34 weeks pregnant following a motor traffic accident. A decision to deliver the baby by caesarean section was taken and shortly afterwards she told the midwife and doctor

---

[14] PDG Skegg. Living Wills and New Zealand Law, *Bioethics Re search Centre Newsletter,* vol. II No. III, September 1993 p. 2

[15] (1990) 47 DLR 18.

[16] PDG Skegy, *above* n. 14 and F. Rouse, Advance Directive: Where are We Heading after *Cruzan*? (1990) 18 *Law Med. Hlth Care* 353.

[17] 497 US 261 (1990); 100 S Ct 2841 (1990). For a discussion on *Cruzan* case, see F. Rouse, Advance Directive: Where are We Heading after *Cruzan* (1990) 18 *Law Med. Hlth Care* 353 and A. Meisel, A Retrospect on Cruzan (1992) 20 *Law Med. Hlth Care* 340.

[18] [1992] WLR 782; [1993] 1 All ER 821; (1993) 12 BMLR 64. See especially, per Lord Donaldson at 792, approving Briston J in *Chatterton* v. *Gerson* [1981] QB 432.

[19] Ibid.

[20] [1992] 4 All ER 649.

of her opposition to blood transfusion. She later signed a form provided by the hospital signifying her refusal of consent to blood transfusion. Blood transfusion on her was authorised by the court on the ground that her refusal was not effective in that it was diminished by illness especially in circumstances where it appeared that she was overborne by her mother's undue influence. The court found the refusal of blood transfusion was only in form, not real. It was informed by third party influence. In the circumstance there was sufficient basis to override her refusal. Lord Donaldson said:

> "Persuasion based upon religious belief can also be much more compelling and the fact that arguments based on religious beliefs are being deployed by someone in very close relationship with the patient will give them added force and should alert the doctor's to the possibility...no more...that the patient's capacity or will to decide has been overborne. In other words the patient may not mean what she says."[21]

If vitiated, as in *Re T* because it is not real, it can be overridden or completely ignored by the doctor with no liability for trespass. Lord Donaldson said:

> "This situation gives rise to a conflict between two interest, that of the patient and that of the society in which he lives. The patient, interest consist of his right to self-determination...his right to live his own life how he wished, even if it will damage his health or lead to his premature death. Society's interest is in upholding the concept that all human life is sacred and that it should be preserved if at all possible. It is well established that in the ultimate the right of the individual is paramount. But this merely shifts the problem where the conflict occurs and calls for a very careful examination of whether and if so the way in which, the individual is exercising that right. In case of doubt, that doubt falls to be resolved in favour of the preservation of life for if the individual is to override the public interest, he must do so in clear terms'"[22]

Incompetent adult

Incompetent adult are persons who though are of full age suffer from a disease of the mind or natural mental infirmity which impairs their reasoning powers. Whether such persons can legally choose alternative treatment or refuse treatment depends on whether the illness is of such a nature as to seriously impair reasoning to the extent that the patient cannot sufficiently understand the nature purpose and effects of the medical treatment proposed. That was the point made by Thorpe J in *Re C*.[23] The court granted an injunction preventing Heatherwood Hospital from amputating C's leg without his express consent. C, a 68 year-old man, was diagnosed

---

[21] [1992] 4 All ER 649 at.796.

[22] Ibid., at p.797.

[23] Unreported, *The Independent* of 15 October 1993 p. 341; Re C adult required of treatment (1994) 1 ALLER819, (1993) 15 BMLR77

with gangrene in the right foot and the hospital considered amputation. C refused and sought an injunction to restrain the amputation. The hospital argued that by virtue of C's chronic mental illness, he had no capacity to make an informed choice. The court held that in considering capacity the important question to be decided is whether it has been established that C's illness prevented him from understanding the nature, purpose and effect of the proposed amputation. To arrive at this His Lordship used as decision-making analysis, the three-stage enquiry, namely: (i) the patient's ability to comprehend and retain treatment information; (ii) believe in the treatment; and (iii) balance of risks and benefit ratio. Applying these three decision-making analyses, the court found that C's mental illness had not displaced his right of self-determination and his choice was informed. Accordingly the hospital was directed to respect his treatment choice. An injunction was ordered in his favour. The conclusion is supportable because even though C's general capacity was impaired by his mental illness – schizophrenia, he still could understand the nature, purpose and effect of the treatment method he refused. Thus the right of C did not evaporate by his illness. It remained intact and there was no jurisdiction whatsoever for the hospital substituting its judgment to his under wardship or *paren patriae* jurisdiction.

The court may authorise medical treatment for an incompetent adult who cannot appreciate the nature effect and purpose of medical treatment. The authorisation of medical treatment or overriding refusal to treatment by the court would usually be based on its *paren patriae* or wardship jurisdiction, even though such a jurisdiction is now legally doubtful.[24]

Minors

A minor is a person yet to attain maturity. The age of maturity varies from country to country. A minor has some qualified legal rights. He can enter into contracts even though they are voidable at his instance until maturity. He is only bound by a contract to supply necessaries.[25] Treatment of minor raises several ethical problems. Parents are their primary care-givers, concerned with their welfare, including medical treatment. In furtherance of parental duties and or rights, parents may make decisions on treatment that others (the community/state, may be hospital authorities) consider unreasonable. It is not uncommon to hear parents tell hospital authorities that as result of their customary and or religious belief they may not accept certain medical procedures such as blood transfusion for their children. Such situations are capable of creating ethical dilemma for hospital, especially if the health condition of the minor patient makes it imperative to apply blood therapy. Hospitals faced with such challenges are required to make balanced decisions considering the

---

[24]Ed Freedman, *Medicine, Ethics and The Law*, London: Stevens & Sons, 1988

[25] Sagay, *Law of Contract*

concern of the parents, its duty to save life, the law and the general position of ethics in this area.

The natural starting point is the position taken by principal care-givers, the parent. The reason is obvious. The family unit is fundamental to all systems of law. According to the *World Book Encyclopaedia*. 'Family is the oldest human institution. In many ways it is the most important. It is society's most basis unit.'[26] This fact was recognised by the Supreme Court of America in *Parham* v. *JR*. The court said:

> "Our jurisprudence historically has reflected western civilization concept of the family as a unit with broad parental authority over minor children. Our cases have consistently followed that course; our constitutional system long ago rejected any notion that a child is "the mere creature of the state", and on the contrary asserted that parents generally have the right coupled with the high duty, to recognize and prepare their children for additional obligations...The law's concept of the family rests on the presumption that parents possess what a child lacks in maturity, experience and capacity for judgment required for making life difficult decisions. More important, historically it has recognized that natural bounds of affection lead parents to act in the best interest of their children"'[27]

For example, section 300 of the Criminal Code states:

> "It is the duty of every persons having charge of another who is unable by reason of age, sickness, unsoundness of mind, detention or any other cause to withdraw himself from such charge, and who is unable to provide for himself with the necessaries of life, whether the charge is undertaken under a contract, or is imposed by law, or arises by reason of any act, whether lawful or unlawful, of the person who has such charge, to provide for that other person the necessaries of life; and he is held to have caused any consequences which result to the life or health of the other person by reason of any omission to perform that duty."[28]

Thus the general rule is that except in cases of emergency, hospital authorities must not treat a minor without the consent of the parents.[29] Statute rests squarely on the feet of parents to provide their minor with necessaries. The Criminal Code provides that if they fail to provide necessaries, they would be held liable for any consequences that results to the health or life of their minor. Necessaries for a minor no doubt include medical treatment. Therefore if a parent refuses to provide medical treatment he could be liable for the natural consequences to the child's health and life. If death results, they may be charged for manslaughter or murder depending on the facts of the particular case.[30] In *R* v. *Nicholls* [31] the defendant was charged for

---

[26] Encyclopaedia.

[27] 442 US 584 (1979).

[28] Criminal Code Law, Cap. LFN, 2004.

[29] *Banks* v. *Medical University of South Caroline* 444 SE 2d 519 (S.G. 1994).

[30] See *R* v. *Izood* (1902) 20 Cox C.C. 690; *R.* v. *Bonny man* (1942) 28 G. App. R 131; *R.* v. *Nicholls* (1874) 13 Cox C.C. 75.

the murder of an aged and infirm woman, because he confined her against her will. He also did not provide her with necessaries – good clothing and medicines. The jury was directed by the judge to find for murder or manslaughter on facts whether the defendant actions were deliberate or careless in the circumstances of the case. In some jurisdictions child protection laws have focused attention on parental responsibilities.[32] In such jurisdictions parents are obliged in positive terms to provide necessaries, including provision for adequate treatment for their children.

If parents, however, make adequate arrangement for the treatment for their children, but refuse a particular management method suggested by the hospital authority, questions may be raised whether in the circumstance it would be proper for hospitals to override parents refusal? And importantly, should it be treated as abandonment of parental responsibility? If the answer is no, would the parents be held liable for any consequences that result from their refusal of medical treatment? If we answer "yes", then one can imagine manslaughter or murder prosecution against parent where death results. If the answer is in the affirmation, then is the law implicated in a process that allows parents to make martyrs of their children? How far can parents ride the horse of self-determination as proxies or surrogates of their minor? Should not the state, as *parens patriae*, have a say in this issue?

These are troublesome ethical questions for which the law gives conflicting answers. Generally where there is no emergency, hospital authorities should respect the treatment choice by parents.[33] The limits are cases of emergency and state intervention for the safety of the child. The Illinois Supreme Court in *Prince* v. *Massachusetts* stated that

> 'parents may be free to become martyrs themselves. But it does not follow they are free, in identical circumstances, to make martyrs of their children before they have reached the age of full and legal discretion when they can make that choice for themselves.'[34]

Though *Prince* was not a case decided where parental right to choose and or refuse medical treatment for their minor was directly in issue, its principle accords with good reasoning. Parents' rights evaporate when they have to choose for their minor the right to die – martyr. The Court however must be able to draw the line between parents subscribed martyrdom and the exercise of a bona fide right of choosing how their minor should live. The distinctions drawn on this point by Lord Denning in *Re T*[35] is instructive and must not be blurred. The court ought to

---

[31] (1874) 13 Cox C.C.75.

[32] See the Children's Code of South Caroline.

[33] *Jehovah's Witness* v. *King Country Hospital* 278 F. Supp. 488 (N.D Wash. 1967) affirmed *per incuriam* in 390 US 598 (1968).

[34] 321 US 158 (1944).

[35] [1992] WLR 782. (1992) 4 ALL ER 649, (1992) 9 BMLR 46 See also Donald T. Ridey, Accommodating Jehovah's Witness Choice of Non-blood Management: Perspectives in Health Risk Management,

examine the facts very critically before reaching a decision because the invisible line between the right to die and the right to choose how is live may prove elusive if great care is not taken to draw the lines of difference. Let us use a classical example, blood transfusion which often occupies the centre burner. The court must be critical in examining the real issue. In litigation around it the critical question ought not to be whether parents refusal to transfusion treatment is rational, but whether parents refusal of blood and request for non-blood management will adequately meet the minor's health requirement. If the non-blood management would meet the minor's health need, the court should uphold parents request for non-blood management. The real focus should not be the reason for the parent's refusal, but whether alternative treatment will meet the minor's health needs. If the alternative treatment is adequate, the wishes of the parents should be respected and only overridden by the state, as *paren patriae* if the court considers that the parents have crossed the invisible line from choosing how their minor shall live to choosing a right to die. Only then should the court short–circuit the parents wishes.

In *Bank* v. *Medical University of South Carolina*,[36] the plaintiff one of Jehovah's Witnesses brought the action against the hospital for wrongful death and battery for non consensual administration of blood on her eight year old daughter, Phaedra. She was admitted in the hospital for respiratory distress and hip pain. The hospital performed surgery on her and notwithstanding plaintiff's refusal, administered blood plasma on her. She did not survive. The court stated that though the plaintiff had no authority to withhold necessary medical treatment for Phaedra even if such treatment was contrary to her religious views, notwithstanding the transfusion amounted to battery in that it was not consented to by the parent when no emergency arose.[37]

Another ethical question that can arise in this respect is whether or not parents can prevent their wishes from being frustrated in an emergency situation by executing in advance a directive prohibiting some form of medical treatment. *Malette* v. *Shulman*[38] decided that an unsigned but witnessed, dated medical alert card prohibiting blood transfusion carried by the patient was binding on all hospital authorities even in life threatening emergency. Though a case dealing with the effect of an alert card on an adult choice, there is good reason why it should apply to a minor.

There are however some minor whose choice need not be made by their parents. If it is shown that a minor is mature enough to appreciate the consequences of his action the court would treat him as a mature minor with the common law right of

---

Winter issue 1990 pp. 17-21; and John J. Paris; Compulsory Medical Treatment and Religious Freedo: Whose law Shall Prevail? [1975]10 No.1 *Univ. of San Francisco L. Rev.* 25 (summer 1978).

[36] 444 S.E. 2d 519 (S.C. 1994).

[37] Jehovah's Witness in the *State of Washington* v. *King Country Hospital* 278 F. Supp. 488 (D. Wash. 1967) affirmed 390 US 598.

[38] (1990) 67 DLR (4th 321, [1991] 2 Med LR 162 (Supreme Court of Ontario). See also PDG Skegg, Living Wills and New Zealand Law, *Bio-Ethics Research Centre Newsletter* vol. II No.3 September 1993 p. 23.

self-determination as though he were an adult.[39] The rationale for this is that 'chronological age is not necessarily a suitable yardstick to determine maturity and capacity to give informed consent. Development criteria can tell when applied on an individual basis.'[40] Maturity age is not an impenetrable barrier that magically precludes a minor from possessing and exercising certain right normally associated with adulthood. So if a minor is mature to possess understanding and appreciation for the nature, extent and probable consequences of his action, he will be treated as a mature minor at common law with the full right of self-determination.

In *Re Ernestine Gregory*[41] the Illinois Supreme Court recognised the mature minor principle. Ernestine a Jehovah's Witness was hospitalised for leukaemia. She was 17 year old. The age of maturity in the state of Illinois was 18. He refused blood transfusion against the hospital's recommendation. Because of his refusal of blood therapy supported by his mother, the child welfare officials in Chicago pressed medical neglect charge against his mother. The court thus authorised transfusion despite the fact that it was clearly shown that the patient was a mature young girl of 17 capable of making informed, intelligent medical decisions for herself consistent with her deeply held values and conviction. The order was appealed to the Illinois Appellate Court. It overruled the transfusion order by the trial court on the ground that the patient having demonstrated sufficient maturity to make informed decision could not be forced to submit to forced transfusion. The court drew a parallel between the patient's case and those where the court has permitted pregnant minor's to abort as part of federal constitutional right of privacy.[42] The decision was further appealed by the child welfare officials to the Supreme Court of Illinois. The Supreme Court affirmed the Appellate Court's decision. It held that though the patient was a minor she had the right of self-determination at common law because in the circumstance she had demonstrated sufficient maturity. The court in reviewing the 'maturity age 18 rule' concluded that there is no reason why the right of dominion over one's owns person should not extend to mature minors. It said,

> 'if the evidence is clear and convincing that the minor is mature to appreciate the consequences of her actions, and that the minor is mature enough to exercise the judgment of an adult, then the mature minor doctrine affords her common law right to consent to or refuse medical treatment.'

---

[39] Illinois Supreme Court decision in *Re Ernestine Gregory* 133 IU 2d 98, 549 NE 2d 322 (1989) US Congress, Office of Technology Assessment, Adolescent Health – vol. III: *Cross-cutting Issues in the Delivery of Health and Related Sciences* 136 (1991); See *Gillick* v. *West Norfolk and Wisbech* AHA(1986)AC112, (1985)3 All ER402, on the mature minor principle.

[40] See in *Re Ernestine Gregory* (*supra*) at 327-328, in Re Swan 569 A 2d 1202 (Me. 1990); *State* v. *Hassey* 521 A 2d 278 (Me. 1987), in *Re Rosebush* 491 NW 2d 633 (Mich ct. App 1992); *Cruzan* v. *Missouri Department of Health* 497 US 261 (1990) at 278.

[41] *Re Ernestine Gregory* 133 IU 2d 98, 549 NE 2d 322 (1989).

[42] See *Hodgson* v. *Minnesota* 110 S. et 2926 at 2937 (1990) *Hellotti* v. *Baird* 443 US 622, 643 (1979) which decide that mature minors may choose to continue or abort their pregnancies regardless of parental consent.

Similarly in *Re Wendell Melvin Jnr*,[43] the Missouri Court of Appeal criticised the trial court for refusing to receive evidence from a 17 year-old patient about his ability to make mature decision about the alleged need of blood. Wendell suffered from leukaemia. The hospital obtained an order from court to transfuse him blood because his red cells and platelet counts were low as a result of chemotherapy, despite his refusal. After the order, Wendell made arrangement for non-blood treatment with a favourable doctor in Houston, Texas. When he was receiving treatment as out-patient in the hospital, he arranged to travel from St. Louis to Houston. Upon knowing of his travel plans, the hospital sought authority to again transfuse him blood because they believed he was unfit to travel to Houston. At the hearing the trial court ruled that its previous order to transfuse still applied. Based on the order he was taken by the Police to the hospital in St. Louis and forcibly transfused despite his resistance. Wendell appealed the decision to the Missouri Court of Appeal. The main plank of his appeal was that he was denied the right to a hearing about his capacity to make mature treatment decisions consistent with his values or about the safety to travel to Houston to receive non-blood management for his ailment. In view of the fact that Wendell was just 3 months to maturity age of 18 and had received bloodless treatment which was effective the court ruled that the appeal was moot and otiose. Notwithstanding it criticise the summary denial of his hearing when the patient was a mature minor.

The English case of *Gillick*[44] establishes without doubt the validity of the mature minor principle. Hospitals are enjoined to respect the wishes of mature minors in the context of self-determination. However under its *parens patria* or wardship jurisdiction the court can override their decision. For example in *Re J*[45] it permitted the force-feeding of an anorexic and in *Re R*[46] it authorized forcible medication of a disturbed teenager.

Pregnancy cases

The Appeal Court of Illinois in *Re Doe*[47] summarised the governing principles this way:

> "A woman's right to refuse invasive medical treatment derives from her rights to privacy bodily integrity and religious liberty. They are not diminished during pregnancy. The woman retains the same right to refuse invasive treatment, even of lifesaving or other beneficial nature, that she can exercise when she is not pregnant. The potential impact on the foetus is not legally relevant...A

---

[43] John J. Paris, *Compulsory Medical Treatment and Religious freedom: Whose law Should Prevail (1995)1 Univ. San Francisco Law Rev. 25*

[44] *Gillick* v. *West Norfolk and Wisbech Area Health Authority* [1986] AC112, [1985] 3 All ER A402.

[45] *Re J (a minor) (wardship: medical treatment) [1990] 3 All ER 930.*

[46] *Re R* (a Minor)(Blood Transfusion) [1993] 2 FCR 544.

[47] *Re Doe* 632 NE 2d 326 (Ill. App. Ct. 1994).

> woman...cannot be compelled to do or not do any thing merely for the benefit of her unborn child."[48]

The above quoted passage succinctly summarises the common law position on the pregnant woman. Her right of bodily self-determination as those of an adult person does not become extinct as a result of pregnancy. In *Roe* v. *Wade* [49] the American Supreme Court held that a woman's right to privacy entitled her to abort a foetus until the third trimester when the foetus becomes viable. Medical deontological code affirms the propriety of respect for the wishes of the pregnant woman. Maternal-foetal conflicts are resolved in favour of the paramount interest of the mother because foetuses have no legal right in law.[50] There is therefore no legal basis for the argument that if a pregnant woman refuses medical treatment deemed necessary for the welfare of her foetus, the state acquires a *parens patriae* interest in the foetus that can override the mother's bodily right. A consequentialist ethos that need justifies means and ends is an unsatisfactory reason for subordinating her rights to that of the foetus.[51]

There can be nothing ethical or legal as using her body to rescue. Our jurisprudence has long frowned at the view that a person should be used to rescue another without his consent. Patients are not be treated as 'means' but rather as 'ends'.[52] In *S* v. *McC* [53] the House of Lords held that it amounts to an unnecessary invasion to body right to have a blood test without a patient's consent. If in minor medical matters as blood test consent is required, then no logical reason can be advanced to use one life to support another without that other's consent. In *McFall* v. *Shimp*,[54] an application to force a man to give live-saving bone marrow tissue for transplant to his anaemic cousin (he being the only available compatible donor) was rejected by the court. The court said:

> "For our law to compel defendant to submit to an intrusion of his body would change every concept and principle upon which our society is founded. To do so would defeat the sanctity of the individual and would impose a rule which would know no limits, and could not imagine where the line would be drawn."[55]

---

[48] 632 NE 2d 326 (1994) at 300at 300.

[49] 410 US 113, 93 S Ct 705, 35 L Ed 2d 147 (1973).

[50] *Paton* v. *Trustees of British Pregnancy Services (supra)* See also *Burton* v. *Islington Health Authority* [1992] 3 All ER 833.

[51] Babara Hawson Ethical Triumph; or Surgical Rape? (1993) 137 *SoJ.* 1182.

[52] Ibid.

[53] [1972] AC 24.

[54] (1978) Pa Dac 3d 90.

[55] Ibid at 91.

Using the pregnant woman as a rescue means against her consent may well be the beginning of gradual erosion of personal liberties.[56] The necessary implications of allowing such gross invasion in the treatment of women was put succinctly by the court in *McFall* case this way:

> "For a society which respects the rights of one individual to sink its teeth into the jugular bone or neck of one of its members and suck from it substance for another member, is revolting to our hard wrought concepts of jurisprudence. Foreseeable extraction of life-saving tissue causes revulsion to the judicial mind. Such would raise the spectre of the Swastika and the Inquisition, reminiscent of the horrors these portend."'[57]

No one is obliged to use his body to rescue another. It is therefore fallacious to argue that a pregnant woman should on the argument that she has chosen freely to use her body to bring a child to the world. The foetus can not acquire superior rights over its mother.[58] In *Re AC* [59] i.e. (Angela Carder), this complex issue arose for determination before the District of Colombia Court of Appeals. In 1987 Angela Carder, a survivor of childhood cancer became pregnant. The cancer reappeared. The hospital without telling her of the reappeared cancer withheld life-saving chemotherapy and radiation in order to protect her 26 weeks pregnancy. As a result of this her health deteriorated more rapidly. The hospital later sought court order for a caesarean despite the fact that they knew this would shorten her life. The trial court granted the order, reasoning that whatever, she was bound to die and the operation would maximise the chances of her foetus surviving. Unfortunately, the foetus did survive for only 2½ hours and she died 2 days later. Her death was attributed to status post-Caesarean section. In 1990, the District of Colombia Court of Appeal reversed the 1987 order of the trial court. It held that terminally ill pregnant woman should not be forced to undergo Caesarean that could maximise the chances of her foetus. It stated further that in virtually all cases the patient is the sole determiner of what treatment is to be administered, in this case the pregnant woman. She is the proper person to make decisions for herself and invariably her foetus. Only in extremely rare and truly exceptional cases may the state as *parens patriae* acquire truly exceptional or compelling rights to override her choice of treatment. This is so because the proposition that a person's body may be invaded for the benefit of another person is 'jarring alien to our Anglo-American legal tradition.'[60]

> The court observed: 'There are practical consequences to consider. What if (the patient) had refused to comply with court order that she submit to a

---

[56] Gallogher, Prenatal Invasions and Interventions: What's wrong with Fetal Rights (1987) 10 *Harv. Women's LJ* 9 at 23 D. Brahams, A Baby's Life or a Mothers's Liberty: A United States Case (1986) 56 *Med Leg J.* 156; M.A. Field, Controlling the Woman to Protect the Fetus (1989) 17 *Law Med Hlth Care* 114.

[57] (1978) Pa Dac 3d 90 .

[58] *Paton* v. *British Pregnancy Advisory Service Trustee* [1979] QB 276; [1978] 2 All ER 987.

[59] 573 A. 3d 1235 (D.C. 1990).

[60] *In Re AC* 573 A. 3d 1235 (D.C. 1990) at 1244.

> Caesarean? Under the circumstances, she obviously could not have been held in civil contempt and imprisoned or required to pay a daily fine until compliance. Enforcement could be accomplished only through physical force or its equivalent. The patient would have to be fastened with restraints... or perhaps involuntarily rendered unconscious by forcibly injecting her with an anaesthetic and then subjected to unwanted major surgery. Such actions would surely give one pause in a civilized society, especially when (the patient) has done no wrong.[61]

This same point was made in *Re Doe*.[62] The patient, a member of a pentecostal church, refused to submit to a caesarean section for her 36 weeks pregnancy on religious grounds. Her doctor testified that chances that the foetus would survive a natural labour was close to zero and that if the child was to survive natural birth it would be retarded. The Illinois Court of Appeal affirmed the trial court ruling that the patient cannot be compelled to submit to a Caesarean. The court observed that the right to withhold consent and refuse treatment incorporates all types of medical treatment including life-saving or life sustaining treatments. It said:

> 'A woman's right to refuse invasive medical treatment derived from her rights to privacy, bodily integrity, and religious liberty, is not diminished during pregnancy. The woman retains the same right to refuse invasive treatment even of life-saving or other beneficial nature that she can exercise when she is not pregnant. The potential impact on the foetus is not legally relevant...A woman cannot be compelled to do or not do anything merely for the benefit of her unborn child.'[63]

The court further frowned at bodily invasion under any circumstances no matter how minor or major such invasion may be from a medical standpoint. It said:

> 'There is no such thing in 'trivial interference' with personal sovereignty; nor is it simply another value to be weighed in a cost-benefit comparison. In this respect, if not others, a trivial interference with sovereignty is like minor invasion of virginity: the logic of each concept is such that a value is respected in its entirety or not at all.'[64]

Thus no surgery, blood transfusion, injection or pill or any medical treatment whatsoever can be forced on a woman whether pregnant or not. It is absolutely

---

[61] Ibid.

[62] Re Doe 632 NE 2d 326 (Ill. App. Ct. 1994) Even though medical evidence was that the 'chances that the foetus would survive a natural labour were close to zero' and that 'if the child were to somehow survive natural child birth he would be retarded,' 632 NE 2d 326 at 328, about two weeks thereafter the mother gave birth naturally to an apparent healthy baby boy. Id. At 329. See also Kennedy, Courts Refuse Request for C-section and Boy is Born Apparently Healthy [1994] 3 ABAJ 27.

[63] Ibid at 332.

[64] Ibid.

unethical.[65] Any judicial authorised force in this respect is not only improper but counterproductive, unprincipled, sexist, repressive and immoral.[66]

Unfortunately there are some disturbing cases which suggest the contrary,[67] the exact opposite to the ratios in *Re AC*[68] and *Re Doe*.[69] In *Re S*,[70] the President of the Family Division declared that a hospital could perform a Caesarean on a pregnant woman in labour against her will. The defendant a Nigerian, refused Caesarean in her previous labour and yet delivered a healthy baby. This time however, her foetus was in transverse position and so could not be delivered vaginally. Surgery was the only medical procedure to save her and the baby. But she refused it claiming that Almighty God will provide a solution. To save her and her foetus, the court ordered forced Caesarean. It is respectfully suggested that the case does not properly represent the law for many reasons.

Re S,[71] is contrary to a long line of established cases that recognise that 'English law would go at great length to protect a person of full age and capacity from interference with his personal liberty.'[72] A pregnant woman is not less competent as a result of pregnancy. To think otherwise is suspect and discriminatory to women.[73] The case has been criticism as a consequentialist decision that ought not to create precedent in law.[74] Coercion on women is repressive. For example the 1992 English House of Common's Health Committee Report on maternity services recommended that pregnant women right of informed choice to all treatment should be

---

[65] Babara Hawson, Ethical Triumph, or Surgical Rape? (1993) 133 *SJ* 1182. Showalter, Decisions to Forgo Medical Treatment: The Preferred Medical, Ethical, and Legal Approach (1984) 29 *Cath. Law* 286.

[66] Feinberg, Autonomy, Sovereignty, and Privacy: Moral Ideals in the Constitution? (1983) 58 *Notre Dame L. Rev.* 445 at 492. See also *Cruzan* v. *Missouri Dep't of Health* (1990) 110 S. Ct. 2841 at 2851and 2853 ('it cannot be disputed that the [United States Constitution] protects an interest in life as well as an interest in refusing life-sustaining medical treatment.').

[67] The cases are *Raleigh Fitkin-Paul Morgan Memorial Hospital* v. *Anderson* 201 A 2d 537 (NJ 1964)(court authorised transfusion on a pregnant woman in the thirty-second week of pregnancy if necessary to ensure safe delivery of her foetus) ; *Jefferson* v. *Griffin Spalding Country Hospital Authority* 247 SE 2d 45 (Ga 1981)(authorised Caesarean section and use of blood if deemed necessary by hospital on a thirty-nine weeks pregnant woman with *placenta previa* challenges) ; *Crouse Irving Memorial Hospital* v. *Paddock* 485 NYS 2d 443 (Sup. Court Onondaga County 1985)(authorised transfusion of mother and child); *In Re Jamaica Hospital* 491 NYS 2d 898 (Sup. Ct. Queen Country 1985).

[68] 573 A. 3d 1235 (D.C. 1990).

[69] *Re Doe*, 632 NE 2d 326 (Ill. App. Ct. 1994).

[70] [1992] 3 WLR 806, [1992] 4 All ER 671, (1992) 9 BMLR 69.

[71] *Supra*.

[72] Per Lord Reid LJ in *S* v. *McC*. [1972] AC 24,43. See also *Sidaway* v. *Bethlehem Royal Hospital* [1985] AC 871, *Airedale* v. *Bland* [1993] 2 WLR 316; Re F. (Mental Patient: Sterilisation) [1990] AC I; *Gillick* [1986] AC 112.

[73] Gallagher, Prenatal Invasions and Interventions: What's Wrong With Foetal Rights (1987) 10 *Harv. Women's LJ* Johnson, The creation of Fetal Rights: Conflict with Women's Constitutional Rights to Liberty, Privacy and Equal Protection (1986) 95 *Yale LJ* 599; Field, Controlling the Woman To Protect the Fetus (1989) 17 *Law, Medicine and Health Care* 114, but cf. Cawley, Criminal Liability in Faith Healing (1954) 39 *Minn. L Rev.* 48. Case Comment-Constitutional Law-Transfusion Ordered for Dying Women over Religious Objection (1964) 113 *U Pa Rev.* 291.

[74] Babara Hawson, Ethical Triumph, or Surgical Rape? (1993) 133 *SJ* 1182

respected.[75] Also the American Medical Association in its reviewed ethical code enjoined members to prevent any forcible treatment on pregnant woman.[76] Not to be overlooked is the fact that forced caesarean may force women out of regulated healthcare system.[77] It produces unacceptable harm and infringes our dear concept of right. Nancy Rhoden summaries it thus:

> 'The court that orders a Caesarean will have wronged the woman. Indeed, it will have decided for her what medical risks she should run. This is a very significant and presumptuous step...Because an objective third party must weigh individual beliefs without believing them, imposing an objective decision on the woman to treat her as if she were not a unique individual entitled to make life choices according to her belief...If it does not matter very much who she is, then she has in a very real sense been wronged.'[78]

To permit 'obstetricians to cut open woman's bodies against their will, as the means of saving their foetuses, is open to powerful moral and legal objection.'[79] Legal objection that may arise range from questions involving matters of fair trial, *locus standi* and the objectionable mode of executing court forced treatment orders. The shortness of time associated with such applications may deprive the court a fair opportunity to adequately hear evidence, evaluate same to be able to arrive at a rationale decision. Constrain of time often prevents the court from hearing both sides on material issues before reaching a decision. The potential of admitting prejudicial evidence against the patient can be real as is usually the case with most pre-emptive applications.[80] Therefore application by hospitals or persons who claim to know better should be strongly discouraged.

It is difficult to imagine how the refusal of treatment by a pregnant woman can infringe on the right of the hospital or other who claim to have an interest more than the patient herself. Only a person who can be directly affected by a cause acquires an interest to sue. All other persons are treated as busy-bodies (traffickers in litigation). They acquire no locus.[81] A hospital interest to preserve life of a patient can hardly be said to constitute sufficient interest to give it locus are an applicant for a declaration to force treatment on a pregnant woman.[82]

More objectionable will be the mode for enforcing court orders for forcible treatment. If the patient refuses or objects to a court order, what will the court do? Imprison her? Forcibly fasten her with restraint to have her invaded? If she flees,

---

[75] Feinberg, Autonomy, Sovereignty, and Privacy: Moral Ideals in the Constitution? 58 *Notre Dame L. Rev.* 445, 414 (1983)

[76] Annas, Foreclosing the Use of Force: *Re AC* Reversed, [1990] 7-8 *Hastings Centre Rep*27 at 29.

[77] Babara Hawson, Ethical Triumph, or Surgical Rape? (1993) 133 *SJ* 1182.

[78] Nancy Rhode: The Judge in the Delivery Room (1986) *Calif. L Rev.* 1951.

[79] Ibid.

[80] See the Supreme Court case of *Kotoye* v. *CBN* [1989] 1 All NLR 76 on fair hearing. See also *Sheldon* v. *Bromfied Justices* [1964] 2 QB 573 at 578.

[81] *Senator Adesanya* v. *Gani Fawehemmi* v. 86; *Re F (Mental Patient: sterilisation)* [1990] AC 1 at 64.

[82] Babara Hawson, Ethical Triumph, or Surgical Rape? (1993) 133 *SJ* 1182.

should she be captured and taken into captivity? .A street chase to bring her in custody would not be funny. It could bring to mind horrors of the Swastika and Inquisition.[83]

It is submitted that to the extent that *Re S* and some cases attempt to put viable foetus ahead of the treatment choices of pregnant women they represent bad law and should be treated as out of alignment with current legal medical ethics. The New Jersey and Georgia Supreme Courts decision in *Raleigh Fitkin-Paul Morgan Memorial Hospital* v. *Anderson* [84] and *Jefferson* v. *Griffin Spalding County Hospital Authority* [85] respectively are the only appellate decision in America which places foetus ahead of pregnant women choices. In the later case, (*Griffin Spalding*)[86] the patient a pregnant woman in her 39 weeks of pregnancy had *placenta previa*. For religious reasons she refused a Caesarean and blood transfusion. The Georgian Supreme Court upheld the trial court order authorising forced Caesarean and blood transfusion on her. In arriving at this decision the court cited (but did not discuss) three cases, namely: (i) *Roe* v. *Wade*[87] where; the United State Supreme held that for extreme and compelling reasons the court may override a pregnant women choice (ii). *Raleigh Fitkin* [88] and (iii) *Struck* v. *Struck* [89]in which the Kentucky Supreme Court ruled that a parent could consent to harvesting of an organ from their incompetent child. The parents gave consent for the kidney of an incompetent child to be harvested for transplant purposes for the benefit of their competent child.

The lack of any discussion of the principles in the cited three cases leaves much to be desired. Let us consider the cases on their merit with a view of determining whether they constitute sound basis for the conclusion in *Griffin Spadling*.[90] Let us begin with *Roe*.[91] The United States Supreme Court held that for extreme and compelling reasons the court may override a pregnant woman's choices. In *Strunk v Strunk* [92] the Kentucky Supreme Court authorised organ harvest from an incompetent adult child on request by his parents. These authorities it is suggested do not support the conclusions in *Griffin Spadling*[93]for the following reasons: (i) the fact that *Roe* v. *Wade* decides that the state has an interest in potential viable foetuses hardly explains how that interest overrides bodily self-determination and freedom of religion of a competent adult, especially when the same Supreme Court

---

[83] *McFall* v. *Shimp* (1978) Pd. 2A 3rd 90, 92, in *Re AC* 573, A 2d 1235 (1990) at 1244.

[84] 201 A 2d 537 (NJ 1964).

[85] 274 S.E. 2d 457 (Ga. 1981).

[86] Ibid.

[87] 401 US 113 (1973).

[88] 201 A 2d 537 (NJ 1964).

[89] 445 SW 2d 145 (Ky. 1969) (court held that parents could consent to the removal of a kidney from their incompetent adult son for transplant into their other competent adult son suffering from kidney failure). But cf. *Lausier* v. *Pescinski* 226 NW 2d 180 (Wise, 1975).

[90] 274 S.E. 2d 457 (Ga. 1981).

[91] 632 NE 2d 326 (Ill. App. Ct. 1994).

[92] 445 SW 2d 145 (Ky. 1969).

[93] 274 S.E. 2d 457 (Ga. 1981).

has previously held that a mother cannot be exposed to increased medical risk for the sake of her foetus.[94] (ii) inexplicable is the reference to *Struck* v. *Struck*. That case has no bearing with the issue for determination in *Griffin Spadling*. The question in *Griffin Spalding* was whether or not a pregnant woman retains her right to choice medical treatment and if so how far it extends. It was not a question on transplant and who can consent to its harvesting. It is respectfully submitted that the fact that the Georgian Supreme Court referred to *Struck* v. *Struck* gives the impression that a pregnant woman who refuses medical treatment was legally equated with an invalid mentally retarded incompetent person whose choice is treated irrelevant or at best permissibly overridden by his care-givers or parents. If that is the case, it is respectively suggested that it is a display of legal ignorance defying description.

Raleigh Fitkin[95] decision by the New Jersey Supreme Court is no better. The only authority cited in support of the court order that a pregnant woman in the 32 week of pregnancy could be transfused despite her refusal to ensure the safe delivery of her baby was a case where a third party, (not the mother) who negligently injured a foetus while in its mother's womb was held liable to the child after delivery for injuries suffered as a result of the negligence.

The ratio of *Raleigh* case is difficult to find because of the brevity of the judgment. Even at that, it would appear that the court equated and viewed a mother's informed choice about the delivery of her baby as no different from a negligent third party who has no connection with the mother or pregnancy except for his negligent injury to her foetus. It is respectfully suggested that a non-negligent mother should not be legally equated with a negligent third party.[96]

Both *Raleigh Fitkin* and *Griffin Spalding* are no doubt at variance with *Re AC*[97] and to *Re Doe*[98] (decisions from state appellate courts, subordinate to state Supreme Court to which *Fitkin* and *Spalding* belong). Nonetheless the state appellate decisions in *Re AC* and *Re Doe* align better with current medical law and ethics, the common law concept of bodily right and the American Supreme Court decision in *Roe* v. *Wade*.[99]

It is suggested that the body rights of a pregnant woman should be respected, not subject to any invasion whatsoever under any guise. She is the final arbiter of what has to be done to her body. If we thinks that she should use her body to

---

[94] *Thornburgh* v. *American College of Obstetricians And Gynaecologist* 476 US 747at 768-71 (1986); *Planned Parenthood of Southern Pennsylvania* v. *Casey* 112 S. Ct. 2791at 2804 (1992) (state's interest in potential life of foetus is insufficient to override woman's interest in preserving her health).

[95] 274 S.E. 2d 457 (Ga. 1981).

[96] See *Sallmen* v. *Youngguist*, 531 NE 2d 355 (Ill 1988) and *In Re Valerie* 623 A 2d. 748 (Conn.1992) where the Illinois Supreme Court discussed the troublesome public policy issues of equating a non-negligent pregnant woman with a negligent third party.

[97] 573 A 2d 1235 (1990).

[98] 632 NE 2d 326 (Ill. App. Ct. 1994).

[99] 401 US 113 (1973), 93 S Ct 705 (1973). For case discussion, see, J.H Ely, The Wages of Crying Wolf: A Comment on *Roe* v. *Wade* (1973) 82 *Yale L.J.* 920.

support her foetus, then there is no reason why court orders of injunction should not also issue against pregnant woman who drink, smoke and engage in other harmful activities. No one would dispute that such injunctive orders are uncalled for and would be considered too invasive. Contemplating it is frightening. If the law will not contemplate it why should the pregnant woman's right to choose medical treatment diminish immediately she enters a maternity ward?

> Boyd graphically put the matter this way: 'The refusal of patient to accept 'good advice' should be put in perspective. We encounter patients, on a daily basis who smoke, drink alcohol, use drugs, overeat, or refuse treatment for degenerative or malignant disease. The unwillingness of all such patients to accept our recommendations is not met with threat of court action, isolation from relatives and ministers of their faith, and refusal to treat on moral grounds.'[100]

Mother-foetus conflict can also raise public policy issues. The emotional appeal of 'saving babies' should not legally require sacrifice of fundamental, constitutional and long cherished rights. The idea of invading the body of a person for the benefit of another person is unwholesome. If the wish of a corpse respecting cadaveric organ donation and general testamentary dispositions are worthy of respect,[101] there should be no logical reason why the wish of a pregnant woman should not with regard to medical treatment. A posture that respects wills of deceased as speaking ambulatory and yet disregards the informed wishes of women is nothing but sheer hypocrisy.

Unwarranted invasion on pregnant woman have been justified by some on the basis that where treatment is uncommon, it is obligatory. That is to say the least another sloppy thinking. Such a distinction in treatment choices in the context of other areas in medicine, as previously discussed in sterilisation treatments have been rejected as unhelpful and it is submitted that it so in the context of informed consent. It sweeps underground the real ethical questions involved. More importantly the proposition does not enjoy general acceptance by commentators[102] and authorities, such as *Re Doe* and the likes. In *Re Doe* the court was emphatic that 'there is no such thing as a 'trivial interference' with personal sovereignty..a trivial

---

[100] Boyd, The Obstetrician and Gynaecologist and the Jehovah's Witness, [1992] 5-6 *Jo. of Socy of Obstetricians & Gynaecologist Canada* 7.

[101] See Wills Act, 1894. For comparison see, generally, Uniform Anatomical Gift Act, Art 3, 8A U.L.A. 13 (Supp. 1990)

[102] Feinberg, Autonomy, Sovereignty, and Privacy: Moral Ideals in the Constitution? 58 *Notre Dame L. Rev.* 445at 492 (1983) stated that no competent pregnant woman's decision ought to be overruled by a judge not only in matters of surgery, 'but blood transfusions, injections, and even forcing a pill down a woman's throat, are to be prohibited.' See also US President's Commission for the Study of Ethical Problems in Medicine, 1983, para. 87, Deciding to Forgo Life-Sustaining Treatment, which states: 'Whether care is ordinary or extraordinary should not determine whether a patient must accept or may decline it..To avoid misunderstanding, public discussions should focus on the underlying reasons for or against a therapy rather than on a simple categorization as ordinary or extraordinary.'

interference with sovereignty is like a minor invasion of virginity: the logic of each concept is such that a value is respected in its entirety or not at all.'[103]

There certainly is good sense in not drawing any line of distinction between ordinary and extraordinary treatment as basis for obligation or otherwise. The principle is clear. 'A competent patient has a right to decline any medical treatment.'[104] There is no basis for holding whether a treatment is common or unusual as significant to a moral analysis of whether the treatment is warranted or obligatory.[105] Patients view of what is acceptable or unacceptable medical treatment differ from person to person in ways that do not necessarily correlate with others view.[106] The reason is obvious. Each patient is different. Each has his or her own attitudes towards serious sickness. So what is considered beneficial to one may be burdensome to another. So decision of what is common or uncommon must be made by or for the patient based on a thorough consideration of all the facts of the case with the patient's best interests foremost in mind.[107]

According to one commentator, it is not just the ethicists and commentators who see the unprincipled weakness in the medical distinction between major or minor, or ordinary or extraordinary intervention:[108]

> The New Jersey Supreme Court also stated that the distinction is unnecessary, when in In re Conroy it said: 'We... find unpersuasive the distinction relied upon by some courts, commentators, and theologians between ordinary treatment, which they would always require, and extraordinary treatment, which they deem optional...To draw a line on this basis for determining whether treatment should be given leads to a semantical milieu that does not advance the analysis...The ordinary/extraordinary distinction is irrelevant except insofar as the particular patient would have made the distinction...A competent patient has the right to decline any medical treatment.'[109]

---

[103] 632 N.E. 2d 326 at 333.

[104] *In re Conroy* 486 A. 2d 1209 (N.J. 1985) New Jersey Supreme Court.

[105] US President's Commission for the Study of Ethical Problems in Medicine, 1983, para. 87, Deciding to Forgo Life-Sustaining Treatment.

[106] US President's Commission for the Study of Ethical Problems in Medicine, 1983 at 62. 'Extraordinary treatment is that which in the patient's view, entails significantly greater burdens than benefit and is therefore undesirable and not obligatory, while ordinary treatment is that which, in the patient's view, produces greater benefits than burdens and is therefore reasonably desirable and undertaken. The claim, then, that the treatment is extraordinary is more of an expression of the conclusion than a justification for it..Clarity and understanding in this area will be enhanced if laws, judicial opinions, regulations, and medical policies speak instead in terms of the proportionate benefits and burdens of treatment as viewed by particular patients.

[107] US President's Commission for the Study of Ethical Problems in Medicine, 1983 at 88-89.

[108] Showalter, Decisions to Forgo Medical Treatment: The Preferred Medical, Ethical, and Legal Approach (1984) 29 *Cath. Law* 286.

[109] 486 A 2d 1209 at 1234-1235 (N.J. 1985) SC. See also *In re Guardianship of Browning*, 568 So. 2d 4 at 11 (Fla. 1990) where the court said there is 'no reason to qualify [the right to refuse treatment] on the basis of the denomination of a medical procedure as major or minor, ordinary or extraordinary.'

Some commentators graphically put matters in perspective why the pregnant woman's right of autonomy must be respected this way:

> 'The refusal of patients to accept 'good advice' should be put in perspective. We encounter patients, on a daily basis, who smoke, drink alcohol, use drugs, overeat, or refuse treatment for degenerative or malignant disease. The unwillingness of all such patients to accept our recommendations is not met with threat of court action, isolation from relatives and ministers of their faith, and refusal to treat on moral grounds.'[110]

Since both *Re AC* and *Doe* are the cases that thoroughly examine the complex social and ethical issues involved in pregnant women's refusal to treatment, especially in the context of maternal-foetal conflict, they are respectfully suggested the leading and preferred authorities in the area. Although both involved Caesarean sections, as a matter of principle there is no difference between a Caesarean section and blood transfusion if the law truly respects a woman's right of autonomy and (religious) freedom. The pregnant woman should be the sole determiner to make the uncertain, highly subjective, value-laden decision about the destiny of her pregnancy. Courts must critically examine medical facts in dispute over 'appropriate medical care.' For instance, if forcibly treatment is not truly needed to advance the welfare of the foetus but is simply the standard course of treatment that is popular or preferred by liability-conscious doctors, the pregnant woman should by allowed to make the treatment choices. Whatever the suggestion, the baseline ought to remain as the New Jersey Supreme Court stated: 'A competent patient has the right to decline any medical treatment.'[111]

Parents (competent) with children

To a large extent the legal position here is no different from what has been discussed above on pregnancy. There is no justification to force treatment on any adult reasoning that it is for the sake of innocent third parties, i.e., his children. An adult refusal of treatment should not be equated with abandonment. No patient's body can be subject or subordinate to that of another person. Neglect and or abandonment of a child is certainly criminal. Section 341 of the Criminal Code provides that

> 'any person who unlawfully abandons or exposes a child under the age of seven in such a manner that grievous harm is likely to be caused the child shall be guilty of a felony, liable to imprisonment for five years.'

By no stretch of imagination should a competent adult parent who refuses treatment be said to have abandoned his children. In cases of abandonment the law

---

[110] Nelson and Milliken, Compelled Medical Treatment of Pregnant Women (1988) 259 JAMA 1060 at 1065. See also Boyd, The Obstetrician and Gynaecologist and the Jehovah's Witness, [1992] 5-6 *Jo. of Socy of Obstetricians & Gynaecologist Canada* 7.

[111] *In re Conroy* 486 A 2d 1209 at 1234-1235 (N.J. 1985) SC.

punishes acts or omission by parents failing to provide necessaries, including medical treatment for their children. The requirements of law relate directly to provision *to* children. It does not cover provision of what is treated as necessary to the parent, even in a manner that may indirectly affect children. It is therefore faulty reasoning to say that if a parent exercises his right to refuse treatment he is implicitly or otherwise embarking on a course that leads to his death and so is invariably choosing the path of abandoning his children. Forcing a parent to receive treatment on that basis is to say the least, reasoning devoid of common sense, causation principles, talk more of its totalitarianisms.

It is respectfully submitted that it is not within the province of law to intervene. One commentator put it this way:

> 'States do not ordinarily force individuals to fulfil their obligation, rather states force individuals to suffer the legal consequences of non-fulfilment. The state does not escort a parent to work to ensure child support, how then, can a court justify forcing an unwilling parent to stay alive in order to achieve the same goal? Finally, the ultimate sanction for child abandonment is court ordered termination of parental rights. In refusing treatment the parent is simply applying this ultimate sanction against himself or herself.'[112]

Therefore the dependent third party argument is faulty legal reasoning. Its application runs contrary to common law right of self-determination and constitutional freedom.[113] For example, consider this hypothesis: Would anyone justify compelling say a Muslim to eat pork meat because it is considered cure for a patient's sickness so that he would stay alive for his children when that offends his strongly held religious beliefs? Would it be proper to compel say a devote Catholic to a force abortion for the sake of his dependants? After all, do we prevent parents from harmful conducts or employment for the sake of their wards? If the answer is no, then why should the law compel a parent to receive medical treatment against his wish under the guise that refusal may amount to abandonment? To the contrary,

> 'parents take all sort of health risks, from sky diving, to drugs or alcohol, to joining the United States Army, that are not subject to state intervention. It is

[112] Note, The Refusal of Life-Saving Medical Treatment vs The State's Interest in the Preservation of Life: A Clarification of the Interests at Stake (1980) 58 *Wash. Univ. L.Q.* 85 at 102. If going by statistic according to the US National Safety Council, (*Accident Facts*, 1988at 34-35 and 44-45) white collar workers have a drastically lower incidence of accidental death and occupational injury than do fire-fighters, coal miners, or those who work in steel foundries , should the law prohibit adults with dependants from such employment? See Note (1980) 58 *Wash. Univ. L.Q.* 85 at 105 n. 110.

[113] Rhoden, Litigating Life and Death (1988) 102 *Harv. LR* 375; Jonsen, Blood Transfusion and Jehovah's Witnesses (1986) 2 *Critical Care Clinics* 91; Note, The Refusal of Life-Saving Medical Treatment vs The State's Interest in the Preservation of Life: A Clarification of the Interests at Stake (1980) 58 *Wash. Univ. L.Q.* 85; The Refusal of Blood Transfusion: An Ultimate Challenge for Law and Morals (1964) 77 *Harv. LR* 1539, (1964) 113 Univ. Pa. LR 290, (1965) 18 *Vand. LR* 772, (1964) 39 *Tul. LR* 125, (1964) 26 *Mont. LR* 95, (1964) *S.C.L. LR* 552; Clarke, The Choice to Refuse or Withhold Mesdical Treatment: The Emerging Technology and Medical-Ethical Consensus (1980) 13 *Creigton LR* 795 at 816-817.

> puzzling that parenthood should vitiated the right to refuse treatment when it leaves intact the freedom to act in other ways equally detrimental to a child.'[114]

In *Public Health Trust* v. *Wons*,[115] the hospital applied to court to transfuse a patient suffering from chronic defectional uterine bleeding. She was anaemic. The application was supported on the grounds that she is the mother of two teenage children. The trial court authorised transfusion. The Florida District Court of Appeal reversed the order, stating that it was wrong and faulty legally. On further appeal the Florida Supreme Court affirmed the decision of the Court of Appeal. The court held that dependant third party basis should not be compelling reasons enough to override a competent patient's right to refuse treatment.

Similarly, in *Fosmire* v. *Nicoleau*,[116] the hospital sought to transfuse a patient who gave birth to a child after a Caesarean. The trial court ordered transfusion because it was concerned about the welfare of her newborn child. The ex-parte order authorising transfusion was vacated by the New York Supreme Court and severely criticised. It said:

> 'Ex-parte applications are generally disfavoured by the courts unless expressly authorised by statute, because of the attendant due process implications caused by preceding without notice ...Under no circumstances however should; the court issue an order authorising medical treatment which is known to be in violation of the patient's expressed wishes and or religious beliefs without first making every effort to communicate with the patient or his or her representatives and to fully comprehend the patients state of mind and wishes.'[117]

It said that the primary duty of the state is to preserve and promote liberty and autonomy of the individual.[118] 'The notion that the individual exist for the good of the state is, of course antithetical to our fundamental thesis that the role of the state is to ensure a maximum of individual freedom of choice and conduct.'[119] The patient is the only person to decide the course of his or her medical treatment. It is not in any way conditioned by considerations of whether she has dependants or not. Self-determination and autonomy do not evaporate because an adult patient has minor dependants. State *paren patrae* interest in the dependant child is no reason for overriding the adult patient informed choice.[120]

---

[114] *Fosmire* v. *Nicoleau* 551 N.E. 2d 77 at 84 (NY 1990) New York Court of Appeals.

[115] 541 So 2d 96 (Fla. 1989) off 500 so 2d 679 (Fla. Dis. Ct. App. 1987).

[116] 75 N.Y 2d 218, 551 NE 2d 77,551 NYS 2d 876 (1990), 551 N.E. 2d 77 at 84 (NY 1990). See also *Norwood Hospital* v. *Minor* 2 409 Mass. 116, 564 NE 2d 1017 (1991) where the Supreme Judicial Court of Massachusetts held that a patients fundamental right of religious freedom and common law right of bodily self-determinism is superior to the state *parens patriae* interest in the welfare of a child.

[117] Ibid.

[118] *Fosmire* v. *Nicoleau* 551 N.E. 2d 77 at 82 (NY 1990).

[119] *In re Osborne* 294 A. 2d. 372 at 375 (DC 1972).

[120] The third party dependant argument as basis for abandonment litigation does not consider the weighty fact that many persons other than parents have dependents. If others do, then the logical strength of third party argument will mean that the state should also vigorously protect such dependents in all

This legal position was put beyond doubt in *Re Dubreuil*.[121] The patient who was pregnant had to undergo a Caesarean. She gave consent to it but refused the use of blood in her treatment. After safe delivery, she experienced severe blood loss and in the opinion of the hospital needed blood. She still refused transfusion. Noteworthy is the fact that her husband did not support her refusal. The trial court ordered transfusion if deemed necessary by the hospital administration. On appeal, the Florida District Court of Appeal affirmed the trial court's ruling. But the Supreme Court of Florida, quashed and set-aside the decision of both courts. It rejected the argument that a parent's right of self-determination is subordinate to the rights of her children on grounds of parental responsibilities. It said:

> 'Parenthood, in and of itself, does not deprive one of living in accord with ones own beliefs. Society does not for example, disparage or preclude one from performing an act of bravery resulting in the loss of that person's life simply because that person has parental responsibility.'[122]

---

similar situations in which their welfare is threatened. According to A Meisel, *The Right to Die*, 1989, 103, 'other close relatives, including adult offsprings of the patient and perhaps even other persons emotionally close to the patient but not related by blood or marriage, might be able to assert a substantial interest in the patient's continued life.'

[121] 629 So. 2d 819 (Fla. 1993). See also *Norwood Hosp.* v. *Munoz*, 564 NE 2d 1017 (Mass. 1991); *Randolph* v. *City of New York*, 507 NE 2d 298 (NY 1987); *Mercy Hosp. Inc.* v. *Jackson*, 489 A 2d 1130 (Md. Ct. Spec. App. 1985). But cf. *In re President and Directors of Georgetown College Inc.*, 331 F 2d 1000 (Wright, J., in chambers) cert. denied, 331 F 2d1010 (DC Cir.), cert. denied, 337 US 978 (1964), Skelly Wright J reasoning that patient's refusal of transfusion was tantamount to voluntary abandonment of her child authorised blood transfusion. Over the years however, the value of the Georgetown case as good precedent has been doubted. For instance, in *In re Dubreuil*, 629 So. 2d 819 at 824 (Fla. 1993), the court described it as having 'little precedential value,' and Warner J, dissenting at 543-544 said it 'serves as scant authority' and 'presents little precedential or analytical authority.' *Fosmire* v. *Nicoleau* 551 N.E. 2d 77 at 83 (NY 1990), states that it 'extends the concept of abandonment far beyond the boundaries recognised in this state, and into areas where it would conflict with other substantial interests.' In *Public Health Trust* v. *Wons*, 541 So. 2d 96 at 99 (Fla. 1989), Ehrlich, CJ, concurring specially states that it is 'not very persuasive' authority. Also in *In re Estate of Brooks*, 205 NE 2d 435 at 439-440 (Ill.1965) Georgetown was described as 'an altogether unique proceeding.' It is respectfully suggested that there is no question about it, Georgetown is indeed unique and strange, illustrating not only the wayward course a single judicial officer may take when he is without the benefit of a full evidentiary hearing but also the need for judicial restraint and thorough, non-emotional examination of the substantial interest at play. It was a case where a hospital orally appealed a district court refusal to transfuse blood to the federal court of appeal. Acting alone in a *nisi prius* as opposed to an appellate capacity, the judge made the order sought, issuing an opinion five months later explaining his actions. Unfortunately, his Lordship did not in his explanation opinion cite ant District of Columbia statute or case law as authority for his action in which he reasoned that the patient's refusal of blood was tantamount to voluntary abandonment of her child. His Lordship merely said at 331 F 2d 1008 is that 'the people' (presumably of the District of Colombia) would not allow such an abandonment. It is further reasoned that, as the denial of the Georgetown patient's petition for rehearing en banc shows, nine of the ten federal court judges would have affirmed the federal district court's denial of the hospital's petition (allowed by Wright J.). In fact the opinion of Miller and Warren Burger JJ (the latter became Chief Justice of the US) at 331 F 2d 1015, highlight the procedural peculiarity and dubious merits of his Lordship's action.

[122] 629 So. 2d 819 (Fla. 1993).

On the question whether the court ought to consider the fact that her husband did not support her refusal to transfusion, the court said: 'marriage does not destroy ones constitutional right to personal autonomy.'[123] The issue here is not what other people think about the patient's refusal, but rather what the patient's wishes. That is what should be respected. On the question of whether the patient's refusal was tantamount to abandonment of her young child, in that her refusal may result in her death and subsequent abdication of her love to the child, the court stated that such presumption was gender discrimination. The place of mother is not just to deliver and tend children. It said:

> 'The rationale in the judgment of the trial court and the Court of Appeal could be read by some to perpetuate the damaging stereotype that a mother's role is one of caregiver, and the father's role is that of an apathetic, irresponsible, or unfit parent...The law has evolved to move away from inappropriate gender–based distinction...we do not want the district's courts rationale misinterpreted to reinforce these outdated ideas in a manner that effectively denies a woman her constitutional right to refuse medical treatment.[124]

Hospital authorities and doctors were accordingly advised by the court not to allow themselves drawn into any ugly, awkward position of having to zealously argue against the interest their patients. The reason is simple. It would be tantamount to abdicating on their duty to provide care and treatment in accordance with the patient's wishes and best interest. A doctor who refuses to heed the advice could expose himself to civil and criminal liability.[125]

When the matter in question has to do with alleged neglect or abandonment of dependent minor, the state *parens patriae* interest is usually ascertainable from its codified laws on child protection. Most statute simply, like our Criminal Code[126] simply requires parents to provide necessaries. If parents fail in this respect the state may intervene to protect the children. Ultimately, such parents will lose parental rights. This is what makes it dubious to resort to statute as providing for the protection of third party dependents as basis for abandonment litigation. If state interest in ensuring support for dependents is that compelling, then the state prophylactic intervention should not be limited to blood transfusion cases.

> 'Why should not a fifty-five-year old man caring for his elderly mother or retarded son be forced to submit to coronary bypass surgery to ensure his continuing ability to provide for these dependents? Consistent application of the dependent-third rule would require intervention whenever any adult's ability to provide support for dependents is threatened.'[127]

---

[123] 629 So. 2d 819 (Fla. 1993).

[124] Ibid.

[125] *Airedale National Health Service* v. *Bland* [1993] 1 All ER 821.

[126] S. 227 of Criminal code

[127] Clarke, The Choice to Refuse or Withhold Medical Treatment: The Emerging Technology and Medical-Ethical Consensus (1980) 13 *Creighton LR* 795 at 817.

To the extent that justification to the dependent-third party rule is somewhat limited to cases of refusal of blood transfusion, to that extent it smells discrimination on religious grounds. Would any doctor be right to compel a Catholic woman to undergo abortion for the sake of minor children she already has? If for instance, her obstetrician advises her (within her first trimester) that she will suffer serious, possibly debilitating injury or death if she takes her pregnancy to term, would doctor, child protection agency or court force her to abort her pregnancy so as to ensure her continuing ability to care for her existing children? If not, there has to be a better reason than that the state respects her autonomy or religious freedom. Medically, the abortion is the safer procedure, legally an embryo is not a person. So either state *parens patriae* interest in the support of the dependent-third party rule overrides the patient's self-determination or religious freedom or both or it does not. There should not be one rule for members of mainstream religions and another for members of religious minorities.[128]

Also not to be overlooked is the fact that non-blood medical treatment has proved successful in many cases where blood therapy has been suggested by doctors, and the inappropriate gender-based stereotype distinction inherent in the dependent-third party rule, which views a mother as caregiver and the man as an apathetic, irresponsible parent. Or how else do we interpret the rule having force on the mother, without it also applying with same force to the father?[129] Health care providers are therefore under obligation to provide treatment in accord with their patient's (or parents) wishes.

State *parens patriae*/wardship jurisdiction

In most jurisdictions, infants are regarded as special persons under the protection of the State or Crown. In England the function is delegated to the Lord Chancellor, a jurisdiction now exercised by the Chancery Division. When an infant is made a ward of court, the court may exercise special jurisdiction in the nature of parental personal and administrative control over him. The underpinning is that the power of wardship exists to supplement, override or replace the powers and the responsibilities of parents.[130] The ancient wardship jurisdiction has been remarkable in England since the Second World War due to the expansive nature of state powers and control over many social relations.[131]

---

[128] Hospital Liason Committee Seminar, 1996, of the Watchtower Society Nigeria.

[129] *In re Dubreuil*, 629 So. 2d 819 (Fla. 1993). See the Florida Supreme Court response to implied argument that the mother as patient has greater responsibility to care for her children than did her husband. It considered such stereotype of gender 'outdated ideas in a manner that effectively denies a woman her constitutional right to refuse medical treatment.'

[130] Brenda Hoggett, The Royal Prerogative in Relations to the Mentally Disordered: Resurrection, Resuscitation or Rejection? In p. 84 at 89.

[131] The sophistication of local authority activities has greatly supplemented the courts jurisdiction in the protection of children in recent times. On the attitude of court to the prerogative of wardship see J v.C [1970] AC 668 and *Re D (a minor wardship: sterilisation)* [1976] Fam 185.

Prerogative powers of wardship is said to be founded on the right of the feudal Lord to the wardship of a tenant who could not carry out his required services to him, a right later taken over by the Crown either by general assent or statute towards the end of the reign of Henry III.[132] This right was later referred to as prerogative and conferred by statute on the Crown.[133] In part it provides as regards idiots the following: 'The King shall have the custody of the lands of natural fouls, taking the profits of them without waste or destruction.' The effect of this is that wardship jurisdiction that originally covered infants came to be construed as extending to persons with mental deficiencies. In *Beall* v. *Smith* [134] it was recognised that infancy gives the Court of Chancery jurisdiction of wardship.

The Crown as *parens patriae* takes upon itself the duty to care for those who cannot care for themselves. Generally children, except mature minor within the bracket of *Gillick* competence, are incompetent.[135] They lack capacity to give consent in law because of lack of understanding. Since their treatment also requires consent, the law requires others to be their consent givers. In the case of minors, their parents or the court and the local authority, if there exists a statutory justification for it.[136]

Essentials of Informed Consent

It is a fundamental principle in medical ethics that every person has a right to self-determination. This is essentially expressed in the notion of consent to medical treatment – a concept through which the patient's right to decide what happens to him is protected and preserved. A paternalist will certainly quarrel with this fundamental principle because to him there are many situations where treatment ought to proceed even without consent. His reason proceeds this way: a patient after all knows less about medicine than the doctor. The doctor's opinion about a treatment procedure ought to override that of the patient. He is the expert. What is more, good health for the patient should be preferred to ill health and insistence on rights of the patient to choose treatment. His analysis may also find support in economics, when couched in social terms. Illness can be costly to the community.[137] Viewed from this perspective there may appear justification in restricting the patient's right of autonomy. Take for example, if the patient choice results in death, the community or the state may come under obligation to maintain his surviving family, a course which may be economically inefficient.[138]

---

[132] Hoggett, *op. cit*, above n. 130.

[133] De Prerogative Regis, 17 Edward II. C 9 and 11.

[134] (1873) 9 Ch App. 80 at 92, per James LJ and *Wellesley* v. *Duke of Baaufor L* (1827) 38 E.R. 236 at 243 per Lord Eldon.

[135] *Gillick* v. *West Norfolk and Wisbech Area Health Authority* [1986] AC 112; [1985] 3 All ER 402.

[136] For example in England, the Children Act 1989 provides that local authorities may acquire parental responsibility over a child.

[137] For general discussion on an economic analysis of law, see R Posner, *An Economic Analysis of Law.*

[138] For example there exist cases such as *In Re President and Directors of Georgetown College*, Inc 331 F 2d 1000 (DC Cir 1964) where Wright J override a patient consent for the sake of innocent third parties'

Such argument notwithstanding, there exists legal justification for respect of patient's right. While it can be conceded that arguments framed in the bracket of abandonment and social cost do have their place, we cannot overlook the damage that can result from coercion in modern democracy. In *Re C*[139] the court observed:

> 'There is no such thing as a trivial interference with personal sovereignty, nor is it simply another value to be weighed in a cost-benefit comparison. In this respect, if not others, a trivial interference with sovereignty is like a minor invasion of virginity. The logic of each concept is such that a value is respected in its entirety or not at all.'[140]

The common law have long recognised that things may not be done to a person without his consent merely on the ground that it is for his benefit. It protects a person from busybodies who think they know what is good for others. This is what is reflected in the libertarian philosophy expounded by J.S Mill in this term:

> 'The sole end for which mankind are warranted, individually or collectively, in interfering with the liberty of action of any of their number is self protection...the only purpose of which power can be rightfully exercised over any member of a civilised community against his will, is to prevent harm to others. His own good, either physical or moral, is not sufficient warrant. He cannot rightfully be compelled to do or forbear because it will be better for him to do so, because it will make him happier, because in the opinion of others, to do so would be wise or even right. These are good reasons for remonstrating with him, or reasoning with him, or persuading him, or entreating him, but not for compelling him, or visiting him with evil in case he does otherwise. To justify that, the conduct from which it is desired to deter him must be calculated to produce evil to someone else...The only freedom which deserves the name is that of pursuing our own good in our own way so long as we do not attempt to deprive others or impede their efforts to obtain it. Each is the proper guardian of his own health, whether bodily, or mental and spiritual.'[141]

---

defendants, on argument framed in terms of abandonment. A closer analysis of the proposition however now reveals that it lacks sound legal or public policy basis. The law hardly justifies the subordination of a patient's bodily self-determination and personal privacy for another. See *McFall* v. *Shimp* 10 Pa. D & C 3d 90 at 91 (1978); Feinberg, Autonomy, Sovereignty and privacy: Moral Ideals in the constitution (1983) 58 *Notre Dame L. Rev.* 445.

[139] 537 A 2d 1235 (D.D 1990).

[140] Ibid., at 1244 n.8.

[141] J.S. Mill, *On Liberty* (1859) Everyman edition p. 72-73, 75; see also *Schloendorff* v. *Society of New York Hospital* (1914) 105 NE 92 at 93, per Cardozo J; Gavin Thurston, Problems of Consent (1966) 6 *BMJ* 1406 Declaration of Lisbon, 1981 Statement of the World Medical Association; *O. Okonkwo* v. *MDPDT*; *Collins* v. *Wilcock* (1984) 1 WLR 1172 at 1177-8, per Goff LJ; *Wilson* v. *Pringle* [1986] 2 All ER 440 at 446 per Croom-Johnson LJ; *Sidaway* v. *Governors of Bethlehem Royal Hospital* [1985] AC 871 at 876, per Scarman LJ; *Malette* v. *Shulman* (1990) 67 DLR (4th) 321 [1991] 2 Med. LR 162; *Re. F* [1989] 2 WLR 1025 at 1040 per Donalson MR; *Airedale National Health Service Trust* v. *Bland* [1993] 2 WLR 316, but cf. *In Re T (Adult: Refusal of Treatment)* [1992] 3 WLR 782. For general reading see Note, The Refusal of Life Saving Medical Treatment v. The State Interest in the Preservation of Life: A Clarification of the Interest at Stake (1980) 58 *Wash. Univ. Law Quarterly* 85; Clarke, The Choice to Refuse or Withhold Medical Treatment: The Emerging Technology and Medical-Ethical Consensus (1980) 13 *Creighton L.*

Noteworthy of mention is the fact that the issue of consent to medical treatment may arise from three main heads:
(i) in relation to the crime of battery and assault;
(ii) in the context of the tort of battery; and
(iii) in the tort of negligence.

Our concern however will be that within the structure of (ii) and (iii), because (i) is well discussed in criminal law text.[142] A doctor who proceeds to treat without consent exposes himself to liability in tort, prosecution for the crime of battery and possibly for professional breach of rules of ethics before his professional colleague.[143]

The fact of consent is concerned with the following three essentials: (i) it must be given by a competent person-capacity; (ii) it must be real in the sense of being voluntary-voluntariness of consent; and (iii) it must qualify as informed-informed consent. What this means in the context of medical law is that the courts emphasise not just the non-consensual nature of treatment but the quality of information given a patient from which consent to medical treatment is grounded.[144] The legal requirement of consent rest on the law's respect for the patient's right to decide. In effect the patient has the right to say yes or no to medical treatment. Let us now consider the essentials of medical consent.

(i) Capacity

Capacity calls to question the competence of the patient to give consent. Flowing from this we can analyse capacity and the related issue of competence from two perspectives – age and understanding.[145] By common law rule on age or status as operational in Nigeria a person above age 21 is taken as having attained majority and accordingly is competent to give or require consent to medical treatment. It is assumed by law that a person who has attained majority can act autonomously. From this premises it can be argued that since autonomy is the root of the

---

Rev 795; Jansen, Blood Transfusion and Jehovah's Witnesses (1986) 2 *Critical care clinics* 91; John J. Paris, Compulsory Medical Treatment and Religious Freedom: Whose Law Shall Prevail? (1973) 10 *Univ. of San Francisco L. Rev.* 25; Showwalter, Decisions to Forego Medical Treatment: The Preferred Medical, Ethical and Legal Approach (1984) 29 *Cath.Law* 286.

[142] *Okonkwo* v. *MDPDT* (1999) 6NMLR (pt. 786)1(SC)

[143] In Okonkwo v. *MDPDT* the doctor was prosecuted before the Medical and Dental Practitioners Disciplinary Tribunal; though convicted, the conviction was eventually quashed by the Supreme Court. In *Malette* v. *Shulman* (1990) 67 DLR (4th0 321 the Ontario Court of appeal assessed the doctor to pay $22,000 for transfusing blood to the patient against her consent. See also PDG Skegg, *Law, Ethics and Medicine* (1984) p.79, A. McCoid, A Reappraisal of Liability for Unauthorised Medical Treatment (1957) 41 *Minnesota LR* 381.

[144] G. Robertson, Informed Consent to medical Treatment (1981) 97 1 *LQR* 102, see also *Pridham* v. *Nash* (1986) 33 DLR (4th) 304 (Ont. H. Ct)) consent form to treatment and unexpected situations); *Davis* v. *Barking, Haverig & Brentwood HA* [1993] 4 Med LR 85.

[145] Generally traditional understanding of capacity hardly focuses on understanding because it is taken as given if patient has attained majority. According to Kennedy & Grubb, *op. cit*, p.106, by so doing two distinct concepts are merged into one by confusing that which goes to actual capacity and that which goes to demonstrate its presence in a particular case.

presumption, it ought to follow that the emphasis should not be on age simpliciter, but sufficient understanding by the individual. Invariably the notion of capacity turns largely on the related question of understanding. If this analysis is taken as correct, then capacity takes on an individual-oriented bent. This is the position suggested by commentaries and case law development. Questioning the rationale of equating capacity with status or age, Skegg stated as follows:

> 'The view that at common law all minors are incapable of consenting to medical procedures results from a fundamental misconception of the position of such procedures in relation to the criminal and civil law. Medical procedures are not in a different category from other bodily touching. If minors are incapable by reason of their age alone of consenting to medical procedures, it would follow that they are incapable of consenting to other touching. This would have interesting consequences. There would not have been any need for the Tattooing of Minors Act 1989, for tattooist who tattooed a minor with only that minor's consent would commit a battery. So too would anyone who embraced a girl who had not attained the majority – unless on one view, the consent of her parents had just been obtained. Furthermore, a minor would not be able to give a legally effective consent to a haircut. There is no reason to believe that this is so, and cases have been decided on the assumption that minors can consent to medical touching and other applications of force.'[146]

The underlining reasoning of Professor Skegg was implicitly recognised by Addy J of the Ontario High Court in *Johnson* v. *Wellesley Hospital.* His Lordship rejected capacity as synonymous with age. He said:

> 'I can find nothing in any of the old reported cases, except where infants to tender age or young children were involved, where the courts have found that a person under 21 years of age was legally incapable of consent to medical treatment. If a person under 21 were unable to consent to medical treatment, he would also be incapable of consenting to other types of bodily interference. A position purporting to establish that any bodily interference acquiesced in by a youth of 20 years would nevertheless constitute an assault would be absurd...I feel that the law on this point is well expressed in the volume on Medical Negligence (1957) by Lord Nathan, p. 16: It was suggested that the most satisfactory solution to the problem is to treat an infant who is capable of appreciating fully the nature and consequences of a particular operation or particular treatment capable of giving an effective consent thereto.[147]

Gillick case[148] explicitly establishes that capacity is individual–oriented, and should be judged in the context of autonomy and understanding. The case established the

---

[146] Skegg, *Law, Ethics and Medicine* (1984) p. 512.

[147] (1970) 17 DLR (3d) 139 at 144-145, per Addy J; see also *Re W (a minor) (medical treatment)* [1992] 4 All ER 627 where s. 8 (i) of the English Family Law Reform Act, 1969 was considered in relation to the provision that majority is irrelevant in determining capacity to consent to Medical treatment.

[148] *Gillick* v. *West Norfolk and Wisbech AHA* [1986] AC 112; [1985] 3 All ER 402 [1985] 2 BMLR 11 per Lord Fraser; see also R v. Howard [1965] 3 All ER 684 at 685; [1986] 1 WLR 13 at 15, per Lord Parker CJ statement on capacity in the context of prosecution for rape where the victim is a minor.

'mature minor' principle in English medical jurisprudence. By it a patient who is a minor capable of understanding a proposed medical treatment and can express his own wishes could validly and effectively authorise the doctor to make examination or give treatment. In the light of the 'mature minor' principle, it can be boldly suggested that capacity has more to do with whether a patient has sufficiently understanding and intelligence to enable him understand what medical treatment is proposed.[149]

Applying the status analysis, it would prima facie be that a mentally disordered person is incompetent and so lacks capacity to give consent to medical treatment. However if it is understood as rooted in understanding, autonomy and self-determination then it would not be implausible to question the conclusion that a mentally retarded is always incompetent. Whether such a person can give consent would depend upon whether he understands and can come to a decision upon what is involved in medical treatment.[150] There is no doubt that most patients in mental hospitals, including those compulsorily detained can sufficiently understand and give legally effective consent. Competence requires the ability of the patient to understand rationally the nature of procedure, its risk and other relevant information.

The English Mental Health Act explicitly recognises that a mentally disordered patient may have capacity in law to consent or refuse treatment if he has sufficient understanding. [151] In *Re Maida Yetter*,[152] an application was made for the purpose of appointing a guardian to the patient so that the guardian can give consent to the performance of diagnostic and corrective surgery on the patient. The patient who was compulsorily detained pursuant to the Mental Health and Mental Retardation Act, 1966 was diagnosed of schizophrenia and chronic undifferentiated. She was discovered to have a breast discharge indicating the possible presence of carcinoma or breast cancer. The doctors recommended that a surgical biopsy with corrective surgery be performed on her. But she refused, stating that she was afraid because the death of her aunt followed such a surgery. William J held that her unwillingness to give consent should not be overridden because even though her position was irrational, it was a competent decision. His Lordship said:

> 'She has been consistent in expressing the fear that she would die if surgery were performed... are we then to force her to submit to medical treatment because some of her present reasons for refusal are delusional and the result of mental illness? Should we now override her original understanding but irrational decision?...Although we recognised the advise of medical experts as

[149] The mature minor principle is widely applied in many common law jurisdictions, including USA. See *C* v. *Wren* (1987) 35 DLR (4th) 419 (Alta CA).

[150] Skegg, *op. cit*, p. 56-57.

[151] Section 57 and 58 of Mental Health Act, 1983 (England).

[152] (1973) 96 D & C 2d 619 (CP Northampton PA), See also *Re Quackenbush* 383 A 2d 785 (1978) where a patients refusal for 40 year of medical surgery was upheld Re. L adult refusal of medical treatment (1994) All ER 819 See also Waltz & Scheuneman, Informed Consent to Therapy (1969) 64 *Northwestern L. Rev.* 628.

> to the need for early detection and treatment of cancer symptoms, upon reflection, balancing the risk involved in our refusal to act in favour of compulsory treatment against the greatest possible protection of the individual in furtherance of his own desires, we are unwilling now to overrule Mrs. Jetter's original irrational but competent decision.'

However in *Kaimowitz* v. *Michigan Department of Mental Health*,[153] the Michigan Circuit Court applied *simpliciter* the status analysis to hold that a mentally retarded patient has no capacity to give or refuse consent. The court adopted the view that even though an involuntarily detained patient may have sufficient IQ, the very nature of his incarceration diminishes his capacity to make a medical decision. It is suggested that the approach adopted by the honourable court on a compulsorily detained mental patient as incapable of giving consent is unfortunate. It is a position that does not enjoy the support of commentaries, case law and legislation.

It is clear that *Gillick* is an authority that rejects the status approach and in its stead, introduces the notion of capacity rooted in understanding. This is the position recommended by the English Law Commission.[154] Problems however surround how the word 'understanding' is construed. The operative test of understanding requires that we make clear (i) whether it is satisfied if the mental disordered patient or any patient for that matter understands all of what is involved in a medical treatment or (ii) whether it simply means that the patient though generally capable of understanding may not understand in sufficient detail what is involved in a particular case. It requires us to make clear whether the patient should exhibit a detailed or mere peripheral understanding i.e. simply ability to appraise treatment and its consequences. The speeches of the Law Lords in *Gillick* contain many inconsistencies in this respect, with no clear indication of which of the two views ought to more properly represent the law. It is however suggested that the second understanding is more aligned to authorities. An analysis of *Gillick* itself reveals that the Law Lords endorsed the general understanding test. It was clear that the mature minor in the case only had a general understanding of contraceptive, but could not in the particular circumstance be said to have detailed knowledge.

This would appear the only basis on which we can justify the conclusions of William J in *Re Maida Yetter*.[155] Her fear of death resulting from surgery based on the death of her aunt some fifteen years was certainly irrational. The evidence of conversation with the case worker attached to her (as shown in the record of proceeding on what basis a decision was reached not to override her refusal to surgery) did not show that she did understand all what was involved in the treatment and its consequence. If she did. William J would not have made reference that he had considered and recognised the advise and advantages of medical experts

[153] (1973) 42 USLW 2063, cited in Kennedy & Grubb, *op. cit*, p. 117.

[154] See Law Commission Consultative Paper, Mentally Incapacitated Adults and Decision – Making: A New Jurisdiction (Cmnd. No 128, 1993) and Mentally Incapacitated Adult and Decision-Making: Medical Treatment and Research (Cmnd. No 129, 1993) where in recommends cognition is the operating test for capacity.

[155] (1973) 96 D & C 2d 619 (CP Northampton PA).

request for surgery, but would turn it down on the basis of the patient's 'irrational but competent decision.' His Lordship must have said so because the patient did not understand in detail particulars all what was involved. She nonetheless had a peripheral understanding. This must be the preferred way to construe the word 'understanding'. For example in *Gillick* the statement by Lord Frazer that 'I do not believe that a person aged 15, who may be living away from home, is incapable of applying on his own behalf for inclusion in the list of a doctor for medical service of an ordinary kind not listed with contraception,'[156] is an indication that to qualify as a mature minor all the patient need exhibit is clear and convincing evidence that he is minor enough to appreciate the consequences of his action and exercise the judgment of an adult in general terms.[157]

Even when an adult exercises the right of consent he is not required to understand all that is involved.[158] All that is required is capacity for general understanding. This is not surprising. Not trained as a doctor the patient can hardly appreciate medical treatment procedures as a doctor. That notwithstanding the law requires that his treatment decisions should be respected. To require from mature competent patients general understanding and a higher standard for mature minors or mentally retarded person would certainly be paradoxical to say the least. It is therefore suggested that the *Gillick* case in general endorsed the peripheral understanding notion.

Understanding in this context is not confined to medical procedure, though it is central. The example of a child living outside employed by Lord Frazer certainly will include knowledge and understanding of general 'worldly matters'. In some jurisdictions conscientious judges have had to quiz patients who for example refuse medical treatment. Report has it that the practice of these judicial officers has proceeded on the basis of quizzing patients on many, though related questions, bordering on their refusal. For example, when a young man refused medical blood transfusion on the grounds of religion, the judge quizzed him about his religious belief, also asking him other basis questions to determine conviction such as the names of the first five books of the Bible. Certainly these are questions designed to test general intelligence and conviction. Therefore sufficient understanding can be made purposive to mean general understanding.

Not to be missed is the important difference that exists between actual knowledge and general knowledge, i.e. an analysis of understanding in category (i) and (ii) above. There is no doubt that (ii) represents the law better. The distinction between both categories also brings to fore notion of capacity rooted in understanding and autonomy. It is conceivable that a person with actual understanding only arrives at a medical decision based on what he is told, i.e., information given to him. This would mean that the patient's understanding can be coloured by what others, whether his parent, friends or doctor give to him. In effect

[156] *Gillick* v. *West Norfolk & Wisbech AHA* [1986] AC 112.
[157] *Johnston* v. *Wellesley Hospital* (1970) 17 DLR (3d) 139.
[158] *Okonkwo* v. *MDPDT* (1999)6 NWLR (pt. 786)1.

the patient's refusal on consent to treatment can hardly be considered real. For example if a doctor gives scanty information about a medical procedure, consent or otherwise of the patient would naturally be based on the quality of the information offered. It would be absurd to make competence dependent on such a preposterous ground. If anything, *Re T (adult: refusal of treatment)*[159] is indicative that actual understanding ought not be the proper way to construe the word 'understanding'. The case involved a mature minor 24 weeks pregnant, involved in a road traffic accident. Although she was brought up by her mother, a fervent Jehovah's Witness, she was not a member of the faith. She executed a form of refusal to blood transfusion. When her condition deteriorated and she was transferred to an intensive case unit, Ward J granted a declaration that in the circumstances then prevailing, it would not be unlawful for the hospital to administer a blood transfusion on ground that it would be in her best interest. The English Court of Appeal was of the view that her decision on no-blood was only in form, not real because she took the decision in circumstances that suggested that her autonomy was overridden by the influence of her mother. Even though the decision has been criticised and possible explained on the ground that 'the court adopted the undue influence approach out of a desire that the patient should not die',[160] it is an authority suggestive of depreciation of the actual understanding approach. This should be so because it can be said that the patient did have actual knowledge, in the sense that she did not desire a blood transfusion based of course on what her mother had told her, but her understanding was deemed unreal in that it was held in ignorance. Perhaps the preferred position is general understanding or capacity to understand approach.

Even though there appears some statement in *Gillick* case that understanding ought to be restricted to the nature of medical treatment, there is good reason to suggest that its scope is more. Lord Scarman, was sure that understanding is not necessarily limited to the nature of medical procedure. He stated that understanding involves and includes moral and family questions, especially relationship with parents, problems associated with pregnancy, its termination and the risk resulting from sexual intercourse.[161] This is suggestive that the scope of understanding can and does include general matters. If that be the case, as is suggested, then the general understanding approach fits more into analysis of understanding than the actual understanding approach.

(ii) Voluntariness of Consent

Next after establishing capacity, the doctor must show that the patient's consent is real in terms of its voluntariness. By the 'rationality' approach, voluntariness is judged and justified by reference to the patient's reasoning on medical treatment. In effect the patient's conclusion to accept or refuse a particular medical procedure

---

[159] [1992] 4 All ER 649 [1992] 9 BMLR 46 (CA).

[160] Kennedy & Grubb, *op cit* 238.

[161] *Gillick* v. *West Norfolk & Wisbech AHA* [1986] AC 112 at per Lord Scarman.

must reflect proper reasoning. When it does, the patient is said to exhibit real consent. The rationality approach is itself social and legal. It requires us to draw an often omitted distinction between consent borne out of belief or values uncommonly held by the patient and those that are based on a misperception of reality. Take for example, a case having to do with two patients who refuse say blood transfusion. One does on grounds of religion, the other on grounds that because blood is red it must be poisonous. Both do not fall in the same category. Given that some find refusal of blood transfusion on both grounds irrational, but that is where the similarities between the two end. The patient in the first case draws a conclusion based on his value system. Provided the patient's decision is consistent with it, we can only challenge it by refusing to accept his value system, a stance the law does not allow us take. By contrast, the second example can be faulted if we can show that it is based upon a false foundation of fact. In this case we can treat the patient as one who does not understand what is involved in treatment. Unlike the first patient who understands what is involved but rejects the treatment nonetheless based on his values, the second's refusal can be considered unreal and should be overridden.[162] According to Kennedy & Grubb, the court in respecting autonomy in this context must draw the line of difference between situations one and two. As stated the patient's wish in the first category is the product of a belief or a value system. In the second case it is a misperception of reality. Only in cases of misconception of reality will it be proper to override the patient view because then the decision not to respect the patient's autonomy does not undermine his right of autonomy. The patient this category cannot be said to understand what is involved in the proposed medical procedure.[163]

In *Re T (adult: refusal of treatment)*[164] the English Court of Appeal held that the patients decision on blood was not real because it was based solely on the persuasion or undue influence of her mother. Interestingly, the court was of the view that if the patient had been a witness her refusal and or consent would have been legally effective. Though most of the cases having to do with refusal to consent to a particular medical procedure have had to do with religious beliefs, especially of Jehovah's witnesses and Christian Scientist, it is not impossible to conceive of cases where it may arise outside the context of religious belief, as was the case in *Re Maida Yetter*.[165] The patient's refusal of a proposed breast surgery was based on fear that some fifteen years ago her aunt died from a similar operation.

In determining the reality of consent courts have had to consider how the patient weighed and balanced the relevant facts, and the circumstances of the patient. In *Re T* the close relationship between the patient and her mother and the fact that her illness made her more susceptible to her persuasion weighed against her

---

[162] Kennedy & Grubb, *op. cit*, 137.

[163] Ibid, see also Law Commission Consultation Paper No. 129 (Cmmd. No 129 of 1993) para. 2.14 – 2.16.

[164] [1992] 4 All ER 649, See also *R* v. *Blaue* [1975] 1 WLR 141; *Re W (a minor)(medical treatment)* [1992] 4 All ER 627.

[165] (1973) 96 D & G 2d 619.

refusal. No doubt patients who come under severe illness may experience more readily undue influence of others, especially from close relatives that would require a more careful scrutiny of their treatment choices. They can under such condition be easily overreached.[166]

(iii) Informed Consent

Though some commentaries equate a valid consent with the concept of informed consent, it must be stated in the outset that they mean different things, especially in the context of our discussion. The requirement of informed consent is merely one of the essential ingredients of a valid consent. Informed consent is related to the scope and nature of information given the patient by the doctor and how the patient's subsequent consent relate to it. *Chatterton* v. *Gerson*[167] provided a classical illustration of it. The plaintiff was treated by the defendant specialist for chronic pains. The treatment however rendered her right leg completely numb and so impaired her mobility. Her claim for battery and medical negligence were dismissed by Bristow J. because she was informed in broad terms of the nature of the procedure intended and she gave consent. He however stated that if in appropriate cases (inapplicable to the facts of the case before him) it were shown that information is withheld in bad faith from the patient, then consent would be vitiated.

Similar question arose for determination in *Sidaway* v. *Bethlehem Royal Hospital Governors*.[168] The patient underwent an operation to relieve her pains in the neck and shoulders. She was informed of possible disturbance of a nerve root and the resultant risk. After the operation her spinal cord was damaged. She alleged that she was not told of the possible risk to spinal cord and so she sued for negligence. Her claim was dismissed. The court stated the law from a paradigm drawn from the tort of battery. According to Donaldson MR:

> 'Consent is not vitiated by a failure on the part of the doctor to give the patient sufficient information before the consent is given. It is only if the consent is obtained by fraud or misrepresentation of the nature of what is to be done that it can be said that an apparent consent is not a true consent.'[169]

By so doing the court approved the scope of the ratio in *R* v. *Clarence*[170] and *R* v. *Flattery*[171] as raising equal application in the context of medical treatment. This

---

[166] *Re T (adult: refusal of treatment)* [1992] 4 All ER 649, per Donaldson LJ stated that capacity may be deprived or reduced by temporary factors such as confusion, shock, fatigue, pain or drugs used in treatment.

[167] [1981] QB 432, [1981] 1 All ER 257, *Hills* v. *Potter* [1983] 3 All ER 716, see also MA Somerville, Structuring the Issues in Informed Consent (1981) 24 *McGill L.J.* 730; J Keown, The Ashes of AIDS and the Phoenix of Informed Consent (1989) 52 *MLR* 790, G Robertson, Informed Consent to Medical Treatment (1981) 97 *LQR* 102.

[168] *Sidaway* v. *Bethlehem Royal Hospital* [1984] 1 All ER 1018 (CA); [1985] AC 871, [1985] 1 All ER 643 (HL). See also *Freeman* v. *Home Office* (No 2) [1984] 1 All ER 1026.

[169] Ibid.

[170] (1888) 22 QB.D 23; *R* v. *Boldue* (1967) 63 DLR (2d) 82 (CanSupSt).

[171] (1877) 2 QB.D 410; *Papadimitropoulos* v. *R* (1957) 98 CLR 249.

analogy with the tort of assault and battery was however criticised as unwarranted by Lord Scarman (on appeal to the House of Lords). His Lordship expressed the view that 'it would be deplorable to base the law in medical cases of this kind on the tort of assault and battery.'[172] Equating defective consent action in the tort of battery with medical negligence is unfortunate. It is a mixture of two concepts that ought to be distinct. True, an action for defective consent may square in any or all of the two grounds, but that does not make them the same. In the context of medical treatment they exhibit differences in such matters as 'onus of proof, causation, the importance of medical evidence, the significance of medical judgment, proof of damage and, most important, of course, the substantive basis upon which liability is rooted.'[173]

Unfortunately the *Sidaway* case and all the authorities built on it have failed to draw the line between information going to the 'nature and purpose' of a proposed medical treatment and information relating to possible risk from a medical procedure. While the former properly squares in the tort of battery, it is not central to a claim based on negligence which makes central the disclosure of attendant risk from treatment. Where the essence of a patient's complaint is that he has suffered from a risk undisclosed or insufficiently disclosed, even though he consented to medical treatment, the claim ought to be one for negligence not battery. In a claim for battery the important question at stake is the amount of information that the patient need have to be able to understand the nature and purpose of a proposed medical treatment; a matter not necessarily coterminous with information concerning risks attending it.

Battery and negligence go to the root of the ingredient of informed consent in that they reveal whether or not there exist consent to the nature and purpose of medical treatment and whether a patient consent to an attendant risk results from treatment. In the context of the later i.e. negligence, it is crucial to determine what information will do and whether there is a positive duty on the doctor to keep his patient informed of all aspects of treatment, even if the patient does not ask question.

This was one of the issues considered by the House of Lords in *Sidaway* v. *Bethlehem Royal Hospital*.[174] Lord Bridge for his part divided the doctor's duty into three (i) diagnosis (ii) advice and (iii) treatment. According to his Lordship the test applied for (i) and (iii) is the *Bolam* test, i.e., that the doctor should exhibit the skill of an ordinary skilled man exercising and professing to have that special skill. The law however remains controversial as to the standard test for (ii) i.e. advice. The statements of the Law Lords (Lords Bridge, Templeman, Scarman, Diplock and Keith) reveal different standard test on matters of non-disclosure. Lord Diplock expressed the view that *Bolam* test constitutes the benchmark for determining whether a doctor's non-disclosure is negligence i.e. whether he has acted in

[172] *Sidaway* v. *Bethlehem Royal Hospital* [1984] 1 All ER 643, at 650, per Lord Scarman.
[173] M A Somerville, Structuring the Issues in Informed Consent (1981) 26 *McGill L.J.* 760.
[174] [1984] 1 *All ER* 1018 (CA); [1985] AC 871, [1985] 1 All ER 643 (HL).

accordance with standard practice recognised by a body of competent doctors. Lord Scarman however rejected the *Bolam* test as applicable. Neither did Lord Bridge (with whom Lord Keith concurred) and Lord Templeman go as far as to reject *Bolam* explicitly,They also did not rely on it wholly. Lord Bridge started that a doctor would be liable for negligent non-disclosure if disclosure of a particular risk was so obviously necessary for an informed choice on the part of the patient that no reasonably prudent doctor will fail to make it. For Lord Templeman, he drew a distinction between risk of a general nature and special risk. The former is one that should be known to the patient and so no duty to disclose will arise. The later may require specific information.

This leaves the law in a confused state and some pessimist may resort to commend Dunn LJ statement in *Sidaway* that 'the concept of informed consent forms no part of English law.' [175] But that will be more a thinking that is wrong than right. The concept is undoubtedly part of today's medical philosophy. A doctor has a duty to disclose to his patient 'any fact which is necessary to form the basis of an intelligent consent by him to a proposed treatment.'[176] If the concept is analysed from the two perspectives of 'patient standard' and 'professional standard,' the former is more squared in battery and the later in negligence and the professional requirement of disclosure.

A careful reading of *Sidaway* suggested two specific aspects on disclosure. One, that risk of procedure must be disclosed subject only to therapeutic reasons which may justify non-disclosure. Two, there exist therapeutic or professional privilege to withhold information that might be psychologically damaging to the patient. Interestingly, Lord Bridge also said that 'when questioned specifically by a patient of apparently sound mind about risk involved in a particular treatment proposed a doctor's duty in my opinion, is to answer both truthfully and as fully as the questioner requires.'[177]

This must be so. The fact that the patient ask question is likely to be connected with that he apprehend a certain degree of risk and it would be unethical if the doctor fails to make the needed disclosure. Unlike the rather cautious approach in England, progress in America has steadily moved in the direction of the patient's autonomy. The result is that the American jurisdiction witnesses more malpractice litigation. Though the present state of law in England is more doctor oriented and can encourage a more therapeutic atmosphere for doctor—patient relationship in which doctors would increasing involve their patients in decision-making, there still remains a need to make the standard required clearer. It is suggested that the Nigerian courts should follow the more therapeutic approach of England as traced out in *Sidaway*, rather than the American patient autonomy swing.

---

[175] (1985)AC 871, (1985)1 *All ER* 643

[176] I Kennedy, The Patient on the Clapham Omnibus (1984)47 MLR 454

[177] (1985) AC871

Voluntariness of Consent

In this context the law is concerned about the willingness of the patient in giving consent. To use the words of Lord Donaldson MR in *Re T (adult: refusal of medical treatment)* the real question for determination turns on

> 'does the patient really mean what he says or is he merely saying it for a quiet life to satisfy someone else or because the advise and persuasion to which he has been subjected is such that he can no longer think and decide for himself?'[178]

If the patient is clear as to his consent or refusal, it must be respected by the doctor. Sometimes however, the doctor may misinterpret the fact of consent especially in cases where the patient does not really mean what he says. To determine the reality the doctor in a clinical treatment may need to do factual evaluation of the situation to arrive at a reasonable conclusion.[179] Mistake in this circumstance cannot be ruled out. A doctor acting in good faith may wrongly interpret the data received from a patient. If in that state he, for example, proceed to treatment without consent interpreting the data received as mistakenly authorising treatment, it is suggested that he will not come under liability for either battery or negligence.[180] It is only an unreasonable mistake that should prima facie give rise liability.[181]

Limits on Consent to Treatment

Generally in the area of criminal law the law does not justify every invasion on a person's body on the ground of consent. While consent may be a valid defence to an assault, the Criminal Code does not make such exception to serious assault-occasioning harm.[182] In the context of medicine, Lord Griffiths in *Re F*[183] stated that in the interest of the public, consent should not provide a blanket to every medical treatment. The facts of the case concerned the sterilisation of a mentally retarded adult woman. In the views of his Lordship, it is too blanket to state that because an individual is master over his body that the law will not impose certain constrains on the right to consent. The law imposes certain constrains on the type of harm a person can inflict on himself.

Since surgery and other invasive medical procedure can involve hurt it may be imagined that these should also be pigeonholed in the same mould as assault occasioning harm. But there is good reason for treat it different. Medical treatment may occasion hurt, but in a beneficial manner, in the sense that it benefits the body.

---

[178] [1992] 4 *All ER* 649; *Freeman* v. *Home Office (No 2)* [1984] QB 524, [1984] 1 All ER 1036.

[179] *Malette* v. *Shulman.* (1990)67 DLR(4th) 321

[180] Noteworthy of mention is that the juridical basis for battery and negligence are different. In the former the patient does not need to prove damage while in the later he must do so.

[181] Kennedy & Grubb, *op. cit.*, p. 241, see also *Fletcher* v. *Fletcher* (1859) 1 E & E 420.

[182] See Sections 189-190 of the Criminal Code.

[183] [1990] 2 AC 1, [1989] 4 BMLR 1; see also *A-Gs Reference (No 6 of 1980)* [1981] 2 All ER 1057, per Lord Lane CJ.

This is why it is legally possible to give consent to say surgery. But we must admit that invasive treatments may not always be geared to better health.[184] In fact, certain surgery is designed to make a patient less well. Consider for a moment. If a patient for purposes of organ transplant consents to the removal of an organ, say one of his kidneys, would we classify the treatment as battery or one within the bracket for which the law should exclude from that bracket? Can we logically treat the removal of the organ as beneficial to the patient? Since the ultimate benefit is a third party and generally the law is reluctant to use a third party benefit as the basis for reaching a decision on a patient's informed consent,[185] would it be consistent to treat such treatment as one for which a patient can effectively give legal consent? According to Skegg, such treatment should be considered not unreasonably dangerous in that its benefit to the recipient third party outweighs possible detriment to the donor patient. On this basis the operation should not be treated as battery. A similar reasoning will also apply to some non-therapeutic medical experimentation and treatment e.g. bodies plastic surgery. If the court consider an activity socially acceptable, it is unlikely that it will question it and treat it as a procedure for which consent will not cover.[186] In *Corbett* v. *Corbett (otherwise Ashley)* a sex reassignment operation, Ormred J said,

> 'there is obviously room for differences of opinion on the ethical aspects of such operation but, if they are undertaken for genuine therapeutic purposes, it is a matter for the decision of the patient and the doctors concerned in his case.'[187]

The public policy perspective of the *Corbett*-type of operation was however questioned in *R* v. *Tan*.[188] But that does not derogate from our early proposition that if judges regard an activity as socially acceptable they are unlikely to question its propriety. In addition to the common law there exist certain statutes that limit consent, e.g., the (English) Prohibition of Female Circumcision Act, 1985. The Act prohibits female circumcision even by a consenting adult.[189]

Prerogative Powers

The court's jurisdiction over a child may be in the form of wardship or its inherent jurisdiction. Wardship jurisdiction according to Latey J derives from allegiance to

---

[184] P D G Skegg, *Law, Ethics and Medicine* (1984) p. 43; Kennedy & Grubb, *op cit* p. 245.
[185] *McFall* v. *Shimp* (1978) 10 Pd Dac 3d 90.
[186] Skegg, *op. cit*; see also *A-G Reference (No 6 of 1980)* [1981] 2 All ER 1057.
[187] [1970] 2 All ER 33.
[188] [1983] QB 1053; *Rees* v. *United Kingdom* [1987 2 FLR 111 (Ect HR); *Cossey* v. *United Kingdom* (1990) 13 EH RR 622.
[189] See ss. 1 and 2 of the Prohibition of Female Circumcision Act, 1985.

the Crown and the duty of the Crown to protect.[190] This is so especially towards minors because they are generally vulnerable. What the court does is to make a child its ward and thereon make decisions in the interest of it which overrides the rights of the parents. In appropriate cases, the court may also make decisions that affect other third parties which the parents could not themselves have made, e.g., an order of injunction restricting publication about the ward or the ward's family circumstances.[191] Noteworthy of mention is that wardship jurisdiction is restricted by the following limitations: (i) it is a jurisdiction vested in the English court by virtue of the Supreme Court Act.[192] In Nigeria the jurisdiction is governed by the Children and Young Persons Act. It follows from this that the jurisdiction will end when the minor attains majority; and (ii) once a wardship jurisdiction is invoked by the court no decision pertaining the child can be taken without the consent to the court.[193]

Beside the courts wardship jurisdiction that exist by statute, there exist an inherent jurisdiction in the court. This jurisdiction often referred to as the *parens patriae* jurisdiction is exercisable whether a child is or is not a ward of the court.[194] According to Lord Donaldson MR in *Re W (a minor refusal of treatment)* 'the only additional effect of a child being a ward of court stems from its status as such and not from the inherent jurisdiction, e.g., a ward of court cannot marry or leave jurisdiction without the consent of the court.'[195]

It has been suggested that the inherent *parens patriae* jurisdiction is exercisable by the High Court of the power of the state. Theoretically the power is without limit unlike the wardship jurisdiction which derives from statute. [196] When the court invokes its inherent jurisdiction unlike its wardship jurisdiction, the court does not take upon itself to make all decisions regarding the life of the child. The court can only determine certain specific issues relating to the upbringing of the child e.g. his medical care. But under this guise the court cannot make additional decision such as that child should not marry,etc.

Tega Esabunor v. *Faweye* [197] is a Nigerian case that attempted to consider the ambits of the power. In the magistrate court of Lagos State the police sought an

---

[190] *Re X (a minor) (Wardship: restriction on publication* [1975] 1 All ER 697 at 700-701; per Latey J and Lord Donaldson MR in *Re C (a minor) (wardship; medical treatment)* (No 2) [1989] 2 All ER 791 at 793-794; see also Lowe & White, *Wards of Court*, 2nd ed, 1986, chapter 1, cited in Kennedy & Grubb, *op. cit*, p. 253.

[191] See S. 41 of The English Supreme Court Act, 1981 and order 90 of the Supreme Court Rules (RSC) See section 27 and 30 of The Children and Young Persons Law Cap 25 of the Laws of Lagos State and *Esabunor* v. *Faweya*, unreported judgment of Magistrate Court, Lagos in Suit No. M/73/97.

[192] Ibid.

[193] *Re D (a minor) (wardship: Sterilisation)* [1976] Fam 185.

[194] *Re M and N (a minor) (wardship: freedom of publication* (1990) 1 All ER 205 at 210 [1990] Fam 211 at 223.

[195] [1992] 4 All ER 627.

[196] *Re L* [1968] 1 All ER 20 at 25, [1968 P. 119 at 157; *Re X (a minor) (Wardship: restriction on publication)* [1975] 1 All ER 697 at 706.

[197] The Magistrate's Court ruling was delivered on 12 May 1997 in Suit No. M/73/97 (In the matter of Tega Esabunor (a child): *Police* v. *Rita Esabunor*).

application against the minor patient's mother for an order that the medical authorities of the clinic of Chevron Nigeria Limited be allowed to do all and anything necessary for the protection of the life and health of the patient. The minor patient who was a three week baby was alleged to be in critical condition that required blood transfusion refused by the mother. Olokoba, (as he then was) sitting as Chief Magistrate made the order sought. Thereafter the mother brought an application as next of friend for an order of certiorari to quash the order authorising transfusion. She also sought damages against the hospital, its doctor, and the police for battery. The respondent argued that the lower court had no inherent jurisdiction beyond sections 27 (i) and 30 of the Children and Young Person Law Cap 25 of the Laws of Lagos State under which the order was made. Some part of this is missing.

Scope of proxy power on the treatment of a child

If there is a legally effective proxy consent document on the treatment of a child it becomes relevant to determine the scope of the proxy's power. A child's proxy must act in its best interest. That is the direction dictated by various legislation relating to children.[198] The best interest standard invariably would require that medical intervention should only be for therapeutic best result to the child. In *S* v. *S*, and *W* v. *Official Solicitor (or W)*,[199] (both appeals jointly heard) paternity was the issue that arose in the divorce proceedings. Blood test were ordered. On the rationale for it Lord Reid said:

> 'A court can only order a blood test of a child in the exercise of the old Chancery jurisdiction acting on behalf of the sovereign as *parens patriae* and that when exercising that jurisdiction a court must act solely in the interest of the child disregarding all none general consideration.'

With some justification it can be argued that the cases above do not come within the bracket of therapeutic treatment. If anything, a blood test is non-therapeutic. If that be the case, as it respectfully suggested, it follows that if a medical intervention is non-therapeutic the court may nonetheless allow the proxy make a binding decision provided the treatment is not against the interest of the child. But that can be countered on the ground that since the blood test were ordered under the court's inherent jurisdiction, it is not good authorities for the proposition that parents can act as legal proxy for minor children in non-therapeutic treatments or research. There is force in this argument especially if it is admitted that the test were ordered with a view of making available to court relevant evidences on paternity.

---

[198] *Gillick* v. *West Norfolk & Wisbech ANA* [1986] AC 112, per Lord Scarman; *Re B (a minor) (wardship: Sterilisation)* [1987] 2 All ER 206 at 212, per Lord Hailsham.

[199] [1972] AC 24, [1970] 3 All ER 107.

The scope of proxy consent takes on significance with the growth of modern medical procedures that make possible organ transplant. Since such transplant can hardly be within the boundaries of therapeutic treatment, it is important to determine whether parent or caregivers can give effect legal consent to organ harvest from a minor. There are three options open to the law: (i) treat such intervention as absolutely prohibited (ii) prohibit them except with court's authority and (iii) adopt a less restrictive stance by placing safeguards.

In *Hurt* v. *Brown*,[200] the parents of identical twins aged about 7 sought permission to have a kidney taken from the healthy twin transplanted to the other suffering from kidney disease. The defendants were the physician and the hospital where the proposed operation was to take place. They refused the use of their facilities unless the court grants the parents a right to give consent. The court held that a court of equity does have the power to permit the natural parents to give consent. In the view of the court, *Bonner* v. *Moran* was a good authority that non-therapeutic operations can be legally permitted on a minor as long as the parents or guardian consent to the procedure. The court stated:

> 'to prohibit the natural parents and the guardian *ad litem* of the minor children the right to give their consent under these circumstances, where there is supervision by the court and other persons in examining their judgment, would be most unjust, inequitable and injudicious.'[201]

Accordingly the court held that the parents could give consent on behalf of their children. Unfortunately in reaching the decision the court did not consider what the minor would have chosen if he were competent. Rather it was content to hold that the natural parent's could substitute their wishes for that of their children after a close and objective investigation of motives and reasons. This is recognition that whether or not the substituted judgment test is applied the governing principles for non-therapeutic intervention rest on the benefit doctrine to the donor, i.e., the benefit the donor would derive. The theory that the minor would have consented to the treatment if he were competent was made subordinate to the benefit theory. The donor twin was construed to benefit from the good health his brother would derive from the donation.

Little v. *Little* [202]was another American case. The mother of a 14-year mentally incompetent daughter sought court authority for the removal of a kidney from the daughter for a younger son suffering from a kidney disease. The court granted the application because in its view the circumstances were proper for its grant. The court was of the view that there was strong evidence to the effect that the donor daughter will receive substantial psychological benefit especially when there exists a close

---

[200] *Supra*, (1972) 29 Conn Supp. 368, 289 A 2d 386.

[201] (1941) 126 F 2nd 121 (USCA DC) a 15 year old consent to the removal of a skin patch for the benefit of his cousin (without his parents consent) was held ineffective.

[202] 576 SW 2d 493 (Tex Civ. 1979); see also *Struck* v. *Struck* (1969) 445 SW 2d 145 Pescinski 67 Wis 2d at 5, 226 NW 2nd 180; *In Re Guardianship of Eberhardy* 102 Wis 2d 539, 307 NW 2d 881 (1981).

relationship between the proposed donor and her brother. The fact that both parent consented and that the daughter had not been subjected to family pressure, that there was no medically preferable alternative and that the danger of the operation was minimal all added to make the grant easier to degree.

The courts in *Hunt*, *Little* and *Struck* showed that regardless of whether the authority to consent is exercised by the court or the parent or guardian of the minor, the key enquiry turns on the presence or absence of benefit to the potential donor – the best interest of the minor. In all the cases the best interest were thought to arise from the relationship existing between the donor and the recipient. In *Struck*, the donor was a brother to the recipient. In *Hunt* and *Little*, the sibling relationship was even thought to be stronger. In *Hunt* and *Little*, the parents gave consent to the donations.

Generally, in determining best interest of the minor the following requirement ought to be satisfied, namely; (a) the parents as consent-givers should be adequately informed of the risk-benefit to their child; (b) there must exist emotional support for the donor minor; (c) a close relationship must exist between the donor and recipient; and (d) a psychological benefit ought to result to the minor donor. Prima facie, requirement (d) would be satisfied if facts exist to imply (c) — a close relationship between the parties.

Most of these cases were reviewed by the Illinois Supreme Court in *Curran* v. *Bosze*.[203] The applicant who was the husband of the respondent sought an application to find that a medical emergency exist and order the respondent to produce their minor twin children to a blood test to determine their computability as potential bone marrow donors to one Jean. The respondent refused the consent. The facts of the case show that while the twin minor children belong to the parties, Jean was the child of the applicant from another woman. On the basis that there was no evidence that the twin as potential donors and Jean know each other as a family and objection was raised by the respondent who was the care-giver of the twins, the court refused the application. The cases establish that the court will allow for non-therapeutic intervention if it is in the best interest of a child. The word 'best interest' is here used not as a word of art. It requires the court to consider many relevant matters having to do with the welfare of the child or minor.[204]

It is plausible to sometimes question the philosophical basis of court's decisions in this context. For example, it can be asked if in a proxy consent scenario whether it is logical to ascribe to the court the position of decision—maker or that of a reviewer of the parent's proxy consent? If we adopt the first position, then we may well question fundamental ethos of freedom and the basis of civilisation. Arrogating parental powers to courts strike at the root of long cherished basis of civilisation founded on concept of family solidarity. Should not parents be treated as primary

---

[203] (1990) 566 NE 2d 1319.

[204] *Re C (a minor) (wardship: medical treatment)*. [1989] 2 AII ER 782; Re B (a minor) (wardship medical treatment) [1981] 3 AII ER 927; [1981] I WLR 1421; *Re J (a minor) (wardship: medical treatment)* [1990] 3 AII ER 930.

consent givers? After all they decide so many basic things on behalf of their minor without question, such as, what school they attend, the friends they keep, etc. It would therefore be unjust and uncivilised for the courts to arrogate that position to itself. In fact, the cases of *Little*, *Hurt* and *Struck* reveal that basically all the court have done is to review the decision of the parents to make it more rounded in the best interest of the child. The proper role of the court is to review, and not to usurp the role of parents as primary consent givers.[205]

One point requires clarification. If a doctor, against the wish of parents, recommends a medical procedure and the parent's request an available though riskier treatment, it appears that the court will uphold the procedure suggested by parents as primary care givers. The Council of Judges in America in a guideline said the following. 'If there is a choice of procedure which has only a 40% chance of success the doctor must take the medically riskier but parentally unobjectionable course.'[206]

Where however the choice is not between two medical procedures and the child's best interest will be compromised if medical treatment is not administered as recommended by the doctor or local authority, as the case may be, the court will override the parent's objection to the (only) recommended and available medical treatment. It was on this basis that Thorpe J in *Re S* [207]disregarded the parent's objection to blood transfusion for their minor child aged about four suffering from T-cell leukaemia. In *Re S*, the evidence established that there was only one treatment which carried a hope for the child. If it were otherwise, the court would have upheld the parents consent to alternative, even riskier treatment.[208] So the result would have been different if there were two or more therapies available.

Generally in granting an application the order of court is to be couched in the language of authorisation i.e. authorising a particular medical procedure suggested by the interested parties in the litigation process. The court should avoid making specific orders it cannot supervise, more so when in medical cases the last word would best rest with the doctor who is an expert; [209] though in exceptional case there may be wisdom in making positive specific orders.[210]

---

[205] Kennedy & Grubb, *op. cit*, p. 27.

[206] Guides to the Judge in Medical Order Affecting Children, issued by the council of Judges in America, referred to in the judgment of Thorpe J in *Re S (a minor) (medical treatment)* [1993] I FLR 376.

[207] [1993] I FLR 376; *Re E (a minor)* [1990] 9 BMLR 1; *Re O (a minor) (medical treatment)* [1993] 4 Med. LR 272; *Re (a minor)* [1993] 2 FLR 5.

[208] Kennedy & Grubb, *op. cit*, p. 272, see also *Tega Esanubor* v. *F.* (the possibilities of two therapies argument was not part before the court); *Re Hofbauer* (1979) 395 NE 2d 1109 (NYCA) custody of a Minor (1979) 393 NE 2d 836 (Mass Sup Jud Ct) and *Re Hamilton* (1983) 657 SW 2d 425 (Tenn. CA).

[209] M Somerville, Refusal of Medical Treatment in 'Captive' Circumstances (1985) 63 *Can. Bar Rev* 59 at 89; see also *Re J (a minor) (Wardship treatment)* [1992] 4 All ER 614.

[210] *Auckland AHA* v. *A.G* [1993] 1 *NZLR* 235 at 252, per Thomas J.

Adult and proxy consent

The general rule is that no legally effective proxy consent can be given on behalf of a competent adult.[211] It has been suggested in some cases that where the adult is unconscious or otherwise incapable of making a decision, a doctor may attempt to secure the consent of a relative.[212] But these cases appear to be overstatement of the law. In fact even if an adult were incompetent, it would appear that there would be no room for proxy consent. In *T* v *T*,[213] the court held that a guardian appointed for a mentally incompetent adult has no implicit power to consent to treatment on behalf of the patient. This is so no matter how beneficial or necessary the treatment may appear.[214]

The absence of legally effective proxy consent for an adult raises conceptual and practical problems. If a competent adult becomes unconscious, for example, the law must find a way of treating the patient that will be legally permissible. If the patient has previously stated his view about medical treatment, his views will be respected.[215] Where however the law permits proxy consent it becomes relevant to determine the extent to which the views and values of the patient will find expression in the decision of the proxy. This concern has led to the development of the concept of substitute judgment. It requires that the proxy should seek to make a decision that the patient would have made if he were competent in the circumstance. To do this the proxy is expected to reflect the views and values of the patient. In effect the proxy is expected to reflect the subjective values of the patient. This test have been used especially in cases of incompetent adult who become so as a result of mental retardness or become vegetative in the context of terminal illness.[216] It is thought that the substitute judgment test has ingredients of recognising and promoting self dignity, worth and integrity of the patient in the sense that the ultimate decision of the proxy closely aligns with what the patient would have himself made if he were competent. Unlike the 'best interest' test which seeks to decide what is best for the patient it seeks to treat the patient on the basis of this decision making. [217] Best interest test is rooted in what others consider best for the patient in the light of their view of the patient's interest.

---

[211] Skegg, *op. cit.*, 72.

[212] *Canterbury* v. *Spence* (1972) 464 F 2d 772 at 789, per Robinson J; *Bonner* v. *Moran* (1941) 126 F 2d 121 at 122-123; *Wilson* v. *Pringle* [1987] QB 237.

[213] [1988] Fam 52.

[214] Re B [1987] 2 All ER 206 at 210 per Dillion LJ, but cf. *Re Eve* [1986] 2 SCR 388 (Sup Ct. of Canada) where the court held that the ancient prerogative jurisdiction vest in court powers over mentally retarded patient. But cf Brenda Hoggett, The Royal Prerogative in Relation to the Mentally Disordered: Resurrection, Resuscitation or Rejection, in *Medicine, Ethics and Law* (MDA Freeman, ed.1988).

[215] *Malette* v. *Shulman* (1990) 67DLR(4th) 321.

[216] *Airedale NHS Trust* v. *Bland* [1993] 1 All ER 821, *Re Moe* [1982] 432 NE 2d 712; see also G Dworkin, Law and Medical Experimentation (1987) 13 *Monash Univ. Law Rev* 189 at 200; J Robertson, Organ Donation by Incompetents and Substituted Judgment Doctrine (1976) 76 *Columbia Law Rev.* 48.

[217] Robertson, above n. 216.

It is reasoned that if a patient were to make in advance a 'living will' he most likely would have chosen a scheme that will be in many respect close to what the substituted judgment test would dictate. Since the law will respect the choices of a competent adult even if others think that it irrational, it would logically follow that if a person becomes incompetent the substituted judgment test and not the best interest test will more closely accord with his dignity, value and wishes. To use the example of Robertson,

> 'the fact that a Jehovah's Witness is unconscious does not justify transfusing blood to save his life if he has previously made it clear that under no circumstances would he want a transfusion... nor should an unconscious person be maintained on an artificial life support system contrary to previously expressed preference if he would have been permitted to refuse treatment when conscious.'[218]

Where however the incompetent person is one who has never been competent before it may be argued that the premises for the application of substituted judgment evaporates in the sense that he had never at any time had a treatment wish.[219] To treat the substitute decision as his own would amount to mere conjunction and an illogical reason. Even that stance can be countered on the ground that it takes the argument too far. An argument on that premises would be suggestive of treating the incompetent as a non-thinking, non-choosing, irrational person. It can be argued that if the basis for applying the substituted judgment test is an attempt to know what choices a competent person with the characteristics, values, taste, preference of the incompetent would make to maximise his interests rather than treat him as a nobody then respect for the incompetent dictates nothing less.
Re Lucille Royal[220] was a case where a hospital sought to administer psychotropic drugs on a mentally ill patient who had rejected any use of medication on religious grounds when not mentally ill. The court held that her refusal should be respected unless compelling state interest justify overriding her refusal. Ferren, (Associate judge) recognised the philosophy of respect as the root for the substituted judgment concept, explicitly stating that it also applies to incompetents. He said;

> 'The court as surrogate for the incompetent, is to determine as best as it can what choice that individual if competent, would make with respect to medical procedures...we believe this approach is sound, whether religious preferences or other factors are involved, for it is the only way to pay full respect to the individuality and dignity of a person who has expressed clear, deeply felt, even sacred preferences while competent, but no longer has the capacity.'

---

[218] Robertson, *above* n. 6;; D. Brahams, Unwanted Life-sustaining Treatment (1990) 335 *Lancet* 1209; D. Lanham, The Right to Choose to Die with Dignity (1990) 14 *Crim. L.J.* 401; F. Rouse, Advance Directive: Where Are We Heading after Cruzan? (1990) 18 *Law Med Hlth Care* 353. See also *Malette* v. *Shulman* (1990) 67 DLR (4th) 321; *Airedale NHS Trust* v. *Bland* [1993] 1 All ER 821.

[219] *Re Eve* [1986] 2 SCR 388 (Sup Ct. of Canada); *Curran* v. *Bosze* (1990) 566 NE 2d (Illinois Sup. Ct).

[220] (1979) 403 A 2d 744 (DC Cir.); see also *Superintendent of Belchertown State School* v. *Saikewicz* 370 NE 2d 417 at 428 (Sup Jud Ct of Mass. 1977).

Some have doubted the applicability of the principle in England. Reference was made to it by Lord Donaldson MR in *Re T (adult: refusal of treatment)* [221] though his Lordships speech seemed to treat it as an aspect of the best interest test. In *Airedale NHS Trust* v. *Bland*, [222] both Lord Goff and Mustill doubted its incorporation in English law. As the law stands in England, unlike in America, it is difficult to say if substituted judgment notion is part of English law. It is however suggested that the principle should be applied by the Nigerian courts because it promotes respect for the dignity and values of the patient and it more represents the general philosophy that underline contemporary medical law and ethics. Writers has suggested that the English jurisdiction by not explicitly recognising substituted judgment leaves open three options for a logical development of proxy consent in this respect. They are: (i) that the law should allow the patient appoint his chosen health care proxy (ii) that the law should pressure those close to the patient to act as the patient's health proxy and (iii) if no one so stand in the position, the law should recognise that the doctor by necessity should act as he sees fit in the best interest of the patient.[223] The English Law Commission has suggested the addition of establishing a formal-decision making body.[224]

A vexed question that sometimes arises in the context of proxy has had to do with whether or not the court can act as sole substitute judgment decision maker. Connected with this is the prerogative powers of court.[225] Statutorily children may be made wards of court. Once that is done the court will have exclusive power to make all significant decisions relating to the child's treatment. The same would be applicable if the court invokes its *parens patriae* jurisdiction over a child. The difference between wardship and *parens patriae* is that while the court acting in the exercise of the former can make many other significant decisions about a child including medical treatment, the later is necessarily restricted to medical treatment decisions.

It is obvious that the court cannot invoke wardship jurisdiction over an adult. Whether it can invoke *parens patriae* jurisdiction over adult remains controversial. Even though Lord Templeman thought it could, the majority of the House suggested that the court has no such jurisdiction over adults.[226] As has been earlier

---

221 [1992] 4 *All ER* 649, *Re J (a minor) (Wardship treatment)* [1990] 3 All ER, 930, per Taylor LJ.

222 [1993] 1 *All ER* 821. The reasons of the Law Lords it has been submitted stems from a misunderstanding of the true nature of substituted judgment. See Kennedy & Grubb, *op. cit*, p. 289.

223 Kennedy & Grubb, *op cit* 293.

224 Consultative Paper: Mentally Incapacitated Adults and Decision-Making; An overview (Cmmd No 119 of 1991) (Cmmd No 129 of 1993) Law Commission England, In some jurisdiction, some hospital maintained ad hoc ethical committees that make several medical decision including matters relating to proxies.

225 On the juridical basis for wardship and the *parens patriae* jurisdiction, see *Re (a minor) (wardship: restriction on publication* [1975] 1 All ER 697 at 700-701, per Latey J; *Re C (a minor) (wardship: medical treatment)* (No 2) [1989] 2 All ER 791 at 793-794, per Lord Donaldson MR.

226 *Re B (a minor) (wardship Sterilisation)* [1988] AC 199 at 205 – 206, per Lord Templeman. Note that Kennedy & Grubb, *op cit* p. 299 have suggested that the question of the courts *parens patriae*

suggested the role of the court in this respect is not to take over decision making, but rather to complement the decision of the other proxy makers.[227]

The justification for proxy decision making, whether by relatives, courts and others, is grounded on its justification or lawfulness. If we begin from the premises that only the individual is sovereign over his body, than it follows that proxy decision making can hardly be an exception to the rule. Legal justification for proxy decision making was directly in issue in *Re F (Mental Patient: Sterilisation)*.[228] The adult patient was mentally retarded with the mental age of a child. She formed a close sexual relationship with a man and the hospital imagined she would be unable to cope with motherhood if pregnancy were to result from the relationship. Because all other form of contraceptive were unsuitable for her due to her peculiar medical condition the hospital suggested sterilisation. In justifying it, the court took the position that proxy finds justification in the common law of necessity.

It therefore follows that it is the necessity principle that justifies treatment given to a patient in circumstances where the patient is temporarily or permanently disabled from consenting. If it were not so it would mean that an incompetent who suffers from say malaria would be left to suffer because there would be no justification in treatment without his consent.

Adult refusal of treatment

It is now time to consider the question whether there is legal justification in overriding an adult refusal of treatment. Traditionally, the adult is sovereign over his body and going by that it can be argued that there can be no justification for forcible treatment, whether on the ground of necessity or emergency for the preservation of life. One early case having a bearing on these connected issues arose for determination in *Leigh* v. *Gladstone*.[229] The prisoner who was in custody refused feeding and so was forcibly fed by the prison authorities. In an action claiming damages for assault and battery, Lord Alverston CJ stated that the authorities have a duty to preserve the health and life of the prisoner in the custody of the Crown and so no action could lie for the forcible feeding. The authority was recently doubted in *A-G of British Columbia* v. *Astaforoff* [230]and *Airedale NHS Trust* v. *Bland* [231] In *Astaforoff,* the court stated that there is no authority whether moral or legal to forcibly feed a prisoner who refuse feeding in order to prevent alleged suicide. In the reasoning of the court, if the prisoner becomes unconscious or incapable of

---

jurisdiction was not an issue in the case, as the real issue was whether the proxy other than the court has decision making power.

[227] *Dept of Health* v. *JWB* (1992) 66 ALJR 300 (Aust. High ct); *Struck* v. *Struck* (1969) 445 SW 2d 145 (KY CA).

[228] [1990] 2 AC 1; [1989] 4 BMLR 1.

[229] (1909) 26 TLR 139 (King's Bench Div), per Lord Alverstone CJ.

[230] [1983] 6 WWR 322, on appeal [1984] 4 WWR 385 (Brit. Columbia ct of App).

[231] [1993] 1 All ER 821.

making a rational decision in which case there is no question of choice by the prisoner, that may warrant a different position. But in *Airedale NHS* v. *Bland*, Lord Keith appeared more unequivocal when he stated that the principle of sanctity of life 'does not authorise forcible feeding of prisoners on hunger strike.'[232]

Be that as it may, it would appear that the ethical questions involved in forcible treatment call to question an anxious balance between the right to self-determination or autonomy and society's interest in the preservation or sanctity of life and health of its member sometimes expressed in the criminalisation of suicide, abandonment crimes etc. These principles no doubt were in conflict in Airedale *NHS* v. *Bland*, and the House of Lords in unequivocal manner stated that the principle of preservation of life or its sanctity must be made subservient to the principle of autonomy. Going by this it would appear preposterous to authorise forcible treatment of a competent adult. Under this category we can class many cases of dying patients or patients at risk because of refusal of a particular treatment, eg., a refusal of blood transfusion.

It appears that a similar position is taken in the American jurisdiction. The right to refuse medical treatment is basic and fundamental. It is recognised as part of the right of privacy and autonomy protected by the common law. It has been said 'its exercise requires no one's approval and not merely one vote subject to be overridden by medical opinion.' [233]

If a doctor performs treatment in the absence of consent, that will be actionable battery. The obvious corollary is that a competent adult patient has the legal right to refuse medical treatment because his interests and desires are the key ingredients in the decision-making process. The right extend to and includes any medical treatment even that which may save or prolong life. [234] In *Bartling* v. *Superior Court*, where the question was whether the patient may refuse even life continuing treatment, Justice Hasting said:

> 'In this case we are called upon to decide whether a competent adult patient with serious illness which are probably incurable but have not been diagnosed as terminal has the right, over the objection of his physician and the hospital to have life-support equipment disconnected despite the fact that withdrawal of such devices will surely hasten his death...The right to have life support equipment disconnected is not limited to comatose, terminally ill patients or representatives acting on their behalf.'[235]

---

[232] Ibid., at 861, per Lord Keith. But cf. *R* v. *Stone* [1977] QB 354, [1977] 2 All ER 341 where the court of Appeal upheld the conviction of defendant who assured a duty of care of the deceased and thereafter failed to provide medical treatment based on the patients wishes that led to death of the patient. Prof Skegg, *Law, Ethics and Medicine* 113 – 114 however submits that it does not follow from the case that a doctor or caregiver is under a duty to provide medical treatment (of food). He submits further that the doctor in *R* v. *Blaue* [1975] 1 WLR 1411 owed a duty of care in the circumstances that was breached. But it is itself no authority that the obligation permits treatment without consent.

[233] *Bonvia* v. *Supreme Court* (1986) 225 Cal. Rptr 297 (Cal CA), per Beach. J.

[234] *Barber* v. *Superior Court* 147 Cal App 3d 1006, 195 Cal Rptr. 484 (1983).

[235] *Supra.*

Authorities and legislation recognise as fundamental the right of an adult to refuse treatment.[236] Some may argue that on plain ethical grounds refusal of treatment is tantamount to suicide. In fact, in *Bonvia* case it was argued that what the patient really wanted was to die, because he had already so expressed the desire. On this point the court held that the right exist and

> 'if a right exist, it matters not what motivates its exercise. The right is not restricted by motive. For it to be valid there is no requirement that it must meet someone else's approval. It is not considered illegal or immoral to prefer natural, albeit sooner, death than drugged life attached to a mechanical device,' according to Beach J.237 His Lordship though not directly distinguishing suicide from the right to refuse treatment, interestingly stated that 'suicide unlike the latter is a crime and its means involve affirmative, assertive, proximate, direct conduct'. Without more, one can state that while suicide is an ending of life, refusal of treatment is merely a choice about how a patient chooses to live. It is not suicide because the patient does not in law cause his death.[238]

Some writers have suggested that the right to refuse treatment is not absolute in character and that it involves the skilful balancing of other competing interest, e.g., societal interest in the preservation of life. This view enjoys judicial support.[239] But there also exist judicial recognition for treating the right as absolute.[240] Majority of the cases where the court chose to override the fundamental right to refuse treatment reveal one disturbing thing – they have to do with overriding the wishes of pregnant woman. It reflects nothing other than the patriarchal bias of law,

---

[236] *Bartling* v. *Superior Court* 163 Cal App 3d 186 at 189, 209.

[237] See for example the state of California Natural Death Act (Health and Safety Code, ss. 7185-7195, though addressed to the terminally ill patient, significantly is a legislation which expresses state policy that adult persons have the fundamental right to control the decisions relating to their medical case. Section 7188 provides the method whereby an adult may execute a medical directive for the withholding or withdrawal of life-sustaining procedures and s. 7193 state that the right will not be in any way impaired as it shall supersede any legal right or responsibility in any lawful manner'. Furthermore, statute gives a patient power to execute an effective legal power of attorney for health care – see s. 2500 of the civil code which state that "Notwithstanding this document, you have the right to make medical and other health care decisions for yourself as long as you can give informed consent with respect to the particular decision. In addition, no treatment may be given to you over your objection at the time.

[238] Argument along this line brings to fore the ethical justification of making a distinction between 'an act' and 'an omission', even if both bring about same consequences, see OF Emiri, Euthanasia and Treatment Cessation: A Paradox *Essence Jour. of Philosophy.*

[239] Kennedy & Grubb, *op. cit*, 340; see also *Re T (adult: refusal of medical treatment)* [1992] 4 All ER 649, per Lord Donaldson MR and Butler–Sloss LJ; *In the matter of Claire Conroy* (1985) 486 A 2d 1209; Re S (adult: refusal of medical treatment) [1992] 4 All ER 671: *Raleigh Fitkin Paul Morgan Memorial Hospital* v. *Anderson* (1964) 201 A 2d 537 (NJ Sup. Ct.), *Jefferson* v. *Griff in Spalding Country Hospital Authority* (1981) 274 GE 2d 457 (Sup Ct. Georgia); see discussion on these cases in which it is suggested that they do not properly represent the law in infra pp. 202 – 209, Emiri, *Medical Jurisprudence.*

[240] *Re AC* (1990) 573 A 2d 1253 (DC CA), referred to by Kennedy & Grubb, *op. cit*, 350, as "perhaps the most significant decision in the United States". See also *Airedale NHS Trust* v. *Bland* [1993] 1 All ER 821, especially Lords Keith, Goff and Mustill.

treating women as though less than men as a result of pregnancy. Majority of these seen to suggest that in 'truly extraordinary or compelling' situations the patient right ought to be subordinate, even though the judges admit that such instances should be rare.

Interestingly, the most significant authority in USA on this matter, *Re C* [241] rejects those exceptions, especially when the court in the guise of the unborn child puts a moral claim ahead of the mother's legal right.[242] In *Re F (in utero)* [243] the English Court of Appeal rejected the essence of *Re S*.[244] The court thought that it was not in line with medical law. This should be so because an unborn child cannot be made a ward of court.[245] On this basis it is submitted that the right to refusal ought to be construed in the light of Lord Mustill's observation in *Airedale NHS Trust* v. *Bland*.

> 'If the patient is capable of making a decision on whether to permit treatment and decide not to permit it his choice must be obeyed, even if on any objective view it is contrary to his best interest. A doctor has no right to proceed on the face of objection, even if it is plain to all, including the patient, that adverse consequences and even death will or may ensue...Thus it is that the patient who undergoing life maintaining treatment and decides that it would be preferable to die must be allowed to die, provided that all necessary steps have been taken to be sure that this is what he or she really desires.'[246]

If the wish is contained in a document, say in the form of a living will, there is sufficient judicial backing that it should be respected. Anticipatory refusal is legally equivalent to contemporaneous refusal. No appeal to 'necessity' can justify overriding it.[247]

Minor

Logically following the *Gillick* principle,[248] it is arguable that a mature minor can also refuse medical treatment regardless of the wishes of others. This is so because the House of Lords recognised that a child or minor in law is competent to make his

---

241 (1990) 573 A 2d 1253 (DC CA).

242 Nancy Rhoden, The Judge in The Delivery Room: The Emergency of Court – Ordered Caesareans (1986) 74 *CalLR* 1951; John Robertson, The Right to Procreate and the Utero Therapy (1982) 3 *J. Legal Med.*

243 [(1988] 2 All ER 193.

244 *Re S (adult: refusal of medical treatment)* [1992] 4 All ER 671.

245 *C* v. *S* (1988) QB 135; (1987) 1 All ER 1230; *Paton* v. *British Pregnancy Advisory Services Trustees* [1979] QB 276, [1978] 2 All ER 987, see also Lowe, Wardship and Abortion Prevention – Further Observations (1980) 96 *LQR* 29 ; 30, but cf. Fortin, Legal Protection for the Unborn child (1988) 51 *MLR* 54.

246 [1993] 1 All ER 821.

247 *Malette* v. *Shulman* (1990) 67 DLR (4th) 321; *Airedale NHS* v. *Bland* [1993] 1 All ER 821 at 860, per Lord Keith, at 866, per Lord Goff and at 892, per Lord Mustill; *Re T (adult's refusal of medical treatment)* [1992] 4 All ER 649.

248 *Gillick* v. *West Norfolk 1 Wisbech AHA* [1986] A C 112, [1985] 3 All ER 402.

own medical decisions if he has 'sufficient understanding and intelligence to enable him or her understand fully what is proposed.'[249] But in *Re R (a minor) (wardship; medical treatment)* [250] and *Re W (a minor) ((wardship; medical treatment)*,[251] the English Court of Appeal suggested that while a mature minor enjoys the right of consent to medical treatment, it would be stating the law too general to hold that his refusal to treatment should have the same force as that of a competent adult.

In *Re R*, the minor was 15 years old so could qualify as a mature minor. She was a ward under the court's wardship jurisdiction. She refused the administration of psychotic drugs on her by the local authority. The English Court of Appeal authorised overriding her refusal. This suggests that even if a child is a mature minor the right to refuse treatment can be limited if he is under the courts wardship jurisdiction. Thus it would invariable follow that if a Nigerian court put a mature minor within its statutory wardship jurisdiction, say under the Children and Young Persons Act, the court can override the child's refusal. While a mature minor may override his parent's choice, the case is different in wardship. The wardship powers of a judge includes power to give consent to medical treatment. So the wardship judge has wider power than a natural parent. Since wardship jurisdiction is not exercisable against an adult it is easy to see why refusal by a competent child does not have the same force as that of an adult.

It can however be counter argued that the case did not make such a proposition and that if it did it would be a decision *per incuriam* because the facts reveal that the patient was incompetent as a result of her mental conditions. Going by this, it would be that all their Lordships said have nothing to do with a competent child or mature minor. By stretch what it said about overriding refusal by a mature minor ought not to so apply, but should be restricted to patients within the bracket of incompetent children. Such counter argument does not really seem to capture the essence of the case. It is respectfully so because all the three judges (Lord Donaldson MR and Staughton, Farquharson LJJ) were in no doubt that their views also extended to the question of overriding the refusal of a competent child.

Lord Donaldson MR was pointed in his view that the court has power to override the refusal of a competent child. He stated:

> 'If Lord Scarman intended to go further than this and to say that in the case of Gillick competent child, a parent has no right either to consent or to refuse consent, his remarks were obiter, because the only question in issue was Mrs Gillick's alleged right to veto. Furthermore I consider that they would have been wrong...If the opinion in law is that upon the achievement of 'Gillick' competence there is a transfer of the right of consent from parents to child and there can never be a concurrent right in both, doctors would be faced with an intolerable dilemma, particularly when the child was nearing the age of 16.'

---

[249] Ibid.
[250] [1986] A C 112 at 188, per Lord Scarman.
[251] [1991] 7 *IBMLR* 147 (1992) Fam 11.

It has been suggested that the courts *parens patriae* jurisdiction (wardship and its inherent powers) were overly stretched in *Re R* and *Re W* because such a jurisdiction does not cover adult (the jurisdiction was founded in the necessity that the law should put under care incompetents, idiots and minor who cannot care for themselves).[252] That being the case there was no justification in applying it to mature minor. Mature minors should be treated as no different from adult.[253] Furthermore, the underlying medical ethos that demand respect for autonomy dictates respect for the wishes of the patient, whether adult or mature minor. If as *Gillick* decides, there is a right to consent to treatment, then by way of corollary, there is also a right to refuse treatment. No distinction should be drawn between consenting to and refusing to. They are merely two ways of exercising the same right. Making decision includes saying yes or no. That is how to see the exercise of the right of autonomy. Whatever, it is suggested that *Re W* and *Re R* do not derogate on the proposition that mature minors refusal to treatment cannot be overridden by the parents. This position is said to be different if the child is made a ward of court. It has been suggested, and rightly too, by Kennedy & Grubb, that the two cases threaten to undermine the gains of *Gillick* and so represents a disorderly development of the law relating to mature minor.[254] The learned writers have thus suggested a reconsideration of the general statements made in the two cases. We suggest that the law on mature adult and mature minor should be harmonised and made the same as to the right to say yes or no to medical treatment. A shift from an overtly paternalistic approach in medicine to one that emphasises choice and autonomy is preferred.[255]

[252] [1992] 4 All ER 627.
[253] *Re Eve* [1986] 2 SCR 388, *Wellesley* v. *Duke of Benufort* (1827) 2 Russ 1 at 20.
[254] Kennedy & Grubb, *op. cit*, 393.
[255] Ibid., p. 395.

Chapter Fifteen

Medical confidentiality and professional secrecy

Introduction

Even in the absence of a specific contractual duty to keep a patient's confidence, the common law puts a doctor under a duty to respect the confidence of his patient.[1] The legal underpinning is located in the fact that doctor-patient relationship is essentially characterised as one of a fiduciary nature. The obligation is supplemented by legislation in some jurisdictions.[2] It has been suggested that the scope of the duty covers information received directly and extends to those received indirectly in so far as they are received in the doctor's character as the patient's doctor.[3] Thus while the duty surely covers information and observation of the patient, it extends to information received from third parties in circumstances where the third party gives the information knowing of the existence of the doctor—patient relationship. Once information is received in his character as the patient's doctor, i.e. cum his professional capacity, it is immaterial whether it was gotten from a professional colleague or from a non-doctor. Both are indistinguishable. The duty of confidentiality applies to both.

Whether the duty will extend to cases where the third party is unaware of the doctor-patient relation remains controversial. In *A-G* v. *Guardian Newspapers Ltd (No 2)*[4] the English Court of Appeal subscribed to the proposition that there is public interest in the legal enforcement and protection of confidences received in circumstances of confidentiality. Flowing from this it can be argued that since a doctor receives information almost always in those circumstances he ought to come under an obligation of confidence. Some have suggested that in the context of information from third parties it must however be shown that the party knows of

---

[1] *Attorney—General* v. *Guardian Newspapers Ltd* (No 2) [1990] 1 AC 109, [1988] 3 AII ER 545 (there exist a public duty to protect confidential information) *Hunter* v. *Mann* [1974] 2 AII ER 114 at 417; WV Egdell [1990]] Ch 359, [1990] 1 AII ER 835 for general reading see D L Kenny, confidentiality; The confusion continues (1982) 307 New Eng. J. Med 1518, J Jacobs, confidentiality: the Danger of Anything weaker than the Medical Ethic (1982) 8 *J Med Ethics* 18; DFH Pherby, changing Practice on confidentiality. A case for concern (1982) 8 *J. M ed Ethics* 12 MH Kottow, Medical Confidentiality: An intransigent and Absolute Obligation (1986) 12 *J. Med. Ethics* 117.

[2] See Francis Gurry, *Breach of Confidence* (1985) cited in Kennedy & Grubb, *Medical Law* 2nd ed. London: Butterworth, 1994 at 637 and 639.

[3] Kennedy & Grubb, *op. cit*, p. 639 – 410.

[4] [1988] 3 All ER 545, [1990] 1 AC 109.

the doctor-patient relationship to raise obligation on the part of the doctor. Such an interpretation however puts too much force on the matter of third party's knowledge, a thing which ought to be general irrelevant to the philosophical reasons for the protection of secrets between the doctor and his patient.

The patients trust that information about his person will be kept secret unless he permits disclosure. It means in effect that confidentiality turns around how the patient perceives the trust held by the doctor. That being the case, it is the circumstance in which the doctor receives the information and not the knowledge of the informant of his status that ought to determine whether a duty does exist or not. That point was implicitly recognised by Lord Goff when he stated:

> "...a duty of confidence arises when confidential information comes to the knowledge of a person (the confidant) in circumstances, where he has notice or is held to have agreed, that the information is confidential, with the effect that it would be just in all the circumstances that he should be protected from disclosing the information to others."[5]

The statement puts beyond doubt that the enquiry ought to turn not on the knowledge of the informant, but rather on the knowledge of the confidant. In our case the doctor, whether the circumstances are such that he knows or ought to know that the information comes to him in confidence that makes it unfair to make disclosure. Accordingly, the better view will be that a duty is owed once the doctor is aware of the confidential nature of the information notwithstanding that the third party informant is unaware of his professional relationship with the patient.

From the days of Hippocrates until the present, doctors have bound themselves not to divulge professional secrets. A doctor ought to keep silent as to any thing he sees or hears while visiting or treating the sick which is improper to divulge.[6] The basis for this was well summarised by Lord Riddel. He said:

> 'A doctor being in fiduciary capacity must preserve his patients confidence unless relieved from the obligation by some lawful excuse of legal compulsion, the patients consent, the performance of a moral or social duty, or protection of the doctors interest. A doctor shares with other citizens the duty to assist in the detection and arrest of a person who have committed a serious crime. Everyone recognises the necessity and importance of medical confidence, but we must recognise also that the rules regarding them exist for the welfare of the community and not for the aggrandisement or convenience of a particular class. We must recognise also that they must be modified to meet the inevitable changes that occur in the necessities of various generation." [7]

---

[5] *AG* v. *Guardian Newspapers (No 2)*[1988] 3 All ER 545 at 658, per Lord Goff.
[6] John Glaister, *op. cit*, at 60.
[7] Lord Riddel, *Medico-Legal Problem*, London, Lewis & Co. Ltd, 1929

> Rule 16 sets out the ambits of the principle of confidentiality.[8] The principle is fundamental and a necessary precondition for the doctor-patient relationship. It is an obligation a doctor owes his patient.

John Glaister reports that the principle form part of the declaration oath sworn to by medical graduate of the University of Glasgow. It states in part: 'And I further declare that I will keep silent as to anything l have seen or heard while visiting the sick which is usual improper to divulge."[9]

The Hippocratic Oath has a similar provision. By virtue of the new Code on ethics operational in Nigeria, allegiance to the Oath is now an integral part of induction ceremony for new doctors. The Rules state as follows: 'Whatever thing l see or hear concerning the life of men in my attendance of the sick or even apart therefrom, which ought not to be raised abroad, l will keep silence thereon, counting such thing to be as sacred secrets.'

The obligation applies not to only medical information but any confidential information. Lord Goff said in *A.G.* v. *Guardian Newspapers (No. 2)*[10]

> 'I start with the broad principle...that a duty of confidence arise when confidential information comes to the knowledge of a person (confidant) in circumstances where he has notice, or is held to have agreed, that the information is confidential with the effect that it will be just in all the circumstances that he should be precluded from disclosing the information to others...The existence of this broad general principle reflects the fact that there is such a public interest in the maintenance of confidences that law will provide remedies for their protection.'[11]

To succeed in an action for breach of confidence the patient must show conclusively two things, namely (i) that the information in the circumstances given or received was meant to be treated as confidential (ii) that the obligation to keep the information confidential was breached by the doctor. The obligation to maintain confidence applies to all fiduciaries—priests, lawyers, company directors and doctors inclusive. Hence the observation of Boreham J in *Hunter* v. *Mann*. 'The second preposition is this: that in common with other professional men, for instance a priest and there are of course others, the doctor is under a duty not to disclose without the consent of his patient information which he, the doctor, has gained in his professional capacity.' [12]

---

[8] See Rules appendix.

[9] John Glaister, *op. cit.*, pp. 60-61. See also current advice of the British General Medical Council to the medical profession pursuant to s.35 of the Medical Act1983. Rule 30 made thereunder provides that "it is a doctors duty except in the cases mentioned below, strictly to observe the rule of professional secrecy by refraining from disclosing voluntarily to any third party information about a patient which he has learnt directly or indirectly in his professional capacity as a registered medical practitioner.

[10] [1988] 3 All ER 545.

[11] [1988] 3 All ER 545 at 658.

[12] [1974] 2 All ER 414 at 417-418, [1974] QB 767 at 777. See also *Goddard* v. *National Building Society* [1986] 3 All ER 264, at 271- per Nourse LJ.

Summarising the obligation, Binghan LJ in *W* v. *Egdell* said:

> 'It has never been doubted that the circumstances here were such as to impose on Dr. Egdell a duty of confidence owed to W. He could not lawfully sell the contents of his report to a newspaper as the judge held. Nor could he without a breach of the law as well as professional etiquette discuss the case in a learned article or in his memoirs or in gossiping with friends, unless he took appropriate steps to conceal the identity of W.'[13]

The fundamental nature of the obligation is responsible for its inclusion as part of the provisions of secondary legislation on doctor's ethics in Nigeria. [14] A similar practice is traced in England.[15] The remedy for its breach is either intra-professional.[16] or extra-professional as by way of civil action for damages. Breach of confidence is criminalised in some jurisdictions. For example, in some Continental countries as France and Belgium, the principle is protected by criminal legislation.[17]

Scope of the rule

The principle is not absolute in nature. Lord Riddel [18] in his work admits that the fundamental obligation must make way for the interest of society. Implicit admission of this, the Declaration of Geneva modifies the strict stance of the Hippocratic Oath that the physician shall 'keep secret' information. Rather it states 'I will respect the secrets which are confided in me.' It is respectfully submitted that the phrase 'respect' makes less sacrosanct the doctor obligation as against the wordings of the Hippocratic Oath – 'to keep secret.'

Whatever the case, medical opinion, case law and legislation now admit that the obligation is qualified. It admits of limitation and exceptions. In this respect the views of His Lordship, Jeffries J of the New Zealand High Court in *Duncan* v. *Medical Practitioners Disciplinary Committee* is instructive:

> 'The platform support of a description of medical confidence is to identify the doctor-patient relationship as a fiduciary. Without trust it would not function properly so as to allow freedom for the patient to disclose all manner of confidences and secrets in the practical certainty they would repose with the doctor. There rests with a doctor a strong ethical obligation to observe strict confidentiality by holding inviolate the confidences and secrets he receives in the course of his professional ministering. If he adheres to that ethical principle

[13] 1990] 1 All ER 835, [1990] Ch 359, [1989] 4 BMLR 96 (CA).

[14] See Rule of Professional conduct for Medical and Dental practitioners in Nigeria, made pursuant to the 1988 Act.

[15] See s. 33 of Human fertilisation and Embryology Act. 1990.

[16] An aggrieved plaintiff may make his case before the council which through its Investigation Panel and Tribunal may sanction the doctor if found guilty.

[17] France: Art. 378 of Penal Code; Belgium: Art 458 of Penal Code.

[18] Lord Riddel, *op. cit*, ft. nt. 2.

then the full scope of his ability to administer medical assistance to his patient will develop.'[19]

Confidentiality is not breached by private discussions with colleagues in pursuance of treatment, but this may require the consent of the patient, which may be waived by the patient. This notwithstanding, a doctor may be required by law to make disclosure, in which case no breach of confidentiality would be said to occur. He also may in a group practice where common filing system is used disclose certain medical aspects of what he sees in examination of a patient without breaching a duty of confidence. If other staff have access to such information it would be proper to impress them with the requirement of confidence. Limited information to some outside agencies may be permissible for purposes of statistics, accounting, data processing or other legitimate information. If a patient is treated by other doctors in the course of treatment, it would be expected that doctors would exchange information about the patient for purposes connected with further treatment or research. Here however a degree of caution and prudence must be observed and consent obtained. A doctor may also reveal confidences and secrets if he is required to present it before a court or tribunal, say if he has to defend himself or others against accusation of wrongful conduct. There may be rare occasions when a doctor who receives information about a dangerous patient that can endanger the lives of others. He would in that circumstance be expected to use good professional judgment to determine if there exist a need to warn those at danger from the patient. If he comes to a conclusion that there is need for such warning then he must act unhesitatingly to prevent injury or loss of life even if that would amount to a breach of confidentiality.[20]

Exception to the Rule

i) Consent to disclose to others

The obligation of a doctor to maintain confidentiality is relaxed or released if there is express or implied consent of the patient to make disclosure.[21] The proviso to Rule states that 'disclosure of information on the patient by the doctor can only be made following an informed consent, preferably written, of the patient.'[22] Consent may be implied from the circumstances of treatment, in which case even though there is a technical breach the court would consider the overall interest of hospital management and the general public. A typical example would be a case where a

---

[19] [198]) 1 NZLR 513 (NZH Ct).

[20] *Tarasoff* v. *Regents of the University of California* (1976) 131 Cal Rptr 14 (Cal Sup. Ct.), per Tobriner J; *Gammil* v. *United States* (1984) 727 F 2d 950 (10th Cir); *W* v. *Egdell* [1989] 1 All ER 1089. But cf. *Rice* v. *Cannolly* [1966] 2 QB 414, (1966) 2 All ER; See also Herman & Gagliano, AIDS, Therapeutic confidentiality and Warning Third Parties (1989) *Maryland Law Rev.* 55. For general reading; M. Junes, *Medical Negligence* (1992) p. 262-8.

[21] See Brigtham LJ in *W* v. *Egdell* [1990] 1 All ER 835, 848 Kennedy & Grubb, *op. cit.*, at. 644.

[22] Rule 16.

patient consults a consultant who has besides him young doctors or students from medical college on pupilage. The circumstances could be good reason to imply consent to disclosure, at least to the medical team. The implication is necessary to shield an otherwise technical breach in that the consulting procedure is expedient for the training of new doctors. It may also enhance proper clinical team management. Another common example would be where a patient is in the care of more than one doctor. Here the patient is assumed to give consent to all the doctors and nurses with a view for better treatment so that they can function as a medical team.[23] The caveat however is that the confidence is not breached so long as the information is used for the performance of their respective duties in the clinical management. Disclosure to person outside the team would constitute a breach.

(ii) Public Interest

Sometime it may be in the public interest to disclose confidential information. This would be so if disclosure would help in investigation of disgraceful conduct, preventing criminality, protect public health, further medical research, or is required for judicial evidence and the protection of the family. In the view of Lord Ridden, the doctor shares with the citizenry a share duty to assist in the detection and arrest of criminals. On this Griffiths LJ in *Lion Laboratories* v. *Evans* had this to say: 'I believe that the so-called iniquity rule evolved because in most cases where the facts justified a publication in breach of confidence the plaintiff had behaved disgracefully or criminally that it was judged in the public interest that his behaviour should be exposed.'

Rule 81(g) of the English Medical Profession Rules states: 'Rarely disclosure may be justified on ground that it is in the public interest which in certain circumstances such as for example, investigation by the public of a grave or very serious crime might override the doctors duty to maintain his patients confidence.' *W* v. *Egdell*, recognises that if a serious crime is committed the obligation to maintain confidentiality will be overridden.[24] Confidentiality would also be overridden if the information is required by a statutory authority.

In *W* v. *Egdell*,[25] W was detained as a prisoner in a secure hospital without limit of time as a potential treat to public safety after he shot and killed five people and wounded two others. Ten years after he had been first detained he applied to the mental health review tribunal for a review of his case so that he could be transferred to a regional secure unit with a view to his eventual discharge or

[23] [1984] 2 All ER 417 (CA).

[24] Rules made pursuant to s. 35 of the English Medical Act. 1983. This was the exception that the judge appeared to have upheld in *W* v. *Egdell* [1989] 1 All ER 1089 at 1104, [1989] 2 WLR 689 at 713 where Bingham LJ stated that; "may view a doctor called on, as Dr, Egdell was, to examine a patient such as woman a duty not only to his patient but also a duty to the public. His duty to the public would require him, in my opinion, to place before the proper authorises the result of his examination if, in his opinion, the public interest so require. This would be so, in my opinion, whether or not; the patient instructed him not to do so."

[25] [1989] 1 All ER 1089 at 1104.

immediate discharge. His application was supported by the medical officer report responsible for his treatment, but opposed by the Secretary of State. As a result his solicitor instructed E, a consultant, to examine W and report on his mental state with a view to using the report to support his clients (W) application to the tribunal. E report was unfavourable. It strongly opposed W's transfer, recommending further test and treatment drawing attention to W's long-standing interest in firearms and explosives. E sent the report to W's solicitor believing that he would place it before the tribunal. W then withdrew his application for review of his case. E knowing of this fact sent a copy of his report to the Medical Director of the hospital where W was detained. At his prompting the hospital sent a copy of the report to the Secretary of State who in turn forwarded the report to the tribunal.

Discovering that the report has been disclosed, W issued a writ against E, and the recipients of the report, seeking injunction to restrain the Secretary of State, Tribunal and hospital from disclosing or using the report, and for damages for breach of duty of confidence. The trial judge, Scott J held that the duty of confidence owed by E to W as his patient was not breached, because he had a duty to disclose the result of his examination to the authorities responsible for W. The disclosure was necessary to ensure that the authorities became fully informed of W's condition when reaching a decision concerning his future. Accordingly W's claim against E and the recipients of the report was dismissed. He appealed to the Court of Appeal (composed of Stephen Brown P. Bingham and Sir John May LJJ). The English Court of Appeal unanimously dismissed the appeal. Bingham LJ in the course of his judgement said:

> 'Where a man has committed multiple killings under the disability of serious mental illness, decision which may lead directly or indirectly to his release from hospital should not be made unless a responsible authority is properly able to make an informed judgment that the risk of repetition is so small to be acceptable. A consultant psychiatrist who became aware, even in the course of a confidential relationship, of information which leads him, in the exercise of what the court considers a sound professional judgment, to fear that such decision may be made on the basis of inadequate information and with a real risk of consequent danger to the public is entitled to take steps as one reasonable in all the circumstance to communicate the grounds of his concern to the responsible authorities. I have no doubt that the judge's decision in favour of Dr. Egdell was right on the facts of this case.'[26]

The ratio of the case places a higher duty on the doctor to make disclosure even if he breaches the duty of confidence to his patient if it is in the interest of the public to do so, especially where the information would assist a statutory authority in reaching decision on matters of public welfare, morality, defence, order and health. In R v. *Crozier*[27] the court held that the action of a psychiatrist in tendering

[26] Contrast *Rice* v. *Cannolly* [1966] 2 QB 414, (1966) 2 All ER 649.

[27] [1990] Ch. 359, [1990] 1 All ER 835.

medical evidence against the defendant's wish was a responsible and reasonable act as his obligation to maintain confidence was subordinate to public interest.

Where however the doctor breaches the patient's confidence on ground of public interest, he must ensure that the disclosure of information is to the relevant statutory body and not to a mere interested persons. He must ensure that he properly chooses the relevant and responsible authority to make disclosure, failing which he would be guilty of professional misconduct. In the New Zealand case of *Duncan* v. *Medical Practitioners Disciplinary Committee*,[28] Mr. Henry, a bus driver for 30 years, was required to furnish a medical certificate of fitness annually for the renewal of his license. He underwent a successful triple coronary by-pass operation for his heart and cardiac problems. Thereafter he consulted Dr. Maar, as an out-patient, whom he asked to issue him a medical certificate of fitness to enable him procure renewal of his license so that he could drive passenger service vehicle. Dr. Maar was of the opinion that he should not apply for a license. However since she was not heart specialist, she asked him to see one Mr. Hill of Greenlane Hospital. After examining him he issued him the necessary certificate to enable him obtain the license. Mr. Henry then proposed to take his bus to Auckland on a charter trip. The night before the trip, his general practitioner Dr. Duncan asked that Mr. Henry's license be withdrawn, and further he phoned one Mrs. Ada Verney, a passenger for the trip informing her that Mr. Henry was not fit to drive and could have a heart attack at any time. Mr. Henry petitioned against Dr. Duncan before the Medical Disciplinary Committee, complaining that his action amounted to professional misconduct. The Committee found him guilty on the basis that he disclosed his patient's confidence to lay persons. Dr. Duncan sought judicial review of the case before the High Court. Jeffries J while acknowledging the propriety of the rule that duty of confidence is subordinate to public interest, refused Dr. Duncan application for judicial review on the ground that it was improper to disclose to lay persons.[29]

Disclosure may be permitted if it aims at the protection of family life. Stable and happy family life is a cherished goal. Society has an interest to promote its happiness. However, there are certain aspects of family life which may prove worrisome to society at large and immediately to the doctor in the discharge of his duty. Cases of family mental, physical and sexual abuses may come to his attention in the course of treatment. Children in the family may request advice and treatment on moral matters like abortion, sterilisation, etc. How a doctor resolves these issue is by no means simple. Where for example, a doctor becomes aware of reported domestic violence which severely effects his patient it would be the course of wisdom to advise clinical mental treatment or counselling of the aggressive partner. If the abuse is extensive, e.g. of a sexual nature on a minor, he may choose to make a report to the appropriate persons for necessary notion. In USA and Canada, statute provides for compulsory reporting of suspected child abuse. The rational for this is

---

[28] [1990] 8 BMLR 128.

[29] [1980] 1 NZLR 513 (NZH Ct) per Jeffries J. [1986] 1 NZLR 513, p. 521.

founded in the belief that victims are usually defenceless and should be protected against repeated abuses.

A doctor would need to balance the confidence of a child patient against parents' desire for disclosure. In this respect *Gillick* case [30] ought to set the guiding principle. If the child is not mature, the parents right to know or disclosure is paramount to any duty of confidence owed by the doctor. Where however the child is a mature minor, the duty owed him is preserved. A doctor in that situation can only make disclosure with the relevant mature minor's consent.

As to whether there is an obligation on the doctor's part to disclose confidential information about a spouse to his partner, the answer is no. There is no such obligation. A married person is a competent adult with rights of autonomy. Generally the broad principle in *Paton* case applies here.[31]

The duty of confidence is not breached if disclosure is for purposes of medical research and teaching. This would be so provided the identity of the patient is concealed. Where however, it is possible to know and identify the patient by description only the patient's consent will do if a breach is not to be raised from the circumstances.

Public health purposes may also provide exception to the obligation of confidence. Take as example the need for warning on AIDS. The mortality rate for full blown AIDS is possibly 100 per cent. Because of its usual spread through unprotected sexual activities the disease is often associated with immorality. Though connection between HIV (human immune deficiency virus) and AIDS (acquired immune deficiency syndrome) remains controversial, public reaction for the disease has been to equate carriers with infectious diseases even though that should not be. As a result the public seeks positive actions to curtail its spread. It is for this reason that HIV, AID and other sexual transmitted disease (STD) attracts concern of confidentiality. It raises question whether it is in the interest of community health to disclose information about the carrier's status for the protection of the life and health of persons proximate to the sufferer. In balancing the question of whether or not to permit a breach of patient's confidence it is necessary to consider not only the proximate person to the carrier, but also the public at large who are concerned about the rapid spread of the disease. Whether disclosure is permissible is generally governed by practice directive of the profession.[32]

Prior to *X* v. *Y* [33] for example the English General Medical Council (GMC) regulation 15 to 17 gives the following guideline: Regulation 15, provides that if HIV infection or AIDS is diagnosed the doctor would be required to do the following

---

[30] [1984] QB 581, [1984] 1 All ER 365 on appeal [1986] AC 112, [1985] 1 All ER 533 reversed in 1986 in [1985] 3 All ER 402 (HL). See also Re 112 discussion on pp.

[31] [1979] QB 276, [1978] 2 All ER 987, per Sir George Baker P.

[32] See General Medical Council (England) Guidance concerning; HIV infection 1988 (amended in June 1993).

[33] [1988] 2 All ER 648, [1987] 3 BMLR 1; *Lion Laboratories* v. *Evans* [1984] 2 All ER 417; *W* v. *Egdell* [1990] All ER 835, [1989] 4 BMLR 96. *Duncan* v. *Medical Practitioner's Disciplinary Committees* [1986] 1 NZLR 513.

three things: (i) discuss openly and frankly with the patient the implications of his condition (ii) discuss the need to secure the health of others and (iii) discuss the need for continued medical care. By Regulation 16, if the patient is diagnosed by a specialist, the specialist shall explain to him that the state of his health ought to be notified to his general practitioner (GP) to enable him provide adequate continuing medical care. He is enjoined to persuade him to consent to the notification. Regulation 17, stipulates what the specialist should do if the patient refuses to give consent. He is required to explain the consequence of patient's refusal of consent to him and that it would effect the provision of his continuing treatment If he still refuses, the specialist is obliged to do no more, save that he may disclose information about the patient's confidence to a medical team that treats the patient if in his opinion non-disclosure would put the medical team at serious risk. So much for the protection of the medical team! The GMC further shows its concern for the proximate sexual partners of the carries by providing in Regulation 19 that the carriers should be encouraged to inform them spouses or other sexual partner. If he refuses to cooperate, the doctor may inform the partner to safeguard him or her from possible infection.

Commendable as these regulations are, they yet appear insufficiently positive in preventive context and fail to address some wider issues. How for example, does the doctor get to know the identity of a patient's sexual partner? Is he expected or under a duty to find and make inquiries on this subject? If yes, from whom? The regulations do not seem to impose a positive duty to disclose on the doctor even in cases where he considers possible fatal infection. The use of the term 'may consider it a duty,' begs the seeming important obligation to disclose for public protection. Furthermore, the language used in Regulation 15-19 seeks to persuade the patient to agree about his health implication to the community. Some may consider this a kid-gloves solution to a pandemic situation requiring disclosure, at a minimum if not requiring draconian measures of quarantine.

In *X* v *Y*[34] the plaintiff is a health authority. The defendants were the reporter of a national newspaper and its publishers. Sometime in February 1987, employees of the plaintiff supplied it with information obtained from the plaintiff hospital record that identified two doctors practising as general practitioners in the plaintiff's employment despite having contacted AIDS. The news was published by the defendant under the headline 'Scandal of Docs with AIDS.' It implied that there were doctor in Britain who continued practice despite having contacted AIDS and that the Health Department was suppressing the fact. The defendants intended to publish a further article identifying the doctors. It was on this basis that the plaintiff sought an injunction to restrain its further publication. It also sought an order compelling the defendants to disclose the source of their information. The court (Rose J), ordered a permanent injunction restraining the defendants from making further publication.

[34] Ibid.

The case suggests that it is unethical to disclose to the public that a doctor has AIDS. Its conclusion can be supported on the grounds that a doctor with AIDS, of course, knowing the grave implication of the state of his health would take precaution to prevent transmission much more than a lay man. To that extent, the public need have no fear consulting him. But is this not too simplistic a viewpoint? Would the public not consider such a condition incompatible with the nature of a doctor calling? Who ensures that the doctor does observe due care and skill in clinical treatment cognisant with their AIDS status? Who can vouch that he may not become mischievous and deliberately infect others for some reasons or no-reason at all - e.g. because he feels like getting 'even' with society by making others 'potential cabbage'? These fears are real to imagine. May be a withdrawal of his services from hospital duties could better conform with the nature of doctor-patient relationship of trust, notwithstanding the stance of the British GMC to the effect that only in exceptional cases for the protection of patient is there a duty to disclose the identity of a doctor without his consent if he has HIV or AIDS.[35] The English position therefore is that there is no common law or statutory duty to inform those at risk. Disclosure is only authorised in exceptional circumstances.

This contrast with the legal position in some jurisdictions in America and Canada that adopt a positive duty to inform persons at risk as shown in *Tarasoff* v. *Regents of the University of California* [36] and *Gammil* v. *United States*.[37] Both cases resulted from concern about warning others of the danger about violent psychiatric. In *Tarasoff's*, the facts were that P killed T. Plaintiffs, who were T's parents alleged that two months earlier before killing T, P confided his intention to kill him to Dr. Lawrence Moore, a psychologist employed by Cowell Memorial Hospital at the University of California at Berkeley. They also alleged that at Dr. Moore's request the campus police detained P, who was later released when he appeared rational. No one warned T's parents of the peril. The plaintiffs predicated liability on the ground that the defendant failed to warn the plaintiffs of impending danger and failed to confine P. The defendant therapist was held liable. Tobriner J observed: 'When a therapist determines, or pursuant to the standards of his profession should determine, that his patient presents a serious danger of violence to another, he incurs an obligation to use reasonable care to protect the interested victim against such danger.'[38]

In Gammill, the plaintiff contacted infectious hepatitis because as alleged the doctor treating him previously contacted the disease. The Circuit Judge dismissed the claim on the ground that the doctor did not know the plaintiff neither was he aware of the risk of their exposure. Noteworthy, the court observed that failure to warn a

---

[35] GMC Guideline: HIV infection and AIDS; the Ethical considerations (Revised 1993).

[36] (1976) 131 Cal Rptr 14 (Cal Sup. Ct.), per Tobriner J see also Herman & Gagliano, AIDS, Therapeutic Confidentiality and Warning third Parties (1989) *Maryland Law Rev.* 55 for general reading; M. Junes *Medical Negligence* (1992) p. 262-8.

[37] (1984) 727 F 2d 950 (10th Cir) per Barrett, Circuit Judge.

[38] (1976) 131 Cal Rptr 14 at (Cal Sup. Ct.). See also *Davis* v. *Lhim* (1983) 335 NW 2d 481 (Mich Sup.Ct.) and; *Thompson* v. *Country Alameda* (1980) 614 P.2d 728 (Cal. Sup.Ct.).

patient's family, treating attendants or other persons likely to be exposed to the infections patient disease could be the basis of liability, though in the present case, this was not the case.

The law does not permit privilege against disclosure of medical confidences in legal proceedings or litigation. Sir John Donaldson MR states:

> 'Nowadays, the general rule is that while a party is entitled to privacy in seeking out the cards for his hands, once he has put his hand together the litigation is to be conducted with all the cards face up in the table. Furthermore, most of the cards have to be put down well before the hearing.'[39]

If statute requires information for purposes of statistics, disease control etc, the duty is not breached if a doctor makes available information to meet the requirement of statute. If disclosure is not in a court proceeding but to a party when proceeding is commenced a claim for breach of confidentiality can be raised. For example in *AB* v *CD*[40] where a doctor disclosed that a pursuers wife had given birth six months after marriage he was held liable. Also in *AB* v. *CD (No.2)*[41] a doctor who revealed certain information about a wife to her husband after examination was held to have breach a duty of confidence to the wife.

Remedies for breach of confidence may be by way of (i) equitable injunction (ii) for damages in tort for distress, loss and harm caused and possibly for defamation.

(iii) Damages for breach of contract

Furniss v. *Fitchett*[42]is a New Zealand case that illustrates the remedies that can arise from a breach of confidence litigation. The defendant doctor, at the request of the plaintiff's husband wrote a letter to the husband stating that his wife exhibited symptoms of paranoia and he suggested an examination by a psychiatrist. The husband later used the letter in separation proceedings against the plaintiff. That was the first time she knew of the existence of the letter. She sued the defendant doctor for breach of confidence. Barrow Clough CJ of the New Zealand High Court held the defendant liable for breach notwithstanding the truth of the document. He said: 'I am of the opinion that on the principle of *Donoghue* v. *Stevenson* (1932) AC 562, there rose a duty of care on his (doctor's) part. While I have not forgotten that the certificate was true and accurate, but I see no reason for limiting the duty to one of care in seeing that it is accurate. The duty must extend also to the exercise of care in deciding whether it should be put in circulation in such a way that it is likely to cause harm to another.'

While the patient may recover for physical harm, it is still controversial whether he may also recover for distress. Scott J in *W* v. *Egdell*[43] was of the view that it is still open to question whether shock and distress caused by unauthorised disclosure can properly be reflected in the assessment of damages. Unfortunately this point was not examined on

---

[39] *Naylor* v. *Preston Area Health Authority* [1987] 2 All ER 353 at 360 [1987] 1 WLR 958, 967, per Donaldson MR.

[40] (1851) 14 D 177 (Scottish case).

[41] (1904) 7 F 72: (Scotland case).

[42] [1958] NZLR 396.

[43] [1989] 1 AII ER 1089.

appeal.[44] It is suggested that there ought to be no bar to such recovery. In fact the English Law Commission thinks it should. Mental distress is a foreseeable loss that can arise from the breach.[45]

Special categories

The dead

Noteworthy of mention, if there exists a duty of confidence, it does not evaporate simply because the patient is dead.[46] If there exists breach during the lifetime of the patient but he dies before vindication it is a claim his survivors can only recover if they can show that disclosure has brought injury to his estate. By some form of ingenuity that the deceased right to confidence can be constructed as an chose in action to which his estate can vindicate.

The obligation of confidence being personal in nature should end at death of the patient. But there are exceptions to the general rule. For example the GMC of England directive on the matter states that a patient's death does not release a doctor from the obligation.[47] Where publicity about a patient's health condition may offend his survivors it would be ethical to disclosure.

Incompetent adult

Even though there is generally no obligation of confidence owed incompetents, it is arguable that the fiduciary nature of doctor-patient relationship from where the non-disclosure principle originates should make unlawful non-consensual disclosure. It will only be excused based on the best interest of the incompetent patient weighed against other relevant factors. If the patient is an incompetent adult, no duty of confidence would be owed because the patient going by our capacity analysis will generally be incompetent to enter a relationship of confidence, talk more of understanding what secrecy entails. The fact that no duty of confidence is owed the incompetent adult is no reason for the doctor to make disclosure to anyone. As in the case of a minor, disclosure can and ought rightly be to the parent because that is what serve the child best interest. Following this analogy, it is suggested that the court can prevent disclosure to a third party if it is not in the interest of the incompetent.[48] Not to be forgotten is the decision in *Re C*[49] By analogy, the no-duty owed incompetents would not cover cases where he can understand the nature of medical treatment proposed. It may be argued, though

---

[44] *W* v. *Egdell* (on appeal) [(1990] 1 All ER 835.

[45] Breach of Confidence Cmnd. 838,, 1981) Law Commission Report No 110.

[46] Advise on standards of Professional conduct and Medical Ethics contained in the General Medical Council's 'Blue Book' on professional conduct and discipline, paragraph 9.

[47] GMC Guideline: Blue Book paragraph 91.

[48] Kennedy & Grubb, *op. cit*, p. 642 – 3. Note the court's *parens patriae* powers of wardship no longer applies to adult in England since 1960 and it remains controversial whether it applies at all to incompetent adult, see B. Hoggett, the Royal Prerogative in Relation to the Mentally Disordered: Resurrection, Resuscitation or Rejection in MDA Freeman (ed*) Medicine Ethics and the Law* London, Steven & Sons 1988 p. 85.

[49] *Re. L (adult : refusal of medical treatment)* (1994) 1 ALL ER 819, (1993) 15 BMLR 77

doubtfully, that such minimum capacity ought to raise a duty of confidence in the circumstance.

Children

The position with children may be somewhat controversial. It requires the balance of many moral issues. It is suggested that two distinct approaches determine the circumstances under which a duty may be owed. They are the 'status' approach and the 'capacity' approach. The status approach is a proposition that once a child is taken to a doctor for treatment by his parent, he becomes the doctor's patient and that relationship is what raises the status of a patient—doctor relationship underlined with the duty of confidence. By this analysis, the doctor is required to observe the child's confidence. The doctor comes under a duty of confidence and if he must make any disclosure of the child's confidence, he must demonstrate that his disclosure comes within one of the recognised exception that justifies disclosure of confidential information.

An analysis along the lines of status is not without conceptual and practical difficulties. The duty of confidence must not be carried too far. The legal underpin is trust and confidence that arises between the doctor and patient. Only a patient who places trust or confidence can come within the parameters of protection. What is more, due to minority and inexperience of a child, the doctor is required by law to bring to the notice of the parent what he discovers in order to seek consent for further or more appropriate treatment of the child. It would therefore be legally and practical paradoxical for the doctor to maintain a stance of status in the protection of a child's confidence. The approach in substance removes the right of parents as 'consent – givers' to children treatment, a position that enjoys little or no case law support, the *Gillick* rule excepted.

The alternative and preferred approach is the capacity analysis. This proposition states that the legal obligation of confidence can only arise if a child is mature enough to form a relationship of confidence. In other words, a child will not enjoy the legal duty unless he can appreciate what is involved in confidence and professional secret. This approach no doubt aligns with the general tenor of the 'mature minor' principles of *Gillick*[50] If it is clear and convincing that the minor child is mature enough to appreciate the consequences of his actions and can exercise the judgement of an adult then he invariable would understand what secrecy entails. Going by this, a doctor will only come under a duty to disclose to a child's parent if the child is *prima facie* incompetent.

It can however be argued that since the fundamental ethos governing the treatment of children is the 'best interest' principle, law should create a strong presumption in favour of disclosure to the parent even if the child is a mature minor especially in cases where the doctor suspects a risk of harm to the child. It will only be proper for the doctor to disclose to those (preferably the parent) who can best protect the child from the risk or harm.[51] Where however it is suspected that the child may come under risk from the parent, a doctor acting in the best interest of the child may determine who best other than the parent to make disclosure.

---

[50] (1986) AC 112, (1985)3 All ER 402 (HL)

[51] *Re C (a Minor Evidence: confidential Information)* [1991] 7 BMLR 138, but cf *Re W (A Minor medical Treatment)* [1992] 4 All ER 627.

PART THREE

General Medicine

Chapter Sixteen

Special cases: allocation of health resources

Issues of allocation of health resources implicate how public resources are allocated by government to the health sector and how doctors allocate their time and care in the treatment of patients. These issues deserve a place in ethics because these resources, whether of government or that of doctors are not limitless. Accordingly they bring to fore priority questions and planning, eg., budgetary allocation. Resource allocation to health can be sizeable. Medical hardware is increasing in demand as new cures are found to hitherto debilitating diseases. Their procurement may cost much in terms of money. The permissiveness of our modern society as demonstrated in loose life style of many would invariable throw on society more health burden. The rising rate of sexually transmitted diseases is already raising ethical questions whether scare national resources allocated to the health sector should be used to sustain 'bad life-style illnesses.' Paradoxically present improved health care would translate to more senior citizens. Since age make people more susceptible to sickness, medical health resources are bound to go up. In developing countries, where the average citizen does not practice the culture of small family, increased population can make matters worse. Sadly most developing economics make little allocation to the sector.[1] Even the little has proved grossly inadequate in the face of ethnic and national wars and commotion.

Allocation of care by doctors to patients also deserves attention. Patient population in developing countries often outstrip doctors and medical facilities, thereby presenting dilemma of prioritising treatment and treatment methods. The state of facilities available in the health care system to certain degree can have a bearing on the quality of care that a patient receives. A combination of these has forced doctors to practice selective treatment of patients raising questions as to what should be the proper basis for selection.

Some however have questioned the morality of selection on the grounds that the state owes a duty of care to its citizens to make adequate provision for their health care. From that premises it makes no sense to talk about selection of what should be of general entitlements. Though some commentators argue that health care ought to be classified as a basis human right issue, the view does not enjoy judicial

[1] For example, the government of Chief Olusegun Obasanjo of Nigeria in a supplementary budget submitted to the National Assembly in July 1999 showed the health was allocated only 5% of the budget, while defence for the law share of 30%

support.[2] Cases where litigants have sorted to impose a duty on the state to provide adequate health care for its citizens have met with low chances of success.[3] The cases explicitly state that the court would not interfere in matters of health resources allocation and schedule of treatment list of hospital. In *R* v. *Secretary of State for Social Services ex. P. Hincks*,[4] the patient's complaint was that failure of the Secretary of State and the health authority to construct a new block in the hospital because of unavailability of resources which resulted in unreasonable time loss for treatment owing to shortage of facilities constituted a breach of duty. Wien J dismissed the action on the ground that it is not a juristic function for the court to direct Parliament what funds should be allocated to health care or a particular hospital. The court could only act on a complaint if it is shown that a government official acted in a manner that breaches a relevant health laws. The decision was affirmed by the English Court of Appeal. It said: 'The courts of this country cannot arrange the lists in the hospital…and should not be asked to intervene.'[5]

Since resources are scare some sort of selective distribution is inevitable.[6] Though the general trend does not classify medical treatment as a fundamental right owed a people by government, the recent introduction of the National Health Insurance Scheme (NHIS) in Nigeria is likely to raise the status of the right to a hybrid. A purposive construction of the NHIS legislation[7] requires that the Minister of Health should come under a statutory duty to at least provide that which is necessary to meet the reasonable requirements of the scheme.[8]

It puts beyond debate that government does not owe a duty to provide adequate health in the form of making sufficient allocation to the sector or in providing

---

[2] The emphasis on a national and global scale is to guarantee more of political and civil rights. Attempt was made in the Nigerian 1979 and 1999 constitution to upgrade social, medical rights from mere rhetoric's some concrete policy for which the state/government ought to strive to provide. However, it must be noted, that these "rights" are to serve as pointers to government and no more – they are not justiciable.

[3] Mason & Smith, *op. cit*, p.254.

[4] (1979) 123 Sol Jo 436. See also the remark of Lord Donaldson.

[5] *Re Walker's Application* [1987] *Times*, 26 Nov. [1987] 3 BMLR 32 (CA); see also *Wilsher* v. *Essex AHA* [1986] 3 All ER 801

[6] For general reading on allocation of scare health resources, see R Klein, Dimensions of Rationing: Who Should Do What (1993) 307 *BMJ* 306; J Charlton, Making Access to Health Care More Equal: The Role of General Medical Services (1987) 295 *BMJ* 764; MA Somerville, Shall the Grandparents Die?: Allocation of Medical Resources with an Ageing Population (1986) 14 *Law Medical Health Care* 158; P A Lewis & M Charny, which of Two Individuals Do you Treat When Only Their Ages Are Different and you can't Treat Both? (1989) 15 *J Med Ethics* 28, A Williams, Cost effectiveness Analysis: Is it Ethical (1992) 18 *J. Med Ethics* 7; M J Garland, Justice, Politics and Community: Expanding Access and Rationing Health Services in Oregon (1992) 20 *Law Med Hlth Care* 67; J Dixon & H G Welch, Priority Setting Lessons from Oregon (1990) 337 *Lancet* 891.

[7] National Health Insurance Service (NHIS) Act, 2005.

[8] See ss of NHIS; see also *R* v. *Secretary of State for Social Services, exp. Hincks* [1980] 1 BMLR 93; (1979) 123 *Col. Jo* 436, for general reading, see F H Miller, Denial of Health Care and Informed Consent in English and American Law (1992) 18 *Amer. J Law Med.* 37; D Brahams, Seeking Increased NHS Resources through the courts (1988) 1 *Lancet* 133; Enforcing A Duty of Care for Patients in the NHS (1984) 2 *Lancet* 1224; C Dyer, Going to Law to Get Treatment (1987) 295 *BMJ* 1554.

facilities. That notwithstanding, it is expected that a responsible government would strive to make adequate allocation to the sector. Though a patient on a waiting list cannot sustain an action against the hospital prioritisation scheme, some American authorities suggest that in matters of transplant courts can interfere on grounds of due process breaches.[9] It is for this reason that selective treatment can be a bad option out of the dilemma facing the health sector. If selection is inevitable, then we must consider the various arguments on priority. They are as follows:

i) Women and Child Priority

It has been suggested that because women are weaker, bear children, have a more vital role to play in procreation and the tending of children priority ought to be given to their treatment. Children selective model proceeds on the ground that paediatric medicine should be given priority because children are more venerable to exploitation, therefore requiring protection even in the area of health provision. This may be the legal underpin for the requirement that parents, person in *locus parentis* and masters, owe a duty to provide necessaries for children under their care.[10]

ii) Cost-Benefit Theory

The argument proceeds on the basis that in making selection we ought to access the gains to society of saving one life against the others. For example, it is argued to save the life of a scientist is better than that of a labourer or menial unskilled worker. Some would raise objection to this model of selection on the ground that no human has the might to decide which of his fellows should live or die, especially when basis for selection is considered value created by society on unempirical criteria. On this basis, the morality of cost-benefit model of selection is open to reservation.

iii) Medical Benefit

Medical care is traditionally expected to bring about prevention of sickness, cure sickness when it occurs, if no cure is possible prevent deterioration and relieve the body and mind of pains and suffering.[11] Therefore if treatment is not aimed at producing any of the four objectives it is considered useless. At that point continued treatment should amount to waste of the scare health resources.

That point was recognised by Balcombe LJ in *Re J (a minor) (wardship: medical treatment)*. He said:

> 'I would stress the absolute undesirability of the court making an order which may have the effect of compelling a doctor or health authority to make available scares resources (both human and material) to a particular child, without knowing whether or not there are other patients to whom the resources might more advantageously be devoted ...(It might) require the

[9] See discussion on organ transplant, *supra*.
[10] S 227 of the Criminal Code makes it an offence not to provide the necessaries to a child.
[11] Per Sir Thomas Bingham MR in *Airedale NHS* v. *Bland* (CA) [1993] 2 WLR 316 at 335.

> health authority to put J on a ventilator in an intensive care unit, and thereby possibly to deny the benefit of those limited resources to a child who was much more likely than J to benefit from them.'[12]

The problem here, however, is how the doctor can discontinue care without exposing himself to criminal and civil sanctions.[13]

iv) Concept of Quality Adjusted Life Years (QALY)

Some commentators suggest that this is perhaps the concept of selection with greatest influence in medicine.[14] By it a year of healthy life expectancy is scored 1, a year of unhealthy life scored less than 1, death scored as zero. Using this mathematically method the doctor measures in numerical strength the values of the patient's life with a view of aiding him in selecting who to treat if there are competing interests. This method of selection has been criticised on grounds that it is basically subjective, determined by each doctor's preference, eg., age and viewpoint of life. He may score certain age more worthy than others. Placing a higher premium on the quality of life also does injustice to the value of life.

v) Lottery selection

This school is of the view that where the competing interest cannot all be satisfied a resort to ballot method of selection is preferred. The danger in the method lies not only in the *modus operandum* for the balloting, but the procedure ignores completely the well being of patients, paying unnecessary allegiance to methods of securing justice. It resembles more of knowledge without wisdom. The adoption of it as a selection method is tantamount to treating humans more as 'things' or 'commodity'.

vi) Just Dessert

This method advocate that those who have brought upon themselves preventable suffering by their free will life style should be less deserving of medical care. Examples of persons who would readily fit into the category are drunkards, prostitutes and smokers. Religionist may subscribe to it on the ground that it is a recompense mechanism; A person reaps what he sows. But not to be forgotten is that some of the above self-inflicted illnesses can be attributed to environmental factors. Possibly some may result from addiction which ought to elicit our sympathy. The method is nothing than society's punishment of a patient for his considered vices, but religion teaches the very opposite, forgiveness.

vii) Purchase Power Ability

Some others argue that the basis for selection ought to be the ability of the patient to pay for services and care. The 'money power' method however should remind us of

---

[12] [1992] 2 FLR 165 at 176, [1992] 9 BMLR 10 at 20.
[13] See the discussion on euthanasia, *supra*.
[14] Mason & Smith, *op. cit.*, p. 261.

the danger of today's materialism. Further the morality of say keeping a rich patient on a ventilator simply because he can pay for its services and denying its benefit to others who are more likely to benefit from it but cannot pay is callous.

So far it would appear that no single selection method is without ethical pitfalls. Faced with the dilemma of selection therefore, the first practical moral guide for the doctor is to consider his conscience or common sense which can roughly be described as moral intuition. In reaching his conclusion, he is however expected to consider matters such as public conscience and probably the principles of utility—benefit derivable from the care. The sum total of these will roughly dictate his conclusion. Provided there is no bad faith in his choice, the court would consider it 'social policy', or political question, a non-juristic matter.[15]

Geriatric medicine

Geriatric medicine is likely to become a contemporary issue in developing countries in the near future. Improved medical and health services are likely to shore-up the number of persons who would become senior citizens. The gradual erosion of the African—Asian communal living and the increasing demands on government to provide social security may gradually give birth to some form of institutional care and treatment. In advanced countries where institutional care is the norm the struggle has been between the competing ethos of autonomy and paternalism. The former dictates respect for the wishes of a patient while the later requires institutional protection of the aged, if need be by methods not agreeable to them. The desirability of this demands a resolution of these competing values.[16] Though this method of care is alien to our culture, it is noteworthy to mention, that there is no obligation (statutory or common law) which requires children to care for their parents.[17]

Re Dinnerstein[18] illustrates certain ethical questions that can arise from treatment of the aged. The patient was a 67-year old woman who suffered from Alzheimer disease, a degenerative disease of the brain of unknown origin, also describe as presenile dementia, resulting in destruction of brain tissue and consequently deterioration in brain function. The condition is progressive, leading to disorientation, loss of memory, personality disorganisation, loss of intellectual function and loss of all motor function. There is no known scientific cure for the disease and no treatment can slow or arrest its course. As a result of the disease her health deteriorated and she was confirmed in a nursing home. She was fed through naso-gastric tube. She was paralysed with high blood pressure which was difficult to control. Her condition was hopeless. Though it was difficult to predict when she would die her life expectancy was no more than a year. She could therefore go into

[15] Dworkin, Taking Rights Seriously,

[16] For a fuller discussion see Mason & Smith, *op. cit*, p. 267-278.

[17] The contrary is true. Parents are enjoined by statute to care for their children. See 227 of Criminal Code.

[18] 380 NE 2d 134 (1978) (App Ct. Mass) a case decided by the Appeal Court of Massachusetts in USA.

a cardiac arrest or stroke at any time which would result in her death. The attending doctor recommended a 'no-code order', i.e., an order not to resuscitate. Her family, consisting of a son, who was a physician practising in New York, and a daughter, with whom the patient lived prior to her hospitalisation supported the doctor and the hospital in bringing an action for declaration that the doctor enters a 'no-code order', or alternatively, if authorisation is a legal prerequisite to the validity of a no-code order, that the authorisation be given. Justice Armstrong took the position that doctors were under no obligation to defy clinical judgment in attempts to rescue patient dying naturally. In his Lordship's view authorisation from the court was unnecessary.

Her type of sickness show that the aged are susceptible to many sicknesses, in some case though with or with no scientific medical cures. Presenile dementia is one of such common diseases. That may be why in some indigenous societies people say a person becomes a child twice in a normal life course – at birth and when aged. Dementia is a common sickness associated with aging. The 67-year old patient in *Re Dinnerstern*[19] was disorientation, lost her memory, intellectual and motor function. Such a state can be distressing for the care-giver making some opt for institutional care or request to hospital for selective non-treatment. Whatever the stress these may cause, it is suggested that this an area of medicine requiring circumspection in the resolution of the many moral issues raised.

While the debate on autonomy and paternalism rages on in treatment decision of the aged,[20] it is expected that with advancement in our society institutional treatment nursing homes would become pronounced. This itself will not be without its ethical implications connected with care-giving and the question of whether nursing homes are better environment for our senior citizens than the general African family setting.[21] Some jurisdictions have a legal regime for compulsory institutionalisation of the age who are not mentally ill but suffer from grave chronic disease of being aged, or being infirm or physically incapacitated live in unsanitary condition and are unable to care for themselves and do not receive from others proper care and attention.[22] Ethical questions can be raised if the aged desirous of independence resists removal to an institution. An elderly person compulsory institutionalised in a nursing or hospital facility may well refuse to accept treatment. At this point all compulsion must cease because like all competent persons an elderly can choose to refuse treatment. It is at this stage that the doctor may need to do some persuasion either himself or through the relatives of the aged to ensure compliance with medical treatment.[23] However under the relevant mental health legislation an

---

[19] *Supra.*

[20] E S Cohen, Autonomy and Paternalism: Two Goals in Conflict (1985) 13 *Law Med Hlth Care* 145.

[21] Family setting in Africa.

[22] A C Homer & C Gillard, Abuse of Elderly by Their Carers (1990) 301 *BMJ* 1359; B Pitt, Abusing Old People (1992) 305 *BMJ* 968; J G Evans, Institutional Care and Elderly People (1993) 306 *BMJ* 806.

[23] See s. 47 of (English) National Assistance Act, 1948. For an analysis of the provision, see JAM Gray. Section 47 (1981) 7 *J Med Ethics* 146; Section 47 – Assault on or Protection of the Freedom of the

incompetent patient compulsorily admitted may be treated for his mental disorder which forms the basis of his institutionalised admission. Other treatment may not be administered save if appropriate for the mental disorder.[24]

Commonly euthanasia issues are likely to rear its head because a lot many old may suffer from degenerative physical disease and intellectual. Not unconnected with the peculiar nature of the elderly much of geriatric medicine is concerned with the management of incurable, though not necessarily terminal diseases. In those circumstances, the yardstick for therapeutic treatment must be the best interest of the elderly. That means that the criteria is likely to be subjective-their best interest judged by persons who are aged. What the world of geriatric view as a happy, contented life may not be how younger person view matters from their youthful perspective. Since these are the ones who determine the aged best interest it is likely that the standard meant to be objective in the perspective of the aged is turned to an objective standard of the young. The demented elderly could by the subjective criteria enjoy a contented life and so a policy of his non-treatment on grounds of the 'quality of cognitive life,' judged objectively must be suspect.[25] *Re Dinnerstein*[26] recognises that matters of selective non-treatment of the elderly should be based on the individual's circumstances rather than an 'unfeeling demographic rationalisation'.[27]

The elderly deserve sufficient allocation of health resources like any other demographic group because ageing is part of living and so society must carry out its duty to the elderly be means designed to prevent their premature death and if possible *deteriorate* ageing. It has been suggested that the very way a society designs its senior citizens quality of life and deals with its vulnerable members, the elderly inclusive, ultimately reflects its civilisation.[28]

While it is beyond doubt that the elderly if competent can like all competent patients refuse treatment, the difficulty of drawing the line between competent and incompetent due to ageing must be appreciated.[29] Compulsory treatment while legally limited to the mentally ill in practice extends to matters of nutrition and

---

Individual (1991) 17 *J Med Ethics* 195; D A Greaves, can compulsory Removal Ever Be Justified for Adults who are Mentally Competent (1991) 17 *J Med Ethics* 189; J D Fear, P Hatton & E B Renvoize, Section 47 of National Assistance Act: A Time for Change (1988) 296 *BMJ* 860.

[24] E Murphy, What to Do with a Sick Elderly Woman who refuses to go to Hospital (1984) 289 *BMJ* 1435. Mental Health Act 1983, s. 7 (England). See also *Re F (mental patient: sterilisation)* [1990] 2 AC 1 at 55: E v. *West Berkshire Health Authority* [1989] 2 All ER 545 at 551, per Lord Brandon: *Re W (EEM)* [1971] Ch 123; See also M J. Gum, Treatment and Mental Handicap (1987) 16 *Anglo-Amer L. Rev.* 242.

[25] See *Re Dinnerstein* 380 NE 2d 134 (Mass. 1978); Do Doctors Short-change old people (1993) 342 *Lancet* 1; CS Robertson, Ethical Dilemmas of Brain Failure in the Elderly (1983) 287 *BMJ* 1775; J E Robb, 1 Murray. In & C Mackay, Is Elective Surgery in the Elderly Worthwhile (1987) 32 *Scot. Med. J* 79; MA Somerville, *above* n. 40.

[26] 380 NE 2d 134 (Mass. 1978).

[27] Ibid.

[28] Mason & Smith, *op. cit*, p. 276.

[29] Re Conroy 464 A 2d 303 (NJ, 1983)

feeding.[30] It is often taken for granted that most old persons' refusal to eat is non-volitional and that some form of force is nothing but an expression of compassion to them. Thus in practice force treatment may be employed for trivial medication such as feeding and nutrition on utilitarian grounds even though it is legally suspect. Refusal in cases of major treatment by an old competent patient clearly deserves respect by the medical team. The American courts have in very positive terms upheld the right of refusal under the long cherished principle of the 'right to be let alone'.[31] What this translates to is that the competent elderly may in fact choose suicide by way of deliberate starvation in preference to medical care. As in the *Conroy*,[32] we should not allow the right to refuse treatment enter a slippery slope of enforcing a duty to die.[33] Ethical principles are implicated by objective thinking that no valid purpose is served by needlessly prolonging a useless life. An aged life is not useless simply because by youthful standards it is consider so. Loss of dignity or low quality of life do not necessarily arise from degenerative illnesses associated with ageing, but rather from the way that we show our care for the sufferers. That they 'have few friends and cast fewer votes'[34] is no reason to treat the aged any less favourable in medical decisions and the allocation of health resources.

Gender medicine

Ethic in medicine makes possible an enabling environment for patient and doctors to talk. It is gradually removing medicine from on era of confrontation. In medicine's quest for maintaining it primal position it is bound to consider not only 'patient's rights versus doctors know best dilemma', but also matter of patient's consumerism and gender. Gender issues are no doubt topical and contemporary. All over the world there is a global concern for women.[35] Gender rights of women raise especially ethical issues in the area of reproductive medicine. We shall only do an outline here because the main points in this respect have been discussed in chapters dealing with reproductive medicine, especially in the areas of surrogacy, abortion, fertility control and informed consent. Ann Oakley, for example, had this to say on one of such areas:

> 'Reproduction has come to be recognised as one area in which women are either liberated or oppressed, either free to determine and control their own

---

[30] E Murphy, Ethical Dilemmas of Brain Failure in the Elderly (1984) 288 *BMJ* 61

[31] For a description of the right, see *Grisworld* v. *Connecticut* (1965) 381 US 479

[32] 464 A 2d 303 (NJ, 1983), CA; 486 A 2d 1209 (NJ, 1985) SC

[33] N Rhoden, How Should We View the Incompetent (1989) 17 *Law Med Health Care* 264

[34] M B Kapp, Financing Long term Care for the Elderly; Am I your Parents Keepers? (1985) 13 Law Med Health Care 188; E Murphy, What to do with a Sick Elderly Woman who Refuses to go Hospital (1984) 289 BMJ 1435; M.A Somerville: Should The Grandfather Die? Allocation of Medical Resources with an Aging Population (1986) 14 Law Med Health Care 158

[35] Burlett, *Feminist Jurisprudence*

> individual or collective destines or compelled to have them chosen and directed by others.'[36]

Gender issues in medicine may arise in the context of abortion. It is now trite that foetus has no legal right. The philosophical foundation for most decision in medicine is the paramount allegiance to patient's right of autonomy or self-determination. This would reasonably dictate that a woman alone is the decision maker on the fate of an unborn child. It is therefore a seeming paradox that abortion is still criminalised in some jurisdictions, including Nigeria. Pressed to logical conclusion the right of autonomy ought to be the basis for de-criminalising abortion. Continued criminalisation appears discriminatory. But it can run into counter-argument that the stretch to logical conclusion of value judgment only reveals the limitation of philosophical argument on logical lines being applied to morals.[37]

From our discussion on compulsory sterilisation we noted that the right to reproduce is gradually being elevated to a basis human right. Freeman[38] has criticised the decision in *Re B* [39] where the court authorised the compulsory sterilisation of a 17 years old girl. In his view, the court would not have authorised it for a boy of 17. His argument proceeds on the basis that sterilisation of a girl or woman is suspect gender discrimination. There is no doubt that Freeman's argument has much moral force. Obvious the court would not have made the order if the patient was a boy or man. But the court's order may find justification on grounds unconnected with gender, especially in the construction of social reality. If the 17-year old was a boy dangers of future pregnancy would be nil. Unless we construe 'future pregnancy' fears to mean fear of a boy impregnating another which would not be as grievous to his development as it would be for the girl, we can begin to place the decision in proper social context. This point must not be missed. Whatever, the fact that sterilisation would not readily be ordered for a boy ought to be circumspective reason for restrain in the court authorising it for girls Unfortunately the authorities paint a picture that gives the impression that courts are too willing to abridge women's right to reproduce on less serious grounds. If they have been that careful cases such as *Re B*, would have be decided otherwise.

Gender issues also have arisen in the context of certain invasive surgical operations. In *Re S*[40] the court authorised a Caesarean on a competent adult in labour against her wishes. The case has provoked condemnation as gender surgical rape and invasion of the body of a woman. The defendant in the case was a Nigerian. Her baby was in transverse lie, so it could not be born vaginally and would die without surgery. She however refused surgery, saying God was in control. The court authorised a forced surgery on her. The decision is hard to reconcile with the principle of autonomy. It is more worrisome in that the court by implication

---

[36] Ann Oakley, *Subject Woman* (1985 ed) pp.198-200.

[37] For a discussion of the logic fits into the question of value, see Toulim, *Place of Reason in Ethics*.

[38] M Freeman, For Her Own Good (1987) 84 *LS Gaz* 949.

[39] [1980] AC 199, [1987] 2 All ER 206 (HL).

[40] [1992] 3 WLR 806.

endorsed the consequentialist ethics, i.e., the end justified the means by requiring that a mother should use her body to save or rescue a 'no person,' the foetus. That was the very thing the court refused in *McFall* v. *Shimp*,[41] an organ donation case. The *McFall* court reasoned that a society which respect the rights of individual would not subscribe to forcible extraction of living tissue to save another, liking it to an act reminiscent to the horror of Swastika and Inquisition. Why did those hard-wrought concepts of jurisprudence suddenly vanish into thin air when the issue turn on treatment of a pregnant women? It gives the impression that pregnant women are equated with incompetents, a sad conclusion. It puts her under a legal obligation to use her life to rescue a foetus. In the views of Nancy Rhoden,[42] the court that orders a forced Caesarean surgery on a woman has wronged her, taken a presumptuous step in deciding for her what medical risk she should run. The hidden subtle reasoning for *Re S*, is that the law still looks for opportunity to treat women as incompetents. It is on this ground that the case is no good law. There are therefore good grounds to resist *Re S*.

The three areas discussed above call for more affirmative class action by women organisations. The observation of Lord Reid in *S* v. *McC*[43] signpost the dangers of silence:

> 'We have too often seen freedom disappear in other countries not only by coup detat but by gradual erosion, and often it is the first step that counts. So it would be unwise to make even minor concessions.'[44]

HIV and AIDS

This section of our discussion has a bearing with medical confidentiality which is already discussed.[45] That notwithstanding the usual struggle between autonomy and paternalism take themselves head long in the management of HIV and AIDS cases. The pendulum continues to swing between appeal to autonomy and paternalism depending on public opinion. Fear of possible transmission is responsible for stigmatising carriers. The current sexual, religious and political undertone given to the disease has aggravated discrimination against patients. How the conflict between autonomy, society and paternalism is resolved to a large extent depends on the how it sees HIV positive patient. Some jurisdictions have taken extreme paternalist methods, quarantining HIV positive patients. That is the practice in Cuba. The basis for this confinement is a fear that a carrier poses threat to the safety of others. But some other countries have had the pendulum swing more on the side of autonomy—opting for compulsory institutional treatment. In many western European countries

---

41 [1978] P & D & C 3d 90 at 92.

42 Nancy Rhoden, The judge in the delivery room (1986) *Calif. L Rev.* 1951.

43 [1972] AC 24.

44 Ibid., at. 43.

45 See discussion on chapter 15.

and America public health authorities encourage empathy for carriers, urging education and understanding as the preferred method for dealing with HIV, AIDS cases. It is therefore not unusual to see famous persons who are confirmed carriers setting up AIDS or health foundation aimed at education and continuing a possible search for the disease.

Discrimination arising from AIDS is real. An employer may refuse to hire a carrier. States may also discourage them as tourist or residents. These policies are to say the least inhuman as they amount to discrimination. The fact that a patient is a carrier does not in any way make him less competent. Thus to restrict his economic potentials and free movement is to obstruct his fundamental human right to respect, family life etc. Most of the reasons for public fear about carriers are founded on the wrong premises that AIDS is an infectious disease. AIDS is not infectious. So there is no reason why carriers of the disease should be excluded from things that non-carriers do. However to control the epidemic continuous education and other safeguards should be encouraged by government.

Court processes and medical decisions

In the doctor-patient relationship, our discussion revealed that the evolving ethos in this field have been largely shaped by decisions of the courts. Hence we shall now consider how the litigation process is commenced. Usually decisions in medical ethics require prompt attention. For example in *Re S*,[46] at the time the case came up before the court she was near delivery. Her foetus was in transverse lie, so the baby could not be born vaginally and would die without surgery. Her life was in danger, but she refused surgery saying that God would provide. Faced with such grave situation the medical team seeking legal intervention would expect the court processes to travel fast because delay may jeopardise the chances of survival of the patient and child. Hearing and judgment in such cases are expected to take sometimes just a few days or even hours. Speedy proceeding are however susceptible to error of judgment and abuse of human rights. For example, in *Re S*, when the court arrived at the forced Caesarean she was not given a chance to attend proceedings, neither was she represented. The proceeding no doubt raises question of possible abuse of due process more so when it is considered from the backdrop that the courts should not be too ready to make unopposed declaration.[47] The decision can still be attacked on the ground that the hospital seeking to authorise forced Caesarean hardly has *locus standi* in the treatment choice of the patient.[48]

It is trite law that urgency of itself cannot and does not confer jurisdiction on any court. Jurisdiction is generally founded on statute.[49] Generally an action is commenced in the high court by a writ of summons, originating summons,

[46] [1992] 3 WLR 806.
[47] See *Re F (Mental Patient: Sterilisation* [1990] AC 1.
[48] Barbara Hewson, Ethical Triumph or Surgical Rape? (1993) 137 SJ 1182.
[49] See *Victor Rossek* v. *African Continental Bank Ltd* (1993) 8 NWLR (pt312) 382 at 392.

originating motion or petition endorsed with a statement of the nature of the claim and relief sought.[50] Application for use of petition is usually prescribed by statute for special cases, e.g. election petition, company winding up proceedings, matrimonial causes, etc. Originating motion is employed if a statute provides for its application without specifying the form in which it is to be made, especially where rules of court do not specify any special procedure.[51] Originating summon on the other hand is principally used for construction of documents and cases where facts are not likely to be in dispute. The writ of summons is the general form for the commencement of most types of action. If a claim is against a doctor and the grounds of the complaint is founded in tort or contract the proper form of action would be a writ of summons.[52] It is the appropriate form that enables the parties put oral evidence before the court. It is expected that most malpractice cases would be contentious, requiring oral evidence.

If the issue sought to be submitted to court has to do with selecting an appropriate medical regime for a patient, the emergency situation makes inappropriate writ of summons. The reasons are that the writ system requires accompanying statement of claim, oral and documentary evidence, protracted litigation process leading to judgment, at which time death or serious damage may have occurred. Averagely, litigation process through the writ system takes about five (5) years in the high courts in Nigeria. The speed of originating motion and the novelty of its procedure—requiring only affidavit (documentary) evidence would be most appropriate. For example if a child is in dire need for medical treatment but the parent and doctor disagree on the method of management, or both parties agree, but are not sure what to do, an application to court by originating motion can be brought under sections 300 to 302 of the Criminal Code or the court's civil jurisdiction for direction. It is suggested that the same rules would apply if the patient is incompetent. The range of persons covered by the section includes persons who are unable by reason of age, sickness, unsoundness of mind and detention from providing themselves necessaries.[53]

---

[50] See 0.3 r.1 of High Court of Lagos State (Uniform) Civil Procedure) Rules 1987 enacted as High Court (Civil Procedure) Rules 1994, applicable in Lagos State.

[51] *Re Meister, Lucius and Bruning* [1914] W N 390.

[52] 03 r.2 (1) (a) and (c) of the Rules, *op. cit*, stipulates that proceedings shall be commenced by writ if the claim is for a remedy for any tort or other civil wrong and if the claim is for a breach of duty (whether raising from a contract or a provision of law or independent of any contract or provision of law) or where damages consist of death of a person or in respect of personal injuries to a person.

[53] S. 300-302 of the Criminal code, Laws of Nigeria 1990 stipulate that anyone in charge of an incompetent person or child shall provide necessaries for the incompetent person or child, either as a result of contract, filial relationship or parental responsibility. To extent that a breach the duty to provide necessaries capable of causing death or ill health, the term "necessaries" must be understood to include medical care and attention. See also s.339- 341 make it criminal felony for person under a duty to provide necessaries, filing to observe the duty of supplying necessaries.

With hindsight of the section it is suggested that *Police* v. *Rita Esuabunor*[54] was wrongly decided under the Children and Young Person Law, Cap 25 of Lagos State. The applicant sought an interim order for the protection of the life of an infant, Tega Esuabunor. The purpose was to enable the medical facility of Chevron Nigeria Limited, Lekki Peninsula, Lagos treat and do all necessary things for the protection of the child. By order of the Chief Magistrate, the clinic was authorised if need be against the wishes of the mother of the child to have custody for purpose of treatment. By so doing the court it is respectfully suggested misapplied the law. It adopted a wrong procedure. The Children and Young Persons Law is a statute enacted to make provision for the welfare of the young and the treatment of young offenders. It was not enacted to care for the provision of medical treatment of young person. Its section 27 (1) stipulates that if a parent or guardian of a child prove to a juvenile court that he is unable to control the child, a court would make a corrective order respecting the child. Thus section 27 only applies to cases where a child is of ungovernable behaviour requiring correction. By no logical stretch does it apply to give hospital custody to treat a child against the wishes of the parent. It is therefore suggested that the decision in *Esuabunor* was reached *per incuriam*.

If there was a complaint about the parent neglect of a child's treatment the proper proceeding would be to bring an originating motion under the relevant provision of the Criminal Code. Where however circumstances of a case are close to the facts as in *Re S* an application for forceful treatment can be hinged on the provision of the Criminal Code which criminalises suicide.[55] It must however be said that refusal of treatment by an adult is not synonymous with suicide and it may indeed by very difficult to establish an attempt to kill oneself to warrant the use of courts coercive power to forcibly treat a patient. Since the court recognise a patient's right to refuse medical treatment even if that is the product of a sensible, insensible, rational or irrational decision, it would be difficult to raise conviction within the necessary provisions of the Criminal Code. Good a thing the line of difference between suicide and the right to decide how to live or be treated is a cherished principle in medicine.[56] In emergency cases whether the patient is competent, incompetent or minor originating motion would be most appropriate.

However, we must not forget to take care of the legal issues that may themselves arise in such proceedings. Proceeding where the patient is excluded from hearing leading to judgment are susceptible to attack on due process grounds.[57] It is for this reason that it is suggested that if it is impossible for the patient to be represented the court should appoint an *amicus curia* on his behalf.

---

[54] Unreported suit No. M/73/97 judgment delivered by Chief Magistrate M Olokoba Esq. on 12th May, 1997.

[55] See s.327 which provides that any person who attempt to skill himself is guilty of a misdemeanour and is liable to imprisonment of one year.

[56] *Sidaway* v. *Board of Governors of the Bethlehem Royal Hospital* [1985] AC 871, 904-905 *Malette* v. *Shulman* (1990) 67 DLR (4th) 321, per Robins JA at p. 336.

[57] *Okonkwo* v. *Chinwenka* (1992) I NWLR (pt216) 175 where the court stated that a breach of fair hearing renders court processes a nullity.

Also is the question of *locus standi.* [58] It is difficult to see how a hospital facility or doctor could be affected adversely to vest in him the right to institute action to compel treatment. Such right in our considered view can only so vest in cases where the refusal of treatment amounts to a crime, in which case the observation of Kayode Esho JSC may apply. He said:

> 'Though Cain challenged the *locus standi* of being questioned as to the whereabout of his brother Abel, it was his reason that he was not his brother's keeper. That might have been at the outskirts of the Garden of Eden. In Nigeria it would be an unacceptable phenomenon. And when it comes to the law of crime, everyone is certainly his brother's keeper.'[59]

Wherever there is need to institute an action via the originating motion method, in cases of emergency, it is desirable to include as part of the documentary evidence an affidavit of urgency, so that the matter can be quickly set down for determination. Medical law litigation is emerging in Nigeria and the procedure to be followed is somewhat ambivalent. With literacy improving it is expected that the rate of litigation is bound to increase and there would be a need for guidance on the best procedure to be employed. It is hoped that in the near future specialised division of the high court, such as the present English Family Division would be established to hear cases connected with matters of medical treatment.[60]

---

[58] See *Senator Abraham Adesanya* v. *The President of the Federal Republic of Nigeria* [1981] 1 SC. 40 and *Chief Gani Fawehinmi* v. *Akilu & Ors* (1987) 1 NWLR (pt. 67).

[59] See Kayode Esho JSC in *Fawehinmi* v. *Akilu* (*supra*).

[60] The Lagos High Court is blazing the trail with specialised divisions, with a Family Division established.

Chapter Seventeen

Psychiatry and Toxicology

Introduction

Nigeria has a few psychiatric hospitals, mostly financed by the World Health Organisation. Psychiatric cases raise moral questions connected with treatment of vulnerable persons. A physician is expected to protect persons of weak intellect, mentally unsound persons, idiots, and several other abnormal persons. Treatment of these ones may require the pronouncement of the physician's medical opinion and certificates for the purpose of determining legal capacity[1] or responsibility for their act and omission.[2]

In *Re C*[3] the applicant, C, aged 68 years was serving a seven-years prison sentence in 1963 when he was diagnosed as mentally ill and transferred to Broadmoor. In September 1963, he was diagnosed with gangrene in the right foot and it was considered that he would die if his leg were not amputated below the knee. It was considered medical opinion that his chances of survival with conservative treatment would be no better than 15 per cent. C refused to consider the medical opinion. He refused amputation. Rather he only gave consent to a more conservative treatment. Fortunately as against medical opinion he got better and the feared death was averted. However the hospital refused to give C an undertaking that it would not amputate in any future circumstances. On this basis, C sought an injunction to restrain the hospital from amputating his right leg without his prior consent in the event his right leg in future threatened his life. On the application medical evidence showed that the condition of C's foot would again threaten his life and that below-knee amputation carried a 15 per cent mortality risk. C still refused, objecting to future amputation. The question for determination were therefore whether C wishes should take precedent over the physician considered opinion and if his mental illness was sufficient to remove his decision–making capacity. It was also in issue if a court

[1] See generally, John Glaister, *Medical Jurisprudence and Toxicology*, 9th edn London: E & S Livingstone, 1953

[2] See s. 24 of Criminal Code.

[3] (1994), All ER 819, (1993) 15 BMLR 77. Thorpe J at 824 noteworthy of mention stated that a refusal to medical treatment can take the form of a declaration of intention never to consent in the future.

could in exercise of its jurisdiction grant an equitable relief of injunction beyond present to future circumstance. Justice Thorpe of the English Family Division answered the last question in the affirmative. On the question of decision–making capacity, he said: 'The decision-making process could be analysed into three stages...

> first, comprehending and retaining the treatment information; second, believing it and third, weighing the information, balancing risks and needs, to arrive at a choice. Applying that list, the presumption that C has the right of self– extermination had not been displaced. Although his general capacity was impaired by schizophrenia it had not been established that he did not sufficiently understand the nature, purpose and effects of the treatment he refused. He understood and had arrived at a clear choice.'[4] Accordingly the court granted the injunctive order in C's favour respecting future medical treatment.

That is explicit recognition that in the treatment of a psychiatric patient a physician must be careful to draw the line between a patient who has lost decision–making capacity for whom his medical decisions would bind, and those who still retain capacity despite mental illness for whom he must seek consent. Drawing the line is not the least easy. Psychiatric cases differ in degree and nature. There is no general agreement even amongst medical doctors on degree of impairment that is sufficient to displace mental capacity. In *C* case the court held that schizophrenia was insufficient. *Re C* merely illustrates that classification of what amounts to psychiatric illness that deprive a patient of capacity is more of policy consideration.

Psychiatric illness bears some resemblance with the description of insanity under the Criminal Code. Section 28 of the Criminal Code states that mental disease or natural mental infirmity which (i) deprives a person of capacity to understand what he is doing or (ii) deprives a person capacity to control his action or (iii) deprives a person of capacity to know that he ought not to do the act or make the omission will raise defence of insanity to a criminal charge. The proviso to the section states that delusion may also qualify as a form of insanity. Proof of insanity in the bracket of (i) to (iii) provides a complete defence to any charge, although the court would then order the detention of the offender under the relevant statutory law in an institutional place at the pleasure of the Governor or President as the case may be. Proof of delusion provides limited defence, in the sense that the offender is criminally responsible for his act and omission to the same extent as if the real state of things had been such as he was induced by the delusion to believe.[5]

The law to a large extent does not consider psychiatric normal members of society. Their mental state make them either very excitable or criminal. There is therefore a need to quarantine them to ensure the safety of others and sometimes the safety of the patient. The justification for compulsory, institutional protection aims to protect society from dangers. In *W* v. *Egdell*[6] and *Tarasoff* v. *Regents of*

[4] *Supra*
[5] Glaister, above n. 1, chapter 15
[6] [1990] 1 AII ER 835.

the University of California [7] the court recognised the good of their compulsory protection. If an offender is shown to be insane the court will make an order under sections. 229 and 401 of the Criminal Procedure Act confining him to prison at the pleasure of the Governor.

The practice of compulsory detention for cases of psychiatric patient can raise human rights issues in certain quarters. Critics of compulsory detention argue that detention constitute unwanted intervention in the lives of psychiatric patients who have a right to live their lives undisturbed though their behaviour is considered cynical. The libertarian philosophy of Mill only justifies an interference with rights for the protection of society from harm. On this ground psychiatric patients who do not constitute harm to society ought to be allowed unfettered freedom no matter how bizarre their lifestyle may be.[8]

Toxicology

This is the branch of medicine that deals with the knowledge, character, nature of poison, the consequence of its use, measures employed to combat its consequences and the rules that regulate sale, and administration of poison.[9] *Poison* is defined to include substances enumerated in the first schedule of the Poisons and Pharmacy Act of 1964.[10] It includes things like lead, mercury, phenol, snake poisons, zinc phosphate, amongst several others. This is by no means an exhaustive definition. The Criminal Code [11] does not also attempt to define the term poison. However the Western Nigeria Criminal Code [12] contains four sections which are equivalent to sections 58-61 of the Poisons And Pharmacy Act, which provide that the term poison and poisonous matter shall mean and include all animal, vegetable and mineral poisons.

By virtue of the Poisons Pharmacy Act only the following persons can mix, compound, prepare, dispense, import and export, i.e., deal in poisons, pharmacist, medical practitioner for the immediate use of his patient, veterinary and dental surgeon for veterinary and dental use respectively, medical and allied studies students who of necessity must handle drug and poison. The Act constitutes the main basis for regulating the handling of drug and poison until the Food and Drug Act 1974 was enacted, to further empower food and drug officers to seize toxicant

---

[7] 529 P 2d 55 (Cal, 1974). See also, T. Groves, PrisonPolicies on HIV under Review (1990) 303 *BMJ* 1354; S.A.M. Gore and A.G. Bird, No Escape: HIV Transmission in Jail (1993) 307 *BMJ* 147. See Mason & Smith *op. cit.* p 385-401.

[8] For related/anological discussion on AIDS see, L. Gostin and A. Ziegler, Review of AIDS-related Legislative and Regulatory Policy in the United States (1987) 15 *Law Med Hlth Care* 5.

[9] Glaister *op. cit.*, p. 499.

[10] See Poison and Pharmacy Act, law of the Federation Vol 2004.

[11] Criminal Code Cap. Vol. of Laws of Federation 2004.

[12] P O Okonkwo, *Forensic Toxicology in the Tropics*, p. 175.

and prosecute offenders.[13] The Act empowers the Food and Drug Council to make regulation on foods, drugs, cosmetics and devices.

Differentiating between a drug and cosmetic may sometimes be difficult to draw. In an attempt to do this the Act provides that the term 'drug' shall include any substance or mixture or substances manufactured, sold or advertised for use in (a) the diagnosis, treatment, mitigation or prevention of any disease, disorder, abnormal physical state, or the symptoms thereof in man or in animals; (b) restoring, correcting or modifying organs functions in man and in animals; (c) disinfecting, or the control of vermin, insects or pests; or (d) contraception. From the use of the term above, it would appear that a substance is classified as a drug if it leads to physiological or psychological changes in man or animals.[14]

The National Drug Law Enforcement Agency Act 1989[15] supplements the position by defining narcotics or dangerous drug to mean mind-affecting drugs. Thus, poison as opposed to drug can be described as 'a substance which when taken into the mouth or stomach, or when absorbed into the blood is capable of affecting seriously the health or of destroying life by its action on the tissues with which it immediately, or after absorption it comes into contact with.'[16] This is in consonance with the context of sections 228, 229, 336 and 338 of the Criminal Code where the word poison is construed by implication to mean any substance calculated to injure health and or life.[17] That is why the law punishes anyone who has in his possession anything described as poison who is not authorised by law to possess or administer it.[18]

Poison can kill or destroy tissues it comes in contact with in the human body. Its effect may be adverse or mild, depending on quantity administered, idiosyncrasy of the person, condition of administration, and its cumulative effect. A common form of abuse of poison in our society is the abuse of alcohol, usually referred to as ethyl alcohol. The rules regulating criminal responsibility arising from alcohol is section 28 and 29 of the Criminal code. As a general rule, intoxication does not constitute a defence to a criminal charge,[19] but it may in certain circumstances provide limited defence if it is shown to be involuntary to the extent of producing insanity in the offender. Its abuse may also constitute defence if it is shown to negate an intention specific or general to commit a crime.[20]

Toxin sometimes does not only mean those substances taken into the human body in form of consumption. It includes objects, things that come in contact with us, most times involuntary. To curtail environmental poison, and safeguard factory

---

[13] Nimi Wilson-Jack, Drug Trafficking and the Law in Nigeria p. 2.

[14] Glaister, *op. cit.*

[15] S. 44 of NDLEA Act, 1989, LFN 2004

[16] Glaister, *op. cit.*, 499.

[17] See *R* v. *Cramp* (1880) 5 QB D 307, *State* v. *Njoku* [1973] 3 ECSLR 638 and S.23 of Offences Against the Persons Act.

[18] Ibid.

[19] *DPP* v. *Beard* [1920] AC 479, *Egbe Nkonu* v. *State* [1980] 3-4 SC 1. See *R* v. *Omoni* (1949) 12 WACA 511.

[20] *Kofi Mensah* v. *R* 14 WACA 174 generally Okonkwo & Naish, *Criminal Law in Southern Nigeria.*

premises and employee, the Factories Act 1956 enjoins factories to minimise dust, fumes or other impurities. Factories are also mandated to provide protective clothing and appliances for its workers. Under the Factories Act the Minister is empowered to make regulations for heat, safety and welfare of workers in factories. Factory inspectors are by the Act empowered to inspect factories and all deaths from occupational diseases must be notified to the government inspectors.

The various statutes regulating dealing in poison are by no means co-ordinated. For example, the Poison and Pharmacy Act still maintains provision that 'persons holding missionary permit' would be permitted to deal in poison. One only wonders how being a missionary or holding a permit from a missionary can qualify a person to be a safe custodian or dispenser of poison, especially when the person has no medical training. The reason for this provision is hard to justify, especially so when the Act came into effect after the dismantling of colonialism with its associated missionary paraphernalia. May be it is founded on the charitable character of the missionary calling, that by virtue of their humanitarian work in society they ought to be allowed to deal in poison. The advantages of such permission to a rural community may of course be real. The definition of drug under the Food and Drugs Act 1974 as any substance of vegetable, animal or mineral origin or any preparation or mixture thereof used for internal or external application to the human body for treatment of disease does not take into cognisance substances used to maintain the human body from deteriorating. Medicine is not only concerned with the treatment of human. It also aims (i) to prevent the occurrence of illness (ii) to cure illness (iii) where illness cannot be cured, to prevent or retard deterioration (iv) to relieve pain and suffering in body and mind.[21] Thus the definition of drug in the Act is not expansive enough to cover all function of medicine and use of drugs.

Regulation of the use of dangerous drugs has long attracted international concern. The Economic and Social Council of the United Nations functioning through the International Narcotics Control Board, controls dealing in import, export, production, manufacture, transportation or otherwise of narcotics drugs. It is the agency for co-ordinating the various international agreements among United Nations members on dangerous and narcotic drugs. In 1961 however the United Nations harmonised the various international agreement by adopting a single convention on narcotic drugs.[22] The 1961 single convention brought to an end and replaced all international agreement on narcotic, namely the following:[23]

1. 1925 Agreement signed at Geneva in 1925, as amended by Protocol at Lake Success, New York in 1946, controlling the manufacture of internal trade in and use of opium.
2. 1925 International Convention signed in Geneva, as amended at Lake Success, New York in 1946.

---

[21] See *Airedale NHS Trust* v. *Bland* (*supra*) at 335.

[22] Single connection on Narcotic Drug 1961, Resolution 689 J (xxvi) of 28th July 1958 of the Economic and Social Council (Ecosoc) of the United Nations.

[23] See Andrew A Egboh, *Textbook of Forensic Pharmacy in Nigeria* (Literamed Publicaction) pp. 56-67.

3. 1931 Convention for limiting the manufacturing and regulating the distribution of narcotic drugs.
4. 1931 Agreement for the Control of Opium smoking in the Far East, signed at Bangkok
5. 1946 Convention for the suppression of the illicit trafficking in dangerous drugs.
6. 1946 Protocol amending the agreements, conventions and protocols on Narcotic Drugs concluded at the Hague on 23 January 1912, at Geneva on 11th February 1925 and 19th February 1925 and 13th July 1931, at Bangkok on 27th November 1931 and at Geneva on 26th June, 1936 signed at Lake Success, New York, on 11th December 1946.
7. 1948 Protocol signed at Paris in 1948 incorporating under international control, drug outside the scope of the convention of 13th July, 1931.
8. 1953 Protocol for limiting and regulating the cultivation of poppy plant, the production of and use of opium.

The single convention enjoins members to establish drug control agency. After the single convention 1961, the United Nations have extended International control to new types of psychoactive drugs such as LSD by the Convention on Psychotropic Substance 1971.[24] The Convention Against Illicit Traffic in Narcotics Drug and Psychotropic Substances 1988 seeks to galvanise the international community to fight the growing menace of the drug trade. Provision is thus made to smash illicit international drug trade with provision to confiscate their proceeds thereto.[17]

It is in response to this international concern that Nigeria enacted the National Drug law Enforcement Agency Act 1989 to fight illegal dealing in narcotics. The preamble sets out the aim of the legislation – namely, government grave concern for the increase in demand and trafficking in narcotics and its determination to eradicate same. The Act established the National Drug Law Enforcement Agency (NDLEA) with the responsibilities of achieving the aims set out the Act. The Agency is also empowered to investigate life style of individual, and where it appears that such lifestyle are ostentatious, to make inquiry on whether it is a result of money laundered from drugs. Under the guise of this power, the Agency has liquidated several moneybags, rightly or otherwise. The Act stipulates punishment for the manufacture, export, import, trafficking in hard drug, as well as laundering the proceeds thereto. The penalty for contravention is placed as life imprisonment.[25]

Possession or use of drugs known as LSD, cocaine or heroin attracts term of imprisonment not less than 15 years, but not exceeding 20 years. The provision on assets seizure and confiscation for money laundering from drug is an innovation in Nigeria drug legislation. For the first time the State acting through the Agency is empowered to seize and or confiscate assets derived from unlawful activities connected with hard drugs. The underpinning for this provision is the supposition that this draconian measure would discourage offenders from dealing in hard drug

[24] Nimi Walson-Jack, *op. cit*, p. 64-67.
[25] S. 4. (1) (a) Ibid.

and incapacitate the offender's re-entry into the trade.[26] The Agency in course of its investigation is empower to require suspects to make frank and full disclosures to it of all or any assets.[27] Initially, drug offenders were tried in special courts/tribunal established pursuant to the Tribunal Miscellaneous Offence Decree 1988, a jurisdiction now transferred to the federal High Courts.

With a view of improving health of Nigerians, it is suggested that toxicology laboratories be established in many states to facilitate diagnosis and legislation be put in place to regulate the level of toxins and poisons in our environment.[28]

---

[26]. S. 26 (I) & (2) make it an offence to refuse to make full disclosure of owns assets.

[27] P O Okonkwo, *Francis Toxicology in the tropics, op. cit.*

[28] Glaister, *op. cit.*

Chapter Eighteen

Commentary on Rules: framework of modern medicine

In the management of a patient's illness, doctors and nurses play a primary role in the health care services. Others also may well have specific roles to play. These other professionals may include pharmacist, dentist, counsellors, social workers, physiotherapist, midwives, medical recorders, radiographers, etc. All of these professions are relegated by statute and rules of professional ethics regulating their professions. The scope of this book has focused on the institutional framework of doctor's treatment, and so shall be the basis of our discussion. As our discussion has so far revealed, a analysis of ethics in the context of doctor-patient relationship can serve as rough map showing the way regulation for the other medical related professions ought to be structured. In fact in Nigeria, the rules of ethics for medical doctors and dental practitioners are same.

The practice of medicine in Nigeria is regulated by the Medical and Dental Practitioners Act No. 23 of 1988, which set up the Medical and Dental Council of Nigeria (MDC called the Council) charged with the following responsibilities.

(i) determining the standard of knowledge and skill to be attained by persons seeking to become members of the medical and dental profession and reviewing those standards from time to time as circumstances may permit.

(ii) Securing in accordance with the provision of the Act the establishment and maintenance of registers of persons entitled to practice as members of the professions and the publication from time to time of lists of those persons,

(iii) Reviewing and proposing from time to time, a statement as to the code of conduct which MDC considers desirable for the practice of the professions in Nigeria and

(iv) Performing the other function conferred on the Council.

By virtue of the powers (iii) the Council enacted the Rules of Professional Conduct for Medical and Dental Practitioners in Nigeria (hereafter called the Code), set up the Medical and Dental Practitioners Disciplinary Tribunal (Tribunal) and the Medical and Dental Practitioners Investigating Panel (Investigating Panel) for the enforcement of its rules. The rules were enacted to enable the professionals maintain universally accepted professional standard of practice and conduct.

In accordance with legislation the Council maintains a register of all persons entitled to practice as members of the medical profession. This naturally raised the question who is a doctor? Though any one can refer to himself as a doctor a medical practitioner is one whose name is in the register of the Council. Registration function is assigned to the Registrar of the Council. The Tribunal of the Council acts as the court for medical discipline. When acting in that capacity it is empowered to conform its practice and procedure to that of the High Court. It is also vested with powers to compel attendance of witnesses, admit documents and administer oath. In its proceedings an assessor, is appointed to advise it on questions of law. For every charged before it, it is empowered to enter a verdict of 'guilty of infamous conduct in a professional respect' or 'not guilty of infamous conduct in a professional respect.' Where the verdict entered in the former, the doctor stands the risk of being suspended or having his name erased from the register. According to Lord Pearson of the Privy Council in the case of *Tamesby* v. *General Medical Council*,[1] the court attaches great weight to the decisions of Medical Council, because of the calibre of professionals it represents. Infamous conduct has been described by the English Court of Appeal in *Hennessey case* to mean such a conduct by a medical man in the pursuit of his profession that reveal that he 'has done something with regard to it which would be reasonably regarded as disgraceful or dishonourable by his professional brethren of good repute and competence.'[2]

Article 1:

Merely states the underlying reasons for the Code of medical ethics, namely to preserve the high esteem of the profession.

Article 2:

States the obvious. The ambit of 1(c) is restrictive. The Tribunal of the Council is established by s. 5 of the Act with jurisdiction to try cases of infamous conduct in a professional respect. By s. 1(2) (c) of the Act, the Council is empowered to prescribe standards of behaviour or rules of ethics for practitioners, which has been so enacted as the Rules herein. Furthermore, the rule states that any practitioner who 'is found to have contravened the Code by the Disciplinary Tribunal of the Medical and Dental Council of Nigeria shall be guilty of professional misconduct.' It is therefore submitted that the combined effect of the above is that the jurisdiction of the Tribunal is necessarily limited and circumscribed to trying only charges alleging a contravention of specific rules made pursuant to s. 1(2) (c). This mean that the degree of infamous conduct is limited to those breaches prescribed by the Code, and to that extent is not open but close by the Code, save where new rules are made extending the categories of infamous conducts. Thus for a charge to succeed against a practitioner the prosecution must show clearly what specific rule in the Code the practitioner has contravened. If the Code is not satisfactory, the Tribunal cannot fill

[1] Unreported (20 July 1970).

[2] [1946] 1 Lancet 616 at 622, 862.

the gaps. Only the Council is vested with the power to make and amend rules.[3] This is the only reasonable way to give effect to the Act and Rules.

However, by virtue of the Council power to review from time to time the statement of conduct desirable for the practice of the profession in Nigeria,[4] it can be said that the scope of matters embraced within the meaning of the term 'infamous conduct in a professional respect' are not closed. The Council may open and expand the scope. But until it is done the present Code represent its scope. Interestingly, the General Medical Council, 'Blue Book' (in England) at paragraph 65 makes as reminder: 'It must be emphasized that the categories of misconduct described in part II cannot be regarded as exhaustive. Any abuse by doctors of any of the privileges and the opportunities afforded to them, or any grave dereliction of professional duty or serious breach of medical ethics, may give rise to a charge of serious professional misconduct.'

A clause like this in our present Code is desirable so that the rules on ethics for practitioners can continue to develop along practice line than the present situation that require express extension or amendment of the Code by the Council when a need for it arises.

Article 2

Requires all practitioners swear to the Physician Oath before being registered by the Council. The Oath is a modernised version of the Hippocratic Oath, introduced by the World Medical Association at the Declaration of Geneva, as amended at Sydney in 1968.

RULE 5

The Hippocratic Oath as modified by the Physician Oath provided the basis of the International Code of Medical Ethics.

RULE 6

(1) The doctor should avoid degrading treatment mindful that s.34 of the 1999 constitution protects the right to dignity of human person. Thus any treatment no matter how perceived by the practitioner as being in a patient's best interest is to be undertaken if it would produce in a patient loss of his esteem or depreciation in life.[5] A practitioner is under obligation to treat the 'whole man,' the patient's body, mind and spirit; for healing of the body in the face of a broken mind or spirit is but partial victory, if not, altogether a defeat of medical treatment.[6]

(2) Generally governed by health resource allocation.[7]

(4) Is our law ripe for changes especially in its construction of the of death, right of personal autonomy and other gray areas to bring it in line with international practice

---

[3] *IBWA* v. *Imano Ltd* (1988) 3 NWLR (pt.85) 633.

[4] See s.1(2) (c) of Act.

[5] *R* v. *Hallstran ex. parte W (No. 2)* [1986] 3 All ER 306 at 314.

[6] See Dr. Mewin A. Gasbery, *Journal of American Medical Association*, July 3, 1967 p. 150 and Dr. G.F. Begley, Texas Medicine, December 1970, p 25.

[7] See discussion on allocation of health resources in chapter 17 and Balcombe observation in *Re J (a minor) wardship: Medical Treatment)* [1992] 2 FLR 165 at 176, [1992] 9 BMLR 10 at 20.

in medicine? Should social and cultural factors not be taken into consideration in this respect?
(6) This should be compared also with rule 16 of the Code.[8]
(7) It puts a duty on a practitioner in all cases of emergency to treat a patient. However, he may refuse to take part in a treatment management he considers objectionable to his conscience. A similar provision is contained in s.4 of the English Abortion Act 1967, which excuses the 'conscientious objector.'[9]
(9) A practitioner should strive for excellence by reading medical journals and articles to deepen his medical knowledge. In *Crawford* v. *Charing Cross Hospital*, the English Court of Appeal was of the opinion while an anaesthetist would failed to read an article in the lancet describing certain risks in an operation may not necessarily be negligent, Lord Denning said: 'It would be putting too high a burden on a medical man to say that he must read every article in the medical press...the medical man's duty is limited to taking reasonable steps to keep himself abreast of modern developments in technique...failure to read a particular article may well be excusable, while disregard of series of warning in the medical press could perhaps be cogent evidence of negligence.'[10]
(10) In the medical case of a patient the practitioner is the primary custodian or against other para-medicals in treatment and management of the patient.
(11) Doctors are by the nature of their job enjoined to issue medical certificate, medical report, post-mortem reports and the like. The doctor must only do so on matters he has personally verified.
(12) Regulates research and experiments.[11]
(14) Is similar to rule 32. Where new procedures or discoveries are made the doctor must be circumspect in the use of the procedure or discoveries.[12]

RULE 7

For example a doctor practising in a remote place is not expert to have the surgical resources of an urban doctor. All the law requires of him is to possess and exercise such amount of skill and care as that of an average doctor. Medical insurance would help a doctor cover litigation damages in the event of negligence, it is therefore desirable. The courts must be mindful of the fact that increase in litigation will inevitably had to the practice of defensive medicine and so can damage the doctor-patient relationship.

---

[8] See discussion in chapter.

[9] *Janaway* v. *Sanford Area Health Authority* [1989] AC 537, [1988] 3 All ER 1079 (HL).

[10] [1953] TLR 1.

[11] See discussion on human research and experimentation in chapter 16.

[12] *Allison* v. *GMC* [1894] QB 750 and *R* v. *GMC ex. parte Kyneston* [1930] 1 KB 562. See also *Allbutt* v. *General Council of Medical Education and Registration* (1989) 23 QBD 400 and *Ex. parte La Mert* (1863) 33 LJ QB 69, 4 B & S 582, where the court was of the view that a doctor's published book on contraception being too low in price made it available to the young to the detriment of public moral thereby constituting infamous conduct. Contra with the modern view expressed in *Gillick* v. *West Norfolk & Wisbeeh Area Health Authority* [1986] AC 112, [1985] 3 All ER 402 (HL)

RULE 8

The range of conduct which amount to infamous conduct in a professional respect is limited to those declared by the Council in the Code.[13]

The term infamous conduct refers to conduct which relate to the pursuit of the professional that incur the strong reprobation of professional brethren of good repute and competence.[14]

The penalties for infringing the rules of the Code are clearly spelt out. It does not include payment of compensation to a patient or his family for any losses suffered.

RULE 10

On para. 1 – See the warning of Lord Denning in *Crawford* v. *Charing Cross Hospital*.[15]

On para. 2 – See comments by Tony Weir that 'those who come to help must not make things worse, the kiss of life should not be the kiss of death. But first aid need not be first class and the emergency may justify incompetence.'[16] The same standard would apply to doctors.

Para. 3 – states the obvious limitation on health resources.

Para. 4 – attempts to classify treatment that amount to professional negligence.

(a) Promptness of attention to some degree depends on the availability of resources.

(b) is more a question of problem of a novice or an inexperienced person.[17] Thus a consultant who delegates his duty to an incapable junior exposes himself to a claim in negligence.

(c) misdiagnosis will not be considered negligence if the proper standard of care is observed. But where the doctor fails to exercise proper skill, eg. fails to conduct test which a competent doctor would, misdiagnosis shall amount to negligence.[18]

(d) A line between this and innovative therapy must be drawn. Seller LJ in *Landau* v. *Werner* state that: 'A doctor might not be negligent if he tried a new technique but if he did he must justify it before the court. If his novel or exceptional

---

13 *IBWA* v. *Imano Ltd* (1988) 3 NWLR (pt.85)33.

14 *Allison* v. *General Council of Medical Education and Registration* [1894] QB 750 at 760-1, per Lord Esher MR; *Re a Solicitor, Ex. parte Law Society* [1912] 1 KB 302; *Grahame* v. *A-G of Fiji* [1936] 2 All ER 992; *Ex. parte Meehan* [1965] NSWR30; *Legal Practitioners Disciplinary Tribunal* v. *Idowu* [1971] NLR 128 at 137- 138, per Ademola; *R* v. *General Council by Medical Education and Registration of the UK* [1930] 1 KB 562 at 569, *Felix* v. *General Dental Council* [1960] AC 794.

15 [1953] TLR 1.

16 *A Case Book on Tort* (4th Ed.) *Windfied on Torts*. See also Wilmer LJ in *Tojo Maru* [1970] P. 21 at 40 'It is well established that the court recognizing the need to encourage salvers should take a lenient view where negligence or lack of skill is alleged against salvers.'

17 *Wilsher* v. *Essex Area Health Authority* [1987] QB 730, [1986] 3 All ER 801 (CA) and *Jones* v. *Manchester Corporation* [1952] 2 QB 852 at 871, [1952] 2 All ER 125 at 133 per Lord Denning.

18 *Chin Keow* v. *Government of Malaysia* [1967] 1 WLR 813 (failure to enquire as to the possibility of penicillin surgery; *Whiteford* v. *Hunter* [1948] 2 Lancet 232, (1950) 94 SJ 758 (HL) (misdiagnosis of bladder complaint as cancer); *Wilsher* v. *Essex Area health Authority* (*supra*); *Coles* v. *Reading and District Hospital Management Committee* (1963) 107 SJ 115 (failure to immunise); *Gardiner* v. *Mounfield & Lincoln Shire Area Health Authority* [1990] 1 Med. LR 205.

treatment has failed disastrously he could not complain if it was held that he went beyond the bounds of due care and skill as recognized generally.' [19]

(e) – If an error in treatment is one for which a man acting with ordinary care might avoid, it is evidence of negligence.[20]

(f) – See the ratio in *Dickson Igbokwe* v. *UCH*.[21]

RULE 11

Sometimes also termed 'malpractice,' means a failure in the exercise of a reasonable degree of care and skill on the part of a doctor in the treatment of his patient.

RULE 12

(a) As with legal practitioner, doctors ought to observe rules of precedence and accord senior members respect.[22]

RULE 15

This is an exception to the rule prohibiting advertisement.

RULE 16

See discussion on Medical Confidentiality.[23]

RULE 18

The right to withdraw service must arise only from good cause. A doctor must not relinquish the management of his patient to the detriment of the patient, that would amount to a 'death sentence' in severe cases. The proper course for the doctor is to refer the patient to another doctor for further management.[24]

RULE 19

Lord Ridell, stated that 'a doctor shares with other citizens the duty to assist in the detection an arrest of a person who has committed a serious crime.'[25] So if a doctor becomes aware of a crime he is authorised to breach the duty to maintain confidence of the offender.

RULE 22

In *McCoan* v. *General Medical Council*,[26] the Privy Council was invited to consider a case of a doctor whose name had been erased off the register on grounds of infamous or disgraceful conduct in a professional respect after he had sexual relationships with one of his patients. Lord Upjohn summarising the legal position stated, 'sexual intercourse with a patient has always been regarded as a most serious breach of the proper relationship between doctor and patient and their lordship do not see how the finding of the Committee on the facts of this case, that the appellant

---

[19] (1961) 105 Sol Jo 1008 (CA). See also *Tonkins* v. *Bexley Area Health Authority* (1993) 4 Med. LR 235

[20] *Whitehouse* v. *Jordan* [1981] 1 All ER 267, [1981] IWLR 246 (HL); *Dickson Igbokwe* v. *University College Hospital Board of Management* [1961] WNLR 173 and *Kanu Okoro Ajegbu* v. *Dr. E.S. Etuk* [1962] 6 ENLR 196.

[21] *Supra.*

[22] *AG* v. *Lord Advocate* [1834] 2 CC & Fin 481.

[23] See chapter 15.

[24] *Okonkwo* v. *MDPT* (1999) 6 NWLR (pt 786) 1 (SC)

[25] Riddel, *Medico-legal Problems*, London: Lewis & Co. Ltd. 1929.

[26] [1964] 3 All ER 143, [1964 1 WLR 1107.

was guilty of infamous conduct in a professional respect can be successfully challenged before their Lordship.'[27]

RULE 23

Deal with matters of abortion.[28]

RULE 25

Re Dinnerstein[29] succinctly summaries the legal position on 'no-code order' record in a patient's hospital case note file.

RULE 34

Discourages the practice of incorporating hospitals as limited liability companies so as not to give a semblance of doctors acting as though are common business persons doing business. No doubt, that is the motive, but it must not be forgotten that the directive can exclude doctors from the obvious advantages of incorporated limited liability companies.

RULE 35-40

Described the nomenclature of health institution.

RULE 41-44

Are regulations bearing on general etiquettes

RULE 45

At one time it was debatable whether or not the Council should only take cognisance of a doctor's conviction pronounced in a professional respect or in the pursuit of his calling as a doctor. This was the burning issue in *Marten* v. *Royal College of Veterinary Surgeon's Disciplinary Committee*.[30] A practising veterinary surgeon had a farm. During winter months a number of his cattle died on his farm from husk. He was charged before the committee of the Council of the Royal College of Veterinary Surgeons 'for disgraceful conduct in that he failed to provide adequate nursing for sick animals under his care, a situation that was likely to bring disgrace on the profession. The Committee found him guilty and he appealed to the Queen Bench Division, contending that a conduct cannot be said to be disgraceful unless it is done in pursuit of his profession. In the judgment of Lord Parker CJ, such an argument was absurd. He said for my part in I see no valid ground for limiting the words in the manner suggested. If of course, the conduct complained of is equally reprehensible in any way, whether a professional or not, as for example, conduct constituting some traffic offence, that conduct would nor come within the expression. If the conduct, however, though reprehensible in anyway is in the cases of the professional man so much more reprehensible as to be defined as disgraceful, it seem to me that it may, depending on the circumstances, amount to conduct disgraceful to him in a professional respect in the sense that it tends to bring disgrace on the profession which he practices. Thus, the disgrace need not arise from a professional calling. For relevant conviction to afford discipline by the Council, it

---

[27] Supra.

[28] See *R* v. *Bourne* (1952) 36 Cr. App. Rep. 125.

[29] 380 NE 2d 134 (1978).

[30] [1966] 1 QB 1, [1965] 1 All ER 499.

needs not to have arisen from the doctor's act or omission relating to his professional calling.'

Even without a conviction, *McEniff* v. *General Dental Council*[31] establishes the rule that medical negligence can itself amount to misconduct.

RULE 46

The prohibition against practising until the practice fees are paid as provided under the rule is observed more in breaches than in compliance.

RULE 47-48

Require the doctors to cooperate with the Investigation Panel and Tribunal to ensure speedy disposition of cases.

[31] [1980] 1 All ER 461, [1980] I WLR 328.

WORLD MEDICAL ASSOCIATION DECLARATION OF LISBON
ON
THE RIGHT OF THE PATIENT

Appointed by the 34th World Medical Assembly
Lisbon, Portugal, September/October 1981

and amended by the 47th General Asembly
Bali, Indonsia, September 1995

PREAMBLE

The relationship between physicains, their patient and broader society has undergone significant changes in recent times. While a physician should always act according to his concience, and alwaysin the best interest of the patient, equal effort must be made to guarantee patient autonomy and justice. The following Declaration represents some of the principle rights of the patient which the medical profession endorses and promotes. Physician and other persons or bodis involved in the provision of health care have a joint responsibility to regonize and uphold these rights.

Whenever legislation, goverment acyion or any other administratio or institution denies patient these rights, physicians should pursue appropriate means to assure or to restore them. In the context of boimedical research involving human subject – including non therapeutic biometical research – the subject is entitled to the same rights and consideration as any patient in a normal therapeutic situation.

PRINCIPLES

1 **Right to medical care of good quality**

Every person is entitled without discrimination to appropriate medical care.

a. Every patient has the right to be cared for by the physician whom he/she knows to be fre to make clinical and ethical without any outside interface.
b. The patient shall always be treated in accordance with his/her best interest. The treatment applied shall be in accordance with generally approved medical principle.
c. Quality assurance always should be apart of human care. Physicans, in particular should accept responsibility for being guardians of the quality of medical services
d. In circumstances where a choice must be made betwen potential patients for a particular treatment which is limited supply, all such patients are entitled to fair selection procedure for that treatment. The choice must be based medical criteria and made without discrimination
e. The patient has the right of continuity of health care. The physician has a obligation to cooperate in the coordination of medically indicated care with other health care provider treating the patient. The physicain may not discontinue treatment of the patien as long as further treatment is medically indicated, without giving the patient reasonable assistance and sufficient opportunity to make alternative arrangement for care.

2 **Right to freedom of choice**

a. The patien has the right to choose freely and change his/her physician anh hospital or health service institution, regardless of whether they are based in the private or public sector.
b. The patien has the right to ask for the opinion of another phsician at any stage.

3 **Right to self-determination**

a. The patient has the right to self-determine, to make free decisions regarding himself/herself. The physician will inform the patient of the consequences of his/her decisions.
b. A mentally competent adult patient has the right to give or withhold consent to any diagonstic procedure or theraphy. The patient has the right to the information necessary to make his/her decisions. The patient should understand clearly what the purpose of any test or treatment, what the results will imply, and what would be the implications of withholding consent.
c. The patient has the right to refuse to participate in research or the teaching of medcine.

4 The unconscious patient

a. If the patient is unconcious or otherwise unable to express his/her will, informed consent must be obtained whenever possible, form a legally entitled representative where legally relevant.
b. If a legally entitled representative is not available, but a medical intervention is urgently needed,consent of the patient may be presumed, unless it is obvious and beyond any doubt on the basis of the patient's previous firm expression or conviction that he/she would refuse consnt to the intervention in that situation.
c. However, physicians should always try to save the life of the patient unconscious due to sucide attempt.

5 The legally incompetent patient

a. If a patient is a minor or otherwise legally incopetent the consent of a legally entitled representative, where legally relevant, is required. Nevertheless the patient must be involved in the decision making to the fullest extent allowed by his/her capacity.
b. If the legally incompetent patient can make rational decision, his/her decision must be respected, and he/she has the right to forbid the disclosure of the information to his/her legally entitled represntative.
c. If the patient legally entitled representative, or a person authorized by the patient, forbids treatment which is, in the opinion of the physician, in the patients best interest, the physician should challenge this decision in the relevant legal or other institution . in case of emergency, the physician will act in the patients best interest.

6 Procedure against the patients will

Diagnostic procedures or treatment against the patients will can be carried out only in exceptional cases, if specifically permitted by law and conforming to the principles of medical ethics.

7 Right to information

a. The patient has the right to recieve about himself/herself record in any of his/her medical records, and to be fully informed about his/her health status including the medical facts about his/her condition. However, confidential information in the patients record about a third party should not be given to the patient without the consent of the third patry.

b. Exceptionally, information may be withheld from the patient when there is good reason to believe that this information would create a serious hazard to his/her life or health.

c. information must be given in a way appropriate to the local culture and in such a way that the patient can understand.

d. The patient has the right not to be informed on his/her explicit request, unless required for the protection of another person's life.

e. The patient has the right to choose who, should be informed on his/her behalf.

8 Right to confidentiality

a. All identifiable information about the patient'shealth status, medical condition, diagnosis, prognosis and treatment of all other information of a personal kind, must be kept confidential, even afetr death. Exceptionally, decendants may have a right to access to information that would inform them of their health risks.
b. Confidential information may be disclosed if the patient's gives explicit consent or if expressly provided by the law. Information can be disclosed to other health care provider only on a strictly "need to know" basis unless the patient has given explicit consent.
c. All identifiable patient data must be protected. The protection of data must be appropriate to the manner of its storage. Human substances from which identifiable data can be derived must be likewise protected.

9 Right to Healt Education

Every person has the right to health education that will assist him/her in making informed choices about personal health and about available health services. The education should include information about healthy livestyles and about methods of prevention and early detection of illnesses. The personal responsibility for everybody for his/her own health should be stressed. Physicians have an obligation to participate actively in educational efforts.

10 Right to dignity

a. The patient's dignity and right to privacy shall be resoected at all times in medical care and teaching, as shall his/her culture and values.

b. The patent is entitled to relief of his/her suffering according to the current state of knowledge.
c. The patient is entitled to humane care nad to be provided with all available assistance in making dying as dignified and confortable as possible.

11 Right to religious assistance

The patient has the right to recieve or decline spritual and moral confort includibg the help of a minister of his/her choice.

Appendix 2

Medical and Dental Practitioners Act

CHAPTER 221

MEDICAL AND DENTAL PRACTITIONERS ACT

ARRANGEMENT OF SECTIONS
SECTION

CHAPTER 221

MEDICAL AND DENTAL PRACTITIONERS ACT

1988 No. 23 An Act to establish the Medical and Dental Council of Nigeria for the registration of medical practitioners and dental surgeons and to provide for a disciplinary and for the discipline of members.

Commencement [28th June, 1998]

Establishment, etc. of the Medical and dental Council of Nigeria

1. There is hereby established a body to be known as the Medical and Dental Council of Nigeria (hereafter in this Act referred to as "the Council") which shall be a body corporate with perpetual succession and a common seal and may sue or be sued in its corporate name.

(2) The Council shall have responsibility for __

(a) determining the standards of knowledge and skill to be attained by persons seeking to become members of the medical or dental profession and reviewing those standards from time to time as circumstances may permit;

(b) securing in accordance with the provisions of this Act, the establishment and maintenance of registers of persons entitled to practise as members of the medical or dental profession and the publication from time to time of lists of those persons;

(c) reviewing and preparing from time to time, a statement as to the code of conduct which the Council considers desirable for the practice of the professions in Nigeria; and

(d) performing the other functions conferred on the Council by this Act.

2. 1) The Council shall consist of a Chairman to be appointed by the President, and the following other members, that is __

(a) two representatives of the Federal Ministry of Health both of whom shall be fully registered medical practitioners or dental surgeons;

(b) the Chief Medical Officer (or however called) of the Ministry of Health of each State of the Federation;

(c) one representatives of the National Post-graduate Medical College;

(e) three representatives of Colleges or Faculties of Medicine of Universities in the country to be appointed by the Minister in rotation from among the provosts or deans of such Colleges or Faculties, so however that no two of such persons shall be from the same University;

(f) two representatives of the Medical and dental professions to be appointed by the Minister; and

(g) eleven members with the Nigeria Dental Association having at least two representatives in the Council.

(2) The provisions of the First Schedule to this Act shall have effect with respect to the qualifications and tenure of the Council and the other matters therein mentioned.

3. (1) Subject to subsection (2) of this section and to any directions given to the Council under this Act, the Council shall have power to do anything which in its opinion is calculated to facilitate the carrying out of its activities under this Act.

(2) The Council shall, with the prior consent of the Minister, have power to borrow money, acquire or dispose of any property and shall have power to pay remuneration (including pensions), allowances or expenses to any member, officer or servant of the Council or to any other person in accordance with scales approved by the Council.

Powers of
the Council

4. (1) The Minister may give to the Council directions of a general character or relating generally to particular matters (but not to any individual person or case) with regard to the exercise by the Council of its functions under this Act and it shall be the duty of the Council to comply with the directions.

(2) Before giving a direction under subsection (1) of this section, the Minister shall serve a copy of the proposed direction on the Council and shall afford the Council an opportunity of making representations to him with respect to the direction.

(3) The Minister may, after considering any representations made to him in pursuance of subsection (2) of this section, give the direction either without modification or with such modifications as appear to him to be appropriate having regard to the representations.

Financial
provisions.

5. (1) The Council shall prepare and submit to the Minister, not later than the 30th day of July of the year in which this Act comes into force and of each subsequent year, an estimate of its expenditure and income during the next succeeding financial year.

(2) The Council shall keep proper accounts in respect of each financial year, and proper records in relation to those accounts and shall cause its accounts to be audited as soon as may be after the end of the financial year to which the accounts relate by a firm of auditors approved, as respect that year, by the Council.

(3) The Minister shall out of moneys provided by the Federal Government, make to the Council either by way of grant or by way of loan, payments of such amounts as the National Council of Ministers may from time to time determine.

Appointment
of Registrar.
preparation and
maintenance of registers.

6. (1) It shall be the duty of the Council to appoint a fit medical practitioner or dental surgeon to be the Registrar for the purposes of this Act.

(2) It shall be the duty of the registrar to prepare and maintain, in accordance with rules made by the Council under this section, registers of the names, addresses and approved qualifications, and of such other particulars as may be specified, of all persons who are entitled in accordance with the provisions of this Act to be registered as medical practitioners or dental surgeons and who apply in the specified manner to be so registered.

(3) Separate registers shall be maintained for medical practitioners and dental surgeons respectively, each of which shall be divided into the following parts __

(a) one part for fully registered persons;

(b) one part for provisionally registered persons, in the case of medical practitioners; and

(c) one part for persons who have been granted limited registration under section 13 of this Act.

(4) Subject to the following provisions of this section, the Council shall make rules with respect to the form and keeping of the registers and the making of entries therein and in particular___

(a) regulating the making of applications for registration and providing for the evidence to be produced in support of the applications;

(b) providing for the notification to the Registrar, by the person to whom any registered particulars relate of any change in those particulars;

(c) authorising a registered person to have any qualification which is, in relation to the relevant profession, either an approved qualification or an accepted qualification for the purposes of this Act, registered in relation to his name in addition to or, as he may elect, in substitution for any other qualifications so registered;

(d) specifying the fees to be paid to the Council in respect of the entry of names on the registers and authorising the Registrar to refuse to enter a name on a register until any fee specified for the entry has been paid; and

(e) specifying anything failing to be specified under the foregoing provisions of this section, but rules made for the purposes of paragraph (d) of this subsection shall not come into force until they are confirmed by order of the Council.

(5) It shall be the duty of the Registrar__

(a) to correct, in accordance with the directives of the Council, any entry in the register which the Council directs him to correct as being in the opinion of the Council, an entry which was incorrectly made;

(b) to make any necessary alterations in the registered particulars of registered persons from time to time;

(c) to remove from the part of the relevant register which relates to provisionally registered persons all particulars relating to a person registered in that part of the register;

(d) to remove from the part of the relevant register which relates to limited registration, all particulars relating to a person whose limited registration has ceased; and

(e) to remove from the relevant register the name of any registered person who has died or become insane.

(6) If the Registrar___

(a) sends by post to any registered persons a registered letter address to him at his address on the register reminding him of any duty or enquiring whether the registered particulars relating to him are correct and receives no reply to the letter within a period of three months from the date of posting it,

the Registrar may remove the particulars relating to the person in question from the relevant register but the Council may direct the Registrar to restore to the appropriate part of the register, any particulars removed therefrom under this subsection.

(7) For the avoidance of doubt it is declared that a person shall not be entitled to have his name included in more than one part of the relevant register; and the Council may direct the removal of the name of any person to give effect hereto, so however that if the person is a citizen of Nigeria, his name shall not be removed from the part of the register which relates to fully registered person under the authority of this subsection.

(8) The Registrar shall give notice in writing by registered post to any medical practitioner or dental surgeon concerned of any directive of the Council given under subsection (7) of this section, and thereafter no appeal shall lie against the removal.

7. (1) It shall be the duty of the Registrar __

Publication of registers and list of corrections.

(a) to cause the registers to be printed, published and put on sale to members of the public not later than two years from the beginning of the year in which this Act comes into force;

(b) in each year after that in which a register is first published under paragraph (a) of this subsection, to cause to be printed, published and put on sale as aforesaid either a corrected edition of the register or a list of alterations made to the register since it was last printed; and

(c) to cause a print of each edition of the register and of each list of corrections to be deposited at the principal offices of the Council.

(2) It shall be the duty of the Council to keep the registers and lists of corrections deposited under subsection (1) of this section open at all reasonable times for inspection by members of the public.

(3) A document purporting to be a print of an edition of a register published under this section by authority of the Registrar in the current year, or documents purporting t be prints of an edition of a register so published in a previous year and of a list of corrections to that edition so published in the current year, shall (without prejudice to any other mode of proof) be admissible in any proceedings as evidence that any person specified in the document, or the documents read together, as being fully or provisionally registered or as being registered for a limited period as a medical practitioner or as a dental surgeon, is so registered and that any person not so specified is not so registered.

Registration

Full registration of medical practitioners and of dental surgeons.

8. (1) Subject to section 16 and to Rules made under section 6 (4) of this Act, a person shall be entitled to be fully registered as a practitioner or as a dental surgeon if __

(a) he has attended a course of training approved by the Council under section 9 of this Act as respects the medical or dental profession, as the case may be:

(b) the course was conducted at an institution so approved, or partly at one such institution and partly at another or others;

(c) he holds a qualification so approved; and

(d) he holds a certificate of experience issued in pursuance of section 11 of this Act.

(2) Subject as aforesaid, a person shall be entitled to register any post-graduate qualification if the qualification is approved by the Council in a specialised branch of medicine or dental surgery.

Approval of courses, qualifications and institutions.

9. (1) Subject to subsection (2) of this section, the Council may approve for the purpose of the Act.__

(a) any course of training which is intended for persons who are seeking to become, or are already members of the medical or dental profession and which the Council considers is designed to confer on persons completing it sufficient knowledge and skill for the practice of that profession or for practice as members of a specialised branch of that profession;

(b) any institution in Nigeria which the Council considers is properly organised and equipped for conducting the whole or any part of a course of training approved by the Council under this section;

(c) any qualification which, as a result of an examination taken in conjunction with a course of training approved by the Council under this section is granted to candidates reaching a standard at the examination indicating, in the opinion of the Council, that they have sufficient knowledge and skill to practise the profession in question or to practise as members of a specialised branch of that profession.

(2) The Council shall not, in pursuance of subsection (1) of this section, approve a qualification granted by an institution in Nigeria unless the qualification bears one of the following designations (with or without the addition of words indicating specialisation in a particular field), that is to say__

(a) bachelor of medicine and surgery; or

(b) bachelor of dental surgery.

(3) The Council may institute an assessment examination for holders of foreign medical or dental qualifications recognised by the government of the countries from where such qualifications were obtained.

(4) The Council may, if it thinks fit, withdraw any approval given under this section in respect of any course, qualification or institution, but before withdrawing such an approval, the Council shall __

(a) give notice that it proposes to do so to each person by whom the course is conducted or the qualification is granted or the institution is controlled, as the case may be;

(b) afford each such person an opportunity of making to the Council representations with regard to the proposal; and

(c) take into consideration any representations made as respects the proposal in pursuance of paragraph (b) of this subsection.

(5) As respects any period during which the approval of the Council under this section for a course, qualification or institution is withdrawn, the course, qualification or institution shall not be treated as approved under this section; but the withdrawal of such an approval shall not prejudice the registration or eligibility for registration of any person who by virtue of the approval was registered or eligible for registration (either unconditionally or subject to his obtaining a certificate of experience) immediately before the approval was withdrawn.

(6) The giving or withdrawal of an approval under this section shall have effect from such date, either before or after the execution of the instrument signifying the giving or withdrawal of approval, as the Council may specify in the instrument; and the Council shall __

(a) as soon as may be, publish a copy of every such instrument in the Federal Gazette; and

(b) not later than seven days before its publication as aforesaid, send a copy of the instrument to the Minister.

Supervision of instructions and examinations leading to approved qualifications.

10. (1) It shall be the duty of the Council to keep itself informed of the nature __

(a) the instructions given at approved institutions to persons attending approved courses of training; and

(b) the examinations as a result of which approved qualifications are granted,

and for the purposes of performing that duty the Council may appoint, either from among its own members or otherwise, persons to visit approved institutions or to attend such examinations at least once in three years.

(2) It shall be the duty of a visitor appointed under subsection (1) of this section to report to the Council on __

(a) the sufficiency of the instructions given to persons attending approved courses of training at institutions visited by him;

(b) the sufficiency of the examinations attended by him; and

(c) any other matters relating to the institutions or examinations on which the Council may, either generally or in particular case, request him to report,

but no visitor shall interfere with the giving of any instruction or the holding of any examination.

(3) On receiving a report made in pursuance of this section, the Council shall as soon as may be send a copy of the report to he person appearing to the Council to be in charge of the institution or responsible for the examinations to which the report relates requesting that person to make observations on the report to the Council within such period as may be specified in the request, not being less than one month beginning with the date of the request.

11. (1) A person who, after obtaining an approved medical or dental qualification, satisfies he conditions specified in subsection (2) of this section shall be entitled to receive free of charge a certificate of experience in the prescribed form.

(2) The conditions which a person must satisfy under subsection (1) of this section are __

(a) he must have been employed for the prescribed period at a recognised institution in Nigeria with a view to obtaining a certificate of experience and have resided throughout that period either in the institution or near to it in accordance with requirements in that behalf specified in the terms of his employment;

(b) he must have acquired during his employment practical experience under the personal supervision and guidance of one or more fully registered medical practitioners in the practice of surgery, midwifery, medicine or dental surgery, as the case may be, for such periods as may be prescribed in relation to each of those subjects respectively; and

(c) the manner in which he carried out the duties of his employment and his conduct during the period of his employment must have been satisfactory.

(3) Any period spent under subsection (2) of this section by a during his employment in acquiring experience of the techniques for safeguarding and improving the health of children or public health or of the activities carried on in a recognised health centre shall be calculated for the purposes of that subsection as periods in the practice of medicine.

(4) It shall be the duty of the person in charge of a recognised institution at which a person is employed with a view to obtaining a certificate of experience to ensure that the last-mentioned person is afforded proper opportunities of acquiring the practical experience required for the purposes of subsection (2) of this section.

(5) Where after having been employed as mentioned in paragraph (a) of subsection (2) of this section at any institution, a person is refused a certificate of experience he shall be entitled__

(a) to receive from the person in charge of the institution particulars in writing of the grounds of the refusal; and

(b) to appeal against the refusal to a committee of the Council in accordance with Rules made by the Council in that behalf (including Rules as to the time within which appeals are to be brought); and after duly considering any such appeal the committee shall either dismiss the appeal or issue the certificate of experience in question or give such other directive in the matter as it considers just.

(6) The Council may make regulations to provide for the issuance of certificate of experience in respect of employment at institutions outside Nigeria.

(7) In this section and in section 12 of this Act, "recognised" means recognised for the time being for the purposes of those sections by order of the Council.

Provisional registration of medical practitioners and dental surgeons.

12. (1) A person who has obtained an approved medical or dental qualification and satisfies the Registrar that he is of good character and he is about to be employed as mentioned in paragraph (a) of subsection (2) of section 11 of this act shall, subject to the provisions of section 15 and of rules made under section 6 of this Act, be entitled to be provisionally registered as a medical practitioner or dental surgeon.

(2) A person who is provisionally registered shall, for the purposes of employment at any recognised institution with a view to obtaining a certificate of experience, but not for any other purposes, be deemed to be fully registered.

Practitioners for limited registration.

13. (1) Where a person satisfies the Council__

(a) that he has been selected for employment for a specified period in an approved hospital or as the case may be, in any other approved institution in Nigeria in the capacity of a practitioner of medicine, surgery, dental surgery or midwifery, and that he is or intends to be in Nigeria for a limited period for the purposes of serving for that period in the employment in question; and

(b) that he has passed the assessment examination, if any, of the Council following some qualifications granted outside Nigeria which is for the time being accepted by the Council for the purposes of this section as respect the capacity in which, if employed, he is to serve,

the Council may, if it thinks fit, give a direction that he shall be registered for a limited period as a medical practitioner or as a dental surgeon, as the case may be.

(2) The registration of a person for a limited period shall continue only he is in such employment as is mentioned in subsection (1) (a) of this section and shall cease __

(a) on the termination of the period of employment specified to the Council under that subsection; or

(b) on the termination of the said employment before the end of that period,

whichever first occurs.

(3) Nothing in subsection (2) of this section shall preclude he Council from giving a further direction under subsection (1) of this section in respect of a specified period whose commencement coincides with the termination of another such period.

(4) A person registered by virtue of the provisions of this section shall, in relation to his employment as mentioned in subsection (1) (a) of this section, and to things done or omitted to be done in the course of that employment, be deemed to be fully registered, but in relation to all other matters he shall be treated as not so registered.

(5) No person with limited registration shall be allowed to either open or manage on his own a private health institution.

(6) In case of doubt as to whether a person's employment has been terminated, the decision of the Council shall be conclusive for the purposes of subsection (2) of this section.

Practising fees

14. (1) Subject to subsection (2) of this section, no medical practitioner or dental surgeon shall practice as a medical practitioner or dental surgeon, as the case may be, in any year unless he has paid to the Council in respect of that year the appropriate practising fee prescribed hereunder__

(a) in the case of a medical practitioner or dental surgeon of not less than 10 years standing, N100.00;

(b) in the case of a medical practitioner or dental surgeon of less than 10 years standing, N50.00;

(c) in the case of a house officer, N25.00; and

(d) in the case of a medical practitioner or dental surgeon with limited registration, N200.00.

(2) A medical practitioner or dental surgeon during his service year in the National Youth Service Corps Scheme shall be exempted from the payment of practising fee.

(3) The Council may, with the approval of the Minister from time to time, vary the practising fees prescribed under subsection (1) of this section.

(4) The Council shall share the aggregate amount collected as practising fees during the year as follows__

(a) 70 per cent to the Nigeria Medical Association; and

(b) 30 per cent to the Medical and Dental Council of Nigeria.

(5) Any medical practitioner or dental surgeon who in respect of any year and without paying the prescribed practising fee practises as such shall be guilty of an offence and shall be liable on conviction__

(a) in the case of a first offence, to a fine of twice the prescribed practising fee; and

(b) in the case of a second or subscribed practising fee,

and if the medical practitioner or dental surgeon is in the employment of any person, that person shall also be guilty of an offence and punished in like manner as the medical practitioner or dental surgeon unless he proves that the failure to pay the practising fee was without his knowledge, consent or connivance.

Professional discipline
Establishment of disciplinary Tribunal and investigating panel.

15. (1) There shall be established a tribunal to be know

as the Medical and Dental Practitioners Disciplinary Tribunal (hereafter in this Act referred to as "the disciplinary tribunal"), which shall be charged with the duty of considering and determining any case referred to it by the panel established under subsection (3) of this section and any other case of which the disciplinary tribunal has cognisance under the following provisions of this Act.

(2) The disciplinary tribunal shall consist of the Chairman of the Council and ten other members of the Council appointed by the Council who shall include not less than two persons who are fully registered dental surgeons.

(3) There shall be established a body to be known as the Medical and Dental Practitioners Investigating Panel (hereafter in this Act referred to as "the panel") which shall be charged with the duty of __

(a) conducting a preliminary investigation into any case where it is alleged that a registered person has misbehaved in his capacity as a medical practitioner or dental surgeon, or should for any other reason be the subject of proceedings before the disciplinary tribunal;

(b) compelling any person by subpoena to give evidence before it;

(c) deciding, if satisfied that to do so is necessary for the protection of members of the public, to make an order for interim suspension from the medical or dental profession in respect of the person whose case they have decided to refer for inquiry; and for the case to be given accelerated hearing by the disciplinary tribunal within three months; or

(d) deciding, if satisfied that to do so is necessary for the protection of members of the public or is in his interest, to make an order for interim conditional registration in respect of that person, that is to say, an order that his registration shall be conditional on his compliance, during such period not exceeding two months as is specified, as the panel may think fit to impose for the protection of members of the public or in his interest.

(4) The panel shall be appointed by the Council and shall consist of fifteen members, at least three of whom shall be dental surgeons.

(5) The provisions of the Second Schedule to this Act shall, so far as applicable to the disciplinary tribunal and the panel respectively, have effect with respect to those bodies.

Penalties for professional misconduct. etc.

16. (1) Where __

(a) a registered person is adjudged by the disciplinary tribunal to be guilty of infamous conduct in any professional respect; or

(b) a registered person convicted, by any court of law or tribunal in Nigeria or elsewhere having power to impose imprisonment for an offence (whether or not an offence punishable with imprisonment) which in the opinion of the disciplinary tribunal is incompatible with the status of a medical practitioner or dental surgeon, as the case may be; or

(c) the disciplinary tribunal is satisfied that the name of any person has been fraudulently registered,

the disciplinary tribunal may, if it thinks fit, give any of the directions specified in subsection (2) of this section.

(2) The disciplinary tribunal may give a direction under subsection (1) of this section __

(a) ordering the Registrar to strike the person's name off the relevant register or registers; or

(b) suspending the person from practice by ordering him not to engage in practice as a medical practitioner or dental surgeon, as the case may be, for such period not exceeding six months as may be specified in the direction; or

(c) admonishing that person.

(3) The disciplinary tribunal may, if it thinks fit, defer or further defer its decision as to the giving of a direction under subsection (1) of this section until a subsequent meeting of the disciplinary committee; but __

(a) no decision shall be deferred under this subsection for any period exceeding two years in the aggregate; and

(b) no person shall be a member of the disciplinary tribunal for the purposes of reaching a decision which has been deferred or further deferred unless he was present as a member of the disciplinary committee when the decision was deferred.

(4) For the purposes of subsection (1) of this section, a person shall not be treated as convicted as mentioned in paragraph (b) of that subsection unless the conviction stands at a time when no appeal or further appeal is pending or may, without extension of time, be brought in connection with the conviction.

(5) When the disciplinary tribunal gives a direction under subsection (1) of this section, he disciplinary tribunal shall cause notice of the direction to be served on the person to whom it relates.

(6) the person to whom such a direction relates may, at any time within twenty-eight days from the date of service on him of the notice of the direction, appeal against the direction of the Court of Appeal; and the disciplinary tribunal may appear as respondent to the appeal and, for the purposes of enabling directions to be given as to the costs of the appeal and of proceedings before the disciplinary tribunal, the disciplinary shall be deemed to be a party thereto whether or not it appears on the hearing of the appeal.

(7) A direction of the disciplinary tribunal under subsection (1) of this section shall take effect __

(a) where no appeal under this section is brought against the direction within the time allowed for the appeal, on the expiration of that time;

(b) where such an appeal is brought and is withdrawn or struck out for want of prosecution, on the withdrawal or striking out of the appeal;

(c) where such an appeal is brought and is not withdrawn or struck out as aforesaid, if and when the appeal is dismissed.

(8) A person whose name is removed from register in pursuance of a direction of the disciplinary tribunal under this section shall not be entitled to be registered in that behalf given by the disciplinary tribunal on the application of that person.

(9) A direction under this section for the removal of a person's name from the register may prohibit an application under subsection (8) of this section by that person until the expiration of such period from the date of the direction, and where he has duly made such an application, from the date of his last application, as may be specified in the direction.

Miscellaneous and General
Offences and
penalties

17. (1) Subject to subsection (6) and (7) of this section, if any person who is not a registered medical practitioner __

(a) for or in expectation of reward, practises or holds himself out to practise as a medical practitioner; or

(b) takes or uses the title of physician, surgeon, doctor or licentiate of medicine, medical practitioner or apothecary; or

(c) without reasonable excuse takes or uses any name, title, addition or description implying that he is authorised by law to practise as a medical practitioner,

he shall be guilty of an offence.

(2) Subject to subsections (6) and (7) of this section, if any person who is not a registered dental surgeon __

(a) for or in expectation of reward, practises or holds himself out to practise as a dental surgeon; or

(b) takes or uses the title of dental surgeon, dentist or dental practitioner; or

(c) without reasonable excuse takes or uses any name, title, addition or description implying that he is authorised by law to practise as a dentist, he shall be guilty of an offence under this section.

(3) If any person, for the purpose of procuring the registration of any name, qualification or other matter__

(a) makes a statement which he believes to be false in a material particular,

he shall be guilty of an offence under this section.

(4) If the Registrar or any other person employed by the council wilfully make any falsification in any matter relating to the register he shall be guilty of an offence under this section.

(5) A person who is guilty of an offence under this section shall be liable__

(a) on summary conviction, to a fine not exceeding N5,000;

(b) on conviction on indictment, to a fine not exceeding N10,000 or imprisonment for a term not exceeding five years or to both such fine and imprisonment.

(6) Where any person is acknowledged by the members generally of the community to which he belongs as having been trained in the system of therapeutic medicine traditionally in use in that community, nothing in paragraph (a) of subsection (1) or paragraph (a) of subsection (2) of this section shall be construed as making it an offence for that person to practise or to hold himself out to practise that system.

(7) The exemption conferred by subsection (6) of this section shall not extend to any activity involving an incision in human tissue or to administering, supplying or recommending the use of any dangerous drugs within the meaning of Part V of the Dangerous Drugs Act.

Cap. 91

(8) Nothing in subsection (1) or (2) of this section shall be construed as making it an offence for a person employed as a medical practitioner or dental surgeon on any ship, other than a Nigerian ship within the of the Merchant Shipping act, to act as a medical practitioner or dental surgeon in relation to the master, crew and passengers of that ship.

Cap. 224

(9) Where an offence, under this section which has been committed by a body corporate is proved to have been committed with the consent or connivance of, or to be attributable to any neglect on the part of, any director, manager, secretary or other similar officer of the body corporate, or any person purporting to act in any such capacity, he, as well as the body corporate, shall be deemed to be guilty of that offence and shall be liable to be proceeded against and punished accordingly.

18. (1) A person shall not hold an appointment or practise as a medical or dental surgeon in Nigeria unless he is registered with he Council under the provisions of this Act.

(2) A registered medical practitioner or dental surgeon shall be entitled to practise as a medical practitioner or dental surgeon, as the case may be, throughout Nigeria.

(3) A document which is required by any law for the time being in force in Nigeria or any part thereof to be issued or signed by a medical practitioner or a dental surgeon of a particular description shall not, if issued or signed, after this Act comes into force, be valid unless it is issued or signed, as the case may be, by a fully registered medical practitioner or dental surgeon.

(4) Without prejudice to the rule of law whereby a contract may be void if it is inconsistent with the provisions of an enactment: no person other than a fully registered medical practitioner or dental surgeon shall be entitled to bring any proceedings in any court of law for the purpose of recovering any fee or other consideration whatsoever payable in respect of services rendered or facilities or things supplied by him when purporting to act as a medical practitioner or as a dental surgeon.

(5) It shall be the duty of the person in charge of the medical school of the University or similar institution in Nigeria at which there is held a course of training intended for persons who are seeking to become members of the medical or dental profession to furnish to the Registrar, a list of successful candidates immediately after the publication of the pass list.

Regulations, rules and orders.

19. (1) Any power to make regulations, rules or orders conferred by this act shall include he power__

(a) to make provision for such incidental and supplementary matters as the authority making the instrument considers expedient for the purposes of the instrument; and

(b) to make different provision for different circumstances.

(2) The Minister shall lay a copy of all regulations made by the Council before the national Council of Ministers as soon as may be after the regulations are made, and if the National Council of Ministers decides that the regulations be annulled, they shall, without prejudice to anything previously done in pursuance of the regulations, cease to have effect on the day next following the date of the decision.

Repeals, saving, and transfer of assets, liabilities, staff. etc.
1963 No. 9.

20. (1) The Medical and Dental Practitioners Act 1963 (in this section referred to as "the repealed enactment") is hereby repealed and the body established thereunder is hereby dissolved.

(2) Notwithstanding subsection (1) of this section__

(a) any person whose name was immediately before the coming into force of this Act included in the registers maintained under the repealed enactment shall, without further application or payment of any other fee, be deemed to be registered under the appropriate provision of this Act;

(b) any register kept in pursuance of the repealed enactment shall be deemed to be part of the register to be keep in pursuance of this Act;

(c) any document referring to a provision of the repealed enactment shall be construed as a reference to the corresponding provision of this Act; and

(d) where any offence, being an offence for the continuance of which a penalty was provided, has been committed under the repealed enactment, proceedings may be taken under this Act in respect of the continuance of the offence after the commencement of this Act, in the same manner as if the offence had been committed under the corresponding provisions of this Act.

(3) All assets, funds, resources and other movable or immovable property which immediately before the commencement of this Act were vested in the body established by the repealed enactment shall by virtue of this Act and without any further assurances, be vested in the Council.

(4) As from the commencement of this Act__

(a) the rights, interests, obligations and liabilities of the body referred to in subsection (3) of this section existing immediately before the commencement of this Act under any contract or instrument or at law or in equity are hereby assigned to and vested in the Council without further assurance; and

(b) any such contract or instrument shall be of the same force and effect against or in favour of the Council and shall be enforceable as fully and effectively as if instead of the body mentioned in the repealed enactments, the Council has been named therein or had been a party thereto.

(5) Any proceedings or cause of action pending or existing immediately before the commencement of this Act by or against the body mentioned in the repealed enactment in respect of any right, interest, obligation or liability of the body aforesaid may be continued or, as the case may be, commenced and any determination of a court of law, tribunal or other authority or person may be enforced by or against the Council to the same extent that any such proceeding, cause of action or determination could have been continued, commenced or enforced by or against the body aforesaid if this Act had not been made.

(6) Notwithstanding the repeal of the enactment referred to in this section, if the Council thinks it expedient that any vacancy in the Council should be filled by a person holding office at the commencement of this Act in the body dissolved by this section it may employ such person by way of transfer to the Council and the previous service in the dissolved body by such person shall count as service for the purposes of any pension subsequently payable by the Council.

Interpretation, etc.

21. (1) In this Act, unless the context otherwise requires__

"approved" means for the time being approved under section 9 of this Act;

"approved medical or dental qualification" means a qualification which is approved in respect of the medical or dental profession;

"certificate of experience" means a certificate granted in pursuance of section 11 of this Act;

"Chairman" means the Chairman of the Council appointed under section 2 (1) of this act;

"Council" means the Medical and Dental Council of Nigeria established pursuant to section 1 (1) of this Act;

"dentistry" in relation to its practice includes the giving of any advice or treatment or the performance of any operation necessary for the cure or preservation of teeth unusually given by or performed by a dental surgeon and includes all operations necessary or incidental to the preparation and fitting of dentures, artificial teeth or other dental appliances or other maxillo-facial operations so however that__

(a) in case of emergency of which the medical practitioner shall be the sole judge, nothing shall preclude a medical practitioner from extracting teeth; and

(b) a qualified dental therapist or nurse acting under the supervision of a registered dental surgeon may scale and polish teeth, extract and scale, polish and restore teeth respectively, advise on dental care and carry out post operative care on maxillo-facial patients;
"disciplinary tribunal" has the meaning assigned to it by section 15 of this Act__
"Gazette" means the Gazette of the Federal Republic of Nigeria;
"Minister" means the Minister charged with the responsibility for matters relating to health
"panel" has the meaning assigned to it by section 15 of this act;
"prescribed" means prescribed by regulations;
"register" means a register maintained under this Act; and
"Registrar" means the Registrar appointed in pursuance of section 6 of this Act; and
"regulations" means regulations made by the Council.

(2) For the purposes of this Act__

(a) a person is fully registered as a medical practitioner or dental surgeon if his name is for the time being entered in the part of the register of medical practitioners or dental surgeons maintained in respect of fully registered medical practitioners or dental surgeons;

(b) a person is provisionally registered as a medical or dental practitioner if his name is for the time being entered in the part of the register maintained in respect of provisionally registered medical or dental practitioners; and

(c) a person has limited registration as a medical practitioner or dental surgeon if his name is for the time being entered in the part of the register maintained in respect of medical practitioners or dental surgeons with limited registration and his registration has not ceased under section 13 of this Act.

(3) Any approval, consent, direction, notice, observations, report, representation or request authorised or required to be given or made by or under this Act shall be in writing and may, without prejudice to any other method of service but subject to the provisions of rules made under the Second Schedule of this Act, be served by post.

Short title.

22. This Act may be cited as the Medical and Dental Practitioners Act

SCHEDULES

FIRST SCHEDULE

SUPPLIMENTARY PROVISIONS RELATING TO THE COUNCIL

Qualifications and Tenure of Office of Members

1. (1) A person shall not be a member of the Council unless he is a fully registered medical practitioner or dental surgeon.

(2) A person who is a member of the Council otherwise than by office shall, subject to the following provisions of this paragraph, hold office for the period of four years beginning with the date of his appointment or election as a member and shall be eligible for re-appointment for only one further period four years.

(3) Any member of the Council other than an ex-officio member may, by notice to the Council, resign his office.

(4) Where a member of the Council ceases to hold office before the date when his term of office would have expired by the effluxion of time, the body or person by whom he was appointed or elected shall, as soon as may be appoint or as the case may be, elect a person to fill the vacancy for the residue of the term aforesaid, so however that the foregoing provisions of this sub-paragraph shall not apply where a person holding office as a member of the Council in pursuance of this paragraph ceases to hold office at a time when the residue of his term does not exceed one year.

(5) The President shall have the power to remove from office the Chairman or any member of the Council or dissolve the Council at any time, if he is satisfied that it is in the interest of the public so to do.

Vice-Chairman and Secretary

2. (1) The Council shall elect from amongst its members a vice-Chairman of the Council who shall act as the Chairman in the absence of the Chairman.

(2) A Vice-Chairman who ceases to be member shall cease to be Vice-Chairman.

(3) The Registrar shall be the Secretary to the Council and to the disciplinary tribunal.

Proceedings of the Council

3. (1) Subject to the provisions of this Act and of section 27 of the interpretation Act 9which provides for decisions of a body to be taken by a majority of the members of the body and for the Chairman to have a second or casting vote), the Council may make standing orders regulating ——————

(2) The quorum of the Council shall be one-third of the membership and the quorum of any committee of the Council shall be determined by the Council.

(3) At any time while the office of Chairman is vacant or the Chairman is, in the opinion of the Council, permanently or temporarily unable to perform the functions of his office, the Vice-Chairman shall perform those functions and reference in this Schedule to the Chairman shall be construed accordingly

4. (1) Subject to the provisions of any standing orders of the council, the shall meet whenever it is summoned by the Chairman; and if the Chairman is required so to do by notice given to him by not less than six other members, he shall summon a meeting of the Council to be held within fourteen days from the date on which the notice is given.

(2) At any meeting of the Council the Chairman or, in his absence, the Vice-Chairman shall preside, but if both are absent the members present at the meeting shall appoint one of their number to preside at that meeting.

(3) where the Council desires to obtain the advice of any person on a particular matter, the Council may co-opt him as a member for such period as it thinks fit: but a person who is a member by virtue of this sub-paragraph shall not be entitled to vote at any meeting of the Council and shall not count towards a quorum.

(4) Notwithstanding anything in the foregoing provisions of this paragraph, the inauguration of the Council shall be summoned by and presided over by the Minister.

Committees

5. (1) The Council may appoint one or more committees to carry out, on behalf of the Council, such of its function as the Council may determine.

(2) A committee appointed under this paragraph shall consist of the number of persons determined by the Council and not more than one-third of those persons may be persons who are not members of the Council; and a person other than a member of the

Council shall hold office on the committee in accordance with the terms of the letter by which he is appointed.

(3) A decision of a Committee of the Council (other than the committee mentioned in subsection (5) of section 11 of this Act) shall be of no effect until it is confirmed by the Council.

Miscellaneous

6. (1) The fixing of the seal of the Council shall be authenticated by the signature of the Chairman and of some other member authorised generally or specially by the Council to act for that purpose.

(2) Any contract or instrument which, if made or executed by a person not being a body corporate, would not be required to be under seal may be made or executed on behalf of the Council by any person generally or specially authorised to act for that purpose by the Council.

(3) Any document purporting to be a document duly executed under the seal of the Council shall be recieved in evidence and shall, unless the contrary is proved, be deemed to be so executed.

7. The validity of any proceedings of the Council or a committee thereof shall not be affected by any vacancy in the membership of the Council, or a person to serve on the committee, or by reason that a person not entitled to do so took part in the proceedings.

8. Any member of the Council, and any person holding office on a committee of the Council, who has a personal interest in any contract or arrangement entered into or proposed to be considered by the Council or committee thereof shall not shall forthwith disclose his interest to the Council or committee and shall not vote on any question relating to that contract or arrangement.

9. A person shall not, by reason of his membership of the Council, be treated as holding an office in the public service of the Federation.

SECOND SCHEDULE Section15(5)

SUPPLEMENTARY PROVISIONS RELATING TO THE DISCIPLINARY TRIBUNAL AND INVESTIGATING PANEL

The Disciplinary Tribunal

1. The quorum of the disciplinary committee shall be determined by the Council of whom__

(a) all shall be fully registered medical practitioners in a case relating to a registered medical practitioner; and

(b) one at least shall be a registered dental dental surgeon in a case relating to a registered dental surgeon.

2. (1) The Attorney-General of the Federation shall make rules as to the selection of members of the disciplinary tribunal for the purposes of any proceedings and as to the procedure to be followed and the rules of evidence to be observed in proceedings before the disciplinary tribunal.

(2) The rules shall in particular provide __

(a) for securing that notice of the proceedings shall be given, at such time and in such manner as may be specified by the rules, to the person who is the subject of the proceedings;

(b) for determining who, in addition to the quorum aforesaid, shall be a party to the proceedings;

(c) for securing that any party to the proceedings shall, if he so requires, be entitled to be heard by the Council;

(d) for enabling any party to the proceedings to be represented by a legal practitioner;

(e) as to the costs of proceedings before the disciplinary tribunal;

(f) for requiring, in a case where it is alleged that the person who is the subject of the proceedings is guilty of infamous conduct in any professional respect, that where the disciplinary tribunal adjudges that the allegation has not been proved it shall record a finding that the person is not guilty of such conduct in respect of the matter to which the allegation relates;

(g) for publishing in the Federal Gazette notice of any direction of the disciplinary tribunal which has taken effect providing that a person's name shall be struck off a register.

3. For the purpose of any proceedings before the disciplinary tribunal, any member of the disciplinary tribunal may administer oaths and any party to the proceedings may issue out of the registry of the Court of Appeal writs of subpoena ad testificandum et duces tecum; but no person appearing before the disciplinary tribunal shall be compelled __

(a) to make any statement before the disciplinary tribunal tending to incriminate himself; or

(b) to produce any document under such a writ which he could not be compelled to produce at the trial of an action.

Assessors

4. (1) For the purpose of advising the disciplinary tribunal on question of law arising in proceedings before it, there shall in all such proceedings be an assessor to the disciplinary tribunal who shall be appointed by the Council on the nomination of the Chief Justice of Nigeria and shall be a legal practitioner of not less than seven years standing.

(2) The Chief Justice of Nigeria shall make rules as to the functions of assessors appointed under this paragraph, and in particular such rules shall contain provisions for securing __

(a) that where an assessors advises the disciplinary tribunal on any question of law as to evidence, procedure or any other matters specified by the rules, he shall do so in the presence of every party or person representing a party to the proceedings who appears thereat or if the advice is tendered while the disciplinary tribunal is deliberating in private, that every such party or person as aforesaid shall be informed what advice the assessor has tendered;

(b) that every such party or person as aforesaid shall be informed if in any case the disciplinary tribunal does not accept the advice of the assessor on such a question as aforesaid.

(3) an assessor may be appointed under this paragraph either generally or for any particular proceedings or class of proceedings, and shall hold and vacate office in accordance with the terms of the letter by which he is appointed.

The Panel

5. The quorum of the panel shall be five of whom __

(a) all shall be fully registered medical practitioners in a case relating to a registered medical practitioner; and

(b) one at least shall be fully registered dental surgeon in a case relating to a registered dental surgeon.

6. (1) The panel may, at any meeting of the panel attended by not less than seven members of the panel, including not less than one registered dental surgeon, make standing orders with respect to the panel.

(2) Subject to the provisions of any such standing orders, the panel may regulate its own procedure.

Miscellaneous

7. (1) A person ceasing to be a member of the disciplinary tribunal or the panel shall be eligible for re-appointment as a member of that body.

(2) a person may, if otherwise eligible, be a member of both the disciplinary tribunal and the panel: but no person who acted as a member of the panel with respect to any case shall act as a member of the disciplinary tribunal with respect to that case.

8. The disciplinary tribunal or the panel may act notwithstanding any vacancy in its membership; and the proceedings of either body shall not be invalidated by any irregularity in the appointment of a member of that body, or, subject to sub-paragraph (2) of paragraph 7 of this Schedule, by reason of the fact that any person who was not entitled to do so took part in the proceedings of that body.

9. The disciplinary tribunal and the panel may each sit in two or more divisions.

10. Any document authorised or required by virtue of this Act to be served on the disciplinary tribunal or the panel shall be served on the Registrar.

11. Any expenses of the disciplinary tribunal or panel shall be defrayed by the Council.

12. A person shall not, by reason only of his appointment as a legal assessor to the disciplinary tribunal or as a member of the panel, be treated as holding an office in the public service of the Federation.

MEDICAL AND DENTAL PRACTITIONERS ACT
CHAPTER 221
SUBSIDIARY LEGISLATION

List of Subsidiary Legislation

MEDICAL AND DENTAL PRACTITIONERS
(DISCIPLINARY TRIBUNAL AND ASSESSORS)
RULES

APPENDIX 3

ADVANCE MEDICAL DIRECTIVE/RELEASE CARD

Allergie:____
Current medication: ____
____
Medical problems:____
____

MEDICAL DIRECTIVE
(signed document inside)

I,——————————————, make this advance directive as formal statement of my wishes. These instructions reflect my resolute decision.

I direct that no blood transfusions (whole blood, red cells, white cells, platelets, or blood plasma) be given to me under any circumstance, even if physicians deem such necessary to preserve my life or health. I will accept non-blood volume expanders (such as dextran, saline or Ringer's solution, or hetastarch) and other non-blood management.

This legal directive is an exercise of my right to accept or to refuse medical treatment in accord with my deeply held values and convictions. I am——————-
And I make this directive out of obedience to —————————— This is, and has been, my unswerving religious stand for————— years. I am —— years old.

I also know that there are various dangers associated with blood transfusions. So I have decided to avoid such dangers and, instead, to accept whatever risks may seem to be involved in my choice of alternative non-blood management.

I release physicians, anaesthesiologists, and hospitals and their personnel from liability for any damages that might be caused by my refusal of blood, despite their otherwise competent care.

I authorize the person(s) named on the reverse to see that my instructions set forth in this directive are upheld and to answer any questions about my absolute refusal of blood.

Signature
________________________________ ______________________________
Address Date

Telephone

Witness

Witness

IN CASE OF EMERGENCY, PLEASE CONTACT:

Name:____

Telephone: ____

Address: ____

ALTERNATE CONTACT:

Name: ____

Telephone: ____

Address: ____

Appendix 4

FORM OF CONSENT

EXPRESS

Consent is express when the patient explicitly agree to what is proposed by the doctor. It need not have been set out in any specific form and it need not be in writing. Indeed, the vast majority of occasions when patients are touched by doctors take place in a GP's surgery where none of the apparatus of formal consent is present.

Consent forms have, however, long been a part of hospital procedure. The Department of Health (DOH) has published specimen forms in it's a Guide to Consent for Examination or Treatment (NHS Management Executive, 1990) (HC (90) 22).

CONSENT FORM

For medical or dental investigation, treatment or operation
Health Authority..........................Patient's Surname......................
Hospital..................................Other Names........................
Unit Number..............................Date of Birth.........................
Sex: (please tick) Male
Female
DOCTORS OR DENTISTS (This part to be completed by doctor or dentist.)
Type of operation, investigation or treatment for which written evidence of consent is considered appropriate.

I confirm that I have explained the operation, investigation or treatment, and such appropriate options as are available and the type of anaesthetic, if any (general/local/sedation) proposed, to the patient in terms which in my judgment are suited to the understanding of the patient and/or to one of the parents or guardians of the patient.

Signature.............................. Date...............................
Name of doctor or dentist..
PATIENT/PARENT/GUARDIAN
1. Please read this form and the notes overleaf very carefully
2. If there is anything that you don't understand about the explanation, or if you want more information, you should ask the doctor or dentist.
3. Please check that all the information on the form is correct. If it is, and you understand the explanation, then sign the form.
I am the patient/parent/guardian (delete as necessary).
I agree * to what is proposed which has been explained to me by the doctor/dentist named on this form.
to the use of the type of anaesthetic that I have been told about
I understand * that the procedure may not be done by the doctor/dentist who has been treating me so far.

* that any procedure in addition to the investigation or treatment described on this form will only be carried out if it necessary and in my best interests and can be justified for medical reasons.

I have told * the doctor or dentist about the procedures listed below I would not wish to be carried out straightaway without my consent having the opportunity to consider them first.

………………………………………………………………

………………………………………………………………

Signature ………………………………………………………………
Name ………………………………………………………………
Address ………………………………………………………………
(if not the patient) ………………………………………………………………

IN CONFIDENCE
Not to be destroyed within three years of the date of operation.

Apppendix-5

ABORTION CERTIFICATE

ABORTION ACT 1967

CERTIFICATE TO BE COMPLETED IN RELATION TO ABORTION PERFORMED IN EMERGENCY UNDER SECTION 1(4) OF THE ACT

I,..

(Name and qualification of practitioner in block capitals)

of ....

....

(Full address of practitioner)

hereby certify that I *am/was of the opinion formed in good faith that it *is/was necessary immediately to terminate the pregnancy of

....

(Full name of pregnant woman in block capitals)

of ....

....

(Usual place of residence of pregnant woman in block capitals)

in order

(Ring appro- 1. to save the life of the pregnant woman: or
priate 2. to prevent grave permanent injury to the physical or mental
number) health of the pregnant woman.

This certificate of opinion is given——-

(Ring appro- A. before the commencement of the treatment for the termination
Priate of the pregnancy to which it relates; or,
Number) if that is not reasonably practicable, then
B. not later than 24 hours after such termination.

Signed ....

Date ....

*Delete as appropriate.

Index

www.ingramcontent.com/pod-product-compliance
Lightning Source LLC
Chambersburg PA
CBHW031334230926
51848CB00002B/236
* 9 7 8 9 7 8 8 4 2 2 3 3 4 *